P9-BAU-534

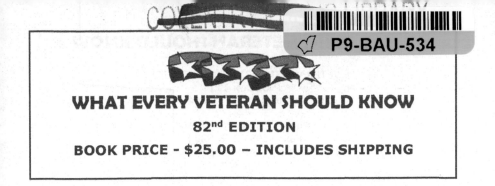

WHAT EVERY VETERAN SHOULD KNOW

82nd EDITION

BOOK PRICE - $25.00 – INCLUDES SHIPPING

This is the 82nd Edition of the book "WHAT EVERY VETERAN SHOULD KNOW," a service officer's guide since 1937.

Monthly supplements are available from the publisher, which provide updates to the information contained in this book. A one-year subscription to the supplement service is $35.00.

The material herein covers veterans' benefits, rights, privileges, and services over which the Department of Veterans Affairs has jurisdiction. All references to "VA" pertain to the Department of Veterans Affairs. Revised and new laws passed by the 115th Congress as of December 31, 2017, are incorporated in this text.

This guide was prepared solely for convenient reference purposes, and does not have the effect of law. Although diligent effort has been made to ensure its accuracy, in the event of any conflict between this book and any regulation, the latter is, of course, controlling.

Veterans and the dependents of deceased veterans are advised to contact their local veterans organization service officers, or the nearest Veterans Administration Office, for help in completing any valid claim.

VETERANS INFORMATION SERVICE
P.O. Box 111
East Moline, Illinois 61244-0111
Telephone: (309) 757-7760
Fax: (309) 278-5304
Email: help@vetsinfoservice.com
www.vetsinfoservice.com

ASK FOR YOUR **FREE** SAMPLE COPY OF THE
MONTHLY SUPPLEMENT,
DESIGNED TO KEEP THIS BOOK UP-TO-DATE.
ONE-YEAR SUPPLEMENT SERVICE: $35.00

WHAT EVERY VETERAN SHOULD KNOW

VETERANS INFORMATION SERVICE
P.O. Box 111
East Moline, Illinois 61244-0111

Phone: (309) 757-7760
Fax: (309) 278-5304
E-mail: help@vetsinfoservice.com
www.vetsinfoservice.com

═══════════════════════════════════

A NOTE TO THE READER:

Revised and new laws passed by the 115th Congress as of December 31, 2017, are incorporated in the text of this book. Chapter 1 of the book contains a brief summary of some of the important legislative changes affecting veterans' benefits during 2017.

You will find a Table of Contents, listing the main subject headings. For your convenience there is also a complete index in the back of the book, as well as an Edge Index on the back cover.

We hope you enjoy this edition of **WHAT EVERY VETERAN SHOULD KNOW**. Any comments or suggestions for future improvements are welcome.

═══════════════════════════════════

© 2018
What Every Veteran Should Know
Library of Congress Cataloging in Serials
ISSN 1532-8112
ISBN 0-9820586-9-1

All rights reserved. Printed in the United States of America. No part of this publication may be reproduced, stored in a retrieval system, or transmitted in any form or by any means, electronic, mechanical, photocopying, recording, or otherwise, without the written permission of the publisher.

Publisher:

Veterans Information Service
P.O. Box 111
East Moline, IL 61244-0111

TABLE OF CONTENTS

VA PHONE NUMBERS

Office	Phone Numbers
Bereavement Counseling	1-202-461-6530
Civilian Health and Medical Program (CHAMPVA)	1-800-733-8387
Education	1-888-442-4551
Federal Recovery Coordination Program	1-877-732-4456
Foreign Medical Program	1-888-820-1756
Headstones and Markers	1-800-697-6947
Health Care	1-877-222-8387
Homeless Veterans	1-877-222-8387
Home Loans	1-877-827-3702
Life Insurance	1-800-669-8477
National Cemetery Scheduling Office	1-800-535-1117
National Suicide Prevention Lifeline	1-800-273-8255
Pension Management Center	1-877-294-6380
Presidential Memorial Certificate Program	1-202-565-4964
Special Health Issues	1-800-749-8387
Spina Bifida/Children of Women Vietnam Veterans	1-888-820-1756

Telecommunication Device for the Deaf (TDD)	1-800-829-4833
VA Benefits	1-800-827-1000
Women Veterans	1-202-461-1070

QUICK GUIDE—
APPLYING FOR BENEFITS

Benefits	How To Apply
Before Leaving Military Service – Pre-Discharge Program for Servicemembers	If you are a member of the armed forces serving on either active duty or full- time National Guard duty, you should apply through the VA Pre-Discharge Program before leaving service.
Vocational Rehabilitation and Employment Benefits for Servicemembers and Veterans	The best way to file for vocational rehabilitation and employment services is to apply online at eBenefits.va.gov. It you don't have an eBenefits account, register today. In eBenefits, apply using the Veterans On-line Application (VONAPP) to complete and submit your application online. The form to use is called VA Form 28-1900, "Disabled Veterans Application for Vocational Rehabilitation." You can also mail the VA Form 28- 1900, "Disabled Veterans Application for Vocational Rehabilitation" to your local regional benefit office. You can locate your local regional benefit office using the VA Facility Locator. You may also visit your local regional benefit office and turn in your application for processing.
Disability Compensation Benefits for Veterans	The best way to file for disability compensation is to apply online at eBenefits.va.gov. If you don't have an eBenefits account, register today. Once you log into your eBenefits account, use Apply for Disability Compensation. VA recommends you appoint an accredited Veterans Service Officer to help you initiate your claim, gather the required medical records and evidence, and submit your claim. You can appoint a Veteran Service Officer while you apply online. If you prefer to file your claim by paper, complete VA Form 21-526EZ, "Application for Disability Compensation and Related Compensation Benefits" and mail the application to your local regional benefit office.

	You can find your local regional benefit office in the VA Facility Locator. You can also visit your local regional office and turn in your application for processing. While there, you can appoint an accredited Veterans Service Officer to help you prepare and submit your claim. You can find an accredited Veteran Service Officer using eBenefits.
Dependency and Indemnity Compensation Benefits for Survivors and Dependents	Download and complete VA Form 21P-534EZ, "Application for DIC, Death Pension, and/or Accrued Benefits"and mail it to your local regional benefit office. You can locate your local regional benefit office using the VA Facility Locator. You may also visit your local regional benefit office and turn in your application for processing. If the death was in service, your Military Casualty Assistance Officer will assist you in completing VA Form 21P- 534a, "Application for Dependency and Indemnity Compensation, Death Pension and Accrued Benefits by a Surviving Spouse or Child" and in mailing the application to the Philadelphia Regional Benefit Office.
Pension Benefits for Veterans	The best way to apply for your pension benefits is using Veterans On-Line Application (VONAPP). If you have never used VONAPP before you can create an account. You may also download and complete VA Form 21-527EZ, "Application for Pension." You can mail your application to your local regional benefit office. You can locate your local regional benefit office using the VA Facility Locator. You may also visit your local regional benefit office and turn in your application for processing.
Pension Benefits for Survivors	Download and complete VA Form 21-534EZ, "Application for DIC, Death Pension, and/or Accrued Benefits" and mail it to your local regional benefit office. You can locate your local regional benefit office using the VA Facility Locator. You may also visit your local regional benefit office and turn in your application .

Education Benefits for Veterans	The best way to apply for your education benefits is online at Vets.gov . You can also submit a paper application. To do this, download and complete VA Form 22-1990, "Application for VA Education Benefits" and mail it to a VA Regional Processing Office. You can mail the form to the region of your home address or to the VA Regional Processing Office for the region of your school's physical address, if you know what school you want to attend. Also, you can call a VA Education Case Manager (1-888- GIBill1) to ask for help.

CHAPTER 1

2017 UPDATES

Following is a brief summary of some of the important legislative changes, as well as VA policy changes, affecting veterans' benefits during 2017.

VALOR Act- H.R. 3949 Became Public Law No. 115-89 on 11/21/2017

Veterans Apprenticeship and Labor Opportunity Reform Act or the VALOR Act

(Sec. 2) This bill provides that the state approving agency for a multi-state non-federal apprenticeship program is: (1) for program approval purposes, the state approving agency for the state in which the headquarters of the apprenticeship program is located; and (2) for all other purposes, the state approving agency for the state in which the apprenticeship program takes place.

(Sec. 3) The bill eliminates the requirement that the veteran or other eligible person enrolled in an apprenticeship or other on-job training program must certify such person's program attendance to receive a training assistance allowance.

Department of Veterans Affairs Expiring Authorities Act of 2017 Became Public Law 115-62 on 9/27/2017

The Department of Veterans Affairs Expiring Authorities Act of 2017 extends a number of expiring authorities impacting veterans' benefits, health care, and homeless programs, including nursing home care, support services for caregivers, transportation, child care assistance, adaptive sports programs and housing and home loan services.

This bill extends the assisted living pilot program for veterans with traumatic brain injury for five additional months to allow extra time for VA to fully transition the veterans currently participating in that pilot into other existing programs more suitable for their ongoing support and rehabilitation. It would also make a number of technical corrections to the *Harry W. Colmery Veterans Educational Assistance Act of* 2017 that have been requested by the administration.

Harry W. Colmery Veterans Educational Assistance Act of 2017- Became Public Law No. 115-48 on 8/16/2017

Section 1. Short Title This section cites the short title of this bill as the *"Harry W. Colmery Veterans Educational Assistance Act of 2017."*

Section 101. Consideration of Certain Time Spent Receiving Medical Care from Secretary of Defense as Active Duty for Purposes of Eligibility for Post-9/11 Educational Assistance. This section would add time spent on active duty under orders authorized by section 12301(h) of title 10, U.S.C., as qualifying time for the Post-9/11 GI Bill. These particular orders are used when a National Guardsman or Reservist is receiving medical care or is recovering from active duty injuries.

Section 102. Consolidation of Eligibility Tiers under Post-9/11 Educational Assistance Program of the Department of Veterans Affairs. This section would authorize additional GI Bill funding for members of the National Guard and Reserve. This section would increase the amount of money/eligibility that individuals receive who serve at least 90 days but less than 6 months on active duty – it would increase from 40% to 50% benefit payable.

It would also increase the amount of money/eligibility that individuals receive who serve at least 6 months but less than 12 months – it would increase from 50% to 60% benefit payable. For a student attending a private school, this would result in approximately $2300 more a year in tuition than they are receiving now and would receive more money for their housing allowance.

Section 103. Educational Assistance Under Post-9/11 Educational Assistance Program for Members of the Armed Forces Awarded the Purple Heart. This section would extend full eligibility for the Post-9/11 GI Bill to any Purple Heart recipients since September 11, 2001.

Section 104. Eligibility for Post-9/11 Educational Assistance for Certain Members of Reserve Components of Armed Forces who Lost Entitlement to Educational Assistance under Reserve Educational Assistance Program. This section would allow certain members of the Reserve component to transfer into the Post-9/11 GI Bill who lost educational assistance benefits when Congress repealed the Reserve Educational Assistant Program (REAP).

Section 105. Calculation of Monthly House Stipend under Post-9/11 Educational Assistance Program Based on Location of Campus where Classes are Attended. This section would change the way living stipend amounts are calculated, from the current rule that says the living stipend payment is based on where the school is located to instead having the payment calculated based on where the student attends the majority of their classes.

Section 106. Charge to Entitlement for Certain Licensure and Certification Tests and National Tests under Department of Veterans' Affairs Post-9/11 Educational Assistance. This section would change the current rules that require that a veteran be charged a whole month of entitlement to pay for any national test (GMET, GRE, SAT etc.) or test that is required for state licensing. Instead of a full month of entitlement this bill would require that the test be pro-rated to the amount of the actual cost of the test.

Section 107. Restoration of Entitlement to Post-9/11 Educational Assistance for Veterans Affected by Closures of Educational Institution. This section would restore entitlement to individuals when their school closes in the middle of a semester. This section would also authorize additional living stipend payments to be paid to students whose school closes in the middle of the semester for no more than 4 months, or the length of the semester, where they were attending training.

Section 108. Inclusion of Fry Scholarship Recipients in Yellow Ribbon GI Education Enhancement Program. This section would extend the Yellow Ribbon Program to students receiving GI Bill payments through the Fry Scholarship program and those who received a Purple Heart after September 11, 2001. Fry recipients are surviving dependents of servicemembers who died while serving on active duty.

Section 109. Additional Authorized Transfer of Unused Post-9/11 Educational Assistance Benefits to Dependents upon Death of Originally Designated Dependent. This section would allow a veteran to transfer remaining months of GI Bill entitlement to another dependent if the dependent who originally received the transferred benefits dies before they can use all of the benefits. The section would also allow a dependent to transfer remaining months of GI Bill entitlement to another dependent after the death of the servicemember or veteran.

Section 110. Edith Nourse Rogers STEM Scholarship. This section would authorize VA to provide additional GI Bill funds to help a student veteran complete a STEM degree. They would be eligible to apply for the program, which would pay for the lesser of nine additional months of Post-9/11 GI Bill or a lump sum of $30,000. The amount of money that could be spent on this program would not exceed $100,000,000 in any one fiscal year. These additional benefits would be known as the 'Edith Nourse Rogers STEM Scholarship'.

Section 111. Honoring National Service of the Members Elimination of Time Limitation for use of Entitlement. This section would eliminate the current time limitation to use the GI Bill for new members of the Armed Forces. Student veterans currently have 15 years from the date of their last active duty discharge to use the benefit.

Section 112. Monthly Stipend for Certain Members of the Reserve Components of the Armed Forces Receiving Post-9/11 Educational Assistance. This section would require VA to pro-rate the GI Bill housing stipend provided to Reservists who get called up for active duty during the middle of a month. Current law prohibits them from pro-rating the stipend so if the reservist is on active duty orders for even one day of a month then they would lose the entire months' worth of VA housing allowance.

Section 113. Improvement of Information Technology of the Veterans Benefits Administration of the Department of Veterans Affairs. This section would authorize $30 million to improve GI Bill claims processing and complete their rules-based processing system for these claims.

Section 114. Department of Veterans Affairs High Technology Pilot Program. This section would authorize VA to conduct a 5-year pilot program that would provide veterans the opportunity to enroll in high technology courses (coding boot camp, IT certifications etc.). VA would enter into contracts with these schools or programs and would provide tuition and fees payments on a sliding scale that incentivizes the schools to graduate the student and ensure they find a job in their field of study. The section would also authorize a living stipend payment equal to the Post-9/11 rate to students while they are using the benefit.

Section 201. Work Study Allowance This section would repeal the sunset date in the law that allows VA work study benefits for outreach to student veterans and to assist State approving agencies.

Section 202. Duration of Educational Assistance under Survivors' and Dependent' Educational Assistance Program. This section would change the number of months of entitlement for individuals who become eligible for the Survivors' and Dependents' Educational Assistance Program from 45 months to 36 months. This would re-align this program with other GI Bill programs that provide 36 months of eligibility for educational assistance. This change would only apply to individuals that become entitled to this program on or after August 1, 2018.

Section 203. Olin E. Teague Increase in the Amounts of Educational Assistance Payable Under Survivors' and Dependent' Educational Assistance Program. This section would increase the monthly payment for educational assistance provided under Survivors' and Dependent' Educational Assistance Program by $200 a month.

Section 301. State Approving Agency Funding. This section would increase the funding out VA's mandatory account for the State Approving Agencies (SAA) from $19 million a year to $21 million a year. This section would also authorize VA to provide an additional $3 million a year to the SAAs out of the Department's discretionary account. This section would also, beginning in fiscal year 2019, require VA to provide a cost of living adjustment increase to the SAAs budget in an amount that equals the same percentage increase as benefits provided under the Social Security Act.

Section 302. Authorization for Use of Post-9/11 Educational Assistance to Pursue Independent Study Programs at Certain Educational Institutions that are Not Institutions of Higher Learning. This section would allow an eligible individual to use their GI Bill benefit for an accredited independent study program (including open circuit television) at an educational institution that is an area career and technical education school or a postsecondary vocational school providing postsecondary level education.

Section 303. Provision of Information on Priority Enrollment for Veterans in Certain Courses of Education. This section would require VA to include on its GI Bill Comparison Tool, information on whether a school has a priority enrollment system in place that allows veterans to enroll in courses earlier than other students attending the school.

Section. 304. Limitation on Use of Reporting Fees Payable to Educational Institutions and Sponsors of Programs of Apprenticeship. This section would allow VA to provide a fee to schools or a sponsor of a program of apprenticeship for the reports or certifications that these institutions are required to submit to VA about the individuals at their school receiving GI Bill benefits. This section would require VA to provide $16 to the institution for each individual that they certify as using GI Bill benefits at their institution. This section would also require that schools with 100 or more enrollees using GI Bill benefits, may not use the funds received by the institution from the reporting fees for the institution's general fund and that these funds may only be used for veterans programs at that institution.

Section. 305. Training for School Certifying Officials. This section would require VA, in consultation with the SAA's, to provide requirements for training for school certifying officials at educational institutions that are approved for GI Bill benefits. This section would also allow VA to disapprove a course of education if a school does not ensure that the school certifying official meets the training requirements.

Section 306. Extension of Authority for Advisory Committee on Education. This section would extend the authority for VA's Advisory Committee on Education from December of 2017 through to December of 2022.

Section 307. Department of Veterans Affairs Provision of On-Campus Educational and Vocational Counseling for Veterans. This section would codify VA's Veterans Success on Campus (VSOC) program, which is administered and overseen by the Vocational Rehabilitation and Employment Service (VS&E). There are currently 94 schools with a VSOC program, which provides a VR&E counselor at each school to assist veterans with their transition from military to college life as well as who provide the support and assistance needed to pursue their educational and employment goals.

Section 308. Provision of Information Regarding Veteran Entitlement to Educational Assistance. This section would require VA to make available to educational institutions, the ability to view the remaining benefit amount for each veteran attending that institution. This section would also allow the veteran or their dependent (if they are a beneficiary of their GI Bill benefits) to opt out of the school's ability to receive such information from VA.

Section 309. Treatment, for Purposes of Educational Assistance Administered by the Secretary of Veterans Affairs, of Educational Courses that Begin Seven or Fewer Days after the First Day of an Academic Year. This section would provide more flexibility to the school certifying officials if the first day of a course does not start on the first day of an academic term, by allowing the school certifying official to certify the course as beginning on that day first day of the academic term for purposes of certifying a veteran for GI Bill benefits.

Section 401. Eligibility of Reserve Component Members for Post 9/11 Educational Assistance. This section would make individuals eligible for Post-9/11 GI Bill benefits who have served and who will serve on 12304, 12304(a) and 12304(b) orders. Any active duty service under these Reserve component orders since the enactment of the Post-9/11 Veterans Educational Assistance Act of 2008 would apply for such benefits going forward.

Section 402. Time Limitation for Training and Rehabilitation for Veterans with Service-Connected Disabilities. This section would also make the 12304, 12304(a) and 12304(b) orders eligible for benefits under the Vocational Rehabilitation and Employment program in chapter 31 of title 38, U.S.C.

Section 501. Repeal Inapplicability of Modification of Basic Allowance for Housing to Benefits under Laws Administered by Secretary of Veterans Affairs. This section would be the offset for the package by realigning the living stipend payments for those using the Post 9/11 GI Bill (E-5 with dependents rate) to the same Basic Allowance for Housing (BAH) payments currently paid to active duty servicemembers at the E-5 with dependents rate.

Several years ago, the annual percentage increase to active duty BAH payments were reduced by 1% a year for five years but GI bill payments were exempt. This bill would re-align these payments so that a GI Bill recipient would receive the same living stipend per month as an E-5 active duty servicemember with dependents. This section also stipulates that these decreases to the annual percentage increase would only be in effect for individuals who first begin using their education benefits on or after January 1, 2018

Veterans Appeals Improvement and Modernization Act of 2017—Became Public Law No. 115-55 8/23/2017

Any time a veteran files a claim for disability that the Department of Veterans Affairs (VA) rejects, they have the right to appeal. But the average wait before a final decision is six years—and one service member has even waited 25 years. As a result, the number of pending appeals has increased sharply, rising in the past two years alone from 380,000 to now 470,000 pending appeals.

The Department of Veterans Affairs (VA) currently spends about $63.7 billion per year on 4.1 million veterans with disabilities related to their time in service.

The law established three new "lanes" for veterans appeals, to separate them out into separate categories and hopefully ease the speed with which they go through, rather than all funneling them together into one bureaucratic catch-all as before.

The "Board lane" instantly moves a pending appeal over to the Board of Veterans' Appeals and skips the intervening layers of VA hierarchy.

"The local higher level review lane" moves a rejected claim to another adjudicator higher up on the VA hierarchy to take a second look at.

The "new evidence lane" allows veterans to submit new evidence related to their disability claim.

While the legislation directs the VA to create this structure for appeals, it does not include specific plans for implementation. Rather, the VA is directed to define which appeals will go in which lane and to implement that structure. The legislation was introduced as H.R. 2288 in the House by Rep. Mike Bost (R-IL12), and as S. 1024 in the Senate by Sen. Johnny Isakson (R-GA).

Veterans' Compensation Cost-of-Living Adjustment Act of 2017—Became Public Law No. 115-75 on 11/2/2017

This bill directs the Department of Veterans Affairs (VA) to increase, as of December 1, 2017, the rates of veterans' wartime disability compensation by 2.0%, additional compensation for dependents, the clothing allowance for certain disabled veterans, and dependency and indemnity compensation for surviving spouses and children. Each such increase shall be the same percentage as the increase in benefits provided under title II (Old Age, Survivors and Disability Insurance) of the Social Security Act, on the same effective date.

Veteran's Choice Accountability Act—Became Public Law No. 115-46

The program had been set to expire in August, but President Trump signed an extension in April. This law, introduced by Sen. Dean Heller (R-NV) in the Senate as a bill labeled S. 114, provides $2.1 billion in funding for the extension.

President Trump's proposed budget would increase the VA's budget by 7 percent, one of the only agencies which would receive an increase rather than a cut. President Obama also significantly increased the VA's budget and cut the patient backlog, though not eliminating it entirely.

New Regulation Decreases Outpatient Copays

The VA previously charged non-exempt veterans $8 or $9 for each 30-day or less supply of outpatient medicine, and the calculation was based on the Medical Consumer Price Index. It was announced in 2017 they would be moving to a tiered system to reduce out-of-pocket costs. The system includes three tiers, with co-pays set at $5, $8 and $11.

VA Introduces Pre-Need Eligibility Determinations

It was announced in 2017 that the Department of Veterans Affairs will now provide eligibility determinations for internment in a VA national cemetery before the time of need. Interested individuals can submit the VA Form 40-10007, Application for Pre-Need Determination of Eligibility for Burial in a VA Cemetery.

Expanded TRICARE Coverage

Effective January 1, 2017, TRICARE Coverage added new services and screenings. TRICARE now covers annual preventative office visits for all Prime beneficiaries, six years and older. TRICARE Standard beneficiaries can receive preventative services with no cost-share or co-pay through disease prevention exams.

The annual well-woman exam will still continued to be covered for all Prime and Standard beneficiaries under age 65, with no cost-share or co-pay requirements.

VA Announces Expansion of Mental Health Care To Veterans with Less-Than-Honorable Discharges

The VA finalized plans to provide emergency mental health coverage to former service members with other-than-honorable administrative discharge. Former service members with an OTH discharge may receive care for their mental health emergency for an initial period of up to 90 days, including inpatient, residential or outpatient care.

VA Introduces Decision Ready Claims (DRC) Program

The Decision Ready Claim (DRC) Program is the fastest way to get your claim processed. With the DRC Program, you can get a decision on your claim within 30 days when you work with an accredited Veterans Service Organization (VSO). Your VSO will help you gather and submit all relevant records and evidence, including federal and medical records and Disability Benefits Questionnaires (DBQs), and will request your VA claim exam, so your claim is ready for VA to make a decision when you submit it.

CHAPTER 2

BENEFITS FOR ELDERLY VETERANS

BENEFIT DESCRIPION

According to the 2012 U.S. Census brief, veterans age 65 or older numbered in excess of 12.4 million. These veterans served in conflicts around the world including World War II, the Korean War, the Vietnam War, and even in the Persian Gulf War. As veterans age, the Department of Veterans Affairs (VA) will provide benefits and services that address a variety of issues including the changing health risks they face, as well as financial challenges through VA benefits and health services.

VA BENEFITS

There are a wide variety of benefits available to all military veterans, including benefits for elderly veterans. Some of these benefits include disability compensation, pension, education and training, health care, home loans, insurance, vocational rehabilitation and burial.

Key Takeaways:

There are many general benefits for veterans age 65 or older including disability compensation, pension and long-term care options

Other options for elderly veterans include Aid and Attendance which is additional monthly pension for veterans already receiving pension as well as Housebound, which is an increased monthly pension amount paid if a veteran is confined to their immediate premises

AID AND ATTENDANCE

Aid and Attendance (A&A) is a monthly pension that's paid if veterans meet certain conditions, listed below. This VA program is designed to provide an additional amount of money for elderly veterans who are eligible for or are receiving a VA Pension benefit.

Eligibility conditions include:

- The veteran is required to have help performing daily functions including bathing, eating or dressing

- The veteran is bedridden

- The veteran is a patient in a nursing home

- The veteran has eyesight limited to a corrected 5/200 visual acuity or less in both eyes, or concentric contraction of the visual field to 5 degrees or less

13

HOUSEBOUND

Housebound is an increased monthly pension amount paid if a veteran is substantially confined to their immediate premises because of a permanent disability.

HOW TO APPLY FOR AID AND ATTENDANCE AND HOUSEBOUND BENEFITS

A veteran may apply for Aid and Attendance or Housebound benefits by writing to the Pension Management Center (PMC) that serves their state. Veterans can also visit their local regional benefit office to file a request.

Copies of included evidence should include, if possible, a report from an attending physician validating the need for Aid and Attendance or Housebound-type care.

The report should include sufficient detail to determine whether there is a disease or injury producing physical or mental impairment, loss of coordination, or conditions affecting the ability to dress and undress, feed oneself, attend to sanitary needs, and to keep oneself ordinarily clean and presentable.

Regardless of whether the claim is for Aid and Attendance or Housebound, the report should indicate how well the applicant gets around, where the applicant goes and what the applicant is able to do during a typical day. It's also important to determine whether the claimant is confined to the home or immediate premises.

VA HEALTH CARE FOR ELDERLY VETERANS

OVERVIEW

Geriatrics is health care for elderly Veterans with complex needs. Extended care – also known as long term care – is a program for Veterans of all ages who need the daily support and assistance of another individual. Elderly Veterans can receive geriatric and long term care programs at home, at VA medical centers, or in the community.

GERIATRICS AND EXTENDED CARE SERVICES

Geriatrics and Extended Care Services (GEC) is committed to optimizing the health and well-being of Veterans with multiple chronic conditions, life-limiting illness, frailty or disability associated with chronic disease, aging or injury. Below are some of the main options for care in these categories.

Adult Day Care

Adult Day Health Care is a veterans program that can include daytime care, social activities, peer support, companionship and recreation. It's designed for veterans who need skilled services, case management and help with activities of daily living. Health services including care from nurses, therapists, social workers, and others may be available.

Adult Day Care can provide respite care for a family caregiver and can help veterans and their caregiver gain skills to manage the veteran's care at home.

The program may be provided at VA medical centers, State Veterans Homes or community organizations.

Home Based Health Care

Home Based Primary Care is health care services provided to veterans in their home, with supervision from a VA physician who manages a health care team delivering services. Home Based Primary Care is for Veterans who have complex health care needs for whom routine clinic-based care isn't effective.

14

The program is for veterans who need skills services, case management and help with activities of daily living. The program is also for veterans who are isolated or who have a caregiver experiencing burden.

Hospice Care

Hospice Care is comfort care provided to you and your family if you have a terminal condition, with less than 6 months to live, and are no longer seeking treatment other than palliative care. Hospice Care can be provided at home, in an outpatient clinic or in an inpatient setting.

Hospice is a benefit that the VA offers to qualified veterans who are in the final phase of their lives, typically six months or less. This multi-disciplinary team approach helps Veterans live fully until they die. The VA also works very closely with community and home hospice agencies to provide care in the home.

Other geriatric care options include: homemaker and home health aide care, palliative care, respite care, skilled home health care and telehealth care.

RESIDENTIAL SETTINGS AND NURSING HOMES

Another option for elderly veterans in terms of long-term care are residential settings. These can include community residential care, medical foster homes, adult family homes and assisted living.

There are also nursing homes including community living centers and community nursing homes, as well as State Veterans Homes.

State Veterans Homes are facilities providing nursing home, domiciliary or adult day care. They're owned, operated and managed by state governments. To participate in the State Veterans Home program, the VA has to formally recognize and certify a facility as a State Veterans Home. The VA then surveys all facilities each year to make sure they meet VA standards.

Eligibility for State Veterans Homes is based on clinical need and setting availability, and each individual state establishes eligibility and admissions criteria for the homes. Some State Veterans Homes may admit non-Veteran spouses and gold star parents, while others may admit only veterans.

PAYING FOR LONG TERM CARE

Home and Community Based Services are part of the VA Medical Benefits Package. All enrolled Veterans are eligible for these services. However, to get the service you must have a clinical need for it, and the service must be available in your location.

VA Standard Benefits Package include:

- Geriatric Evaluation to assess your care needs and to create a care plan

- Adult Day Health Care

- Respite Care

- Skilled Home Health Care

Some Home and Community Based Services may be prioritized based on your level of VA service-connected disability. Nursing Home and Residential Settings have different eligibility requirements for each setting. The VA does not pay for room and board in residential settings such as Assisted Living or Adult Family Homes. However, you may receive some Home and Community Based Services while you are living in a residential setting.

The VA will provide Community Living Center (VA Nursing Home) or community nursing home care IF you meet certain eligibility criteria involving your service connected status, level of disability, and income.

SERVICE-CONNECTED DISABILITY

A "service-connected disability" is a disability that is related to your active military service. Your disability is assigned a rating (0% to 100%) based on how severely it impacts your daily life. The greater your disability, the higher your rating.

VA DISABILITY COMPENSATION

VA Disability Compensation is a monthly tax-free payment to Veterans who have a service-connected disability. The higher your rating, the higher monthly payments will be.

However, having a disability caused by your active military service does NOT automatically start disability compensation payments. You need to APPLY for those benefits. It is important to do this because your service-connected disability status has an effect on how much you pay for VA health care services, what programs you are eligible for, and your priority in receiving certain services

HOW DO I APPLY FOR VA DISABILITY COMPENSATION?

There are several ways to apply for your service-connected disability status. You can:

- Complete and mail VA Form 21-526EZ to your Veterans Benefits Administration (VBA) regional office. To find your VBA regional office, visit the facility locator site, or

- Complete the application online using an eBenefits account, or

- Work with a representative, such as a Veterans Service Officer. You can search for a representative here, or visit your local VBA office for assistance.

Your disability needs to be reviewed by staff at VBA and assigned a rating before you can receive payments.

Other Available Monthly Compensation

If you receive VA compensation for a service-connected disability, you may be eligible to receive additional monthly monetary benefits if you ALSO:

- Require significant help with your personal care needs by another person because of your disability, or

- Are bedridden because of your disability

Veterans Pension

Veterans Pension is a sometimes tax-free monetary benefit paid to low-income war-time Veterans who are ALSO:

- 65 or older, or

- Totally and permanently disabled, or

- Living in a nursing home receiving skilled nursing care, or

- Receiving Social Security Disability Insurance, or

- Receiving Supplemental Security Income Low-income guidelines are set by Congress. Additional income is allowed if you have dependents.

How much does it pay?

Your payments will raise your income to the Maximum Annual Pension Rate, and not exceed it. Pension benefits are paid monthly.

How do I apply?

Complete and mail VA Form 21P-527EZ to your Veterans Benefits Administration (VBA) regional office. To find your VBA regional office, visit the facility locator site, or

Complete the application online using an eBenefits account, or

Work with an accredited representative or agent, such as a Veterans Service Officer. You can search for representatives here, or visit your local VBA office for assistance.

WORLD WAR II VETERANS

World War II (WWII) was the most widespread war in history with more than 100 million people serving in military units. About 16 million Americans served during WWII, and many of those Veterans are now receiving VA benefits including Pension and Health Care. WWII Veterans who were a part of the Occupation Forces assigned to Hiroshima and Nagasaki, Japan soon after the detonation of Atomic-Bombs over those respective cities, and those American prisoners of war (POW's) who were housed in close proximity to those cities are sometimes called "Atomic Veterans.

VA BENEFITS

World War II Veterans may be eligible for a wide variety of benefits available to all U.S. military Veterans. VA benefits include disability compensation, pension, education and training, health care, home loans, insurance, vocational rehabilitation and employment, and burial.

The following sections provide information tailored to the experiences of World War II Veterans to help you better understand specific VA benefits for which you may qualify.

Benefits for World War II Veterans Exposed to Ionizing Radiation

World War II era Veterans may qualify for health care and compensation benefits if you were exposed to ionizing radiation during military service. Health care services include an Ionizing Radiation Registry health exam and clinical treatment at VA's War Related Illness and Injury Study Centers. You may also be entitled to disability compensation benefits if you have certain cancers as a result of exposure to ionizing radiation during military service.

Benefits for World War II Veterans Who Participated in Radiation-Risk Activities

World War II era Veterans may qualify for health care and compensation benefits if you participated in certain radiation-risk activities, such as nuclear weapons testing, during military service. These Veterans may be informally referred to as "Atomic Veterans". Health care services include an Ionizing Radiation Registry health exam and clinical treatment at VA's War Related Illness and Injury Study Centers. You may also be entitled to disability compensation benefits if you have certain cancers as a result of your participation in a radiation-risk activity during military service

Benefits for Survivors of Veterans with Radiation Exposure

Surviving spouses, dependent children, and dependent parents of Veterans who died as the result of diseases related to radiation exposure during military service may be eligible for survivors' benefits.

KOREAN WAR VETERANS

Approximately 5.7 million Veterans served in the Korean War. Korean War Veterans are more prone to suffer from disabilities related to cold injures as a result of exposure to severe cold climates. Cold weather accounted for 16% of Army non-battle injuries and over 5,000 U.S. casualties of cold injury required evacuation from Korea during the winter of 1950-1951. In many instances, Servicemembers could not seek or were unable to obtain medical care for cold injuries because of battlefield conditions.

VA BENEFITS

Korean War veterans may be eligible for a range of benefits available to all U.S. military veterans including disability compensation, pension, education and training, health care, home loans, insurance, vocational rehabilitation and employment and burial.

Benefits For Veterans Who Experience Cold Injuries

Veterans who experienced cold injuries may have medical conditions resulting from a cold-related disease or injury.

Examples of cold-related medical conditions include:
*   Skin cancer in frostbite scars;
*   Arthritis;
*   Fallen arches;
*   Stiff toes;
*   Cold sensitization.

These cold-related problems may worsen as Veterans grow older and develop complicating conditions such as diabetes and peripheral vascular disease, which place them at higher risk for late amputations.

Benefits for Korean War Veterans Exposed to Ionizing Radiation

Korean War era Veterans may qualify for health care and compensation benefits if you were exposed to ionizing radiation during military service. Health care services include an Ionizing Radiation Registry health exam and clinical treatment at VA's War Related Illness and Injury Study Centers. You may also be entitled to disability compensation benefits if you have certain cancers as a result of exposure to ionizing radiation during military service. Korean War era Veterans may qualify for health care and compensation benefits if you participated in certain radiation-risk activities, such as nuclear weapons testing, during military service. These Veterans may be informally referred to as "Atomic Veterans".

Health care services include an Ionizing Radiation Registry health exam and clinical treatment at VA's War Related Illness and Injury Study Centers. You may also be entitled to disability compensation benefits if you have certain cancers as a result of your participation in a radiation-risk activity during military service.

VIETNAM VETERANS

United States military involvement in the Vietnam War officially began on August 5, 1964; however, the first U.S. casualty in Vietnam occurred on July 8, 1959.

Approximately 2.7 million American men and women served in Vietnam. During the war, over 58,000 U.S. military members lost their lives and 153,000 were wounded. There were 766 prisoners of war of which 114 died in captivity.

VA Benefits for Vietnam Veterans

Vietnam Veterans may be eligible for a wide-variety of benefits available to all U.S. military Veterans. VA benefits include disability compensation, pension, education and training, health care, home loans, insurance, vocational rehabilitation and employment, and burial.

Disability Compensation for Veterans Exposed to Agent Orange

VA *presumes* that some disabilities diagnosed in certain Veterans were caused by exposure to Agent Orange during military service.

Children of Veterans with Exposure to Agent Orange

Children of Veterans exposed to Agent Orange who have a birth defect including spina bifida, a congenital birth defect of the spine, and certain other birth defects may be entitled to VA benefits. These include monetary benefits, health care, and vocational rehabilitation services.

CHAPTER 3

BENEFITS FOR YOUNGER VETERANS

BENEFIT DESCRIPTION

Younger veterans are often referred to as Gulf War Veterans. More than 650,000 Service members served in Operation Desert Shield and Desert Storm from August 2, 1990 to July 31, 1991. For VA benefits eligibility purposes, the Gulf War period is still in effect. This means that anyone who served on active duty from August 2, 1990, to present is considered a Gulf War Veteran. For example, the Veterans Pension benefit requires service during a wartime period. Therefore, any Veteran who served on active military service for any period from August 2, 1990, to the present meets the wartime service requirement.

VA BENEFITS

Gulf War veterans may be eligible for a wide variety of benefits available to all U.S. military veterans including disability compensation, pension, education and training, health care, home loans, insurance, vocational rehabilitation and employment, and burial.

> **Key Takeaways:**
>
> Younger veterans are often also referred to as Gulf War Veterans
>
> The Gulf War Period started on August 2,1990 and for benefits purposes is still in effect
>
> There are certain defined Gulf War Veterans' Illnesses including ALS, and unexplained illnesses called "Gulf War Syndrome"
>
> The VA offers not only benefits such as disability compensation and the Post-9/11 GI Bill for younger veterans, but also options for vocational training, transitional benefits and substance and mental health counseling

GULF WAR VETERANS' ILLNESSES

Certain illnesses and diseases are presumed by the VA to be related to military service in designated areas of Southwest Asia and may entitle the veteran to VA disability compensation benefits. For Gulf War veterans, these presumptive diseases include:

- Medically unexplained illnesses often called "Gulf War Syndrome"

- Certain infectious diseases

- Amyotrophic lateral sclerosis (ALS) diagnosed in all veterans who had 90 days or more continuous active military service

Veterans discharged under conditions other than dishonorable who served in the Southwest Asia theater of military operations, which includes the areas specified by regulation, but not Afghanistan, may be entitled to disability compensation for certain undiagnosed illnesses, certain diagnosable chronic disability patterns, and certain presumptive diseases (as described below) even though these disorders did not become manifest during qualifying service.

Veterans who served in Afghanistan on or after September 19, 2001, may be entitled to disability compensation for certain presumptive diseases.

ELIGIBILITY REQUIREMENTS

Qualifying undiagnosed illnesses or diagnosable chronic disability patterns, that appeared either during a qualifying period of active service or prior to December 31, 2021, must meet the following conditions:

- There must be no other cause for your disability or illness than service in the Southwest Asia theater of military operations.

- Your disability existed for 6 months or more, AND

- If your disability or illness did not appear during active duty in the Southwest Asia theater of military operations, then it must have appeared prior to December 31, 2021, to a degree that is at least 10-percent disabling (for VA rating purposes).

The disability must be one or more of the following:

- **Undiagnosed illnesses.** These are illnesses that may include but are not limited to: abnormal weight loss, fatigue, cardiovascular disease, muscle and joint pain, headache, menstrual disorders, neurological and psychological problems, skin conditions, respiratory disorders, and sleep disturbances.

- **Diagnosable functional gastrointestinal disorders.** Functional gastrointestinal disorders are a group of conditions characterized by chronic or recurrent symptoms that are unexplained. These disorders may include but are not limited to irritable bowel syndrome, functional dyspesia, functional vomiting, functional constipation, functional bloating, functional abdominal pain syndrome, and functional dysphagia.

- Diagnosable Chronic Fatigue Syndrome

- Diagnosable Fibromyalgia

Certain presumptive diseases, which will be considered to have been incurred in or aggravated by service even if there is no evidence of such disease during active service. With three exceptions (see asterisks), one of the following must have become manifest to a degree of 10 percent or more within 1 year of the date of separation from a qualifying period of active service:

- Burcellosis
- Campylobacter jejuni
- Coxiella burnetii (Q fever)
- Malaria* (if not 10 percent or more within one year of separation, may be 10 percent or more at a time when standard or accepted treatises indicate that the incubation period commenced during qualifying period of service)
- Mycobacterium tuberculosis* (no time limit)
- Nontyphoid Salmonella
- Shigella
- Visceral leishmaniasis* (no time limit)

21

- West Nile Virus

Evidence Requirements

- The evidence must show you served in the Southwest Asia theater of military operations, as defined by regulation or served in Afghanistan on or after September 19, 2001, for benefits associated with certain presumptive diseases.
- Medical evidence of treatment of the claimed disability or illness.
- If there is no medical evidence that you have been previously treated for a disability pattern and the only significant evidence is a lay statement describing the disability pattern, a VA examination may be needed (VA will request an examination).
- For undiagnosed illness claims, the evidence may be medical evidence or nonmedical indications that can be independently observed or verified such as lost time from work, changes in appearance, changes in physical abilities, and changes in mental or emotional attitudes (**Note:** Independently verified means it must be possible for VA to obtain verification of the nonmedical indicators from an independent source).

2017 UPDATE: BLENDED RETIREMENT GOES INTO EFFECT

A new retirement system was introduced in 2017, which is known as the "Blended Retirement System" or BRS. The blending is of two primary sources of retirement income. One of these is the existing annuity provision for people retiring after 20 or more years of service, in addition to the Thrift Savings Plan (TSP), which is a government-operated 401(k) retirement account allowing members to invest their own money in stocks or government securities and also receive a contribution to that account from their employer.

BRS will use the annuity formula currently in place: the average of the servicemember's highest 36 months of basic pay times 2.5% of their years of service -- but the 2.5% is adjusted downward by half of a percentage point, from 2.5 to 2%.

To make up for this reduction the government will contribute to a member's TSP. After the first 60 days in the service, all members will be enrolled in TSP and receive an automatic government contribution of 1% of basic pay into their account each month. Additionally, the servicemember will be automatically enrolled to contribute 3% of their basic pay to the TSP each month.

After two years of service, the government will match the member's contributions up to an additional 4%. So, after 2 years members can get up to a 5% government contribution on top of what they contribute each month.

Therefore if a member contributes 5% of their basic pay the government will match it, making a total contribution to the TSP of 10% of their basic pay.

BRS also includes a mid-career continuation pay at about 12 years of service, as a further incentive to continue serving toward the traditional 20 years to qualify for monthly military retired pay.

When you retire (at age 60 for guard/reserve members), you will be given the option to take your full retirement pay or you can take a lump-sum payment of either 25% or 50% of your gross estimated retired pay and receive a reduced monthly annuity until the age of 67 when your retirement pay goes back up to the full amount.

Current members who have less than 12 total years of service when the new plan is effective in 2018 will be able to switch over to the new system. There will be no back pay but matching contributions will begin on enrollment.

Active Duty Eligibility for the New Retirement System

If you joined active duty:

- Before January 1, 2006 - you will remain in your current retirement system
- After December 31, 2005 but before January 1, 2018 - you can choose either your current retirement system or the BRS
- After December 31, 2017 - you will be enrolled in the BRS

The opt-in/election period for the Blended Retirement System begins January 1, 2018, and concludes on December 31, 2018.

Reserve Component Member Eligibility

Reserve Component members with more than 4,320 retirement points will remain under their current retirement system. Reserve Component members with less than 4,320 retirement points as of December 31, 2017, will have the choice of whether to opt into the new Blended Retirement System or remain in the legacy retirement system. New accessions after January 1, 2018, will automatically be enrolled in the new Blended Retirement System. The opt-in/election period for the Blended Retirement System begins January 1, 2018, and concludes on December 31, 2018.

The mid-career continuation pay for reserve component members is 0.5x monthly basic pay (of active duty).

TRANSITION ASSISTANCE PROGRAM

Overview

The Transition Goals, Plans, Success program, known as Transition GPS, was created by the Department of Defense along with the Department of Defense and other partnering agencies. The goal is to provide in-depth services to servicemembers as they transition to work, life and home after the military.

EARNED SERVICES

Transition GPS delivers information about the benefits and services servicemembers have earned. Some of the offerings include:

- Pre-Separation Counseling: Before leaving the military servicemembers can receive individual assessments and one-on-one counseling with military service representatives who specialize in the transition process.

- Enhanced VA benefits briefings: Training sessions are led by trained instructors to cover what the VA offers to servicemembers, veterans, family members and services.

- Education and employment programs are offered to strengthen job skills and jump-start careers.

- VA benefits and services are offered to improve overall quality of life.

- There are other benefits designed to help transitioning service members maintain a stable home environment.

PERSONALIZED PLANS

The Transition GPS program is designed to make adjusting to post-military life easier, and all transitioning servicemembers are required to participate in the program. This includes Guard and Reserve members demobilizing after 180 days or more of active service.

Services include individual transitioning planning to create a customized roadmap that will outline career goals and steps necessary to achieve them.

Employment workshops are designed to show transitioning service members what civilian employers are looking for in applicants.

There are tailored tracks that include three optional workshops to prepare servicemembers for separation or retirement.

Through two briefings—VA Benefits I and II—learn what you need to know about VA benefits and services in a highly interactive, activity-based class attended by your peers. Information is provided through these briefings:

VA Benefits I. This is a four-hour briefing providing information on education, health care, compensation, life insurance, and home loans, as well as vocational rehabilitation and employment benefits information and counseling. The program assists you in developing a personal plan of action for using VA benefits. It's open to 50 attendees per class; spouses and family members are encouraged to attend.

VA Benefits II. This two-hour supplemental briefing with video presentations provides an overview of the eBenefits portal and further information on VA health care benefits and services and the disability compensation process.

PRE-DISCHARGE

The VA recommends disability compensation claims are submitted before separation, retirement, or release from active duty or demobilization. Processing times tend to be significantly shorter for claims submitted pre-discharge as opposed to after discharge. Pre-discharge programs provide servicemembers with the chance to file claims for disability compensation up to 180 days before separation or retirement from active duty or full-time National Guard or Reserve duty.

Benefits Delivery at Discharge (BDD)

Benefits Delivery at Discharge (BDD) lets a service member submit a claim for disability compensation 60 to 180 days before separation, retirement or release from active duty or demobilization. BDD can help veterans receive VA disability benefits sooner, with the goal of within 60 days after release or discharge.

BDD requires a minimum of 60 days to allow sufficient time to complete the medical examination process (which may involve multiple specialty clinics) prior to separation from service. If you are closer than 60 days to separation from service, you can submit a Quick Start claim. BDD is available nationwide and open to all Servicemembers on full time active duty, including members of the National Guard and Reserve. Members of the Coast Guard may also participate.

To file a pre-discharge claim under BDD, do one of the following:

- Submit your application online using eBenefits and follow the instructions about where to submit your service treatment records

- Complete the VA Form 21-526EZ, Application for Disability Compensation and Related Compensation Benefits, and submit it with copies of your service treatment records to the VA location nearest you.

- Call VA toll free at 1-800-827-1000 to have the claim form mailed to you

- Visit your local VA regional office. For the VA regional office nearest you, call VA toll-free at 1-800-827-1000.

Quick Start Program

Quick Start lets a servicemember submit a claim for disability compensation 1 to 59 days before separation, retirement or release from active duty or demobilization. Submitting a claim before discharge makes it possible to receive VA disability benefits as soon as possible after separation, retirement or demobilization.

Servicemembers with 1-59 days remaining on active duty or full time Reserve or National Guard service or servicemembers who don't receive BDD criteria requiring availability for all examinations before discharge may apply through Quick Start.

The program is available nationwide and open to all servicemembers on full time active duty including members of the National Guard and Reserves.

INTEGRATED DISABILITY EVALUATION SYSTEM

The "Integrated Disability Evaluation System (IDES) Examination" is used to determine a Servicemember's fitness for duty. The Departments of Defense (DoD) and Veterans Affairs (VA) worked together to make disability evaluation seamless, simple, fast and fair. If the Servicemember is found medically unfit for duty, the IDES gives them a proposed VA disability rating before they leave the service. IDES participants may be entitled to Vocational Rehabilitation and Employment services.

POST 9/11 GI BILL

The Post 9/11 GI-Bill can help pay for education and housing to those who:

- Have been discharged honorably.
- Have at least 90 days of aggregate service on or after September 11, 2001.
- Discharged with a service-connected disability after 30 days.

What Does the Bill Cover?

- Tuition and fees paid directly to the school is based on the maximum in-state tuition rate at a public institution of higher learning. That is the maximum coverage, unless Yellow Ribbon comes into play.
- Monthly housing allowance.
- Living expense stipend based on E-5 BAH with dependents based on the zip code of your school.
- Annual books and supplies stipend up to $1,000 paid proportionately based on enrollment.
- Can transfer to eligible dependents.

If you have served on or called to active duty after Sept. 11, 2001:

- **100%** benefit if you have at least 36 months of duty
- **100%** benefit if you have 30 days service and were discharged with a service-connected disability
- **90%** 30 to 36 month of duty
- **80%** 24 to 30 months of duty
- **70%** 18 to 24 months of duty
- **60%** 12 to 18 months of duty
- **50%** 0 to 12 months of duty

25

- **40%** 90 days to 6 months of duty

READJUSTMENT COUNSELING SERVICES

The VA operates 300 community-based counseling Vet Centers. Many providers at Vet Centers are Veterans of combat themselves. Vet Centers provide readjustment counseling and outreach services to all Veterans who served in any combat zone. Military sexual trauma counseling and bereavement counseling are also provided. Services are available for family members for military related issues, and bereavement counseling is offered for parents, spouses, and children of Armed Forces, National Guard, and Reserves personnel who died in the service of their country. Veterans have earned these benefits through their service, and all are provided at no cost to the Veteran or family.

SUBSTANCE ABUSE PROGRAMS

Some Veterans who return from combat have problems with use of alcohol, tobacco or drugs. This can include use of street drugs as well as using prescription medications in ways they weren't prescribed. Such substance use can harm health, cause mood and behavior problems, hurt social relationships, and cause financial problems. Available treatments address all types of problems related to substance use, from unhealthy use of alcohol to life-threatening addictions.

A patient coming to VA can expect to find the following types of care:
- First-time screening for alcohol or tobacco use in all care locations;
- Short outpatient counseling including focus on motivation;
- Intensive outpatient treatment;
- Residential (live-in) care;
- Medically managed detoxification (stopping substance use safely) and services to get stable;
- Continuing care and relapse prevention;
- Marriage and family counseling;
- Self-help groups;
- Drug substitution therapies and newer medicines to reduce cravings.

How To Get Help

- Speak with your existing VA healthcare provider;
- Contact the OEF/OIF Coordinator at your local VA Medical Center;
- Contact your local Vet Center;
- Call 1-800-827-1000, VA's general information hotline;

HOME LOANS

VA helps Servicemembers, Veterans, and eligible surviving spouses become homeowners. As part of our mission to serve you, VA provide a home loan guaranty benefit and other housing-related programs to help you buy, build, repair, retain, or adapt a home for your own personal occupancy.

VA Home Loans are provided by private lenders, such as banks and mortgage companies. VA guarantees a portion of the loan, enabling the lender to provide you with more favorable terms.

Benefits

Purchase Loans help you purchase a home at a competitive interest rate often without requiring a down payment or private mortgage insurance. Cash Out Refinance loans allow you to take cash out of your home equity to take care of concerns like paying off debt, funding school, or making home improvements.

Interest Rate Reduction Refinance Loan (IRRRL): also called the Streamline Refinance Loan can help you obtain a lower interest rate by refinancing your existing VA loan.

Native American Direct Loan (NADL) Program: helps eligible Native American Veterans finance the purchase, construction, or improvement of homes on Federal Trust Land, or reduce the interest rate on a VA loan.

Adapted Housing Grants: help Veterans with a permanent and total service- connected disability purchase or build an adapted home or to modify an existing home to account for their disability.

Other Resources: many states offer resources to Veterans, including property tax reductions to certain Veterans.

CHAPTER 4

DISABILITY COMPENSATION FOR SERVICE-CONNECTED DISABILITIES

BENEFIT DESCRIPTION

In grateful recognition of their dedication and sacrifice, the United States, through the Veterans Administration has provided its former servicemen and women with compensation and pension programs designed to assist disabled veterans and their dependents. The disability compensation program provides financial assistance to veterans with service-connected disabilities to compensate them for the loss of, or reduction in earning power resulting from comparable injuries and disease in civil life.

Disability compensation payments vary in amount, depending on the impairment of earning capacity suffered by the veteran. The degree is assessed in multiples of 10, from 10 percent to 100 percent, with special statutory rates for such disabilities as blindness and loss of use of limbs.

The VA shall adopt and apply a schedule of ratings in reductions in earning capacity from specific injuries or combination of injuries.

> **Key Takeaways:**
> There was a 2.0% COLA increase in 2017
>
> Disability claims ratings are based on the impairment of earning capacity suffered by veteran
>
> The Fully Developed Claim program is relatively new and lets veterans and survivors receive faster claims decisions from the VA
>
> For any veteran who served for 90 days or more during a period of war, there are certain diseases and conditions that are considered to have been incurred or aggravated during service

The rating shall be based, as far as practicable, upon the average impairments of earning capacity resulting from such injuries in civil occupations. The Administrator shall from time to time readjust this schedule or ratings in accordance with experience.

The rates of compensation payments are not automatically adjusted for inflation, and they can be increased only if Congress passes specific enabling legislation.

However, almost without exception, each Congress has acted to grant an increase equal to the consumer price in that determine the social security old-age increases.

If a veteran is evaluated as having a service-connected disability of 30 percent or more, the veteran is entitled to additional allowances for his or her dependents. In addition, in cases where a veteran has suffered certain severe disabilities, the veteran may be entitled to *special monthly compensation* (SMC), which can provide compensation payments at a rate much greater than the 100 percent rate.

Severely disabled veterans in need of regular aid and attendance, or daily health-care services may be eligible for additional compensation.

2017 Update: Decision Ready Claims

The Decision Ready Claim (DRC) Program is the fastest way to get your claim processed. With the DRC Program, you can get a decision on your claim within 30 days when you work with an accredited Veterans Service Organization (VSO).

Your VSO will help you gather and submit all relevant records and evidence, including federal and medical records and Disability Benefits Questionnaires (DBQs), and will request your VA claim exam, so your claim is ready for VA to make a decision when you submit it.

Currently, the DRC Program is available for the following types of compensation claims:

- Direct Service Connection Claims
- Presumptive Service Connection Claims
- Secondary Service Connection Claims
- Increased Disability Claims
- Dependency and Indemnity Compensation (DIC) Claims
- Pre-Discharge Claims

To file a DRC, you must have previously filed a VA claim and received a rating decision from VA on that claim (this does not include Pre-Discharge or DIC claims). You also cannot file your claim through the DRC Program if you currently have another disability claim pending, if you have an appeal pending for the condition you are claiming, or if your claim is related to pension or special monthly compensation (SMC).

You will need copies of your federal records, medical records, completed Disability Benefits Questionnaires (DBQs), and any other evidence that supports your claim. Depending on the type of DRC you're filing, you may also need copies of your Service Treatment Records (STRs), the Veteran's death certificate, and all of the Veteran's relevant medical records. Your VSO can also help you gather any medical information you are missing to make sure your claim is complete. As part of the DRC Program, VSOs can now quickly request a VA claim exam, also called a Compensation & Pension (C&P) exam, for you, if needed, before you submit your claim. Providing all relevant evidence when you submit your DRC allows VA to process your claim faster.

The DRC Program allows you to submit VA compensation claims that are decision-ready so you can get your claim processed as fast as possible.

To submit a DRC, you must:

- Appoint and work with an accredited Veterans Service Organization (VSO),
- Gather all relevant and required evidence to support your claim, and
- Attend a VA claim exam, if needed, before submitting your claim.

When you work with an accredited VSO and provide all the necessary evidence with your application, you can get a decision on your claim in 30 days or less.

The Types of Claims That Can Be Filed Through the DRC Program

Currently, the DRC Program is available for the following types of compensation claims:

- Direct Service Connection Claims: Claims for conditions that began during your military service or were caused by an event while serving.
- Presumptive Service Connection Claims: Claims for conditions that are presumed to have been caused by an event during your military service, even if there is no specific evidence showing a connection between your condition and your military service in your service records. This includes conditions related to Agent Orange, chronic disabilities, and the following conditions tied to service during the Gulf War: fibromyalgia, chronic fatigue syndrome, and functional gastrointestinal disorders.
- Secondary Service Connection Claims: Claims for conditions that were caused or aggravated by a service-connected disability.
- Increased Disability Claims: Claims for existing service-connected conditions that you have medical evidence to show have gotten worse.
- Dependency and Indemnity Compensation (DIC) Claims: Claims for surviving spouses of Veterans whose death resulted from a service-related injury or disease or who was rated 100% disabled due to service-connected conditions (including entitlement to Individual Unemployability) for 10 years prior to their death. To learn more about DIC, including eligibility requirements, go to the Dependency and Indemnity Compensation page.
- Pre-Discharge Claims: Claims for disability compensation filed by Servicemembers who have less than 90 days remaining before their separation from military service.

To file a DRC, you must have previously filed a VA claim and received a rating decision from VA on that claim (this does not include DIC and Pre-Discharge claims).

Disability Compensation DRC Eligibility

The following exclusions apply for DRC claims.
1. Waiting for a decision on a pending disability claim, unless the claim was submitted via the Benefits Delivery at Discharge (BDD) program
2. Currently appealing the condition you want to file a DRC for
3. Filing a claim for a previously denied condition
4. Rated at 100% for your condition
5. Filing a direct service connection DRC for Posttraumatic Stress Disorder (PTSD), Traumatic Brain Injury (TBI), Camp Lejeune Contaminated Water (CLCW), and conditions related to Mustard Gas or as a Former Prisoner of War (FPOW)
6. Exception: Pre-Discharge claims involving PTSD, and/or TBI may be processed under the DRC program if an in-service diagnosis has been documented on examination
7. Filing a claim for a disability incurred during a prior period of active duty for training or inactive duty for training, unless you are a Service member filing a VA claim prior to discharge
8. Filing a claim for Pension
9. An incarcerated Veteran
10. Claiming Individual Unemployability
11. Seeking Special Monthly Pension
12. Seeking only Special Monthly Compensation
13. Living outside of the U.S.
14. Submitting a DRC application without a Veteran signature
15. Filing for Chapter 18 (Spina Bifida) and any other birth defects for dependent children
16. Filing a restricted access claim (includes VBA employees, relatives of VBA

30

employees, National Service Officers, or high-ranking government officials)

Pre-Discharge DRCs
The following are exclusions from the DRC program that will lead to a Pre-Discharge claim being disqualified.

1. claims involving one or more of the factors outlined above
2. claims in which the Service member has more than 90 days remaining on active duty, unless there is a pending BDD claim
3. claims in which the Service member is currently enrolled in IDES
4. awaiting discharge while hospitalized in a VA or military treatment facility, or pregnant
5. claims requiring a character of discharge determination, and/or claims for aggravation of a condition that pre-existed service or was noted at the time of entry into service (unless evidence of pre-service baseline severity is provided).

VA Expands Provision of TBI Benefits

The VA has officially put new regulations in place, making it easier for some veterans diagnosed with traumatic brain injury (TBI) to receive additional disability compensation. The VA announced the implementation of a new regulation that impacts some veterans living with TBI who also have Parkinson's disease, certain types of dementia, depression, unprovoked seizures or certain diseases of the hypothalamus and pituitary glands.

Elimination of Income Reporting Requirement

The VA announced the removal of the annual income reporting requirement for most veterans enrolled in the VA healthcare system. Beginning in March 2014, the VA began utilizing income information as reported from the IRS and Social Security administration.

Same-Sex Married Couples

The Obama administration announced a decision to extend veteran benefits to same-sex married couples, as a result of the Supreme Court's decision to strike down the *Defense of Marriage Act*. Veterans' spouses are now eligible to collect benefits, regardless of sexual orientation.

Veterans with Spinal Cord Injuries

There are 24 VA-operated Spinal Cord Injury Centers (SCI) that provide services for Veterans with spinal cord injuries and disorders (SCI/D). Comprehensive rehabilitation, SCI/D specialty care, medical, surgical, primary, preventive, psychological, respite, and home care are provided at these centers by interdisciplinary teams which include physicians, nurses, therapists (physical, occupational, kinesio therapists, therapeutic recreation), psychologists, social workers, vocational counselors, dieticians, respiratory therapy, and other specialists as needed.

There are five SCI centers that provide long-term care for Veterans with SCI/D. In VA facilities that do not have SCI centers, there is a designated team that consists of a physician, nurse, and social worker to address primary care needs for Veterans with SCI/D and to make referrals to SCI Centers. These SCI Centers and the teams in facilities that do not have centers, comprise VA SCI System of Care. Some of the services provided in this system of care include rehabilitation, prosthetics and durable medical equipment, orthotics, sensory aids, assistive technology, environmental modifications, telehealth, ventilator weaning and care, chronic pain management, mental health treatment, drivers training, peer counseling, substance abuse treatment, vocational counseling, and caregiver training and support.

There is a long-standing memorandum of agreement between VA and the Department of

Defense (DoD) to provide specialized care at VA medical facilities for Active Duty Servicemembers who have sustained a spinal cord injury. Ongoing collaboration and education between VA and DoD ensures continuity of care and services.

WAR TIME DISABILITY COMPENSATION

Eligibility

A veteran may be entitled to VA disability compensation for any medical condition or injury that was incurred in, or aggravated by his or her military service. The veteran must have been discharged or released under conditions other than dishonorable from the period of service in which the injury or disease was incurred or aggravated. No compensation shall be paid if the disability is a result of the person's own willful misconduct or abuse of alcohol or drugs.

There is no time limit for applying for VA disability compensation. However, veterans are encouraged to apply within one year of release from active duty. If a claim is filed within this period, entitlement may be established retroactively to the date of separation from service. If a claim is filed beyond one year of release from active duty, the effective date of eligibility for benefits will be based upon the date of the claim, not the date of separation.

Individual Unemployability

There is a benefit administered by the U.S. Department of Veterans Affairs (VA) that is payable under certain conditions when a veteran has one or more service connected disabilities rated less than 100% that interfere with his or her ability to secure or retain employment. This benefit is known as Individual Unemployability (I.U.). I.U. must be established on a factual basis. establishes entitlement to compensation at the 100% disability rate even though a veteran's combined disabilities are less than a scheduler 100% rating.

Eligibility Requirements

* You must be a veteran

* You must have at least one service-connected disability rated at least 60% or

* Two or more service-connected disabilities at least one disability ratable at 40 percent or more with a combined rating of 70 percent or more

* You must be unable to maintain substantially gainful employment as a result of service-connected disabilities (marginal employment, such as odd jobs, is not considered substantial gainful employment for VA purposes)

Evidence Requirements

* Evidence of at least one service-connected disability AND

* That the service-connected disability or disabilities are sufficient, without regard to other factors, to prevent performing the mental and/or physical tasks required to get or keep substantially gainful employment AND

* That one disability is ratable at 60% or more OR

* If more than one disability exists one disability is ratable at 40% or more with a combined rating of 70% or more.

Under exceptional circumstances this benefit may be granted with a lower disability rating than noted above provided the evidence shows the service-connected disability or disabilities present such an exceptional or unusual disability picture, due to such factors as marked interference with employment or frequent periods of hospitalization, that applying the normal disability requirements is impractical.

To apply for I.U. benefits VA form 21-8940, Application for Increased Compensation Based on Unemployability, must be submitted to the VA with current medical evidence on the extent of the service connected disabilities.

VA's definition of substantial gainful employment is basically any amount earned above the annual poverty limit for one person set by the U.S. Census Bureau.

Amounts earned below the Census Bureau annual poverty limit are considered marginal employment and do not affect receipt of I.U. benefits.

Each year after the U.S. Census Bureau sets the new poverty limit, VA publishes notice in the Federal Register.

VA PENSION BENEFITS

Occasionally, a veteran may be entitled to both VA Compensation benefits, and VA Pension benefits. The VA is prohibited from paying both benefits concurrently. In the event a veteran is entitled to both, the VA will typically pay the higher of the monetary amount of the two.

SELECTED RESERVE AND NATIONAL GUARD

Since September 11, 2001, numerous members of the Armed Forces Reserves have been called to active duty. Some of these individuals had already filed claims for VA compensation, based on earlier periods of active service. In September 2004, the VA General Counsel issued a precedent opinion that discussed the effect of a return to active service on a pending disability compensation claim.

In general, a veteran's return to active duty does not affect his or her claim for VA benefits, and does not alter either the veteran's right or the VA's duty to develop and adjudicate the claim. If the veteran is temporarily unable to report for a medical examination, or take some other required action because of his or her return to active duty, the VA must defer processing the claim until the veteran can take the required action. The VA cannot deny a claim because a veteran is temporarily unavailable due to a return to active duty.

A veteran is not entitled to receive both active duty pay and VA disability compensation for the same period of time. However, the higher monetary benefit is usually paid. If a veteran with a pending claim dies on active duty before the claim is decided, an eligible survivor may be entitled to any accrued benefits payable.

FULLY DEVELOPED CLAIMS

The Fully Developed Claims (FDC) program is an optional new initiative that offers Servicemembers, Veterans, and survivors faster decisions from VA on compensation, pension, and survivor benefit claims.

Veterans, Servicemembers, and survivors simply submit all relevant records in their possession, and those records which are easily obtainable, such as private medical records, at the time they make their claim and certify that they have no further evidence to submit. VA can then review and process the claim more quickly.

By filing an FDC, Veterans, Servicemembers and survivors take charge of their claim by providing all the evidence at once. By then certifying that there is no more evidence, VA can issue a decision faster.

File an FDC without risk. Participation will not affect the attention your claim receives from qualified VA rating staff or the benefits to which you're entitled. If VA determines other records exist and are required to decide a claim, VA will simply remove the claim from the FDC program and process it through the traditional claims process. Once you initiate your FDC, you'll have up to one year to complete it. Should VA approve your claim, you'll be paid back to the day you initiated your claim.

TYPES OF CLAIMS

33

There are many types of claims for disability compensation. For example, if you're filing a VA claim for the very first time, you have an **original claim**. A **reopened claim** means you have new *and* material evidence and you want VA to reconsider a claim it once denied. There are also **new claims**, **secondary claims**, and **special claims**.

WHO CAN FILE A CLAIM

Veterans may file an FDC for disability compensation for the following reasons:

• An injury, disability, or condition believed to have occurred or been aggravated by military service.
• A condition caused or aggravated by an existing service-related condition.
• Servicemembers may use the Benefits Delivery at Discharge (BDD) program at eBenefits.va.gov to submit a Fully Developed Claim before discharge.

The BDD program is available nationwide to all Servicemembers on full-time active duty, including members of the National Guard, Reserve, and Coast Guard.

Servicemembers who do not meet the BDD criteria or have 1-59 days remaining in service should submit a Quick Start claim on eBenefits.va.gov.

WHAT'S THE BEST WAY TO FILE AN FDC?

The best way to file an FDC is electronically at eBenefits.va.gov. Once you log on to your account, VA recommends you appoint an accredited Veterans Service Officer to help you initiate your claim, gather the required medical records and evidence, and submit your claim.

If you prefer to file your FDC by paper, complete VA Form 21-526EZ and visit your local regional office. While there, you can appoint an accredited Veterans Service Officer to help you prepare and submit your claim. You can also appoint your accredited Veterans Service Officer online at eBenefits.va.gov.

MILITARY RETIRED PAY

Historically, veterans were not permitted to receive *full* military retirement pay and VA compensation benefits at the same time. Veterans who were entitled to both had to either elect one of the benefits, or waive the amount of retirement pay which equaled the amount of VA disability compensation to which he or she was entitled. This issue was commonly known as "concurrent receipt".

Because there was often a tax advantage to receive VA disability compensation, which is tax free, rather than military retirement pay, most disabled retirees chose to have a $1 reduction in their retired pay for each $1 of VA disability compensation they received. Since this type of rule against "concurrent receipt" does not apply to any other group of federal or state retirees, many individuals and service organizations felt this was unfair discrimination against disabled military retirees.

This has been a very hot topic for the last several years, and Congress and the President have taken several steps toward eliminating the bar to concurrent receipt of full military retired pay and full disability compensation.

DETAILS OF CRSC PAYMENTS

As a result of the current disability process, a retiree can have both a DOD and a VA disability rating and these ratings will not necessarily be the same percentage. The percentage determined by DOD is used to determine fitness for duty and may result in the medical separation or disability retirement of the service member. The VA rating, on the other hand, was designed to reflect the average loss of earning power.
CRSC is not subject to taxation. Individuals must apply for CRSC.

For detailed information, individuals should contact the following:

ARMY:
DEPARTMENT OF THE ARMY
U.S. Army Physical Disabilities Agency/ Combat Related Special Compensation (CRSC)
200 Stovall Street
Alexandria, VA 22332-0470
(866) 281-3254

NAVY AND MARINE CORPS:
Department of Navy Naval Council of Personnel Boards Combat-Related Special
Compensation Branch
720 Kennon Street S.E., Suite 309
Washington Navy Yard, DC
20374-5023
(877) 366-2772

AIR FORCE:
United States Air Force Personnel Center Disability Division (CRSC)
550 C Street West, Suite 6
Randolph AFB TX 78150-4708
(800) 525-0102

DETAILS OF CONCURRENT RECEIPT

As veterans, military retirees can apply to the VA for disability compensation. A retiree may (1) apply for VA compensation any time after leaving the service and (2) have his or her degree of disability changed by the VA as the result of a later medical reevaluation, as noted above. Many retirees seek benefits from the VA years after retirement for a condition that may have been incurred during military service but that does not manifest itself until many years later. Typical examples include hearing loss, some cardiovascular problems and conditions related to exposure to Agent Orange.

Until 2004, the law required that military retired pay be reduced dollar-for-dollar by the amount of any VA disability compensation received. This procedure was generally referred to as an "offset." If, for example, a military retiree who received $1,500 a month in retired pay and was rated by the VA as 70% disabled (and therefore entitled to approximately $1,000 per month in disability compensation), the offset would operate to pay $500 monthly in retired pay and the $1,000 in disability compensation.

WHAT IF A RETIREE IS ELIGIBLE FOR BOTH THE CRSC AND CONCURRENT RECEIPTPROGRAMS?

Retirees eligible for both programs will be able to make an election between the two programs, depending on which one is more advantageous.

Because the CRSC program provides full payment immediately, versus the 10—year phase in for concurrent receipt, the election can be changed each year. (This recognizes that a retiree who is 100% disabled, but only 60% of that is due to combat-related conditions, may find it advantageous to elect full CRSC payments for a few years until the concurrent receipt payment rises to a level that exceeds the CRSC payment. Because CRSC payments are tax-free, and non-disability retired pay is not, this could also figure into a retiree's election decision.

**DETAILED RATES OF DISABILITY COMPENSATION—RATES
EFFECTIVE DECEMBER 1,2017**

DISABILITY RATING

DEPENDENT STATUS	10%	20%	30%	40%	50%	60%	70%	80%	90%	100%
Veteran Alone	136.24	269.30	417.15	600.90	855.41	1083.52	1365.48	1587.25	1783.68	2973.86
Veteran & Spouse	136.24	269.30	466.15	666.90	937.41	1182.52	1481.48	1719.25	1932.68	3139.67
Veteran & Spouse & 1 Child	136.24	269.30	503.15	714.19	998.41	1255.52	1566.48	1816.25	2041.68	3261.10
Veteran & No Spouse & 1 Child	136.24	269.30	450.15	644.90	910.41	1149.52	1442.48	1675.25	1882.68	3084.75

DEPENDENT STATUS	10%	20%	30%	40%	50%	60%	70%	80%	90%	100%
Veteran & Spouse & No Children and 1 parent	136.24	269.30	505.15	719.90	1003.41	1261.52	1574.48	1825.25	2051.68	3272.73
Veteran & Spouse & 1 Child & 1 parent	136.24	269.30	542.15	767.90	1064.41	1334.52	1659.48	1922.25	2160.68	3394.16
Veteran & Spouse & No Child & 2 Parents	136.24	269.30	544.15	772.90	1069.41	1340.52	1667.48	1931.25	2170.68	3405.79
Veteran & Spouse & 1 Child & 2 Parents	136.24	269.30	581.15	820.90	1130.41	1413.52	1752.48	2028.25	2279.68	3527.22
Veteran & No Spouse & No Children & 1Parent	136.24	269.30	456.15	653.90	921.41	1162.52	1458.48	1693.25	1902.68	3106.92
Veteran & No Spouse & 1 Child & 1 Parent	136.24	269.30	489.15	697.90	967.41	1228.52	1535.48	1781.25	2001.68	3217.81
Veteran & No Spouse & No Children & 2 Parents	136.24	269.30	495.15	706.90	987.41	1241.52	1551.48	1799.25	2021.68	3239.98
Veteran & No Spouse & 1 Child & 2 Parents	136.24	269.30	528.15	750.90	1042.41	1307.52	1628.48	1887.25	2120.68	3350.87

BENEFIT RATES FOR SERVICE CONNECTED DISABILITY COMPENSATION

VA compensation and pension benefits cost of living allowance (COLA) is paid based on the Social Security Administration (SSA) COLA. By statue, compensation COLA may not be more than the SSA COLA; and pension COLA is equal to the SSA COLA.

This year SSA increased COLA by 2.0%

BASIC RATES OF DISABILITY COMPENSATION – RATES EFFECTIVE DECEMBER 1, 2017:		
Title 38, USC 1114 subsection:	Disability Rating	Monthly Benefit
(a)	10 percent	$136.24
(h)	20 percent	$269.30
(c)	30 percent	$417.15
(d)	40 percent	$600.90
(e)	50 percent	$855.41
(f)	60 percent	$1083.52
(g)	70 percent	$1365.48
(h)	80 percent	$1587.25
(i)	90 percent	$1783.68
(j)	100 percent	$2973.86

ADDITIONAL AMOUNT PAYABLE FOR SPOUSE REQUIRING AID & ATTENDANCE-RATES EFFECTIVE DECEMBER 1, 2017							
Disability Rating	30%	40%	50%	60%	70%	80%	90%	100%
Monthly Benefit	$46	$61	$76	$91	$106	$122	$137	$152.06

ADDITIONAL AMOUNT PAYABLE FOR EACH ADDITIONAL CHILD UNDER AGE 18- RATES EFFECTIVE DECEMBER 1, 2017							
Disability Rating	30%	40%	50%	60%	70%	80%	90%	100%
Monthly Benefit	$24	$32	$41	$49	$57	$65	$74	$82.38

ADDITIONAL AMOUNT PAYABLE FOR EACH ADDITIONAL CHILD OVER AGE 18 ATTENDING SCHOOL RATES EFFECTIVEDECEMBER 1, 2017							
Disability Rating	30%	40%	50%	60%	70%	80%	90%	100%
Monthly Benefit	$79	$106	$133	$159	$186	$212	$239	$266.13

Notes:

Rates for Children over age 18 attending school are shown separately in the above chart. All other entries in the above charts reflect rates for children under age 18, or helpless.

All references in the preceding charts to parents refer to parents who have been determined to be dependent by the Secretary of Veterans Affairs.

HIGHER STATUTORY AWARDS FOR CERTAIN MULTIPLE DISABILITIES

ADDITIONAL COMPENSATION FOR DEPENDENTS

(38 USC 1115)

TITLE 38, USC 1114 SUBSECTION (K)

If a veteran, as the result of a service-connected disability, has suffered the anatomical loss or loss of use of one or more creative organs, or one foot, or one hand, or both buttocks, or 25 percent or more tissue from a single breast or from both breasts in combination (loss by mastectomy or partial mastectomy or following radiation treatment), or blindness of one eye, having only light perception, or has suffered complete organic aphonia with constant inability to communicate by speech, or deafness of both ears, having absence of air and bone conduction, the rate of compensation shall be $105.61 per month for each such loss or loss of use.

In the event the veteran has suffered one or more of the disabilities previously specified in this subsection, in addition to the requirement for any of the rates specified in subsections (l) through (n), described below, the rate of compensation shall be increased by $103.61 per month for each such loss or loss of use.

TITLE 38, USC 1114 SUBSECTION (L)

If the veteran, as the result of a service-connected disability, has suffered the anatomical loss or loss of use of both feet, or of one hand and one foot, or is blind in both eyes, with 5/200 visual acuity or less, or is permanently bedridden or so helpless as to be in need of regular aid and attendance, the monthly compensation shall be $3,700.43

TITLE 38, USC 1114 SUBSECTION (M)

If the veteran, as the result of a service-connected disability, has suffered the anatomical loss or loss of use of both hands, or of both legs at a level, or with complications, preventing natural knee action with prostheses in place, or of one arm and one leg at levels, or with complications, preventing natural elbow and knee action with prostheses in place, or has suffered blindness in both eyes, having only light perception, or has suffered blindness in both eyes, rendering such veteran so helpless as to be in need of regular aid and attendance, the monthly compensation shall be $4,083.79.

TITLE 38, USC 1114 SUBSECTION (N)

If the veteran, as the result of a service-connected disability, has suffered the anatomical loss or loss of use of both arms at levels, or with complications, preventing natural elbow action with prostheses in place, has suffered the anatomical loss of both legs so near the hip as to prevent the use of prosthetic appliances, or has suffered the anatomical loss of one arm and one leg so near the shoulder and hip as to prevent the use of prosthetic appliances, or has suffered the anatomical loss of both eyes, or has suffered blindness without light perception in both eyes, the monthly compensation shall be $4,645.60.

TITLE 38, USC 1114 SUBSECTION (O)

If the veteran, as the result of a service connected disability, has suffered disability under conditions which would entitle such veteran to two or more of the rates provided in one or more subsections (l) through (n) of this section, no condition being considered twice in the determination, or if the veteran has suffered bilateral deafness (and the hearing impairment in either one or both ears is service connected) rated at 60% or more disabling, and the veteran has also suffered service-connected total blindness with 5/200 visual acuity or less, or if the veteran has suffered service-connected total deafness in one ear or bilateral deafness (and the hearing impairment in either one or both ears is service connected) rated at 40% or

39

more disabling, and the veteran has also suffered service- connected blindness having only light perception or less, or if the veterans has suffered the anatomical loss of both arms so near the shoulder as to prevent the use of prosthetic appliances, the monthly compensation shall be $5,192.65.

TITLE 38, USC 1114 SUBSECTION (P)

In the event a veteran's service-connected disabilities exceed the requirements for any of the rates previously prescribed in this section, the Secretary of Veterans Affairs may allow the next higher rate, or an intermediate rate, but in no event in excess of $5,192.65.

In the event a veteran has suffered service-connected blindness with 5/200 visual acuity or less, and (1) has also suffered bilateral deafness (and the hearing impairment in either one or both ears is service connected) rated at no less than 30% disabling, the Secretary of Veterans Affairs shall allow the next higher rate, or (2) has also suffered service- connected total deafness in one ear or service-connected anatomical loss or loss of use of one hand or one foot, the Secretary shall allow the next intermediate rate, but in no event in excess of$5,192.65.

In the event a veteran has suffered service-connected blindness, having only light perception or less, and has also suffered bilateral deafness (and the hearing impairment in either one or both ears is service-connected) rated at 10 or 20% disabling, the Secretary shall allow the next intermediate rate, but in no event in excess of $5192.65.

In the event a veteran has suffered the anatomical loss or loss of use, or a combination of anatomical loss and loss of use, of three extremities, the Secretary shall allow the next higher rate or intermediate rate, but in no event in excess of $5,192.65

Any intermediate rate under this subsection shall be established at the arithmetic mean, rounded down to the nearest dollar, between the two rates concerned.

TITLE 38, USC 1114 SUBSECTION (R)

If a veteran is entitled to compensation under (o) of this section, at the maximum rate authorized under (p) of this section, or at the intermediate rate authorized between the rates authorized under subsections (n) and (o) of this section and at the rate authorized under subsection (k) of this section, is in need of regular aid and attendance, then, in addition to such compensation:

The veteran shall be paid a monthly aid and attendance allowance at the rate of $7,419.88; or $8,510.79.

If the veteran, in addition to such need for regular aid and attendance, is in need of a higher level of care, such veteran shall be paid a monthly aid and attendance allowance at the rate of $152.06, in lieu of the allowance authorized in the previous paragraph. Need for a higher level of care shall be considered to be need for personal health-care services provided on a daily basis in the veteran's home by a person who is licensed to provide such services or who provides such services under the regular supervision of a licensed health-care professional. The existence of the need for such care shall be determined by a physician employed by the VA, or in areas where no such physician is available, by a physician carrying out such function under contract or fee arrangement based on an examination by such physician.

TITLE 38, USC 1114 SUBSECTION (S)

- If a veteran has a service-connected disability rated as total, and:
- Has additional service-connected disability or disabilities independently ratable at 60% or more; or
- By reason of such veteran's service-connected disability or disabilities, is permanently housebound, and then the monthly compensation shall be $3,328.70.

For the purposes of this subsection, the requirement of "permanently housebound" will be considered to have been met when the veteran is substantially confined to such veteran's house (ward or clinical areas, if institutionalized) or immediate premised due to a service-connected disability or disabilities which it is reasonable certain will remain throughout such veteran's lifetime.

Adjustment to Individual VA Awards

There will be no adjustment of VA awards. Special Compensation paid under 10 USC 1413 is provided under chapter 71, title 10, USC, "Computation of Retired Pay." However, it is NOT RETIRED PAY. It is to be paid from funds appropriated for pay and allowances of the recipient member's branch of service. Eligible retirees in receipt of VA disability compensation may receive this special compensation in addition to their VA disability compensation.

PRESUMPTIONS

Presumption of Sound Condition

Every veteran will be assumed to have been in sound medical condition when examined, accepted, and enrolled for service, except any defects, infirmities, or disorders noted at the time of the examination, acceptance, and enrollment, or if there is clear and unmistakable evidence showing that the injury or disease did exist before acceptance and enrollment, and the injury or disease was not aggravated by such service.

Presumptions of Service-Connection Relating to Certain Chronic Diseases and Disabilities

In the case of any veteran who served for 90 days or more during a period of war, any of the following shall be considered to have been incurred in, or aggravated by such service, notwithstanding there is no record of evidence of such disease during the period of service:

A chronic disease (detailed below), becoming manifest to a degree of 10% or more within one year from the date of separation from such service.

A tropical disease (detailed below), and the resultant disorders or disease originating because of therapy, administered in connection with such diseases, or as a preventative thereof, becoming manifest to a degree of 10% or more within one year from the date of separation from such service. Additionally, if it is shown to exist at a time when standard and accepted treatises indicate that the incubation period thereof commenced during active service, it shall be deemed to have incurred during such service.

Active tuberculosis disease developing a 10% degree of disability or more within 3 years from the date of separation from such service.

Multiple sclerosis developing a 10% degree of disability or more within seven years from the date of separation from such service.

Hansen's disease developing a 10% degree of disability or more within three years from the date of separation from such service.

CHRONIC DISEASES:
* Amyotrophic lateral sclerosis (ALS)
* Anemia, primary
* Arteriosclerosis
* Arthritis
* Atrophy, progressive muscular
* Brain hemorrhage
* Brain thrombosis
* Bronchiectasis

41

- Calculi of the kidney, bladder, or gallbladder
- Cardiovascular-renal disease, including hypertension
- Cirrhosis of the liver
- Cocidiodomycosis
- Diabetes mellitus
- Encephalitis lethargica residuals
- Endocarditis
- Endocrinopathie
- Epilepsies
- Hansen's disease
- Hodgkin's disease
- Leukemia
- Lupus erythematosus, systemic
- Myasthenia gravis
- Myelitis Myocarditis
- Nephritis
- Organic diseases of the nervous system
- Osteitis deformans (Paget's disease)
- Osteomalacia
- Palsy, bulbar
- Paralysis agitans
- Psychoses
- Purpura idiopathic, hemorrhagic
- Raynaud's disease
- Sarcoidosis
- Scleroderma
- Sclerosis, amyotrohpic lateral Sclerosis,
- multiple Syringomyelia
- Thromboangiitis obilterans (Buerger's disease)
- Tuberculosis, active
- Tumors, malignant, or of the brain or spinal cord or peripheral nerves
- Ulcers, peptil (gastric or duodenal)
- Other chronic diseases the Secretary of Veterans Affairs may add to this list.

TROPICAL DISEASES:
- Amebiasis
- Blackwater fever
- Cholera
- Dracontiasis
- Dysentery
- Filiariasis
- Hansen's disease
- Leishmaniasis, including kala-azar
- Loiasis
- Malaria
- Onchocerciasis
- Oroya fever
- Pinta
- Plague Schistosomiasis
- Yaws
- Yellow fever
- Other tropical diseases the Secretary of Veterans Affairs may add to this list.

Presumptions of Service-Connection Relating to Certain Diseases and Disabilities for Former Prisoners of War

In the case of any veteran who is a former prisoner of war, and who was detained or interned for not less than thirty days, any of the following which became manifest to a degree of 10% or more after active military, naval or air service, shall be considered to have been incurred in or aggravated by such service, notwithstanding that there is no record of such disease during the period of service:

In the case of any veteran who is a former prisoner of war, and **who was detained or interned for not less than thirty days,** any of the following which became manifest to a degree of 10% or more after active military, naval or air service, shall be considered to have been incurred in or aggravated by such service, notwithstanding that there is no record of such disease during the period of service:

- Avitaminosis
- Beriberi (including beriberi heart disease, which includes Ischemic Heart Disease-coronary artery disease-for former POWs who suffered during captivity from edema-swelling of the legs or feet- also known as "wet" beriberi)
- Chronic dysentery
- Helminthiasis
- Malnutrition (including optic atrophy associated with malnutrition)
- Pellagra
- Any other nutritional deficiency
- Peripheral neuropathy, except where directly related to infectious causes
- Irritable bowel syndrome
- Peptic ulcer disease
- Cirrhosis of the liver (This condition was added as part of *Public Law 108- 183, The Veterans Benefit Act of 2003*.)
- Atherosclerotic heart disease or hypertensive vascular disease (including hypertensive heart disease) and their complications (including myocardial infarction, congestive heart failure and arrhythmia). These conditions were added as part of *Public Law 109-233*.
- Stroke and its complications; this condition was added as part of *Public Law 109-233.*
- The *Veterans Benefits Improvement Act* added osteoporosis to the list of disabilities presumed to be service-connected (and therefore compensable through VA disability compensation) in the case of veterans who are former prisoners of war, if the Secretary determines that such veteran has post- traumatic stress disorder (PTSD).

In the case of any veteran who is a former prisoner of war, and **who was detained or interned for any period of time,** any of the following which became manifest to a degree of 10% or more after active military, naval or air service, shall be considered to have been incurred in or aggravated by such service, notwithstanding that there is no record of such disease during the period of service:

- Psychosis
- Any of the anxiety states
- Dysthymic disorder (or depressive neurosis)
- Organic residuals of frostbite, if the VA determines the veteran was interned in climatic conditions consistent with the occurrence of frostbite
- Post-traumatic osteoarthritis

Presumptions Relating to Certain Diseases Associated with Exposure to Radiation

VA may pay compensation for radiogenic diseases under two programs specific to radiation-exposed veterans and their survivors:

Statutory List

Veterans who participated in nuclear tests by the U.S. or its allies, who served with the occupation forces in Hiroshima or Nagasaki, Japan, between August 1945 and July 1946, or who were similarly exposed to ionizing radiation while a prisoner of war in Japan, are eligible for compensation for cancers specified in legislation.

The definition of radiation-risk activities was expanded in March 2002 to include service at Amchitka Island, Alaska, prior to January 1, 1974, if a veteran was exposed while performing duties related to certain underground nuclear tests.

The new definition also included service at gaseous diffusion plants located in Paducah, Ky., Portsmouth, Ohio and an area known as K25 at Oak Ridge, Tenn.

The types of cancer covered by these laws are:

All forms of leukemia

Cancer of the thyroid,

Cancer of the breast,

Cancer of the pharynx,

Cancer of the esophagus,

Cancer of the stomach,

Cancer of the small intestine,

Cancer of the pancreas,

Cancer of the bile ducts,

Cancer of the gall bladder,

Cancer of the salivary gland,

Cancer of the urinary tract,

Lymphomas (except Hodgkin's disease),

Multiple myeloma,

Primary liver cancer.

Bone Cancer

Brain Cancer

Colon Cancer

Lung Cancer

Ovary Cancer

The rules apply to those veterans who participated in "radiation-risk activities" while on active duty, during active duty for training or inactive duty training as a member of a reserve component.

Regulatory List

Disability compensation claims of veterans who were exposed to radiation in service and who develop a disease within specified time periods not specified in the statutory list are governed by regulation. Under the regulations, various additional factors must be considered in determining service-connection, including amount of radiation exposure,

44

duration of exposure, and elapsed time between exposure and onset of the disease. VA regulations identify all cancers as potentially radiogenic, as well as certain other non-malignant conditions: posterior subcapsular cataracts; non-malignant thyroid nodular disease; parathyroid adenoma; and tumors of the brain and central nervous system.

A final rule that expanded the regulatory list from more than a dozen specific cancers to add "any other cancer" (any malignancy) was published Sept. 24, 1998. The rulemaking began following a 1995 review of the radiogenicity of cancer generally by the Veterans Advisory Committee on Environmental Hazards. It concluded that, on the basis of current scientific knowledge, exposure to ionizing radiation can be a contributing factor in the development of any malignancy. VA also will consider evidence that diseases other than those specified in regulation may be caused by radiation exposure

Presumptions of Service-Connection for Diseases Associated with Exposure to Certain Herbicide Agents

A disease specified below, becoming manifest in a veteran, who, during active military, naval, or air service, served in the Republic of Vietnam during the period beginning on January 9, 1962, and ending on May 7, 1975 shall be considered to have been incurred in or aggravated by such service, notwithstanding that there is no record of evidence of such disease during the period of such service.

In 2011, the Department of Veterans Affairs published a final regulation expanding the dates when illnesses caused by herbicide exposure can be presumed to be related to Agent Orange.

Under the final regulation, published in the *Federal Register,* the VA will presume herbicide exposure for any Veteran who **served between April 1, 1968 and August 21, 1971 in** an area in or near the Korean demilitarized zone in which herbicides were applied.

The diseases referred to above are:

Acute and Subacute Peripheral Neuropathy

A nervous system condition that causes numbness, tingling, and motor weakness. Under VA's rating regulations, it must be at least 10% disabling within 1 year of exposure to Agent Orange and resolve within 2 years after the date it began.

AL Amyloidosis

A rare disease caused when an abnormal protein, amyloid, enters tissues or organs.

B Cell Leukemias

Cancers which affect B cells, such as hairy cell leukemia.

Chloracne (or Similar Acneform Disease)

A skin condition that occurs soon after dioxin exposure and looks like common forms of acne seen in teenagers. Under VA's rating regulations, chloracne (or other acneform disease similar to chloracne) must be at least 10% disabling within 1 year of exposure to Agent Orange.

Chronic Lymphocytic Leukemia

A disease that progresses slowly with increasing production of excessive numbers of white blood cells.

Diabetes Mellitus (Type 2)

A disease characterized by high blood sugar levels resulting from the body's inability to respond properly to the hormone insulin.

Hodgkin's Disease

A malignant lymphoma (cancer) characterized by progressive enlargement of the lymph nodes, liver, and spleen, and by progressive anemia.

Ischemic Heart Disease

A disease characterized by a reduced supply of blood to the heart.

Multiple Myeloma

A cancer of specific bone marrow cells that is characterized by bone marrow tumors in various bones of the body.

Non-Hodgkin's Lymphoma

A group of cancers that affect the lymph glands and other lymphatic tissue.

Parkinson's Disease

A motor system condition with symptoms that include trembling of the limbs and face and impaired balance.

Porphyria Cutanea Tarda

A disorder characterized by liver dysfunction and by thinning and blistering of the skin in sun-exposed areas. Under VA's rating regulations, it must be at least 10% disabling within 1 year of exposure to Agent Orange.

Prostate Cancer

Cancer of the prostate; one of the most common cancers among men

Respiratory Cancers

Cancers of the lung, larynx, trachea, and bronchus.

Soft Tissue Sarcoma (other than Osteosarcoma, Chondrosarcoma,

Kaposi's sarcoma, or Mesothelioma

A group of different types of cancers in body tissues such as muscle, fat, blood and lymph vessels, and connective tissues.

Each additional disease (if any) that the Secretary of the VA determines warrants a presumption of service-connection by reason of having positive association with exposure to an herbicide agent, becomes manifest within the period (if any) prescribed in such regulations in a veteran who, during active military, naval, or air service, served in the Republic of Vietnam during the period beginning on January 9, 1962 and ending on May 7, 1975, and while so serving was exposed to that herbicide agent.

Veterans having a disease referred to above, shall be presumed to have been exposed during such service to an herbicide agent containing dioxin or 2,4-dichlorophenoxyacetic acid, and may be presumed to have been exposed during such service to any other chemical compound in an herbicide agent, unless there is affirmative evidence to establish that the veteran was not exposed to any such agent during that service.

If the Secretary of the VA later determines that a previously established presumption of service-connection for one of the above diseases is no longer warranted, all veteran currently awarded compensation on the basis of the presumption shall continue to be entitled to receive compensation. Additionally, all survivors of any such veterans who were awarded dependency and indemnity compensation shall continue to be entitled to receive dependency and indemnity compensation on that basis.

Presumptions of Service-Connection for Illnesses Associated with Service in the Persian Gulf During the Persian Gulf War

Like all other veterans, veterans of the Persian Gulf War can receive service-connected compensation for mental and physical disabilities that were incurred during, or aggravated by their service in the armed forces

Recent legislation also authorized disability compensation for Persian Gulf veterans with chronic, **undiagnosed** illness resulting in a permanent disability that developed after they left the Persian Gulf.

Congress created this legislation after many Persian Gulf War veterans reported they were suffering from multi-symptom disabilities that are poorly understood by the medical profession, and may be classified as "undiagnosed" by one physician, or referred to as "chronic fatigue syndrome" by another physician.

Public Law 107-103, signed by then-President Bush on December 27, 2001, extended the presumptive period for disabilities associated with Persian Gulf War service until December 31, 2011, or such later date as prescribed by VA.

To be entitled to disability compensation due to an undiagnosed illness, the claimant must meet the following requirements:

The veteran must qualify as a Persian Gulf War veteran.

VA considers an individual to be a Persian Gulf War veteran if he or she served on active military, naval, or air service in the Southwest Asia theater of operations during the Persian Gulf War. This includes service in Iraq, Kuwait, Saudi Arabia, the neutral zone between Iraq and Saudi Arabia, Bahrain, Qatar, the United Arab Emirates, Oman, the Gulf of Aden, the Gulf of Oman, the Persian Gulf, the Arabian Sea, the Red Sea, and the airspace above these locations.

The veteran's period of service must have included service in the designated area after August 2, 1990. Since members of the armed services are still serving in the area of operations, they qualify as Persian Gulf veterans because the end date for the Persian Gulf War has not been set.

The veteran must suffer from a "qualifying chronic disability."

A "qualifying chronic disability" can be any of the following (or combination of the following):

An undiagnosed illness; A medically unexplained chronic multi-symptom illness (such as chronic fatigue syndrome, fibromyalgia, or irritable bowel syndrome) that is defined by a cluster of signs or symptoms;

Any diagnosed illness that the VA Secretary determines warrants a presumption of service connection.

VA considers disabilities to be chronic if they have existed for 6 months or more, or if they have exhibited intermittent episodes of improvement and worsening over a 6- month period. The 6-month period is measured from the earliest date that the signs or symptoms manifested.

The "qualifying chronic disability" must have appeared either during active duty in the Southwest Asia Theater of Operations during the Gulf War or it must have manifested to a degree of at least 10 percent during the presumptive period.

The following symptoms may be manifestations of an undiagnosed illness:

Fatigue

Skin disorders

Headaches

Muscle pain

Joint pain

Neurological symptoms

Neuropsychological symptoms

Symptoms involving the respiratory system

Sleep disturbances

Gastrointestinal symptoms

Cardiovascular symptoms

Abnormal weight loss

Menstrual disorders

Any poorly defined chronic multi-symptom illness of unknown etiology characterized by 2 or more of the above symptoms.

Rates of compensation depend upon the degree of disability, and follow a payment schedule that is adjusted annually and applies to all veterans. Please refer to the charts detailed earlier in this chapter for the current rates payable.

Presumptive Illnesses in Iraq, Afghanistan

In late 2010, VA the VA established new presumptions of service connection for nine specific infectious diseases associated with military service in Southwest Asia beginning on or after the start of the first Gulf War on August 2, 1990, through the conflict in Iraq and on or after September 19, 2001, in Afghanistan.

The nine diseases are: Brucellosis, Campylobacter jejuni, Coxiella burnetii (Q fever), Malaria, Mycobacterium tuberculosis, Nontyphoid Salmonella, Shigella, Visceral leishmaniasis and West Nile virus.

A veteran now only has to show service in Southwest Asia or Afghanistan and that he or she had one of the nine diseases within a certain time after service, and has a current disability as a result of that disease, subject to certain time limits for seven of the disease

LOU GEHRIG'S DISEASE AMYOTROPHIC LATERAL SCLEROSIS (ALS)

ALS is a rapidly progressive, totally debilitating, and irreversible motor neuron disease that results in muscle weakness leading to a wide range of serious disabilities, including impaired mobility. VA adapted its rules so Veterans with service- connected ALS no longer have to file multiple claims with VA for increased benefits as their condition progresses.

Prior to the new Specially Adapted Housing (SAH) regulatory change, many Veterans and Servicemembers who were rated by VA for service connected ALS, but who did not yet have symptoms debilitating enough to affect their mobility to the degree required for SAH grant eligibility, were unable to begin the process of modifying their homes to accommodate their often rapidly progressing conditions. Veterans with Lou Gehrig's or ALS are eligible for monthly VA disability compensation benefits because of a presumption of service connection established in 2008. VA amended its disability rating scale in January 2012 to assign a 100% disability evaluation for any veteran with service-connected ALS.

In 2014 the VA announced military personnel and veterans with service-connected ALS would also be presumed medically eligible for grants up to $81,080 to adapt their homes, making them eligible for the maximum grant amount.

PRESUMPTIONS REBUTTABLE

If there is affirmative evidence to the contrary, or evidence to establish that an intercurrent injury or disease which is a recognized cause of any of the diseases or disabilities mentioned in the above sections, has been suffered between the date of separation from service and the onset of any such diseases or disabilities, or if the disability is due to the veteran's own willful misconduct, payment of compensation shall not be made.

SPECIAL PROVISIONS RELATING TO CLAIMS BASED UPON EFFECTS OF TOBACCO PRODUCTS

Effective June 10, 1998, a veteran's death or disability will not be considered to have resulted from personal injury suffered, or disease contracted in the line of duty if the injury or disease is attributable to the use of tobacco products by the veteran during the veteran's service.

PEACETIME DISABILITY COMPENSATION

Basic Entitlement

A veteran may be entitled to VA disability compensation for any medical condition or injury that was incurred in, or aggravated by his or her military service, during any period other than a period of war. The veteran must have been discharged or released under conditions other than dishonorable from the period of service in which the injury or disease was incurred or aggravated.

No compensation shall be paid if the disability is a result of the person's own willful misconduct or abuse of alcohol or drugs.

Presumption of Sound Condition

Every person employed in the active military, naval, or air service during any period other than a period of war, for 6 months or more, will be assumed to have been in sound medical condition when examined, accepted, and enrolled for service, except any defects, infirmities, or disorders noted at the time of the examination, acceptance, and enrollment, or if there is clear and unmistakable evidence showing that the injury or disease did exist before acceptance and enrollment, and the injury or disease was not aggravated by such service.

Presumptions Relating to Certain Diseases

If a veteran who served in the active military, naval, or air service after December 31, 1946, during any period other than a period of war, for 6 months or more, contracts any of the following, it shall be considered to have been incurred in, or aggravated by such service, notwithstanding there is no record of evidence of such disease during the period of service:

- A chronic disease, becoming manifest to a degree of 10% or more within one year from the date of separation from such service.
- A tropical disease, and the resultant disorders or disease originating because of therapy, administered in connection with such diseases, or as a preventative thereof, becoming manifest to a degree of 10% or more within one year from the date of separation from such service. Additionally, if it is shown to exist at a time when standard and accepted treatises indicate that the incubation period thereof commenced during active service, it shall be deemed to have incurred during such service.

49

- Active tuberculosis disease developing a 10% degree of disability or more within 3 years from the date of separation from such service.
- Multiple sclerosis developing a 10% degree of disability or more within seven years from the date of separation from such service.
- Hansen's disease developing a 10% degree of disability or more within three years from the date of separation from such service.

In the case of any veteran who served for 90 days or more during a period of war, service-connection will not be granted in any case where the disease or disorder is shown by clear and unmistakable evidence to have had its inception before or after active military, naval, or air service.

Presumptions Rebuttal

If there is affirmative evidence to the contrary, or evidence to establish that an intercurrent injury or disease which is a recognized cause of any of the diseases or disabilities mentioned in the above sections, has been suffered between the date of separation from service and the onset of any such diseases or disabilities, or if the disability is due to the veteran's own willful misconduct, payment of compensation shall not be made.

Rates of Peacetime Disability Compensation

The compensation payable shall be the same as the compensation payable for Wartime Disability Compensation. Please refer to the charts presented earlier in this chapter.

Additional Compensation for Dependents

Any veteran entitled to peacetime disability compensation, and whose disability is rated as 30% or greater, will be entitled to additional monthly compensation for dependents in the same amounts payable for Wartime Disability Compensation. Please refer to the charts presented earlier in this chapter

GENERAL DISABILITY COMPENSATION PROVISIONS

How to Apply for Disability Compensation Benefits

The Department of Veteran Affairs (VA) has announced the elimination of the need for veterans to complete the Eligibility Verification Report (EVR), annually. According to the VA, this is a way of cutting the red tape for veterans, and working toward eliminating the claims backlog. The VA reports that it will implement a new process to confirm veterans benefits eligibility, and staff members that had previously been responsible for processing the old form will now focus on eliminating the compensation claims backlog.

Previously, beneficiaries had been required to complete an EVR each year in order to ensure the continuation of pension benefits. With the new change in eligibility confirmation, the VA says it will work with the Internal Revenue Service (IRS) and the Social Security Administration (SSA), to confirm eligibility for benefits.

In order to apply for disability compensation benefits from the VA, **Form 21-526EZ, Application for Disability Compensation and Related Compensation Benefits**, must be completed and returned to the VA Regional Office serving the veteran's area (refer to Chapter 36 for a listing of regional offices). In addition to the application, the following documents must be submitted:

- Service Medical Records: In order to expedite processing of the claim, if an applicant has his or her service medical records, they should be submitted with the application. If not included with the application, VA will contact the veteran's service department to obtain them.

- Other Medical Records: Any medical records from private doctors or hospitals pertaining to the claim should be submitted along with the application.

- Dependency Documents: Copies of pertinent birth, marriage, death and divorce certificates should be submitted along with the application.

- Military Discharge / DD Form 214-Copy 4-Member Copy: In order to expedite processing of the claim, if an applicant has a copy of his or her DD-214, it should be submitted with the application. If not included with the application, VA will attempt to obtain verification from the veteran's service department. Copies of missing DD Forms 214 may be obtained from:

  National Personnel Records Center

  1 Archives Dr.

  St. Louis, MO 63138

If any of the pertinent supporting evidence is not immediately available, the applicant should send in the application anyway. The date VA receives the application is important! If VA approves the claim, benefit payments usually begin from the date the application is received, regardless of when the claim is approved.

Adjudication

Adjudication means a judicial decision made by the Veterans Administration in claims filed within their jurisdiction. There is an Adjudication Division in each regional office, under the direction of an adjudication officer, who is responsible for the preparation of claims.

Upon the receipt of an original application in the Adjudication Division, it will be referred to the Authorization Unit for review and development in accordance with established procedures. All reasonable assistance will be extended a claimant in the prosecution of his or her claim, and all sources from which information may be elicited will be thoroughly developed prior to the submission of the case to the rating board. Every legitimate assistance will be rendered a claimant in obtaining any benefit to which he or she is entitled, and the veteran will be given every opportunity to substantiate his or her claim. Information and advice to claimants will be complete, and will be given in words that the average person can understand.

VA personnel must at all times give to claimants and other properly interested and recognized individuals courteous and satisfactory service which is essential to good public relations. It is incumbent upon the claimant to establish his or her case in accordance with the law. This rule, however, should not be highly technical and rigid in its application. The general policy is to give the claimant every opportunity to substantiate the claim, to extend all reasonable assistance in its prosecution, and to develop all sources from which information may be obtained. Information and advice to claimants will be complete and expressed, so far as possible, in plain language, which can be easily read and understood by persons not familiar with the subject matter.

Benefits for Persons Disabled by Treatment or Vocational Rehabilitation

Compensation shall be awarded for a qualifying additional disability or a qualifying death of a veteran in the same manner as if such additional disability or death were service-connected, provided:

The disability or death was caused by hospital care, medical or surgical treatment, or examination was furnished under any law administered by the VA, either by a VA employee, on a VA facility, and the proximate cause of the disability or death was:

- Carelessness, negligence, lack of proper skill, error in judgment, or similar

51

instance of fault on the part of the VA in furnishing the hospital care, medical treatment, surgical treatment, or examination; or

• An event not reasonably foreseeable.

• The disability or death was proximately caused by the provision of training and rehabilitation services by the VA (including a service-provider used by the VA) as part of an approved rehabilitation program.

Effective December 1, 1962, if an individual is awarded a judgment against the United States in a civil action brought pursuant to Section 1346(b) of Title 28, or enters into a settlement or compromise under Section 2672 or 2677 of Title 28 by reason of a disability or death treated pursuant to this section as if it were service-connected, then no benefits shall be paid to such individual for any month beginning after the date such judgment, settlement, or compromise on account of such disability or death becomes final until the aggregate amount of benefits which would be paid out for this subsection equals the total amount included in such judgment, settlement, or compromise.

LGBT VETERANS

The Obama administration announced a decision to extend veteran benefits to same-sex married couples, as a result of the Supreme Court's decision to strike down the *Defense of Marriage Act*. Veterans' spouses are now eligible to collect benefits, regardless of sexual orientation.

> If you have questions about services for LGBT veterans, contact the LGBT coordinator at local facilities.

LGBT Veterans are eligible for the same VA benefits as any other Veteran and will be treated in a welcoming environment. Comprehensive health services are available to LGBT Veterans including primary care, specialty care, mental health care, residential treatment and reproductive health care services. VA provides management of acute and chronic illnesses, preventive care, contraceptive and gynecology services, menopause management, and cancer screenings.

Transgender Veterans will be treated based upon their self- identified gender, including room assignments in residential and inpatient settings. Eligible transgender Veterans can receive cross- sex hormone therapy, gender dysphoria counseling, preoperative evaluations, as well as post-operative and long-term care following sex reassignment surgeries.

PERSON HERETOFORE HAVING A COMPENSABLE STATUS

The death and disability benefits outlined in this chapter, shall, notwithstanding the service requirements thereof, be granted to persons heretofore recognized by law as having a compensable status, including persons whose claims are based on war or peacetime service rendered before April 21, 1898.

AGGRAVATION

A preexisting injury or disease will be considered to have been aggravated by active military, naval, or air service, if there is an increase in disability during such service, unless there is a specific finding that the increase in disability is due to the natural progress of the disease.

CONSIDERATION TO BE ACCORDED TIME, PLACE AND CIRCUMSTANCES OF SERVICE

Consideration shall be given to the places, types, and circumstances of each veteran's service. The VA will consider the veteran's service record, the official history of each organization in which such veteran served, such veteran's medical records, and all pertinent medical and lay evidence. The provisions of *Public Law 98-542 – Section 5 of the Veterans' Dioxin and Radiation Exposure Compensation Standards Act* shall also be applied.

In the case of any veteran who engaged in combat with the enemy in active service with a military, naval, or air organization of the United States during a period of war, campaign, or expedition, the Secretary shall accept as sufficient proof of service- connection of any disease or injury alleged to have been incurred in or aggravated by such service, if consistent with the circumstances, conditions, or hardships of such service. This provision will apply even if there is no official record of such incurrence or aggravation in such service. Every reasonable doubt in such instance will be resolved in favor of the veteran.

Service-connection of such injury or disease may be rebutted only by clear and convincing evidence to the contrary. The reasons for granting or denying service-connection in each case shall be recorded in full.

DISAPPEARANCE

If a veteran who is receiving disability compensation disappears, the VA may pay the compensation otherwise payable to the veteran to such veteran's spouse, children, and parents. Payments made to such spouse, child, or parent shall not exceed the amounts payable to each if the veteran had died from a service-connected disability.

COMBINATION OF CERTAIN RATINGS

If the VA finds that a veteran has multiple disability they use a Combined Ratings Table to calculate combined disability rating. Disability ratings are not additive, meaning that if a veteran has one disability rated 60% and a second disability 20%, the combined rating is not 80%. This is because subsequent disability ratings are applied to an already disabled veteran, so the 20% disability is applied to a veteran who is already 60% disabled. The following outlines how the VA combines ratings for more than one disability:

- The disabilities are first arranged in the exact order of their severity, beginning with the greatest disability combined with use of the Combined Ratings Table.
- The degree of one disability will be read in the left column of the table, and the degree of the other in the top row, whoever is appropriate.
- The figures appearing in the space where the column and row intersect will represent the combined value of the two.
- This combined value is rounded to the nearest 10%.
- If there are more than two disabilities, the combined value for the first two will be found as previously described for two disabilities.
- The exact combined value—without yet rounding—is combined with the degree of the third disability.
- The process continues for subsequent disabilities and the final number is rounded to the nearest 10%.

Example of Combining Two Disabilities: If a Veteran has a 50 percent disability and a 30 percent disability, the combined value will be found to be 65 percent, but the 65 percent must be converted to 70 percent to represent the final degree of disability.

Similarly, with a disability of 40 percent, and another disability of 20 percent, the combined value is found to be 52 percent, but the 52 percent must be converted to the nearest degree divisible by 10, which is 50 percent.

Example of Combining Three Disabilities: If there are three disabilities ratable at 60 percent, 40 percent, and 20 percent, respectively, the combined value for the first two will be found opposite 60 and under 40 and is 76 percent. This 76 will be found in the left column, then the 20 rating in the top row. The intersection of these two ratings is 81. Thus, the final rating will be rounded to 80%.

TAX EXEMPTION

Compensation and pension may not be assigned to anyone, and are exempt from taxation (including income tax). No one can attach, levy, or seize a compensation or pension check either before or after receipt. Property purchased with money received from the government is not protected.

Disabled veterans may be eligible to claim a federal tax refund based on: an increase in the veteran's percentage of disability from the Department of Veterans Affairs (which may include a retroactive determination) **or** the combat-disabled veteran applying for, and being granted, Combat-Related Special Compensation, after an award for Concurrent Retirement and Disability.

To do so, the disabled veteran will need to file the amended return, Form 1040X, Amended U.S. Individual Income Tax Return, to correct a previously filed Form 1040, 1040A or 1040EZ. An amended return cannot be e-filed. It must be filed as a paper return. Disabled veterans should include all documents from the Department of Veterans Affairs and any information received from Defense Finance and Accounting Services explaining proper tax treatment for the current year.

Please note: It is only in the year of the Department of Veterans Affairs reassessment of disability percentage (including any impacted retroactive year) or the year that the CRSC is initially granted or adjusted that the veteran may need to file amended returns.

Under normal circumstances, the Form 1099-R issued to the veteran by Defense Finance and Accounting Services correctly reflects the taxable portion of compensation received. No amended returns would be required, since it has already been adjusted for any non-taxable awards.

If needed, veterans should seek assistance from a competent tax professional before filing amended returns based on a disability determination. Refund claims based on an incorrect interpretation of the tax law could subject the veteran to interest and/or penalty charges.

PROTECTION OF SERVICE CONNECTION

Service connection for any disability or death granted under this title which has been in force for ten or more years shall not be severed on or after January 1, 1962, unless it is shown that the original grant of service connection was based on fraud, or it is clearly shown from military records that the person concerned did not have the requisite service or character of discharge. The mentioned period shall be computed from the date determined by the VA as the date on which the status commenced for rating purposes.

PRESERVATION OF RATINGS

Public Law 88-445, approved August 19, 1964, effective the same date, amends Section 110, Title 38, U.S. Code as follows:

The law provides that a disability which has been continuously rated at or above a given percentage for 20 years or longer for the purpose of service connection compensation under laws administered by the VA shall not thereafter be rated at any lesser percentage except upon showing that the rating was based on fraud.

SPECIAL CONSIDERATION FOR CERTAIN CASES OF LOSS OF PAIRED ORGANS OR EXTREMITIES

If a veteran has suffered any of the following, the VA shall assign and pay to the veteran the applicable rate of compensation, as if the combination of disabilities were the result of a service-connected disability:

- Blindness in one eye as a result of a service-connected disability, and blindness in the other eye as a result of a non-service-connected disability not the result of the veteran's own willful misconduct; or

- The loss or loss of use of one kidney as a result of a service-connected disability, and involvement of the other kidney as a result of a non-service connected disability not the result of the veteran's own willful misconduct; or

- Total deafness in one ear as a result of a service-connected disability, and total deafness in the other ear as the result of non-service-connected disability not the result of the veteran's own willful misconduct; or

- The loss or loss of use of one hand or one foot as a result of a service-connected disability and the loss or loss of use of the other hand or foot as a result of non-service-connected disability not the result of the veteran's own willful misconduct; or

- Permanent service-connected disability of one lung, rated 50% or more disabling, in combination with a non-service-connected disability of the other lung that is not the result of the veteran's own willful misconduct.

If a veteran described above receives any money or property of value pursuant to an award in a judicial proceeding based upon, or a settlement or compromise of, any cause of action for damages for the non-service-connected disability, the increase in the rate of compensation otherwise payable shall not be paid for any month following a month in which any such money or property is received until such time as the total of the amount of such increase that would otherwise have been payable equals the total of the amount of any such money received, and the fair market value of any such property received.

PAYMENT OF DISABILITY COMPENSATION IN DISABILITY SEVERANCE CASES

The deduction of disability severance pay from disability compensation, as required by Section 1212(c) of Title 10, shall be made at a monthly rate not in excess of the rate of compensation to which the former member would be entitled based on the degree of such former member's disability, as determined on the initial Department rating.

TRIAL WORK PERIODS AND VOCATIONAL REHABILITATION FOR CERTAIN VETERANS WITH TOTAL DISABILITY RATINGS

The disability rating of a qualified veteran who begins to engage in a substantially gainful occupation after January 31, 1985, may not be reduced on the basis of the veteran having secured and followed a substantially gainful occupation unless the veteran maintains such an occupation for a period of 12 consecutive months.

("Qualified Veteran" means a veteran who has a service-connected disability or disabilities, not rated as total, but who has been awarded a rating of total of disability by reason of inability to secure or follow a substantially gainful occupation as a result of such disability or disabilities.)

Counseling services, placement, and post placement services shall be available to each qualified veteran, whether or not the veteran is participating in a vocational rehabilitation program.

ASBESTOS EXPOSURE

Veterans who were exposed to asbestos while in service and developed a disease related to asbestos exposure may receive service-connected compensation benefits.

If you served in any of the following occupations, you may have been exposed to asbestos:

mining, milling, shipyard work, insulation work, demolition of old buildings, carpentry and construction, the manufacturing and installation of products such as flooring, roofing, cement sheet, pipe products, or the servicing of friction products such as clutch facings and brake linings.

Additionally, if you served in Iraq or other countries in that region, you could have been exposed to asbestos when older buildings were damaged and the contaminant was released into the air.

Eligibility Requirements

• You must be a Veteran who was discharged under conditions other than dishonorable.

• You must have been exposed to asbestos while in military service.

• You must have a disease or disability related to the asbestos exposure that occurred in military service.

Evidence Requirements

The evidence must show asbestos exposure while in military service. This may include your military occupation specialty and/or where you were stationed

The evidence must show you have a disease or disability related to asbestos and a relationship exists between the exposure to asbestos in military service and the disease/disability.

Note: You must claim a disease or disability. Exposure, in and of itself, is not a condition that is subject to service connection.

Normally, VA will initiate a VA medical examination and request an opinion regarding the relationship of the disease or disability to asbestos exposure that occurred during military service.

NATURILIZATION

Veterans who served prior to September 11, 2001, are eligible to file for naturalization based on their U.S. military service. An applicant who served three years in the U.S. military and is a lawful permanent resident is excused from any specific period of required residence, period of residence in any specific place, or physical presence within the United States if the application for naturalization is filed while the applicant is still serving in the military or within six months of honorable discharge. Applicants who file for naturalization more than six months after termination of three years of U.S. military service may count any periods of honorable service as residence and physical presence in the United States.

Aliens and non-citizen nationals with honorable service in the U.S. armed forces during specified periods of hostilities may be naturalized without having to comply with the general requirements for naturalization. This is the only section of the Immigration and Nationality Act, as amended, which allows persons who have not been lawfully admitted for permanent residence to file an application for naturalization.

Any person who has served honorably during qualifying time may file an application at any time in his or her life if, at the time of enlistment, reenlistment, extension of enlistment or induction, such person shall have been in the United States, the Canal Zone, American Samoa or Swain's Island, or, on or after November 18, 1997, aboard a public vessel owned or operated by the United States for non-commercial service, whether or not lawful admittance to the United States for permanent residence has been granted. Certain applicants who have served in the U.S. Armed Forces are eligible to file for naturalization based on current or prior U.S. military service. Such applicants should file the N-400 Military Naturalization Packet.

CHAPTER 5

MISCELLANEOUS BENEFITS—

AUTOMOBILES, ADAPTIVE EQUIPMENT, HOUSING GRANTS, CLOTHING ALLOWANCE AND MEDAL OF HONOR PENSION

AUTOMOBILE ASSISTANCE PROGRAM

The VA offers an automobile assistance program for eligible veterans, or eligible members of the Armed Forces serving on active duty who are suffering from a disability as described below, if such disability is the result of an injury incurred or disease contracted in or aggravated in the line of duty in the active military, naval, or air service. Following are highlights of the VA program:

Financial Assistance

Qualified veterans may receive a *one-time* payment from VA of up to **$20,577.18** to be used toward the purchase of an automobile or other conveyance. The law requires that this amount be adjusted annually by the percentage increase in the Consumer Price Index.

This is available beginning 10/01/17. You must have VA approval before purchasing an automobile or adaptive equipment

> ### Key Takeaways
> Special grants are available to certain veterans with service-connected losses. These can be used for things such as making adaptations to houses and vehicles.
>
> A clothing allowance is available and is available for veterans who wear or use a prosthetic or orthopedic appliance for a service-connected disability. It's also available for veterans with certain service-connected skin conditions.
>
> The Medal of Honor Pension is a special pension a veteran receives beginning on the first day of the first month beginning after the date of the act the person was awarded the Medal for.

Eligibility Requirements for Receipt of One-Time Payment

Veterans or service members who are entitled to Disability Compensation under Chapter 11 of Title 30 due to one of the following service-connected losses:

- The loss or permanent loss of use of one or both feet; or
- The loss or permanent loss of use of one or both hands; or

- The permanent impairment of vision of both eyes of the following status:

  o Central visual acuity of 20/200 or less in the better eye, with corrective glasses, or central visual acuity of more than 20/200 if there is a field defect in which the peripheral field has contracted to such an extent that the widest diameter of visual field subtends an angular distance no greater than twenty degrees in the better eye.

Adaptive Equipment

In addition to the one-time payment described above, VA will also pay for installation of adaptive equipment deemed necessary to insure that the eligible veteran will be able to safely operate the vehicle, and to satisfy the applicable state standards of licensure.

VA will also repair, replace, or reinstall adaptive equipment determined necessary for the operation of a vehicle acquired under this program, or for the operation of a vehicle an eligible veteran may previously or subsequently have acquired.

Eligibility Requirements for Receipt of Adaptive Equipment

- The loss or permanent loss of use of one or both feet; or
- The loss or permanent loss of use of one or both hands; or
- The permanent impairment of vision of both eyes of the following status:
- Central visual acuity of 20/200 or less in the better eye, with corrective glasses, or central visual acuity of more than 20/200 if there is a field defect in which the peripheral field has contracted to such an extent that the widest diameter of visual field subtends an angular distance no greater than twenty degrees in the better eye; or
- Ankylosis (immobility) of one or both knees; or
- Ankylosis (immobility) of one or both hips.

Adaptive Equipment Available For Installation

The term adaptive equipment, means generally, any equipment which must be part of or added to a vehicle manufactured for sale to the general public in order to make it safe for use by the claimant, and to assist him or her in meeting the applicable standards of licensure of the proper licensing authority.

Following is a partial list of adaptive equipment available under this program:
- Power steering;
- Power brakes;
- Power window lifts;
- Power seats;
- Special equipment necessary to assist the eligible person into and out of the automobile or other conveyance;
- Air-conditioning equipment, if such equipment is necessary to the health and safety of the veteran and to the safety of others, regardless of whether the automobile or other conveyance is to be operated by the eligible person or is to be operated for such person by another person;
- Any modification of the size of the interior space of the automobile or other conveyance if necessary for the disabled person to enter or operate the vehicle;
- Other equipment, not described above, if determined necessary by the Chief Medical Director or designee in an individual case.

Eligible veterans are not entitled to adaptive equipment for more than 2 vehicles at any one time during any four-year period. (In the event an adapted vehicle is no longer available for use by the eligible veteran due to circumstances beyond his or her control, loss due to fire, theft, accident, etc., an exception to this four-year provision may be approved.

SPECIALLY ADAPTED HOUSING GRANT

There are three types of grants that may be payable:

Specially Adapted Housing Grants (SAH)
Special Housing Adaptations Grants (SHA)
Temporary Residence Adaptation Grants (TRA)
Specially Adapted Housing Grant (SAH)

The VA may approve a grant of not more than 50% of the cost of building, buying, or remodeling adapted homes, or paying indebtedness on homes previously acquired, up to a maximum of **$81,080.**

Public law 110-289 directed that the maximum grant amount will be adjusted annually. The amount will either increase or stay the same each year – it cannot decrease.

To qualify for this grant, veterans must be entitled to compensation for permanent and total service-connected disability due to:

- Loss or loss of use of both lower extremities, which prevents movement without the aid of braces, crutches, canes, or a wheelchair; or

Disability which includes:

- Blindness in both eyes, having only light perception; **with** Loss or loss of use of one lower extremity; or
- Loss or loss of use of one lower extremity together with:
- Residuals of organic disease or injury; **or**
- The loss or loss of use of one upper extremity, which so affects the functions of balance or propulsion as to preclude locomotion without using braces, canes, crutches, or a wheelchair.
- Loss of, or loss of use, of both upper extremities such as to preclude use of the arms at or above the elbows.
- A severe burn injury (as so determined.)

ELIGIBILITY FOR ACTIVE DUTY MEMBERS

Public Law 108-183, *The Veterans Benefits Act of 2003*, which became law on December 16, 2003, extended eligibility for the $81,080 grant to members of the Armed Forces serving on active duty who are suffering from a disability as described above, if such disability is the result of an injury incurred or disease contracted in or aggravated in the line of duty in the active military, naval, or air service.

Public Law 110-289, the *Economic and Housing Recovery Act of 2008*, dated July 30, 2008, extended eligibility for active duty servicemembers to the same extent, and made them subject to the same limitations, as veterans.

An eligible veteran or active duty service member can use his or her benefit up to three times, as long as the aggregate amount of assistance does not exceed the maximum amounts allowable.

This benefit extends to previous grant recipients, however, they cannot obtain a subsequent grant(s) to pay for adaptations made prior to June 15, 2006, or to reduce an existing mortgage principal balance for properties acquired prior to June 15, 2006.

SPECIAL HOUSING ADAPTATION GRANT (SHA)

VA may approve a grant for the actual cost, up to a maximum of $16,217, for adaptations to a veteran's residence that are determined by VA to be reasonably necessary. Public Law 110-289 directed that the maximum grant amount will be adjusted annually, based on a cost-of-construction index. The amount will either increase or stay the same each year- it cannot decrease.

The grant may also be used to assist veterans in acquiring a residence that already has been adapted with special features for the veteran's disability.

To qualify for this grant, veterans must be entitled to compensation for permanent and total service-connected disability due to:

* Blindness in both eyes, with 5/200 visual acuity or less; or

* Anatomical loss or loss of use of both hands.

TEMPORARY RESIDENCE ADAPTATIONS GRANT (TRA)

Eligible veterans and servicemembers who are temporarily residing in a home owned by a family member may also receive a Temporary Residence Adaptation (TRA) grant to help the veteran or servicemember adapt the family member's home to meet his or her special needs. While the SAH and SHA grants require ownership and title to a house, in creating the TRA, Congress recognized the need to allow veterans and active duty members who may not yet own homes to have access to the adaptive housing grant program.

VA may provide a TEMPORARY RESIDENCE ADAPTATION GRANT of up to

$35,593 (for those eligible for the $81,080 to assist a veteran in adapting a family member's home to meet the veteran's special needs.

VA may provide a TEMPORARY RESIDENCE ADAPTATION GRANT of up to

$6,355 (for those eligible for the $16,217 grant) to assist a veteran in adapting a family member's home to meet the veteran's special needs.

SUPPLEMENTAL FINANCING – LOAN GUARANTY

Veterans who have available loan guaranty entitlement may also obtain a guaranteed loan or possibly a direct loan from VA to supplement the grant to acquire a specially adapted home.

CLOTHING ALLOWANCE

In 2011, a final regulation was published in the Federal Register expanding the eligibility criteria for veterans with multiple prosthetic and orthopedic devices or those who use prescription medications for service-related skin conditions.

The new regulation provides the criteria for more than one annual clothing allowance in situations where distinct garments are affected. Payment for more than one clothing allowance for eligible veterans began in 2012.

The VA shall pay a clothing allowance of $795.21 per year (rate effective December 1, 2017 and payable beginning August 1, 2018) to each veteran who:

* Because of a service-connected disability, wears or uses a prosthetic or orthopedic appliance (including a wheelchair) which the VA determines tends to wear out or tear the clothing of the veteran; or

* Uses medication prescribed by a physician for a skin condition that is due to a service-connected disability, and which the VA determines causes irreparable damage to the veteran's outer garments.

The law further states that VA shall pay, in a lump sum, to each person who is in receipt of the Medal of Honor Pension, an amount equal to the total amount of special pension that the person would have received during the period beginning on the 1st day of the 1st month beginning after the date of the act for which the person was awarded the Medal of Honor, and ending on the last day of the month preceding the month in which the person's special pension commenced.

For each month of a period referred to in the previous paragraph, the amount of special pension payable shall be determined using the rate of special pension that was in effect for such month.

The Secretary of the Department of the Army, the Department of the Navy, the Department of the Air Force, or the Department of Transportation will determine the eligibility of applicants to be entered on the Medal of Honor Roll and will deliver to the Secretary of the Department of Veterans Affairs a certified copy of each certificate issued in which the right of the person named in the certificate to the special pension is set forth. The special pension will be authorized on the basis of such certification.

The special pension will be paid in addition to all other payments under laws of the United States. However, a person awarded more than one Medal of Honor may not receive more than one special pension.

The Medal of Honor Pension rate was changed 12/01/2017 to $1,329.52

CHAPTER 6

PENSION: NON-SERVICE CONNECTED DISABILITY

BENEFIT DESCRIPTION

Non-Service Connected Disability Pension is a Department of Veterans Affairs benefits program that provides financial support to wartime veterans having limited income. The amount payable under this program depends on the type and amount of income the veteran and family members receive from other sources. Monthly payments are made to bring a veteran's total annual income (including other retirement and Social Security income) to an established support level. (Unreimbursed medical expenses may reduce countable income.)

DEFINITIONS

Indian Wars: means the campaigns, engagements, and expeditions of the United States military forces against Indian tribes or nations, service in which has been recognized heretofore as pensionable service.

Key Takeaways

VA Pension programs are available for certain low-income veterans

Pensions are based on annual income limitations set each year. Annual income limitations for veterans alone start at $13,166 for 2018.

Pension programs covered in this chapter include Improved Pension, Section 306 Pensions, and Old Law Pensions

---

World War I: means the period April 6, 1917, through November 11, 1918. In the case of a veteran who served with the United States military forces in Russia, the ending date is April 1, 1920. Service after November 11, 1918 and before July 2, 1921 is considered World War I for compensation or pension purposes, if the veteran served in the active military, naval, or air service after April 5, 1917 and before November 12, 1918

Civil War Veteran: includes a person who served in the military or naval forces of the Confederate States of America during the Civil War, and the term "active military or naval service" includes active service in those forces

Period of War: means the Mexican border period, World War I, World War II, the Korean conflict, the Vietnam era, the Persian Gulf War, and the period beginning on the date of any future declaration of war by the Congress and ending on the date prescribed by Presidential proclamation or concurrent resolution of the Congress.

Permanently and Totally Disabled: for the purposes of this chapter, a person shall be considered to be permanently and totally disabled if such person is unemployable as a result of a disability reasonably certain to continue throughout the life of the disabled person, or:

- Suffering from any disability which is sufficient to render it impossible for the average person to follow a substantially gainful occupation, but only if it is reasonably certain that such disability will continue throughout the life of the disabled person; or

- Suffering from any disease or disorder determined by the VA Secretary to be of such a nature or extent as to justify a determination that persons suffering are permanently and totally disabled; or

- Is a patient in a nursing home for long-term care because of disability; or

- Is disabled, as determined by the Social Security Administration (SSA) for purpose of benefits administered by the SSA; or

- Is unemployable, as a result of suffering from any disability which is sufficient to render it impossible for the average person to follow a substantially gainful occupation, but only if it is reasonable certain that such disability will continue throughout the life of the person, or otherwise justifying a determination of permanent and total disability.

Regular Aid and Attendance: for the purposes of this chapter, a person shall be considered to be in need of regular aid and attendance if such person is:

- A patient in a nursing home; or

- Helpless or blind, or so nearly helpless or blind as to need or require the aid and attendance of another person.

Permanently Housebound: for the purposes of this chapter, the requirement of "permanently housebound" will be considered to have been met when the veteran is substantially confined to such veteran's house (ward or clinical areas, if institutionalized) or immediate premises due to a disability or disabilities, which it is reasonably certain will remain throughout such veteran's lifetime.

Annual Income: In determining annual income under this chapter, all payments of any kind or from any source (including salary, retirement or annuity payments, or similar income, which has been waived, irrespective of whether the waiver was made pursuant to statue, contract, or otherwise) shall be included except:

- Donations from public or private relief or welfare organizations;

- Payments under this chapter;

- Amounts equal to amounts paid by a spouse of a veteran for the expenses of such veteran's last illness, and by a surviving spouse or child of a deceased veteran for:

- Such veteran's just debts;

- The expenses of such veteran's last illness; and

- The expenses of such veteran's burial to the extent such expenses are not reimbursed through Chapter 23 of Title 38, United States Code (Burial Benefits);

Amounts equal to amounts paid:

- By a veteran for the last illness and burial of such veteran's deceased spouse or child; or

- By the spouse of a living veteran or the surviving spouse of a deceased veteran for the last illness and burial of a child of such veteran;

- Reimbursements of any kind for any casualty loss, but the amount excluded under this clause may not exceed the greater of the fair market value or reasonable replacement value of the property involved at the time immediately preceding the loss;

• Profit realized from the disposition of real or personal property other than in the course of a business;

• Amounts in joint accounts in banks and similar institutions acquired by reason of death of other joint owner;

• Amounts equal to amounts paid by a veteran, veteran's spouse, or surviving spouse, or by or on behalf of a veteran's child for unreimbursed medical expenses, to the extent that such amounts exceed 5% of the maximum annual rate of pension (including any amount of increased pension payable on account of family members but not including any amount of pension payable because a person is in need of regular aid and attendance, or because a person is permanently housebound) payable to such veteran surviving spouse, or child.

   • In the case of a veteran or surviving spouse pursuing a course of education or vocational rehabilitation or training, amounts equal to amounts paid by such veteran or surviving spouse for such course of education or vocational rehabilitation or training, including:

   • Amounts paid for tuition, fees, books, and materials; and

      • In the case of such a veteran or surviving spouse in need of regular aid and attendance, unreimbursed amounts paid for unusual transpiration expenses in connection with the pursuit of such course of education or vocational rehabilitation or training, to the extent that such amounts exceed the reasonable expenses which would have been incurred by a nondisabled person using an appropriate means of transportation (public transportation, if reasonably available); and

In the case of a child, or any current-work income received during the year, to the extent that the total amount of such income does not exceed an amount equal to the sum of:

• The lowest amount of gross income for which an income tax return is required under section 6012(a) of the Internal Revenue Code of 1986, to be filed by an individual who is not married, is not a surviving spouse, and is not a head of household; and

• If the child is pursuing a course of postsecondary education or vocational rehabilitation or training, the amount paid by such child for such course of education or vocational rehabilitation or training, including the amount paid for tuition, fees, books, and materials.

ELIGIBILITY

Veteran was discharged from service under other than dishonorable conditions; and Veteran served 90 days or more of active duty with at least 1 day during a period of war time. However, 38 CFR 3.12a requires that anyone who enlisted after 9/7/80 generally has to serve at least 24 months or the full period for which a person was called or ordered to active duty in order to receive any benefits based on that period of service; and Veteran is permanently and totally disabled, or is age 65 or older; and

Veteran's countable family income is below a yearly limit set by law.

IMPROVED PENSION ANNUAL RATES- EFFECTIVE DECEMBER 1, 2017	
STATUS OF VETERAN:	**ANNUAL LIMIT**
Permanently & totally disabled veterans:	
Veteran alone	$13,166.00
Veteran with one dependent	17,241.00
Each additional dependent child	2,250.00
Veteran – Aid and Attendance:	
Veteran alone	21,962.00
Veteran with one dependent	26,036.00
Each additional dependent child	2,250.00
Veteran –Housebound:	
Veteran alone	16,089.00
Veteran with one dependent	20,166.00
Each additional dependent child	2,250.00
Two veterans married to one another:	17,241.00
Each additional dependent child	2,250.00
Add for Mexican Border Period or World War I Veterans:	2,991.00
Child Earned Income Exclusion effective 1-1-2018 –$10,650	

If eligible, VA pays the difference between a recipient's countable family income and the annual income limit set by law (see following charts) for his or her status. This difference is generally paid in 12 equal monthly installments.

FAMILY INCOME LIMITS

Maximum Annual Income Limitations for Protected Pensions Effective December 1, 2017

Pensioners entitled to benefits as of December 31, 1978, who do not elect to receive a pension under the Improved Pension Program, may continue to receive pension benefits at the rates they were entitled to receive on December 31, 1978 or June 30, 1960, as long as they remain permanently and totally disabled, do not lose a dependent, and their income does not exceed the income limitation, adjusted annually.

PENSION LAW IN EFFECT ON DECEMBER31, 1978 (SECTION306):

The rate entitled to on December 31, 1978 may be continued if the recipients IVAP for 2017 is below the following limits:

STATUS OF RECIPIENT:	ANNUAL INCOME LIMITATION:
Veteran / widow with no dependents	$14,974.00 or less
Veteran / widow with one or more dependent	$20,128.00 or less
Child (no entitled veteran or surviving spouse)	$12,244.00 or less
Veteran with no dependents in receipt of A&A	$15,513.00 or less
Veteran with one dependent in receipt of A&A	$20,666.00 or less
Surviving spouse's income exclusion	$4,782.00

PENSION LAW IN EFFECT ON JUNE30,1960 (OLDLAW):

The rate entitled to on June 30, 1960 may be continued if the recipients IVAP for 2017 is below the following limits:

STATUS OF RECIPIENT:	ANNUAL INCOMELIMITATION:
Veteran / widow with no dependents	$13,112.00
Veteran / widow with one or more dependents	$18,899.00
Child /no entitled veteran or surviving	$13,112.00

Monthly benefit payable to eligible veterans receiving disability pension under laws in effect June 30, 1960 or December 31, 1978

VETERAN'S ENTITLEMENT:	RATE PAYABLE:
Basic Rates	$66.15
10 Years or Age 65	78.75
If Entitled To Aid & Attendance	135.45
If Entitled To Housebound	100.00

66

Veterans can apply for a Pension by completing VA Form 21-527EZ. If available, the applicant should attach copies of dependency records (marriage and children's birth certificates) and current medical evidence (doctor and hospital reports). The completed form should be sent to the veteran's VA Regional Office. If any of the pertinent supporting evidence is not immediately available, the applicant should send in the application anyway. The date VA receives the application is important!

If VA approves the claim, benefit payments usually begin from the date the application is received, regardless of when the claim is approved.

Net Worth Limitation

Net worth means the net value of the assets of the veteran and dependents. It includes such assets as bank accounts, CD's, stocks, bonds, mutual funds, and any real estate other than the personal residence and a reasonable lot area. There is no set limit on how much net worth a veteran and dependents can have, but net worth cannot be excessive. Each case is decided individually. The life expectancy of the claimant, the available income, and the cost of unreimbursed medical and care costs are taken into consideration.

Combination of Ratings

The VA shall provide that, for the purpose of determining whether or not a veteran is permanently and totally disabled, ratings for service-connected disabilities may be combined with ratings for non-service-connected disabilities.

Where a veteran is found to be entitled to a Non-Service-Connected Disability Pension, and is also entitled to Service-Connected Disability Compensation, the VA shall pay the veteran the greater benefit.

Vocational Training for Certain Pension Recipients

In the case of a veteran who is awarded a Non-Service-Connected Disability Pension, the VA shall, based on information on file with the VA, make a preliminary finding whether such veteran, with the assistance of a vocational training program, has a good potential for achieving employment. If such potential is found to exist, the VA shall solicit from the veteran an application for vocational training. If the veteran thereafter applies for such training, the VA shall provide the veteran with an evaluation, which may include a personal interview, to determine whether the achievement of a vocational goal is reasonably feasible.

If the VA, based on the evaluation, determines that the achievement of a vocational goal by a veteran is reasonably feasible, the veteran shall be offered, and may elect to pursue a vocational training program.

If the veteran elects to pursue such a program, the program shall be designed in consultation with the veteran in order to meet the veteran's individual needs, and shall be set forth in an individualized written plan of vocational rehabilitation.

A vocational training program under this section:

- May not exceed 24 months unless, based on a determination by the VA that an extension is necessary in order for the veteran to achieve a vocational goal identified in the written plan formulated for the veteran, the VA grants an extension for a period not to exceed 24 months.
- May not include the provision of any loan or subsistence allowance, or any automobile adaptive equipment.
- May include a program of education at an institution of higher learning, only in a case in which the Secretary of the VA determines that the program involved is predominantly vocational in content.
- When a veteran completes a vocational training program, the VA may provide the veteran with counseling, placement and post-placement services for a period not to exceed 18 months.

A veteran may not begin pursuit of a vocational training program under this chapter after the later of:

- December 31, 1995; or
- The end of a reasonable period of time, as determined by the VA, following either the evaluation of the veteran or the award of pension to the veteran.

In the case of a veteran who has been determined to have a permanent and total non-service-connected disability and who, not later than one year after the date the veteran's eligibility for counseling under this chapter expires, secures employment within the scope of a vocational goal identified in the veteran's individualized written plan of vocational rehabilitation (or in a related field which requires reasonably developed skills, and the use of some or all of the training or services furnished the veteran under such plan), the evaluation of the veteran as having a permanent and total disability may not be terminated be reason of the veteran's capacity to engage in such employment until the veteran first maintains such employment for a period of not less than 12 consecutive months.

Protection of Healthcare Eligibility

In the case of a veteran whose entitlement to pension is terminated after January 31, 1985, by reason of income from work or training, the veteran shall retain for a period of three years, beginning on the date of such termination, all eligibility for care and services that the veteran would have had if the veteran's entitlement to pension had not been terminated.

Disappearance

When a veteran receiving a non-service-connected disability pension from the VA disappears, the VA may pay the pension otherwise payable to such veteran's spouse and children. Payments made to a spouse or child shall not exceed the amount to which each would be entitled if the veteran died of a non-service-connected disability.

CHAPTER 7

SURVIVOR BENEFITS:
DEPENDENCY AND INDEMNITY COMPENSATION FOR SERVICE-CONNECTED DEATHS

Dependency and Indemnity Compensation (DIC) payments may be available for:

Surviving spouses who have not remarried

Surviving spouses who remarry after attaining age 57

Unmarried Children under 18; Helpless children;

Children between 18 and 23, if attending a VA-approved school; and

Low-income parents of deceased servicemembers or veterans.

DEFINITIONS

Veteran: in this chapter, the term includes a person who died in the active military, naval, or air service.

Social Security Increase: in this chapter, the term means the percentage by which benefit amounts payable under Title II of the Social Security Act (42 U.S.C. 401 et seq.) are increased for any fiscal year as a result of a determination under section 215(i) of such Act (42 U.S.C. 415(i)).

Permanently Housebound: for the purposes of this chapter, the requirement of "permanently housebound" will be considered to have been met when the individual is substantially confined to such individual's house (ward or clinical areas, if institutionalized) or immediate premises due to a disability or disabilities, which it is reasonably certain will remain throughout such individual's lifetime.

ELIGIBILITY

To receive Dependency and Indemnity Compensation (DIC), an individual must be an eligible survivor of a veteran who died from:
- A disease or injury incurred or aggravated while on active duty or active duty for training; or

> **Key Takeaways**
>
> DIC is a tax-free benefit paid to eligible survivors of servicemembers or veterans.
>
> To apply, VA Form 21-534EZ must be completed. This form is "Application for Dependency and Indemnity Compensation, Death Pension and Accrued Benefits by a Surviving Spouse or Child."
>
> Effective 12/1/17 the Basic Monthly Rate is $1,283.11

- An injury incurred or aggravated in the line of duty while on inactive duty training; or
- A disability compensable by VA.

The death cannot be a result of the veteran's willful misconduct.

DIC also may be authorized for survivors of veterans who at the time of death, were determined to be totally disabled as a result of military service, even though their service-connected disabilities did not cause their deaths. The survivor qualifies if:
- The veteran was continuously rated totally disabled for a period of 10 or more years immediately preceding death; or
- The veteran was so rated for a period of at least five years from the date of military discharge; or
- The veteran was a former prisoner of war who died after Sept. 30, 1999, and who was continuously rated totally disabled for a period of at least one year immediately preceding death.

To qualify as an eligible survivor, an individual must have proof of the following:
- Proof that he or she was married to the veteran for at least 1 year (Note: If a child was born, there is no time requirement); AND
- Proof that the marriage was VALID; AND
- Proof that he or she lived with the veteran continuously until his/her death or, if separated, the surviving spouse wasn't at fault; AND
- Proof that he or she did not remarry. (Note: The remarriage of the surviving spouse of a veteran shall not bar the furnishing of DIC if the remarriage is terminated by death, divorce, or annulment, unless the VA determines that the divorce or annulment was secured through fraud or collusion.)

Public Law 108-183, The Veterans Benefits Act of 2003, restored DIC eligibility, effective January 1, 2004, for surviving spouses who remarry after age 57. Qualifying spouses who remarried at age 57 or older prior to enactment of this bill had until December 16, 2004 to apply for reinstatement of these benefits. No retroactive benefits will be paid for any period prior to January 1, 2004.

OR

The individual is an unmarried child of a deceased veteran; AND

The individual is under age 18, or between the ages of 18 and 23 and attending school.

Note: Certain helpless adult children and some parents of deceased veterans are entitled to DIC. Call VA at (800) 827-1000 for the eligibility requirements for these survivors.

AMOUNT OF DIC PAYMENTS TO SURVIVING SPOUSES

Surviving spouses of veterans who died after January 1, 1993, receive a basic monthly rate of **$1,283.11 (effective December 1, 2017)**

Surviving spouses entitled to DIC based on the veteran's death prior to January 1, 1993, receive the greater of:

The basic monthly rate of **$1,283.11 or**

An amount based on the veteran's pay grade. (See following sections for Pay Grade tables and Determination of Pay Grade.)

There are additional DIC payments for dependent children. (Refer to the following charts.)

ADDITIONAL ALLOWANCES FOR SURVIVING SPOUSES

Add **$272.46** to the basic monthly rate if, at the time of the veteran's death, the veteran was in receipt of, or entitled to receive compensation for a service- connected disability rated totally disabling (including a rating based on individual unemployability) for a continuous period of at least 8 years immediately preceding death AND the surviving spouse was married to the veteran for those same 8 years.

Add **$317.87** per child to the basic monthly rate for each dependent child under age 18.

If the surviving spouse is entitled to Aid & Attendance, add **$317.87** to the basic monthly rate.

If the surviving spouse is Permanently Housebound, add **$148.91** to the basic monthly rate

SURVIVING SPOUSEDIC RATES IF VETERAN'S DEATH WAS PRIOR TO JANUARY 1, 1993			
	Monthly Rate	Pay Grade	Monthly Rate
E-1*:	$1283.11	W-4**:	1534.46
E-2*:	1283.11	O-1**:	1354.93
E-3*(see footnote#1):	1283.11	O-2**:	1401.40
E-4*:	1283.11	O-3**:	1497.49
E-5*:	1283.11	O-4:	1587.25
E-6*:	1283.11	O-5:	1746.72
E-7**:	1327.47	O-6:	1969.56
E-8**:	1401.40	O-7:	2125.84
E-9**(see footnote#2):	1461.59 OR 1577.76	O-8:	2334.95
W-1**:	1354.93	O-9:	2497.58
W 2**:	1408.78	O-10 (see footnote#3):	2739.41 OR 2940.07
W-3**:	1449.97		

Footnotes to Table:

* Add \$272.46 if veteran rated totally disabled 8 continuous years prior to death, and surviving spouse was married to veteran those same 8years.

A surviving spouse of an Aviation Cadet or other service not covered by this table is paid the DIC rate for enlisted E-3 under 34.

\$1577.76 is for a veteran who served as Sergeant Major of the Army or Marine Corps, Senior Enlisted Advisor of the Navy, Chief Master Sergeant of the Air Force, or Master Chief Petty Officer of the CoastGuard.

\$2940.07 is for a veteran who served as Chairman of the Joint Chiefs of Staff, Chief of Staff of the Army or Air Force, Chief of Naval Operations, or Commandant of the Marine Corps.

DETERMINATION OF PAY GRADE

With respect to a veteran who died in the active military, naval, or air service, such veteran's pay grade shall be determined as of the date of such veteran's death, or as of the date of a promotion after death, while in a missing status.

With respect to a veteran who did not die in the active military, naval, or air service, such veteran's pay grade shall be determined as of:

- The time of such veteran's last discharge or release from active duty under conditions other than dishonorable; or
- The time of such veteran's discharge or release from any period of active duty for training or inactive duty training, if such veteran's death results from service-connected disability incurred during such period, and if such veteran was not thereafter discharged or released under conditions other than dishonorable from active duty.
- If a veteran has satisfactorily served on active duty for a period of six months or more in a pay grade higher than that specified in the previous paragraphs of this section, and any subsequent discharge or release from active duty was under conditions other than dishonorable, the higher pay grade shall be used if it will result in greater monthly payments to such veteran's surviving spouse under this chapter. The determination as to whether an individual has served satisfactorily for the required period in a higher pay grade shall be made by the Secretary of the department in which such higher pay grade washeld.

DIC PAYMENTS TO CHILDREN

Whenever there is no surviving spouse of a deceased veteran entitled to DIC, DIC shall be paid in equal shares to the children of the deceased veteran at the following monthly rates (effective December 1, 2017):

Number of Children	Total Payable (to be divided in equal shares):
1	\$541.76
2	779.37
3	1016.99
4	1210.26

5	1403.53
6	1596.80
7	1790.07
8	1983.34

If DIC is payable monthly to a person as a surviving spouse, and there is a child (of such person's deceased spouse) who has attained the age of 18, and who, while under such age, became permanently incapable of self-support, DIC shall be paid monthly to each such child, concurrently with the payment of DIC to the surviving spouse, in the amount of **$541.76.**

If DIC is payable monthly to a person as a surviving spouse, and there is a child (of such person's deceased spouse) who has attained the age of 18 and who, while under the age of 23, is pursuing a course of instruction at a VA-approved educational institution, DIC shall be paid monthly to each such child, concurrently with the payment of DIC to the surviving spouse, in the amount of **$269.30**

DIC PAYMENTS FOR PARENTS

Parents whose child died in-service or from a service-connected disability may be entitled to DIC if they are in financial need. Parents may be biological, step, adopted, or *in loco parentis*. The monthly payment for parents of deceased veterans depends upon their income. The following 3 charts outline the monthly rates payable, **effective December 1, 2017,** under various conditions.

Chart #1 Sole Surviving Parent Unremarried or Remarried Living With Spouse			
Income Not Over:	*Monthly*	*Income Not Over:*	*Monthly Rate:*
$ 800	$634	$ 2,500	$ 498
900	626	2,600	490
1,000	618	2,700	482
1,100	610	2,800	474
1,200	602	2,900	466
1,300	594	3,000	458
1,400	586	3,100	450
1,500	578	3,200	442
1,600	570	3,300	434

1,700	562	3,400	426
1,800	554	3,500	418
1,900	546	3,600	410
2,000	538	3,700	402
2,100	530	3,800	394
2,200	522	3,900	386
2,300	514	4,000	378
2,400	506	4,100	370

Income Not Over:	Monthly Rate:	Income Not Over:	Monthly Rate:
$4,200	$362	$6,300	$194
4,300	354	6,400	186
4,400	346	6,500	178
4,500	338	6,600	170
4,600	330	6,700	162
4,700	322	6,800	154
4,800	314	6,900	146
4,900	306	7,000	138
5,000	298	7,100	130
5,100	290	7,200	122
5,200	282	7,300	114
5,300	274	7,400	106
5,400	266	7,500	98
5,500	258	7,600	90
5,600	250	7,700	82

5,700	242	7,800	74
5,800	234	7,900	66
5,900	226		
6,000	218	If A&A add:	343
6,100	210	If living w/ spouse: 20,128	
6,200	202	**If not living w/ spouse: 14,974	

Chart#2- One of Two Parents Not Living With Spouse			
Income Not Over:	*Monthly Rate:*	*Income Not Over:*	*Monthly Rate:*
$800	$459	$3,600	$235
900	451	3,700	227
1,000	443	3,800	219
1,100	435	3,900	211
1,200	427	4,000	203
1,300	419	4,100	195
1,400	411	4,200	187
1,500	403	4,300	179
1,600	395	4,400	171
1,700	387	4,500	163
1,800	379	4,600	155
1,900	371	4,700	147
2,000	363	4,800	139
2,100	355	4,900	131
2,200	347	5,000	123
2,300	339	5,100	115
2,400	331	5,200	107
2,500	323	5,300	99
2,600	315	5,400	91
2,700	307	5,500	83
2,800	299	5,600	75
2,900	291	5,700	67

76

3,000	283	5,800	59
3,100	275	5,900	51
3,200	267	6,000	43
3,300	259	6475 to 14,974	5
3,400	251		
3,500	243	If A&A add:	$343

Chart #3 1 of 2 Parents Living with Spouse or Other Parent			
Income Not Over:	*Monthly Rate:*	*Income Not Over:*	*Monthly Rate:*
$1,000	$431	$4,000	$252
1,100	420	4,100	244
1,200	417	4,200	236
1,300	414	4,300	228
1,400	411	4,400	220
1,500	408	4,500	212
1,600	404	4,600	204
1,700	400	4,700	196
1,800	396	4,800	188
1,900	392	4,900	180
2,000	387	5,000	172
2,100	382	5,100	164
2,200	377	5,200	156
2,300	372	5,300	148
2,400	367	5,400	140
2,500	361	5,500	132
2,600	355	5,600	124
2,700	349	5,700	116
2,800	343	5,800	108
2,900	337	5,900	100

3,000	330	6,000	92
3,100	323	6,100	84
3,200	316	6,200	76
3,300	308	6,300	68
3,400	300	6,400	60
3,500	292	6,500	52
3,600	284	6,600	44
3,700	276	6,800	28
3,800	268	6,900	20
3,900	259	If A&A add:	343

Miscellaneous Information Regarding Income Limitations for Parents

The VA may require, as a condition of granting or continuing DIC to a parent that such parent, other than one who has attained 72 years of age, and has been paid DIC during 2 consecutive calendar years, file for a calendar year with the VA, a report showing the total income which such parent expects to receive in that year, and the total income which such parent received in the preceding year. The parent or parents shall notify the VA whenever there is a material change in annual income.

In determining income under this section, all payments of any kind, or from any source shall be included except:
- Payments of a death gratuity;
- Donations from public or private relief or welfare organizations;
- Payments under this chapter (DIC), Chapter 11 of *Title 38, United States Code* (Disability Compensation), and *Chapter 15 of Title 38, United States Code* (Non-Service Connected Disability/Death Pension);
- Payments under policies of servicemembers group life insurance, United States Government life insurance, or national service life insurance, and payments of servicemen's indemnity;
- 10% of the amount of payments to an individual under public or private retirement, annuity, endowment, or similar plans or programs;

- Amounts equal to amounts paid by a parent of a deceased veteran for:
    - A deceased spouse's just debts;
    - The expenses of the spouse's last illness, to the extent such expenses are not reimbursed under Chapter 51 of Title 38 of the United States Code;
    - The expenses of the spouse's burial to the extent that such expenses are not reimbursed under Chapter 23 or Chapter 51 of *Title 38 of the United States Code*;
    - Reimbursements of any kind for any casualty loss (as defined in regulations which the VA shall prescribe), but the amount excluded under this clause may not exceed the greater of the fair market value or the reasonable replacement value of the property involved at the time immediately preceding the loss;
- Amounts equal to amounts paid by a parent of a deceased veteran for:
    - The expenses of the veteran's last illness, and expenses of such veteran's burial, to the extent that such expenses are not reimbursed under Chapter 23 of *Title 38 of the United States Code*;
    - Profit realized from the disposition of real or personal property other than in the course of a business;
    - Payments received for discharge of jury duty or obligatory civic duties;
    - Payments of annuities elected under Subchapter I of Chapter 73 of *Title 10*.

Where a fraction of a dollar is involved, annual income shall be fixed at the next lower dollar. The VA may provide by regulation for the exclusion from income under this section of amounts paid by a parent for unusual medical expense

SPECIAL PROVISIONS RELATING TO SURVIVING SPOUSES

No Dependency and Indemnity Compensation shall be paid to the surviving spouse of a veteran dying after December 31, 1956, unless such surviving spouse was married to such veteran:
- Before the expiration of 15 years after the termination of the period of service in which the injury or disease causing the death of the veteran was incurred or

aggravated; or
- For one year or more; or
- For any period of time if a child was born of the marriage, or was born to them before the marriage.

APPLYING FOR DEPENDENCY AND INDEMNITY COMPENSATION

Eligible surviving spouses and dependent children can apply for DIC by completing VA Form 21P-534ez, "Application for Dependency and Indemnity Compensation or Death Pension by Surviving Spouse or Child". If available, copies of dependency records (marriage records, divorce records, & children's birth certificates) should be attached to the application. A copy of the veteran's DD Form 214 and a copy of the veteran's death certificate should also be included with the completed application.

> **Note:**
> If any of the pertinent supporting evidence is not immediately available, the applicant should send in the application anyway. The date VA receives the application is important!
> If VA approves the claim, benefit payments usually begin from the date the application is received, regardless of when the claim is approved.

The completed form should be sent to the applicable VA Regional Office (refer to Chapter 36 for a listing of all VA regional offices.)

CHAPTER 8

SURVIVOR BENEFITS: DEATH PENSIONS

A Death Pension is a benefit paid to eligible dependents of deceased wartime veterans.

DEFINITIONS

Veteran: as used in this chapter, includes a person who has completed at least 2 years of honorable active military, naval, or air service, as certified by the appropriate authority, but whose death in such service was not in line of duty.

Indian Wars: means the campaigns, engagements, and expeditions of the United States military forces against Indian tribes or nations, service in which has been recognized heretofore as pensionable service.

World War I: means the period April 6, 1917, through November 11, 1918. In the case of a veteran who served with the United States military forces in Russia, the ending date is April 1, 1920. Service after November 11, 1918 and before July 2, 1921 is considered World War I for compensation or pension purposes, if the veteran served in the active military, naval, or air service after April 5, 1917 and before November 12, 1918.

> **Key Takeaways**
>
> Certain eligible dependents may qualify for a death pension
>
> Pension rates are based on a Maximum Annual Pension Rate
>
> The MAPR for 2017 starts at an annual income requirement of less than $8,830.00 for a surviving spouse alone

Civil War Veteran: includes a person who served in the military or naval forces of the Confederate States of America during the Civil War, and the term "active military or naval service" includes active service in those forces.

Period of War: means the Mexican border period, World War I, World War II, the Korean conflict, the Vietnam era, the Persian Gulf War, and the period beginning on the date of any future declaration of war by the Congress and ending on the date prescribed by Presidential proclamation or concurrent resolution of the Congress.

Regular Aid and Attendance: for the purposes of this chapter, a person shall be considered to be in need of regular aid and attendance if such person is:

- A patient in a nursing home; or
- Helpless or blind, or so nearly helpless or blind as to need or require the aid and attendance of another person.

Permanently Housebound: for the purposes of this chapter, the requirement of "permanently housebound" will be considered to have been met when the surviving spouse is substantially confined to such surviving spouse's house (ward or clinical areas, if institutionalized) or immediate premises due to a disability or disabilities, which it is reasonably certain will remain throughout such surviving spouse's lifetime.

ELIGIBILITY REQUIREMENTS

Eligible dependents may qualify for a Death Pension if:
* For service on or before September 7, 1980, the veteran must have served at least 90 days of active military service, with at least one day during a war time period
* If he or she entered active duty after September 7, 1980, generally he or she must have served at least 24 months or the full period for which called or ordered to active duty with at least one day during a war time period
* Was discharged from service under other than dishonorable condition
* The dependent is the surviving spouse (spouse must not have remarried), or the unmarried child of the deceased veteran (children must be under age 18, or under age 23 if attending a VA-approved school); **AND**
* The dependent's countable income is below an annual limit set by law (See below for 2017 annual income limitations.)

(Children who become incapable of self-support because of a disability before age 18 may be eligible for a pension as long as the condition exists, unless the child marries or the child's income exceeds the applicable limit.)

ANNUAL INCOME LIMITATIONS

DEATH PENSION RATE TABLE FOR SURVIVING SPOUSES & CHILDREN- Rates Effective December 1, 2017	
Maximum Annual Pension Rate (MAPR)Category	Annual Income Must Be Less Than:
Surviving Spouse Alone (No Dependent Child):	$8,830.00
Surviving Spouse With One Dependent Child:	11,557.00
Child Alone:	2,250.00
Housebound Spouse Without Dependents:	10,792.00
Housebound Spouse With One Dependent:	13,514.00
Surviving Spouse In Need Of Aid And Attendance (No Dependent Child):	14,113.00
Surviving Spouse In Need Of Aid And Attendance With One Dependent Child:	16,837.00
For Each Additional Child:	2,250.00
Child Earned Income Exclusion Effective 1/1/2018:	10,650.00

MAXIMUM ANNUAL INCOME LIMITATIONS FOR PROTECTED PENSIONS

Effective December 1, 2017

Pensioners entitled to benefits as of December 31, 1978, who do not elect to receive a pension under the Improved Pension Program, may continue to receive pension benefits at the rates they were entitled to receive on December 31, 1978 or June 30, 1960, as long as they remain permanently and totally disabled, do not lose a dependent, and their income does not exceed the income limitation, adjusted annually.

PENSION LAW IN EFFECT ON DECEMBER 31,1978 (SECTION306):

The rate entitled to on December 31, 1978 may be continued if the recipient's IVAP for 2017 is below the following limits:

STATUS OF RECIPIENT:	ANNUAL INCOME LIMITATION:
Surviving spouse with no dependents	$14,974.00
Surviving spouse with one or more dependents	$20,128.00
Child (no entitled veteran or surviving spouse)	$12,244.00

PENSIONLAW IN EFFECT ON JUNE 30,1960 (OLDLAW):

The rate entitled to on June 30,1960 may be continued if the recipient's IVAP for 2017 is below the following limits:

STATUS OF RECIPIENT:	ANNUAL INCOME LIMITATION:
Surviving spouse with no dependents	13,112.00
Surviving spouse with one or more dependents	18,899.00
Child only (no entitled veteran or surviving spouse)	13,112.00

Note: Some income is not counted toward the yearly limit (for example, welfare benefits, some wages earned by dependent children, and Supplemental Security Income).

In determining the annual income of a surviving spouse, if there is a child of the veteran in the custody of the surviving spouse, that portion of the annual income of the child that is reasonably available to or for the surviving spouse shall be considered to be income of the surviving spouse, unless in the judgment of the VA, to do so would work a hardship on the surviving spouse.

NET WORTH LIMITATION

The VA shall deny or discontinue payment of pension to a surviving spouse when the corpus of the estate of the surviving spouse is such that under all the circumstances, including consideration of the income of the surviving spouse and the income of any child from whom the surviving spouse is receiving increased pension, it is reasonable that some part of the corpus of such estate be consumed for the surviving spouse's maintenance.

The VA shall deny or discontinue the payment of increased pension on account of a child when the corpus of such child's estate is such that under all the circumstances, including consideration of the income of the surviving spouse and such child and the income of any other child for whom the surviving spouse is receiving increased pension, it is reasonable that some part of the corpus of the child's estate be consumed for the child's maintenance. During the period such denial or discontinuance remains in effect, such child shall not be considered as the surviving spouse's child for purposes of this chapter.

The VA shall deny or discontinue payment of pension to a child when the corpus of the state of the child is such that under all the circumstances, including consideration of the income of the child, the income of any person with whom such child is residing who is legally responsible for such child's support, and the corpus of the estate of such person, it is reasonable that some part of the corpus of such estate be consumed for the child's maintenance.

APPLYING FOR DEATH PENSION BENEFITS

Eligible surviving spouses and dependent children can apply for Death Pension benefits by completing VA Form 21P-534EZ, "Application for Dependency and Indemnity Compensation or Death Pension by Surviving Spouse or Child". If available, copies of dependency records (marriage & children's birth certificates) should be attached to the application. A copy of the veteran's DD Form 214 and a copy of the veteran's death certificate should also be included with the completed application.

The completed forms should be sent to the applicable VA Regional Office.

CHAPTER 9

SURVIVOR BENEFITS:
MISCELLANEOUS BENEFITS FOR
SURVIVING SPOUSES AND CHILDREN

SURVIVOR BENEFIT PLAN (SBP)

Military retired pay stops upon death of retiree, and the Survivor Benefit Plan (SBP), allows a retiree to ensure after death a continuous lifetime annuity for their dependents. The annuity is based on a percentage of retired pay and is called SBP—which is paid to an eligible beneficiary. It pays your eligible survivors an inflation-adjusted monthly income.

A military retiree pays premiums for SBP coverage upon retiring. Premiums are paid from gross retired pay, so they don't count as income. This means less tax and less out-of-pocket costs for SBP. The premiums are partially funded by the government and the costs of operating the program are absorbed by the government, so the average premiums are well below the cost for a conventional insurance policy. For most retirees, SBP is a good choice, but the government contribution is based on assumptions in average cases and may not apply equally to every situation.

The maximum SBP annuity for a spouse is based on 55 percent of the member's retired pay (or in the case of a member who retires under REDUX, the retired pay the member would have received if under the high-three retirement system). However, a smaller amount may be elected.

> **Key Takeaways**
>
> The Survivor Benefit Plan is an elective program providing monthly income to survivors of retired military personnel.
>
> The Special Survivor Indemnity Allowance (SSIA) was increased in 2016, but expires in 2018.
>
> Certain surviving spouses of military retirees who didn't participate in the Survivor Benefit plan and who died before September 21, 1973 are eligible for the SBP-MIW.
>
> There are benefits available for the children of women Vietnam veterans born with certain birth defects. The monthly allowance paid to the child is determined through a schedule rating defects and disabilities.

Your base amount can be any amount from full coverage down to as little as $300 a month. Full coverage is based on your full retired pay meaning your spouse will receive **55%** of your retirement pay. If you select lesser coverage then your spouse will receive 55% percent of your elected "base amount."

Note: A surviving spouse's SBP annuity is reduced when they reach age 62 and become eligible for Social Security. This is called the Social Security offset. In the past the offset reduced the SBP annuity to 35 percent of the base amount. The offset created a need for members to purchase a Supplemental Survivor Benefit Plan (SSBP) policy. Fortunately the *National Defense Authorization Act of 2005* established a phase out of the offset by 2008, thus eliminating the need for the SSBP. Details of the *National Defense Authorization Act of 2005* are described below.

PHASED-IN INCREASE IN BASICANNUITY

One major provision of the Ronald W. Reagan FY2005 *National Defense Authorization Act* included an increase in the minimum SBP annuity for survivors age 62 and older from 35% to 55% over a 3-yearperiod.

The FY 2005 *Defense Authorization Act* included provisions to eliminate the social security offset under SBP by increasing the annuities paid to survivors of military retirees who are 62 or older from 35 percent of retired pay to the percentages indicated below:

For months after:

September 2005 and before April 2006:	40%
For months after March 2006 and before April 2007:	45%
For months after March 2007 and beforeApril2008:	50%
For months after March 2008:	55%

Note: *Public Law 108-183, The Veterans Benefits Act of 2003* provided that, for surviving spouses who remarry after attaining age 57, Dependency and Indemnity Compensation (DIC) be paid with no reduction of certain other Federal benefits to which a surviving spouse might be entitled. This provision, in essence eliminates the requirement for DIC to offset military SBP annuities, as was required under prior law. In other words, concurrent receipt of DIC and SBP without an offset of either is now allowed for surviving spouses who remarry after attaining age 57.

WHAT IS THE DIFFERENCE BETWEEN DIC AND SBP?

Dependents Indemnity Compensation (DIC), is an entitlement benefit paid to eligible survivors including spouses and married children of certain deceased servicemembers and veterans. The DIC benefit is managed by the Department of Veterans Affairs, and is dispersed to surviving family members that meet specific criteria. The Survivor Benefit Program is a voluntary annuity program managed by the Department of Defense.

WHAT IS THE SBP/DIC OFFSET?

DIC is a payment made by the Department of Veteran Affairs (DVA) to the spouse of a member who dies due to a service-connected illness or injury. The DVA determines entitlement to and the amount of the DIC award. If DIC is awarded, the SBP/RCSBP annuity must be reduced by the amount of the DIC award. The SBP/RCSBP annuity is terminated if the DIC is greater than the SBP/RCSBP. However, if an annuitant receives DIC based on a member other than the one providing SBP/RCSBP, there will not be a DIC reduction.

Each annuitant signs a DIC authorization statement when they submit their annuity application. This allows DFAS to establish their SBP/RCSBP annuity prior to notification from the DVA regarding their entitlement to DIC. This prevents delays in SBP/RCSBP payments.

If DIC is awarded, the following conditions apply:

• If the monthly DIC benefit exceeds the SBP/RCSBP monthly annuity, the amount of thesBP/RCSBP annuity paid prior to notification of the DIC award, not including the month of death, is an overpayment. If the DIC monthly benefit does not exceed the SBP/RCSBP monthly annuity, the amount of SBP overpayment will be the amount of DIC awarded prior to notification. See number 3 for more information on overpayments.

• Once Defense Finance and Accounting Services (DFAS) receives all of the necessary information from the DVA, the annuitant will be due a refund of all or part of the SBP/RCSBP costs paid into the plan by the member (SBP/RCSBP cost refund) if the DIC award is made retroactive to the date of death. The SBP/RCSBP cost refund will be applied to any SBP/RCSBP overpayment or other indebtedness, and a check for the remaining balance, if any, will be forwarded to the annuitant. The SBP/RCSBP cost refund may be taxable if the retiree paid the SBP/RCSBP costs from the retired pay taxable income. Any taxable portion of the cost refund will be included as taxable income on the TD Form 1099-R annuitants receive at the end of the year.

• Depending on the amount of the overpayment, it will either be collected from the SBP/RCSBP cost refund, referred to the DVA for collection from the annuitant's DIC payment, or combination of both. Annuitants will be advised of the method of collection and sent an account statement showing the SBP/RCSBP cost refund less any overpayment collected when the SBP/RCSBP cost refund is processed.

• Annuitant's taxable income will be increased by the taxable portion of the cost refund and reduced by the amount applied to the overpayment. The taxable income will be adjusted when the overpayment is collected. An annuitant may receive a tax deduction or tax credit, as appropriate, if the overpayment occurred.

• Since SBP/RCSBP costs are not paid by members who die while on active duty, or by Reservist who dies before retirement, there will be no refund of costs. The overpayments will be referred to the DVA for collection from the annuitant's DIC.

• Annuitants can reduce the amount of the SBP/RCSBP overpayment by notifying DFAS at once when DIC has been awarded. Please furnish DFAS a copy of the award letter from the DVA.

• Since DIC benefits are nontaxable, VA encourages annuitants to apply for DIC if they have not done so.

• If the DIC effective date is past the first day of the month after the member's death and the annuitant has received benefit from receipt of the SBP/RCSBP, no cost refund is due.

SPECIAL SURVIVOR INDEMNITY ALLOWANCE (SSIA)

Section 644 of the *National Defense Authorization Act (NDAA) for Fiscal Year 2008* created the Special Survivor Indemnity Allowance (SSIA). This allowance is payable to all Survivor Benefit Plan (SBP) annuitants whose annuity has been offset for receipt of Dependency and Indemnity Compensation (DIC) from the Department of Veterans Affairs (DVA). The benefit increased from $275 to $310 in October 2016. **SSIA Payments terminate after FY 2018.**

This allowance is taxable. Your DIC payment address will be used for your SSIA payment. If you are currently receiving your DIC payment from the DVA at your home address, your SSIA payment will also be sent there. If your DIC payment is paid via electronic funds transfer (EFT) by the DVA, your DIC electronic payment address will be used for the SSIA payment.

Questions concerning this allowance may be directed to the Cleveland Center at 1-800- 321-1080, between 7 a.m. and 7:30 p.m., Eastern Time, Monday through Friday, or write to Defense Finance and Accounting Service, U.S. Military Annuitant Pay, P.O. Box 7131, London, KY 40742-7131.

SURVIVOR BENEFIT PLAN – MINIMUM INCOME ANNUITY

Eligible surviving spouses of military retirees who did not participate in the plan, and who died prior to September 21, 1973 are eligible for SBP-MIW (Survivor Benefit Plan – Minimum Income Annuity). To be eligible the surviving spouse must not be remarried, must be eligible for VA death pension, and must have income for VA purposes, excluding any SBP annuity, of less than the MIW- SBP annuity limitation. **Effective December 1, 2017, the SBP-MIW annuity limitation is $8,830.00**

BENEFITS FOR CHILDREN OF WOMEN VIETNAMVETERANS BORN WITH CERTAIN BIRTH DEFECTS

Section 401 of *P.L. 106-416*, which became law on November 1, 2000 directed the Secretary of VA to identify birth defects of children of female Vietnam veterans that: (1) are associated with service during the Vietnam era; and (2) result in the permanent physical or mental disability of such children. The law excludes from such defects familial or birth- related defects or injuries. The law further directs the Secretary to provide to such children necessary health care to address the defect and any associated disability. It authorizes the Secretary to provide vocational training to such a child if the achievement of a vocational goal is reasonably feasible. The law also directs the Secretary to pay a monthly allowance to such a child, the amount to be determined through a schedule rating the various defects and disabilities and their degrees. The receipt of such allowance shall not infringe upon the right to receive any other benefit to which the individual is entitled. Such allowance shall not be considered income for purposes of other veterans' benefits for which income limitations exist. In the case of an eligible child whose only covered birth defect is spina bifida, a monetary allowance shall be paid under these provisions only. An eligible individual shall be provided only one program of vocational training.

The monthly allowance is set at four levels, depending upon the degree of disability suffered by the child.

CHILDREN OF WOMEN VIETNAM VETERANS BORN WITH CERTAIN BIRTH DEFECTS (P.L 106-419)- RATES EFFECTIVE 12-01-2017	
Disability Level	*Monthly Allowance*
Level I	$148.00
Level II	$321.00
Level III	$1097.00
Level IV	$1869.00

SURVIVORS' FREQUENTLY ASKED QUESTIONS

1. How do I apply for benefits?

The application for VA Survivors Benefits involves the claimant completing the appropriate forms and supplying the necessary documentation. Applications are then sent to the appropriate VA Regional Office or Pension Management Center for processing.

It is strongly recommended that claimants make duplicate copies of their application for their own records.

2. How do I reinstate my previous benefit?

If your DIC benefit as a surviving spouse was terminated because you remarried, but the subsequent marriage has since ended due to death, divorce, or annulment, you may file to have your previous Survivor's benefit reinstated.

To do so, you will be asked to complete VA form 21-4138 and submit it to your local VA Regional Office along with documentation supporting the claim that your subsequent marriage has ended (i.e., divorce decree or death certificate). After doing so, call the Veterans Benefits Administration directly at **800-827-1000** to confirm that your materials have been received and to find out the status of your reinstatement.

3. Is there someone that can help me file my claim?

Yes. You have two options available. You may seek assistance at your local VA regional office. Another option is to locate a Veteran Service Organizations (VSO) or County Veteran Service Officers (CVSO) throughout the United States. Many VSOs offer to surviving families' benefits counseling and assistance with the application process, and often have local chapters.

It is strongly recommended that surviving family members consult with the VSO of their choice when applying for VA Survivor Benefits.

4. As a survivor, am I eligible for my loved one's month of death compensation?

The Department of Veterans Affairs (VA) announced immediate actions to quickly identify and pay surviving spouses who are eligible to receive the deceased veteran's VA compensation or pension benefit for the month of the veteran's death.

This benefit is only payable to surviving spouses of veterans who were receiving VA compensation or pension benefits at the time of their death.

Because VA does not always know if a veteran is survived by a spouse, some surviving spouses have not received the month-of-death benefit to which they are entitled.

5. As a surviving spouse, am I eligible for VA medical care?

The Department of Veterans Affairs offers CHAMPVA healthcare coverage to family members that meet specific eligibility criteria. The Civilian Health and Medical Program of the Department of Veterans Affairs (CHAMPVA) is a comprehensive health care program in which the VA shares the cost of covered health care services and supplies with eligible beneficiaries. The program is administered by Health Administration Center and our offices are located in Denver, Colorado.

Due to the similarity between CHAMPVA and the Department of Defense (DoD) TRICARE program (sometimes referred to by its old name, CHAMPUS) the two are often mistaken for each other. CHAMPVA is a Department of Veterans Affairs program whereas TRICARE is a regionally managed health care program for active duty and retired members of the uniformed services, their families, and survivors.

In some cases a veteran or survivor may look to be eligible for both/either program on paper. However, if you are a military retiree, or the spouse of a veteran who was killed in action, you are and will always be a TRICARE beneficiary, you cannot choose between the two.

CHAPTER 10

BURIAL AND MEMORIAL BENEFITS

BURIAL, HEADSTONE & PLOT RATE TABLES EFFECTIVE 10/1/2017

Benefits	Rate	Date Rate Changed	Public Law
Headstone/Marker	$137	10-01-2008	PL 95-476
	$136	10-01-2007	
	$132	10-01-2006	
	$128	10-01-2005	
	$113	10-01-2004	
	$112	10-01-2003	
	$101	10-01-2002	
	$109	10-01-2001	
	$94	10-01-2000	
Service-Connected Burial	*$2,000	12-1-2001	PL 107-103
	$1,500	04-01-1988	PL 100-322
Non-Service Connected Burial	$762	10-01-2017	PL 111-275
	$749	10-01-2016	PL 111-275
	$747	10-01-2015	PL 100-322
	$745	10-01-2014	
	$734	10-01-2013	
	$722	10-01-2012	
	$700	10-01-2011	
	$300	04-01-1988	
Plot Allowance	$762	10-01-2017	PL 111-275
	$749	10-01-2016	PL 107-103
	$747	10-01-2015	PL 100-322
	$745	10-01-2014	
	$734	10-01-2013	
	$722	10-01-2012	
	$700	10-01-2011	
	$300	12-01-2001	
	$150	04-01-1988	

State Cemetery	$762	10-01-2017	PL 111-275
Plot Allowance	$749	10-01-2016	PL 107-103
	$747	10-01-2015	PL 100-322
	$745	10-01-2014	
	$734	10-01-2013	
	$722	10-01-2012	

Note 1: The P.L. 107-103 service-connected burial rate applies in cases where death occurred on or after 9/11/01.

Note 2: The headstone/marker allowance is payable only if the veteran died between 10/18/78 and 11/1/90. The rate payable is determined by when the headstone/marker was purchased.

Note 3: For non-service connected deaths, VA will pay up to $749 toward burial and funeral expenses (if hospitalized by VA at time of death), or $300 toward burial and funeral expenses (if not hospitalized by VA at time of death).

2017 UPDATE:
PRE-NEED BURAL ELIGIBILITY

The Department of Veterans Affairs (VA) implemented the pre-need burial eligibility determination program to assist anyone who would like to know if they are eligible for burial in a VA national cemetery. VA is promoting pre-need eligibility determinations to encourage Veterans and their eligible family members to plan in advance to use VA burial benefits that Veterans have earned through their military service. Planning in advance for a Veteran's or loved-one's final resting place can eliminate unnecessary delays and reduce stress on a family at a difficult time. Veteran families will have increased confidence that their loved ones are eligible for burial in a VA national cemetery at their time of need.

Upon request VA will make eligibility determinations for burial in a VA national cemetery in advance of need. Eligible individuals are entitled to burial in any open VA national cemetery which includes opening/closing of the grave, a government-furnished grave liner, perpetual care of the gravesite, and a government-furnished upright headstone or flat marker or niche cover all at no cost to the family. Veterans are also eligible for a burial flag and Presidential Memorial Certificate.

Burial in a VA national cemetery is open to all members of the armed forces and Veterans who have met minimum active duty service requirements, as applicable by law and were discharged under conditions other than dishonorable. Members of the reserve components of the armed forces who die while on active duty under certain circumstances or who die while on training duty are also eligible for burial, as are service members and former service members who were eligible for retired pay at the time of their death. Spouses, minor children and, under certain conditions, dependent unmarried adult children are also eligible for burial even if they predecease the Veteran.

The Department of Veterans Affairs (VA) has implemented this pre-need eligibility program so that Veterans, spouses and unmarried dependent adult children may better prepare for burial in a VA national cemetery prior to the time of need. Interested individuals may submit VA Form 40-10007, Application for Pre-Need Determination of Eligibility for Burial in a VA National Cemetery, along with a copy of supporting documentation of military service such as a DD214, if readily available, by: toll-free fax at 1-855-840-8299; or mail to the National Cemetery Scheduling Office, P.O. Box 510543, St. Louis, MO 63151.

Authorized representatives can also apply on behalf of eligible claimants. An authorized agent or representative is an individual authorized by the claimant to make decisions on the claimant's behalf. An authorized representative first needs to be recognized by VA as an authorized representative or agent by filing a VA Form 21-22 Appointment of Veterans Service Organization As Claimant Representative or VA Form 21-22a Appointment of Attorney Or Agent As Claimant Representative. You can access the forms at www.vba.va.gov/pubs/forms/VBA-21-22-ARE.pdf and VA Form 21-22a at www.vba.va.gov/pubs/forms/VBA-21-22A-ARE.pdf. Written authorization should be included with the VA Form 40-10007, Application for Pre-Need Determination of Eligibility for Burial in a VA National Cemetery, if available. A notarized statement is not required.

VA will review pre-need burial applications and provide written notice of a determination of eligibility. VA will store the pre-need application, supporting documentation, and the decision letter to expedite burial arrangements at the time of need. We encourage you to keep the decision letter with supporting documentation with your important papers in a safe place and to discuss you burial wishes and final arrangements with your loved ones or other representatives. Submission of a pre-need burial eligibility application does not obligate the Veteran or family member to burial in a VA national cemetery.

Applicants may indicate a preference for a VA national cemetery on the application form, but a pre-need determination of eligibility does not guarantee burial in a specific VA national cemetery or a specific gravesite. VA assigns gravesites in cemeteries with available space once death has occurred and the burial is scheduled.

At your time of need, your next-of-kin, funeral home or other representative responsible for making your final arrangements should contact the National Cemetery Scheduling Office at (800) 535-1117 to request burial. VA will locate your pre-need decision letter and validate our determination. Because laws affecting VA burial eligibility and individual circumstances may change, upon receipt of a burial request, VA will verify pre-need decisions in accordance with the laws in effect at that time including bars to receipt of burial benefits.

BURIAL BENEFITS

Beginning July 7, 2014 VA changed its monetary burial benefits regulations to simplify the program and pay eligible survivors more quickly and efficiently. These regulations will authorize VA to pay, without a written application, most eligible surviving spouses basic monetary burial benefits at the maximum amount authorized in law through automated systems rather than reimbursing them for actual costs incurred.

The new burial regulations will permit VA to pay, at a flat rate, burial and plot or interment allowances thereby enabling VA to automate payment of burial benefits to most eligible surviving spouses and more efficiently process other burial benefit claims. The burial allowance for a non-service-connected death is $300, and $2,000 for a death connected to military service.

BENEFIT
Service-related Death

VA will pay up to $2,000 toward burial expenses for deaths on or after September 11, 2001, or up to $1,500 for deaths prior to September 11, 2001. If the Veteran is buried in a VA national cemetery, some or all of the cost of transporting the deceased may be reimbursed.

Non-service-related Death

VA will pay up to $762 toward burial and funeral expenses for deaths on or after October 1, 2017 (if hospitalized by VA at time of death), or $300 toward burial and funeral expenses (if not hospitalized by VA at time of death), and a $762 plot-interment allowance (if not buried in a national cemetery).

For deaths on or after December 1, 2001, but before October 1, 2011, VA will pay up to $300 toward burial and funeral expenses and a $300 plot-interment allowance. For deaths on or after April 1, 1988 but before October 1, 2011, VA will pay $300 toward burial and funeral expenses (for Veterans hospitalized by VA at the time of death).

An annual increase in burial and plot allowances for deaths occurring after October 1, 2011 begins in fiscal year 2013 based on the Consumer Price Index for the preceding 12- month period.

Eligibility Requirements

- You paid for a Veteran's burial or funeral, AND
- You have not been reimbursed by another government agency or some other source, such as the deceased Veteran's employer,AND
- The Veteran was discharged under conditions other than dishonorable, AND
- The Veteran died because of a service-related disability, OR
- The Veteran was receiving VA pension or compensation at the time of death,
- OR The Veteran was entitled to receive VA pension or compensation, but decided not to reduce his/her military retirement or disability pay, OR
- The Veteran died while hospitalized by VA, or while receiving care under VA contract at a non-VA facility, OR
- The Veteran died while traveling under proper authorization and at VA expense to or from a specified place for the purpose of examination, treatment, or care, OR
- The Veteran had an original or reopened claim pending at the time of death and has been found entitled to compensation or pension from a date prior to the date or death, OR
- The Veteran died on or after October 9, 1996, while a patient at a VA-approved state nursing home.

NOTE: VA does not pay burial benefits if the deceased:

- Died during active military service,OR
- Was a member of Congress who died while holding office, OR
- Was a Federal prisoner

Evidence Requirements:

- Acceptable proof of death as specified in 38 CFR 3.211, AND
- Receipted bills that show that you made payment in whole or part, OR
- A statement of account, preferably on the printed billhead of the funeral director or cemetery owner.

The statement of account must show:

- The name of the deceased Veteran for whom the services and merchandise were furnished, AND
- The nature and cost of the services and merchandise,AND
- All credits, AND
- The amount of the unpaid balance, if any

You can apply online at Vets.gov or submit a paper application by completing VA Form 21P-530, Application for Burial Allowance. When completed, mail it to the Pension Management Center that serves your state. You can also work with an accredited representative or go to your local regional benefit office.

DIGNIFIED BURIAL OF UNCLAIMED VETERANS ACT

On December 30, 2012, the *Dignified Burial of Unclaimed Veterans Act of 2012* was sent the President for signature into law. The law contains the following provisions:

Cemetery Matters: The bill authorizes the Secretary of Veterans Affairs (VA) to furnish a casket or urn for a deceased veteran with no known living kin.

Veterans Freedom of Conscience Protection: Under the bill, in cases where family or the next of kin of a deceased veteran can be identified, the bill requires the VA to ensure that the expressed wishes of the next of kin are met with regards to memorial service, funeral or interment at a national cemetery.

Improved Communication Between Department of Veterans Affairs And Medical Examiners and Funeral Directors: The bill requires the VA to obtain information from the relevant medical examiner, funeral director, service group or other entity regarding the steps taken to determine if the deceased has no next of kin.

Identification and Burial of Unclaimed or Abandoned Human Remains: The VA will be required to cooperate with veterans service organizations to assist entities in possession of unclaimed or abandoned remains of veterans, with the department authorized to determine whether such remains are eligible for burial in a national cemetery.

Restoration, Operation and Maintenance of Clark Veterans Cemetery by American Battle Monuments Commission: The bill authorizes the appropriation of $5 million for site preparation and construction at the Clark Veterans Cemetery located in the Philippines. The bill directs the American Battle Monuments Commission to restore and operate the cemetery once a cooperative agreement is reached with the government of the Philippines.

REIMBURSEMENT OF BURIAL EXPENSES

The Veterans Benefits Administration administers a burial benefits program designed to assist claimants in meeting the funeral and burial costs of a deceased veteran. The type and amount of benefits payable depends on the veteran's individual service record and cause of death.

SERVICE-CONNECTED DEATH

If a veteran's death is service-connected, the VA will pay a burial allowance of up to $2,000 (*for deaths on or after 9-11-2001 - prior to 9-11-2001, the burial allowance was $1,500*). If the veteran is buried in a VA national cemetery, some or all of the cost of moving the deceased to the national cemetery nearest the veteran's home may also be reimbursed. There is no time limit for applying for a service-connected burial allowance. The person who bore the veteran's burial expense may claim reimbursement from any VA regional office.

UNPAID BALANCE DUE PERSONS WHO PERFORMED SERVICES

If there is an unpaid balance due the person who performed burial, funeral, and transportation services, such claim as a creditor for the statutory burial allowance will be given priority over any claim for reimbursement based on use of personal funds, unless there is executed by such creditor a waiver in favor of the person or persons whose personal funds were used in making the partial payment of the account.

No reimbursement may be made to a State, County, or other governmental subdivision.

VETERAN'S ESTATE

The representative of a deceased person's estate may file a claim for reimbursement, if estate funds were used to pay the expenses of the veteran's burial, funeral, and transportation. Accordingly, if otherwise in order, reimbursement may be made to the estate, regardless of whether such person pre-deceased the veteran or was deceased at the time the expenses were incurred or paid, or burial of the veteran actually occurred.

DEATH OF ACTIVE DUTY PERSONNEL

The VA does not pay a burial or plot interment allowance if a veteran dies while on active military duty. However, such veteran is entitled to certain benefits from the military. Information should be obtained from the branch of the armed forces in which the person served at time of death.

CORRECTION OF DISCHARGE TO HONORABLE CONDITIONS

Public Law 88-3 (H.R. 212) provides that where burial allowance was not payable at the time of a veteran's death because of the nature of his discharge from service, but after death his discharge is corrected by competent authority so as to reflect a discharge under conditions other than dishonorable, claim may be filed within two years from the date of correction of the discharge.

LEGAL EXECUTION

The execution of a veteran as a lawful punishment for a crime does not of itself preclude a payment of the statutory burial allowances.

STATE BURIAL ALLOWANCE

There are some burial allowances allowed by states or counties for the burial of needy veterans, and in some instances, of their dependents. Check with the veteran's state or county of residence for specific information.

ASSISTANCE TO CLAIMANTS

It is incumbent upon the claimant to establish his case in accordance with the law. This rule, however, will not be highly technical or rigid in its application. The general policy of the VA is to give the claimant every opportunity to substantiate his claim, to extend all reasonable assistance in its prosecution, and develop all sources from which information may be obtained. Assistance may also be secured from post, state, and national service officers or veterans' organizations

MISCELLANEOUS

If the deceased veteran is entitled to payment in full of burial expenses by the Employees' Compensation Commission, Workman's Compensation, or employer, the Veterans Administration will make no payment.

APPEAL

An appeal may be made within one year from the date of denial of a claim. The appeal must be sent to the regional VA office that denied the claim

BURIAL FLAGS

The VA shall furnish a United States flag, at no cost, for burial or memorial purposes in connection with the death of an eligible veteran who served honorably in the U.S. Armed Forces.

Public Law 105-261, added eligibility for former member of the Selected Reserve who:

- Completed at least one enlistment as a member of the Selected Reserve or, in the case of an officer, completed the period of initial obligated service as a member of the Selected Reserve; or
- Was discharged before completion of the person's initial enlistment as a member of the Selected Reserve or, in the case of an officer, period of initial obligated service as a member of the Selected Reserve, for a disability incurred or

aggravated in line of duty; or
* Who died while a member of the Selected Reserve.

Burial flags may not be furnished on behalf of deceased veterans who committed capital crimes.

After the burial of the veteran, the flag shall be given to his next of kin. If no claim is made for the flag by the next of kin, it may be given, upon request, to a close friend or associate of the deceased veteran. If a flag is given to a close friend or associate of the deceased veteran, no flag shall be given to any other person on account of the death of such veteran.

When burial is in a national, state or post cemetery, a burial flag will automatically be provided. When burial is in a private cemetery, an American flag may be obtained by a service officer, an undertaker or other interested person from the nearest Veterans Administration office or most U.S. Post Offices. VA Form 2008, "Application for United States Flag for Burial Purposes", must be completed and submitted along with a copy of the veteran's discharge papers. Generally, the funeral director will help the next of kin with this process.

The proper way to display the flag depends upon whether the casket is open or closed. VA Form 2008 provides the proper method for displaying and folding the flag. The burial flag is not suitable for outside display, because of its size and fabric.

After burial of a veteran, the flag should be folded in military style and presented to the next of kin at the cemetery. Local veteran organizations, when presenting the flag, usually say something like this:

"In the name of the United States government and name of veterans organization, (such as A.L., D.A.V., V.F.W., and American Veterans of World War II, etc.) we present you this flag, in loving memory of our departed comrade."

Presenting of the flag is sometimes a difficult task when there is a disagreement in the family. However, the Veterans Administration gives the following order of preference to be followed:
* Widow or widower (even if separated but not divorced)
* Children according to age (minor child may be issued flag on application signed by guardian)
* Father, including adopted, step and foster father
* Mother, including adopted, step and foster mother
* Brothers or sisters, including brothers and sisters of half blood. Uncles or aunts
* Nephews or nieces
* Cousins, grandparents, etc. (but not in-laws)
* If two relatives have equal rights, the flag will be presented to the elder one.

Following a veteran's burial, the United States flag received by the next of kin may be donated to the VA, for use on national holidays at VA national cemeteries. If the next of kin chooses to make such a donation, it should be given or mailed to the Director of any national cemetery selected by the donor with a written request that the flag be flown at that location. If the flag is brought into a Veterans Service Division, it will be accepted and forwarded to the cemetery chosen by the donor. A Certificate of Appreciation is presented to the donor for providing their loved ones' burial flag to a national cemetery. Please note that VA cannot provide flag holders for placement on private headstones or markers. These flag holders may be purchased from private manufacturing companies.

The law allows the VA to issue one flag for a veteran's funeral. The VA cannot replace it if it is lost, destroyed, or stolen. However, if this occurs, a local veteran's organization or other community group may be able to assist you in obtaining another flag.

HEADSTONES AND MARKERS IN PRIVATE CEMETERIES

Ordering Grave Marker Medallion

In 2012 the VA introduced a new form, **VA Form 40-1330M**, which is now used as the sole form for families to order a grave marker medallion. Prior to the change, families of the deceased used a form to order the medallion that was the same as the form used to order a government headstone or grave marker. The medallion is given instead of a traditional government headstone or marker, specifically for veterans whose death occurred on or after November 1, 1990. The medallion is intended for use for those veterans whose grave is located in a private cemetery, and marked with a privately purchased headstone or marker.

The VA is required to furnish an appropriate headstone or marker for the graves of eligible veterans buried in private cemeteries, whose deaths occur on or after December 27, 2001, regardless of whether the grave is already marked with a non-government marker. Headstones or markers may not be furnished on behalf of deceased veterans who committed capital crimes.

For all deaths occurring prior to September 11, 2001, the VA may provide a headstone or marker only for graves that are not marked with a private headstone.

Spouses and dependents buried in a private cemetery are not eligible for a Government-provided headstone or marker.

Flat markers in granite, marble, and bronze; and upright headstones in granite and marble are available. The style chosen must be consistent with existing monuments at the place of burial. Niche markers are also available to mark columbaria used for cremated remains.

Government-furnished headstones and markers must be inscribed with the name of the deceased, branch of service, and the year of birth and death, in this order. Headstones and markers also may be inscribed with other items, including an authorized emblem of belief and, space permitting, additional text including military grade, rate or rank, war service such as "World War II", complete dates of birth and death, military awards, military organizations, and civilian or veteran affiliations. To apply, and to obtain specific information on available styles, contact the cemetery where the headstone or marker is to be placed.

When burial occurs in a private cemetery, an application for a government-furnished headstone or marker must be made to VA. The government will ship the headstone or marker free of charge, but will not pay for its placement. To apply, complete VA Form 40-1330M **(application form updated in 2012)**, and forward it along with a *copy* of the veteran's military discharge documents (do not send original discharge documents, as they will not be returned) to:

Memorial Products Service (41B)
Department of Veterans Affairs
5109 Russell Road
Quantico, VA 22134-3903

BRONZE MEDALLION

VA made available a new medallion to be affixed to an existing privately purchased headstone or marker to signify the deceased's status as a veteran.

If requested, the medallion will be furnished in lieu of a traditional government headstone or marker for veterans that died on or after November 1, 1990, and whose grave is marked with a privately purchased headstone or marker.

The medallion is currently available in three sizes, 5 inches, 3 inches, and 1 ½ inches. Each medallion will be inscribed with the word VETERAN across the top and the Branch of Service at the bottom. Appropriate affixing adhesive, instructions and hardware will be provided with the medallion.

Important: This benefit is only applicable if the grave is marked with a privately purchased headstone or marker. In these instances, eligible veterans are entitled to __either__ a traditional government-furnished headstone or marker, or the new medallion, but not both.

ELIGIBILITY RULES FOR A GOVERNMENT HEADSTONE OR MARKER IN A PRIVATE CEMETERY

Veterans and Members of the Armed Forces (Army, Navy, Air Force, Marine Corps, Coast Guard):

- Any veterans or members of The Armed Forces who dies while on active duty.
- Any veteran who was discharged under conditions other than dishonorable. With certain exceptions, service beginning after September 7, 1980, as an enlisted person, and service after October 16, 1981, as an officer, must be for a minimum of 24 months or the full period for which the person was called to active duty. (Examples include those serving less than 24 months in the Gulf War or Reservists that were federalized by Presidential Act.) Undesirable, bad conduct, and any other type of discharge other than honorable may or may not qualify the individual for veterans benefits, depending upon a determination made by a VA Regional Office. Cases presenting multiple discharges of varying character are also referred for adjudication to a VA Regional Office

Members of Reserve Components and Reserve Officers' Training Corps:
- Reservists and National Guard members who, at time of death, were entitled to retired pay under Chapter 1223, Title 10, United States Code, or would have been entitled, but for being under the age of 60.
- Members of reserve components who die while hospitalized or undergoing treatment at the expense of the United States for injury or disease contracted or incurred under honorable conditions while performing active duty for training or inactive duty training, or undergoing such hospitalization or treatment.
- Members of the Reserve Officers' Training Corps of the Army, Navy, or Air Force who die under honorable conditions while attending an authorized training camp or on an authorized cruise, while performing authorized travel to or from that camp or cruise, or while hospitalized or undergoing treatment at the expense of the United States for injury or disease contracted or incurred under honorable conditions while engaged in one of those activities.
- Members of reserve components who, during a period of active duty for training, were disabled or died from a disease or injury incurred or aggravated in the line of duty or, during a period of inactive duty training, were disabled or died from an injury incurred or aggravated in the line of duty.

Commissioned Officers, National Oceanic and Atmospheric Administration:
- A commissioned Officer of the National Oceanic and Atmospheric Administration (formerly titled the Coast and Geodetic Survey and the Environmental Science Services Administration) with full-time duty on or after July 29, 1945
- A commissioned Officer who served before July 29, 1945, and:
- Was assigned to an area of immediate military hazard while in time of war, or of a Presidentially declared national emergency as determined by the Secretary of Defense; or
- Served in the Philippine Islands on December 7, 1941, and continuously in such islands thereafter; or

- Transferred to the Department of the Army or the Department of the Navy under the provisions of the Act of May 22, 1917 Public Health Service
- A Commissioned Officer of the Regular or Reserve Corps of the Public Health Service who served on full-time duty on or after July 29, 1945. If the service of the particular Public Health Service Officer falls within the meaning of active duty for training, as defined in section 101(22), title 38, United States Code, he or she must have been disabled or died from a disease or injury incurred or aggravated in the line of duty.

A Commissioned Officer of the Regular or Reserve Corps of the Public Health Service who performed full-time duty prior to July 29, 1945:
- In time of war;
- On detail for duty with the Army, Navy, Air Force, Marine Corps, or Coast Guard; or,
- While the Service was part of the military forces of the United States pursuant to Executive Order of the President.
- A Commissioned Officer serving on inactive duty training as defined in section 101(23), title 38, United States Code, whose death resulted from an injury incurred or aggravated in the line of duty.

World War II Merchant Mariners

United States Merchant Mariners with oceangoing service during the period of armed conflict, December 7, 1941, to December 31, 1946. Prior to the enactment of *Public Law 105-368*, United States Merchant Mariners with oceangoing service during the period of armed conflict of December 7, 1941, to August 15, 1945, were eligible.

With enactment of *Public Law 105-368*, the service period is extended to December 31, 1946, for those dying on or after November 11, 1998. A DD-214 documenting this service may be obtained by submitting an application to Commandant (G-MVP- 6), United States Coast Guard, 2100 2nd Street, SW, Washington, DC 20593.

Notwithstanding, the Mariner's death must have occurred after the enactment of *Public Law 105-368* and the interment not violate the applicable restrictions while meeting the requirements held therein.

PERSONS NOT ELIGIBLE FOR A HEADSTONE OR MARKER

Disqualifying Characters of Discharge

A person whose only separation from the Armed Forces was under dishonorable conditions or whose character of service results in a bar to veterans' benefits.

- Discharge from Draft

- A person who was ordered to report to an induction station, but was not actually inducted into military service.

- Person Found Guilty of a Capital Crime

- Eligibility for a headstone or marker is prohibited if a person is convicted of a federal capital crime and sentenced to death or life imprisonment, or is convicted of a state capital crime, and sentenced to death or life imprisonment without parole. Federal officials are authorized to deny requests for headstones or markers to persons who are shown by clear and convincing evidence to have committed a Federal or State capital crime but were not convicted of such crime because of flight to avoid prosecution or by death prior to trial.

- Subversive Activities

  o Any person convicted of subversive activities after September 1, 1959, shall have no right to burial in a national cemetery from and after the date of commission of such offense, based on periods of active military service commencing before the date of the commission of such offense, nor shall another person be entitled to burial on account of such an individual. Eligibility will be reinstated if the President of the United States grants a pardon.

- Active or Inactive Duty for Training

  o A person whose only service is active duty for training or inactive duty training in the National Guard or Reserve Component, unless the individual meets the following criteria.

Reservists and National Guard members who, at time of death, were entitled to retired pay under Chapter 1223, title 10, United States Code, or would have been entitled, but for being under the age of 60. Specific categories of individuals eligible for retired pay are delineated in section 12731 of Chapter 1223, title 10, United States Code.

Members of reserve components who die while hospitalized or undergoing treatment at the expense of the United States for injury or disease contracted or incurred under honorable conditions while performing active duty for training or inactive duty training, or undergoing such hospitalization or treatment.

Members of the Reserve Officers' Training Corps of the Army, Navy, or Air Force who die under honorable conditions while attending an authorized training camp or on an authorized cruise, while performing authorized travel to or from that camp or cruise, or while hospitalized or undergoing treatment at the expense of the United States for injury or disease contracted or incurred under honorable conditions while engaged in one of those activities.

Members of reserve components who, during a period of active duty for training, were disabled or died from a disease or injury incurred or aggravated in line of duty or, during a period of inactive duty training, were disabled or died from an injury incurred or aggravated in line of duty.

Other Groups

Members of groups whose service has been determined by the Secretary of the Air Force under the provisions of Public Law 95-202 as not warranting entitlement to benefits administered by the Secretary of Veterans Affairs.

BURIAL IN NATIONAL CEMETERIES

In 2012 the VA announced plans to move forward with plan to provide burial options for veterans who live in rural areas, where no national, state or tribal cemeteries are available. The plan is part of the Rural Initiative Plan, in which the VA will work to build small National Veterans Burial Grounds that will be located inside existing rurally-located public or private cemeteries. These burial grounds will also be located where the un- served veteran population is 25,000 or less, within a 75-mile radius.

The VA announced plans to open eight National Veteran Burial Grounds. A National Veterans Burial Ground will consist of a small area of three to five acres, located within an existing public or private cemetery that will be managed by the VA. The VA will provide a full range of burial options and be responsible for the maintenance and operation of the burial lots. These sections will be held to the national shrine standards that are in place at VA national cemeteries.

The National Cemetery Administration honors Veterans with a final resting place and lasting memorials that commemorate their service to our nation.

Veterans and service members who meet the eligibility requirements and their eligible dependents may be buried in one of the VA's national cemeteries. The National Cemetery Administration currently includes 122 national cemeteries. The Department of the Army administers 2 national cemeteries, and the Department of the Interior administers 14 national cemeteries. There are also numerous state cemeteries for veterans throughout the U.S. For a listing of all national cemeteries as well as state veterans cemeteries refer to the listing at the end of this chapter.

Effective under *Public Law 112-154*, reservations for more than one space at Arlington National Cemetery will no longer be accepted, and reservations will not be honored until the time of death, unless there is a case of extraordinary circumstances.

HONORING AMERICA'S VETERANS AND CARING FOR CAMP LEJEUNE FAMILIES ACT OF 2012

Became Public Law 112-154 on August 5, 2012

This law, signed into effect by President Obama, provided sweeping legislation for veterans, including limitations on protestors at military funerals. The law prohibits protestors at military funerals from protesting two hours before or after a military funeral, and the must hold their protests at least 300 feet from the site of the funeral.

RESPECT FOR AMERICA'S FALLEN HEROES ACT

Became Public Law 109-228 on May 29, 2006

On May 29, 2006, then-President Bush signed the *Respect For America's Fallen Heroes Act* into law. This law does the following:

Prohibits a demonstration on the property of a cemetery under the control of the National Cemetery Administration or on the property of Arlington National Cemetery unless the demonstration has been approved by the cemetery superintendent or the director of the property on which the cemetery is located.

Prohibits, with respect to the above cemeteries, a demonstration during the period beginning 60 minutes before and ending 60 minutes after a funeral, memorial service, or ceremony is held, which:

- Takes place within 150 feet of a road, pathway, or other route of ingress to or egress from such cemetery property; or
- Is within 300 feet of such cemetery and impedes access to or egress from such cemetery.

The term "Demonstration" includes the following:

- Any picketing or similar conduct.
- Any oration, speech, use of sound amplification equipment or device, or similar conduct that is not part of a funeral, memorial service, or ceremony.
- The display of any placard, banner, flag, or similar device, unless the display is part of a funeral, memorial service, or ceremony.
- The distribution of any handbill, pamphlet, leaflet, or other written or printed matter other than what is distributed as part of a funeral, memorial service, or ceremony. Amends the federal criminal code to provide criminal penalties for violations of such prohibitions.
- Express the sense of Congress that each state should enact similar legislation to restrict demonstrations near any military funeral.

ELIGIBILITY

The VA national cemetery directors have the primary responsibility for verifying eligibility for burial in VA national cemeteries. A dependent's eligibility for burial is based upon the eligibility of the veteran. To establish a veteran's eligibility, a copy of the official military discharge document bearing an official seal or a DD 214 is usually sufficient. The document must show that release from service was under conditions other than dishonorable. A determination of eligibility is usually made in response to a request for burial in a VA national cemetery.

The cemeteries administered by the National Cemetery Administration and the Department of the Interior use the eligibility requirements that follow. The Department of the Interior can be contacted at:

Department of the Interior National Park Service
1849 C Street, N.W.
Washington, D.C. 20240
(202) 208-4621

The Department of the Army should be contacted directly for inquiries concerning eligibility for interment in either of the two cemeteries under its jurisdiction (call (703) 695-3250).

Eligibility requirements for burial in state veterans cemeteries are the same, or similar, to the eligibility requirements that follow. However, some states also have residency and other more restrictive requirements. Please contact the specific state cemetery for its eligibility requirements.

The following veterans and members of the Armed Forces (Army, Navy, Air Force, Marine Corps, Coast Guard) are eligible for burial in a VA national cemetery:

- Any member of the Armed Forces of the U.S. who dies on active duty.

- Any citizen of the U.S. who, during any war in which the U.S. has been engaged, served in the Armed Forces of any U.S. ally during that war, whose last active service was terminated honorably by death or otherwise, and who was a citizen of the U.S. at the time of entry into such service and at the time of death.

- Any veteran discharged under conditions other than dishonorable, and who has completed the required period of service. With certain exceptions, service beginning after September 7, 1980, as an enlisted person, and service after October 16, 1981, as an officer, must be for a minimum of 24 months or the full period for which the person was called to active duty.

MEMBERS OF RESERVE COMPONENTS AND RESERVE OFFICERS' TRAINING CORPS

- Reservists and National Guard members with 20 years of qualifying service, who are entitled to retired pay, or would be entitled, if at least 60 years of age.
- Members of reserve components who die under honorable conditions while hospitalized or undergoing treatment at the expense of the U.S. for injury or disease contracted or incurred under honorable conditions, while performing active duty for training, or inactive duty training, or undergoing such hospitalization or treatment.
- Members of the Reserve Officers' Training Corps of the Army, Navy, or Air Force who die under honorable conditions while attending an authorized training camp or cruise, or while traveling to or from that camp or cruise, or while hospitalized or undergoing treatment at the expense of the U.S. for injury or disease contracted or incurred under honorable conditions while engaged in one of those activities.
- Members of reserve components who, during a period of active duty for training, were disabled or died from a disease or injury incurred or aggravated in the line of duty, or, during a period of inactive duty training, were disabled or died from an injury incurred or aggravated in the line of duty.

COMMISSIONED OFFICERS, NATIONAL OCEANIC AND ATMOSPHERIC ADMINISTRATION

- A Commissioned Officer of the National Oceanic and Atmospheric Administration with full-time duty on or after July 29, 1945.
- A Commissioned Officer of the National Oceanic and Atmospheric Administration who served before July 29, 1945, and:
- Was assigned to an area of immediate hazard described in the Act of December 3, 1942 (56 Stat. 1038; 33 U.S.C. 855a), as amended
- Served in the Philippine Islands on December 7, 1941, and continuously in such islands thereafter.

PUBLIC HEALTH SERVICE

- A Commissioned Officer of the Regular or Reserve Corps of the Public Health Service who served on full-time duty on or after July 29, 1945. If the service of such Officer falls within the meaning of active duty for training, he must have been disabled or died from a disease or injury incurred or aggravated in the line of duty.
- A Commissioned Officer of the Regular or Reserve Corps of the Public Health Service who performed full-time duty prior to July 29, 1945:
- In time of war; or
- On detail for duty with the Army, Navy, Air Force, Marine Corps, or Coast Guard; or While the service was part of the military forces of the U.S. pursuant to Executive Order of the President.
- A Commissioned Officer of the Regular or Reserve Corps of the Public Health Service serving on inactive duty training as defined in Section 101 (23), title 39, U.S. Code, whose death resulted from an injury incurred or aggravated in the line of duty.

WORLD WAR II MERCHANT MARINERS

U.S. Merchant Mariners with oceangoing service during the period of armed conflict, December 7, 1941 to December 31, 1946. Prior to the enactment of Public Law 105-368, United States Merchant Mariners with oceangoing service during the period of armed conflict of December 7, 1941, to August 15, 1945, were eligible. With enactment of Public Law 105-368, the service period is extended to December 31, 1946, for those dying on or after November 11, 1998.

Merchant Mariners who served on blockships in support of Operation Mulberry during WWII.

THE PHILIPPINE ARMED FORCES

Any Philippine veteran who was a citizen of the United States or an alien lawfully admitted for permanent residence in the United States at the time of their death; and resided in the United States at the time of their death; and:

Was a person who served before July 1, 1946, in the organized military forces of the Government of the Commonwealth of the Philippines, while such forces were in the service of the Armed Forces of the United States pursuant to the military order of the President dated July 26, 1941, including organized guerilla forces under commanders appointed, designated, or subsequently recognized by the Commander in Chief, Southwest Pacific Area, or other competent authority in the Army of the United States who dies on or after November 1, 2000; or

Was a person who enlisted between October 6, 1945, and June 30, 1947, with the Armed Forces of the United States with the consent of the Philippine government, pursuant to Section 14 of the Armed Forces Voluntary Recruitment Act of 1945, and who died on or after December 16, 2003.

SPOUSES AND DEPENDENTS

The spouse or surviving spouse of an eligible veteran is eligible for interment in a national cemetery even if that veteran is not buried or memorialized in a national cemetery. In addition, the spouse or surviving spouse of a member of the Armed Forces of the United States whose remains are unavailable for burial is also eligible for burial.

The surviving spouse of an eligible veteran who had a subsequent remarriage to a non-veteran and whose death occurred on or after January 1, 2000, is eligible for burial in a national cemetery, based on his or her marriage to the eligible veteran.

The minor children of an eligible veteran. For the purpose of burial in a national cemetery, a minor child is a child who is unmarried and:

- Under 21 years of age; or
- Under 23 years of age and pursuing a full-time course of instruction at an approved educational institution.
- An unmarried adult child of an eligible veteran if the child became permanently physically or mentally disabled and incapable of self-support before reaching 21 years of age, or before reaching 23 years of age if pursuing a full-time course of instruction at an approved educational institution.
- Any other persons or classes of persons as designated by the Secretary of Veterans Affairs or the Secretary of the Air Force.

  The *Veterans' Benefits Act of 2010* contains a provision which allows a parent whose child gave their life in service to our country to be buried in a national cemetery with that child when their veteran child has no living spouse or children.

The following are not eligible for burial in a VA National Cemetery:

- A former spouse of an eligible individual whose marriage to that individual has been terminated by annulment or divorce, if not otherwise eligible.
- Family members other than those specifically described above.
- A person whose only separation from the Armed Forces was under dishonorable conditions, or whose character of service results in a bar to veterans benefits.
- A person ordered to report to an induction station, but not actually inducted into military service.
- Any person found guilty of a capital crime. Interment or memorialization in a VA cemetery or in Arlington National Cemetery is prohibited if a person is convicted of a federal capital crime and sentenced to death or life imprisonment, or is convicted of a state capital crime, and sentenced to death or life imprisonment without parole. Federal officials are authorized to deny burial in veterans' cemeteries to persons who are shown by clear and convincing evidence to have committed a federal or state capital crime but were not convicted of such crime because of flight to avoid prosecution or by death prior to trial. The Secretary is authorized to provide aid to states for the establishment, expansion and/or improvement of veterans cemeteries on the condition that the state is willing to prohibit interment or memorialization in such cemeteries of individuals convicted of federal or state capital crimes, or found by clear and convincing evidence to have committed such crimes, without having been convicted of the crimes due to flight to avoid prosecution or death prior to trial.
- Any person convicted of subversive activities after September 1, 1959, shall have no right to burial in a national cemetery from and after the date of commission of such offense, based on periods of active military service commencing before the date of the commission of such offense, nor shall another person be entitled to burial on account of such an individual. Eligibility will be reinstated if the President of the United States grants a pardon.

REQUESTS FOR GRAVESITES IN NATIONAL CEMETERIES

Under Public Law 112-154 the Secretary of the Army will be responsible for decisions regarding organizations wishing to place monuments honoring the service of a group or individual at Arlington. This became law in 2012.

An eligible veteran or family member may be buried in the VA national cemetery of his choice, provided space is available. A veteran may not reserve a gravesite in his name prior to his death. However, any reservations made under previous programs will be honored. The funeral director or loved one making the burial arrangements must apply for a gravesite at the time of death. No special forms are required when requesting burial in a VA national cemetery. The person making burial arrangement should contact the national cemetery in which burial is desired at the time of need.

If possible, the following information concerning the deceased should be provided when the cemetery is first contacted:

- Full name and military rank;

- Branch of service;

- Social security number;

- VA claim number, if applicable;

- Date and place of birth;

- Date and place of death;

- Date of retirement or last separation from active duty; and

- Copy of any military separation documents (such as DD-214)

When a death occurs and eligibility for interment in a national cemetery is determined, grave space is assigned by the cemetery director in the name of the veteran or family member

One gravesite is permitted for the interment of all eligible family members, unless soil conditions or the number of family decedents necessitate more than one grave. There is no charge for burial in a national cemetery.

The availability of grave space varies among each National Cemetery. In many cases, if a national cemetery does not have space for a full-casket burial, it may still intern cremated remains. Full-casket gravesites occasionally become available in such cemeteries due to disinterment or cancellation of prior reservations. The cemetery director can answer such questions at the time of need.

Most national cemeteries do not typically conduct burials on weekends. However, weekend callers trying to make burial arrangements for the following week will be provided with the phone number of one of three strategically located VA cemetery offices that remains open during weekends.

BURIAL AT SEA

The National Cemetery Administration cannot provide burial at sea. For information, contact the United States Navy Mortuary Affairs office toll-free at 866-787-0081.

FURNISHING AND PLACEMENT OF HEADSTONES AND MARKERS

In addition to the gravesite, burial in a VA national cemetery also includes furnishing and placement of the headstone or marker, opening and closing of the grave, and perpetual care. Many national cemeteries also have columbaria or gravesites for cremated remains. (Some state veterans' cemeteries may charge a nominal fee for placing a government-provided headstone or marker.)

SPECIAL NOTES:

For persons with 20-years service in the National Guard or Reserves, entitlement to retired pay must be subsequent to November 1, 1990 in order to qualify for a government-provided headstone or marker. A copy of the Reserve Retirement Eligibility Benefits Letter must accompany the application. Active duty service while in the National Guard or Reserves also establishes eligibility.

Service prior to World War I requires detailed documentation to prove eligibility such as muster rolls, extracts from State files, military or State organizations where served, pension or land warrants, etc.

Flat bronze, granite, or marble grave markers and upright marble or granite headstones are available to mark graves in the style consistent with existing monuments in the national cemetery. Niche markers are also available for identifying cremated remains in columbaria. The following is a brief description of each type:

- Upright Marble and Upright Granite: 42 inches long, 13 inches wide, 4 inches thick, approximately 230 pounds.

- Flat Bronze: 24 inches long, 12 inches wide, ¾ inch rise, approximately 18 pounds. Anchor bolts, nuts and washers for fastening to base are supplied with marker. The government does not provide the base.

- Flat Granite and Flat Marble: 24 inches long, 12 inches wide, 4 inches thick, approximately 130 pounds.

- Bronze Niche: 8 ½ inches long, 5 ½ inches wide, 7/16 inch rise, approximately 3 pounds. Mounting bolts and washers are supplied with marker.

There are also two special styles of upright marble headstones and flat markers available - one for those who served with the Union Forces during the Civil War or the Spanish-American War; and one for those who served with the Confederate Forces during the Civil War.

INSCRIPTIONS

Headstones and markers are inscribed with the name of the deceased, branch of service, year of birth, and year of death.

The word "Korea" may be included on government headstones and markers for the graves of those members and former members of the United States Armed Forces who served within the areas of military operations in the Korean Theater between June 27, 1950 and July 27, 1954; and for headstones and markers for active duty decedents who lost their lives in Korea or adjacent waters as a result of hostile action subsequent to the 1953 Armistice

The word "Vietnam" may be included on government headstones and markers for the graves of those members and former members of the United States Armed Forces who died in Vietnam or whose death was attributable to service in Vietnam, and on the headstones and markers of all decedents who were on active duty on or after August 5, 1964

108

The words "Lebanon" or "Grenada" may be included on government headstones and markers for those killed as a result of those military actions.

The words "Panama" and "Persian Gulf" may be included on government headstones and markers for those killed as a result of those military actions

If desired, the following inscriptions can also be made (space permitting):
Military grade
Military rank
Military rate
Identification of war service
Months and days of birth and death
An authorized emblem of religious belief (see following list of available emblems)
Military awards (documentation of award must be provided)
Military organizations
Civilian or veteran affiliations

With the VA's approval, terms of endearment that meet acceptable standards of good taste may also be added. Most optional inscriptions are placed as the last lines of the inscription. No other graphics are permitted on government-provided headstones and markers, and inscriptions will be in English text only. Civilian titles such as "Doctor or Reverend" are not permitted on the name line of government-provided headstones and markers.

AVAILABLE EMBLEMS OF BELIEF FOR PLACEMENT ON GOVERNMENT HEADSTONES AND MARKERS:

Christian Cross
Buddhist (Wheel of Righteousness)
Hebrew (Star of David)
Presbyterian Cross
Russian Orthodox Cross
Lutheran Cross
Episcopal Cross
Unitarian Church (Flaming Chalice)
United Methodist Church
Aaronic Order
Church Mormon (Angel Moroni)
Native American Church of North America
Serbian Orthodox
Greek Cross
Bahai (9 Pointed Star)
Atheist
Muslim (Crescent and Star)
Hindu
Konko-Kyo
Faith Community of Christ
Sufism Reoriented Tenrikyo Church
Seicho-No-Ie
Church of World Messianity (Izunome)
United Church of Religious Science
Christian Reformed Church
United Moravian Church
Eckankar
Christian Church United Church of Christ
Christian & Missionary Alliance
Humanist Emblem Of Spirit
Presbyterian Church (USA)

Izumo Taishakyo Mission Of Hawaii
Soka Gakkai International - USA Sikh (Khanda)
Christian Scientist (Cross and Crown)
Muslim (Islamic 5 Pointed Star)

ORDERING A HEADSTONE OR MARKER

For burial of a veteran in a national, state veteran, or military post cemetery, the cemetery will order the headstone or marker, and can give loved ones information on style, inscription, and shipment. Shipment and placement of the headstone or marker is provided at no cost.

When burial is in a private cemetery, VA Form 40-1330, "Application for Standard Government Headstone or Marker" must be submitted by the next of kin or a representative, such as funeral director, cemetery official or veterans' counselor, along with the veteran's military discharge documents, to request a Government-provided headstone or marker. Do not send original documents, as they will not be returned.

HEADSTONES AND MARKERS FOR SPOUSES AND CHILDREN

The VA will issue a headstone or marker for an eligible spouse or child buried in a national, state veteran or military post cemetery. However, the VA cannot issue a headstone or marker for a spouse or child buried in a private cemetery.

The applicant can, however, request to reserve inscription space below the veteran's inscription, so that the non- veteran's commemorative information can be inscribed locally, at private expense, when the non-veteran is buried. The applicant may also choose to have his/her name and date of birth added at Government expense, when the headstone or marker is ordered. The date of death may then be added, at private expense, at the time of his/her death.

COMMEMORATION OF UNIDENTIFIED REMAINS

Many national cemeteries have areas suitable to commemorate veterans whose remains were not recovered or identified, were buried at sea, or are otherwise unavailable for interment. In such instances, the VA will provide a memorial headstone or marker to be placed in that section of the cemetery. The words *"In Memory of"* must precede the authorized inscription.

CHECKING ORDER STATUS

To check the status of a previously ordered headstone or marker for placement in a private cemetery, applicants may call the VA's Applicant Assistance Line at (800) 697- 6947. The line is open weekdays, from 8:00 A.M. to 5:00 P.M., Eastern Standard Time

REPLACEMENT OF HEADSTONES AND MARKERS

The government will replace a previously furnished headstone or marker if it: becomes badly damaged, is vandalized, is stolen, becomes badly deteriorated, the inscription becomes illegible, is different from that ordered by the applicant, becomes damaged in transit, or the inscription is incorrect.

Government headstones or markers in private cemeteries damaged by cemetery personnel will not be replaced at government expense.

If a marble or granite headstone or marker is permanently removed from a grave, it must be destroyed. Bronze markers must be returned to the contractor.

MILITARY HONORS

The rendering of Military Funeral Honors is a way to show the nation's deep gratitude to those who have faithfully defended our country in times of war and peace. It is the final demonstration a grateful nation can provide to the veterans' families.

The following service members are eligible for Military Funeral Honors:
- Military members on active duty or in the Selected Reserve at time of death;
- Former military members who served on active duty and departed under conditions other than dishonorable;
- Former military members who completed at least one term of enlistment or period of initial obligated service in the Selected Reserve, and departed under conditions other than dishonorable;
- Former military members discharged from the Selected Reserve due to a disability incurred or aggravated in the line of duty.

All eligible veterans receive basic Military Funeral Honors, if requested by the deceased veteran's family. As provided by law, an honor guard detail for the burial of an eligible veteran shall consist of not less than two members of the Armed Forces. One member of the detail shall be a representative of the parent Service of the deceased veteran. The honor detail will, at a minimum, perform a ceremony that includes the folding and presenting of the American flag to the next of kin, and the playing of Taps. Taps will be played by a bugler, if available, or by electronic recording.

The ceremonial bugle consists of a small cone-shaped device inserted deep into the bell of a bugle that plays an exceptionally high-quality rendition of Taps that is virtually indistinguishable from a live bugler.

The ceremonial bugle will be offered to families as an alternative to the pre-recorded Taps played on a stereo, but will not be used as a substitute for a live bugler when one is available. Live buglers will continue to play at veterans' funerals whenever available.

Funeral Directors have the responsibility of assisting loved ones in requesting military honors. A toll-free telephone number has been established for funeral directors requesting military honors. That number is 1-800-535-1117.

The Department of Defense (DOD) has provided registered funeral home directors with a military funeral honors kit and information on how to contact the appropriate military organization to perform the honors ceremony.

Questions about the Military Funeral Honors program should be sent to:
Deputy Assistant Secretary of Defense
(Military Community and Family Policy)
4000 Defense Pentagon, Room 5A726
Washington DC 20380

PREPARATIONS WHICH CAN BE MADE PRIOR TO DEATH

It is suggested that veterans and their families prepare in advance by discussing cemetery options, collecting the veteran's military information (including discharge papers), and by contacting the cemetery where the veteran wishes to be buried. If burial will be in a private cemetery and a government headstone or marker will be requested, VA Form 40- 1330 can be completed in advance and placed with the veteran's military discharge papers for use at the time of need.

BURIAL LOCATION ASSISTANCE

The VA National Cemetery Administration can provide limited burial location assistance to family members and close friends of descendants thought to be buried in a VA national cemetery.

The National Cemetery Administration will research its records to determine if the decedent is buried in one of VA's national cemeteries. A request can include a maximum of ten specific names to locate. The National Cemetery Administration does not have information on persons buried in cemeteries other than its national cemeteries. Its records do not contain any personal, military or family information – only information regarding whether or not an individual is buried in a VA national cemetery, and if so, where, can be provided

The "Gravesite Locator" tool is available online at the VA's website.

If the online tool is not available or helpful, you may submit a written request. No form is required to request this information, and no fee is charged. The following information should be provided.

- Full name, including any alternate spellings, of descendent;
- Date and place of birth;
- Date and place of death;
- State from which the individual entered active duty;
- Military service branch;
- Mailing address and phone number of individual requesting the information.

Allow approximately 4 weeks for a reply.

Requests should be sent to:
U.S. Department of Veterans Affairs
National Cemetery Administration (41C1)
Burial Location Request
810 Vermont Avenue, N.W.
Washington, D.C. 20420

U.S. MILITARY CEMETERIES AND MONUMENTS OVERSEAS

The *American Battle Monuments Commission(ABMC)* a small, independent agency of the government's executive branch, maintains 24 American military cemeteries, and 27 memorials, monuments, or markers. (The VA is not responsible for maintaining cemeteries and monuments honoring deceased veterans buried on foreign soil.)

ABMC SERVICES

The ABMC can provide interested parties with:

Name, location, and information on cemeteries and memorials.

Plot, row and grave number or memorialization location of Honored War Dead.

Best in-country routes and modes of travel to cemeteries or memorials.

Information on accommodations near cemeteries or memorials.

Escort service for relatives to grave and memorial sites within the cemeteries.

Letters authorizing fee-free passports for members of the immediate family traveling overseas to visit a grave or memorialization site.

Black and white photographs of headstones and Tablets of the Missing on which the names of dead or missing are engraved.

Arrangements for floral decorations placed at graves and memorialization sites.

An Honor Roll Certificate containing data on a Korean War casualty suitable for framing.

Polaroid color photographs of donated floral decorations in place.

THE ANDREWS PROJECT

The commission also provides friends and relatives of those interred in its cemeteries or memorialized on its Tablets of the Missing with color lithographs of the cemetery or memorial on which is mounted a photograph of the headstone or commemorative inscription. The Andrews Project, named in honor of its sponsor, the late Congressman George W. Andrews, is ABMC's most popular service.

For further information, contact the ABMC at:
American Battle Monuments Commission
Arlington Court House Plaza II
2300 Clarendon Blvd., Suite 500
Arlington, VA 22201
(703) 696-6897

PASSPORTS TO VISIT OVERSEAS CEMETERIES

Family members who wish to visit overseas graves and memorial sites of World War I and World War II veterans are eligible for "no-fee" passports. Family members eligible for the "no-fee" passports include surviving spouses, parents, children, sisters, brothers and guardians of the deceased veteran buried or commemorated in American military cemeteries on foreign soil. For further information contact the American Battle Monuments Commission at the address and phone number indicated in the previous section.

PRESIDENTIAL MEMORIAL CERTIFICATES

Under *Public Law 112-154*, service members who die on active-duty are eligible for Presidential Memorial Certificates. A Presidential Memorial Certificate is an engraved paper certificate that has been signed by the current president, honoring the memory of any honorably discharged deceased veteran. Presidential Memorial Certificates may be distributed to a deceased veteran's next of kin and loved ones. More than one certificate can be provided per family, and there is no time limit for applying for the certificate.

Presidential Memorial Certificates may not be furnished on behalf of deceased veterans who committed capital crimes.

Requests for a Presidential Memorial Certificate can be made in person at any VA regional office, by faxing the request and all supporting documents (copy of discharge and death certificate) to (202) 565-8054, or by U.S. Mail.

There is no form to use when requesting a certificate. A copy of the veteran's discharge documents and a return mailing address should be included with any request. Written requests should be sent to:
Presidential Memorial Certificates (41A1C)
Department of Veterans Affairs
5109 Russell Road
Quantico, VA 22134-3903

LISTS OF NATIONAL CEMETERIES

Some national cemeteries can bury only cremated remains or casketed remains of eligible family members of those already buried. Contact the cemetery director for information on the availability of space

DEPARTMENT OF VETERANS AFFAIRS NATIONAL CEMETERIES

ALABAMA

Alabama National Cemetery
3133 Highway 119
Montevallo, AL 35115
(205) 665-9039

Fort Mitchell National Cemetery
553 Highway 165
Ft. Mitchell, AL 36856
(334) 855-4731

Mobile National Cemetery
1202 Virginia Street
Mobile, AL 36604
(850) 453-4635
Burial Space- Closed

ALASKA

Fort Richardson National Cemetery
Building #58-512,
Davis Highway
Fort Richardson, AK 99505
(907) 384-7075

Sitka National Cemetery
803 Sawmill Creek Road
Sitka, AK 99835
(907) 384-7075

ARIZONA

National Memorial Cemetery of Arizona
23029 North Cave Creek Road
Phoenix, AZ 85024
(480) 513-3600
Prescott National Cemetery
500 Highway 89 North

Prescott, AZ 86303
(928) 717-7569
Cremation Only

ARKANSAS

Fayetteville National Cemetery
700 Government Avenue
Fayetteville, AR 72701
(479) 444-5051

Fort Smith National Cemetery
522 Garland Avenue
Fort Smith, AR 72901
(479) 783-5345

Little Rock National Cemetery
2523 Springer Blvd.
Little Rock AR 72206
(479) 783-5345
Closed

CALIFORNIA

Baker National Cemetery
30338 East Bear Mountain Blvd.
Arvin, CA 93203
(661) 867-2250

Fort Rosecrans National Cemetery
Cabrillo Memorial Dr.
San Diego, CA 92106
(619) 553-2084
Closed

Golden Gate National Cemetery
1300 Sneath Lane
San Bruno, CA 94066
(650) 589-7737
Closed

Los Angeles National Cemetery
950 South Sepulveda Boulevard
Los Angeles, CA 90049
(310) 268-4675
Closed

Miramar National Cemetery
5795 Nobel Dr.
San Diego, CA 92122
(858) 658-7360

Riverside National Cemetery
22495 Van Buren Boulevard
Riverside, CA 92518
(951) 653-5233

Sacramento Valley National Cemetery
5810 Midway Road
Dixon, CA 9562
(707) 693-2460
Closed

San Francisco National Cemetery
1 Lincoln Blvd.
Presidio of San Francisco
San Francisco, CA 94129
(650) 589-7737
Closed

San Joaquin Valley National Cemetery
32053 West McCabe Road
Santa Nella, CA 95322
(209) 854-1040

COLORADO

Fort Logan National Cemetery
4400 W. Kenyon Ave.
Denver, CO 80236
(303) 761-0117

Fort Lyon National Cemetery
15700 County Road HH
Las Animas, CO 81054
(303) 761-0117

FLORIDA

Barrancas National Cemetery
1 Cemetery Rd.
Pensacola, FL 32508
(850) 453-4108

Bay Pines National Cemetery
1000 Bay Pines Boulevard North
St. Petersburg, FL 33708
(727) 319-6479
Cremation Only

Florida National Cemetery
6502 SW 102nd Avenue
Bushnell, FL 33513
(352) 793-7740

Jacksonville National Cemetery
4083 Lannie Road
Jacksonville, FL 32218-1247
(904) 766-5222

Sarasota National Cemetery
9810 State Hwy 72
Sarasota, FL 34241
(877) 861-9840
South Florida National Cemetery

6501 S. State Road
Lake Worth, FL 33449
(561) 649-6489

St. Augustine National Cemetery
104 Marine Street
St. Augustine, FL 32084
(904) 766-5222
Closed

Tallahassee National Cemetery
5015 Apalachee Parkway
Tallahassee, FL 32311
(850) 402-8941

GEORGIA

Georgia National Cemetery
1080 Scott Hudgens Drive
Canton, GA 30114
(866) 236-8159

Marietta National Cemetery
500 Washington Avenue
Marietta, GA 30060
(866) 236-8159
Closed

HAWAII

National Memorial Cemetery of the
Pacific
2177 Puowaina Drive
Honolulu, HI 96813-1729
(808) 523-3720
Cremation Only

ILLINOIS

Abraham Lincoln National Cemetery
20953 W. Hoff Road
Elwood, IL 60421
(815) 423-9958

Alton National Cemetery
600 Pearl Street
Alton, IL 62003
(314) 845-8320

Camp Butler National Cemetery
5063 Camp Butler Road
Springfield, IL 92707-9722
(217) 492-4070

Danville National Cemetery
1900 East Main Street
Danville, IL 61832
(217) 554-4550

115

Mound City National Cemetery
141 State Highway 37
Mound City, IL 62963
(618) 748-9107

Quincy National Cemetery
36th and Maine Street
Quincy, IL 62301
(309) 782-2094
Closed

Rock Island National Cemetery
Bldg. 118
Rock Island Arsenal
Rock Island, IL 61299-7090
(309) 782-2094

Confederate Mound
Oak Woods Cemetery
1035 E. 67th St.
Chicago IL 60637
(815) 423-9958
Closed

North Alton Confederate Cemetery
635 Rozier St.
Alton, IL 62003
(314) 845-8355
Closed

Rock Island Confederate Cemetery
Rodman Avenue
Rock Island Arsenal
Rock Island, IL 61299
(309) 782-2094
Closed

INDIANA

Crown Hill National Cemetery
700 West 38th
Street Indianapolis, IN 46208
(765) 674-0284
Closed

Marion National Cemetery
1700 East 38th Street
Marion, IN 46952
(765) 674-0284

New Albany National Cemetery
1943 Ekin Avenue
New Albany, IN 47150
(502) 893-3852
Cremation Only

Crown Hill Cemetery Confederate Plot
700 West 38th St.

Indianapolis, IN 46208
(765) 674-0284
Closed

Woodlawn Monument site
North 3rd St. and 4th Avenue
Terre Haute, IN 47802
(815) 423-9958
Closed

IOWA

Keokuk National Cemetery
1701 J Street
Keokuk, IA 52632
(319) 524-1304

KANSAS

Fort Leavenworth Natl Cemetery
395 Biddle Blvd.
Fort Leavenworth, KS 66027
(913) 758-4105
Cremation Only

Fort Scott National Cemetery
900 East National Avenue
Fort Scott, KS 66701
(620) 223-2840

Leavenworth National Cemetery
150 Muncie Rd.
Leavenworth, KS 66048
(913) 758-4136

Baxter Springs City Cemetery
Baxter Springs, KS 66713
(913)758-4136
Closed

Mound City Cemetery Soldiers' Lot
Woodland Cemetery
Mound City, KS 66506
(913) 758-4105
Closed

KENTUCKY

Camp Nelson National Cemetery
6980 Danville Road
Nicholasville, KY 40356
(859) 885-5727

Cave Hill National Cemetery
701 Baxter Avenue
Louisville, KY 40204
For information please contact:
Zachary Taylor National Cemetery
(502) 893-3852

116

Closed

Danville National Cemetery
277 North First Street
Danville, KY 40442
(859) 885-5727
Closed

Lebanon National Cemetery
20 Highway 208
Lebanon, KY 40033
(270) 692-3390

Lexington National Cemetery
833 West Main Street
Lexington, KY 40508
(859) 885-5727
Closed

Mill Springs National Cemetery
9044 West Highway 80
Nancy, KY 42544
(859) 885-5727

Zachary Taylor National Cemetery
4701 Brownsboro Road
Louisville, KY 40207
(502) 893-3852
Closed

Evergreen Cemetery Soldiers' Lot
25 South Alexandria Pike
Southgate, KY 41071
(859) 885-5727
Closed

LOUISIANA

Alexandria National Cemetery
209 East Shamrock Street
Pineville, LA 71360
(601) 445-4891
Closed

Baton Rouge National Cemetery
220 North 19th Street
Baton Rouge, LA 70806
(225) 654-1988
Closed

Louisiana National Cemetery
303 W. Mount Pleasant Rd.
Zachary, LA 70791
(225) 654-1988

Port Hudson National Cemetery
20978 Port Hickey Road
Zachary, LA 70791

(225) 654-3767
Cremation Only

MAINE

Togus National Cemetery
VA Medical and Regional Office Center
Togus, ME 04330
(508) 563-7113
Closed

MARYLAND

Annapolis National Cemetery
800 West Street
Annapolis, MD 21401
(410) 644-9696
Closed

Baltimore National Cemetery
5501 Frederick Avenue
Baltimore, MD 21228
(410) 644-9696
Cremation Only

Loudon Park National Cemetery
3445 Frederick Avenue
Baltimore, MD 21228
(410) 644-9696
Closed

MASSACHUSETTS

Massachusetts National Cemetery
Connery Ave.
Bourne, MA 02532
(508) 563-7113

MICHIGAN

Fort Custer National Cemetery
15501 Dickman Road
Augusta, MI 49012
(269) 731-4164

Great Lakes National Cemetery
4200 Belford Road
Holly, MI 48842
(866) 348-8603

MINNESOTA

Fort Snelling National Cemetery
7601 34th Avenue
South Minneapolis, MN 55450-1199
(612) 726-1127

117

MISSISSIPPI

Biloxi National Cemetery
400 Veterans Avenue
Bld. 1001
Biloxi, MS 39535-4968
(228) 388-6668

Corinth National Cemetery
1551 Horton Street
Corinth, MS 38834
(901) 386-8311

Natchez National Cemetery
41 Cemetery Road
Natchez, MS 39120
(601) 445-4981

MISSOURI

Jefferson Barracks National Cemetery
2900 Sheridan Road
St. Louis, MO 63125
(314) 845-8320

Jefferson City National Cemetery
1024 East McCarty Street
Jefferson City, MO 65101
(314) 845-8320
Closed

Springfield National Cemetery
1702 East Seminole Street
Springfield, MO 65804
(417) 881-9499
Cremation Only

NEBRASKA

Fort McPherson National Cemetery
12004 South Spur 56A
Maxwell, NE 69151
(308) 582-4433

Omaha National Cemetery
14250 Schram Rd.
Omaha, NE 68138
(402) 253-3949

NEW JERSEY

Beverly National Cemetery
916 Bridgeboro Rd.
Beverly, NJ 08010
(215) 504-5610
Closed

Finn's Point National Cemetery
454 Fort Mott Road,

Pennsville, NJ 08070
(215) 504-5610
Cremation only

NEW MEXICO

Fort Bayard National Cemetery
200 Camino De Paz
Fort Bayard, NM 88036
(505) 988-6400

Santa Fe National Cemetery
501 North Guadalupe Street
Santa Fe, NM 87501
(505) 988-6400

NEW YORK

Bath National Cemetery
San Juan Avenue
Bath, NY 14810
(607) 664-4853

Calverton National Cemetery
210 Princeton Boulevard
Calverton, NY 11933-1031
(631) 727-5410

Cypress Hills National Cemetery
625 Jamaica Avenue
Brooklyn, NY 11208
(631) 454-4949
Closed

George B.H. Solomon Saratoga
National Cemetery
200 Duell Rd.
Schuylerville, NY 12871
(631) 454-4949
Cremation Only

Long Island National Cemetery
2040 Wellwood Avenue
Farmingdale, NY 11735-1211
(631) 454-4949
Cremation Only

Woodlawn National Cemetery
1825 Davis Street
Elmira, NY 14901
(607) 732-5411
Cremation Only

NORTH CAROLINA

New Bern National Cemetery
1711 National Avenue
New Bern, NC 28560
(252) 637-2912

Closed

Raleigh National Cemetery
501 Rock Quarry Road
Raleigh, NC 27610
(252) 637-2912d
Closed

Salisbury National Cemetery
501 Statesville Blvd.
Salisbury, NC 28144
(704) 636-2661

Wilmington National Cemetery
2011 Market Street
Wilmington, NC 28403
(910) 815-4877
Closed

OHIO

Dayton National Cemetery
4400 West Third St.
Dayton, OH 45428-1008
(937) 268-2221

Ohio Western Reserve National
Cemetery
10175 Rawiga Road
Seville, OH 44273
(330) 335-3069

OKLAHOMA
Fort Gibson National Cemetery
1423 Cemetery Road
Fort Gibson, OK 74434
(918) 478-2334

Fort Sill National Cemetery
2648 NE Jake Dunn Rd.
Elgin, OK 73538
(580) 492-3200

OREGON

Eagle Point National Cemetery
2763 Riley Road
Eagle Point, OR 97524
(541) 826-2511

Roseburg National Cemetery
913 NW Garden Valley Blvd.
Roseburg, OR 97471
(541) 671-3152

Willamette National Cemetery
11800 S.E. Mt. Scott Boulevard
Portland, OR 97086
(503) 273-5250

PENNSYLVANIA

Indiantown Gap National Cemetery
Indiantown Gap Rd.
Annville, PA 17003-9618
(717) 865-5254

National Cemetery of the Alleghenies
1158 Morgan Road
Bridgeville, PA 15017
(724) 746-4363

Philadelphia National Cemetery
Haines Street and Limekiln Pike
Philadelphia, PA 19138
(215) 504-5611
Closed

PUERTO RICO

Puerto Rico National Cemetery
Avenue Cementario Nacional
#50 Bayamon, PR 00960
(787) 798-8400

SOUTH CAROLINA

Beaufort National Cemetery
1601 Boundary Street
Beaufort, SC 29902
(843) 524-3925

Florence National Cemetery
803 East National Cemetery Road
Florence, SC 29501
(843) 669-8783

Fort Jackson National Cemetery
4170 Percival Rd
Columbia, SC 29229
(866) 577-5248

SOUTH DAKOTA

Black Hills National Cemetery
20901 Pleasant Valley Dr.
Sturgis, SD 57785
(605) 347-3830

Fort Meade National Cemetery
Old Stone Road
Sturgis, SD 57785
(605) 347-3830
Closed

Hot Springs National Cemetery
VA Medical Center
Hot Springs, SD 57747
(605) 347-3830

Closed

TENNESSEE

Chattanooga National Cemetery
1200 Bailey Avenue
Chattanooga, TN 37404
(423) 855-6590

Knoxville National Cemetery
939 Tyson Street, N.W.
Knoxville, TN 37917
(423) 855-6590
Cremation Only

Memphis National Cemetery
3568 Townes Avenue
Memphis, TN 38122
(901) 386-8311
Cremation Only

Mountain Home National Cemetery
53 Memorial Avenue
Mountain Home, TN 37684
(423) 979-3535

Nashville National Cemetery
1420 Gallatin Road S
Madison, TN 37115-4619
(615) 860-0086
Cremation Only

TEXAS

Dallas-Fort Worth National Cemetery
2000 Mountain Creek Parkway
Dallas, TX 75211
(214) 467-3374

Fort Bliss National Cemetery
5200 Fred Wilson Road
El Paso, TX 79906
(915) 564-0201

Fort Sam Houston National Cemetery
1520 Harry Wurzbach Road
San Antonio, TX 78209
(210) 820-3891

Houston National Cemetery
10410 Veterans Memorial Drive
Houston, TX 77038
(281) 447-8686

Kerrville National Cemetery
3600 Memorial Boulevard
Kerrville, TX 78028
(210) 820-3891

Closed

San Antonio National Cemetery
517 Paso Hondo Street
San Antonio, TX 78202
(210) 820-3891
Cremation Only

VIRGINIA

Alexandria National Cemetery
1450 Wilkes Street
Alexandria, VA 22314
(703) 221-2183
Cremation Only

Balls Bluff National Cemetery
Route 7
Leesburg, VA 22075
(540) 825-0027
Closed

City Point National Cemetery
10th Avenue and Davis Street
Hopewell, VA 23860
(804) 795-2031
Closed

Cold Harbor National Cemetery
6038 Cold Harbor Rd.
Mechanicsville, VA 23111
(804) 795-2031
Closed

Culpeper National Cemetery
305 U.S. Avenue
Culpeper, VA 22701
(540) 825-0027

Danville National Cemetery
721 Lee Street
Danville, VA 24541
(704) 636-2661
Cremation Only

Fort Harrison National Cemetery
8620 Varina Road
Richmond, VA 23231
(804) 795-2031
Closed

Glendale National Cemetery
8301 Willis Church Road
Richmond, VA 23231
For information please contact:
Fort Harrison National Cemetery
(804) 795-2031

Hampton National Cemetery Road at
Marshall Avenue
Hampton, VA 23667
(757) 723-7104

Hampton National Cemetery
VA Medical Center
Emancipation Drive
Hampton, VA 23667
(757) 723-7104

Quantico National Cemetery
P. O. Box 10
18424 Joplin Road (Route 619)
Triangle, VA 22172
(703) 221-2183 (local)

Richmond National Cemetery
1701 Williamsburg Road
Richmond, VA 23231
For information please contact: Fort
Harrison National Cemetery
(804) 795-2031

Seven Pines National Cemetery
400 East Williamsburg Road
Sandston, VA 2315
For information please contact: Fort
Harrison National Cemetery
(804) 795-2031

Staunton National Cemetery
901 Richmond Avenue
Staunton, VA 24401
(540) 825-0027

Winchester National Cemetery
401 National Avenue
Winchester, VA 22601
For information please contact:
Culpeper National Cemetery
(540) 825-0027

WASHINGTON

Tahoma National Cemetery
18600 Southeast 240th Street
Kent, WA 98042-4868
(425) 413-9614

WEST VIRGINIA

Grafton National Cemetery
431 Walnut Street
Grafton, WV 26354
For information please contact:
West Virginia National Cemetery
(304) 265 2044

West Virginia National Cemetery
Route 2, Box 127
Grafton, WV 26354
(304) 265-2044

WISCONSIN

Wood National Cemetery
5000 W National Ave, Bldg 1301
Milwaukee, WI 53295-4000
(414) 382-5300

**DEPARTMENT OF THE
INTERIOR NATIONAL
CEMETERIES**

DISTRICT OF COLUMBIA

Battleground National Cemetery
C/O Superintendent,
Rock Creek Park
3545 Williamsburg Lane, NW
Washington, DC 20008
(202) 282-1063

GEORGIA

Andersonville National Historic Site
Route 1, Box 800
Andersonville, GA 31711
(912) 924-0343

LOUISIANA

Chalmette National Cemetery C/O Jean
Lafitte National Historical Park and
Preserve
365 Canal Street, Suite 2400
New Orleans, LA 70130
(504) 589-3882
(504) 589-4430

MARYLAND

Antietam National Battlefield
Box 158
Sharpsburg, MD 21782-0158
(301) 432-5124

MISSISSIPPI

Vicksburg National Military Park
3201 Clay Street
Vicksburg, MS 39180
(601) 636-0583

MONTANA

Little Bighorn Battle National
Monument Custer National Cemetery
P. O. Box 39
Crow Agency, MT 59022

PENNSYLVANIA

Gettysburg National Military Park
97 Taneytown Road
Gettysburg, PA 17325-2804
(717) 334-1124

TENNESSEE

Andrew Johnson National Historic Site
P. O. Box 1088
Greeneville, TN 37744
(423) 638-3551

Fort Donelson National Battlefield
P. O. Box 434
Dover, TN 37058
(615) 232-5348

Shiloh National Military Park
Route 1, Box 9
Shiloh, TN 38376-9704
(901) 689-5275

Stones River National Battlefield
3501 Old Nashville Highway
Murfreesboro, TN 37129
(615) 893-9501

VIRGINIA

Fredericksburg and Spotsylvania
County Battlefields Memorial National
Military Park
120 Chatham Lane
Fredericksburg, VA 22405
(540) 371-0802

Poplar Grove National Cemetery
Petersburg National Battlefield
1539 (Yorktown Battlefield Cemetery
Colonial National Historical Park
P. O. Box 210
Yorktown, VA 23690
(757) 898-3400

**DEPARTMENT OF THE ARMY
NATIONAL CEMETERIES**

United States Soldiers' &
Airmen's Home National
Cemetery

21 Harewood Road, NW
Washington, DC 20011
(202) 829-1829

STATE VETERANS CEMETERIES

ALABAMA

Alabama State Veterans Memorial
Cemetery At Spanish Fort
34904 State Highway 225
Spanish Fort, AL 36577

ARIZONA

Southern Arizona Veterans Memorial 1
14317 Veterans Drive
Camp Navajo
PO Box 16419
Bellemont, AZ
(928) 214-3474

ARKANSAS

Arkansas Veterans Cemetery
1501 W Maryland Avenue
North Little Rock, AR 72120
(501) 683-2259

CALIFORNIA

Veterans Memorial Grove Cemetery
Veterans Home of California
Yountville, CA 94599
(707) 944-4600

Northern California Veterans Cemetery
P.O. Box 76
11800 Gas Point Road
Igo, CA 96047
(866) 777-4533

COLORADO

Colorado State Veterans Cemetery At
Homelake
3749 Sherman Avenue
Monte Vista, CO 81144
(719) 852-5118

Veterans Memorial Cemetery Of
Western Colorado
2830 D Road
Grand Junction, CO 81505
(970) 263-8986

CONNECTICUT

Colonel Raymond F. Gates Memorial

122

Cemetery Veterans Home and Hospital
287 West Street
Rocky Hill, CT 06067
(860) 721-5838

Spring Grove Veterans Cemetery
Darien, CT C/O Veterans Home and
Hospital
287 West Street
Rocky Hill, CT 06067
(860) 721-5838

Middletown Veterans Cemetery C/O
Veterans Home and Hospital
287 West Street
Rocky Hill, CT 06067
(860) 721-5838

DELAWARE

Delaware Veterans Memorial Cemetery
2465 Chesapeake City Road
Bear, DE 19701
(302) 834-8046

Delaware Veterans Memorial
Cemetery-Sussex County
RD 5 Box 100
Millsboro, DE 19966
(302) 934-5653

GEORGIA

Georgia Veterans Memorial Cemetery
2617 Vinson Highway
Milledgeville, Georgia 31061
(478) 445-3363

Georgia Veterans Memorial Cemetery
8819 U.S. Highway 301
Glennville, Georgia 30427
(912)-654-5398

HAWAII

Director, Office of Veterans Services
459 Patterson Road
E-Wing, Room 1-A103
Honolulu, HI 96189
(808) 433-0420

Hawaii State Veterans Cemetery
45-349 Kamehameha Highway
Kaneohe, HI 96744
(808) 233-3630

East Hawaii Veterans Cemetery
No. I County of Hawaii
25 Aupuni Street

Hilo, HI 96720
(Island of Hawaii)
(808) 961-8311

East Hawaii Veterans Cemetery
-No. II
County of Hawaii
25 Aupuni Street
Hilo, HI 96720
(Island of Hawaii)
(808) 961-8311

Kauai Veterans Cemetery County of
Kauai Public Works
3021 Umi Street
Lihue, HI 96766
(Island of Kauai)
(808) 241-6670

Maui Veterans Cemetery
1295 Makawao Avenue,
Box 117
Makawao, HI 96768 (Island of Maui)
(808) 572-7272

Hoolehua Veterans
Cemetery (Molokai)
P. O. Box 526
Kauna Kakai, HI 96748
(Island of Molokai)
(808) 553-3204

Lanai Veterans Cemetery Maui County
(Island of Lanai)
PO Box 630359
Lanai City, Hawaii 96763

IDAHO

Idaho Veterans Cemetery
10101 North Horseshoe Bend Road
Boise, ID 83714
(208) 334-4796

ILLINOIS

Sunset Cemetery Illinois Veterans
Home
1707 North 12th Street
Quincy, IL 62301
(217) 222-8641

INDIANA

Indiana State Soldiers Home Cemetery
3851 North River Road
West Lafayette, IN 47906-3765
(765) 463-1502

123

Indiana Veterans Memorial Cemetery
1415 North Gate Road
Madison, IN 47250
(812) 273-9220

IOWA

Iowa Veterans Home and Cemetery
13th & Summit Streets
Marshalltown, IA 50158
(641) 753-4309

Iowa Veterans Cemetery
34024 Veterans Memorial Drive
Adel, Iowa 50003-3300
(515) 996-9048

KANSAS

Kansas Veterans Cemetery At Fort
Dodge
714 Sheridan, Unit #66
Fort Dodge, KS 67801
(620) 338-8775

Kansas Veterans Cemetery At
Wakeeney
P.O. Box 185
4035 13th Street
Wakeeney, KS 67672
(785) 743-5685

Kansas Veterans Cemetery At Winfield
1208 North College
Winfield, KS 67156
(620) 229-2287

KENTUCKY

Kentucky Veterans Cemetery
Central
1111 Louisville Road
Frankfort, Kentucky
(502) 564-9281

Kentucky Veterans Cemetery
North 205 Eibeck Lane
P.O. Box 467
Williamstown, Kentucky 41097
(859)-823-0720

Kentucky Veteran's Cemetery West
5817 Fort Campbell Boulevard
Hopkinsville, Kentucky 42240
(270) 707-9653

LOUISIANA

Northwest Louisiana Veterans

Cemetery
7970 Mike Clark Road
Keithville, Louisiana 71047
(318) 925-0612

MAINE

Maine Veterans Memorial
Cemetery (Closed)
Civic Center Drive
Augusta, Maine

Maine Veterans Memorial Cemetery--
Mt. Vernon Rd.
163 Mt. Vernon Road
Augusta, ME 04330
(207) 287-3481

Northern Maine Veterans Cemetery-
Caribou
37 Lombard Road
Caribou, ME 04736
(207)-492-1173

MARYLAND

Maryland State Veterans Cemeteries
Federal Building- 31 Hopkins Plaza
Baltimore, MD 21201
(410) 962-4700

Cheltenham Veterans
Cemetery
11301 Crain Highway
P. O. Box 10
Cheltenham, MD 20623
(301) 372-6398

Crownsville Veterans Cemetery
1080 Sunrise Beach Road Crownsville,
MD 21032
(410) 987-6320

Eastern Shore Veterans Cemetery
6827 East New Market Ellwood Road
Hurlock, MD 21643
(410) 943-3420

Garrison Forest Veterans Cemetery
11501 Garrison Forest Road
Owings Mills, MD 21117
(410) 363-6090

Rocky Gap Veterans Cemetery
14205 Pleasant Valley Road, NE
Flintstone, MD 21530
(301) 777-2185

124

MASSACHUSETTS

Massachusetts State Veterans Cemetery
(Agawam & Winchendon)
1390 Main Street
Agawam, MA 01001
(413) 821-9500

Winchendon Veterans Cemetery
111 Glenallen Street
Winchendon, MA 01475
(978) 297-9501

MICHIGAN

Grand Rapids Home for Veterans
Cemetery
3000 Monroe, NW
Grand Rapids, MI 49505
(616) 364-5400

MINNESOTA

MN State Veterans Cemetery
15550 HWY 15
Little Falls, MN 56345
(320) 616-2527

MISSOURI

St. James Missouri Veterans Home
Cemetery
620 North Jefferson
St. James, MO 65559
(573) 265-3271

Missouri Veterans Cemetery -
Higgensville, MO
20109 Bus. Hwy. 13
Higgensville, MO 64037
(660) 584-5252

Missouri Veterans Cemetery –
Springfield. MO
5201 South Southwood Road
Springfield, MO 65804
(417) 823-3944

Missouri State Veterans Cemetery
Bloomfield
17357 Stars and Strips Way Bloomfield,
Missouri 63825
(573) 568-3871

Missouri State Veterans Cemetery -
Jacksonville
1479 County Road 1675
Jacksonville, Missouri 65260
(660) 295-4237

MONTANA

State Veterans Cemetery
Fort William H. Harrison Box 5715
Helena, MT 59604
(406) 324-3740

State Veterans Cemetery Miles City
Highway 59
Miles City, MT 59301
(406) 324-3740

Montana Veterans Home Cemetery
P. O. Box 250
Columbia Falls, MT 59912
(406) 892-3256

NEBRASKA

Nebraska Veterans Home Cemetery
Burkett Station
Grand Island, NE 68803
(308) 385-6252, Ext. 230

NEVADA

Commissioner of Veterans Affairs
1201 Terminal Way, Room 108
Reno, NV 89520
(775) 688-1155

Northern Nevada Veterans
Memorial Cemetery
14 Veterans Way
Fernley, NV 8940
(775) 575-4441

Southern Nevada Veterans Memorial
Cemetery
1900 Buchanan Boulevard
Boulder City, NV 89005
(702) 486-5920

NEW HAMPSHIRE

NH State Veterans Cemetery
110 Daniel Webster Hwy, Route 3
Boscawen, NH 03303
(603) 796-2026

NEW JERSEY

Brigadier General William C. Doyle
Veterans Memorial Cemetery
350 Provenceline Road,
Route #2
Wrightstown, NJ 08562
(609) 758-7250

New Jersey Memorial Home Cemetery
(Closed)
524 N.W. Boulevard
Vineland, NJ 08360
(609) 696-6350

NORTH CAROLINA

Western Carolina State Veterans
Cemetery
962 Old Highway 70,
West Black Mountain, NC 28711
(828) 669-0684

Coastal Carolina State Veterans
Cemetery
P. O. Box 1486
Jacksonville, NC 28541
(910) 347-4550 or 3570

Sandhills State Veterans Cemetery
P. O. Box 39
400 Murchison Road
Spring Lake, NC 28390
(910) 436-5630 or 5635

NORTH DAKOTA

North Dakota Veterans Cemetery
1825 46ᵗʰ Street
Mandan, ND 58554
(701) 667-1418

OHIO

Ohio Veterans Home Cemetery
3416 Columbus Avenue
Sandusky, OH 44870
(419) 625-2454, Ext. 200

OKLAHOMA

Oklahoma Veterans Cemetery Military
Department (OKFAC)
3501 Military Circle N.E.
Oklahoma City, OK 73111-4398
(405) 228-5334

PENNSYLVANIA

Pennsylvania Soldiers and Sailors
Home Cemetery
P. O. Box 6239
560 East Third Street
Erie, PA 16512-6239
(814) 871-4531

RHODE ISLAND

Rhode Island Veterans Cemetery
301 South County
Trail Exeter, RI 02822-9712
(401) 268-3088

SOUTH CAROLINA

M.J. "Dolly" Cooper Veterans Cemetery
140 Inway Drive
Anderson, SC 29621
(864) 332-8022

SOUTH DAKOTA

SD Veterans Home Cemetery
2500 Minnekahta Avenue
Hot Springs, SD 57747
(605) 745-5127

TENNESSEE

East Tennessee State Veterans
Cemetery
5901 Lyons View Pike
Knoxville, TN 37919
(865) 594-6776

Middle Tennessee Veterans Cemetery
7931 McCrory Lane
Nashville, TN 37221
(615) 532-2238

West Tennessee Veterans Cemetery
4000 Forest Hill/Irene Road
Memphis, TN 38125
(901) 543-7005

TEXAS

Central Texas State Veterans Cemetery
11463 South Highway 195
Killeen, Texas 76542
(512) 463-5977

Rio Grande Valley
State Veterans Cemetery
2520 South Inspiration Road
Mission, TX 78572
(956) 583-7227

UTAH

Utah State Veterans Cemetery
Utah Parks and Recreation
17111 South Camp Williams Road
Bluffdale, UT 84065
(801) 254-9036

VERMONT

Vermont Veterans Home War
Memorial Cemetery
325 North Street
Bennington, VT 05201
(802) 442-6353

Vermont Veterans Memorial Cemetery
120 State Street
Montpelier, VT 05602-4401
(802) 828-3379

VIRGINIA

Virginia Veterans Cemetery
10300 Pridesville Road
Amelia, VA 23002
(804) 561-1475

Albert G. Horton, Jr. Memorial
Veterans Cemetery

5310 Milner's Road
Suffolk, Virginia 23434
(757) 334-4731

WASHINGTON

Washington Soldiers Home Colony and
Cemetery
1301 Orting-Kapowsin Highway
Orting, WA 98360
(360) 893-4500

Washington Veterans Home Cemetery
PO. Box 698
Retsil, WA 98378
(360) 895-4700

WISCONSIN

Northern Wisconsin Veterans
Memorial Cemetery
N4063 Wildcat Road QQ
Spooner, WI 54801
(715) 635-5360

Wisconsin Veterans Memorial Cemetery
Wisconsin Veterans Home
N2665 Highway QQ
King, WI 54946
(715) 258-5586

Southern Wisconsin Veterans Memorial Cemetery
21731 Spring Street
Union Grove, WI 53182
(262) 878-5660

WYOMING

Oregon Trail Veterans Cemetery
89 Cemetery Road, Box 669
Evansville, WY 82636
(307) 235-6673

TERRITORIES

Guam Veterans Cemetery
490 Chalan Palayso Agatna Heights
Guam 96910
(671) 475-4225

SAIPAN
CNMI Veterans Cemetery Military/Veterans Affairs
Box 503416
Saipan, MP 96950
(670) 664-2650

NOTE:
All state cemeteries (except Nevada, Pennsylvania,
Wyoming and Utah) restrict burials to state residents.

CHAPTER 11

HEALTHCARE BENEFITS

Individuals are encouraged to contact the nearest VA benefits or healthcare facility to obtain the latest information regarding healthcare benefits. Legislation often changes the specific regulations regarding healthcare and nursing home care.

HEALTH ID CARDS

The VA announced the rollout of secure veterans health identification cards. The new cards are designed to have additional security features. The card is called the Veterans Health Identification Card, which is similar to a traditional health insurance ID card. It displays the veteran's member and plan ID, and demonstrates their enrollment in VA healthcare.

CHOICE PROGRAM

If you are already enrolled in VA health care, the Choice Program allows you to receive health care within your community. Using this program does NOT impact your existing VA health care, or any other VA benefit.

AM I ELIGIBLE?

If you are already enrolled in VA health care, you may be able to receive care within your community, instead of waiting for a VA appointment or traveling to a VA facility.

You are eligible if any of these situations apply to you:

	Key Takeaways

Key Takeaways

The main factor used to determine eligibility to receive VA health care benefits is veteran status.

Status is determined by active duty in the military, and a discharge or release from active military service under other-than-dishonorable conditions.

Many veterans qualify for cost-free health care services based on a compensable service-connected condition or other qualifying factors.

Some veterans may be required to pay a copay for treatment of their non-service connected conditions.

- You have been (or will be) waiting more than 30 days for VA medical care.
- You live more than 40 miles away from a VA medical care facility or face one of several excessive travel burdens.

ADDITIONAL PROGRAM INFORMATION

The Choice Program does not impact your existing VA health care or any other VA benefit.

If you did not receive a Choice Card or if you cannot find your card, please call 1-866-606-8198 to learn more about eligibility for the Veterans Choice Program. If you are satisfied with your wait time at a VA facility and wish to continue waiting for VA care, there is nothing you need to do at this time.

Care in the community is only covered by VA for medical needs which have been approved by your VA physician. The VA can schedule an appointment for other medical needs, but we can only cover the cost of care related to your VA-approved health needs. The Veteran Choice Program is part of the Veterans Access, Choice, and Accountability Act of 2014 (VACAA).

VETERAN HEALTH REGISTRIES

Certain veterans can participate in a VA health registry and receive free medical examinations, including laboratory and other diagnostic tests, when determined necessary by an examining clinician.

GULF WAR REGISTRY:

For veterans who served in the Gulf War and Operation Iraqi Freedom

DEPLETED URANIUM REGISTRIES:

VA maintains two registries for veterans possibly exposed to depleted uranium. The first is for veterans who served in the Gulf War, including Operation Iraqi Freedom. The second is for veterans who served elsewhere, including Bosnia and Afghanistan.

AGENT ORANGE REGISTRY:

For veterans possible exposed to dioxin or other toxic substances in herbicides used during the Vietnam War, while serving in Korea in 1968 or 1969, or as a result of testing, transporting, or spraying herbicides for military purposes.

IONIZING RADIATION REGISTRY:

For veterans possibly exposed to atomic radiation during the following activities:

Atmospheric detonation of a nuclear device;

Occupation of Hiroshima or Nagasaki from August 6, 1945 through July 1, 1946;

Internment as a prisoner of war in Japan during WWII

Serving in official military duties at the gaseous diffusion plants at Paducah, KY; Portsmouth, OH; or the K-25 area at Oak Ridge, TN for at least 250 days before February 1, 1992, or in Longshot, Milrow or Cannikin underground nuclear tests at Amchitka Island, Alaska, before January 1, 1974; or

Treatment with nasopharyngeal (NP) radium during military service.

ELIGIBILITY

The primary factor in determining a veteran's eligibility to receive VA health care benefits is "veteran status." "Veteran status" is established by active duty service in the military ,naval, or air service and a discharge or release from active military service under other than dishonorable conditions.

The veteran's length of service may also matter. It depends on when he or she

served. There is no length of service requirement for:

- Former enlisted persons who started active duty before September 8, 1980; or
- Former officers who first entered active duty before October 17, 1981.
- All other veterans must have 24 months of continuous active duty military service or meet one of the exceptions described below.

EXCEPTIONS TO THE 24-MONTH ACTIVE DUTY RULE

The 24 continuous months of active duty service requirement does not apply to:

- Reservists who were called to Active Duty and who completed the term for which they were called, and who were granted an "other than dishonorable" discharge; or
- National Guard members who were called to Active Duty by federal executive order, and who completed the term for which they were called, and who were granted an "other than dishonorable" discharge; or
- Veterans requesting a benefit for, or in connection with, a service-connected condition or disability; or
- Veterans who were discharged or released from active duty under section 1171 or 1173 of title 10; or
- Veterans who were discharged or released from active duty for a disability incurred or aggravated in line of duty; or
- Veterans who have been determined by VA to have compensable service-connected conditions; or
- Veterans requesting treatment for and/or counseling of sexual trauma that occurred while on active military service, for treatment of conditions related to ionizing radiation or for head or neck cancer related to nose or throat radium treatment while in the military.

ENROLLMENT

The very first step in obtaining access to your VA Health Benefits is to apply for enrollment. Effective immediately, veterans who served in a theater of combat operations after November 11, 1998, can complete applications for enrollment in VA health care by telephone without the need for a signed paper application.

All other Veterans may apply by phone effective since July 5, 2016.

When veterans choose to enroll, VA offers an enhancement to their enrollment experience through "Welcome to VA" (W2VA). W2VA enhances communication by reaching out to newly enrolled veterans through personal phone calls upon enrollment, providing assistance with health care inquiries and assisting with their initial appointment at their preferred VA healthcare facility.

In addition, VA sends each new enrollee an introductory letter and personalized Veterans Health Benefits Handbook in the mail.

All veterans seeking VA healthcare are required to be enrolled unless they are in one of the following categories:

- VA rated the individual as having a service-connected disability of 50% or more;
- It has been less than one year since the veteran was discharged from military service for a disability that the military determined was incurred or aggravated in the line of duty, and has not yet been rated by VA;
- Veteran is seeking care from VA for a service-connected disability only.

As part of the enrollment process, a veteran may select any VA health care facility to serve as his or her primary treatment facility.

There are three ways a veteran can apply to enroll in healthcare benefits. The first is to obtain the enrollment form, "10-10EZ" from their local VA Medical Center or Clinic, in person. The second way is telephone; by calling (877) 222-VETS (8387) Monday through Friday between 8:00 a.m. and 8:00 p.m. Eastern Time. The third way to apply is online, through the VA's website.

The application will be processed and forwarded to the VA Health Eligibility Center in Atlanta, GA. The Health Eligibility Center will notify the veteran of his or her status.

Once enrolled, most veterans will remain enrolled from year to year without further action on their part. However, certain veterans are required to provide income information to determine their priority level. These veterans will be mailed a "VA Form 10-10 EZ" for completion for re-enrollment on an annual basis, or they can renew their benefits by visiting the VA's website.

A veteran may choose not to be re-enrolled, or changes in VA funding may reduce the number of priority groups VA can enroll in a given fiscal year. If VA cannot renew enrollment for another year, the veteran will be notified in writing before their enrollment period expires.

PRIORITY GROUPS

The number of veterans who can be enrolled in the health care program is determined by the amount of money Congress gives VA each year. Since funds are limited, VA set up priority groups to make sure that certain groups of veterans are able to be enrolled before others.

Once a veteran applies for enrollment, his or her eligibility will be verified. Based on the individual's specific eligibility status, he or she will be assigned a priority group.

The priority groups range from 1-8 with 1 being the highest priority for enrollment. Some veterans may have to agree to pay copay to be placed in certain priority groups.

A veteran may be eligible for more than one Enrollment Priority Group. In that case, VA will always place him or her in the highest priority group that he or she is eligible for. Under the Medical Benefits Package, the same services are generally available to all enrolled veterans.

The priority groups are complicated and some reference financial thresholds.

PRIORITY GROUP 1

Veterans with service-connected disabilities rated 50% or more disabling; or Veterans determined by VA to be unemployable due to service-connected conditions.

PRIORITY GROUP 2

Veterans with service-connected disabilities rated 30% or 40% disabling.

PRIORITY GROUP 3

Veterans who are former POWs;

Veterans whose discharge was for a disability that was incurred or aggravated in the line of duty;

Veterans with service-connected disabilities rated 10% or 20% disabling;

Veterans who are Purple Heart recipients (unless eligible for a higher Priority Group);

Veterans who are Medal of Honor Recipients;

Veterans awarded special eligibility classification under Title 38, U.S.C., Section 1151, "benefits for individuals disabled by treatment or vocational rehabilitation".

PRIORITY GROUP 4

Veterans who are receiving aid and attendance or housebound benefits from VA; Veterans who have been determined by VA to be catastrophically disabled.

PRIORITY GROUP 5

Nonservice-connected veterans and service-connected veterans rated 0% disabled whose annual income and net worth are below the established dollar threshold. (Veterans in this priority group must provide VA with information on their annual income and net worth in order to determine whether they are below the "means test" threshold; or agree to co-payment requirements.

The threshold is adjusted annually, and announced in January. In making the assessment, the veteran's household income is considered.);

Veterans receiving VA pension benefits; Veterans eligible for Medicaid benefits.

PRIORITY GROUP 6

Veterans with 0% service-connected conditions, but receiving VA compensation benefits Veterans exposed to ionizing radiation during atmospheric testing or during the occupation of Hiroshima and Nagasaki.

Project 112/SHAD participants.

Veterans who served in the Republic of Vietnam between January 9, 1962 and May 7, 1975.

Veterans who served in the Southwest Asia theater of operations from August 2, 1990 through November 11, 1998.

Veterans who served in a theater of combat operations after November 11, 1998 as follows:

Veterans discharged from active duty on or after January 28, 2003, for five years post discharge.

PRIORITY GROUP 7

Veterans with incomes below the geographic means test (GMT) income thresholds and who agree to pay the applicable copayment

PRIORITY GROUP 8

Veterans with gross household incomes above the VA national income threshold and the geographically-adjusted income threshold for their resident location and who agrees to pay copays

Veterans eligibility for enrollment:
- Noncompensable 0% service-connected and:
- Subpriority a: Enrolled as of January 16, 2003, and who have remained enrolled since that date and/or placed in this subpriority due to changed eligibility status
- Subpriority b: Enrolled on or after June 15, 2009 whose income exceeds the current VA National Income Thresholds or VA National Geographic Income

thresholds by 10% or less

Veterans eligibility for enrollment:
- Non-service-connected and:
- Subpriority c: Enrolled as of January 16, 2003, and who remained enrolled since that date and or/placed in this subpriority due to changed eligibility status
- Subpriority d: Enrolled on or after June 15, 2009 and whose income exceeds the current VA National Income Thresholds or VA National Geographic Income thresholds by 10% or less

Veterans not eligible for enrollment: veterans not meeting the criteria below:
- Subpriority e: Noncompensable 0%service-connected
- Subpriority f: Non-service-connected

SPECIAL ACCESS TO CARE

SERVICE-DISABLED VETERANS

Veterans who are 50 percent or more disabled from service-connected conditions, unemployable due to service-connected conditions, or receiving care for a service-connected disability receive priority in scheduling of hospital or outpatient medical appointments.

MEANS TEST

Most veterans who do not receive a VA disability or pension payment or have a VA special eligibility, such as a recently discharged combat veteran must complete "VA form 10-10EZ." These veterans must provide information on their prior income year total gross household income and net worth to determine eligibility status, and copay responsibility for VA health care and/or prescription medication. Total gross household income includes income of the veteran, spouse and dependent children.

EXISTING HEALTHCARE COVERAGE

Since VA health care depends primarily on annual congressional appropriations, veterans are allowed to keep their current healthcare coverage and are encouraged to do so. Veterans with private insurance or other coverage such as DoD, Medicare, or Medicaid may find these coverages to be a supplement to their VA enrollment. The use of other available healthcare coverage does not affect a veteran's enrollment status. VA does not charge the veteran for insurance company co-payments and deductibles.

When applying for medical care, all veterans will be asked to provide information pertaining to health insurance coverage, including policies held by spouses. VA is obligated to submit claims to insurance carriers for the recovery of costs for medical care provided to nonservice-connected veterans and service-connected veterans for nonservice-connected conditions.

COPAYMENT REQUIREMENTS

While many veterans qualify for free healthcare services based on a VA compensable service-connected condition or other eligibilities, most veterans are required to complete a financial assessment or means test at the time of enrollment to determine if they qualify for free health care services. Veterans whose income exceed VA income limits as well as those who choose not to complete the financial assessment at the time of enrollment must agree to pay required copays for health care services to become eligible for VA health care services.

Veterans Not Required to Make Copays

Some veterans qualify for free healthcare and/or prescriptions based on special eligibility factors including but not limited to:
- Former Prisoner of War status
- 50% or more compensable VA service connected disabilities (0-40% may take copay test to determine prescription copay status)
- Veterans deemed catastrophically disabled by a VA provider

Services Exempt From Inpatient and Outpatient Copays

- Special registry exams offered by VA to evaluate health risks associated with service
- Compensation and Pension exams
- Counseling and care for Military Sexual Trauma
- Care related to a VA-rated service-connected disability
- Readjustment counseling and related mental health services
- Care that is part of a VA research project
- Care for cancer of head or neck caused by nose or throat radium treatments received while in the military
- Care potentially related to combat service for veterans that served in a theater of combat operations after November 11,1998
- Laboratory and electrocardiograms
- Hospice care

Copayment Rates – Current as of January 2017

OUTPATIENT SERVICES	
Basic Services – Services provided by a primary care clinician	$15/visit
Specialty Care Services –services provided by a clinical specialist such as surgeon, radiologist, audiologist, optometrist, cardiologist, and specialty tests such as magnetic resonance imagery (MRI), computerized axial tomography (CAT) scan, and nuclear medicine studies	$50 /visit
Footnotes for outpatient services: *Copayment amount is limited to a single charge per visit regardless of the number of health care providers seen in a single day. The copayment amount is based on the highest level of service received.* *There is no copayment requirement for preventive services such as screenings and immunizations.)*	
MEDICATIONS	
Veterans in Priority Groups 2-6, for each 30-day supply of medication for treatment of nonservice-connected conditions	$8/prescription

(The total amount paid annually by veterans in Priority Groups 2 through 6 is limited to $960.)	
Effective July 1, 2010, Veterans in Priority Groups 7-8, , for each 30- day supply of medication for treatment of nonservice-connected conditions	$9/prescription
(Veterans in Priority Groups 7-8 do not qualify for medication copay annual cap.)	
Veterans in Priority Group 1 do not pay for medications.	
INPATIENT SERVICES	
Priority Group 8 and certain other Veterans are responsible for VA's full inpatient copay rate. Inpatient Copay for the first 90 days of care during a 365-day period	$1,288.00
Priority Group 8 and certain other Veterans are responsible for VA's full inpatient copay rate. Inpatient Copay for each additional 90 days of care during a 365-day period	$644.00
Per Diem Charge Daily Charge for Priority Group 8 and Other Certain Veterans	$10/day $10/day
Priority Group 7 and certain other Veterans are responsible for paying 20 percent of VA's inpatient copay rate. Inpatient Copay for the first 90 days of care during a 365-day period	$267.50
Priority Group 7 and certain other Veterans are responsible for paying 20 percent of VA's inpatient copay rate. Inpatient Copay for each additional 90 days of care during a 365-day period	$128.00
Priority Group 7 And Other Certain Veterans Daily Charge	$2/day
LONG-TERM CARE	
Nursing Home Care / Inpatient Respite Care / Geriatric Evaluation	Maximum of $97/day Adult

Day Health Care / Outpatient Geriatric Evaluation / Outpatient Respite Care	Maximum of $15/day
Domiciliary Care	Maximum of $5/day
Footnote for inpatient services: **Copayments for Long-Term Care services start on the 22nd day of care during any 12-month period — there is no copayment requirement for the first 21 days. Actual copayment charges will vary from Veteran to Veteran depending upon financial information submitted on VA Form 10-10EC.	

HARDSHIP DETERMINATION

If gross household income decreases, a veteran may be eligible for a hardship which may qualify them for copayment exemption for the remaining calendar year and enrollment in a higher priority group.

To request a hardship determination, veterans should send a letter explaining the financial hardship their copayment charges will cause them and a completed Request For Hardship Determination (**VA Form10-10HS**).

Letters and forms can be submitted in person at a local Veteran Affairs Medical Center Business Office or Health Administration Office.
They can also be sent by mail to the Business Office/Health Administration Service at a local VA medical Center.

INFORMATION FOR VETERANS ABOUT MEDICARE PRESCRIPTION DRUG BENEFITS

Beginning January 1, 2006, Medicare prescription drug coverage (Medicare Part D) became available to everyone with Medicare Part A or B coverage. The Medicare prescription drug coverage is wholly voluntary on the part of the participant. Each individual must decide whether to participate based on his or her own circumstances.

How This Affects Veterans:

Each veteran must decide whether to enroll in a Medicare Part D plan based on his or her own situation. An individual's VA prescription drug coverage will not change based on his or her decision to participate in Medicare Part D. VA prescription drug coverage is considered by Medicare to be at least as good as Medicare Part D coverage. (Therefore, it is considered to be creditable coverage. Refer to following section for more information regarding creditable coverage. If an individual's spouse is covered by Medicare, he or she must decide whether to enroll in a Medicare Part D plan regardless of the veteran's decision to participate.

CREDITABLE COVERAGE

Most entities that currently provide prescription drug coverage to Medicare beneficiaries, including VA, must disclose whether the entity's coverage is "creditable prescription drug coverage."

Enrollment in the VA health care system is creditable coverage. This means that VA prescription drug coverage is at least as good as the Medicare Part D coverage.

Because they have creditable coverage, veterans enrolled in the VA health care program who chose not to enroll in a Medicare Part D plan before May 15, 2006 will not have to pay a higher premium on a permanent basis ("late enrollment penalty") if they enroll in a Medicare drug plan during a later enrollment period.

However, if an individual un-enrolls in VA health care or if he or she loses his or her enrollment status through no fault of his/her own (such as an enrollment decision by VA that would further restrict access to certain Priority Groups), he or she may be subject to the late enrollment penalty unless he or she enrolls in a Medicare Part D plan within 62 days of losing VA coverage.

If a veteran becomes a patient or inmate in an institution of another government agency (for example, a state veterans home, a state institution, a jail, or a corrections facility), he or she may not have creditable coverage from VA while in that institution. For further information, individuals should contact the institution where the veteran resides, the VA Health Benefits Service Center at (877) 222-VETS, or the local VA medical facility.

COVERED SERVICES – STANDARD BENEFITS

VA's medical benefits package provides the following health care services to all enrolled veterans:

PREVENTIVE CARE SERVICES
- Immunizations
- Physical Examinations (including eye and hearing examinations)
- Health Care Assessments
- Screening Tests
- Health Education Programs

AMBULATORY (OUTPATIENT) DIAGNOSTIC AND TREATMENT SERVICES
- Emergency outpatient care in VA facilities
- Medical
- Surgical (including reconstructive/plastic surgery as a result of disease or trauma)
- Chiropractic Care
- Bereavement Counseling
- Mental Health
- Substance Abuse

HOSPITAL (INPATIENT) DIAGNOSTIC AND TREATMENT
- Emergency inpatient care in VA facilities
- Medical
- Surgical (including reconstructive/plastic surgery as a result of disease or trauma)
- Mental Health
- Substance Abuse

LIMITED BENEFITS
The following is a partial listing of acute care services which may have limitations and special eligibility criteria:
- Ambulance Services
- Dental Care (refer to Chapter 11 of this book for additional details.)
- Durable Medical Equipment
- Eyeglasses (see footnote below)
- Hearing Aids (see footnote below)
- Home Health Care
- Homeless Programs
- Maternity and Parturition Services—usually provided in non-VA contracted hospitals at VA expense, care is limited to the mother (costs associated with the care of newborn are not covered)

NON-VA HEALTHCARE SERVICES

- Orthopedic, Prosthetic, and Rehabilitative Devices
- Rehabilitative Services
- Readjustment Counseling
- Sexual Trauma Counseling

Footnote: To qualify for hearing aids or eyeglasses, the individual must have a VA service- connected disability rating of 10% or more. An individual may also qualify if he or she is a former prisoner of war, Purple Heart recipient, require this benefit for treatment of a 0% service-connected condition, or are receiving increased pension based on the need for regular aid and attendance or being permanently housebound.

GENERAL EXCLUSIONS

The following is a partial listing of general exclusions:

- Abortions and abortion counseling
- Cosmetic surgery except where determined by VA to be medically necessary for reconstructive or psychiatric care
- Gender alteration
- Health club or spa membership, even for rehabilitation
- Drugs, biological, and medical devices not approved by the Food and Drug Administration unless part of formal clinical trial under an approved research program or when prescribed under a compassionate use exemption.
- Medical care for a veteran who is either a patient or inmate in an institution of another government agency if that agency has a duty to provide the care or services.
- Services not ordered and provided by licensed/accredited professional staff
- Special private duty nursing

EMERGENCY CARE

A medical emergency is defined as a condition of such nation that it would be expected that a delay in immediate medical attention would be life-threatening. With VA medical care, a veteran may receive emergency care at a non-VA health care facility at VA expense when a VA facility or other federal health care facility with which the VA has an agreement can't furnish economical care due to your distance from the facility, or when the VA is unable to furnish the needed emergency services.

VA Payment For Emergency Care

Since payment may be limited to the point when your condition is stable enough for you to travel to a VA facility, you need to contact the nearest VA medical facility as possible. VA may pay for your non-VA emergency care based on the following situations

If you are service-connected: The VA may pay for your non-VA emergency care for a rated service-connected disability, or for your nonservice-connected condition associated with and held to be aggravating for your service- connected condition, or any condition if you are an active participant in the VA Chapter 31 Vocational Rehabilitation program, and you need treatment to make possible your entrance into a course of training or to prevent interruption of a course of training or other approved reason for any condition, if you ware rated as having a total disability permanent in nature resulting from your service-connected disability

VA Payment for Emergency Care of Non-Service- Connected Conditions Without Prior Authorization

VA may pay for emergency care provided in a non-VA facility for treatment of a non-service-connected condition only if all the following conditions are met:

If you are service-connected, not permanently and totally disabled, or nonservice-connected, then the VA may pay for your non-VA emergency care for treatment of a non-service-connected condition if all of the following conditions are met:
- The episode of care can't be paid for under another VA authority, and
- Based on an average knowledge of health and medicine you reasonably expected that a delay in seeking immediate medical attention for have been hazardous to life or health and
- A VA or other federal facility/provider wasn't feasibly available and
- You receive VA medical care within a 24-month period preceding the non VA

139

emergency care and
- The services were furnished by an emergency department or similar facility held out to provide emergency care to the general public and
- You are financially liable to the health care provider for the emergency care and
- You have no other coverage under a health plan including Medicare, Medicaid and Worker's Compensation and
- You have no contractual or legal recourse against a third party that would, in whole, extinguish your liability

FAQs About Veteran Emergency Care

What is An Emergency?

A medical emergency is defined as an injury or illness so severe that without immediate treatment, it threatens your life or health. Your situation is an emergency if you believe your life or health is in danger. If you believe your life or health is in danger, call 911 or go to the ER immediately. You don't need to call the VA before calling an ambulance or going to the ER.

When Should I Contact the VA About An ER Visit?

You, your family, friends or hospital staff should call the closest VACM as possible, and it's best if this happens within 72 hours of an emergency. The VA will need information about your emergency and the services being provided, and the VA can provide guidance on what charges are covered.

If the Doctor Wants Me To Be Admitted to the Hospital, Do I Need Advance Approval from the VA?

If you are being admitted because of an emergency an advanced approval isn't required, but prompt VA notification is important.

If I Am Admitted to the Hospital As a Result of An Emergency, How Much Will VA Pay?

Depending on your VA eligibility, VA may pay all, some or none of the charges. Since payment may be limited to the point when your condition is stable enough for you to travel to a VA facility, you need to contact the nearest VA medical facility as soon as possible. An emergency is deemed to have ended at the point when a VA provider has determined that, based on sound medical judgment, you should be transferred from the non-VA facility to a VA medical center.

If you are service-connected the VA may pay for your non-VA emergency care for a rated Service-connected disability, or for your Nonservice-connected condition associated with and held to be aggravating your Service-connected condition, or any condition, if you are an active participant in the VA Chapter 31 Vocational Rehabilitation program, and you need treatment to make possible your entrance into a course of training or to prevent interruption of a course of training or other approved reason or any condition, if you are rated as having a total disability permanent in nature resulting from your Service-connected disability.

If you are service-connected, not permanently and totally disabled, or non-service connected, then VA may pay for non-VA emergency care for treatment of a nonservice-connected condition if all the following conditions are met:

- The episode of care can't be paid under another VA authority and
- Based on an average knowledge of health and medicine, you reasonably expected

that delay in seeking immediate medical attention would have been hazardous to your life or health and
- A VA or other federal facility or provider was not feasibly available and
- You received VA medical care within a 24-month period preceding the non-VA emergency care and
- The services were furnished by an Emergency Department or similar facility held out to provide emergency care to the general public and
- You have no other coverage under a health plan including Medicare, Medicaid and Worker's Compensation and
- You have no contractual resource against a third party that would in whole extinguish your liability

Preauthorized Non-VA Inpatient/Outpatient Medical Care

This Care in the Community program provides payment authorization for eligible Veterans to obtain routine outpatient or inpatient medical services through community providers. An authorization may be granted when it has been determined that direct VA services are either geographically inaccessible or VA facilities are not available to meet a Veteran's needs. All community services must be preapproved before a Veteran receives treatment.

However, it may not be possible to contact VA prior to treatment in emergency situations.

Each individual Veteran's eligibility status and medical care needs are reviewed to decide whether payment for community treatment can be approved. The VA also requires a 72-hour notification of emergency room care.

Individual eligibility determinations are difficult, and therefore outside the scope of this general information. Please contact your local VA health care facility for individual Veteran eligibility questions or concerns.

A local VA Medical Center may request medical documentation to support adjudication of a submitted claim from a community health care provider. In addition, standard billing forms such as the UB-04 CMS-1450* or CMS-1500 are required.

Eligibility for VA payment of emergency care, as well as deadlines for filing claims, depend upon whether or not you have a service-connected condition and your specific eligibility for non-VA medical care. It is important to inform the non-VA medical facility treating you that you are a veteran. If inpatient care is required and you desire VA care and payment consideration, always inform the non-VA medical facility treating you that you are a veteran. If inpatient care is required and you desire VA care and payment consideration, always inform the non-VA medical facility staff that you want to transfer to a VA facility when your medical condition stabilizes. It's important to contact the closest VA facility as soon as possible to find out more about VA payment of your emergency care.

AMBULANCE TRANSPORT

The Department of Veterans Affairs may provide or reimburse for land or air ambulance transport of certain eligible veterans in relation to VA care or VA-authorized community care.

VA pays for ambulance transport when the transport has been preauthorized and in certain emergency situations without preauthorization. Two criteria must be met for the VA to pay for ambulance transport.

First, the claimant must meet appropriate administrative eligibility, and a VA provider must determine medical need for ambulance transport.

VA must be providing medical care or paying a community care provider for medical care in order to pay for the transport in relation to that care.

PREAUTHORIZED AMBULANCE TRANSPORT

Transport is arranged for eligible veterans before inpatient or outpatient care. To qualify a veteran must meet the following administrative requirements:

- Has a single or combined service-connected rating of 30 percent or more, or
- Veteran is in receipt of VA pension, or
- Previous calendar year income does not exceed maximum VA pension rate, or
- Projected income in travel year does not exceed maximum VA pension rate, or
- Projected income in travel year does not exceed maximum VA pension rate, or
- Travel is in connection with care for a service-connected disability, or
- Travel is for a Compensation and Pension exam, or
- Travel is to obtain a service dog, and
- A VA clinician must determine and document that special mode transportation is medically required

UNAUTHORIZED AMBULANCE TRANSPORT

Transport must be preauthorized by VA unless it is in relationship to a medical emergency. Veterans do not have to contact VA in advance of a medical emergency and are encouraged to call 911 or go to the nearest medical emergency room.

VA may pay for ambulance transport that's not preauthorized in the following situations:

- Transport from point of community emergency to a VA facility if the veteran meets administrative and eligibility criteria noted under "Preauthorized ambulance transport"
- Transport from point of community emergency to a community care facility if VA pays for the emergency care in the community care facility under the nonservice-connected or service-connected authorities detailed below
- VA is contacted within 72 hours of care at a community care facility and retroactively authorizes the community care, and the veteran meets administrative and medical travel eligibility noted under "preauthorized ambulance transport."

In order for VA to pay for unauthorized ambulance transport, the care associated with the transport must meet one of the following authorities for VA payment:

Emergent care for nonservice-connected conditions (38 United States Code (U.S.C.) 1725 ["Mill Bill"])

- Based on average knowledge of health and medicine, it is reasonably expected that a delay in seeking immediate medical attention would have been hazardous to life or health and
- The episode of care can't be paid under another VA authority and
- A VA or other federal facility/provider was not feasibly available and
- VA medical care was received within 24 months prior to the episode of emergency care and
- The services were furnished by an Emergency Department or similar facility that provides emergency care to the general public and
- Veteran is financial liable for the emergency care and
- Veteran has no other coverage under a health care plan including Medicare, Medicaid or Worker's Compensation, and
- There is no contractual or legal recourse against a third party that could, in whole, extinguish liability

Emergent Care For Service-Connect Conditions (38 U.S.C. 1728)

- Care is for a service-connected disability or
- Care is for a nonservice-connected condition associated with and aggravating a service-connected condition or
- Care is for any condition of an active participant in the VA Chapter 31 Vocational Rehabilitation program and is needed to make possible entrance into a course of training or to prevent interruption of a course of training, or
- Care is for any condition of a veteran rated as having a total disability permanent in nature resulting from a service-connected disability and
- Based on an average knowledge of health and medicine, it is reasonably expected that delay in seeking immediate medical attention would have been hazardous to life or health and
- A VA or other federal facility/provider was not feasibly available

Retroactive Preauthorization (38 CFR 17.54)

In case of an emergency which existed at the time of treatment, VA may retroactively preauthorize the care if:
- An application for VA payment of care provided is made within 72 hours after the emergency care initiated and
- Veteran meets the eligibility criteria for community care at VA expense of 38 U.S.C. 1703

Reimbursement Considerations

- If the emergency room visit and/or admission meets eligibility for VA reimbursement, and the veteran meets beneficiary travel requirements, the ambulance will be paid from the scene of the incident to the first community care facility providing necessary care
- If a veteran arrives via ambulance but leaves the hospital before being treated by a physician, the ambulance is not guaranteed to be covered by VA regardless of eligibility
- Accepted VA payments are payments in full. Balance due billing of VA or veterans is prohibited. VA pays the authorized amount or not at all.

Documents Needed To Process Claims

In order to consider a claim for VA payment of emergency care provided and associated ambulance transport, VA needs the following documents:
- Documented request or application for VA payment of emergency transportation (usually a Health Care Financing Administration form or a bill). Unless transport is preauthorized, the application must be made within 30 days of transport.
- Ambulance trip report documenting circumstances of medical event and care provided by the ambulance service.
- Invoice from ambulance service and community care provider.
- Community care facility records of care provided to the veteran—VA will request these from facility.

All required documents must be received prior to payment consideration. Payment for associated ambulance transport can't occur unless VA is providing or paying for the emergency care.

Appeals

If a claim does not meet VA payment criteria (is not payable,) then it's denied and both the community care provider and veteran are provided an explanation of denial and notified of the right to appeal the decision (VA Form 4107, Notification of Rights to Appeal Decision).

PATIENT-CENTERED COMMUNITY CARE (PC3)

Patient-Centered Community Care is a Veterans Health Administration (VHA) nationwide program that utilizes health care contracts to provide eligible Veterans access to primary care, inpatient/outpatient specialty care, mental health care, limited emergency care, and limited newborn care for enrolled female Veterans following birth of a child.

In instances where you require primary and specialty care that is not readily available through your VA Health Care Facility (HCF), your HCF may use a Patient-Centered Community Care (PC3) contract to purchase your care. Your HCF's clinical and Non-VA care teams coordinate to determine if the care is available at your HCF, a nearby HCF or another health care partner. If not, they will look to the PC3 contract to buy the care. If you need care, you should always start with your VA health care provider at your local facility.

If your VA provider has authorized health care for you through a PC3 contract, you should receive a flyer from your HCF for your respective contractor at the time of referral.

Contracts have been awarded to Health Net Federal Services and TriWest Healthcare Alliance in the following regions:

Health Net Federal Services:

- Region 1: VISNs 1, 2, 3 and 4
- Region 2: VISNs 5, 6, 7 and 8
- Region 4: VISNs 10, 11, 12, 19 and 23

TriWest Healthcare Alliance

- Region 3: VISNs 9, 15, 16 and 17
- Region 5AL VISNs 18, 20 (excluding Alaska), 21 (excluding Hawaii and Pacific Islands), and 22
- Region 5B: VISN 21—Hawaii and Pacific Islands (Philippines not covered)
- Region 6: VISN 20—Alaska

STEP 1: An eligible Veteran visits their VA primary care provider and requires primary or specialty health care that is not readily available at the local VA Medical Center (VAMC).

STEP 2: The Non-VA Medical Care Office authorizes the Veteran for care through PC3 if care is not available through another VAMC, sharing agreement, Academic Affiliate or pilot.

STEP 3: The Veteran is contacted by a regional contractor within five days of authorization to set up an appointment. (The contractor should ensure that the Veteran's commute is within the standard.) VA sends the medical information to the non-VA provider.

STEP 4: The Veteran sees the local PC3 provider within 30 days of appointment scheduling.

STEP 5: The Veteran's records are returned to the VAMC within 14 days for an outpatient visit or within 30 days for an inpatient visit.

STEP 6: VA continues to provide and coordinate patient care. Veterans may be surveyed about their health care experience to give patient feedback which helps ensure PC3 meets Veterans' needs.

PC3 sets contractual requirements that benefit Veterans and the VA Medical Centers. These contracts:
- Ensure quality as providers and facilities meet quality standards

- Provide efficiency as providers help the VA Medical Centers (VAMC) manage high volumes of one type of care. Contractors set appointments and authorizations do not require additional contracting review
- Convenient for Veterans who can be seen quickly and within required commute times
- Decrease improper payments as payment rates are defined by the contract and contractors perform an additional level of review to ensure services performed match the authorization and were billed correctly to VA
- Support care coordination by providing medical documentation back to the VAMC in a timely manner
- Standardize processes by providing national contract administration and oversight from the VHA Office of Community Care, and integrating into Non-VA Care Coordination processes
- Support reimbursement as appointment information provided by the contractor allows for review of third party payer precertification

VETERANS TRANSPORTATION PROGRAM

VA Veterans Transportation Program (VTP) offers veterans travel solutions to and from VA health care facilities. These services include Beneficiary Travel (BT), Veterans Transportation Service (VTS), and Highly Rural Transportation Grants (HRTG).

Veterans Transportation Service

The Veterans Transportation Service (VTS) provides safe and reliable transportation to veterans who require assistance traveling to and from VA health care facilities and authorized non-VA health care appointments. VTS also partners with service providers in local communities to serve veterans transportation needs. Partners include Veterans Service Organizations (VSOs), local and national non-profit groups, and federal, state and local transportation services.

VA recognizes Veterans who are visually impaired, elderly, or immobilized due to disease or disability, and particularly those living in remote and rural areas face challenges traveling to their VA health care appointments. Veterans Transportation Service (VTS) is working to establish Mobility Managers at each local VA facility to help Veterans meet their transportation needs.

VTS has established a network of transportation options for Veterans through joint efforts with VA's Office of Rural Health and organizations, such as Veterans Service Organizations (VSOs); community transportation providers; federal, state and local government transportation agencies; non-profits and Veterans Transportation Community Living Initiative (VTCLI) grantees.

Veterans who are eligible for VA health care benefits and have a VA-authorized appointment are eligible for transportation through the VTS program based on the availability and guidelines in place at their local facility. Each local VA authorized facility has ridership guidelines based on their capabilities.

Highly Rural Transportation Grants

Highly Rural Transportation Grants (HRTG) is a grant-based program that helps veterans in highly rural areas travel to VA or VA-authorized health care facilities. This program provides grant funding to Veteran Service Organizations and State Veterans Service Agencies to provide transportation services in eligible counties

HRTGs provide transportation programs in counties with fewer than seven people per square mile. There is no cost to participate in the program for veterans who live in an area where HRTG is available.

Grantee Organization Name	Details
North Dakota Department of Veterans Affairs	Eligible Counties: Adams, Billings, Bottineau, Bowman, Burke, Cavalier, Divide, Dickey, Dunn, Emmons, Foster, Golden Valley, Grant, Griggs, Hettinger, Kidder, Lamoure, Logan, McHenry, McIntosh, McKenzie, McLean, Mountrail, Nelson, Oliver, Pierce, Renville, Sargent, Sheridan, Sioux, Slope, Steele, Towner Call for Transportation Services: 1-800-920-9595
North Dakota-Robert Tovsrud VFW Post 757	Eligible Counties: Benson, Eddie, Wells Call for Transportation Services: 701-438-2192
South Dakota-American Legion Stanley Post 20	Eligible Counties: Clark, Dewey, Hand, Hyde, Haakon, Jerauld, Jones, Kingsbury, Lyman, Miner, Potter, Sandborn, Spink, Stanley, Sully, Ziebach. Call for Transportation Services: 605-945-2360 or Toll Free at 1-877-587-5776 Eligible Counties: Butte, Custer, Fall River Call for Transportation Services: 605-642-6668 or Toll Free at 1-877-673-3687
Washington State Department of Veterans Affairs	Eligible County: Skamania Call for Transportation Services: 509-427-3990 Eligible County: Ferry Call for Transportation Services: 1-800-776-9026 or 509-684-2961
Nevada Department of Veterans Services	Eligible County: Elko Call for Transportation Services: 775-777-1428 Eligible County: Nye Call for Transportation Services: 775-572-VETS (8387)
California-VFW Post 8988	Eligible County: Mono, Inyo Call for Transportation Services: 760-873-7850
Texas Veterans Commission	Eligible County: Duval Call for Transportation Services: 361-279-6219

	Eligible County: Hansford Call for Transportation Services: 806-659-4100 Eligible County: Kimble Call for Transportation Services: 325-396-4682 Eligible County: Jim Hogg Call for Transportation Services: 361-527-5845 Eligible County: McMullen Call for Transportation Services: 361-279-6219 Eligible County: Briscoe Call for Transportation Services: 806-823-2131 Eligible County: Cochran Call for Transportation Services: 806-266-5508 Eligible County: Kent Call for Transportation Services: 806-237-3373 Eligible County: Menard Call for Transportation Services: 325-396-4682
Texas-American Legion Post 142	Eligible Counties: Baylor, Cottle, Foard, Hardeman Call for Transportation Services: 1-800-633-0852
Texas VFW Post 7207	Eligible Counties: Borden, Crane, Glasscock, Loving, Martin, Pecos, Reeves, Terrell Call for Transportation Services: 1-800-245-9028 Eligible counties: Brewster, Culberson, Hudspeth, Jeff Davis, Presidio Call for Transportation Services: 1-855-879-8729
Maine Veterans of Foreign Wars of the U.S	Eligible County: Piscataquis Call for Transportation Services: Bangor Clinic: 207-561-3637 or Lincoln Clinic: 207-403-2012
Montana-American Legion Rocky Boy Post 67	Eligible Counties: Blaine, Chouteau, Hill Call for Transportation Services: 406-395-5610

Idaho-American Legion Post 12	Eligible County: Boise Call for Transportation Services: 208-392- 9934 or 9935
Oregon Department of Veterans Affairs	Eligible Counties & the number to call for Transportation Services: Baker, 541-523-6591 Gilliam, 541-384-2252 Grant, 541-575-2721 Malheur, 541-881-0000 Morrow, 541-922-6420 Sherman 541-565-3553 Wallowa, 541-426-3840 Wheeler 541-468-2859
Alaska Department of Military and Veterans Affairs	Interior Alaska Bus Eligible County: Southwest Fairbanks Call for Transportation Services: 1-800-770-6652 Valley People Mover Eligible County: Matanuska-Susitna Call for Transportation Services: 907-892-8800 Alaska Marine Highway System Eligible Counties: Kodiak Island, Kenai Peninsula Call for Transportation Services: 1-800-642-0066 Inter-Island Ferry Eligible County: Prince of Wales- Hyder Call for Transportation Services: 1-866-308-4848

BENEFICIARY TRAVEL

The Beneficiary Travel program provides eligible veterans and other beneficiaries mileage reimbursement, common carrier, or when medically indicated, special mode transport for travel to and from VA health care or VA authorized non-VA healthcare for eligible veterans.

A veteran may be eligible for Beneficiary Travel Service if the following criteria are met:

- You have a service-connected rating of 30 percent or more, or
- You are traveling for treatment of a service-connected condition, or
- You receive a VA pension or your income does not exceed the maximum annual VA pension rate, or
- Your income does not exceed the maximum annual VA pension rate, or
- You are traveling for a scheduled compensation or pension

You qualify for special mode transportation (ambulance, wheelchair, van, etc.) if:

- You meet one of the eligibility criteria above, and
- Your medical condition requires an ambulance or specially equipped van as determined by a VA clinician, and

148

- The travel is pre-authorized (authorization is not required for emergencies if a delay would be hazardous to life or health)

In Vitro Fertilization (IVF)

The VA recently announced its fertility regulations would be expanded to include in vitro fertilization. The new benefit makes IVF available as an option for eligible veterans with service-connected disabilities that result in infertility. The benefit also provides spouses of eligible veterans with access to assisted reproductive technologies including IVF.

The Office of Women's Health Services (10P4W) is responsible for the contents of this VHA directive. Questions may be referred to the Director of Reproductive Health at 202-461-0373.

This Veterans Health Administration (VHA) directive establishes policy and procedures for Department of Veterans Affairs (VA) health care systems for the evaluation and treatment of infertility as authorized under the VA medical benefits package for eligible Veterans enrolled in the VA health care system.

NOTE: Except for certain Veterans who have a service-connected disability that results in their inability to procreate without the use of assisted reproductive technology (ART), and their spouses, VA cannot perform or pay for in vitro fertilization (IVF) because it is specifically excluded from the VA medical benefits package (Title 38 Code of Federal Regulations (CFR) 17.38). VA may also provide ART and fertility counseling and treatment that is available under the medical benefits package to spouses of Veterans authorized to receive IVF.

AUTHORITY: Title 38 United States Code (U.S.C.) 7301(b), Public Law 114-223 section 260, 38 CFR §§ 17.38, 17.380, and 17.412.

The Office of Women's Health Services (Reproductive Health), in collaboration with experts designated by the National Surgery Office (NSO), will be available to assist with Veterans Integrated Service Network (VISN) level consultations when the medical standards for providing services and treatment related to gamete (sperm or oocyte) cryopreservation or other infertility services are unavailable or unclear. Women's Health Services (WHS) may need to involve Spinal Cord Injury/Disorders (SCI/D) National Program Office, National Center for Ethics in Health Care and the NSO).

Eligibility

Veterans eligible to receive health care under the medical benefits package may receive VA-covered infertility evaluation, management, and treatment. IVF is specifically excluded from the medical benefits package.

However, ART including IVF, is authorized under 38 CFR 17.380 for certain Veterans who have a service-connected disability that results in the inability of the Veteran to procreate without the use of assisted reproductive technology (ART).

The spouse of a Veteran authorized to receive IVF may be provided with fertility counseling and treatment that is available under the medical benefits package, as well as ART, including IVF (38 CFR 17.412). The aforementioned ART/IVF benefit for certain Veterans and their spouse is further delineated in VHA Directive 1334, Assisted Reproductive Technology (ART) Services for the Benefit of Veterans with Service-Connected Illness or Injury Resulting in Infertility, pending publication.

Otherwise, non-Veteran partners (spouses or significant others), if applicable, are not eligible to receive infertility treatment services from VA unless they are eligible for the Civilian Health and Medical Program of the Department of Veterans Affairs (CHAMPVA), which allows VA to provide infertility services and treatment to certain family members of

Veterans under 38 CFR 17.270- 278.

In cases where a non-Veteran partner is not eligible for VA-covered infertility services, the Veteran and non-Veteran partner must be informed that payment for such service to the community provider is the responsibility of the Veteran and non-Veteran partner. These requirements must be discussed with the Veteran before any treatment course is undertaken.

Exclusions

The following procedures or services are not covered VA medical benefits: (1) Gestational surrogacy treatment; (2) Costs of obtaining, transporting, and storing donor sperm and oocytes; (3) IVF procedures, except for certain Veterans who have a service-connected disability that results in the inability of the Veteran to procreate without the use of assisted reproductive technology (ART) (38 CFR 17.380). The spouse of a Veteran authorized to receive IVF may be provided with fertility counseling and treatment that is available under the medical benefits package, as well as IVF (38 CFR 17.412). (4) Costs of cryopreservation, storage, and transport of embryo(s), except for certain Veterans who have a service-connected disability that results in the inability of the Veteran to procreate without the use of ART and their non-Veteran spouses. (38 CFR 17.380 and 17.412); and (5) Infertility, evaluation, and management of non-Veteran partners except for the spouse of certain Veterans who have a service-connected disability that results in the inability of the Veteran to procreate without the use of assisted reproductive technology (ART), including IVF.

CHAPTER 12

NURSING HOME AND LONG-TERM CARE BENEFITS

STANDARD BENEFITS

The following long-term care services are available to all enrolled veterans:

Geriatric Evaluation

A geriatric evaluation is the comprehensive assessment of a veteran's ability to care for him/herself, his/her physical health, and social environment, which leads to a plan of care. The plan could include treatment, rehabilitation, health promotion, and social services. These evaluations are performed by inpatient Geriatric Evaluation and Management (GEM) Units, GEM clinics, geriatric primary care clinics, and other outpatient settings.

> **Key Takeaways**
>
> Nursing and long-term care options are available for some veterans
>
> Nursing care decisions are based on factors including priority group and financial assessments
>
> Other care options include state veterans homes and Community Living Centers

Adult Day Health Care

The adult day health care (ADHC) program is a therapeutic day care program, providing medical and rehabilitation services to disabled veterans in a combined setting.

Respite Care

Respite care provides supportive care to veterans on a short-term basis to give the caregiver a planned period of relief from the physical and emotional demands associated with providing care. Respite care can be provided in the home or other noninstitutionalized settings.

Home Care

Skilled home care is provided by VA and contract agencies to veterans that are homebound with chronic diseases and includes nursing, physical/occupational therapy, and social services.

Hospice/Palliative Care

Hospice/palliative care programs offer pain management, symptom control, and other medical services to terminally ill veterans or veterans in the late stages of the chronic disease process. Services also include respite care as well as bereavement counseling to family members.

FINANCIAL ASSESSMENT FOR LONG-TERM CARE SERVICES

For veterans who are not automatically exempt from making copayments for long-term care services, a separate financial assessment must be completed to determine whether they qualify for cost-free services or to what extent they are required to make long term care copayments. For those veterans who do not qualify for cost-free services, the financial assessment for long term care services is used to determine the copayment requirement. Unlike copayments for other VA health care services, which are based on fixed charges for all, long-term care copayment charges are individually adjusted based on each veteran's financial status.

LIMITED BENEFITS

NURSING HOME CARE

While some veterans qualify for indefinite nursing home care services, other veterans may qualify for a limited period of time. Among those that automatically qualify for indefinite nursing home care are veterans whose service-connected condition is clinically determined to require nursing home care and veterans with a service-connected rating of 70% or more. Other veterans—with priority given to those with service-connected conditions—may be provided short-term nursing home care if space and resources are available.

The Department of Veterans Affairs (VA) provides both short-term and long-term care in nursing homes to veterans who aren't sick enough to be in the hospital but are too disabled or elderly to take care of themselves. Priority is given to veterans with service- connected disabilities.

PRIORITY GROUPS

The VA is required to provide nursing home care to any veteran who

- Needs nursing home care because of a service-connected disability
- Has a combined disability rating of 70% or more, or
- Has a disability rating of at least 60% and is:
- Deemed unemployable, or
- Has been rated permanently and totally disabled.

Other veterans in need of nursing care will be provided services if resources are available after the above groups are taken care of.

TYPES OF NURSING CARE AVAILABLE

Community Living Centers

Some VA Medical Centers have Community Living Centers (these used to be called Nursing Home Care Units or VA Nursing Homes). These centers are typically located within the VA Medical Center itself or in a separate building.

Contract Nursing Home Care

Nursing home care in public or private nursing homes is also available to some veterans. Stays in these nursing homes can be limited, however, for veterans with ratings less than 70% and for veterans who do not need care due to a service-connected disability.

State Veterans Homes

State Veterans Homes are nursing homes run by the state and approved by the VA. Sometimes the VA will pay for part of the care a veteran gets at a state veterans' home.

ELIGIBILITY FOR COMMUNITY LIVING CENTERS (CLCS)

To receive care in a Community Living Center/VA nursing home, a veteran must:
- Be enrolled in the VA Health Care System
- Be psychiatrically and medically stable
- Provide documentation specifying whether short or long-term care is needed, an estimation of how long the stay will be, and when discharge will occur, and
- Show priority for a stay in a CLC.

However, meeting the above criteria does not automatically ensure admission. CLCs make decisions about whether to admit a veteran based on the following factors:

- Availability services in the CLC
- What sort of care the veteran needs, and
- Whether the CLC can competently provide the type of care the veteran needs.

CO-PAYS

Veterans required to make co-pays are typically those:

- Without a service-connected disability rated at least 10%, and
- Whose income is higher than the VA's maximum annual pension rate.

HOW TO APPLY FOR CLC CARE

Typically a veteran's physician will submit the application requesting care in a CLC. Veterans who are not exempt from co-pays must complete VA Form 10-10EC, Application for Extended Care Services.

ELIGIBILITY FOR CONTRACT NURSING HOME CARE

Any veteran who needs Contract Nursing Home Care for a service-connected disability or is receiving VA home health care after discharge from a VA hospital is eligible for direct admission. To be admitted, all that is required is for a VA physician or authorized private physician to determine that nursing home care is needed. Veterans rated 70% or more service-connected should also be eligible.

Other veterans are eligible to be transferred into Contract Nursing Home Care (also called a Community Nursing Home) if the VA determines the care is needed and:
- The veteran is in a VA hospital, nursing home, domiciliary, or has been receiving VA outpatient care, or
- An active member of the Armed Forces who was in a DOD hospital, needs nursing care, and will be an eligible veteran upon discharge.

TIME LIMITS FOR CONTRACT NURSING HOME CARE

Veterans who are not in the priority groups are technically limited to six months of care, but this may be reduced to 30 to 60 days if resources are limited. Veterans in the priority groups are technically entitled to unlimited free care, but again may receive shorter stays due to a lack of funding and resources to accommodate them.

Many veterans can extend their stay by relying on payments from Medicare and Medicaid.

153

HOW TO APPLY FOR CONTRACT NURSING HOME CARE

Typically application will be made by a veterans' doctor, social worker or nurse, using VA Form 10-0415, Geriatrics and Extended Care (GEC) Referral.

ELIGIBILITY FOR STATE VETERANS HOMES

In some cases, the VA will help pay for a veteran's care at a State Veterans Home. The payments the VA will make are called per diem aid. A home must meet the VA standards for nursing home care to receive per diem aid. In addition, the VA will not pay more than half the cost of the veteran's care.

State homes provide hospital care, nursing home care, domiciliary care, and sometimes adult day care. To receive per diem aid, veterans must meet VA eligibility requirements for the type of care they will receive.

States usually have their own eligibility requirements, in addition to the VA's requirements, such as residency requirements. The veterans home will apply for VA aid for a veteran's care by submitting VA Form 10-10EZ, Application for Medical Benefits.

The VA will pay per diem aid for a veteran's care indefinitely.

FY 2017 Basic State Home Per Diem Rates

The Basic State Home Per Diem Rates for Fiscal Year (FY) 2017 are as follows:

Adult Day Health Care: $84.52, per day

Domiciliary: $45.79, per day

Nursing Homes: $106.10, per resident per day

FY 2016 Basic State Home Per Diem Rates

The Basic State Home Per Diem Rates for Fiscal Year (FY) 2016 are as follows:

Adult Day Health Care: $82.54, per day

Domiciliary: $44.72, per day

Nursing Homes: $103.61, per resident per day

FY 2015 Basic State Home Per Diem Rates

The Basic State Home Per Diem Rates for Fiscal Year (FY) 2015 are as follows:

Adult Day Health Care: $81.56, per day

Domiciliary: $44.19, per day

Nursing Homes: $102.38, per resident per day

FY 2014 Basic State Home Per Diem Rates

The Basic State Home Per Diem Rates for Fiscal Year (FY) 2014 are as follows:

Adult Day Health Care: $79.96, per day

Domiciliary: $43.32, per day

Nursing Homes: $100.37, per resident per day

FY 2013 Basic State Home Per Diem Rates

The Basic State Home Per Diem Rates for Fiscal Year (FY) 2013 are as follows:

Adult Day Health Care: $77.33, per day

Domiciliary: $41.90, per day

Nursing Homes: $97.07, per veteran, per day

REDUCTION IN VA PENSION

A veteran who begins to receive nursing home care will have his or her monthly pension payment reduced to $90 if:

- The veteran has no dependents
- The veteran is living in a Medicaid-approved nursing facility, and
- The nursing home care is paid for by Medicaid.

DOMICILIARY CARE

Domiciliary care provides rehabilitative and long-term, health maintenance care for veterans who require some medical care, but who do not require all the services provided in nursing homes. Domiciliary care emphasizes rehabilitation and return to the community. VA may provide domiciliary care to veterans whose annual income does not exceed the maximum annual rate of VA pension or to veterans who have no adequate means of support.

SERVICES AND AIDS FOR BLIND VETERANS

Veterans with corrected central vision of 20/200 or less in both eyes, or field loss to 20 degrees or less in both eyes are considered to be blind.

Blind veterans may be eligible for many of the benefits detailed throughout this book, including, but not limited to: Disability Compensation, Health Insurance, Adaptive Equipment, and Training & Rehabilitation. In addition to these benefits, there are a number of miscellaneous benefits due veterans of all wars who were blinded as the result of their war service. Many individual states offer special programs and benefits for the blind.

Services are available at all VA medical facilities through Visual Impairment Services Team (VIST) coordinators.

The VIST Coordinator is a case manager who has major responsibility for the coordination of all services for legally blind veterans and their families. Duties include providing and/or arranging for appropriate treatment, identifying new cases of blindness, providing professional counseling, resolving problems, arranging annual healthcare reviews, and conducting education programs relating to blindness.

Blind veterans may be eligible for services at a VA medical center, or for admission to a VA blind rehabilitation center or clinic. In addition, blind veterans entitled to receive disability compensation may receive VA aids for the blind, which may include:

- A total health and benefits review by a VA Visual Impairment Services team;
- Adjustment to blindness training;
- Home Improvements and Structural Alterations to homes (HISA Program);
- Specially adapted housing and adaptations;
- Low-vision aids and training in their use;
- Electronic and mechanical aids for the blind, including adaptive computers and computer-assisted devices;
- Guide dogs, including the expense of training the veteran to use the dog, and the cost of the dog's medical care;
- Talking books, tapes, and Braille literature, provided from the Library of

Congress.

GUIDE DOGS / SERVICE DOGS

As previously mentioned, VA may provide guide dogs to blind veterans. Additionally, *Public Law 107-135* (signed by then-President Bush January 23, 2002) states that VA may provide:

- Service dogs trained for the aid of the hearing impaired to veterans who are hearing impaired, and are enrolled under Section 1705 of Title 38; and
- Service dogs trained for the aid of persons with spinal cord injury or dysfunction or other chronic impairment that substantially limits mobility to veterans with such injury, dysfunction, or impairment who are enrolled under section 1705 of Title 38.
- VA may also pay travel and incidental expenses for the veteran to travel to and from the veteran's home while becoming adjusted to the dog.

The VA operates nine blind rehabilitation centers in the United States and Puerto Rico. Rehabilitation centers offer comprehensive programs to guide individuals through a process that eventually leads to maximum adjustment to the disability, reorganization of the person's life, and return to a contributing place in the family and community. To achieve these goals, the rehabilitation centers offer a variety of skill courses to veterans, which are designed to help achieve a realistic level of independence. Services offered at rehabilitation centers include:

- Orientation and mobility;
- Living skills;
- Communication skills;
- Activities of daily living;
- Independent daily living program;
- Manual skills;
- Visual skills;
- Computer Access Training Section;
- Physical conditioning;
- Recreation;
- Adjustment to blindness;
- Group meetings.

The VA also employs Blind Rehabilitation Outpatient Specialists (BROS) in several areas, including:

Albuquerque, NM
Ann Arbor, MI
Bay Pines / St. Petersburg, FL
Baltimore, MD
Boston, MA
Cleveland, OH
Dallas, TX
Gainesville, FL
Los Angeles, CA
Phoenix, AZ
Portland, OR
San Antonio, TX
San Juan, PR
Seattle, WA
West Haven, CT

HOME IMPROVEMENTS AND STRUCTURAL ALTERATIONS (HISA)

The HISA program provides funding for disabled veterans to make home improvements necessary for the continuation of treatment or for disability access to the home, essential lavatory and sanitary facilities.

Disabled veterans may be eligible for HISA when it is determined medically necessary or appropriate for the effective and economical treatment of the service-connected disability.

Veterans who are rated 50% or higher are not required to prove their service-connected disability is the reason for their HISA request, although veterans rated less than 50% must demonstrate their disability is the cause of the HISA improvements.

Lifetime home improvement benefits may not exceed $6,800 (U.S.). Any costs that exceed $6,800 (U.S.) will be the veteran's responsibility. This amount is provided to veterans with a service-connected condition or a non-service-connected condition of a veteran rated 50 percent or more service-connected. Home improvement benefits of up to $2,000 may be provided to all other veterans registered in the VA healthcare system.

To apply, veterans must submit the following documentation:
- A letter from describing the physical disability and a description of the request home improvement and/or structural alteration;
- A statement from the attending physician or therapist. This statement should describe the physical condition/disability, why the home modification(s) are medically necessary or appropriate for the effective and economical treatment of the service- connected disabling condition;
- A drawing of the work to be undertaken. This drawing can be hand sketched. It should include the height, width and length dimensions. It does not have to be a formal blueprint or architectural drawing;
- A completed, signed home ownership or a rental lease form with a letter from the landlord agreeing with the modifications if required;
- A completed and signed "VA Form 10-0103", Veterans Application for Assistance;
- Documentation verifying that the provider/contractor is licensed/bonded;
- An itemized cost estimate of the proposed improvement and/or structural alteration from the provider/contractor.

Preauthorization must be obtained before beginning any alterations, otherwise, HISA benefits will be denied.

CHAPTER 13

DENTAL BENEFITS

VA OUTPATIENT DENTAL BENEFITS

Eligibility and benefits for veteran dental care are restricted by law and categorized into VA dental classifications or classes. If you just got out of the service, you may be entitled to a one-time course of dental care. You must apply for dental care within 180 days of your discharge, and your discharge must be under conditions under than dishonorable, from a period of active duty of 90 days of more.

If not eligible for VA Dental Care, the national VA Dental Insurance Program gives enrolled Veterans and CHAMPVA beneficiaries the opportunity to purchase dental insurance at a reduced cost.

OUTPATIENT DENTAL PROGRAM

The eligibility for outpatient dental care isn't the same as for most other VA medical benefits and is categorized into classes. If you are eligible for VA dental care under Class I, IIA, IIC or IV, you are eligible for any necessary dental care to maintain or restore oral health and masticatory function, including repeat care. Other classes have time and/or service limitations.

If You:	You Are Eligible For:	Through:
Have a service connected compensable dental disability or condition	Any needed dental care	Class I
Are a former prisoner of war	Any needed dental care disability, convalescence or pre-stabilization are not eligible for comprehensive outpatient dental services based on this temporary rating)	Class IIC

Apply for dental care within 180 days of discharge or release (under conditions other than dishonorable) from a period of active duty of 90 days or more during the Persian Gulf War era	One-time dental care if your DD214 certificate of discharge does not indicate that a complete dental examination and all appropriate dental treatment had been rendered prior to discharge	Class II
Have a service-connected noncompensable dental condition or disability resulting from combat wounds or service trauma	Any dental care necessary to provide and maintain a functioning dentition. A Dental Trauma Rating (VA Form 10-564-D) or VA Regional Office Rating Decision Letter (VA Form 10-7131) identifies the tooth/teeth/conditions that are trauma rated	Class IIA
Have a dental condition clinically determined by VA to be associated with and aggravating a service-connected medical condition	Dental care to treat the oral conditions that are determined by a VA dental professional to have a direct and material detrimental effect to your service connected medical condition	Class III
Are actively engaged in a 38 USC Chapter 31 vocational rehabilitation program	Dental care to the extent necessary as determined by a VA dental professional to: Make possible your entrance into a rehabilitation program Achieve the goals of your program Prevent interruption of your program Hasten the return to a rehabilitation program if you are in interrupted or leave status Hasten the return to a rehabilitation program of a veteran placed in discontinued status because of illness, injury or a dental condition, or secure and adjust to employment during the period of employment assistance, or enable you to achieve maximum independence in daily living	Class V

Are receiving VA care or are scheduled for inpatient care and require dental care for a condition complicating a medical condition currently under treatment	Dental care to treat the oral conditions that are determined by a VA dental professional to complicate your medical condition currently under treatment	Class VI
Are an enrolled veteran who may be homeless and receiving care under VHA Directive 2007-039	A one-time course of dental care that is determined medically necessary to relieve pain, assist you to gain employment, or treat moderate, severe or complicated and severe gingival and periodontal conditions	Class IIB

VA DENTAL INSURANCE PROGRAM

VA offers the comprehensive VA Dental Insurance Program (VADIP) as a way for enrolled veterans and CHAMPVA beneficiaries the chance to purchase dental insurance through Delta Dental and MetLife at a reduced cost. Participation is voluntary and purchasing a dental plan doesn't impact veteran's eligibility for VA dental services and treatments. Covered services include diagnostic, preventative, surgical, emergency and endodontic/restorative treatment. Delta Dental and MetLife offering multiple plans.

Each participant pays the fixed monthly premiums for coverage and any copayments required, depending on the type of plan selected.

Dependents of veterans, except for those eligible under CHAMPVA are not authorized to participate in VADIP. These individuals may be eligible for separate dental insurance coverage offered by these carriers.

TRICARE RETIREE DENTAL PROGRAM

The TRICARE Retiree Dental Program (TRDP) is for Uniformed Services pre-retirees, retirees, retired members of the National Guard/Reserve components and their eligible family members.

It's a program offered by the Federal Government Programs division of Delta Dental under contract with the U.S. Department of Defense.

The TRDP covers more than 1.5 million enrollees in the U.S., D.C., U.S. territories, Canada and overseas.

ELIGIBILITY REQUIREMENTS:

Eligibility requirements for enrollment in the TRDP are set forth by the federal government in the law that established the program. Applicants may be required to submit additional information if it is needed by Delta to verify eligibility. To enroll in the enhanced program, an individual must be one of the following:
- A member of the Uniformed Services who is entitled to Uniformed Services retired pay, even if you are 65 or older;

- A current spouse of an enrolled member;
- A member of the retired Reserve/Guard, including a "gray-area" reservist, who is entitled to retired pay but does not actually begin receiving it until age 60;
- A child of an enrolled member, up to age 21 (to age 23 if a full-time student, or older if disabled before losing eligibility);
- An unremarried surviving spouse or eligible child of a deceased member who died on retired status or while on active duty;
- A Congressional Medal of Honor recipient and eligible family members, or an unremarried surviving spouse/eligible family members of a deceased recipient;
- A current spouse and/or eligible child of a non-enrolled member with documented proof the member is:
    o Eligible to receive ongoing, comprehensive dental care from the Department of Veterans Affairs;
    o Enrolled in a dental plan through employment and the plan is not available to family members; or
    o Unable to obtain benefits through the TRDP due to a current and enduring medical or dental condition.

Those who are not eligible for this program are:
- Former spouses of eligible members;
- Remarried surviving spouses of deceased members;
- Family members of non-enrolled retirees who do not meet one of the three special circumstances noted above.

PREMIUMS
- Premiums are automatically deducted each month from your retirement pay
- A prepayment of two months' premiums is required with enrollment
- If retirement pay is unavailable/insufficient, electronic funds transfer or recurring credit card payment of your monthly premiums is required
- Premium rates are subject to change on January 1 of each contract year
- Monthly premiums vary by ZIP code. Specific rates can be found on trdp.org

COVERAGE
In-network routine services are covered at 100% and deductibles and maximums don't apply. You can coordinate your TRDP benefits with other dental plans to lower or eliminate out-of-pocket costs on major services. Three annual cleanings are available for enrollees with diagnosed Type 1/Type 2 diabetes. Emergency treatment is covered worldwide.

Generous maximums include a $1,300 annual maximum, $1,200 dental accident maximum, and a $1,750 lifetime maximum for braces.

When you see a TRDP network dentist, you get two annual cleanings (or three with diagnosed Type 1/Type 2 diabetes), two annual exams and an annual x-ray with no cost share. Network dentists submit all your claims paperwork and bill Delta Dental directly for the care you receive. Network dentists will not charge you more than your applicable cost share and deductible.

This chart provides an overview of coverage under the TRICARE Retiree Dental Program for patients who visit a participating network dentist

Benefits available during the first 12 months of enrollment:	*Delta Pays:
Diagnostic services and Preventative exams, x-rays cleanings, fluoride treatments	100%
Other Preventative (sealants, space maintainers)	80%
Basic Restorative services (fillings, including certain tooth-colored fillings on back teeth)	80%
Endodontics	60%
Periodontics	60%
Oral Surgery	60%
Emergency	80%
Dental Accident Coverage	100%

Additional services available after 12 months of continuous enrollment:	
Cast Crowns, Onlays & Bridges	50%
Partial/Full Dentures	50%
Dental Implants	50%
Orthodontics	50%

Annual Deductible	$50 per person, limit $150 per family per contract year
Annual Maximum	$1300
Orthodontic Maximum	$1,750
Dental Accident Maximum	$1,200
Benefit Year: January 1-December 31	

*The percentage paid by Delta is based on the allowed amount for each procedure. Out-of- pocket costs may be higher if care is received from a non-participating provider.

NATIONAL GUARD AND RESERVE PERSONNEL

Effective February 1, 2005, officials authorized a waiver from requiring retired National Guard/Reserve men and women who meet the criteria to be enrolled in the TRDP for 12 months prior to gaining the maximum allowed benefits for cast crowns, cast restorations, bridges, dentures and orthodontics for both adults and children.

Additionally, this waiver can be applied retroactively to February 1, 2004 for any Guard and Reserve enrollees who can document their enrollment in the TRDP within 120 days after their retirement effective date.

All new enrollees seeking to obtain the waiver should submit a copy of their retirement orders together with their application.

TRICARE SELECTED RESERVE DENTAL PROGRAM BENEFITS

Individuals with at least one year of service commitment remaining who are serving in the Army Reserve, Naval Reserve, Air Force Reserve, Marine Corps Reserve, Coast Guard Reserve, Army National Guard or Air National Guard, may be eligible to enroll in the Tricare Selected Reserve Dental Program(TSRDP).

The Department of Defense works in conjunction with Humana Military Healthcare Services to offer and administer the TRICARE Selected Reserve Dental Program.

Coverage remains available as long as an individual maintains his or her Reserve status, and is shown as eligible on the DEERS record.

The information provided in this section is intended only as a brief overview. Humana Military Healthcare Services has a staff of trained Beneficiary Services Representatives who are available to answer your questions.

TRICARE Dental Program Survivor Benefit Plan

If your sponsor died while serving on active duty, you may qualify for the TRICARE Dental Program Survivor Benefit Plan.

This includes 100% payment of monthly premiums, and TRICARE pays for cost shares for covered service.

If you were using the TRICARE Dental Program when your sponsor died, you're automatically transferred to the Survivor Benefit Plan. If not, you can enroll at any time. After three years, surviving spouses lose eligibility for the TRICARE Dental Program. They can purchase the TRICARE Retiree Dental Program only if their sponsor died while on active duty for more than 30 days.

Surviving children can remain enrolled in the TRICARE Dental Plan until they lose TRICARE eligibility for other reasons.

CHAPTER 14

CHAMPVA

The Civilian Health and Medical Program of the Department of Veterans Affairs (CHAMPVA), is a comprehensive health care program where the VA shares the cost of covered health care services and supplies with eligible beneficiaries. The program is administered by the Veterans Health Administration Office of Community Care (VHA CC) in Denver, Colorado.

CHAMPVA is similar to the Department of Defense TRICARE program, but CHAMPVA is a VA program, while TRICARE is a regionally managed care program for active duty and retired members of the military, their family and their survivors.

> **Key Takeaways**
>
> CHAMPVA is a healthcare program where the VA shares the cost of covered health care and services with beneficiaries.
>
> CHAMPVA covers most health care services and supplies that are medically and psychologically necessary.
>
> To be eligible for CHAMPVA you can't be eligible for TRICARE.

Under CHAMPVA, VA shares the cost of covered healthcare services and supplies with eligible beneficiaries.

ELIGIBILITY REQUIREMENTS

To be eligible for CHAMPVA, you cannot be eligible for TRICARE/CHAMPUS and you must be in one of these categories:

- The spouse or child of a veteran who has been rated permanently and totally disabled for a service-connected disability by a VA regional office; or

- The surviving spouse or child of a veteran who died from a VA-rated service connected disability; or The surviving spouse or child of a veteran who was at the time death rated permanently and totally disabled from a service connected disability ;or

- The surviving spouse or child of a military member who died in the line of duty, not due to misconduct (in most of these cases, these family members are eligible for TRICARE, not CHAMPVA).

An eligible CHAMPVA sponsor may be entitled to receive medical care through the VA health care system based on his or her own veteran status. Additionally, as the result of a recent policy change, if the eligible CHAMPVA sponsor is the spouse of another eligible

164

CHAMPVA sponsor, both may now be eligible for CHAMPVA benefits. In each instance where the eligible spouse requires medical attention, he or she may choose the VA health care system or coverage under CHAMPVA for his/her health care needs. If you have been previously denied CHAMPVA benefits and you believe you would now be qualified, please call (800)733-8387.

BENEFITS

In general, CHAMPVA covers most healthcare services and supplies that are medically and psychologically necessary. Upon confirmation of eligibility, applicants will receive program material that specifically addresses covered and non-covered services and supplies.

CHAMPVA General Exclusions

- Services determined by VA to be medically unnecessary;
- Care as part of a grant, study, or research program;
- Care considered experimental or investigational;
- Care for persons eligible for benefits under other government agency programs, except Medicaid and State Victims of Crime Compensation programs;
- Care for which the beneficiary is not obligated to pay, such as services obtained at a health fair;
- Custodial, domiciliary, or rest cures;
- Dental care (except treatment related to certain covered medical conditions);
- Medications that do not require a prescription (except insulin);
- Personal comfort and convenience items;
- Services rendered by providers suspended or sanctioned by other Federal entities.

Retention of CHAMPVA For Surviving Spouses Remarrying After Age 55

Eligibility for CHAMPVA ends at midnight on the date of your remarriage if you remarry prior to age 55. However, *Public Law 107-330* (signed by then-President Bush on December 6, 2002) contained a provision stating that:

"For marriages occurring on or after February 4, 2003, the remarriage after age 55 of the surviving spouse of a veteran shall not bar the furnishing of benefits under CHAMPVA to such person as the surviving spouse of the veteran".

The law also contained a provision allowing those widows who remarried prior to February 4, 2003, and were over the age of 55 and lost their CHAMPVA benefits, to apply to have their medical benefits reinstated. However, such widows had to apply for reinstatement of benefits by February 4, 2004. (The deadline was later extended to December 16, 2004.)

Termination of Remarriage:

If a widow(er) of a qualifying sponsor remarries, and the remarriage is later terminated by death, divorce, or annulment he or she may reestablish CHAMPVA eligibility. The beginning date of re-eligibility is the first day of the month after termination of the remarriage or December 1, 1999, whichever date is later. To reestablish CHAMPVA eligibility, copies of the marriage certificate and death, divorce, or annulment documents (as appropriate) must be provided.

Applying for CHAMPVA and Filing Claims

To apply for CHAMPVA, applicants should submit the following documents

- Application for CHAMPVA Benefits, VA Form 10-10d
- Other Health Insurance (OHI) Certification, VA Form 10-7959c or Forma 10- 7959c
- For individuals who are eligible for Medicare for any reason, a copy of their

165

Medicare card is also needed
* If you are 65 or older and not entitled to Medicare you must send documentation from the Social Security Administration confirming you're not entitled to Medicare benefits under anyone's Social Security number

Optional Documents

If you want to speed up the processing of your application, you can send copies of the following:
* Birth certificate/adoption papers for children.
* The page from the VBA rating decision showing permanent and total disablement or death rating for a survivor
* If you are a remarried widow/widower and are again single, provide a copy of the legal documentation terminating the marriage. The document may be a divorce decree, death certificate or annulment decree.
* Veteran's DD214 or if a WWII or Korean Veteran, the Report of Separation.
* School certification of full-time enrollment for children ages 18-23 Sign and date the application, and send it to the following address:

VHA Office of Community Care
CHAMPVA Eligibility PO Box 469028
Denver, CO 80246-9028
Fax: (303) 331-7809

CHAMPVA AS SECONDARY PAYER

CHAMPVA is intended to serve as a safety net in the event other coverage is not available—rather than being the primary carrier. While families with other health insurance are not disqualified from CHAMPVA benefits, CHAMPVA's safety net protection only kicks in after the application of all other policies—including benefits available from the enrollment in a health maintenance organization (HMO).

Exceptions to CHAMPVA's secondary payer status are supplemental CHAMPVA policies, Medicaid, and State Victims Compensation Programs—CHAMPVA assumes primary payer in these cases.

Beneficiaries enrolled in an HMO cannot elect to waive the HMO benefits without forfeiting their CHAMPVA benefits. CHAMPVA benefits, however, do apply to covered services that are not covered by the HMO.

HEALTHCARE SERVICES AT VA FACILITIES

Under the CHAMPVA In-house Treatment Initiative (CITI for short), CHAMPVA beneficiaries may receive cost-free healthcare services at participating VA facilities.

Although some VA facilities are not CITI participants due to the volume of veterans they are responsible for serving, most are. **The CITI program is not available to beneficiaries with Medicare or with an HMO insurance plan.**

CHAMPVA AND THE AFFORDABLE CARE ACT

The Affordable Care Act designates CHAMPVA as fulfilling the minimum essential coverage requirement. If you are enrolled in CHAMPVA you don't need to take additional steps to meet health care coverage standards. The ACA does not change CHAMPVA benefits or out-of-pocket costs. CHAMPVA will send IRS Form 1095-B, Health Coverage annually.

MEDICARE IMPACT

If a person is eligible for CHAMPVA, under age 65 and enrolled in both Medicare Parts A & B, SSA documentation of enrollment in both Parts A&B is required.

CHAMPVA is always the secondary payer to Medicare.

For benefits to be extended past age 65, the individual must meet the following conditions:

- If he or she turned 65 before June 5, 2001, and only has Medicare Part A, he or she will be eligible for CHAMPVA without having to have Medicare Part B coverage.
- If he or she turned 65 on/or before June 5, 2001, and has Medicare Parts A and B, he or she must keep both Parts to be eligible.
- If he or she turned 65 on or after June 5, 2001, he or she must be enrolled in Medicare Parts A and B to be eligible.

CHAPTER 15

TRICARE AND TRICARE FOR LIFE

TRICARE is the Department of Defense's worldwide health care program for active duty and retired uniformed services members and their families. TRICARE offers several health plan options to meet your specific needs.

TRICARE For Life
TRICARE Global Remote Overseas
TRICARE Prime
TRICARE Prime Overseas
TRICARE Prime Remote
TRICARE Reserve Select
TRICARE Standard and Extra
TRICARE Standard Overseas
Family HealthPlan
TRICARE Young Adult

TRICARE FOR LIFE

TRICARE For Life (TFL) is TRICARE's Medicare- wraparound coverage available to *all* Medicare-eligible TRICARE beneficiaries, regardless of age, provided they have Medicare Parts A and B.

> **Key Takeaways**
>
> TRICARE For Life is available to all Medicare-eligible TRICARE beneficiaries
>
> TRICARE Prime is a managed care option that's considered the most comprehensive and most affordable
>
> TRICARE Standard is a fee-for-service option
>
> The U.S. Family Health Plan is an additional TRICARE PRIME option available through community-based and not-for-profit health care systems

While Medicare is your primary insurance, TRICARE acts as your secondary payer minimizing your out-of-pocket expenses. TRICARE benefits include covering Medicare's coinsurance and deductible.

KEY FEATURES OF TRICARE FOR LIFE INCLUDE:

- Minimal **out-of-pocket costs** (aside from Medicare Part B Premium).
- No enrollment fees for TFL. But, you must purchase Medicare Part B and pay monthly premiums to be eligible for TFL.
- Coordination of benefits between Medicare and TRICARE.
- TRICARE is the secondary payer for all services covered by both TRICARE and Medicare.
- TRICARE is the primary payer for those services covered only by TRICARE. Additional steps may be required in order to coordinate benefits if you have other health insurance in addition to TRICARE and Medicare.

- Freedom to manage your own health care.
- No assigned primary care manager.
- Visit any Medicare provider.
- Receive care at a military treatment facility on a space-available basis.
- No claims to file (in most cases).
- Your provider files your claim with Medicare.
- Medicare processes the claims.
- Medicare forwards it electronically to TRICARE.
- TRICARE pays similarly to TRICARE Standard in those overseas locations where Medicare is not available.

ELIGIBILITY

TFL is available to all Medicare-eligible TRICARE beneficiaries, regardless of age, including retired members of the National Guard and Reserve who are in receipt of retired pay, family members, widows and widowers and certain former spouses. Dependent parents and parents-in-law are not eligible for TFL.

*Note: If you're under age 65, have Medicare Part B, and live in a TRICARE Prime service area, you have the option to enroll in **TRICARE Prime**; TRICARE waives your TRICARE Prime enrollment fee.*

You should confirm that your Medicare status is current in the **Defense Enrollment Eligibility Reporting System** (DEERS). Your uniformed services ID card and your Medicare card, which must reflect enrollment in Medicare Part B, are evidence of your TFL eligibility.

TRICARE GLOBAL REMOTE OVERSEAS

TRICARE Global Remote Overseas (TGRO) is a TRICARE Prime option offered in designated remote overseas locations for active duty service members and their families. TRICARE has partnered with International SOS to identify the best local providers and facilities and develop a network of licensed, qualified physicians in remote overseas areas. The TGRO contractor's careful selection of providers is the first step in ensuring quality care.

Only physicians who are licensed and who have graduated from an accredited medical school are included in the core network. To access a list of TGRO providers please visit the TGRO Provider Directory. The TGRO network is updated daily.

KEY FEATURES OF TGRO INCLUDE:

- Enrollment is required, but there are no enrollment fees.
- Fewer out-of-pocket costs than TRICARE Standard Overseas.
- You receive most care from your primary care manager (PCM).
- Your PCM or TGRO Call Center refers you to specialists when necessary and will tell you when you need to go to another city, country or the U.S. for quality care.
- No claims to file (in most cases).

ELIGIBILITY

In general, TGRO is available to the following beneficiaries:

- Permanently-assigned active duty service members living in designated remote locations.
- Command-sponsored active duty family members living with their active duty sponsors in designated remote locations.
- Activated National Guard and Reserve members living in designated remote locations

when their orders are for more than 30 consecutive days.
- Command-sponsored family members of activated National Guard and Reserve living with their sponsors in designated remote locations.

TRICARE PRIME

TRICARE Prime is a managed care option offering the most affordable and comprehensive coverage. TRICARE Prime is available in Prime Service Areas in each TRICARE Region. To find out if you live in a Prime Service Area, contact your regional contractor. If you don't, you may be eligible for TRICARE Prime Remote, or you may use TRICARE Standard and Extra.

KEY FEATURES INCLUDE:

- Enrollment is required.
- Fewer out-of-pocket costs than other TRICARE options.
- Enhanced vision and preventive coverage.
- Priority access for care at military treatment facilities.
- Receive most care from an assigned primary care manager (PCM).
- Your PCM refers you to specialists when necessary.
- No claims to file (in most cases).
- Easy to transfer enrollment when you move.
- Time and distance access standards for care, including wait times for urgent, routine and specialty care.

ELIGIBILITY

You may enroll in TRICARE Prime as long as you are not entitled to Medicare based on age (65). (At age 65, you become eligible for TRICARE For Life as long as you have Medicare Parts A and B). The following beneficiaries who live in a Prime Service area may enroll in TRICARE Prime:
- Active duty service members* and their families.
- Retired service members and their families.
- Surviving family members (widowed spouses, children)
- Eligible former spouses.
- Activated National Guard/Reserve members* and their families.
- Retired National Guard and Reserve members and their families (upon reaching age 60).
- Medal of Honor recipients and their families.
- *Active duty service members and activated National Guard/Reserve members must enroll in one of the TRICARE Prime options (includes TRICARE Prime, TRICARE Prime Remote, TRICARE Prime Overseas and TRICARE Global Remote Overseas).

TRICARE PRIME OVERSEAS

TRICARE Prime Overseas is a managed care plan for active duty service members and their eligible family members residing together in overseas locations in which TRICARE Prime Overseas is available. Retirees and retiree family members are not eligible for TRICARE Prime Overseas.

KEY FEATURES OF TRICARE PRIME OVERSEAS INCLUDE:

- Enrollment required, but no enrollment fees.
- Fewer out-of-pocket costs than TRICARE Standard Overseas.
- Enhanced coverage for vision and clinical preventive services.
- You receive most care from your primary care manager (PCM).

- Your PCM refers you to specialists when necessary.
- No claims to file (in most cases).
- Easy to transfers from one overseas area to another or back to the United States.
- Time and distance access standards for care, including wait times for urgent, routine and specialty care.
- Point of service option available (in certain circumstances) to receive care without requesting a referral from your PCM (resulting in higher out-of-pocket costs).

ELIGIBILITY

In general, TRICARE Prime Overseas is available to the following beneficiaries:
- Active duty service members residing in overseas areas in which Prime is offered.
- Active duty family members who:
  o Accompany their sponsor;
  o Are command-sponsored on their permanent change of station orders or relocate on service sponsored/funded orders;
  o Are eligible in the Defense Enrollment Eligibility Reporting System; and
  o Enroll through the nearest TRICARE Service Center.

TRICARE PRIME REMOTE

TRICARE Prime Remote (TPR) is a managed care option similar to TRICARE Prime for active duty service members and their eligible family members while they are assigned to remote duty stations in the United States

Remote locations are those that are 50 miles or an hour drive time from a military treatment facility and the ZIP code areas are pre-determined.

Note: TRICARE Global Remote Overseas is a similar program available in remote locations outside of the United States

KEY FEATURES OF TRICARE PRIME REMOTE INCLUDE:

- Enrollment required to participate
- Active duty service members must enroll
- Active duty family members have the option to enroll or use TRICARE Standard and Extra
- Flexible enrollment options:
  o Online via the Beneficiary Web Enrollment Web Site
  o Submit a *TRICARE Prime Enrollment and PCM Change Form* through the mail
  o Receive most care from an assigned network primary care manager (PCM) who will provide referrals for specialty care.
  o If a network PCM is not available, care is received from any TRICARE- authorized provider.
- Fewer out-of-pocket costs.
- Eligible for travel reimbursement if referred for medically necessary care far from home.
- Enhanced coverage for vision and clinical preventive services.
- Time and distance access standards for care.
- No claims to file (in most cases).
- Easy to transfer enrollment when moving to another location in your TRICARE region or to a new TRICARE region.

TRICARE RESERVE SELECT

TRICARE Reserve Select (TRS) is a premium-based health plan that qualified National Guard and Reserve members may purchase. TRS, which requires a monthly premium, offers coverage similar to TRICARE Standard and Extra.

KEY FEATURES OF TRS INCLUDE:

- Available worldwide to most Selected Reserve members (and families) when not on active duty orders or covered under the Transitional Assistance Management Program.
- Must qualify for and purchase TRS to participate.
- Must pay monthly premiums. Failure to pay monthly premiums on time may result in disenrollment and an enrollment lockout.
- Freedom to manage your own health care; no assigned primary care manager.
- Visit any TRICARE-authorized provider or qualified host nation provider (if located overseas).
- Pay fewer out-of-pocket costs when choosing a provider in the TRICARE network.
- Network providers not available overseas.
- No referrals are required, but some care may require prior authorization.
- May have to pay for services when they are received and then seek reimbursement.
- May have to submit health care claims.
- May receive care in a military treatment facility (MTF) on a space-available basis only.
- Offers comprehensive health care coverage including TRICARE's prescription drug coverage.

TRICARE STANDARD AND EXTRA

TRICARE Standard is a fee-for-service option. When you use TRICARE Standard, you have more choice in providers as you can seek care from any TRICARE-authorized provider (network or non-network), but you'll pay higher out-of-pocket costs.

To reduce your out-of-pocket costs, use the TRICARE Extra option by seeking care TRICARE network providers. Using TRICARE Extra is like using a Preferred Provider Option (PPO).

KEY FEATURES INCLUDE:

- Freedom to choose any TRICARE-authorized provider.
- Referrals not required, but some care may require prior authorization.
- Highest out-of-pocket costs.
- You may have to submit health care claims.
- Save time and money with the TRICARE Extra option.
- Visit a TRICARE network provider.
- Pay fewer out-of-pocket costs.
- Network providers will file claims for you.
- Receive care in a military treatment facility on a space-available basis only.
- TRICARE Standard is available worldwide, but Extra option is not available overseas.

ELIGIBILITY

In general, the following are eligible for TRICARE Standard and Extra:

- Active duty family members
- Retirees and their family members

172

- Surviving family members (widowed spouses, children)
- Eligible former spouses
- Family members of activated National Guard or Reserve members
- Retired National Guard and Reserve members and their families (upon reaching age 60)
- Medal of Honor recipients and their families

TRICARE STANDARD OVERSEAS

TRICARE Standard Overseas is a fee-for-service option. TRICARE Standard Overseas gives you more choices in the providers you can see for care, but costs you more in out- of-pocket costs. TRICARE Extra is not available in overseas locations.

KEY FEATURES OF TRICARE STANDARD OVERSEAS INCLUDES:

- Higher out-of-pocket costs than TRICARE Prime Overseas.
- Freedom to choose from any qualified host nation provider.
- Referrals not required, but some care may require prior authorization.
- You may have to pay for services when they are received and then seek reimbursement.
- You may have to submit health care claims.
- There is no assigned primary care manager.
- No enrollment process, which means no enrollment forms to fill out and no annual enrollment fees for retirees and others.
- Receive care in a military treatment facility on a space-available basis only.

In general, TRICARE Standard Overseas is available to the following beneficiaries:

- Active duty family members living overseas with their sponsors and those who have relocated with service sponsored/funded orders.
- Non-command sponsored active duty family members who reside overseas.
- Retirees and their family members who reside overseas.
- Survivors who reside overseas.
- Eligible former spouses who reside overseas.
- National Guard or Reserve family members who are living overseas while their sponsor is on active duty for more than 30 consecutive days.

FAMILY HEALTH PLAN

The US Family Health Plan is an additional TRICARE Prime option available through networks of community-based, not-for-profit health care systems in six areas of the United States. You must be enrolled in the Defense Eligibility Reporting System (DEERS) and reside in the one of the designated US Family Health Plan service areas.

KEY FEATURES OF THE US FAMILY HEALTH PLAN INCLUDE:

- The only TRICARE Prime program that offers benefits to beneficiaries age 65 and over, regardless of whether or not you participate in Medicare Part B. (See "Should I get Medicare Part B" below.)
- Few out-of-pocket costs (similar to TRICARE Prime).
- You do not access Medicare providers, military treatment facilities (MTFs) or TRICARE network providers, but instead receive your care from a primary care

physician that you select from a network of private physicians affiliated with one of the not-for-profit health care systems offering the plan. Your primary care physician assists you in getting appointments with specialists in the area and coordinates your care.

- You will benefit from the same level of prescription coverage as that available under the TRICARE program and at the same costs. However, you may only use your US Family Health Plan's list of retail or on-site pharmacies and the US Family Health Plan mail order service instead of TRICARE retail, mail- order or MTF pharmacies.
- If you move or un-enroll from the US Family Health Plan, you may choose any TRICARE program that you are eligible for and that is available in your area.
- Each US Family Health Plan site offers enhanced benefits and services such as discounts for eyeglasses, hearing aids and dental care. These enhancements will vary by US Family Health Plan site.
- There are no claims to file when plan-approved providers are used.
- Enrollment is required. You may enroll at anytime throughout the year and enrollment is automatically renewed each year unless you take action to un- enroll. Enrollment fees, if applicable, may transfer to another US Family Health Plan location or to TRICARE Prime.
- You are encouraged to enroll in the US Family Health Plan as a complete family unit, but you may enroll on an individual basis. When you enroll in the US Family Health Plan, you are committing to the plan for one year unless moving out of the area or un-enrolling for another qualified reason.

Eligible beneficiaries include:

- Active duty family members.
- Retirees and their eligible family members.
- Survivors.
- Former spouses.
- Medal of Honor recipients and their families.
- Family members of activated National Guard or Reserve Members.

SHOULD I GET MEDICARE PART B?

You do not need to have Medicare Part B to enroll in the US Family Health Plan. However, if you do not enroll in Medicare Part B when first eligible, and subsequently choose to do so, you will pay (in addition to the normal Medicare Part B monthly premium) an annual 10% penalty for each year you were eligible to enroll in Medicare Part B and did not.

In addition, you will only be able to in Medicare Part B enroll during the general enrollment period, January 1-March 31, of each year, and your Part B benefits will not be effective until July 1 of that year. You are encouraged to enroll in Medicare Part B when first eligible.

If you are entitled to Medicare Part A and decide to un-enroll from the US Family Health Plan, you will then be able to use the TRICARE For Life benefit, but only if you also are enrolled in Medicare Part B. Additionally, if you subscribe to Medicare Part B, you pay only copayments for prescription drugs and your annual enrollment fee is waived. Medicare Part B also adds coverage for End Stage Renal Disease, a condition that usually involves kidney failure. Medicare Part B is not required for the US Family Health Plan, but you should carefully consider whether or not it is in your best interest to enroll.

TRICARE YOUNG ADULT

TRICARE Young Adult is a premium-based health care plan that qualified dependents may purchase. TRICARE Young Adult provides medical and pharmacy benefits, but dental coverage is not included. The plan allows dependent adult children to purchase TRICARE coverage after eligibility for "regular" TRICARE coverage ends at age 21 (or age 23 if enrolled in a full course of study at an approved institution of higher learning). There are two options to select from at enrollment; Prime and Standard.

ELIGIBILITY

You may be eligible if you are:

- An adult child of an eligible sponsor.
- Eligible sponsors include:
- Active duty servicemembers
- Retired servicemembers
- Activated Guard/Reserve members
- Non-activated Guard/Reserve members using TRICARE Reserve Select
- Retired Guard/Reserve members using TRICARE Retried Reserve
- Unmarried
- At least age 21, but not yet age 26 (If you are enrolled in a full course of study at an approved institution of higher learning and your sponsor provides 50 percent of your financial support, your eligibility may not begin until age 23 or upon graduation, whichever comes first.)
- Not eligible to enroll in an employer-sponsored health plan based on your own employment
- Not otherwise eligible for TRICARE program coverage

KEY FEATURES OF TRICARE YOUNG ADULT PRIME COVERAGE

- In the United States, the Prime Option is available only in Prime Service Areas to children of active duty and retired service members.
- If you live in an area where the US Family Health Plan is offered, you may enroll in the US Family Health Plan for your prime option.
- If your sponsor is on active duty you may also select the Prime Option when you live with your sponsor:
    - o In remote U.S. Zip Codes if your sponsor is enrolled in TRICARE Prime remote and; Anywhere overseas if you are command- sponsored.
    - o If your sponsor is using TRICARE Reserve Select or TRICARE Retired Reserve, the Prime Option is not available to you.
- With the Prime Option, you will have an assigned primary care manager (PCM), either at a military treatment facility (MTF) or in the TRICARE network, who will provide the majority of your care.
- Your PCM will refer you to a specialist for care when he or she is unable to provide that care. Your PCM will also coordinate with your regional contractor for authorization, to find a specialist in the network, and will file claims on your behalf.
- Other benefits include enhanced vision and preventative services, and travel reimbursement for some specialty care.
- Children of active duty servicemembers pay no out-of-pocket costs for any type of care as long as care is received from PCM or with a referral.

KEY FEATURES OF TRICARE YOUNG ADULT STANDARD OPTION

All dependent children who qualify for TRICARE Young Adult may select the Standard Option.

You may visit any TRICARE-authorized provider, network or non-network. Care at military treatment facilities is available on a space-available basis only. You do not need a referral for any type of care but some services may require prior authorization.

The type of provider determines how much you'll pay out-of-pocket. If you're visiting a network provider you'll pay less out-of-pocket and the provider will file claims for you.

TRANSITIONAL ASSISTANCE MANAGEMENT PROGRAM

The Transitional Assistance Management Program (TAMP) provides 180 days of transitional health care benefits upon separation from active duty service. Service members who meet the criteria below are eligible for TRICARE benefits for themselves and their family members.

- A member who is involuntarily separated from active duty.
- A member of a reserve component who is separated from active duty to which called or ordered in support of a contingency operation if the active duty is for a period of more than 30 days.
- A member who is separated from active duty for which the member is involuntarily retained under Section 12305 (also referred to as "stop loss") of Title 10, U.S.C., in support of a contingency operation.
- A member who is separated from active duty served pursuant to a voluntary agreement of the member to remain on active duty for a period of less than one year in support of a contingency operation.

For those who qualify, the 180-day TAMP period begins upon the sponsor's separation. During TAMP, sponsors and family members are eligible to use one of the following health plan options:

- TRICARE Prime (enrollment required) TRICARE Standard and Extra
- TRICARE Prime Overseas (enrollment required) TRICARE Standard Overseas

CONTINUED HEALTH CARE BENEFIT PROGRAM (CHCBP)

The Continued Health Care Benefit Program (CHCBP) is a premium-based health care program administered by Humana Military Health Care Services, Inc. (Humana Military). CHCBP offers temporary transitional health coverage (18-36 months) after TRICARE eligibility ends. If you qualify, you can purchase CHCBP within 60 days of loss of eligibility for either regular TRICARE or Transitional Assistance Management Program (TAMP) coverage.

CHCBP acts as a bridge between military health benefits and your new civilian health plan. CHCBP benefits are comparable to TRICARE Standard with the same benefits, providers and program rules. The main difference is that you pay premiums to participate.

WHO IS ELIGIBLE?

Under certain circumstances, the following beneficiaries may be eligible:
- Former active duty service members released from active duty (under other than adverse conditions) and their eligible family members. Coverage is limited to 18 months.
- Un-remarried former spouses who were eligible for TRICARE on the day before the date of the final decree of divorce, dissolution or annulment. Coverage is usually limited to 36 months however some un- remarried former spouses may continue coverage beyond 36 months if they meet certain criteria. Contact Humana Military

for details.

- Children who cease to meet the requirements to be an eligible family member and were eligible for TRICARE on the day before ceasing to meet those requirements. Coverage is limited to 36 months.
- Certain unmarried children by adoption or legal custody. Coverage is limited to 36 months.

For more information about CHCBP, call (800) 444-5445. Contact your regional contractor or a Beneficiary Counseling and Assistance Coordinator (BCAC) to discuss your eligibility for this program.

EXTENDED CARE HEALTH OPTION

The TRICARE Extended Care Health Option (ECHO) provides financial assistance to eligible beneficiaries who qualify based on specific mental or physical disabilities and offers an integrated set of services and supplies not available through the basic TRICARE program. TRICARE ECHO doesn't replace basic TRICARE programs; it supplements the benefits of the TRICARE program option that eligible beneficiaries use.

ECHO benefits are only available to qualified active duty family members (including family members of activated National Guard or Reserve members). Active duty family members must qualify for ECHO through ECHO case managers in each TRICARE region.

ELIGIBILITY

The TRICARE Extended Care Health Option (ECHO) is available *only to active duty family members* who have a qualifying condition.

Qualifying conditions include:
- Moderate or severe mental retardation
- A serious physical disability
- An extraordinary physical or psychological condition of such complexity that the beneficiary is homebound
- A diagnosis of a neuromuscular developmental condition or other condition in an infant or toddler that is expected to precede a diagnosis of moderate or severe mental retardation or a serious physical disability
- Multiple disabilities, which may qualify if there are two or more disabilities affecting separate body systems

If you or your provider believes a qualifying condition exists, talk to a case manager or with your regional contractor or TRICARE Area Office (if stationed overseas) to determine eligibility for TRICARE ECHO benefits.

To begin using TRICARE ECHO, qualifying family members must be enrolled in the *Exceptional Family Member Program* and must be registered for TRICARE ECHO with their regional contractor or TRICARE Area Office. There is no enrollment fee for TRICARE ECHO.

PRE-ACTIVATION BENEFIT FOR NATIONAL GUARD AND RESERVE

National Guard and Reserve members who are issued delayed-effective-date active duty orders for more than 30 days in support of a contingency operation may qualify for "early eligibility for TRICARE" beginning on the later of:

- the date their orders were issued; or

- 90 days before they report to active duty.

National Guard and Reserve members who qualify for the pre-activation benefit are covered as "active duty service members" and receive active duty medical and dental benefits.

Additionally, when National Guard or Reserve members qualify for pre-activation benefits, family members who are registered in the Defense Enrollment Eligibility Reporting System are also covered under TRICARE up to 90 days before the sponsor's active duty service begins. Family members become covered by TRICARE as "active duty family members during the pre-activation period and while the sponsor is activated.

The member's Service personnel office will tell members if they are eligible for pre-activation benefits when they receive their delayed-effective-date active duty orders.

PHARMACY BENEFITS

TRICARE prescription drug coverage is available to all TRICARE-eligible beneficiaries who are enrolled in the Defense Enrollment Eligibility Reporting System (DEERS). Prescription drug coverage is the same regardless of which health plan option you are using and it is available worldwide.

Eligible beneficiaries include:
- Active duty service members and their families
- Activated National Guard and Reserve Members and their families (on Title 10 or Title 32 [federal]orders)
- Retired service members and their families
- Retired National Guard and Reserve Members and their families (age 60 and above and receiving retired pay)
- Survivors, widows/widowers and certain former spouses
- Medal of Honor recipients and their families
- Beneficiaries enrolled in TRICARE Reserve Select or the Continued Health Care Benefit Program
- Other beneficiaries listed in DEERS as eligible for TRICARE, including foreign force members and their families.

CHIROPRACTIC CARE

In 2001, the *National Defense Authorization Act* established the Chiropractic Health Care Program. The program is currently available to active duty service members (including activated National Guard and Reserve members) at designated military treatment facilities (MTFs) throughout the United States.

ELIGIBILITY

Active duty service members and activated National Guard or Reserve members must obtain chiropractic care at a designated MTF and must receive a referral from their primary care manager (PCM).

Family members, retirees and their family members, un-remarried former spouses and survivors **are not eligible** for this program. They may be referred to non-chiropractic health care services in the Military Health System (e.g., physical therapy or orthopedics) or may seek chiropractic care in the local community at their own expense.

ACCESS TO CHIROPRACTIC CARE

During the course of treatment, the service member's PCM will determine if specialty care (traditional or chiropractic care) is required. If chiropractic care is considered an option, the service member will undergo a screening process to rule out any medical conditions that would prohibit chiropractic care. If appropriate, the PCM will refer the service member to a chiropractic provider for treatment.

While receiving chiropractic care, the service member will continue to see his or her PCM and the duration/frequency of the chiropractic services will be determined by the PCM and follow the usual referral process.

Chiropractic care received outside of the designated locations is not covered under the Chiropractic Health Care Program.

TRICARE CATASTROPHIC CAP

The TRICARE catastrophic cap limits the amount of out-of-pocket expenses a family will have to pay for TRICARE-covered medical services. The cap applies to the allowable charges for covered services—annual deductibles, Prime enrollment fees, pharmacy co-pays, and other cost shares based on TRICARE-allowable charges. Out-of-pocket expenses paid under the TRICARE Prime point-of-service (POS) option (deductibles and cost-shares) are not applied to the annual enrollment year catastrophic cap. Additionally, any POS charges incurred after the catastrophic cap has been met are the beneficiary's financial responsibility.

The catastrophic cap amount depends on an individual's profile, and should be obtained from TRICARE directly.

TRICARE REGIONS

NORTH

TRICARE's North region includes Connecticut, Delaware, the District of Columbia, Illinois, Indiana, Kentucky, Maine, Maryland, Massachusetts, Michigan, New Hampshire, New Jersey, New York, North Carolina, Ohio, Pennsylvania, Rhode Island, Vermont, Virginia, West Virginia, and Wisconsin (and some zip code areas in Iowa, Missouri, and Tennessee). Health Net Federal Services, Inc. is the new regional contractor providing health care services and network-provider support in the TRICARE North region.

Health Net's customer service representatives are available Monday – Friday, 8 a.m. to 7 p.m. in all North region time zones, at (877) 874-2273.

SOUTH

TRICARE's South region includes Alabama, Arkansas, Florida, Georgia, Louisiana, Mississippi Oklahoma, South Carolina, and Tennessee (excluding 35 Tennessee zip codes in the Fort Campbell, KY area), and Texas (excluding, only, the extreme southwestern El Paso-area). Humana-Military is the regional contractor providing health care services and network provider support in the TRICARE South region.

Humana's customer service representatives are available Monday – Friday, 8 a.m. to 6 in all South region time zones, at (800) 444-5445.

WEST

TRICARE's West region includes Alaska, Arizona, California, Colorado, Hawaii, Idaho, Iowa (except 82 Iowa zip codes that are in the Rock Island, Illinois area), Kansas, Minnesota, Missouri (except the St. Louis area), Montana, Nebraska, Nevada, New Mexico, North Dakota, Oregon, South Dakota, Texas (the southwestern corner, including El Paso, only) Utah, Washington, and Wyoming. TriWest Healthcare Alliance is the regional contractor providing health care services and network-provider support in the TRICARE West region.

TriWest's customer service representatives are available Monday – Friday, 8 a.m. to 6 p.m. in the West Region time zone in which you reside, at (888) 874-9378.

EUROPE AREA

The TRICARE Europe area is managed by the TAO Europe located at Sembach Air Base in Germany, and includes Europe, Africa and the Middle East.

Customer service representatives can be reached at (888) 777-8343.

LATIN AMERICA AND CANADA AREA

The TRICARE Latin America and Canada (TLAC) area is managed by the TAO TLAC located at Fort Gordon, Georgia and includes Central and South America, the Caribbean Basin, Canada, Puerto Rico and the Virgin Islands.

Customer service representatives can be reached at (888) 777-8343.

PACIFIC AREA

The TRICARE Pacific area is managed by the TAO Pacific located at Camp Lester in Okinawa, Japan, and includes Guam, Japan, Korea, Asia, New Zealand, India and Western Pacific remote countries.

Customer service representatives can be reached at (888) 777-8343.

AFFORDABLE CARE ACT

The Affordable Care Act, also known as the health care law, was created to expand access to coverage, control health care costs and improve health care quality and care coordination. The health care law does not change VA health benefits or Veterans' out- of-pocket costs.

Three things you should know:

- VA wants all Veterans to receive health care that improves their health and well-being.
- If you are enrolled in VA health care, you don't need to take additional steps to meet the health care law coverage standards. The health care law does not change VA health benefits or Veterans' out-of-pocket costs.
- If you are not enrolled in VA health care, you can apply at any time.

VETERANS ENROLLED IN VA HEALTH CARE

Veterans enrolled in VA health care programs have health coverage that meets the new health care law's standard. You do not have to take any additional steps to have health coverage.

VETERANS NOT ENROLLED IN VA HEALTH CARE

Veterans not currently enrolled in VA health care program can apply for enrollment at any time.

FAMILY MEMBERS

VA offers health care benefits for certain family members of Veterans through programs such as the Civilian Health and Medical Program of the Department of Veterans Affairs (CHAMPVA) and the Spina Bifida program. Your family members who are not enrolled in a VA health care program should use the Marketplace to get coverage

CHAPTER 16

VA'S FIDUCIARY PROGRAM

PROGRAM DESCRIPTION

VA's Fiduciary Program was established to protect Veterans and other beneficiaries who, due to injury, disease, or due to age, are unable to manage their financial affairs. VA will only determine an individual to be unable to manage his or her financial affairs afterreceipt of medical documentation or if a court of competent jurisdiction has already made the determination.

Upon determining a beneficiary is unable to manage his or her financial affairs, VA will appoint a fiduciary. The fiduciary, normally chosen by the beneficiary, must undergo an investigation of their suitability to serve. This investigation includes a criminal background check, review of credit report, personal interview, and recommendations of character references. Only after a complete investigation is a fiduciary appointed to manage a beneficiaries VA benefits. The fiduciary is responsible to the beneficiary

> **Key Takeaways**
>
> The Fiduciary Program protects veterans who aren't able to manage their financial affairs
>
> The field examination is used to appoint a fiduciary
>
> A fiduciary is responsible to the beneficiary and oversees financial management of VA benefit payments
>
> The determination that you are unable to manage your VA benefits doesn't affect your non-VA finances, or your right to vote or contract

and oversees financial management of VA benefit payments. Generally, family members or friends serve as fiduciaries for beneficiaries; however, when friends and family are not able to serve, VA looks for qualified individuals or organizations to serve as a fiduciary.

WHAT IS THE FIDUCIARY PROGRAM?

The purpose of the Department of Veterans Affairs (VA) Fiduciary Program is to protect Veterans and beneficiaries who are unable to manage their VA benefits through the appointment and oversight of a fiduciary.

If you have been determined unable to manage your VA benefits, the VA will conduct a field examination to appoint a fiduciary to assist you.

THE VA FIELD EXAMINATION

A VA field examination will be scheduled for the purpose of appointing a fiduciary to assist you in managing your VA benefits. During the field examination, please have the following information available for review by the field examiner:

- Photoidentification.
- The source and amount of all monthly bills, recurring expenses (annual, bi-annual, quarterly, etc.), and income.
- A list of all assets, to include bank accounts, owned property, stocks, bonds, life insurance, burial plans,etc.
- A list of all current medications.
- Name, phone number, and address of your primary care doctor. Name, phone number, and address of your next of kin.

SELECTION PROCESS

During the selection process, the VA will first seek to qualify the individual you desire to serve as your fiduciary.

The fiduciary selection is based on an assessment of the qualifications of the proposed fiduciary. When seeking a fiduciary the following individuals may be considered:

- A spouse or family member
- Court-appointed fiduciaries
- Another interested party,or
- A professional fiduciary

An assessment of the qualifications of a proposed fiduciary includes, but is not limited to:

- The willingness to serve and abide by all agreements
- An interview with a VA representative
- Credit report review
- An inquiry into the criminal background, and
- Interviews with character witnesses

WHAT ARE MY RIGHTS

The determination that you are unable to manage your VA benefits does not affect your non-VA finances, or your right to vote or contract.

You have the right to appeal VA's decision finding that you are unable to manage your VA benefits. You also have the right to appeal VA's selection of the fiduciary. If you disagree with the VA on either of these matters you may:

- Appeal to the Board of Veterans' Appeals (Board) by telling them you disagree with their decision and want the Board to review it, or
- Give them evidence we do not already have that may lead us to change our decision.

HOW TO APPLY

To become a fiduciary for a family member or friend, submit a request with the beneficiary's name and VA file number, and your name and contact information to the VA regional office nearest you

To become a professional fiduciary, submit your resume with cover letter to the following e-mail address: VA_Fiduciary@va.gov. Include your name, the name of your organization (if applicable), mailing address, and e-mail address with your request.

SELECTION PROCESS

The fiduciary selection is based on an assessment of the qualifications of the proposed fiduciary. When seeking a fiduciary the following individuals may be considered:

- A spouse or family member
- Court-appointed fiduciaries
- Another interested party
- A professional fiduciary

CHAPTER 17

VOCATIONAL REHABILITATION AND EMPLOYMENT SERVICES FOR VETERANS WITH SERVICE-CONNECTED DISABILITIES

OVERVIEW

You may receive Vocational Rehabilitation and Employment (VR&E) services to help with job training, employment accommodations, resume development, and job seeking skills coaching. Other services may be provided to assist Veterans in starting their own businesses or independent living services for those who are severely disabled and unable to work in traditional employment.

Services that may be provided by the VR&E Program include:

- Comprehensive evaluation to determine abilities, skills, and interests for employment

- Vocational counseling and rehabilitation planning for employment services

- Employment services such as job- training, job-seeking skills, resume development, and other work readiness assistance

- Assistance finding and keeping a job, including the use of special employer incentives and job accommodations

- On the Job Training (OJT), apprenticeships, and non-paid work experiences

- Post-secondary training at a college, vocational, technical or business school

- Supportive rehabilitation services including case management, counseling, and medical

> **Key Takeaways**
>
> Vocational Rehabilitation helps disabled veterans get and maintain suitable jobs
>
> Services include vocational and personal counseling and more
>
> Typically a veteran must first be awarded a monthly VA Disability Compensation Payment
>
> A Subsistence Allowance may be paid each month and is based on rate of attendance and number of dependents

referrals

- Independent living services for Veterans unable to work due to the severity of their disabilities

ELIGIBILITY

Active Duty Servicemembers are eligible if they:

- Expect to receive an honorable or other than dishonorable discharge upon separation from active duty
- Obtain a memorandum rating of 20% or more from the Department of Veterans Affairs (VA), and
- Apply for VR&E services

Or (until December 31, 2017)

- Are participating in the Integrated Disability Evaluation System (IDES) or are certified by the military as having a severe injury or illness that may prevent them from performing their military duties
- Apply for VR&E services, and
- Report for an evaluation with a VR&E counselor before separating from active duty

Veterans are eligible if they:

- Have received a discharge that is other than dishonorable
- Have a service-connected disability rating of at least 10% from VA
- Apply for VR&E services

Basic Period of Eligibility

The basic period of eligibility ends 12 years from the date of notification of one of the following:

- Date of separation from active military service, or
- Date the veteran was first notified by VA of a service-connected disability rating.

The basic period of eligibility may be extended if a Vocational Rehabilitation Counselor (VRC) determines that a Veteran has a Serious Employment Handicap.

What Happens after Eligibility is Established?

The Veteran is scheduled to meet with a VRC for a comprehensive evaluation to determine if he/she is entitled for services. A comprehensive evaluation includes:

- An assessment of the Veteran's interests, aptitudes, and abilities
- An assessment of whether service connected disabilities impair the Veteran's ability to find and/or hold a job using the occupational skills he or she has already developed
- Vocational exploration and goal development leading to employment and/or maximum independence in the Veteran's daily living at home and in the community

What is an Entitlement Determination?

A VRC works with the Veteran to complete a determination if an employment handicap exists. An employment handicap exists if the Veteran's service connected disability impairs his/her ability to obtain and maintain a job. Entitlement to services is established if the veteran has an employment handicap and is within his or her 12-year basic period of eligibility and has a 20% or greater service-connected disability rating.

If the service connected disability rating is less than 20%, or if the Veteran is beyond the 12-year basic period of eligibility, then a serious employment handicap must be found to establish entitlement to VR&E services. A serious employment handicap is based on the extent and complexity of services required to help a Veteran to overcome the significant restrictions caused by his or her service and non-service connected disabilities, permitting the return to suitable employment

What Happens after the Entitlement Determination is Made?

The Veteran and VRC work together to:
- Determine transferable skills, aptitudes, and interests
- Identify viable employment and/or independent living services options
- Explore labor market and wage information
- Identify physical demands and other job characteristics
- Explore vocational options to identify a suitable employment goal
- Select a VR&E program track leading to an employment or independent living goal
- Investigate training requirements
- Identify resources needed to achieve rehabilitation
- Develop an individualized rehabilitation plan to achieve the identified employment or independent living goals

What is a Rehabilitation Plan?

A rehabilitation plan is an individualized, written plan of services, which outlines the resources and criteria that will be used to achieve employment or independent living goals. The plan is an agreement that is signed by the Veteran and the VRC and is updated as needed to assist the Veteran to achieve his/her goals. Depending on their circumstances, veterans will work with their VRC to select one of the following five tracks of services

- Reemployment (with a former employer)
- Direct job placement services for new employment
- Self-employment
- Employment through long term services including OJT, college, and other training
- Independent living services

What Happens after the Rehabilitation Plan is Developed?

After a plan is developed and signed, a VRC or case manager will continue to work with the Veteran to implement the plan to achieve suitable employment and/or independent living. The VRC or case manager will provide ongoing counseling, assistance, and coordinate services such as tutorial assistance, training in job-seeking skills, medical and dental referrals, adjustment counseling, payment of training allowance, if applicable, and other services as required to help the Veteran achieve rehabilitation.

How can I get paid the Post-9/11 GI Bill rate for my Vocational Rehabilitation program?

A Veteran participating in the VR&E Program who qualifies for Post 9/11 GI Bill benefits can elect to receive the GI Bill rate of pay instead of the regular Chapter 31 subsistence allowance. In most cases, the GI Bill rate is higher than the regular Chapter 31 rate of pay. To elect the GI Bill rate, the Veteran must have remaining eligibility for the Post-9/11 GI Bill, and must formally choose (or "elect") the GI Bill rate. Your VRC can help you with election.

Veterans participating in the VR&E Program who elect the Post-9/11 rate are paid at the 100% rate level for their school and training time, even if their Post-9/11 GI Bill eligibility is less than 100%. Additional benefits are also available through the VR&E Program, such as payment of all required books, fees and supplies as well as other supportive services.

AMOUNT OF VA PAYMENTS

If a veteran needs training, VA will pay his or her training costs, such as:

Tuition and fees;
Books;
Supplies;
Equipment; and
Special services (such as prosthetic devices, lip-reading training, or signing for the deaf), if needed

While a veteran is in training, VA will also pay him or her a monthly benefit to help with living expenses, called a subsistence allowance. Details are provided in the next section of this chapter.

SUBSISTENCE ALLOWANCE

In some cases, a veteran requires additional education or training in order to become employable. A Subsistence Allowance may then be paid each month, and is based on the rate of attendance (full-time or part-time) and the number of dependents. The charts on the following page reflect the rates as of October 1, 2017.

The following Subsistence Allowance rates are paid for training in an Institution of Higher Learning

Number Of Dependents	Full Time	Three Quarter Time	One Half Time
No Dependents	$617.40	463.90	310.40
One Dependent	765.83	575.21	384.59
Two Dependents	902.48	674.73	452.06
Each Additional Dependent	65.77	50.59	33.75

Subsistence Allowance is paid for full time training only, in the following training programs:

Nonpay or nominal pay on-job training in a federal, state, local, or federally recognized Indian tribe agency; training in the home; vocational course in a rehabilitation facility or sheltered workshop; institutional non-farm cooperative

Number Of Dependents	Full Time
No Dependents	$617.40
One Dependent	765.83
Two Dependents	902.48
Each Additional Dependent	65.77

The following rates are paid for Work Experience programs:

Nonpay or nominal pay work experience in a federal, state, local or federally recognized Indian tribe agency.

Number Of Dependents	Full Time	Three Quarter Time	One Half Time
No Dependents	$617.50	463.90	310.40
One Dependent	765.83	575.21	384.59
Two Dependents	902.48	674.73	452.06
Each Additional Dependent	65.77	50.59	33.75

Subsistence Allowance is paid for full time training only in the following training programs:

Farm cooperative, apprenticeship, or other on-job training

Number of Dependents	Full Time
No Dependents	$539.81
One Dependent	652.79
Two Dependents	752.34
Each Additional Dependent	48.93

Subsistence Allowance is paid at the following rates for combined training programs:

Combination of Institutional and On-Job Training (Full Time Rate Only).

Number Of Dependents	Institutional Greater than one half	On-The-Job Greater than one half
No Dependents	$617.50	539.81
One Dependent	765.83	652.79
Two Dependents	902.48	752.34
Additional Dependents	65.77	48.93

Subsistence Allowance is paid at the following rates for Non-farm Cooperative Training:

Non-farm Cooperative Institutional Training and Non-farm Cooperative On-Job Training - Full Time Rate Only.

Number Of Dependents	FT Non-farm Coop/Institutional	FT Non-farm Coop/On-The-Job
No Dependents	$617.40	539.81

One Dependent	765.83	652.79
Two Dependents	902.48	752.34
Each Additional Dependent	65.77	48.93

Subsistence Allowance is paid at the following rates for Independent Living programs:

A subsistence allowance is paid each month during the period of enrollment in a rehabilitation facility when a veteran is pursuing an approved Independent Living Program plan. Subsistence allowance paid during a period of Independent Living Services is based on rate of pursuit and number of dependents.

Number Of Dependents	Full Time	Three Quarter Time	One Half Time
No Dependents	$617.40	463.90	310.40
One Dependent	765.83	575.21	384.59
Two Dependents	902.48	674.73	452.06
Each Additional Dependent	65.77	50.59	33.75

Subsistence Allowance is paid at the following rates for Extended Evaluation programs:

A subsistence allowance is paid each month during the period of enrollment in a rehabilitation facility when a veteran requires this service for the purpose of extended evaluation. Subsistence allowance during a period of extended evaluation is paid based on the rate of attendance and the number of dependents.

Number of Dependents	Full Time	Three Quarter Time	One Half Time	One Quarter Time
No Dependents	$617.40	463.90	310.40	155.18
One Dependent	765.83	575.21	384.59	192.32
Two Dependents	902.48	674.73	452.06	226.03
Each Additional Dependent	65.77	50.59	33.75	16.84

PROGRAM FOR UNEMPLOYABLE VETERANS

Veterans awarded 100% disability compensation based upon unemployability may still request an evaluation, and, if found eligible, may participate in a vocational rehabilitation program and receive help in getting a job. A veteran who secures employment under the special program will continue to receive 100% disability compensation until the veteran has worked continuously for at least 12 months.

ELECTION OF ALTERNATE SUBSISTENCE ALLOWANCE UNDER *PUBLIC LAW 111- 377*

This option is included for your use in comparing subsistence allowance rates that may be available to certain Veterans participating in the Chapter 31 program.

The VA is authorized to allow a Veteran, entitled to both a Chapter 31 subsistence allowance and *Post 9/11 GI Bill* Chapter 33 educational assistance, to elect to receive a replacement in an alternate amount instead of the regular Chapter 31 subsistence allowance.

The alternate payment will be based on the military basic allowance for housing (BAH) for an E-5 with dependents residing in the zip code of the training facility. Training in foreign institutions and training that is solely on-line or in-home will be based on the national average BAH.

PARALYMPIC VETERANS BENEFIT

Some veterans in training for the U.S. Paralympics may qualify for a monthly subsistence allowance from VA. The allowance is pegged to the subsistence allowance for participants in a fulltime institutional program under chapter 31 of title 38 of the U.S. Code. According to the new rule, the VA will pay the allowance to a veteran with a service-connected or non-service-connected disability if the veteran is invited by the U.S. Paralympics to compete for a slot on the U.S. Paralympic team or is residing at the U.S. Paralympic training center for training or competition. Applications for the allowance must be submitted through the U.S. Paralympics. Through the program, VA will pay a monthly allowance to a veteran with a service-connected or non-service-connected disability if the veteran meets the minimum military standard or higher (e.g., Emerging, Talent Pool, National Team) in his or her respective sport at a recognized competition. Besides making the military standard, an athlete must also be nationally or internationally classified by his or her respective sport federation as eligible for Paralympic competition within six or 12 months of a qualifying performance.

Athletes must also have established training and competition plans and are responsible for turning in monthly and quarterly reports in order to continue receiving a monthly assistance allowance. The allowance base for an athlete approved for monetary assistance ranges from $566.97 up to $1,084.00 per month, depending on the number of dependent.

VOCATIONAL TRAINING FOR CHILDREN WITH SPINA BIFIDA

To qualify for entitlement to a vocational training program an applicant must be a child:

*   To whom VA has awarded a monthly allowance for spina bifida; and

*   For whom VA has determined that achievement of a vocational goal is reasonably feasible.

A vocational training program may not begin before a child's 18th birthday, or the date of completion of secondary schooling, whichever comes first. Depending on the need, a child may be provided up to 24 months of full-time training.

VOCATIONAL TRAINING FOR CHILDREN OF FEMALE VIETNAM VETERANS BORN WITH CERTAIN BIRTH DEFECTS

Section 401 of *P.L. 106-416*, which became law on November 1, 2000 directed the Secretary of VA to identify birth defects of children of female Vietnam veterans that: (1) are associated with service during the Vietnam era; and (2) result in the permanent physical or mental disability of such children. The law excludes from such defects familial or birth- related defects or injuries. The law further directs the Secretary to provide to such children a monthly monetary allowance, as well as necessary health care to address the defect and any associated disability. It authorizes the Secretary to provide vocational training to such a child if the achievement of a vocational goal is reasonably feasible.

INDEPENDENT LIVING SERVICES

These services can help an individual with disabilities so severe that he or she cannot work. These services can lessen the individual's need to rely on others by giving him or her the skills needed to live as independently as possible at home and in the community.

APPLYING FOR BENEFITS

Interested veterans can apply by filling out "VA Form 28-1900", "Disabled Veterans Application for Vocational Rehabilitation", and mailing it to the VA regional office serving his or her area.

CHAPTER 18

VET CENTERS

Vet Centers serve veterans and their families by providing a continuum of quality care that adds value for veterans, families, and communities. Care includes:

- Professional readjustment counseling;
- Professional counseling for posttraumatic stress disorder;
- Marital and family counseling;
- Substance abuse information and referral;
- Community education;
- Outreach to special populations, including disenfranchised and unserved veterans;
- The brokering of services with community agencies;
- Provides a key access link between the veteran and other services in the U.S. Department of Veterans Affairs;
- Promotion of wellness activities with veterans to help them reach quality health and life goals, and diminish the need for more intensive healthcare.

> **Key Takeaways**
>
> Vet Centers provide assistance to veterans and their families to help them make a successful post-war adjustment
>
> Vet Centers across the country provide counseling, outreach and referral services to combat veterans and their families
>
> Vet Centers may include services related to PTSD, alcohol and drug assessment, and suicide prevention referrals
>
> All services are free and confidential

ELIGIBILITY

Vet Centers serve the following veterans:

WAR ZONE VETERANS- ALL ERAS, INCLUDING:

Vietnam War – February 28, 1961 to May 7, 1975
Vietnam Era Veterans Not In The War Zone – August 5, 1964 to May 7, 1975
Korean War – June 27, 1950 to July 27, 1954 (eligible for the Korean Service Medal)
World War II – There are 3 eligible categories:
- *European-African-Middle Eastern Campaign Medal – December 7, 1941 to November 8, 1945*
- *Asiatic-Pacific Campaign Medal – December 7, 1941 to March 2, 1946*
- *American Campaign Medal – December 7, 1941 to March 2, 1946*

Lebanon – August 25, 1982 to February 26, 1984
Grenada – October 23, 1983 to November 21, 1983
Panama – December 20, 1989 to January 31, 1990
Persian Gulf – August 2, 1990 to a date to be set by law or Presidential Proclamation
Somalia – September 17, 1992 to a date to be set by law or Presidential Proclamation
Operation Joint Endeavor, Operation Joint Guard, & Operation Joint Forge - Vet Center eligibility has been extended to veterans who participated in one or more of the three successive operations in the former Yugoslavia (Bosnia-Herzegovina and Croatia, aboard U.S. Naval vessels operating in the Adriatic Sea, or air spaces above those areas).
Global War on Terrorism – Veterans who serve or have served in military expeditions to combat terrorism on or after September 11, 2001 and before a terminal date yet to be established.

SEXUAL TRAUMA AND HARASSMENT COUNSELING

Veterans of both sexes, all eras. Vet Center services include individual readjustment counseling, referral for benefits assistance, group readjustment counseling, liaison with community agencies, marital and family counseling, substance abuse information and referral, job counseling and placement, sexual trauma counseling, and community education.

At the VA, Veterans can receive free, confidential treatment for mental and physical health conditions related to Military Sexual Trauma (MST). You may be able to receive this MST-related care even if you are not eligible for other VA services. To receive these services, you do not need a VA service-connected disability rating, to have reported the incident when it happened, or have other documentation that it occurred.

Knowing that MST survivors may have special concerns, every VA healthcare facility has an MST Coordinator who can answer any questions you might have about VA's MST services. VA has a range of services available to meet Veterans where they are at in their recovery:

Every VA healthcare facility has providers knowledgeable about treatment for problems related MST. Many have specialized outpatient mental health services focusing on sexual trauma. Vet Centers also have specially trained sexual trauma counselors.

VA has almost two dozen programs nationwide that offer specialized MST treatment in a residential or inpatient settings. These programs are for Veterans who need more intense treatment and support.

Because some Veterans do not feel comfortable in mixed-gender treatment settings, some facilities have separate programs for men and women. All residential and inpatient MST programs have separate sleeping areas for men and women.

VET CENTER LOCATIONS

ALABAMA

Montgomery Vet Center
4405 Atlanta Highway
Montgomery, AL 36109
(334) 273-7796

ALASKA

Anchorage Vet Center
4400 Business Park Blvd.
Suite B-34
Anchorage, AK 99503
(907) 563-6966

Fairbanks Vet Center
542 4th Avenue
Suite 100
Fairbanks, AK 99701
(907) 456-4238

Wasilla Vet Center
851 East Westpoint Ave,
Suite 109
Wasilla, AK 99654
(907) 376-4318

ARIZONA

Lake Havasu Vet Center
1720 Mesquite
Suite 101
Lake Havasu, AZ 86403
928-505-0394

Mesa Vet Center
1303 South Longmore
Suite 5
Mesa, AZ 85202
(480) 610-6727

Phoenix Vet Center
4020 North 20th St.
Suite 110
Phoenix, AZ 85016
(602) 640-2981

Prescott Vet Center
3180 Stillwater Dr.
Suite A
Prescott, AZ 86305
(928) 778-3469
Tucson Vet Center
2525 E. Broadway Blvd.
Suite 100

Tucson, AZ 85716

(520) 882-0333

Yuma County Vet Center
1450 East 16th St.
Suite 103
Yuma, AZ 85365

ARKANSAS

North Little Rock Vet Center
201 West Broadway
Suite A
Little Rock, AR 72114
(501) 324-6395

CALIFORNIA

RCS Pacific District Office
420 Executive Court North, Suite A
Fairfield, CA 94534
(707) 646-2988

Chico Vet Center
280 Cohasset Road
Chico, CA 95926
(530) 899-8549

Concord Vet Center
1899 Clayton Rd, Suite 140
Concord, CA 94520
(925) 680-4526

Corona Vet Center
800 Magnolia Avenue, Suite 110
Corona, CA 92879-8202
(909) 734-0525

East Los Angeles Vet Center
5400 E Olympic Blvd, #140
East Los Angeles, CA 90022
(323) 728-9966

Eureka Vet Center
2830 G Street, Suite A
Eureka, CA 95501
(707) 444-8271

Fresno Vet Center
1320 E. Shaw Ave, Suite 125
Fresno, CA 93710
(559) 487-5660

Los Angeles Vet Center
1045 W. Redondo Beach Blvd., Suite 150
Gardena, CA 90247
(310) 767-1221

Modesto Vet Center
1219 N. Carpenter Rd.,
Suite 12
Modesto, CA 95351
(209) 569-0713

Oakland Vet Center
1504 Franklin St, Suite 200
Oakland, CA 94612
(510) 763-3904

Redwood City Vet Center
2946 Broadway Street
Redwood City, CA 94062
(650) 299-0672

Rohnert Park Vet Center
6225 State Farm Drive Suite
101 Rohnert Park, CA 94928
(707) 586-3295

Sacramento Vet Center
1111 Howe Avenue
Suite 390
Sacramento, CA 95825
(916) 566-7430

San Bernardino Vet Center
155 West Hospitality Lane Suite #140
San Bernardino, CA 92408
(909) 890-0797

San Diego Vet Center
2900 6th Avenue
San Diego, CA 92103
(619) 294-2040

San Francisco Vet Center
505 Polk Street
San Francisco, CA 94102
(415) 441-5051

San Jose Vet Center
278 North 2nd Street
San Jose, CA 95112
(408) 993-0729

San Marcos Vet Center
One Civic Center Dr., Suite 140
San Marcos, CA 92069
(760) 744-6914

Santa Cruz County Vet Center
1350 41st Ave, Suite 102

Capitola, CA 95010
(831) 464-4575

Sepulveda Vet Center
9737 Hascle Street
Sepulveda, CA 91343
(818) 892-9227

Ventura Vet Center
790 E. Santa Clara St., Suite 100
Ventura, CA 93001
(805) 585-1860

West Los Angeles Vet Center
5730 Uplander Way, Suite 100
Culver City, CA 90230
(310) 641-0326

COLORADO

Boulder Vet Center
2336 Canyon Blvd, Suite 130
Boulder, CO 80302
(303) 440-7306

Colorado Springs Vet Center
416 East Colorado Avenue
Colorado Springs, CO 80903
(719) 471-9992

4A Western Mountain Regional Office
789 Sherman Street, Suite 570
Denver, CO 80203
(303) 393-2897

Denver Vet Center
7465 E Academy Boulevard Denver, CO
80220
(303) 326-0645

Ft. Collins Vet Center Outstation 1100
Poudre River Dr. (Lower)
Ft. Collins, CO 80524
(970) 221-5176

Grand Junction Vet Center 2472 F. Road
Unit 16
Grand Junction, CO 81505
(970) 245-4156

Pueblo Vet Center Outstation
509 E. 13th St.
Pueblo, CO 81001
(719) 546-6666

CONNECTICUT

New Haven Vet Center
141 Captain Thomas Boulevard
New Haven, CT 06516
(203) 932-9899

Norwich Vet Center
5 Cliff Street
Norwich, CT 06360
(860) 887-1755

Wethersfield Vet Center
30 Jordan Lane
Wethersfield, CT 06109
(860) 563-2320

DELAWARE

Wilmington Vet Center
1601 Kirkwood Highway
Wilmington, DE 19805
(302) 994-1660

DISTRICT OF COLUMBIA

Washington, D.C. Vet Center
1250 Taylor Street, NW
Washington, DC 20011
(202) 726-5212

FLORIDA

Fort Lauderdale Vet Center
713 NE 3rd Avenue
Fort Lauderdale, FL 33304
(954) 356-7926

Ft. Myers Vet Center
4110 Center Pointe Dr. Unit 204
Ft. Myers, FL 33916
(239) 652-1861

Gainesville Vet Center
105 NW 75th Street, Suite #2
Gainesville, FL 32607
(352) 331-1408

Jacksonville Vet Center
300 East State Street
Jacksonville, FL 32202
(904) 232-3621

Key Largo Vet Center Outstation
105662 Overseas Hwy.
Key Largo, FL 33037
(305) 451-0164

Melbourne Vet Center

2098 Sarno Road
Melbourne, FL 32935
(321) 254-3410

Miami Vet Center
2700 SW 3rd Avenue Suite 1A
Miami, FL 33129
(305) 859-8387

Orlando Vet Center
5575 S Semoran Blvd Suite 36
Orlando, FL 32822
(407) 857-2800

Palm Beach Vet Center
2311 10th Avenue, North #13
Palm Beach, FL 33461
(561) 585-0441

Pensacola Vet Center
4501 Twin Oaks Drive
Pensacola, FL 32506
(850)456-5886

Sarasota Vet Center
4801 Swift Road
Sarasota, FL 34231
(941) 927-8285

St. Petersburg Vet Center
2880 1st Avenue, N.
St. Petersburg, FL 33713
(727) 893-3791

Tallahassee Vet Center
548 Bradford Road
Tallahassee, FL 32303
(850) 942-8810

Tampa Vet Center
8900N Armenia Ave, #312
Tampa, FL 33604
(813) 228-2621

GEORGIA

Atlanta Vet Center
1440 Dutch Valley Place Suite G,
Box 29 188
Atlanta, GA 30324
(404) 347-7264

Macon Vet Center
750 Riverside Drive
Macon, GA 31201
(478) 477-3813

North Atlanta Vet Center
930 River Centre Plaza
Lawrenceville, GA 30043
(770) 963-1809

Savannah Vet Center
8110A White Bluff Road
Savannah, GA 31406
(912) 652-4097

GUAM

Agana Vet Center
222 Chalan Santo Papa Street Reflection
Center, Suite 102
Agana, Guam 96910
(671) 472-7160

Guam Vet Center
222 Chalan Santo Papa Reflection Ctr.
Ste 201
Hagatna, GU 96910
(671) 472-7160

HAWAII

Hilo Vet Center
120 Keawe Street Suite 201
Hilo, HI 96720
(808) 969-3833

Honolulu Vet Center
1680 Kapiolani Boulevard SuiteF3
Honolulu, HI 96814
(808) 973-8387

Kailua-Kona Vet Center Lihue Vet Center
3-3367 Kuhlo Highway
Suite 101
Lihue, HI 96766
(808) 246-1163

Western Oahu Vet Center
885 Kamokila Blvd. Suite 105
Kapolei, HI 96707
(808) 674-2414

Wailuku Vet Center
35 Lunalilo Suite 101
Wailuku, HI 96793
(808) 242-8557

IDAHO

Boise Vet Center
5440 Franklin Road, Suite 100
Boise, ID 83705
(208) 342-3612

Pocatello Vet Center
1800 Garrett Way
Pocatello, ID 83201
(208) 232-0316

ILLINOIS

Chicago Vet Center
2038 West 95th Street Suite 200
Chicago, IL 60643
(773) 881-9900

Chicago Heights Vet Center
1600 Halsted Street
Chicago Heights, IL 60411
(708) 754-0340

East St. Louis Vet Center
1265 North 89th Street, Suite 5
East St. Louis, IL 62203
(618) 397-6602

Evanston Vet Center
565 Howard Street
Evanston, IL 60202
(847) 332-1019

Moline Vet Center
465 Avenue of the Cities, Suite #140
Moline , IL 61244
(319) 383-4782

Oak Park Vet Center
155 S Oak Park Blvd
Oak Park, IL 60302
(708) 383-3225

Peoria Vet Center
3310 North Prospect Street
Peoria, IL 61603
(309) 688-2170

Rockford Vet Center Outstation
4960 E. State St. #3
Rockford, IL 61108
(815)-395-1276

Springfield Vet Center
624 South 4th Street
Springfield, IL 62703
(217) 492-4955

INDIANA

Evansville Vet Center
311 North Weinbach Avenue
Evansville, IN 47711
(812) 473-5993

Fort Wayne Vet Center
528 West Berry Street
Fort Wayne, IN 46802
(260) 460-1456

Gary Vet Center
6505 Broadway Ave.
Merrillville, IN 46410
(219) 736-5633

Indianapolis Vet Center
3833 Meridian, Suite 120
Indianapolis, IN 46208
(317) 927-6440

IOWA

Cedar Rapids Vet Center
1642 42nd Street, N.E.
Cedar Rapids, IA 52402
(319) 378-0016

Des Moines Vet Center
2600 Martin Luther King Jr. Parkway
Des Moines, IA 50310
(515) 284-4929

Sioux City Vet Center
1551 Indian Hills Drive
Sioux City, IA 51104
(712) 255-3808

KANSAS

Manhattan Vet Center
205 South 4th Street, Suite B
Manhattan, KS 66502
(785) 587-8257

Wichita Vet Center
413 South Pattie
Wichita, KS 67211
(316) 265-3260

KENTUCKY

Lexington Vet Center
301 East Vine Street, Suite C
Lexington, KY 40507
(859) 253-0717

Louisville Vet Center
1347 South 3rd Street
Louisville, KY 40208
(502) 634-1916

LOUISIANA

Baton Rouge Vet Center
5207 Essen Lane, Suite 2
Baton Rouge, LA 70809
(225) 757-0042

New Orleans Vet Center
2200 Veterans Blvd, Suite 114
Kenner, LA 70062
(504) 464-4743

Shreveport Vet Center
2800 Youree Drive
Building 1, Suite 105
Shreveport, LA 71104
(318) 861-1776

MAINE
Bangor Vet Center
352 Harlow Street
Bangor, ME 04401
(207) 947-3391

Caribou Vet Center
York Street Complex
Caribou, ME 04736
(207) 496-3900

Lewiston Vet Center Parkway Complex
29 Westminster Street
Lewiston, ME 04240
(207) 783-0068

Portland Vet Center
475 Stevens Avenue
Portland, ME 04103
(207) 780-3584

Sanford Vet Center
628 Main Street
Springvale, ME 04083
(207) 490-1513

MARYLAND

Baltimore Vet Center
1777 Reisterstown Road
Suite 199
Baltimore, MD 21208
(410) 764-9400

Cambridge Vet Center
5510 West Shore Drive
Cambridge, MD 21613
(410) 228-6305

Elkton Vet Center
103 Chesapeake Blvd,
Suite A
Elkton, MD 21921
(410) 394-4485

Harford County Vet Center Outstation
223 W. Bel Avenue
Aberdeen, MD 21001
(410)-272-6771

Silver Spring Vet Center
1015 Spring St, Suite 101
Silver Spring, MD 20910
(301) 589-1073

Towson Vet Center
305 W. Chesapeake Ave Suite 300
Towson, MD 21204
(410) 828-6619

MASSACHUSETTS

Boston Vet Center
665 Beacon Street
Boston, MA 02215
(617) 424-0665

Brockton Vet Center
1041-L Pearl Street
Brockton, MA 02401
(508) 580-2730

Hyannis Vet Center
474 West Main Street
Hyannis, MA 02601
(508) 778-0124

Lowell Vet Center
73 East Merrimack Street
Lowell, MA 01852
(978) 453-1151

New Bedford Vet Center
73 Huttleston Ave., Unit 2
Fairhaven, MA 02719
(508) 999-6920

Springfield Vet Center
1985 Main Street Northgate Plaza
Springfield, MA 01103
(413) 737-5167

Worcester Vet Center
597 Lincoln Street
Worcester, MA 01605
(508) 856-7428

MICHIGAN
Dearborn Vet Center
2881 Monroe Street
Suite 100
Dearborn, MI 48124
(313) 277-1428

Detroit Vet Center
4161 Cass Avenue
Detroit, MI 48201
(313) 831-6509

Escanaba Vet Center
3500 Ludington Street
Suite # 110
Escanaba, MI 49829
(906) 233-0244

Grand Rapids Vet Center
1940 Eastern SE
Grand Rapids, MI 48507
(616) 243-0385

Michigan Upper Peninsula Vet Center
2600 College Ave.
Escanaba, MI 49829
(906) 789-9732

MINNESOTA

Duluth Vet Center
405 East Superior Street Duluth, MN
55802
(218) 722-8654

St. Paul Vet Center
2480 University Avenue St.
Paul, MN 55114
(651) 644-4022

MISSISSIPPI

Biloxi Vet Center
288 Veterans Avenue
Biloxi, MS 39531
(228) 388-9938

Jackson Vet Center
1755 Lelia Dr.
Jackson, MS 39216
Suite 104
(601) 965-5727

MISSOURI

Kansas City Vet Center
3931 Main Street
Kansas City, MO 64111
(816) 753-1866

St. Louis Vet Center
2345 Pine Street
St. Louis, MO 63103
(314) 231-1260

MONTANA

Billings Vet Center
1234 Avenue C
Billings, MT 59102
(406) 657-6071

Missoula Vet Center
500 North Higgins Avenue
Missoula, MT 59802
(406) 721-4918

NEBRASKA

Lincoln Vet Center
920 L Street
Lincoln, NE 68508
(402) 476-9736

Omaha Vet Center
2428 Cuming Street
Omaha, NE 68131
(402) 346-6735

NEVADA

Las Vegas Vet Center
1040 East Sahara Avenue Suite 102
Las Vegas, NV 89104
(702) 388-6368

Reno Vet Center
1155 West 4th Street Suite 101
Reno, NV 89503
(775) 323-1294

NEW HAMPSHIRE

Berlin Vet Center
515 Main Street
Gorham, NH 03581
(603) 752-2571

Manchester Vet Center
103 Liberty Street
Manchester, NH 03104
(603) 668-7060

NEW JERSEY

Jersey City Vet Center
115 Christopher Columbus Drive
Room 200

Jersey City, NJ 07302
(201) 748-4467

Newark Vet Center
45 Academy Street
Suite 303
Newark, NJ 07102
(973) 645-5954

Trenton Vet Center
171 Jersey St., Building 36
Trenton, NJ 08611
(609) 989-2260

Ventnor Vet Center
6601 Ventnor Avenue,
Suite 105
Ventnor, NJ 08406
(609) 487-8387

NEW MEXICO

Albuquerque Vet Center
1600 Mountain Road, NW
Albuquerque, NM 87104
(505) 346-6562

Farmington Vet Center
4251 East Main, Suite B
Farmington, NM 87402
(505) 327-9684

Las Cruces Vet Center
230 S. Water Street
Las Cruces, NM 88001
(575) 523-9826

Santa Fe Vet Center
2209 Brothers Road, Suite 110
Santa Fe, NM 87505
(505) 988-6562

NEW YORK

Albany Vet Center
875 Central Avenue
Albany, NY 12206
(518) 438-2505

Babylon Vet Center
116 West Main Street
Babylon, NY 11702
(631) 661-3930

Binghamton Vet Center
53 Chenango Street
Binghamtom, NY 13901
(866) 716-8213

Bronx Vet Center
226 East Fordham Road
Room 220
Bronx, NY 10458
(718) 367-3500

Brooklyn Vet Center
25 Chapel Street, Suite 604
Brooklyn, NY 11201
(718) 330-2825

Buffalo Vet Center
564 Franklin Street
Buffalo, NY 14202
(716) 882-0505

Harlem Vet Center
55 West 125th Street
New York, NY 10027
(212) 426-2200

Manhattan Vet Center
32 Broadway, 2nd Floor Suite 200
New York, NY 10004
(212) 742-9591

Middletown Vet Center
726 East Main Street, Suite 203
Middletown, NY 10940
(845) 342-9917

Rochester Vet Center
1867 Mount Hope Avenue
Rochester, NY 14620
(585) 232-5040

Staten Island Vet Center
150 Richmond Terrace
Staten Island, NY 10301
(718) 816-4499

Syracuse Vet Center
716 East Washington Street
Syracuse, NY 13210
(315) 478-7127

Watertown Vet Center
210 Court Street
Watertown, NY 13601
(866) 610-0358

White Plains Vet Center
300 Hamilton Avenue
White Plains, NY 10601
(914) 682-6250

Woodhaven Vet Center
75-10B 91st Avenue

Woodhaven, NY 11421
(718) 296-2871

NORTH CAROLINA

Charlotte Vet Center
223 South Brevard Street Suite 103
Charlotte, NC 28202
(704) 333-6107

Fayetteville Vet Center
4140 Ramsey St., Suite 110
Fayetteville, NC 28311
(910) 488-6252

Greensboro Vet Center
2009 South Elm-Eugene Street
Greensboro, NC 27406
(336) 333-5366

Greenville Vet Center
150 Arlington Blvd., Suite B
Greenville, NC 27858
(252) 355-7920

Raleigh Vet Center
1649 Old Louisburg Road
Raleigh, NC 27604
(919) 856-4616

NORTH DAKOTA

Bismarck Vet Center
1684 Capital Way
Bismarck, ND 58501
(701) 244-9751

Fargo Vet Center
3310 Fiechtner Drive,
Suite 100
Fargo. ND 58103
(701) 237-0942

Minot Vet Center
2041 3rd Street, N.W.
Minot, ND 58701
(701) 852-0177

OHIO

Cincinnati Vet Center
801-B West 8th Street
Cincinnati, OH 45203
(513) 763 3500

Cleveland Heights Center
2022 Lee Road
Cleveland Heights, OH 44118
(216) 932-8471

Columbus Vet Center
30 Spruce Street
Columbus, OH 43215
(614) 257-5550

Dayton Vet Center
6th Floor, East Medical Plaza
627 Edwin
Dayton, OH 45408
(937) 461-9150

McCafferty Outstation Vet Center
4242 Lorain Avenue,
Suite 201
Cleveland, OH 44113
(216) 939-0784

Parma Vet Center
5700 Pearl Rd., Suite 102
Parma, OH 44129
(440) 845-5023

Toledo Vet Center
1565 S. Byrne Road, Suite 104
Toledo, OH 43614
(419) 213-7533

OKLAHOMA

Oklahoma City Vet Center
3033 North Walnut,
Suite 101W
Oklahoma City, OK 73105
(405) 270-5184

Tulsa Vet Center
1408 South Harvard
Tulsa, OK 74112
(918) 748-5105

OREGON

Eugene Vet Center
1255 Pearl Street
Eugene, OR 97403
(541) 465-6918

Grants Pass Vet Center
211 S.E. 10th Street
Grants Pass, OR 97526
(541) 479-6912

Portland Vet Center
8383 N.E. Sandy Blvd,

Suite 110
Portland, OR 97220
(503) 273-5370

Salem Vet Center
617 Chemeketa St., N.E.
Salem, OR 97301
(503) 362-9911

PENNSYLVANIA

DuBois Vet Center
100 Meadow Lane
Suite 8
DuBois, PA 15801
(814) 372-2095

Erie Vct Center
1001 State Street Suites 1 & 2
Erie, PA 16501
(814) 453-7955

Harrisburg Vet Center
1500 N 2nd Street, Suite 2
Harrisburg, PA 17102
(717) 782-3954

McKeesport Vet Center
2001 Lincoln Way
McKeesport, PA 15131
(412) 678-7704

Philadelphia Vet Center
801 Arch Street, Suite 102
Philadelphia, PA 19107
(215) 627-0238

Philadelphia Vet Center
101 East Olney Avenue
Philadelphia, PA 19120
(215) 924-4670

Pittsburgh Vet Center
2500 Baldwick Road
Pittsburgh, PA 15205
(412) 920-1765

Scranton Vet Center
1002 Pittston Avenue
Scranton, PA 18505
(570) 344-2676

Williamsport Vet Center
805 Penn Street
Williamsport, PA 17701
(570) 327-5281

PUERTO RICO

Arecibo Vet Center
52 Gonzalo Marin Street
Arecibo, Puerto Rico 00612-4702
(787) 879-4510

Ponce Vet Center
35 Mayor Street
Ponce, Puerto Rico 00730
(787) 841-3260

San Juan Vet Center
Condominio Medical Center Plaza
Suite LC8A and LC9
Rio Piedras, Puerto Rico 00921
(787) 749-4409

RHODE ISLAND

Warwick Vet Center
2038 Warwick Avenue
Warwick, RI 02889
(401) 739-0167

SOUTH CAROLINA

Columbia Vet Center
1513 Pickens Street
Columbia, SC 29201
(803) 765-9944

Greenville Vet Center
14 Lavinia Avenue
Greenville, SC 29601
(864) 271-2711

North Charleston Vet Center
5603A Rivers Avenue
North Charleston, SC 29406
(843) 747-8387

SOUTH DAKOTA

Pine Ridge Vet Center Outstation
P.O. Box 910,
105 E. Hwy 18
Martin, SD 57747
(605) 685-1300

Rapid City Vet Center
621 Sixth Street,
Suite 101
Rapid City, SD 57701
(605) 348-0077

Sioux Falls Vet Center
601 S. Cliff Ave., Suite C Sioux Falls, SD
57104

(605) 330-4552

TENNESSEE

Chattanooga Vet Center
951 Eastgate Loop Road Building 5700,
Suite 300
Chattanooga, TN 37411
(423) 855-6570

Johnson City Vet Center
1615A West Market Street
Johnson City, TN 37604
(423) 928-8387

Knoxville Vet Center
2817 East Magnolia Avenue
Knoxville, TN 37914
(865) 545-4680

Memphis Vet Center
1835Union, Suite 100
Memphis, TN 38104
(901) 544-0173

Nashville Vet Center
1420 Donelson Pike Suite A-5
Nashville, TN 37217
(615) 366-1220

TEXAS

Amarillo Vet Center
3414 Olsen Blvd., Suite E
Amarillo, TX 79109
(806) 354-9779

Austin Vet Center
1110 W William Cannon Dr
Suite 301
Austin, TX 78745
(512) 416-1314

Corpus Christi Vet Center
4646 Corona, Suite 250
Corpus Christi, TX 78411
(361) 854-9961

Dallas Vet Center
5232 Forest Lane, Suite 111
Dallas, TX 75244
(214) 361-5896

El Paso Vet Center
1155 Westmoreland Suite 121
El Paso, TX 79925
(915) 772-0013

Fort Worth Vet Center

1305 West Magnolia, Suite B
Forth Worth, TX 76104
(817) 921-9095

Houston Vet Center
503 Westheimer
Houston, TX 77006
(713) 523-0884

Houston Vet Center
701 N. Post Oak Rd., Suite 102
Houston, TX 77024
(713) 682-2288

Killeen Heights Vet Center
302 Millers Crossing, Suite #4
Harker Heights, TX 76548
(254) 953-7100

Laredo Vet Center
6020 McPherson Road, #1A
Laredo, TX 78041
(956) 723-4680

Lubbock Vet Center
3208 34th Street
Lubbock, TX 79410
(806) 792-9782

McAllen Vet Center
801 Nolana Loop, Suite 115
McAllen, TX 78504
(956) 631-2147

Midland Vet Center
3404 W. Illinois, Suite 1
Midland, TX 79703
(432) 697-8222

San Antonio Vet Center
231 West Cypress Street
San Antonio, TX 78212
(210) 472-4025

UTAH

Provo Vet Center
750 North 200 West
Suite 105
Provo, UT 84601
(801) 377-1117

Salt Lake City Vet Center
1354 East 3300
South Salt Lake City, UT 84106 (801)
584-1294

VERMONT

South Burlington Vet Center
359 Dorset Street
South Burlington, VT 05403
(802) 862-1806

White River Junction Vet Center
222 Holiday Drive
Gilman Office Center
Building #2
White River Junction, VT 05001
(802) 295-2908

VIRGINIA

Alexandria Vet Center
8796 Sacramento Drive
Suites D& E
Alexandria, VA 22309
(703) 360-8633

Norfolk Vet Center
2200 Colonial Avenue, Suite 3
Norfolk, VA 23517
(757) 623-7584

Richmond Vet Center
4202 Fitzhugh Avenue
Richmond, VA 23230
(804) 353-8958

Roanoke Vet Center
350 Albemarle Avenue, S.W.
Roanoke, VA 24016
(540) 342-9726

VIRGIN ISLANDS

St. Croix Vet Center
The Village Mall
Rural Route 2 Box 10553,
Kingshill St. Croix,
Virgin Islands 00850

St. Thomas Vet Center
9800 Buccaneer Mall, Suite 8
St. Thomas, Virgin Islands 00802
(340) 774-6674

WASHINGTON

Bellingham Vet Center
3800 Byron Avenue, Suite 124
Bellingham, WA 98229
(360) 733-9226

Everett Vet Center
3311 Wetmore Avenue
Everett, WA 98201
(425)252-9701

Seattle Vet Center
2030 9thAvenue, Suite 210
Seattle, WA 98121
(206) 553-2706

Spokane Vet Center
100 North Mullan Road, Suite 102
Spokane, WA 99206
(509) 444-8387

Tacoma Vet Center
4916 Center Street, Suite
E Tacoma, WA 98409
(253) 565-7038

Yakima Valley Vet Center
1111 North 1st Street Suite 1
Yakima, WA 98901
(509) 457-2736

WEST VIRGINIA

Beckley Vet Center
101 Ellison Avenue
Beckley, WV 25801
(304) 252-8220

Logan Vet Center Outstation
21 Main Street
West Henlawson, WV 25624
(304) 752-4453

Charleston Vet Center
521 Central Avenue
Charleston, WV 25302
(304) 343-3825

Martinsburg Vet Center
900 Winchester Avenue
Martinsburg, WV 25401
(304) 263-6776

Morgantown Vet Center
1083 Greenbag Road
Morgantown, WV 26508
(304) 291-4303

Parkersburg Vet Center Outstation
2011 Ohio Avenue, Suite D
Pakersburg, WV 26101
(304) 485-1599

Princeton Vet Center
905 Mercer Street

Princeton, WV 24740
(304) 425-5653

Wheeling Vet Center
1206 Chapline Street
Wheeling, WV 26003
(304) 232-0587

WISCONSIN

Madison Vet Center
147 South Butler Street
Madison, WI 53703
(608) 264-5342

Milwaukee Vet Center
5401 North 76th Street
Milwaukee, WI 53218
(414) 536-1301

WYOMING

Casper Vet Center
111 South Jefferson
Casper, WY 82601
(307) 261-5355

Cheyenne Vet Center
2424 Pioneer Avenue, Suite 103
Cheyenne, WY 82001
(307) 778-7370

CHAPTER 19

EDUCATION BENEFITS
OVERVIEW

The Veterans' Administration administers ten educational assistance programs, each with different eligibility criteria. Typically, a veteran's eligibility is based on his or her dates of active duty. Generally, only the VA can determine an applicant's eligibility. Specific information regarding educational benefits can be obtained from the Education Service of the VA (888) GI-BILL-1 or any VA regional office.

An individual can be eligible for more than one of the available education benefits. If so, he or she must elect which benefit to receive. Payments for more than one benefit at a time may not be made.

The VA strongly encourages individuals who qualify for more than one type of education benefit to discuss their education plans with a Veterans Benefits Counselor so that all options can be explored, and maximum benefits can be paid.

> **Key Takeaways**
>
> There are a number of different educational assistance programs including VEAP, the Educational an Assistance Test Program and the Survivors and Dependents Educational Assistance Program
>
> Eligibility varies
>
> If a veteran is eligible for multiple programs they should talk to a benefits counselor to determine which is right for them

2017 EDUCATION UPDATES—*HARRY W. COLMERY ACT*

Section 1. Short Title This section cites the short title of this bill as the *"Harry W. Colmery Veterans Educational Assistance Act of 2017."*

Section 101. Consideration of Certain Time Spent Receiving Medical Care from Secretary of Defense as Active Duty for Purposes of Eligibility for Post-9/11 Educational Assistance. This section would add time spent on active duty under orders authorized by section 12301(h) of title 10, U.S.C., as qualifying time for the Post-9/11 GI Bill. These particular orders are used when a National Guardsman or Reservist is receiving medical care or is recovering from active duty injuries.

Section 102. Consolidation of Eligibility Tiers under Post-9/11 Educational Assistance Program of the Department of Veterans Affairs. This section would authorize additional GI Bill funding for members of the National Guard and Reserve. This section would increase the amount of money/eligibility that individuals receive who serve at least 90 days but less than 6 months on active duty – it would increase from 40% to 50% benefit payable. It would also increase the amount of money/eligibility that individuals receive who serve at least 6 months but less than 12 months – it would increase from 50% to 60% benefit payable. For a student attending a private school, this would result in approximately $2300 more a year in tuition than they are receiving now and would receive more money for their housing allowance.

Section 103. Educational Assistance Under Post-9/11 Educational Assistance Program for Members of the Armed Forces Awarded the Purple Heart. This section would extend full eligibility for the Post-9/11 GI Bill to any Purple Heart recipients since September 11, 2001.

Section 104. Eligibility for Post-9/11 Educational Assistance for Certain Members of Reserve Components of Armed Forces who Lost Entitlement to Educational Assistance under Reserve Educational Assistance Program. This section would allow certain members of the Reserve component to transfer into the Post-9/11 GI Bill who lost educational assistance benefits when Congress repealed the Reserve Educational Assistant Program (REAP).

Section 105. Calculation of Monthly House Stipend under Post-9/11 Educational Assistance Program Based on Location of Campus where Classes are Attended. This section would change the way living stipend amounts are calculated, from the current rule that says the living stipend payment is based on where the school is located to instead having the payment calculated based on where the student attends the majority of their classes.

Section 106. Charge to Entitlement for Certain Licensure and Certification Tests and National Tests under Department of Veterans' Affairs Post-9/11 Educational Assistance. This section would change the current rules that require that a veteran be charged a whole month of entitlement to pay for any national test (GMET, GRE, SAT etc.) or test that is required for state licensing. Instead of a full month of entitlement this bill would require that the test be pro-rated to the amount of the actual cost of the test.

Section 107. Restoration of Entitlement to Post-9/11 Educational Assistance for Veterans Affected by Closures of Educational Institution. This section would restore entitlement to individuals when their school closes in the middle of a semester. This section would also authorize additional living stipend payments to be paid to students whose school closes in the middle of the semester for no more than 4 months, or the length of the semester, where they were attending training.

Section 108. Inclusion of Fry Scholarship Recipients in Yellow Ribbon GI Education Enhancement Program. This section would extend the Yellow Ribbon Program to students receiving GI Bill payments through the Fry Scholarship program and those who received a Purple Heart after September 11, 2001. Fry recipients are surviving dependents of servicemembers who died while serving on active duty.

Section 109. Additional Authorized Transfer of Unused Post-9/11 Educational Assistance Benefits to Dependents upon Death of Originally Designated Dependent. This section would allow a veteran to transfer remaining months of GI Bill entitlement to another dependent if the dependent who originally received the transferred benefits dies before they can use all of the benefits. The section would also allow a dependent to transfer remaining months of GI Bill entitlement to another dependent after the death of the servicemember or veteran.

Section 110. Edith Nourse Rogers STEM Scholarship. This section would authorize VA to provide additional GI Bill funds to help a student veteran complete a STEM degree. They would be eligible to apply for the program, which would pay for the lesser of nine additional months of Post-9/11 GI Bill or a lump sum of $30,000. The amount of money that could be spent on this program would not exceed $100,000,000 in any one fiscal year. These additional benefits would be known as the 'Edith Nourse Rogers STEM Scholarship'.

Section 111. Honoring National Service of the Members Elimination of Time Limitation for use of Entitlement. This section would eliminate the current time limitation to use the GI Bill for new members of the Armed Forces. Student veterans currently have 15 years from the date of their last active duty discharge to use the benefit.

Section 112. Monthly Stipend for Certain Members of the Reserve Components of the Armed Forces Receiving Post-9/11 Educational Assistance. This section would require VA to pro-rate the GI Bill housing stipend provided to Reservists who get called up for active duty during the middle of a month. Current law prohibits them from pro-rating the stipend so if the reservist is on active duty orders for even one day of a month then they would lose the entire months' worth of VA housing allowance.

Section 113. Improvement of Information Technology of the Veterans Benefits Administration of the Department of Veterans Affairs. This section would authorize $30 million to improve GI Bill claims processing and complete their rules-based processing system for these claims.

Section 114. Department of Veterans Affairs High Technology Pilot Program. This section would authorize VA to conduct a 5-year pilot program that would provide veterans the opportunity to enroll in high technology courses (coding boot camp, IT certifications etc.). VA would enter into contracts with these schools or programs and would provide tuition and fees payments on a sliding scale that incentivizes the schools to graduate the student and ensure they find a job in their field of study. The section would also authorize a living stipend payment equal to the Post-9/11 rate to students while they are using the benefit.

Section 201. Work Study Allowance This section would repeal the sunset date in the law that allows VA work study benefits for outreach to student veterans and to assist State approving agencies.

Section 202. Duration of Educational Assistance under Survivors' and Dependent' Educational Assistance Program. This section would change the number of months of entitlement for individuals who become eligible for the Survivors' and Dependents' Educational Assistance Program from 45 months to 36 months. This would re-align this program with other GI Bill programs that provide 36 months of eligibility for educational assistance. This change would only apply to individuals that become entitled to this program on or after August 1, 2018.

Section 203. Olin E. Teague Increase in the Amounts of Educational Assistance Payable Under Survivors' and Dependent' Educational Assistance Program. This section would increase the monthly payment for educational assistance provided under Survivors' and Dependent' Educational Assistance Program by $200 a month.

Section 301. State Approving Agency Funding. This section would increase the funding out VA's mandatory account for the State Approving Agencies (SAA) from $19 million a year to $21 million a year. This section would also authorize VA to provide an additional $3 million a year to the SAAs out of the Department's discretionary account. This section would also, beginning in fiscal year 2019, require VA to provide a cost of living adjustment increase to the SAAs budget in an amount that equals the same percentage increase as benefits provided under the Social Security Act.

Section 302. Authorization for Use of Post-9/11 Educational Assistance to Pursue Independent Study Programs at Certain Educational Institutions that are Not Institutions of Higher Learning. This section would allow an eligible individual to use their GI Bill benefit for an accredited independent study program (including open circuit television) at an educational institution that is an area career and technical education school or a postsecondary vocational school providing postsecondary level education.

Section 303. Provision of Information on Priority Enrollment for Veterans in Certain Courses of Education. This section would require VA to include on its GI Bill Comparison Tool, information on whether a school has a priority enrollment system in place that allows veterans to enroll in courses earlier than other students attending the school.

Section. 304. Limitation on Use of Reporting Fees Payable to Educational Institutions and Sponsors of Programs of Apprenticeship. This section would allow VA to provide a fee to schools or a sponsor of a program of apprenticeship for the reports or certifications that these institutions are required to submit to VA about the individuals at their school receiving GI Bill benefits. This section would require VA to provide $16 to the institution for each individual that they certify as using GI Bill benefits at their institution. This section would also require that schools with 100 or more enrollees using GI Bill benefits, may not use the funds received by the institution from the reporting fees for the institution's general fund and that these funds may only be used for veterans programs at that institution.

Section. 305. Training for School Certifying Officials. This section would require VA, in consultation with the SAA's, to provide requirements for training for school certifying officials at educational institutions that are approved for GI Bill benefits. This section would also allow VA to disapprove a course of education if a school does not ensure that the school certifying official meets the training requirements.

Section 306. Extension of Authority for Advisory Committee on Education. This section would extend the authority for VA's Advisory Committee on Education from December of 2017 through to December of 2022.

Section 307. Department of Veterans Affairs Provision of On-Campus Educational and Vocational Counseling for Veterans. This section would codify VA's Veterans Success on Campus (VSOC) program, which is administered and overseen by the Vocational Rehabilitation and Employment Service (VS&E). There are currently 94 schools with a VSOC program, which provides a VR&E counselor at each school to assist veterans with their transition from military to college life as well as who provide the support and assistance needed to pursue their educational and employment goals.

Section 308. Provision of Information Regarding Veteran Entitlement to Educational Assistance. This section would require VA to make available to educational institutions, the ability to view the remaining benefit amount for each veteran attending that institution. This section would also allow the veteran or their dependent (if they are a beneficiary of their GI Bill benefits) to opt out of the school's ability to receive such information from VA.

Section 309. Treatment, for Purposes of Educational Assistance Administered by the Secretary of Veterans Affairs, of Educational Courses that Begin Seven or Fewer Days after the First Day of an Academic Year. This section would provide more flexibility to the school certifying officials if the first day of a course does not start on the first day of an academic term, by allowing the school certifying official to certify the course as beginning on that day first day of the academic term for purposes of certifying a veteran for GI Bill benefits.

Section 401. Eligibility of Reserve Component Members for Post 9/11 Educational Assistance. This section would make individuals eligible for Post-9/11 GI Bill benefits who have served and who will serve on 12304, 12304(a) and 12304(b) orders. Any active duty service under these Reserve component orders since the enactment of the Post-9/11 Veterans Educational Assistance Act of 2008 would apply for such benefits going forward.

Section 402. Time Limitation for Training and Rehabilitation for Veterans with Service-Connected Disabilities. This section would also make the 12304, 12304(a) and 12304(b) orders eligible for benefits under the Vocational Rehabilitation and Employment program in chapter 31 of title 38, U.S.C.

Section 501. Repeal Inapplicability of Modification of Basic Allowance for Housing to Benefits under Laws Administered by Secretary of Veterans Affairs. This section would be the offset for the package by realigning the living stipend payments for those using the Post 9/11 GI Bill (E-5 with dependents rate) to the same Basic Allowance for Housing (BAH) payments currently paid to active duty servicemembers at the E-5 with dependents rate. Several years ago, the annual percentage increase to active duty BAH payments were reduced by 1% a year for five years but GI bill payments were exempt. This bill would re-align these payments so that a GI Bill recipient would receive the same living stipend per month as an E-5 active duty servicemember with dependents. This section also stipulates that these decreases to the annual percentage increase would only be in effect for individuals who first begin using their education benefits on or after January 1, 2018

VETERANS EDUCATIONAL ASSISTANCE PROGRAM (VEAP)

The Post-Vietnam Veterans' Educational Assistance Program is also known as VEAP.

VEAP provides education and training opportunities to eligible persons who contributed to the program while on active duty. If an individual did not contribute, or received a refund of contributions, he or she is not eligible for VEAP benefits. The initial contribution must have been made by March 31, 1987. The maximum contribution by any individual participant is $2,700. A participating member's contributions are matched on a $2 for $1 basis by the Government.

Since August 1, 2011, break (or interval pay) became no longer be payable under VEAP except during periods your school is closed as a result of an Executive Order of the President or an emergency (such as a natural disaster or strike). For example, if your Fall term ends on December 15th and your Spring term begins January 10th, your January housing allowance will cover 15 days in December and your February housing allowance will cover 21 days in January.

VEAP ELIGIBILITY

To qualify for VEAP benefits, individuals must have:

- Entered active duty for the first time between January 1, 1977 and June 30, 1985; and
- Enrolled in and contributed to VEAP before April 1, 1987; and
- Served for a continuous period of 181 days or more (Individuals may be eligible if discharged from a shorter period of active duty for a service- connected disability.); and
- Been discharged or released from service under conditions other than dishonorable; and
- Completed 24 continuous months of active duty if enlisted for the first time after September 7, 1980, or entered active duty as an officer or enlistee after October 16, 1981. (Individuals meet this requirement if they completed a shorter period of active duty to which the service department called or ordered the individual.)

Individuals may be eligible for VEAP benefits if they did not complete 24 continuous months of active duty if they:

- Received VA disability compensation or military disability retirement; or
- Served a period of at least 24 continuous months of active duty before October 17,

1981; or
- Were discharged or released for early out, hardship, or service-connected disability.

Individuals may be eligible for VEAP benefits while still on active duty if they:

- Entered active duty for the first time after December 31, 1976, and before July 1, 1985; and
- Enrolled in and contributed to VEAP before April 1, 1987, and have at least three months of contributions available (For an elementary or high school program, at least one month of contributions must be available.); and
- Served for a continuous period of 181 days or more; and
- Completed their first active duty commitment.

The following types of active duty do not establish eligibility:

- Time assigned by the military to a civilian institution for the same course provided to civilians;
- Time served as a cadet or midshipman at a service academy;
- Time spent on active duty for training in the National Guard or Reserve

NOTE: Individuals are not eligible for VEAP if they are eligible for the Montgomery GI Bill-Active Duty based on prior eligibility for Vietnam Era Veterans' Educational Assistance.

APPROVED COURSES

VEAP benefits may be received for a wide variety of training, including:

- Training for a high school diploma or the equivalent
- Undergraduate or graduate degrees from a college or university
- Cooperative training programs
- Accredited independent study programs leading to standard college degrees
- Courses leading to certificates or diplomas from business, technical or vocational schools
- Vocational flight training (Individuals must have a private pilot's license and meet the medical requirements for a desired license before beginning training, and throughout the flight training program)
- Apprenticeship or job training programs offered by a company or union
- Correspondence courses
- VA may approve programs offered by institutions outside of the United States, when they are pursued at educational institutions of higher learning, and lead to a college degree. Individuals must receive VA approval prior to attending or enrolling in any foreign programs.

Since March 1, 2001, benefits weren't payable for licensing or certification tests. The tests are those needed to enter, maintain, or advance into employment in a civilian vocation or profession. The eligible veteran or family member may receive payment of the fee charged for the test or $2,000, whichever is less. The tests must be approved for VA benefits.

If an individual is seeking a college degree, the school must admit him or her to a degree program by the start of the third term.

RESTRICTIONS ON TRAINING

- Bartending and personality development courses
- Non-accredited independent study courses

213

- Any course given by radio
- Self-improvement courses such as reading, speaking, woodworking, basic seamanship, and English as a second language
- Any course which is avocational or recreational in character
- Farm cooperative courses
- Audited courses
- Courses not leading to an educational, professional, or vocational objective
- Courses an individual has previously taken and successfully completed
- Courses taken by a Federal government employee under the Government Employees' Training Act
- Courses paid for in whole or in part by the Armed Forces while on active duty
- Courses taken while in receipt of benefits for the same program from the Office of Workers' Compensation Programs
- The VA must reduce benefits for individuals in Federal, State or local prisons After being convicted of a felony.
- An individual may not receive benefits for a program at a proprietary school if he or she is an owner or official of the school.

PART-TIME TRAINING

Individuals unable to attend school full-time should consider going part-time. Benefit rates and entitlement charges are less than the full-time rates. For example, if a student receives full-time benefits for 12 months, the entitlement charge is 12 months. However, if the student receives ½ time benefits for 12 months, the charge is 6 months. VA will pay for less than ½ time training if the student is not receiving Tuition Assistance for those courses.

REMEDIAL, DEFICIENCY AND REFRESHER TRAINING

Remedial and deficiency courses are intended to assist a student in overcoming a deficiency in a particular area of study. In order for such courses to be approved, the courses must be deemed necessary for pursuit of a program of education.

Refresher training is for technological advances that occurred in a field of employment. The advance must have occurred while the student was on active duty, or after release. There is an entitlement charge for these courses.

TUTORIAL ASSISTANCE

Students may receive a special allowance for individual tutoring if they entered school at one-half time or more. To qualify, the student must have a deficiency in a subject. The school must certify the tutor's qualifications, and the hours of tutoring. Eligible students may receive a maximum monthly payment of $100.00. The maximum total benefit payable is $1,200.00. There is no entitlement charge for the first $600.00 of tutorial assistance.

To apply for tutorial assistance, students must submit "VA Form 22-1990t", Application and Enrollment Certification for Individualized Tutorial Assistance. The form should be given to the certifying official in the office handling VA paperwork at the school for completion.

MONTHS OF BENEFITS / ENTITLEMENT CHARGED

Eligible members may be entitled to receive up to 36 months of VEAP benefits. Usually, the number of monthly payments for full- time training is the same as the number of months an individual contributed to VEAP.

Benefits are generally payable for 10 years following a veteran's release from active duty.

Individuals qualifying for more than one VA education program may receive a maximum of 48 months of benefits. For example, if a student used 30 months of Dependents' Educational Assistance, and is eligible for chapter 1606 benefits, he or she could have a maximum of 18 months of entitlement remaining.

Individuals are charged one full day of entitlement for each day of full-time benefits paid.

For correspondence and flight training, one month of entitlement is charged each time VA pays one month of benefits. For cooperative programs, one month of entitlement is used for each month of benefits paid.

For apprenticeship and job training programs, the entitlement charge changes every 6 months. During the first 6 months, the charge is 75% of full time. For the second 6 months, the charge is 55% of full time. For the remainder of the program, the charge is 35% of full time.

RATES OF EDUCATIONAL ASSISTANCE PAY

The total dollar amount of VEAP benefits is:

An individual's total contributions, plus
Matching funds equal to 2 times the individual's contributions, plus
Any additional contributions or kickers made by the Department of Defense

The amount of money an individual receives each month depends on the type of training and the training time.

INSTITUTIONAL TRAINING:

The monthly benefit payment will vary depending on the amount and number of contributions. Divide the total contributions by the number of months contributed, and this equals the full-time institutional rate.

Example: Step 1:
$1,800 individual contributions
+3,600 matching funds (2 times individual contribution)
+ -0- kicker
_____
$5,400 TOTAL ENTITLEMENT

Step 2:
$5,400 divided by 36 months of contributions = $150 monthly full-time institutional rate

(No amount in excess of an individual's total entitlement can be paid.)

CORRESPONDENCE TRAINING

An individual can be reimbursed for the entire established charges paid for a correspondence course. However, no amount in excess of an individual's total entitlement can be paid.

FLIGHT TRAINING

Individuals taking flight training will receive 60% of the approved charges for the course, including solo hours. (VA does not pay for solo hours before October 1, 1992.) No amount in excess of an individual's total entitlement can be paid.

APPRENTICESHIP OR JOB TRAINING

The monthly benefit amount is:

- 75% of the full-time rate for the first 6 months of training;
- 55% of the full-time rate for the second 6 months of training;
- 35% of the full-time rate for the rest of the training.

Monthly payments are reduced if an individual works less than 120 hours a month.

COOPERATIVE TRAINING

Individuals may receive payment at 80% of the rate to which he or she is entitled for institutional training.

ELIGIBILITY PERIODS

Benefits end 10 years from the date of the individual's last discharge or release from active duty.

VA can extend the 10-year period by the amount of time a service member was prevented from training during the period due to a disability or being held by a foreign government or power.

VA may extend the 10-year period if the individual reenters active duty for 90 days or more after becoming eligible. The extension ends 10 years from the date of discharge or release from the later period. Periods of active duty of less than 90 days can qualify for extensions only if discharge or release was due to:

A service-connected disability; or
A medical condition existing before active duty; or Hardship; or
A reduction in force.

If a discharge is upgraded by the military, the 10-year period begins on the date of the upgrade.

MISCELLANEOUS INFORMATION

Any change in educational, professional or vocational objectives is considered a "change of program." The law permits one change of program without prior VA approval, provided an individual's attendance, conduct and progress in the last program were satisfactory. Additional "changes of program" require prior VA approval. VA will not charge a change of program if the individual enrolls in a new program after successful completion of the immediately preceding program.

Once an individual starts receiving benefits, he must maintain satisfactory attendance, conduct and progress. The VA may stop benefits if an individual does not meet the standards set by the school. VA may later resume benefits if the individual reenters the same program at the same school, and the school approves the reentry, and certifies it to VA.

If the individual does not reenter the same program at the same school, VA may resume benefits if the cause of unsatisfactory attendance, conduct or progress has been removed;

and the program that the student intends to pursue is suitable to his or her abilities, aptitudes and interests.

APPLICATION FOR BENEFITS

When the individual finds a school, program, company, apprenticeship or job-training program, there are two important steps that must be followed:

- Make sure the program is approved for VA training. Contact the local VA regional office if there are any questions.
- Compete "VA Form 22-1990", "Application for Education Benefits." The completed form should be sent to the VA regional office with jurisdiction over the State where training will occur. (See the following section for Areas of VA jurisdiction.) Individuals not on active duty should send copy 4 of Form DD- 214 along with the completed "VA Form 22-1990."

Following receipt of an application, VA will review it and advise if anything else is needed.

If an individual has started training, the application and Notice of Basic Eligibility should be taken to the school, employer or union. The certifying official should complete "VA Form 22-1999," Enrollment Certification, and send all the forms to VA.

AREAS OF VA JURISDICTION
Eastern VA Regional Office
PO Box 4616
Buffalo, NY
14240-4616

Connecticut
Delaware
District of Columbia
Maine
Maryland
Massachusetts
New Hampshire
New Jersey
New York
Ohio
Pennsylvania
Rhode Island
Vermont
Virginia
West Virginia
Foreign Schools

Southern VA Regional Office
PO Box 100022
Decatur, GA 30031-7022

Alabama
Florida
Georgia
Mississippi
North Carolina
Puerto Rico
South Carolina
Virgin Islands

Western VA Regional Office
PO Box 8888
Muskogee, OK 74402-8888

Alaska
Arizona
Arkansas
California
Hawaii
Idaho
Louisiana
New Mexico
Nevada
Oklahoma
Oregon
Philippines
Texas
Utah
Washington
American Samoa
Guam

PROCEDURES FOR RECEIPT OF MONTHLY PAYMENTS

After selecting a school and submitting an application to VA, the school official must complete an enrollment certification, and submit it to the appropriate VA regional office. If a student meets the basic eligibility requirements for benefits, and the program or course is approved, VA will process the enrollment based on certified training time.

If a student is enrolled in a degree program at a college or university, he or she will receive payment after the first of each month for the training during the preceding month. If a student is enrolled in a certificate or diploma program at a business, technical, or vocational school, he or she will not receive payment until they have verified their attendance. Students will receive a "Student Verification of Enrollment Form 22-8979" each month, and must complete and return it to the appropriate VA regional office. After processing, VA will release a check.

If an individual is in an apprenticeship or job-training program, he or she will receive a form to report the hours worked each month. The form must be signed and given to the certifying official for the company or union. The certifying official must complete the form and send it to the appropriate VA regional office. After processing, VA will release a check.

If an individual is taking a correspondence course, he or she will receive a form each quarter, on which the student must show the number of lessons completed that quarter. The completed form should be sent to the school for certification of the number of lessons serviced during the quarter. The school will send the form to the appropriate VA regional office. After processing, VA will release a check. Payments are based on the number of lessons serviced by the school.

VA will send flight schools a supply of blank monthly certification of flight training forms. The school must complete the form by entering the number of hours, the hourly rate, and the total charges for flight training received during the month. The student should review and sign the completed form, and send it to the appropriate VA regional office. After processing, VA will release a check.

NOTE: It is against the law for schools to cash VA checks under a Power of Attorney Agreement.

TIMELY RECEIPT OF VERIFICATION FORMS AND CHECKS

Once a completed verification form has been submitted, the student should receive a check within 2 weeks. If a check is not received by then, the VA should immediately be contacted so that appropriate action can be taken.

Students taking courses leading to a degree at a college or university should receive their checks for each month by the fifth of the next month. If it is not received by then, the VA should be immediately contacted so that appropriate action can be taken.

Students taking courses leading to a certificate or diploma from a business, technical, or vocational school should receive their verification forms for each month by the fifth of the following month. If it is not received by then, the VA should be immediately contacted so that another form can be issued.

ADVANCE PAYMENTS

An advance payment for the initial month, or partial month and the following month may be made, if:

- The school agrees to handle advance payments; and
- Training is one-half time or more; and
- A request is made by the individual in writing; and
- The VA receives the enrollment certification at least 30 days prior to the start of classes.

Advance payments are made out to the individual, and sent to the applicable school for delivery to the individual registration. VA cannot issue a check more than 30 days before classes start. Before requesting an advance payment, students should verify with the school certifying official that the school has agreed to process advance payments.

Requests for advance payments must be on "VA Form 22-1999," Enrollment Certification, or a sheet of paper attached to the enrollment certification.

Once a student receives an advance payment at registration, the school must certify to VA that the student received the check. If a student reduces enrollment, or withdraws from all courses during the period covered by an advance payment, he or she must repay the overpayment to VA.

If an individual believes that the amount of a VA check is incorrect, the VA should be contacted before the check is cashed.

DIRECT DEPOSIT

Payments can be sent directly to a student's savings or checking account through Direct Deposit (Electronic Funds Transfer). To sign up for direct deposit by phone, students must call (877) 838-2778.

STUDENT RESPONSIBILITIES

To ensure timely receipt of correct payments, students should be sure to promptly notify the VA of:

Any change in enrollment
Any change in address

In addition, students should use reasonable judgment when accepting and cashing a check. All letters from VA about monthly rates and effective dates should be read carefully. If a student thinks the amount of a VA check is wrong, VA should be contacted *before* cashing the check. Any incorrect checks should be returned to VA.

If a student cashes a check for the wrong amount, he or she will be liable for repayment of any resulting overpayment.

RECOVERY OF OVERPAYMENTS

VA must take prompt and aggressive action to recover overpayments. Students have the right to request a waiver of the overpayment, or verification that the amount is correct. If an overpayment is not repaid or waived, VA may add interest and collection fees to the debt. VA may also take one or more of the following actions to collect the debt:
Withhold future benefits to apply to the debt;

Refer the debt to a private collection agency;
Recover the debt from any Federal income tax refund;
Recover the debt from the salary (if student is a Federal employee);
File a lawsuit in Federal court to collect the debt;
Withhold approval of a VA home loan guarantee.

An individual's reserve component will act to collect penalties caused by unsatisfactory participation in the reserve.

CHANGES IN ENROLLMENT

If a student withdraws from one or more courses after the end of the school's drop period, VA will reduce or stop benefits on the date of reduction or withdrawal. Unless the student can show that the change was due to *mitigating circumstances*, the student may have to repay **all** benefits for the course.

VA defines *mitigating circumstances* as "unavoidable and unexpected events that directly interfere with the pursuit of a course, and which are beyond the student's control.

Examples of reasons VA may accept include:

Extended illness;
Severe illness or death in immediate family;
Unscheduled changes in employment; and
Lack of child care.

Examples of reasons VA may not accept include:

Withdrawal to avoid a failing grade;
Dislike of the instructor; and
Too many courses attempted.

VA may ask the student to furnish evidence to support the reason for change, such as physician or employer written statements.

The first time a student withdraws from up to 6 credit hours, VA will "excuse" the withdrawal, and pay benefits for the period attended.

If a student receives a grade that does not count toward graduation, all benefits for the course may have to be repaid.

If a student receives a non-punitive grade, the school will notify VA, and VA may reduce or stop benefits. The student may not have to repay the benefits if he or she can show that the grades were due to mitigating circumstances.

WORK-STUDY PROGRAMS

Students may be eligible for an additional allowance under a work-study program that allows students to perform work for VA in return for an hourly wage. Students may perform outreach services under VA supervision, prepare and process VA paperwork, work at a VA medical facility or National Cemetery, or perform other approved activities.

Students must attend school at the three-quarter of full-time rate.

VA will select students for the work-study program based on different factors. Such factors include:

* Disability of the student;
* Ability of the student to complete the work-study contract before the end of his or her

221

eligibility for education benefits;
- Job availability within normal commuting distance to the student.

VA will give the highest priority to a veteran who has a service-connected disability or disabilities rated by VA at 30% or more.

The number of applicants selected will depend on the availability of VA-related work at the school or at VA facilities in the area.

Students may work during or between periods of enrollment, and can arrange with VA to work any number of hours during his or her enrollment. However, the maximum number of hours a student may work is 25 times the number of weeks in the enrollment period.

Students will earn an hourly wage equal to the Federal or State minimum wage, whichever is greater. If a student works at a college or university, the school *may* pay the difference between the amount VA pays and the amount the school normally pays other work-study students doing the same job.

Students interested in taking part in a work-study program must complete VA Form 228691, "Application for Work-Study Allowance." Completed forms should be sent to the nearest VA regional office.

EDUCATIONAL COUNSELING

VA can provide services to help eligible individuals understand their educational and vocational strengths and weaknesses and to plan:
- An educational or training goal, and the means by which the goal can be reached; or
- An employment goal for which an individual qualifies on the basis of present training or experience.

VA can also help plan an effective job search. Counseling is available for:
- Service members eligible for VA educational assistance; or
- Service members on active duty and within 180 days of discharge; or
- Veterans with discharges that are not dishonorable, who are within one year from date of discharge.

VOCATIONAL REHABILITATION

Vocational rehabilitation helps disabled veterans become independent in daily living. Veterans may also receive assistance in selecting, preparing for, and securing employment that is compatible with their interests, talents, skills, physical capabilities, and goals.

Veterans may qualify for Training and Rehabilitation if:

- The veteran has a service- connected disability or disabilities rated by VA at 20% or more; and
- The veteran received a discharge from active duty that was not dishonorable; and
- The veteran has an employment handicap.

Veterans may also qualify with a service-connected disability or disabilities rated by VA at 10%, and:

- The veteran has a serious employment handicap; or
- The veteran first applied for vocational rehabilitation benefits before November 1, 1990, reapplied after that date, and has an employment handicap.
- To apply for vocational rehabilitation, VA form 28-1900, Disabled Veterans

Application for Vocational Rehabilitation, must be completed and sent to the nearest VA regional office.

REFUND OF VEAP BENEFITS

If a service member does not wish to use his or her VEAP benefits, he or she must apply to the nearest VA regional office for a refund of his or her contributions.

APPEAL OF VA DECISION

VA decisions on education benefits may be appealed within one year of the date an individual receives notice of a VA decision.

EDUCATIONAL AND ASSISTANCE TEST PROGRAM (SECTION 901)

This program was included as part of the *Department of Defense Authorization Act of 1981*. The test program is funded by the Department of Defense, and administered by the VA. "Section 901" has been used to identify the program since its inception. However, the title "chapter 107" may also be used.

Section 901 is a noncontributory program in which an eligible participant, or in some cases his or her dependent(s), may receive an educational assistance and subsistence allowance while training at an accredited institution.

Basic eligibility to section 901 benefits was limited to a small group of servicepersons who enlisted between September 30, 1980 and October 1, 1981, met strict guidelines and were selected by the Department of Defense. The Waco Regional Office processes all section 901 payments.

Beginning August 1, 2011, break (or interval pay) was no longer be payable under the Educational Assistance Test Program except during periods your school is closed as a result of an Executive Order of the President or an emergency (such as a natural disaster or strike). For example, if your Fall term ends on December 15th and your Spring term begins January 10th, your January housing allowance will cover 15 days in December and your February housing allowance will cover 21 days in January.

EDUCATIONAL ASSISTANCE PILOT PROGRAM

Section 903 is a modified Chapter 32 (VEAP) program, in which the Service Department makes the individual's monthly contributions. Eligibility was limited to a small group of participants, selected by the service department, who enlisted between November 30, 1980 and October 1, 1981. Individuals must have been selected for the pilot program.

SURVIVORS' AND DEPENDENTS EDUCATIONAL ASSISTANCE PROGRAM (DEA)

The Survivors' and Dependents Educational Assistance Program (DEA) was enacted by Congress to provide education and training opportunities to eligible dependents of certain veterans.

The program offers up to 45 months of education benefits.

ELIGIBILITY REQUIREMENTS

To qualify, one must be the son, daughter or spouse of:

- A veteran who died, or is permanently and totally disabled as the result of a service-connected disability, which arose out of active service in the Armed Forces.
- A veteran who died from any cause while such service-connected disability was in existence.
- A service member who is missing in action or captured in the line of duty by a hostile force.
- A service member who is being forcibly detained or interned in the line of duty by a foreign power.
- A service member who is hospitalized or receiving outpatient treatment for a service connected permanent and total disability and is likely to be discharged for that disability. This change became effective December 23, 2006.

ELIGIBILITY PERIOD: SON OR DAUGHTER

As a son or daughter (including stepchild or adopted child), as long as the individual has entitlement left, he or she may generally receive benefits under this program from age 18 to 26 (8 years). However, in certain instances, benefits may begin before age 18 and continue after age 26. In some instances, the individual may choose among possible beginning dates.

EFFECT OF ACTIVE DUTY ON ELIGIBILITY

Following are the effects of active duty on an individual's period of eligibility. (See also Effect of Active Duty on Entitlement.)

Individuals may not receive DEA benefits while on active duty in the Armed Forces. To receive DEA benefits after military service, discharge must not be under dishonorable conditions.

The eligibility period can generally extend for eight years from the date of the individual's first unconditional release from active duty, if his or her service was between ages 18 and 26. But this extension can't go beyond the individual's 31st birthday.

If, on or after September 11, 2001, an individual is called to active duty under title 10, or if he or she was involuntarily ordered to full-time National Guard duty under section 502 (f) of title 32 (State authority), in most cases VA can extend the eligibility period for DEA by the number of months and days spent on active duty plus four months. This extension may go beyond the 31st birthday, depending on the facts in the claim.

OTHER EXTENSIONS OF THE ELIGIBILITY PERIOD

Circumstances Beyond an Individual's Control

If evidence is provided that training had to stop because of conditions beyond an individual's control, in some cases VA can extend eligibility for the period he or she had to stop training.

Circumstances that may be considered beyond control (if verified by evidence) include:
- Service in an official missionary capacity;
- Immediate family or financial obligations that require the individual to stop training, for example, to take employment;
- Unavoidable conditions of employment that require the individual to stop training;
- The individual's illness or death; or illness in his or her immediate family.

IN TRAINING WHEN ELIGIBILITY ENDS

If an individual is enrolled in training when eligibility ends, in most cases VA can extend his or her eligibility to the end of the semester or quarter, or to the end of twelve weeks if the course isn't operated on a semester or quarter basis.

MARRIAGE

As a son or daughter, marriage doesn't affect the period of eligibility.

ELIGIBILITY PERIOD: SPOUSE

If a spouse is eligible because the veteran has a permanent and total service-connected disability, benefits generally end 10 years from one of the following dates:

- Effective date of the veteran's permanent and total disability evaluation;
- Date VA notifies the veteran of the permanent and total disability evaluation;
- Beginning date chosen by the spouse, between the date the spouse become eligible and the date VA notifies the veteran of the permanent and total disability evaluation.
- If the VA rated the veteran permanently and totally disabled with an effective date of 3 years from discharge a spouse will remain eligible for 20 years from the effective date of the rating. This change is effective October 10, 2008 and no benefits may be paid for any training taken prior to that date.

SERVICE MEMBER HELD CAPTIVE OR MISSING

If a spouse is eligible because the veteran or service member is being held or is missing, as:

- A prisoner of war;
- Missing in action; or
- Forcibly held by a foreign government or power;

His or her 10-year period of eligibility begins on the 91st day after the date the service member was listed as a captive or missing.

If the veteran or service member is released from captivity, or is determined to be alive and no longer missing, the spouse's period of eligibility ends on that date. If the spouse is enrolled in training on that date, his or her eligibility may be extended to the end of the term or course.

VETERAN DIED ON ACTIVE DUTY

If a spouse is eligible because the veteran died on active duty, his or her eligibility period is 20 years from the date of death.

EFFECT OF ACTIVE DUTY ON ELIGIBILITY

Following are the effects of active duty on the eligibility period:

- Individuals may not receive DEA benefits while on active duty in the Armed Forces.
- To receive DEA benefits after military service, his or her discharge must not be under dishonorable conditions.
- If, on or after September 11, 2001, the individual was called to active duty under title 10, or involuntarily ordered to full-time National Guard duty under section 502 (f) of title 32 (State authority), in most cases VA can extend the eligibility period for DEA by the number of months and days spent on active duty plus four months.

EFFECT OF DIVORCE ON ELIGIBILITY

If marriage to the veteran ends in divorce, the spouse's eligibility for DEA benefits ends on that date. But if he or she is in training, and the divorce occurs through no fault of him or her, VA can extend the eligibility as explained in the next section under *While in Training.*

EXTENSIONS OF ELIGIBILITY PERIOD

DISABILITY

VA may be able to extend the 10-year eligibility period by the amount of time the spouse was prevented from training during that period because of a disability he or she incurred. WHILE IN TRAINING

If the spouse is enrolled in training when his or her eligibility ends, in most cases VA can extend eligibility to the end of the semester or quarter, or to the end of twelve weeks if the course isn't operated on a semester or quarter basis.

EFFECT OF REMARRIAGE

Before age 57:
- If a surviving spouse remarries before age 57, his or her eligibility ends on the date of remarriage.
- If an individual remarried after November 30, 1999, and the remarriage ends, VA may reinstate eligibility to DEA. The remarriage must be ended by death, divorce, or because the individual stopped living with his or her spouse and stopped holding him or herself out to the public as the person's spouse.
- If a surviving spouse remarried after October 31, 1990, but before November 30, 1999, VA can't reinstate eligibility, even if remarriage ends.

After age 57:

If a surviving spouse remarries on or after January 1, 2004, and is 57 or older, he or she can still be eligible for DEA benefits. (If the surviving spouse remarried after age 57 and before December 16, 2003, *he or she must have applied in writing before December 16, 2004,* for eligibility to be reinstated.)

Note: Remarrying after age 57 doesn't extend the 10-year period of eligibility that was established before remarriage.

Example: A surviving spouse established eligibility for a 10-year period ending on November 15, 2005, which is 10 years from the date of the veteran's death. She remarried in April 2004 at age 58. She will keep her eligibility for DEA through November 15, 2005.

MONTHS OF BENEFITS PAYABLE

The following applies to sons and daughters (including stepchildren and adopted children), spouses and surviving spouses.

Individuals may be entitled to receive up to 45 months of DEA benefits. They may receive a maximum of 48 months of benefits combined if they are eligible under more than one VA education program.

Individuals are charged one full day for each day of full-time benefits paid. Entitlement is charged in months and days. Each month is counted as 30 days. If he or she trains part-time, VA adjusts the entitlement charge according to the training time

EFFECT OF ACTIVE DUTY ON AVAILABLE MONTHS OF BENEFITS

If an individual is called up to active duty under title 10 (federal authority) while he or she is receiving benefits, and has to drop out of school without receiving credit, VA will restore (give back) the months of benefits used for that period of training.

If called up under title 32 (State authority), VA can't restore the months of benefits used.

PENSION, COMPENSATION, AND DIC PROGRAMS

A son or daughter who is eligible for Chapter 35 benefits, as well as pension, compensation, or Dependency & Indemnity Compensation (DIC) based on school attendance, must elect which benefit to receive. An election of Chapter 35 benefits is a bar to further payment of pension, compensation, or DIC after the age of 18.

NOTE: If a program will last longer than 45 months, the son or daughter may find it to his or her advantage to defer Chapter 35 benefits. He or she could continue to receive pension, compensation, or DIC benefits which are payable as a result of school attendance. *The VA strongly encourages individuals who qualify for more than one type of education benefit to discuss their education plans with a Veterans Benefits Counselor so that all options can be explored, and maximum benefits can be paid.*

APPROVED COURSES

A State agency or VA must approve each program offered by a school or company. Individuals may receive benefits for a wide variety of training, including:
- Undergraduate degrees from a college or university
- Graduate degrees from a college or university
- Cooperative training programs
- Accredited independent study programs leading to a college degree
- Courses leading to a certificate or diploma from business, technical, or vocational schools
- Apprenticeship or job training program offered by a company or union
- Correspondence courses (spouses only)
- Farm cooperative courses
- Secondary school programs for individuals who are not high school graduates
- Secondary school deficiency or remedial courses to qualify for admission to an educational institution
- Effective November 1, 2000, persons eligible for DEA became able to receive benefits for VA-approved preparation courses for college and graduate school entrance exams. (The law also allows children to pursue these courses before age 18.)
- Effective March 1, 2001, benefits became payable for licensing or certification tests. The tests are those needed to enter, maintain, or advance into employment in a civilian vocation or profession. The eligible veteran or family member may receive payment of the fee charged for the test or $2,000, whichever is less. The tests must be approved for VA benefits. Contact the VA for a complete list of approved certification tests.

VA may approve programs offered by institutions outside of the United States, when they are pursued at educational institutions of higher learning, and lead to a college degree. Individuals must receive VA approval prior to attending or enrolling in any foreign programs.

An eligible son or daughter who is handicapped by a physical or mental disability that prevents pursuit of an educational program may receive Special Restorative Training. This may involve speech and voice correction, language retraining, lip reading, auditory training,

Braille reading and writing, etc.

An eligible spouse or son or daughter over age 14 who is handicapped by a physical or mental disability that prevents pursuit of an educational program may receive Specialized Vocational Training. This includes specialized courses, alone or in combination with other courses, leading to a vocational objective that is suitable for the person and required by reason of physical or mental handicap.

If an individual is seeking a college degree, the school must admit the individual to a degree program by the start of the individual's third term.

RESTRICTIONS ON TRAINING

Benefits are not payable for the following courses:
- Non-accredited independent study courses
- Bartending and personality development courses
- Correspondence courses (if you are a dependent or surviving child)
- Any course given by radio
- Vocational flight training
- Self-improvement courses such as reading, speaking, woodworking, basic seamanship, and English as a 2nd language
- Any course which is avocational or recreational in character
- Audited courses
- Courses not leading to an educational, professional, or vocational objective
- Courses previously taken and successfully completed
- Courses taken by a Federal government employee under the Government Employee's Training Act
- Courses taken while in receipt of benefits for the same program from the Office of Workers' Compensation Programs
- VA must reduce benefits for individuals in Federal, State, or local prisons after being convicted of a felony.
- An individual may not receive benefits for a program at a proprietary school if her or she is an owner or official of the school.
- An individual may not receive benefits under this program while serving on active duty in the Armed Forces.

PART-TIME TRAINING

Individuals unable to attend school full-time should consider going part-time. Benefit rates and entitlement charges are less than the full-time rates. For example, if a student receives full-time benefits for 12 months, the entitlement charge is 12 months. However, if the student receives 1/2 time benefits for 12 months, the charge is 6 months. VA will pay for less than 1/2 time training if the student is not receiving Tuition Assistance for those courses.

REMEDIAL, DEFICIENCY AND REFRESHER TRAINING

Remedial and deficiency courses are intended to assist a student in overcoming a deficiency in a particular area of study.

Refresher training is available only at the elementary or secondary level. It is for reviewing or updating material previously covered in a course satisfactorily completed.

There is no entitlement charge for these courses for the first 5 months of training.

TUTORIAL ASSISTANCE

Students may receive a special allowance for individual tutoring performed after September 30, 1992, if they entered school at one-half time or more. To qualify, the student must have a deficiency in a subject. The school must certify the tutor's qualifications, and the hours of tutoring. Eligible students may receive a maximum monthly payment of $100.00. The maximum total benefit payable is $1,200.00.

There is no entitlement charge for the first $600.00 of tutorial assistance.

To apply for tutorial assistance, students must submit VA Form 22-1990t, Application and Enrollment Certification for Individualized Tutorial Assistance. The form should be given to the certifying official in the office handling VA paperwork at the school for completion.

You may receive up to 45 months of education benefits. Effective Oct. 1, 2013, some DEA beneficiaries may be eligible for up to 81 months of GI Bill benefits if they use the Survivors and Dependents Educational Assistance program in conjunction with an entitlement from other VA education programs.

RATES OF EDUCATIONAL ASSISTANCE

The following basic monthly rates are effective October 1, 2017

BASIC MONTHLY RATES SURVIVORS' AND DEPENDENTS EDUCATIONAL ASSISTANCE PROGRAM (DEA)					
Type of Training	Full-Time	Three-Quarter Time	One-Half Time	Less than ½ Time, But More Than ¼ Time	One-Quarter Time
Institutional	$1041.00	780.00	519.00	Tuition & Fees, not to exceed $519.00	Tuition & Fees, not to exceed $260.25
Farm Cooperative Training	$837.00	630.00	417.00		
Correspondence Training	Entitlement charged at the rate of one month for each $1041.00 paid.				
Apprenticeship On-The-Job Training -	First six months: $760.00 Second six months: $571.00 Third six months: $375.00 Remainder of program: $191.00				
Special Restorative Training:			$1041.00		
Accelerated Charges: Cost of Tuition & Fees in Excess of:			$322.00		
Entitlement Reduced 1 Day For Each			$34.70 (1/30th of Full-Time Rate)		

CHANGE OF PROGRAM

Any change in educational, professional or vocational objectives is considered a *"change of program."* VA will not charge a change of program when a student enrolls in a new program, provided he or she successfully completed the immediately preceding program.

SPOUSE, WIDOW OR WIDOWER OF VETERAN

A spouse, widow, or widower of a veteran may make one change of program without prior VA approval if attendance, conduct, and progress in the last program were satisfactory. VA may approve additional changes if the proposed programs are suitable to the student's abilities, aptitudes, and interests.

CHILD OF VETERAN

VA may approve a change of program for sons or daughters if it finds that the new program is suitable to the student's abilities, aptitudes, and interests.

ATTENDANCE, CONDUCT AND PROGRESS

Once an individual starts receiving benefits, he must maintain satisfactory attendance, conduct and progress. The VA may stop benefits if an individual does not meet the standards set by the school. VA may later resume benefits if the individual reenters the same program at the same school, and the school approves the reentry, and certifies it to VA.

If the individual does not reenter the same program at the same school, VA may resume benefits if the cause of unsatisfactory attendance, conduct or progress has been removed; and the program that the student intends to pursue is suitable to his or her abilities, aptitudes and interests.

APPLICATION FOR BENEFITS

When the individual finds a school, company or apprenticeship, there are two important steps that must be followed:
- Make sure the program is approved for VA training. Contact the local VA regional office if there are any questions.
- Complete VA Form 22-5490, "Application for Survivors' and Dependents' Educational Assistance." The completed form should be sent to the VA regional office with jurisdiction over the State where training will occur. Sons or daughters under legal age must have the application signed by a parent or guardian. Sons or daughters of age can apply alone.
- Following receipt of an application, VA will review it and advise if anything else is needed.

If an individual has started training, the application and Notice of Basic Eligibility should be taken to the school, employer or union. The certifying official should complete VA Form 22-1999, "Enrollment Certification," and send all the forms to VA.

PROCEDURES FOR RECEIPT OF MONTHLY PAYMENTS

After selecting a school and submitting an application to VA, the school official must complete an enrollment certification, and submit it to the appropriate VA regional office. If a student meets the basic eligibility requirements for benefits, and the program or course is approved, VA will process the enrollment based on certified training time.

If a student is enrolled in a degree program at a college or university, he or she will receive payment after the first of each month for the training during the preceding month. If a student is enrolled in a certificate or diploma program at a business, technical, or vocational school, he or she will not receive payment until they have verified their attendance. Students will receive a "Student Verification of Enrollment Form 22-8979" each month, and must complete and return it to the appropriate VA regional office. After processing, VA will release a check.

If an individual is in an apprenticeship or job-training program, he or she will receive a form to report the hours worked each month. The form must be signed and given to the certifying official for the company or union. The certifying official must complete the form and send it to the appropriate VA regional office. After processing, VA will release a check.

If an individual is taking a correspondence course, he or she will receive a form each quarter, on which the student must show the number of lessons completed that quarter. The completed form should be sent to the school for certification of the number of lessons serviced during the quarter. The school will send the form to the appropriate VA regional office. After processing, VA will release a check. Payments are based on the number of lessons serviced by the school.

NOTE: It is against the law for schools to cash VA checks under a Power of Attorney Agreement.

TIMELY RECEIPT OF VERIFICATION FORMS AND CHECKS

Students taking courses leading to a degree at a college or university should receive their checks for each month by the fifth of the next month. If it is not received by then, the VA should be immediately contacted so that appropriate action can be taken.

Students taking courses leading to a certificate or diploma from a business, technical, or vocational school should receive their verification forms for each month by the fifth of the following month. If it is not received by then, the VA should be immediately contacted so that another form can be issued.

One a completed verification form has been submitted, the student should receive a check within 2 weeks. If a check is not received by then, the VA should immediately be contacted so that appropriate action can be taken.

ADVANCE PAYMENTS

An advance payment for the initial month, or partial month and the following month may be made, if:

* The school agrees to handle advance payments; and Training is one-half time or more; and
* A request is made by the individual in writing; and
* The VA receives the enrollment certification at least 30 days prior to the start of classes.

Advance payments are made out to the individual, and sent to the applicable school for delivery to the individual registration. VA cannot issue a check more than 30 days before classes start. Before requesting an advance payment, students should verify with the school certifying official that the school has agreed to process advance payments.

Requests for advance payments must be on VA Form 22-1999, "Enrollment Certification," or a sheet of paper attached to the enrollment certification.

Once a student receives an advance payment at registration, the school must certify to VA that the student received the check. If a student reduces enrollment, or withdraws from all courses during the period covered by an advance payment, he or she must repay the overpayment to VA.

231

If an individual believes that the amount of a VA check is incorrect, the VA should be contacted before the check is cashed.

DIRECT DEPOSIT

Payments can be sent directly to a student's savings or checking account through Direct Deposit (Electronic Funds Transfer). To sign up for direct deposit by phone, students must call (877) 838-2778.

STUDENT RESPONSIBILITIES

To ensure timely receipt of correct payments, students should be sure to promptly notify the VA of:

- Any change in enrollment;
- Any change in address;
- Any change in marital status (separation from the veteran, divorce from the veteran, or remarriage following the death of the veteran).

In addition, students should use reasonable judgment when accepting and cashing a check. All letters from VA about monthly rates and effective dates should be read carefully. If a student thinks the amount of a VA check is wrong, VA should be contacted **before** cashing the check. Any incorrect checks should be returned to VA.

If a student cashes a check for the wrong amount, he or she will be liable for repayment of any resulting overpayment.

RECOVERY OF OVERPAYMENTS

VA must take prompt and aggressive action to recover overpayments. Students have the right to request a waiver of the overpayment, or verification that the amount is correct. If an overpayment is not repaid or waived, VA may add interest and collection fees to the debt. VA may also take one or more of the following actions to collect the debt:

- Withhold future benefits to apply to the debt;
- Refer the debt to a private collection agency;
- Recover the debt from any Federal income tax refund;
- Recover the debt from the salary (if student is a Federal employee);
- File a lawsuit in Federal court to collect the debt;
- Withhold approval of a VA home loan guarantee.

CHANGES IN ENROLLMENT

If a student withdraws from one or more courses after the end of the school's drop period, VA will reduce or stop benefits on the date of reduction or withdrawal. Unless the student can show that the change was due to *mitigating circumstances*, the student may have to repay **all** benefits for the course.

VA defines *mitigating circumstances* as "unavoidable and unexpected events that directly interfere with the pursuit of a course, and which are beyond the student's control.

Examples of reasons VA may accept include:

- Extended illness;
- Severe illness or death in immediate family;
- Unscheduled changes in employment; and

232

- Lack of child care.

Examples of reasons VA may not accept include:

- Withdrawal to avoid a failing grade;
- Dislike of the instructor; and
- Too many courses attempted.

(VA may ask the student to furnish evidence to support the reason for change, such as physician or employer written statements.)
The first time a student withdraws from up to 6 credit hours, VA will "excuse" the withdrawal, and pay benefits for the period attended.

If a student receives a grade that does not count toward graduation, all benefits for the course may have to be repaid.

If a student receives a non-punitive grade, the school will notify VA, and VA may reduce or stop benefits. The student may not have to repay the benefits if he or she can show that the grades were due to mitigating circumstances.

WORK-STUDY PROGRAMS

Students may be eligible for an additional allowance under a work-study program that allows students to perform work for VA in return for an hourly wage. Students may perform outreach services under VA supervision, prepare and process VA paperwork, work at a VA medical facility or National Cemetery, or perform other approved activities.

Students must attend school at the three-quarter of full-time rate.

VA will select students for the work-study program based on different factors. Such factors include:
- Disability of the student;
- Ability of the student to complete the work-study contract before the end of his or her eligibility for education benefits;
- Job availability within normal commuting distance to the student;
- VA will give the highest priority to a veteran who has a service-connected disability or disabilities rated by VA at 30% or more.

The number of applicants selected will depend on the availability of VA-related work at the school or at VA facilities in the area.

Students may work during or between periods of enrollment, and can arrange with VA to work any number of hours during his or her enrollment. However, the maximum number of hours a student may work is 25 times the number of weeks in the enrollment period.

Students will earn an hourly wage equal to the Federal or State minimum wage, whichever is greater. If a student works at a college or university, the school **may** pay the difference between the amount VA pays and the amount the school normally pays other work-study students doing the same job.

Students interested in taking part in a work-study program must complete VA Form 22,8691, "Application for Work-Study Allowance." Completed forms should be sent to the nearest VA regional office.

EDUCATIONAL COUNSELING

Upon request, VA will provide counseling services, including testing, to help qualified individuals:
- Select an educational, vocational, or professional objective;

- Develop a plan to achieve the above objective;
- Overcome any personal or academic problems that may interfere with the successful achievement of the stated objective.
- Qualified VA personnel are available to provide counseling services free of charge
- to qualified individuals. Individuals must pay the cost of any travel to and from the place at which VA provides counseling.

VA requires and provides counseling for each disabled child who needs special services to pursue a program of education and for certain other eligible children.

VA requires and provides counseling for disabled spouses and those who need specialized programs of vocational training as a result of the handicapping effects of their disabilities.

Individuals should contact the nearest VA regional office to make counseling appointments.

APPEAL OF VA DECISION

VA decisions on education benefits may be appealed within one year of the date an individual receives notice of a VA decision.

RESTORED ENTITLEMENT PROGRAM FOR SURVIVORS (REPS)

The *Restored Entitlement Program for Survivors* (REPS) is authorized by Section 156 of *Public Law 97-377*. This program restores social security benefits that were reduced or terminated *by Public Law 97-35*, the *Omnibus Budget Reconciliation Act of 1981*. This act eliminated the "parent with child in care" benefit when a surviving spouse's last child in care attained age 16. REPS restores the benefit until the youngest child in care attains 18, unless entitled to another Social Security benefit of equal or greater value.

The REPS program is funded by the Department of Defense, based on Social Security rules, and administered by the VA.

REPS benefits are payable to certain spouses and children of veterans who died while on active duty before August 13, 1981, or died from disabilities incurred in active duty before August 13, 1981. If a surviving spouse remarries, his or her benefits are terminated. If the child in care leaves the parent's custody, marries or dies, REPS entitlement ends. REPS benefits are reduced by $1 for each $2 of earned income over the exempt amount for Social Security (announced by Social Security Administration at the beginning of each calendar year).

REPS benefits are payable to unmarried children between the ages of 18 and 22 who are full-time students at approved schools beyond the high school level. Benefits are awarded on a school year basis. Each year verification must be received before any additional benefits can be awarded. If the child marries or reduces to less than full-time attendance, benefits will be discontinued. If the child has earned income or wages, REPS benefits are reduced. REPS benefits are not payable based on service in the commissioned corps of the National Oceanic and Atmospheric Administration, or the Public Health Service.

To apply for REPS benefits, VA Form 21-8924, "Application of Surviving Spouse or Child for REPS Benefits" must be completed and sent to the local VA regional VA office for basic eligibility determination.

Once completed, the application will be forwarded to the St. Louis office for processing. A *Student Beneficiary Report* is mailed to each student receiving REPS benefits each March. The report confirms enrollment, and allows students to report any earnings. For specific information, contact the nearest regional VA office.

OMNIBUS DIPLOMATIC SECURITY AND ANTITERRORISM ACT

Public Law 99-399, The *Omnibus Diplomatic Security and Antiterrorism Act of 1986* (the Antiterrorism Act) became effective January 21, 1981. This program is designed to provide educational assistance for persons held as captives, and their dependents.

Under this Act, VA may provide education benefits to:

- Former captives who were employees of the United States Government. Individuals providing personal services to the United States similar to that provided by civil service employees may also be eligible. This includes foreign nationals and resident aliens of the United States.
- Former captives taken during hostile action resulting from their relationship with the United States
- Family members of individuals in captivity or individuals who die while in captivity.

- VA will provide educational benefits to persons eligible under the *Antiterrorism Act* that are identical to those provided to eligible persons under Chapter 35 of title 38, U.S. Code (Survivors' and Dependents' Educational Assistance Program).

All inquiries regarding this Act should be directed to the nearest VA regional office.

CHAPTER 20

EDUCATION BENEFITS - MONTGOMERY G.I. BILL (MGIB), CHAPTER 30

OVERVIEW

The MGIB-AD Program, also called Chapter 30, is designed to provide education benefits to veterans and servicemembers with at least two years of active duty.

Assistance may be used for anything from college degree and certificate programs.

Benefits are usually payable for 10 years following your release from honorable active service.

The Montgomery G.I. Bill (MGIB) establishes education benefits for four categories of individuals, based on active duty service. The benefits available under each category may vary depending on individual situations and lengths of active duty service.

The eligibility requirements for each category are described below. However, the following two requirements must be met by all individuals, no matter which category his or her eligibility falls under.

> **Key Takeaways**
>
> The MGIB-AD program provides education benefits to veterans and servicemembers with at least two years of active duty
>
> Benefits are usually payable for 10 years following release from honorable active service
>
> Eligible servicemembers may receive up to 36 months of education benefits
>
> Some servicemembers contribute up to an additional $600 to the GI Bill to receive increased monthly benefits

Character Of Discharge

To use MGIB after an individual is separated from active duty, an individual's discharge must be fully honorable. Discharges "under honorable conditions" and "general" discharges don't establish eligibility for MGIB.

Completed High School:

To use MGIB as an active duty member, or after separation from active duty, an individual must obtain a high school diploma or equivalency certificate before applying for benefits.

Completing 12 hours toward a college degree before applying for benefits also meets this requirement. This is a change in eligibility rules that became effective November 1, 2000. If an individual wasn't previously eligible because he or she did not meet the high school requirement, the change provides a second chance.

In addition to the above requirements, individuals must meet requirements from one of the four following categories. (Individuals who entered active duty before July 1, 1985 may only qualify under Categories 2, 3, or 4.)

CATEGORY I

- The veteran must have entered active duty for the first time on or after July 1, 1985.
- The veteran must have enrolled in MGIB (didn't decline MGIB in writing upon entry into active duty). Exception: If an individual declined MGIB in writing, he or she may not change this decision at a later date unless:
  - o The individual qualifies under Category 3; or
  - o The individual withdrew his or her election not to participate during the "open period" for withdrawal (December 1, 1988 through June 30, 1989).
- Individuals who graduated from a service academy and received a commission are not eligible. Individuals who became commissioned upon completing an ROTC scholarship program are not eligible, unless one of the following exceptions applies:
  - o The individual received a commission after becoming eligible for MGIB.
  - o The individual received a commission after September 30, 1996, and received less than $3,400 during any one year of his or her ROTC program.
- Individuals who received loan repayment from the military for their education are not eligible. (Note: Individuals who received loan repayment for one period of active duty, may still be eligible based on another period of active duty, as long as they did not decline MGIB when they first entered active duty.
- To use MGIB while on active duty, an individual must serve two continuous years of active duty.
- To use MGIB after separation from active duty, the individual must have served 3 continuous years of active duty, unless discharged early for one of the following reasons:
  - o Convenience of the government (veteran must have served 30 months if he had a 3-year obligation)
  - o Service-connected disability
  - o Hardship
  - o A medical condition the individual had before service
  - o A condition that interfered with performance of duty
  - o Certain reductions in force(RIF)

Exception: To use MGIB after separation from active duty, the individual may only need 2 years of active duty if:

- He or she first enlisted for 2 years of active duty; or
- The individual has an obligation to serve 4 years in the Selected Reserve (the 2 X 4 program). The individual must enter the Selected Reserve within one year of release from active duty; or
- The individual was separated early for one of the following reasons:
- Convenience of the government (veteran must have served 20 months if he had a

2-year obligation)
- Service-connected disability
- Hardship
- A medical condition the individual had before service
- A condition that interfered with performance of duty
- Certain reductions in force (RIF)

SERVICE IN THE NATIONAL GUARD OR RESERVE

Service in the National Guard or reserve is qualifying as active duty for MGIB benefits only under the following conditions:

- Full-time National Guard or Reserve service authorized under title 10, U.S. Code (Active Guard/Reserve, or AGR) is considered active duty for purposes of qualifying for VA education benefits, unless the service is active duty for training.
- Full-time National Guard service under title 32, U.S. Code (State authority) is considered active duty for purposes of qualifying for VA education benefits, provided the service was first performed after November 29, 1989 (with no previous active duty); and is for the purpose of organizing, administering, recruiting, instructing, or training the National Guard. Duty for the purpose of performing operations (such as drug interdiction, for example) is not considered active duty for MGIB benefits.

CATEGORY II

The veteran had remaining entitlement under the Vietnam Era Veterans' Educational Assistance Program (chapter 34 of Title 38, U.S. Code) on December 31, 1989; and

- The veteran served on active duty for any number of days during the period October 19, 1984 to June 30, 1985, and then continued active duty without a break from July 1, 1985 through: June 30, 1988, or June 30, 1987, and then served four years in the Selected Reserve after release from active duty. The individual must have entered the Selected Reserve within one year of his or her release from active duty.
- The individual wasn't on active duty on October 19, 1984, but reentered active duty after that date, and served three continuous years on active duty on or after July 1, 1985, or two years on active duty followed by four years in the Selected Reserve on or after July 1, 1985. (This option became effective December 27, 2001.)
- Individuals who graduated from a service academy and received a commission after December 31, 1976 are not eligible.
- Individuals who received a commission after September 30, 1996 upon completing an ROTC scholarship program are not eligible, unless one of the following exceptions applies:
  - o the individual received a commission after becoming eligible for MGIB.
  - o The individual completed ROTC without a full scholarship.
  - o The individual received a commission after September 30, 1996, and received less than $3,400 during any one year of his or her ROTC program.

CATEGORY III

A veteran may qualify if:
- The veteran was on active duty on September 30, 1990, and was involuntarily separated after February 2, 1991; or

- The veteran was involuntarily separated on or after November 30, 1993.
- Effective October 23, 1992, the law was expanded to allow the same opportunity to elect MGIB benefits before separation to members voluntarily separated under either the Voluntary Separation Incentive (VSI) or Special Separation Benefit (SSB)program.
- If the member was eligible for the Post Vietnam Era Veterans' Educational Assistance Program (VEAP), he must elect to receive MGIB benefits, and apply for a refund of contributions to Chapter 32.
- The member must have had his military pay reduced by $1,200 before discharge.
- Members qualifying under Category III based on a voluntary or involuntary separation are not eligible for MGIB benefits until the day following discharge.

(If a veteran eligible under Category 3 had a chapter 32 kicker, VA will pay the basic chapter 30 rate and an additional amount based upon the amount of the remaining kicker.)

CATEGORY IV

- Individuals may qualify under Category IV if they were on active duty on October 9, 1996, and were VEAP participants with money in the VEAP fund. These individuals must have elected MGIB, and paid $1,200 by October 9, 1997.
- Individuals may also be eligible if they served on full time active duty in the National Guard between June 10, 1985 and November 29, 1989, and elected to have their National Guard service count toward establishing eligibility for MGIB benefits by July 9, 1997.
- Effective November 1, 2000, VEAP participants, whether they had contributions in their accounts or not, could become eligible for MGIB if they:
  o Made an irrevocable election to receive MGIB; and
  o Were VEAP participants on or before October 9, 1996; and
  o Continuously served on active duty from October 9, 1996 through April 1, 2000; and
  o Made a payment of $2,700. The payment will be made by reducing their basic pay before their discharge from service. If $2,700 is not collected before discharge from pay reductions, veterans must make payments to the military service in the amount needed to bring the total to $2,700. DoD can also collect the additional amount by reducing retired or retainer pay.

(NOTE: This payment, unlike earlier contributions to VEAP is *not refundable*.)

The payment does not go into the VEAP account, it is deposited into the Treasury of the United States as miscellaneous receipts; and

- Met other VEAP eligibility requirements.
- VEAP participants must have made this election on or before October 31, 2001.

TRANSFERABILITY OF GI BILL TO DEPENDENTS

Eligible soldiers may now transfer up to 18 months of their GI Bill to spouses or children. This pilot program is authorized under Title 38, U.S. Code, Chapter 30 (amended by *PL 107-107*), the Montgomery GI Bill (MGIB).

ELIGIBILITY REQUIREMENTS

Participants must ensure they meet the following eligibility requirements and take the following actions to participate in the program:

- MGIB-era Soldiers who are eligible for MGIB must have enrolled in the MGIB upon initial entry to active duty and paid the $1,200 for MGIB enrollment. (Not eligible are Vietnam Ear-Rollover, VEAP conversion, and Involuntary

Separation.)
- Completed at least 6 years of service in the Armed Forces at the time of reenlistment.
- Reenlist for a period of at least 4 years and complete DD Form 2366- 2 with their servicing Army Retention Career Counselor.
- Qualify for a MOS Specific Selective Reenlistment Bonus (SRB) and entitled to a Zone B or Zone C bonus at the time of reenlistment.

The following individuals may receive transfer of entitlement:

- The spouse of the individual making the transfer;
- One or more of the children of the individual making the transfer; or
- A combination of the individuals referred above.

A dependent to whom the entitlement is transferred may not begin using the entitlement until:

Spouse:
- The Soldier has completed at least six years of service in the Armed Forces.

Child:
- The Soldier has completed at least 10 years of service in the Armed Forces, and either:
- The completion by the child of the requirement of a secondary school diploma (or equivalency certificate); or
- The attainment by the child of 18 years of age.

DISCHARGES AND SEPARATIONS

As previously mentioned, if the veteran is separated from active duty, the character of discharge must specifically be listed as "Honorable." "Under Honorable Conditions," or a "General" discharge do not establish eligibility. A discharge for one of the following reasons may result in a reduction of the required length of active duty to qualify for benefits under the MGIB:

- Convenience of the Government; or
- Disability; or
- Hardship; or
- Medical conditions existing before entry into Service; or
- Force reductions; or
- Medical condition which is not a disability due to misconduct, but which prevents satisfactory performance of duty.

CERTAIN TYPES OF ACTIVE DUTY WHICH DO NOT ESTABLISH ELIGIBILITY

The following types of active duty do not establish eligibility for MGIB benefits:
- Time assigned by the military to a civilian institution to take the same course provided to civilians.
- Time served as a cadet or a midshipman at a service academy.
- Time spent on active duty for training in the National Guard or Reserve.

Please note: Time assigned by the military to a civilian institution, and time served at a service academy does not break the continuity of active duty required to establish eligibility for MGIB benefits. Active duty for training does count toward the four years in the Selected Reserve under the 2 by 4 program.

APPROVED COURSES

This program provides veterans up to 36 months of education benefits. The benefits may be used for:

- Undergraduate or graduate degrees from a college or university;
- Cooperative training programs;
- Accredited independent study programs leading to standard college degrees;
- Courses leading to certificates or diplomas from business, technical or vocational schools;
- Vocational flight training (from September 30, 1990 only – Individuals must have a private pilot's license and meet the medical requirements for a desired license before beginning training, and throughout the flight training program);
- Apprenticeship / job training programs offered by a company or union;
- Correspondence courses;

VA may approve programs offered by institutions outside of the United States, when they are pursued at educational institutions of higher learning, and lead to an associate or higher degree, or the equivalent. Individuals must receive VA approval prior to attending or enrolling in any foreign programs;

RESTRICTIONS ON TRAINING

- Bartending and personality development courses
- Non-accredited independent study courses;
- Any course given by radio;
- Self-improvement courses such as reading, speaking, woodworking, basic seamanship, and English as a second language;
- Any course which is avocational or recreational in character;

- Farm cooperative courses;
- Audited courses;
- Courses not leading to an educational, professional, or vocational objective;
- Courses an individual has previously completed;
- Courses taken by a Federal government employee under the Government Employees' Training Act;
- Courses paid for in whole or in part by the Armed Forces while on active duty;
- Courses taken while in receipt of benefits for the same program from the Office of Workers' Compensation Programs.

The VA must reduce benefits for individuals in Federal, State or local prisons after being convicted of a felony.

An individual may not receive benefits for a program at a proprietary school if he or she is an owner or official of the school.

Benefits are generally payable for 10 years following a veteran's release from active duty.

PART-TIME TRAINING

Individuals unable to attend school full-time should consider going part-time. Benefit rates and entitlement charges are pro-rated as follows:

- Individuals who are on active duty or training at less than one-half time, will receive the lesser of:
- The monthly rate based on tuition and fees for the course(s); or
- The maximum monthly rate based on training time.
- Individuals training at less than one-half time will receive payment in one sum for

241

the whole enrollment period.

REMEDIAL, DEFICIENCY AND REFRESHER TRAINING

Remedial and deficiency courses are intended to assist a student in overcoming a deficiency in a particular area of study. In order for such courses to be approved, the courses must be deemed necessary for pursuit of a program of education.

Refresher training is for technological advances that occurred in a field of employment. The advance must have occurred while the student was on active duty, or after release.

There is an entitlement charge for these courses.

TUTORIAL ASSISTANCE

Students may receive a special allowance for individual tutoring, if attending school at one-half time or more. To qualify, the student must have a deficiency in a subject. The school must certify the tutor's qualifications, and the hours of tutoring. Eligible students may receive a maximum monthly payment of $100.00. The maximum total benefit payable is $1,200.00.

There is no entitlement charge for the first $600.00 of tutorial assistance.

To apply for tutorial assistance, students must submit VA Form 22-1990t, "Application and Enrollment Certification for Individualized Tutorial Assistance." The form should be given to the certifying official in the office handling VA paperwork at the school for completion.

MONTHS OF BENEFITS / ENTITLEMENT CHARGED

Individuals who complete their full period of enlistment may receive up to 36 months of MGIB benefits.

Individuals are considered to have completed their full enlistment period if they are discharged for the convenience of the government after completing 20 months of an enlistment of less than three years; or 30 months of an enlistment of three years or more Individuals will earn only one month of entitlement for each month of active duty after June 39, 1985, if they are discharged for other specific reasons (i.e. service- connected disability, reduction in force, hardship, etc.) before completing the enlistment period.

Individuals will earn one month of entitlement for each four months in the Selected Reserve after June 30, 1985.

Individuals qualifying for more than one VA education program may receive a maximum of 48 months of benefits. For example, if a student used 30 months of Dependents' Educational Assistance, and is eligible for chapter 1606 benefits, he or she could have a maximum of 18 months of entitlement remaining.

Individuals are charged one full day of entitlement for each day of full-time benefits paid. For correspondence and flight training, individuals use one month of entitlement each time the VA pays the equivalent of one month of full-time benefits. Individuals pursuing a cooperative program use one month for each month of benefits paid.

For apprenticeship and job-training programs, the entitlement charge during the first 6 months is 75% of full-time. For the second six months, the charge is 55% of full-time. For the rest of the program, the charge is 35% of full-time. VA can extend entitlement to the end of a term, quarter, or semester if the ending date of an individual's entitlement falls within such period. If a school does not operate on a term basis, entitlement can be extended for 12 weeks.

RATES OF EDUCATIONAL ASSISTANCE AFTER SEPARATION FROM ACTIVE DUTY

The basic monthly rates increase October 1 every year with the Consumer Price Index (CPI) increase. While in training, students receive a letter with the current rates when the increase goes into effect each year. The rates may increase at other times by an act of Congress.

BASIC MONTHLY RATES FOR COLLEGE AND VOCATIONAL SCHOOL

For approved programs in college and vocational or technical schools, basic payments are monthly and the rates are based on training time. When students train at less than half time, they will be paid tuition and fees. But if tuition and fees amount to more than would be paid at the half-time rate (or the quarter-time rate if training at quarter-time or less), payments will be limited to the half time (or the quarter-time rate).

For on-the-job training (OJT) and apprenticeship programs, rates are monthly and based on the length of time in the program. MGIB rates decrease as the student's wages increase according to an approved wage schedule.

RATES FOR OTHER TYPES OF TRAINING

For correspondence courses, students receive 55% of the approved charges for the course. For flight training, students receive 60% of the approved charges for the course.

For reimbursement of tests for licenses or certifications, students receive 100% of the charges up to a maximum of $2,000 per test.

RATES OF EDUCATIONAL ASSISTANCE WHILE ON ACTIVE DUTY

If a service member goes to school while on active duty, he or she may have two options for using MGIB benefits. The may be eligible to receive:
- "Regular" MGIB; or
- Tuition Assistance plus MGIB, or
- Tuition Assistance "Top-Up"

USING "REGULAR" MGIB ON ACTIVE DUTY

If a service member uses "regular" MGIB while on active duty, VA can pay whichever is less:
- The monthly rate based on tuition and fees for your course(s); or
- The maximum monthly MGIB rate (basic rate plus any increases he or she may qualify for).

The basic monthly rates increase October 1 every year with the Consumer Price Index (CPI) increase. While in training, students receive a letter with the current rates when the increase goes into effect each year. The rates may increase at other times by an act of Congress.

USING TUITION ASSISTANCE "TOP-UP"

If a student is on active duty, he or she may be eligible to receive Tuition Assistance (TA) from his or her branch of service. If the student has been on active duty for two years, he or she may also be eligible to use MGIB to supplement, or "top up," the TA. Top-up covers the remaining percentage of costs approved for TA that TA alone doesn't' cover—*up to specified limits*. For example, if a student's service authorizes 75% of costs, top-up can pay the remaining 25% of costs approved for TA. **DETAILED RATES OF EDUCATIONAL ASSISTANCE. The rates effective October 1, 2017 are detailed in the following charts:**

BASIC MONTHLY RATES EFFECTIVE OCTOBER 1, 2017 MONTGOMERY G.I. BILL - ACTIVE DUTY (MGIB), CHAPTER 30					
Type of Training	Full-Time	Three-Quarter Time	One-Half Time	Less Thank One-Half Time But More than 1/4	One-Quarter Time
Institutional	$1928.00	1446.00	964.00	964.00	482.00
Cooperative Training	$1928.00 (Full-Time Only)				
Correspondence Training	Entitlement charged at the rate of one month for each $1928.00 paid				
Apprenticeship On-The-Job Training-	First six months: $1446.00 Second six months: $1060.40 Remainder of program: 674.80				
Flight Training	Entitlement charged at the rate of one month for each $1928.00 paid				

BASIC MONTHLY RATES EFFECTIVE OCTOBER 1, 2017 For persons whose initial active duty obligation was less than three years and who served less than three years (excluding 2x4 participants)					
Type of Training	Full- Time	Three-Quarter Time	One- Half Time	Less Than ½ Time But More Than 1/4	One- Quarter Time
Institutional	$1566.00	1174.50	783.00	Tuition & Fees, Not to exceed $783.00	$391.50
Correspondence Training	Entitlement charged at the rate of one month for each $1566.00 paid				
Apprenticeship On-The-Job Training-	First six months: $1174.50 Second six months: $861.30 Remainder of program: $548.10				
Flight Training	Entitlement charged at the rate of one month for each $1566.00 paid				
Cooperative Training	$1566.00 (Full-Time Only)				

BASIC INSTITUTIONAL RATES EFFECTIVE OCTOBER 1, 2017
For persons with remaining entitlement under Chapter 34 of Title 38, U.S.C.

Time	No Dependents	One Dependent	Two Dependents	Each Add'l Dependent
Full	$2116.00	2152.00	2183.00	$16.00
Three-Quarter	$1587.00	1614.00	1637.50	$12.00
One-Half	$1058.00	1076.00	1091.50	$8.50
Less Than 1/2, But More Than 1/4	Tuition and fees, not to exceed the rate of $1058.50			
One-Quarter	Tuition and fees, not to exceed the rate of $529.00			
Cooperative	$2116.00	$2152.00	$2183.00	$16.00

BASIC JOB TRAINING RATES EFFECTIVE OCTOBER 1, 2017
For persons with remaining entitlement under Chapter 34 of Title 38 U.S.C.
Apprenticeship and On-the-Job Training

Time	No Dependents	One Dependent	Two Dependents	Each Add'l Dependent
First six months	$1548.75	$1561.13	$1572.00	$5.25
Second six months	$1116.78	$1126.13	$1133.83	$3.85
Third six months	$698.60	$704.73	$709.45	2.45
Remainder	$686.70	$692.48	$697.73	$2.45

SPECIAL NOTES:
Cooperative Training is full time only.
Individuals taking correspondence courses will receive 55% of the approved charges for the course.
Individuals taking flight training will receive 60% of the approved charges for the course, including solo hours.

INCREASED ABOVE BASIC RATES

Individuals may qualify for the following increases above their basic monthly rates. These increases don't apply to correspondence courses, the test for a license or certification, or flight training.

COLLEGE FUND

Certain branches of service may offer the College Fund. The College Fund money, or "kicker," is an additional amount of money that increases the basic MGIB monthly benefit and is included in the VA payment.

Important: Students can't receive College Fund money without receiving MGIB. A common misunderstanding is that the College Fund is a separate benefit from MGIB. The College Fund is an add-on to the MGIB benefit.

VEAP KICKER

VA pays an additional amount, commonly known as a "kicker," if directed by the Department of Defense (DoD). If an individual is eligible under Category 3 or Category 4 and has a VEAP kicker, he or she can receive the amount of the VEAP kicker contributed by the service department divided by the total months of MGIB eligibility.

ACCELERATED PAYMENTS FOR EDUCATION LEADING TO EMPLOYMENT IN HIGH TECHNOLOGY

One of the provisions contained in the *Veterans Education and Benefits Expansion Act of 2001 (Public Law 107-103)* called for accelerated payments for education leading to employment in high technology, effective October 1, 2002. Following are questions and answers provided by the VA regarding this provision.

What is an accelerated payment?

An accelerated payment is a lump sum payment of 60% of tuition and fees for certain high cost, high tech programs. If a participant does not have sufficient entitlement to cover 60% of tuition and fees, he or she will receive pay based on the actual remaining entitlement.

VA will make accelerated payments for one term, quarter, or semester at a time. However, if the program is not offered on a term, quarter or semester basis, the accelerated payment is paid for the entire program. To qualify, a participant must be enrolled in a high-tech program and must certify that he or she intends to seek employment in a high tech industry as defined by VA. Accelerated payment is paid instead of Montgomery GI Bill benefits that would otherwise have been received.

Who qualifies for accelerated payments?

Only individuals eligible for the Montgomery GI Bill - Active Duty (Chapter 30) qualify for accelerated payments.

How high do the tuition and fees have to be?

To receive accelerated payment, the tuition and fees must be more than double the Montgomery GI Bill benefits that a participant would otherwise receive for that term. For example, if the full-time rate is $732 and a participant is enrolled in a 4-month semester, the tuition and fees must be over $5,856 (4 months x $732=$2,928; $5,856=2 x $2,928) before he or she could receive an accelerated payment.

If a participant receives $900 in monthly benefits, the tuition and fees must be over $7,200 (4 months x $900=$3,600; $7,200= 2 x $3,600).

If a participant receives $1,050 in monthly benefits, the tuition and fees must be over $8,400 (4 months x $1,050 = $4,200; 2 x $4,200 = $8,400).

What programs qualify for accelerated payment?

Both degree and non-degree programs qualify. A participant must be enrolled in a program in one of the following categories:

Life science or physical science (but not social science);
Engineering (all fields);
Mathematics;
Engineering and science technology;
Computer specialties; and·

Engineering, science, and computer management

What industries qualify for accelerated payments?

A participant must intend to seek employment in one of the following industries:

Biotechnology;
Life Science Technologies;
Opto-electronics;
Computers and telecommunications; Electronics;
Computer-integrated manufacturing; Material Design;
Aerospace;
Weapons;
Nuclear technology

How does a participant apply for accelerated payments?

The individual must ask the school to include his or her request for accelerated payment to VA when it sends the enrollment information to VA for processing. The individual's request must include his or her certification of intent to seek employment in a high technology industry.

How is the education entitlement charged?

VA will divide the accelerated payment by the amount of the individual's full-time monthly rate (including kickers and additional contributions) and will reduce the entitlement by the resulting number of months and days. Example: Jill received an accelerated payment of $3,600. Her full-time rate is $900. VA will charge her entitlement as follows: $3,600/$900 = 4months.

When can accelerated payments be made?

Accelerated payments may only be made for terms or other enrollment periods that begin on or after October 1, 2002.

Can school-related expenses (such as books, supplies and living expenses) be counted as tuition and fees for accelerated payments?

No. Only the school's tuition and fees can be considered for accelerated payment.

Can an individual receive accelerated payments for short, non-degree courses?

Yes, as long as they are approved for VA benefits. Short, expensive, IT courses offered by businesses typically are not approved for VA benefits.

Can an individual receive accelerated payments for non-technical courses when taking them as part of a high technology program?

Yes. However, the degree or certificate must require the completion of these other non-technical courses.

Is it possible to receive an accelerated payment check before a school term begins?

No. VA needs to verify that the individual has enrolled before sending out the large payment. VA will pay the student as soon after the start of the term as possible. Individuals will receive payment faster if they receive direct deposit.

Does a student have to verify enrollment each month if he or she receives an accelerated payment?

No. After the individual completes his or her enrollment, VA will ask the student to verify that he or she have received the accelerated payment. VA will also ask the individual to indicate how he or she used the accelerated payment (such as toward tuition, fees and books and supplies). VA is asking the latter question for statistical purposes only because

the law requires them to collect this information. A student's answer will have no bearing on his or her entitlement to the accelerated payment. The student must respond to these questions within 60 days from the end of the enrollment period or VA will create an overpayment equal to the accelerated payment. As with any course, the student must notify VA of any change in his or her enrollment. The student's school must report any changes as well.

Is there any financial risk with accelerated payment?

Yes. If a student receives a grade, which does not count toward graduation requirements, he or she may have to repay all or part of the accelerated payment, depending on the circumstances. This could be a large amount of money.

Do the accelerated payments have to be paid back if the individual fails to find employment in a high technology industry?

No. The fact that he or she intended to find employment in a high technology industry is sufficient.

List of approved high technology programs

1.09 Animal Sciences
01.0901 Animal Sciences, General 01.0902 Agricultural Animal Breeding 01.0903 Animal Health
01.0904 Animal Nutrition
01.0905 Dairy Science
01.0906 Livestock Management
01.0907 Poultry Science

01.10 Food Science and Technology 01.1001 Food Science
01.1002 Food Technology and Processing 01.1099 Food Science and Technology 01.1101 Plant Sciences General
01.1102 Agronomy and Crop Science 01.1103 Horticultural Science
01.1104 Agricultural and Horticultural Plant Breeding 01.1105 Plant Protection and Integrated Pest Management 01.1106 Range Science Management

01.12 Soil Sciences
01.1201 Soil Science and Agronomy General 01.1202 Soil Chemistry and Physics
01.1203 Soil Microbiology
01.1299 Soil Sciences

03.01 Natural Resources Conservation and Research 03.0104 Environmental Science

03.03 Fishing and Fisheries Sciences and Management

Forestry
03.0501 Forestry, General
03.0502 Forest Sciences and Biology
03.0506 Forest Management/Forest Resources Management 03.0508 Urban Forestry
03.0509 Wood Science and Wood Products/Pulp and Paper Technology 03.0510 Forest
Resources Production and Management 03.0511 Forest Technology/Technician

Wildlife and Wildlands Science and Management

09.07 Radio, Television, and Digital Communication 09.0702 Digital Communication and
Media/Multimedia

11.0101 Computer and Information Sciences, General 11.0102 Artificial Intelligence and
Robotics
11.0103 Information Technology
11.0199 Computer and Information Sciences

Computer Programming
11.0201 Computer Programming/Programmer General 11.0202 Computer Programming
Specific Applications

Data Processing
11.0301 Data Process and Data Processing Technology/Technician

Information Science/Studies Computer Systems Analysis Computer Science

Computer Software and Media Application
11.0801 Web Page, Digital/Multimedia and Information Resources Design 11.0802 Data
Modeling/Warehousing and Database Administration 11.0803 Computer Graphics
11.0899 Computer Software and Media Applications, Other.

Computer System Networking and Telecommunications

Computer/Information Technology Administration and Management
11.1001 System Administration/Administrator
11.1002 System, Networking and LAN/WAN Management/Manager 11.1003 Computer and
Information Systems Security
11.1004 Web/Multimedia Management and Webmaster

Engineering.
Instructional program that prepare individuals to apply mathematical and scientific
principles to the solution of practical problems.
*15. Engineering Technologies/Technicians.
Instructional programs that prepare individuals to apply basic engineering principles and
technical skills in support of engineering and related projects.

Biological and Biomedical Sciences.
Instructional programs that focus on the biological sciences and the non-clinical biomedical
sciences, and that prepare individuals for research and professional careers as biologist and
biomedical scientist.

Mathematics and Statistics.
Instructional programs that focus on the systematic study of logical symbolic language and
its applications.

*Military Technologies.
A program that prepares individuals to undertake advanced and specialized leadership and technical responsibilities for the armed services and related national security organizations. Includes instruction in such areas as weapons systems and technology, communications, intelligence, management, logistics and strategy.

30.01 Biological and Physical Sciences

30.06 System Science and Theory

30.08 Mathematics and Computer Science Biopsychology

Gerontology

Accounting and Computer Science Behavioral Sciences

Natural Sciences Nutrition Sciences Neuroscience Cognitive Science

*40. Physical Sciences.
Instructional programs that focus on the scientific study of inanimate objects, processes of matter and energy, and associated phenomena.

*41. Science Technologies/Technicians.
Instructional programs that prepare individuals to apply scientific principles and technical skills in support of scientific research and development.

42.11 Physiological Psychology/Psychobiology

42.19 Psychometrics and Quantitative Psychology

24 Psychopharmacology Forensic Psychology

*51.14 Medical Clinical Sciences/Graduate Medical Studies
51.1401 Medical Scientist (MS, PhD)

NOTE: "*" means all programs are considered high technology programs within that discipline.

ELIGIBILITY PERIODS

Benefits generally end 10 years from the date of an individual's last discharge or release from active duty. The VA may extend the 10-year period by the amount of time an individual is prevented from training due to a disability, or the individual is being held by a foreign government or power.

The VA may extend the 10-year period if an individual reenters active duty for 90 days or more after becoming eligible. The extension ends 10 years from the date of discharge or release from the later period. Periods of active duty of less than 90 days may qualify for extensions, only if the discharge or release was for:
* A service-connected disability; or
* A medical condition existing before active duty; or
* Hardship; or
* A reduction in force.

If an individual's discharge is upgraded by the military, the 10-year period begins on the date of the upgrade.

SPECIAL NOTE FOR INDIVIDUALS ELIGIBLE UNDER THE 2 BY 4 PROGRAM

If an individual is eligible based upon two years of active duty followed by four years in the Selected Reserve, the individual may have 10 years from release from active duty, or 10 years from the completion of the four-year Selected Reserve obligation to use benefits, whichever is later.

MISCELLANEOUS INFORMATION

Any change in educational, professional or vocational objectives is considered a "change of program." The law permits one change of program without prior VA approval, provided an individual's attendance, conduct and progress in the last program were satisfactory. Additional "changes of program" require prior VA approval. VA will not charge a change of program if the individual enrolls in a new program after successful completion of the immediately preceding program.

Once an individual starts receiving benefits, he must maintain satisfactory attendance, conduct and progress. The VA may stop benefits if an individual does not meet the standards set by the school. VA may later resume benefits if the individual reenters the same program at the same school, and the school approves the reentry, and certifies it to VA.

If the individual does not reenter the same program at the same school, VA may resume benefits if the cause of unsatisfactory attendance, conduct or progress has been removed; and the program that the student intends to pursue is suitable to his or her abilities, aptitudes and interests.

APPLICATION FOR BENEFITS

VA Form 22-1990, "Application for Education Benefits" must be completed. The form may be obtained from individual schools, from any VA regional office, or by calling (888) GIBILL-1.

The completed form should be sent to the VA regional office with jurisdiction over the state in which the individual will train.

If an individual is not on active duty, copy 4 of DD Form 214 ("Certificate of Release or Discharge from Active Duty"), must also be sent to the VA. If an individual is on active duty, enrollment must be approved by the Base Education Services Officer, and service must be verified by the Commanding Officer.

If training has already started, the school, employer, or union should complete VA Form 22-1999 ("Enrollment Certification") and submit it along with the application.

PROCEDURES FOR RECEIPT OF MONTHLY PAYMENTS

After selecting a school and submitting an application to VA, the school official must complete an enrollment certification, and submit it to the appropriate VA regional office. If a student meets the basic eligibility requirements for benefits, and the program or course is approved, VA will process the enrollment based on certified training time.

If a student is enrolled in a degree program at a college or university, or a certificate or diploma program at a business, technical, or vocational school, they will not receive payment until they have verified their attendance. Students will receive a "Student Verification of Enrollment Form 22-8979" each month, and must complete and return it to the appropriate VA regional office. After processing, VA will release a check.

If an individual is in an apprenticeship or job-training program, he or she will receive a form to report the hours worked each month. The form must be signed and given to the certifying official for the company or union. The certifying official must complete the form and send it to the appropriate VA regional office. After processing, VA will release a check.

If an individual is taking a correspondence course, he or she will receive a form each quarter, on which the student must show the number of lessons completed that quarter. The completed form should be sent to the school for certification of the number of lessons serviced during the quarter. The school will send the form to the appropriate VA regional office. After processing, VA will release a check. Payments are based on the number of lessons serviced by the school.

VA will send flight schools a supply of blank monthly certification of flight training forms. The school must complete the form by entering the number of hours, the hourly rate, and the total charges for flight training received during the month. The student should review and sign the completed form, and send it to the appropriate VA regional office. After processing, VA will release a check.

NOTE: It is against the law for schools to cash VA checks under a Power of Attorney Agreement.

TIMELY RECEIPT OF VERIFICATION FORMS AND CHECKS

Students should receive their verification forms for each month by the fifth of the following month. If it is not received by then, the VA should be immediately contacted so that another form can be issued.

One a completed verification form has been submitted, the student should receive a check within 2 weeks. If a check is not received by then, the VA should immediately be contacted so that appropriate action can be taken.

ADVANCE PAYMENTS

An advance payment for the initial month, or partial month and the following month may be made, if:

- The school agrees to handle advance payments; and
- Training is one-half time or more; and
- A request is made by the individual in writing; and
- The VA receives the enrollment certification at least 30 days prior to the start of classes.
- Advance payments are made out to the individual, and sent to the applicable school for delivery to the individual registration. VA cannot issue a check more than 30 days before classes start. Before requesting an advance payment, students should verify with the school certifying official that the school has agreed to process advance payments.

Requests for advance payments must be on VA Form 22-1999, "Enrollment Certification," or a sheet of paper attached to the enrollment certification.

Once a student receives an advance payment at registration, the school must certify to VA that the student received the check. If a student reduces enrollment, or withdraws from all courses during the period covered by an advance payment, he or she must repay the overpayment to VA.

If an individual believes that the amount of a VA check is incorrect, the VA should be contacted before the check is cashed.

DIRECT DEPOSIT

Chapter 30 payments can be sent directly to a student's savings or checking account through Direct Deposit (Electronic Funds Transfer). To sign up for direct deposit by phone, students must call (877) 838-2778.

STUDENT RESPONSIBILITIES

To ensure timely receipt of correct payments, students should be sure to promptly notify the VA of:

- Any change in enrollment;
- Any change in address;
- Any change in selected reserve status;
- Any changes affecting a student's dependents (if a student is receiving an allowance which includes an additional amount for dependents).

In addition, students should use reasonable judgment when accepting and cashing a check. All letters from VA about monthly rates and effective dates should be read carefully. If a student thinks the amount of a VA check is wrong, VA should be contacted **before** cashing the check. Any incorrect checks should be returned to VA.

If a student cashes a check for the wrong amount, he or she will be liable for repayment of any resulting overpayment.

RECOVERY OF OVERPAYMENTS

VA must take prompt and aggressive action to recover overpayments. Students have the right to request a waiver of the overpayment, or verification that the amount is correct. If an overpayment is not repaid or waived, VA may add interest and collection fees to the debt. VA may also take one or more of the following actions to collect the debt:

- Withhold future benefits to apply to the debt;
- Refer the debt to a private collection agency;
- Recover the debt from any Federal income tax refund;
- Recover the debt from the salary (if student is a Federal employee);
- File a lawsuit in Federal court to collect the debt;
- Withhold approval of a VA home loan guarantee.

CHANGES IN ENROLLMENT

If a student withdraws from one or more courses after the end of the school's drop period, VA will reduce or stop benefits on the date of reduction or withdrawal. Unless the student can show that the change was due to *mitigating circumstances*, the student may have to repay **all** benefits for the course.

VA defines *mitigating circumstances* as "unavoidable and unexpected events that directly interfere with the pursuit of a course, and which are beyond the student's control.

Examples of reasons VA may accept include:

- Extended illness;
- Severe illness or death in immediate family;
- Unscheduled changes in employment; and
- Lack of child care.

Examples of reasons VA may not accept include:

- Withdrawal to avoid a failing grade;
- Dislike of the instructor; and
- Too many courses attempted.

(VA may ask the student to furnish evidence to support the reason for change, such as physician or employer written statements.)

The first time a student withdraws from up to 6 credit hours, VA will "excuse" the withdrawal, and pay benefits for the period attended.

If a student receives a grade that does not count toward graduation, all benefits for the course may have to be repaid. Affected students should check the school's grading policy with the office handling VA paperwork.

If a student receives a non-punitive grade, the school will notify VA, and VA may reduce or stop benefits. The student may not have to repay the benefits if he or she can show that the grades were due to mitigating circumstances.

WORK-STUDY PROGRAMS

Students may be eligible for an additional allowance under a work-study program that allows students to perform work for VA in return for an hourly wage. Students may perform outreach services under VA supervision, prepare and process VA paperwork, work at a VA medical facility or National Cemetery, or perform other approved activities.

Students must attend school at the three-quarter of full-time rate.

VA will select students for the work study program based on different factors. Such factors include:

- Disability of the student;
- Ability of the student to complete the work-study contract before the end of his or her eligibility for education benefits;
- Job availability within normal commuting distance to the student;
- VA will give the highest priority to a veteran who has a service-connected disability or disabilities rated by VA at 30% or more.

The number of applicants selected will depend on the availability of VA-related work at the school or at VA facilities in the area.

Students may work during or between periods of enrollment, and can arrange with VA to work any number of hours during his or her enrollment. However, the maximum number of hours a student may work is 25 times the number of weeks in the enrollment period.

Students will earn an hourly wage equal to the Federal or State minimum wage, whichever is greater. If a student works at a college or university, the school **may** pay the difference between the amount VA pays and the amount the school normally pays other work-study students doing the same job.

Students may elect to be paid in advance for 40% of the number of hours in the work-study agreement, or for 50 hours, whichever is less. After completion of the hours covered by the first payment, VA will pay the student after completion of each 50 hours of service.

Students interested in taking part in a work-study program must complete VA Form 22-8691, "Application for Work-Study Allowance." Completed forms should be sent to the nearest VA regional office.

EDUCATIONAL COUNSELING

VA can provide services to help eligible individuals understand their educational and vocational strengths and weaknesses and to plan:
- An educational or training goal, and the means by which the goal can be reached; or
- An employment goal for which an individual qualifies on the basis of present training or experience.

VA can also help plan an effective job search. Counseling is available for:
- Service members who are on active duty, and are within 180 days of discharge, and are stationed in the United States; or
- Veterans with discharges that are not dishonorable, who are within one year from date of discharge.

VOCATIONAL REHABILITATION

Veterans may qualify for Training and Rehabilitation under Chapter 31 of Title 38, United States Code, if:
- The veteran has a service-connected disability or disabilities rated by VA at 20% or more; and
- The veteran received a discharge from active duty that was not dishonorable; and
- The veteran has an employment handicap.

Veterans may also qualify with a service-connected disability or disabilities rated by VA at 10%, and:
- The veteran has a serious employment handicap; or
- The veteran first applied for vocational rehabilitation benefits before November 1, 1990, reapplied after that date, and has an employment handicap.

Vocational rehabilitation helps disabled veterans become independent in daily living. Veterans may also receive assistance in selecting, preparing for, and securing employment that is compatible with their interests, talents, skills, physical capabilities, and goals.

To apply for vocational rehabilitation, VA for 28-1900, "Disabled Veterans Application for Vocational Rehabilitation," must be completed and sent to the nearest VA regional office For detailed information on vocational rehabilitation refer to Chapter 14 of this book.

APPEAL OF VA DECISION

VA decisions on education benefits may be appealed within one year of the date an individual receives notice of a VA decision.

CHAPTER 21

EDUCATION BENEFITS: POST-9/11 G.I. BILL, CHAPTER 33

OVERVIEW

The Post-9/11 GI Bill is for servicemembers with at least 90 days of aggregate active duty service after September 10, 2001, whether they are still on active duty or they are an honorably discharged veteran. This education benefit also applies to veterans discharged with a service-connected disability after 30 days.

If you have eligibility for the Post-9/11 GI Bill and any other GI Bill program, you must make an irrevocable election of the Post-9/11 GI Bill before you can receive any benefits.

The Post-9/11 GI Bill has specific components unavailable in other GI Bill programs including Yellow Ribbon Program and the Transfer of Entitlement Option.

For approved programs, the Post-9/11 GI Bill provides up to 36 months of education benefits, generally payable for 15 years following release from active duty.

> **Key Takeaways**
>
> The Pos-9/11 GI Bill is different from other GI Bill programs because it includes the Yellow Ribbon Program and the Transfer of Entitlement Option
>
> Some service members may transfer unused GI Bill benefits to their dependents
>
> Full tuition and fees are paid directly to the school for all public school in-state students
>
> For private schools, tuition and fees are capped at the national maximum rate

Institutions of higher learning participating in the Yellow Ribbon Program may make additional funds available for education programs without an additional charge to GI Bill entitlements.

VETERANS EDUCATIONAL ASSISTANCE IMPROVEMENTS ACT OF 2010

Certain National Guard members mobilized on Title 32 orders on-or-after September 11, 2001 are eligible for the Post-9/11 GI Bill and any qualifying Title 32 mobilization may be used to increase his or her percentage of eligibility.

o   Limits active duty members to the net cost for tuition and fees prorated based on the eligibility tiers (40%-100%) previously established for Veterans. (Same limitations apply to transferee spouses of active duty servicemembers.)

o   *The Post-9/11 GI Bill* will now pay all public school in-state tuition and fees; this includes graduate training, etc.

o   MGIB-AD & MGIB-SR College fund payments will now be paid on a monthly basis instead of a lump-sum at the beginning of the term.

o   Reimbursement is now available for multiple Licensing and Certification Tests.

o   Reimbursement is now available for fees paid to take national examinations used for admission to an institution of higher learning (e.g. SAT, LSAT, ACT, GMAT, etc).

o   Vocational Rehabilitation participants may now elect the higher housing allowance offered by the *Post-9/11 GI Bill* if otherwise eligible for the Post-9/11 GI Bill.

o   If training at greater than ½ time the housing allowance is now prorated according to the training time the individual is enrolled (rounded to the nearest tenth). So, if a student's full housing allowance is $1000, and he or she is attending ¾ time - the housing allowance would be $800 (80% of $1000).

o   Break or interval pay is no longer payable under any VA education benefit program unless under an Executive Order of the President or due to an emergency situation such as a natural disaster or strike. Entitlement which previously would have been used for break pay will be available for use during a future enrollment. This means that if the semester ends December 15, the housing allowance is paid for the first 15 days of December only. Benefits will begin again when the new semester begins (e.g. January 15), and the student will be paid for the remaining days of that month and term.

o   Students using other VA education programs are included in this change. Monthly benefits will be prorated in the same manner.

o   NOAA and PHS personnel are now eligible to transfer their entitlement to eligible dependents

If a student is training at greater than ½ time, his or her housing allowance is now prorated according to the training time he or she is enrolled. For example, if full housing allowance for is $1000, and the student is attending ¾ time - the housing allowance would be $750 (¾ of $1000)

Housing allowance is now payable to students enrolled solely in distance learning. The housing allowance is ½ the national average BAH for an E-5 with dependents (the rate would be $673.50 for 2011).

Non-college degree programs, on-the-job training, and flight training programs are now covered under the Post-9/11 GI Bill. The book stipend is now payable to active duty members.

ELIGIBILITY

If an individual has served a total of at least 90 consecutive days on active duty in the Armed Forces since September 11, 2001, he or she is eligible. However, the amount of benefits received under this program is determined by the actual amount of accumulated post 9/11 service the individual has.

An individual may be eligible if he or she has served at least 90 aggregate days on active duty after September 10, 2001, and is still on active duty, or was honorably:

▪   Discharged from the active duty; or
▪   Released from active duty and placed on the retired list or temporary disability retired list; or
▪   Released from active duty and transferred to the Fleet Reserve or Fleet Marine Corps Reserve; or

- Released from the active duty for further service in a reserve component of the Armed Forces.

Individuals may also be eligible if they were honorably discharged from active duty for a service-connected disability, and served 30 continuous days after September 10, 2001.

Some periods of active duty service are excluded. Periods of service under the following do not count toward qualification for the *Post 9/11 GI Bill*:
- NOAA, PHS, or Active Guard Reserve; ROTC under 10 U.S.C. 2107(b);
- Service academy contract period;
- Service terminated due to defective enlistment agreement;
- Service used for loan repayment; and
- Selected reserve service used to establish eligibility under the *Montgomery GI Bill* (MGIB chapter 30), MGIB for Selected Reserve (MGIB-SR Chapter 1606), or the Reserve Education Assistance Program (REAP chapter 1607).

Under the MGIB, officers who received their commission through a service academy, or an ROTC scholarship were ineligible. There are no such restrictions under the new program. Any officer who was previously ineligible will be eligible for the new program, assuming they have at least 90 days of post 9/11 active duty service.

Similarly, military members who previously declined the MGIB are eligible for the new program.

If, on August 1, 2009, a servicemember was eligible for MGIB-SR or REAP, and he or she qualifies for the *Post-9/11 GI Bill*, he or she must make an irrevocable election to receive benefits under the *Post-9/11 GI Bill*. The individual then loses any right to future MGIB- SR or REAP benefits.

BENEFIT AMOUNT PAYABLE

The new rates depend on the length of post 9/11 active duty service, the state of residence, and the number of courses taken. Like the MGIB, the *Post-9/11 GI Bill* pays 36 months of full time education benefits. So, if an individual goes to school full-time, he or she will receive the full benefit rates for 36 months. If he or she goes to school 1/2 time, he or she will receive half of the monthly entitlement for 72 months, etc.

Based on the length of active duty service, eligible participants are entitled to receive a percentage of the following:
- Cost of tuition and fees, not to exceed the most expensive in-state undergraduate tuition at a public institution of higher education (paid directly to the school);
- Monthly housing allowance equal to the basic allowance for housing payable to a military E-5 with dependents, in the same zip code as the primary school (paid directly to the servicemember or veteran);
- Yearly books and supplies stipend of up to $1,000 per year (paid directly to the servicemember or veteran); and
- A one-time payment of $500 paid to certain individuals relocating from highly rural areas. (The housing allowance and books and supplies stipend are not payable to individuals on active duty. The housing allowance is not payable to those pursuing training at halftime or less or to individuals enrolled solely in distance learning programs.)

The following chart outlines the breakdown of benefits based on amount of service:

Member Serves	Percentage of Maximum Benefit Payable
At least 36 months	100%
At least 30 continuous days on active duty and must be discharged due to service-connected disability	100%
At least 30 months, but less than 36 months	90%
At least 24 months, but less than 30 months	80%
At least 18 months, but less than 24 months	70%
At least 12 months, but less than 18 months	60%
At least 06 months, but less than 12 months	50%
At least 90 days, but less than 06 months	40%

2017-2018 MAXIMUM IN-STATE TUITION & FEES

If an eligible student is attending a public school, they may qualify for all tuition and fee payments for an in-state student.

For private or foreign school attendees, students receive up to $22,805.34 per academic year, based on the National Maximum.

CONTRIBUTIONS

Unlike the MGIB and VEAP, the new MGIB does not require the servicemember to elect or decline, nor make monthly contributions. Unfortunately, if someone has already contributed to the GI Bill, he or she won't get their money back, unless they use all of their new GI Bill entitlements.

If they do, the $1,200 contribution to the MGIB (or a proportional amount, if they used any of their MGIB entitlement) will be added to his or her final new GI Bill education payment. If an individual is currently paying into the MGIB, he or she can stop now, and still be eligible for the new program.

COVERED EXPENSES

The plan covers any approved programs offered by a school in the United States that is authorized to grant an associate (or higher) degree.

You can be reimbursed up to $2,000 per test. Your entitlement will be charged one month for every $1,832.96 paid to you rounded to the nearest non-zero whole month; this means even low-cost tests are charged one month of entitlement per test.

If a servicemember transferred to the *Post-9/11 GI Bill* from MGIB-Active Duty, MGIB-SR, or REAP, he or she may also receive Post-9/11 benefits for flight training, apprenticeship, or on-the-job training programs, and correspondence courses.

COLLEGE FUNDS

If the member is eligible for a "kicker," such as the Army or Navy College Fund, or a Reserve "Kicker," he or she will still receive the extra monthly benefit under the new GI bill. This monthly amount will be paid to the member, not to the university.

COLLEGE LOAN REPAYMENT

Individuals, who were previously ineligible for the MGIB because they elected the College Loan Repayment Program (CLRP), are eligible for the new GI Bill, but only active duty service performed after their initial active duty service obligation counts toward the new benefits. In other words, if they were initially enlisted for five years and received the CLRP, they would have to reenlist or extend their enlistment in order to take advantage of the new GI Bill.

TRANSFERRING BENEFITS TO DEPENDENTS

While the Post-9/11 GI Bill offers a very generous post-service education benefit, a special provision of the program allows career service members the opportunity to share their education benefits with immediate family members.

Allowing career service members to transfer their GI Bill benefits to family members has long been one of the most requested items among military family readiness and advocacy groups.

ELIGIBLE INDIVIDUALS

Any member of the Armed Forces (active duty or Selected Reserve, officer or enlisted) on or after August 1, 2009, who is eligible for *the Post-9/11 GI Bill*, and:

- Has at least 6 years of service in the Armed Forces on the date of election and agrees to serve 4 additional years in the Armed Forces from the date of election.
- Has at least 10 years of service in the Armed Forces (active duty and/or selected reserve) on the date of election, is precluded by either standard policy (service or DoD) or statute from committing to 4 additional years, and agrees to serve for the maximum amount of time allowed by such policy or statute, or
- Is (or becomes) retirement eligible during the period from August 1, 2009, through August 1, 2013. A servicemember is considered to be retirement

eligible if he or she has completed 20 years of active duty or 20 qualifying years of reserve service.

- For those individuals eligible for retirement on August 1, 2009, no additional service is required.
- For those individuals who have an approved retirement date after August 1, 2009, and before July 1, 2010, no additional service is required.
- For those individuals eligible for retirement after August 1, 2009, and before August 1, 2010, 1 year of additional service after approval of transfer is required.
- For those individuals eligible for retirement on or after August 1, 2010, and before August 1, 2011, 2 years of additional service after approval of transfer are required.
- For those individuals eligible for retirement on or after August 1, 2011, and before August 1, 2012, 3 years of additional service after approval of transfer required.

ELIGIBLE FAMILY MEMBERS

An individual approved to transfer an entitlement to educational assistance under this

260

section may transfer the individual's entitlement to:
- The individual's spouse.
- One or more of the individual's children.
- Any combination of spouse and child.

A family member must be enrolled in the Defense Eligibility Enrollment Reporting System (DEERS) and be eligible for benefits, at the time of transfer to receive transferred educational benefits.

A child's subsequent marriage will not affect his or her eligibility to receive the educational benefit; however, after an individual has designated a child as a transferee under this section, the individual retains the right to revoke or modify the transfer at any time.

A subsequent divorce will not affect the transferee's eligibility to receive educational benefits; however, after an individual has designated a spouse as a transferee under this section, the eligible individual retains the right to revoke or modify the transfer at any time.

NATURE OF TRANSFER

An eligible Service member may transfer up to the total months of unused Post-9/11 GI Bill benefits, or the entire 36 months if the member has used none.

Family member use of transferred educational benefits is subject to the following:

SPOUSE:
May start to use the benefit immediately.

May use the benefit while the member remains in the Armed Forces or after separation from active duty.

Is not eligible for the monthly stipend or books and supplies stipend while the member is serving on active duty.

Can use the benefit for up to 15 years after the service member's last separation from active duty.

CHILD:
May start to use the benefit only after the individual making the transfer has completed at least 10 years of service in the Armed Forces.

May use the benefit while the eligible individual remains in the Armed Forces or after separation from active duty.

May not use the benefit until he/she has attained a secondary school diploma (or equivalency certificate), or reached 18 years of age.

Is entitled to the monthly stipend and books and supplies stipend even though the eligible individual is on active duty.

Is not subject to the 15-year delimiting date, but may not use the benefit after reaching 26 years of age.

VEAP & THE POST 9/11 BENEFIT

If someone is eligible for both VEAP and the Post-9/11 GI Bill he or she may un-enroll from VEAP and receive a refund of contributions, or leave the remaining contributions in the VEAP account and remain eligible for both benefit programs.

NOTE: Students may not receive benefits under more than one program at the same time.

EXPIRATION DATE

Eligibility for the new GI Bill expires 15 years from the last period of active duty of at least 90 consecutive days. If released for a service-connected disability after at least 30 days of continuous service, eligibility ends 15 years from when the member is released for the service-connected disability.

YELLOW RIBBON PROGRAM

The Post-9/11 GI Bill pays up to the highest public in-state undergraduate tuition. Tuition and fees may exceed that amount for individuals attending a private institution, graduate school or attending in a non-resident status.

The Yellow Ribbon Program is a provision of the *Post-9/11 Veterans Education Assistance Act of 2008*. Its purpose is to address enrollment at institutions that cost more than the Post-9/11 GI Bill's tuition benefit cap.

This program allows institutions of higher learning (degree granting institutions) in the United States to voluntarily enter into an agreement with VA to fund tuition expenses that exceed the highest public in-state undergraduate tuition rate. The institution can waive up to 50% of those expenses and VA will match the same amount as the institution.

To be eligible, the student must be:
* A veteran receiving benefits at the 100% benefit rate payable; A transfer-of-entitlement eligible dependent child; or
* A transfer-of-entitlement eligible spouse of a veteran. The Institution of Higher Learning (IHL) must agree to:
    o Provide contributions to eligible individuals who apply for the Yellow Ribbon Program on a first-come first-served basis, regardless of the
* Rate at which the individual is pursuing training in any given academic year;
    o Provide contributions during the current academic year and all subsequent academic years in which the student maintains satisfactory progress, conduct, and attendance; Make contributions toward the program on behalf of the individual in the form of a waiver;
    o Choose the percentage that will be waived and waive the same percentage (up to 50%) of established charges that exceed the in- State maximum for each student eligible;
    o State the maximum number of individuals for whom contributions will be made in any given academic year.

WORK-STUDY PROGRAM

Veterans and eligible transfer-of-entitlement recipients who train at the three-quarter rate of pursuit or higher may be eligible for a work study program in which they work for VA and receive hourly wages. Students under the work-study program must be supervised by a VA employee and all duties performed must relate to VA. The types of work allowable include:

* VA paperwork processing at schools or other training facilities
* Assistance with patient care at VA hospitals or domiciliary care facilities.
* Work at national or state veterans' cemeteries.
* Other VA-approved activities.

CHAPTER 22

EDUCATION BENEFITS: RESERVE EDUCATIONAL ASSISTANCE PROGRAM (REAP)—CHAPTER 1607

IMPORTANT CHANGE IN REAP ELIGIBILITY

The *National Defense Authorization Act of 2016* ended REAP on November, 25, 2015. Some individuals will remain eligible for REAP benefits until November 25, 2019, while others are no longer eligible for REAP benefits.

The Post-9/11 GI Bill in many ways has replaced REAP because it also provides educational assistance benefits for Reserve and National Guard members called to active duty on or after September 11, 2001, and in many cases also provides a greater level of benefit than REAP.

The following is a breakdown of how beneficiaries are impacted by the change:

Key Takeaways
The REAP program ended under the *National Defense Authorization Act of 2016*.
Some individuals remain eligible for benefits until November 25, 2019, while others are no longer eligible for benefits.
Many people who were eligible for REAP benefits qualify for Post-9/11 GI Bill benefits.

- Current REAP Beneficiaries: Veterans who were attending an educational institution on November 24, 2015 or during the last semester, quarter or term ending prior to that date are eligible to continue to receive REAP benefits until November 25, 2019.
- REAP Beneficiaries Not Attending School: Veterans who applied for REAP but were not attending an educational institution on November 24, 2015 or during the last semester, quarter, or term ending prior to that date are no longer eligible to receive benefits. These people may be eligible for benefits under the Post 9/11 GI Bill.
- New REAP Applicants: Veterans who have not enrolled in school and applied for REAP benefits prior to November 25, 2015 are no longer eligible for REAP benefits, but in most cases, they are eligible for the Post-9/11 GI Bill.

OVERVIEW

H.R. 4200 created a new education benefit called the **Reserve Educational Assistance Program (REAP)** or Chapter 1607. This new program makes certain individuals who were activated after September 11, 2001 either eligible for education benefits or eligible for increased benefits.

PURPOSE

Chapter 1607 provides educational assistance to members of the reserve components called or ordered to active duty in response to a war or national emergency (contingency operations) as declared by the President or Congress.

Note: "Contingency operations" as defined in title 10 U.S. Code means "military operations that are designated by the Secretary of Defense as an operation in which members of the armed forces are or may become involved in military actions, operations or hostilities against an enemy of the United States or against opposing military force; or results in the call or order to, or retention on active duty of members of the uniformed services...."

ELIGIBILITY

The Secretaries of each military service, Department of Defense, and Department of Homeland Security (Coast Guard) will determine eligibility.

The law requires DoD to give individuals written notification of eligibility for REAP.

Unlike the MGIB-Active Duty, service members do not have to pay anything to participate in Chapter 1607.

A member of a reserve component who serves on active duty on or after September 11, 2001 under title 10 U.S. Code for a contingency operation and who serves at least 90 consecutive days or more is eligible for chapter 1607.

National Guard members also are eligible if their active duty is under section 502(f), title 32 U.S.C. and they serve for 90 consecutive days when authorized   by   the President or Secretary of Defense for a national emergency and is supported by federal funds. Individuals are eligible as soon as they reach the 90-day point whether or not they are currently on active duty. DoD will fully identify contingency operations that qualify for benefits under chapter1607.

Disabled members who are injured or have an illness or disease incurred or aggravated in the line of duty and are released from active duty before completing 90 consecutive days are also eligible.

Note: Members released early for disability incurred or aggravated in the line of duty may receive Chapter 1607 benefits at the 40% rate. The member is entitled to Chapter 1607 benefits for 10 years from the date of eligibility.

CHAPTER 23

EDUCATION BENEFITS - MONTGOMERY G.I. BILL – SELECTED RESERVE (MGIB-SR), CHAPTER 1606

The Montgomery GI Bill-Selected Reserve Program is for members of the Selected Reserve, including the Army Reserve, Navy Reserve, Air Force Reserve, Marine Corps Reserve, Coast Guard Reserve, Army National Guard and Air National Guard. While the reserve components decide who is eligible for the program, VA makes the payments for the program. Chapter 1606 is the first educational program that does not require service in the *active* Armed Forces in order to qualify.

ELIGIBILITY REQUIREMENTS

Member must have signed a 6-year obligation to serve in the Selected Reserve after June 30, 1985. (Officers must have agreed to serve 6 years in addition to his or her original obligation.) For some types of training, it is necessary to have a 6-year commitment that began after September 30, 1990. Call (888) GIBILL-1 for more information;

> **Key Takeaways**
>
> The MGIB-SR program provides education and training benefits to members of the Selected Reserve
>
> You may be entitled to receive up to 36 months of education benefits
>
> Full time institutional training rates for this program begin at $369.00, effective October 1, 2016
>
> Apprenticeship and on-the-job training begins at a rate of $276.75 for the first six months of training

Member must have completed his or her Initial Active Duty for Training (IADT); Member must maintain Selected Reserve Status - Serve in a drilling Selected Reserve unit and remain in good standing;

Member must meet the requirement to receive a high school diploma or equivalency certificate before completing IADT. Member must remain in good standing while serving in an active Selected Reserve Unit;

Effective November 1, 2000, veterans and reservists can apply for MGIB-SR benefits any time after receiving their high school diploma or equivalency certificate. It no longer has to be received prior to the end of the individual's first period of active duty. If an individual enters active duty in the Selected Reserve (AGR, TAR, FTS) after November 29, 1989, he or she must have been eligible *before* November 29, 1989 in order to remain eligible.

ELIGIBILITY RESTRICTIONS

MGIB – AD:

An individual can't be eligible for MGIB – SR if he or she elected to have his or her service in the Selected Reserve credited toward establishing eligibility under the Montgomery GI Bill – Active Duty

ROTC (Reserve Officers' Training Corps) scholarship under section 2107 of title 10, Code:

An individual can't be eligible for MGIB – SR if he or she is receiving financial assistance through the Senior ROTC program under this section of the law.

Note: However, an individual may still be eligible for MGIB – SR if he or she receives financial assistance under *Section 2107a* of title 10, U.S. Code. This financial assistance program is for specially selected members of the Army Reserve and National Guard only. Individuals should check with their ROTC advisor for more information.

Note: There's no restriction on service academy graduates receiving MGIB – SR. Service academy graduates who received a commission aren't eligible under MGIB – AD.

If an individual enters Active Guard and Reserve (AGR) status, his or her eligibility for MGIB – SR will be suspended. He or she may be eligible for MGIB – AD. The individual may resume MGIB – SR eligibility after AGR status ends.

APPROVED COURSES

Individuals may receive benefits for a wide variety of training, including:
* Undergraduate degrees from a college or university;
* Beginning November 30, 1993, graduate degrees from a college or university;
* Accredited independent study programs leading to standard college degrees;
* Technical courses for a certificate at a college or university.

Individuals with 6-year commitments beginning after September 30, 1990 may take the following types of training:
* Courses leading to a certificate or diploma from business, technical, or vocational schools;
* Cooperative training;
* Apprenticeship or job training programs offered by companies;
* Correspondence training;
* Independent study programs;
* Flight training (Individuals must have a private pilot's license, and must meet the medical requirements for the desired license program before beginning training, and throughout the flight training program.)

VA may approve programs offered by institutions outside of the United States, when they are pursued at educational institutions of higher learning, and lead to a college degree. Individuals must receive VA approval prior to attending or enrolling in any foreign programs.

Eligibility for this program is determined by the Selected Reserve components. Payments for the program are made by the VA.

266

A state agency or VA must approve each program offered by a school or company.

If an individual is seeking a college degree, the school must admit the individual to a degree program by the start of the individual's third term.

RESTRICTIONS ON TRAINING

Benefits are not payable for the following courses:
- Courses paid by the military Tuition Assistance program, if student is enrolled at less than ½ time;
- Courses taken while student is receiving a Reserve Officers' Training Corps scholarship;
- Non-accredited independent study courses;
- Bartending and personality development courses;
- Any course given by radio;
- Self-improvement courses such as reading, speaking, woodworking, basic seamanship, and English as a 2nd language;
- Any course which is avocational or recreational in character;
- Farm-cooperative courses;
- Audited courses;
- Courses not leading to an educational, professional, or vocational objective;
- Courses previously taken and successfully completed;
- Courses taken by a Federal government employee under the *Government Employee's Training Act*;
- Courses taken while in receipt of benefits for the same program from the Office of Workers' Compensation Programs.

VA must reduce benefits for individuals in Federal, State, or local prisons after being convicted of a felony.

An individual may not receive benefits for a program at a proprietary school if he or she is an owner or official of the school.

PART-TIME TRAINING

Individuals unable to attend school full-time should consider going part-time. Benefit rates and entitlement charges are less than the full-time rates. For example, if a student receives full-time benefits for 12 months, the entitlement charge is 12 months. However, if the student receives ½ time benefits for 12 months, the charge is 6 months. VA will pay for less than ½ time training if the student is not receiving Tuition Assistance for those courses.

REMEDIAL, DEFICIENCY AND REFRESHER TRAINING

Remedial and deficiency courses are intended to assist a student in overcoming a deficiency in a particular area of study. Individuals may qualify for benefits for remedial, deficiency, and refresher courses if they have a 6-year commitment that began after September 30, 1990. In order for such courses to be approved, the courses must be deemed necessary for pursuit of a program of education.

Refresher training is for technological advances that occurred in a field of employment. The advance must have occurred while the student was on active duty, or after release.

There is an entitlement charge for these courses.

TUTORIAL ASSISTANCE

Students may receive a special allowance for individual tutoring performed after September 30, 1992, if they entered school at one-half time or more. To qualify, the student must have a deficiency in a subject. The school must certify the tutor's qualifications, and the hours of tutoring. Eligible students may receive a maximum monthly payment of $100.00. The maximum total benefit payable is $1,200.00.

There is no entitlement charge for the first $600.00 of tutorial assistance.

To apply for tutorial assistance, students must submit VA Form 22-1990t, "Application and Enrollment Certification for Individualized Tutorial Assistance." The form should be given to the certifying official in the office handling VA paperwork at the school for completion.

MONTHS OF BENEFITS / ENTITLEMENT CHARGED

Eligible members may be entitled to receive up to 36 months of education benefits. Benefit entitlement ends 10 years from the date the member becomes eligible for the program, or on the day the member leaves the Selected Reserve. (If a member's Reserve or National Guard unit was deactivated during the period October 1, 1991 through September 30, 1999, or if the member was involuntarily separated from service during this same period, eligibility for MGIB-SR benefits is retained for the full 10-year eligibility period. Eligibility for MGIB-SR benefits is also retained if a member is discharged due to a disability that was not caused by misconduct. Eligibility periods may be extended if a member is ordered to active duty.)

Individuals qualifying for more than one VA education program may receive a maximum of 48 months of benefits. For example, if a student used 30 months of Dependents' Educational Assistance, and is eligible for chapter 1606 benefits, he or she could have a maximum of 18 months of entitlement remaining.

Individuals are charged one full day of entitlement for each day of full-time benefits paid. For correspondence and flight training, one month of entitlement is charged each time VA pays one month of benefits. For cooperative programs, one month of entitlement is used for each month of benefits paid.

For apprenticeship and job training programs, the entitlement charge changes every 6 months. During the first 6 months, the charge is 75% of full time. For the second 6 months, the charge is 55% of full time. For the remainder of the program, the charge is 35% of full time.

RATES OF EDUCATIONAL ASSISTANCE PAY

The following basic monthly rates are effective October 1, 2017:

BASIC MONTHLY RATES MONTGOMERY G.I. BILL – SELECTED RESERVE (MGIB-SR), CHAPTER 1606				
Type of Training	Full-Time	Three-Quarter Time	One-Half Time	Less than ½ Time
Institutional	$375.00	281.00	187.00	93.75
Cooperative Training	$375.00 (Full-Time Only)			
Correspondence Training	Entitlement charged at the rate of one month for each $375.00 paid (Payment for correspondence courses is made at 55% of the approved charges for the course.)			
Apprenticeship On-The-Job Training -	First six months: $281.25 Second six months: $206.25 Remainder of program: $131.25			
Flight Training	Entitlement charged at the rate of one month for each $375.00 paid (Payment for flight training is made at 60% of the approved charges for the course, including solo hours.)			

ELIGIBILITY PERIODS

Under previous law, benefits typically ended upon separation from the Reserves. Section 530 of the *National Defense Authorization Act of 2008* **increased the time period that a reservist may use SRMGIB benefits to ten years after separation from the Reserves**, as long as the member's discharge characterization is honorable. **This revision is backdated to October 28, 2004.**

For individuals who separated from the Selected Reserve prior to 10/28/2004, generally benefits end the day of separation. For individuals who stayed in the Selected Reserve, generally benefits ended 14 years from the date the individual became eligible for the program.

Exceptions: If an individual stayed in the Selected Reserve, VA could generally extend the 14-year period if:

- The individual couldn't train due to a disability caused by Selected Reserve service; or
- The individual was activated for service in the Persian Gulf Era (which hasn't ended for purposes of VA education benefits); or
- The individual's eligibility expired during a period of his or her enrollment in training.

MISCELLANEOUS INFORMATION

Any change in educational, professional or vocational objectives is considered a "change of program." The law permits one change of program without prior VA approval, provided an individual's attendance, conduct and progress in the last program were satisfactory. Additional "changes of program" require prior VA approval. VA will not charge a change of program if the individual enrolls in a new program after successful completion of the immediately preceding program.

Once an individual starts receiving benefits, he must maintain satisfactory attendance, conduct and progress. The VA may stop benefits if an individual does not meet the standards set by the school. VA may later resume benefits if the individual reenters the same program at the same school, and the school approves the reentry, and certifies it to VA.

If the individual does not reenter the same program at the same school, VA may resume benefits if the cause of unsatisfactory attendance, conduct or progress has been removed; and the program that the student intends to pursue is suitable to his or her abilities, aptitudes and interests.

Effective November 1, 2000, VA education benefits can be paid (with some exceptions) for school breaks, if the breaks do not exceed 8 weeks; and the terms before and after the breaks are not shorter than the break. Prior to November 1 2000, VA education benefits could be paid only if the breaks did not exceed a calendar month.

APPLICATION FOR BENEFITS

When an individual becomes eligible for the program, his or her unit will provide the individual with a "Notice of Basic Eligibility, DD Form 2384," or DD Form 2384-1 (for persons who establish eligibility on or after October 1, 1990). The unit will also code the eligibility into the Department of Defense personnel system.

When the individual finds a school, program, company, apprenticeship or job-training program, there are two important steps that must be followed:
* Make sure the program is approved for VA training. Contact the local VA regional office if there are any questions.
* Complete VA Form 22-1990, "Application for Education Benefits." The completed form should be sent to the VA regional office with jurisdiction over the state where training will occur.

Following receipt of an application, VA will review it and advise if anything else is needed. If an individual has started training, the application of "Basic Eligibility" should be taken to the school, employer or union. The certifying official should complete VA Form 22- 1999, "Enrollment Certification," and send all the forms to VA.

PROCEDURES FOR RECEIPT OF MONTHLY PAYMENTS

After selecting a school and submitting an application to VA, the school official must complete an enrollment certification, and submit it to the appropriate VA regional office. If a student meets the basic eligibility requirements for benefits, and the program or course is approved, VA will process the enrollment based on certified training time.

VA will accept the Notice of Basic Eligibility to pay benefits for 120 days after an individual's eligibility date. If the eligibility date is more than 120 days before the training program starts, VA will not approve the claim unless the Department of Defense personnel system shows that the individual is eligible. Only a student's reserve component can update the DoD personnel system. VA cannot change an individual's eligibility record.

When VA approves a claim, it will issue a letter with the details of the benefits payable. The first payment should be received within a few days of receipt of the letter.

If a student is enrolled in a degree program at a college or university, he or she will receive payment after the first of each month for the training during the preceding month. If a student is enrolled in a certificate or diploma program at a business, technical, or vocational school, he or she will not receive payment until they have verified their attendance. Students will receive a "Student Verification of Enrollment Form 22-8979" each month, and must complete and return it to the appropriate VA regional office. After processing, VA will release a check.

If an individual is in an apprenticeship or job-training program, he or she will receive a form to report the hours worked each month. The form must be signed and given to the certifying official for the company or union. The certifying official must complete the form and send it to the appropriate VA regional office. After processing, VA will release a check.

If an individual is taking a correspondence course, he or she will receive a form each quarter, on which the student must show the number of lessons completed that quarter. The completed form should be sent to the school for certification of the number of lessons serviced during the quarter. The school will send the form to the appropriate VA regional office. After processing, VA will release a check. Payments are based on the number of lessons serviced by the school.

VA will send flight schools a supply of blank monthly certification of flight training forms. The school must complete the form by entering the number of hours, the hourly rate, and the total charges for flight training received during the month. The student should review and sign the completed form, and send it to the appropriate VA regional office. After processing, VA will release a check.

NOTE: It is against the law for schools to cash VA checks under a Power of Attorney Agreement.

TIMELY RECEIPT OF VERIFICATION FORMS AND CHECKS

Students taking courses leading to a degree at a college or university should receive their checks for each month by the fifth of the next month. If it is not received by then, the VA should be immediately contacted so that appropriate action can be taken.

Students taking courses leading to a certificate or diploma from a business, technical, or vocational school should receive their verification forms for each month by the fifth of the following month. If it is not received by then, the VA should be immediately contacted so that another form can be issued.

One a completed verification form has been submitted, the student should receive a check within 2 weeks. If a check is not received by then, the VA should immediately be contacted so that appropriate action can be taken.

ADVANCE PAYMENTS

An advance payment for the initial month, or partial month and the following month may be made, if:
- The school agrees to handle advance payments; and
- Training is one-half time or more; and

- A request is made by the individual in writing; and
- The VA receives the enrollment certification at least 30 days prior to the start of classes.

Advance payments are made out to the individual, and sent to the applicable school for delivery to the individual registration. VA cannot issue a check more than 30 days before classes start. Before requesting an advance payment, students should verify with the school certifying official that the school has agreed to process advance payments.

Requests for advance payments must be on VA Form 22-1999, Enrollment Certification, or a sheet of paper attached to the enrollment certification.

Once a student receives an advance payment at registration, the school must certify to VA that the student received the check. If a student reduces enrollment, or withdraws from all courses during the period covered by an advance payment, he or she must repay the overpayment to VA.

If an individual believes that the amount of a VA check is incorrect, the VA should be contacted before the check is cashed.

DIRECT DEPOSIT

Payments can be sent directly to a student's savings or checking account through Direct Deposit (Electronic Funds Transfer). To sign up for direct deposit by phone, students must call (877) 838-2778.

STUDENT RESPONSIBILITIES

To ensure timely receipt of correct payments, students should be sure to promptly notify the VA of:
- Any change in enrollment;
- Any change in address;
- Any change in selected reserve status (If an individual changes units or components, both the old and new units must report the change to VA through the components' eligibility data systems.)

In addition, students should use reasonable judgment when accepting and cashing a check. All letters from VA about monthly rates and effective dates should be read carefully. If a student thinks the amount of a VA check is wrong, VA should be contacted **before** cashing the check. Any incorrect checks should be returned to VA.

If a student cashes a check for the wrong amount, he or she will be liable for repayment of any resulting overpayment.

If an individual does not participate satisfactorily in the Selected Reserve, his or her eligibility ends. His or her component can require that a penalty be paid, based on a portion of payments received.

RECOVERY OF OVERPAYMENTS

VA must take prompt and aggressive action to recover overpayments. Students have the right to request a waiver of the overpayment, or verification that the amount is correct. If an overpayment is not repaid or waived, VA may add interest and collection fees to the debt. VA may also take one or more of the following actions to collect the debt:
- Withhold future benefits to apply to the debt;

- Refer the debt to a private collection agency;
- Recover the debt from any Federal income tax refund;
- Recover the debt from the salary (if student is a Federal employee);
- File a lawsuit in Federal court to collect the debt;
- Withhold approval of a VA home loan guarantee.
- An individual's reserve component will act to collect penalties caused by unsatisfactory participation in the reserve.

CHANGES IN ENROLLMENT

If a student withdraws from one or more courses after the end of the school's drop period, VA will reduce or stop benefits on the date of reduction or withdrawal. Unless the student can show that the change was due to *mitigating circumstances*, the student may have to repay **all** benefits for the course.

VA defines *mitigating circumstances* as "unavoidable and unexpected events that directly interfere with the pursuit of a course, and which are beyond the student's control.

Examples of reasons VA may accept include:
- Extended illness;
- Severe illness or death in immediate family;
- Unscheduled changes in employment; and
- Lack of child care.

Examples of reasons VA may not accept include:
- Withdrawal to avoid a failing grade;
- Dislike of the instructor; and
- Too many courses attempted.

(VA may ask the student to furnish evidence to support the reason for change, such as physician or employer written statements.)

The first time a student withdraws from up to 6 credit hours, VA will "excuse" the withdrawal, and pay benefits for the period attended.

If a student receives a grade that does not count toward graduation, all benefits for the course may have to be repaid.

If a student receives a non-punitive grade, the school will notify VA, and VA may reduce or stop benefits. The student may not have to repay the benefits if he or she can show that the grades were due to mitigating circumstances.

WORK-STUDY PROGRAMS

Students may be eligible for an additional allowance under a work-study program that allows students to perform work for VA in return for an hourly wage. Students may perform outreach services under VA supervision, prepare and process VA paperwork, work at a VA medical facility or National Cemetery, or perform other approved activities.

Students must attend school at the three-quarter of full-time rate.

VA will select students for the work-study program based on different factors. Such factors include:

- Disability of the student;
- Ability of the student to complete the work-study contract before the end of his or her eligibility for education benefits;
- Job availability within normal commuting distance to the student

273

VA will give the highest priority to a veteran who has a service-connected disability or disabilities rated by VA at 30% or more.

The number of applicants selected will depend on the availability of VA-related work at the school or at VA facilities in the area.

Students may work during or between periods of enrollment, and can arrange with VA to work any number of hours during his or her enrollment. However, the maximum number of hours a student may work is 25 times the number of weeks in the enrollment period.

Students will earn an hourly wage equal to the Federal or State minimum wage, whichever is greater. If a student works at a college or university, the school **may** pay the difference between the amount VA pays and the amount the school normally pays other work-study students doing the same job.

Students interested in taking part in a work-study program must complete VA Form 22-8691, Application for Work-Study Allowance. Completed forms should be sent to the nearest VA regional office.

EDUCATIONAL COUNSELING

VA can provide services to help eligible individuals understand their educational and vocational strengths and weaknesses and to plan:

An educational or training goal, and the means by which the goal can be reached; or An employment goal for which an individual qualifies on the basis of present training or experience.

VA can also help plan an effective job search. Counseling is available for:
* Service members eligible for VA educational assistance; and
* Service members on active duty and within 180 days of discharge; or
* Veterans with discharges that are not dishonorable, who are within one year from date of discharge.

VOCATIONAL REHABILITATION

Veterans may qualify for Training and Rehabilitation under Chapter 31 of Title 38, United States Code, if:
* The veteran has a service-connected disability or disabilities rated by VA at 20% or more; and
* The veteran received a discharge from active duty that was not dishonorable; and
* The veteran has an employment handicap.

Veterans may also qualify with a service-connected disability or disabilities rated by VA at 10%, and:
* The veteran has a serious employment handicap; or
* The veteran first applied for vocational rehabilitation benefits before November 1, 1990, reapplied after that date, and has an employment handicap.

Vocational rehabilitation helps disabled veterans become independent in daily living. Veterans may also receive assistance in selecting, preparing for, and securing employment that is compatible with their interests, talents, skills, physical capabilities, and goals.

To apply for vocational rehabilitation, VA for 28-1900, Disabled Veterans Application for Vocational Rehabilitation, must be completed and sent to the nearest VA regional office.

APPEAL OF VA DECISION

VA decisions on education benefits may be appealed within one year of the date an individual receives notice of a VA decision. Examples of VA decisions include:

- Training time,
- Change of program,
- School or course approval.

If a service member disagrees with a decision about his or her basic eligibility, he or she must contact the unit, National Guard Education Officer, or Army Reserve Education Services Officer. VA does not have authority under the law to reverse eligibility determinations. If the eligibility status is corrected, VA will pay benefits for periods during which the individual was eligible.

CHAPTER 24

LIFE INSURANCE

VA insurance programs were developed to provide insurance benefits for veterans and servicemembers who may not be able to get insurance from private companies because of a service connected disability or because of the extra risks involved in military service.

VA has responsibility for veterans' and servicemembers' life insurance programs. Listed below are the eight life insurance programs managed by VA. The first four programs listed are closed to new issues. The last four are still issuing new policies.

USGLI

In 1917, America entered the war against Germany. Shortly thereafter, Congress approved issuance of Government life insurance to servicemembers under what was known as the War Risk Insurance program. Congress took this action because commercial life insurance companies either excluded protection against the hazards of war or charged premiums that were much higher than normal rates. During World War I, over 4 million policies were issued.

In 1919, Congress established the United States Government Life Insurance (USGLI) program to manage World War I policies and new policies issued thereafter. The program was closed to all new issues on April 25, 1951. USGLI policies could be retained by the insured even after his or her military service ended. Today there are just under 8,000 policies still in force and the average age of policyholders is 88 years.

Policies were issued in a variety of permanent plans and as renewable term insurance. The maximum face amount of a USGLI policy is $10,000. All USGLI policies were declared paid-up as of January 1, 1983 meaning that no further premium payments were due. Annual dividends continue to be paid on these policies.

> **Key Takeaways**
>
> Servicemembers' Group Life Insurance (SGLI) is a low-cost term life insurance program
>
> Veterans' Group Life Insurance (VGLI) allows veterans to convert SGLI to a civilian program of lifetime renewable term coverage after separate from service
>
> Family Servicemembers' Group Life Insurance (FSGLI) insures spouses and children of servicemembers with SGLI coverage

NATIONAL SERVICE LIFE INSURANCE

The National Service Life Insurance (NSLI) program was created on October 8, 1940, to manage the insurance needs of World War II service personnel. Over 22 million NSLI policies were issued from 1940 until the program was closed to new issues on April 25, 1951. Policies were issued under a variety of permanent plans and as renewable term insurance.

Today there are just over 950,000 policies still in force and the average age of policyholders is 81 years. Annual dividends are paid on these policies. The maximum face amount of a policy is $10,000. However, this limit does not include paid-up additional insurance which can be purchased with the annual dividends. Certain disability benefits are available under these policies for policyholders who become totally disabled before their 65th birthday.

VETERANS' SPECIAL LIFE INSURANCE (KOREAN WAR PROGRAM)

The *Insurance Act of 1951* established a program to meet the insurance needs of Korean War service personnel and veterans. During this period, all service members on active duty were covered by $10,000 of free insurance under a program known as Servicemen's Indemnity.

They remained covered under Servicemen's Indemnity for 120 days after their discharge. Newly discharged veterans could then apply for Veterans Special Life Insurance (VSLI) which was renewable term insurance. The VSLI program was closed to new issues at the end of 1956. Effective January 1, 1959, VSLI term policies could be converted to permanent plans of insurance or exchanged for a limited convertible term policy. Today there are 181,000 policies still in force and the average age of policyholders is 75 years. Annual dividends are paid on these policies.

The maximum face amount of a policy is $10,000. However, this limit does not include paid-up additional insurance which can be purchased with the annual dividends. Certain disability benefits are available under these policies for policyholders who become totally disabled before their 65th birthday.

SERVICE-DISABLED VETERANS INSURANCE-S-DVI (1951- PRESENT) (POLICY PREFIX - RH OR ARH)

The only new insurance issued between 1957 and 1965 to either servicemembers or veterans was Service-Disabled Veterans Insurance. This insurance was (and still is) available to veterans with a service-connected disability.

S-DVI, also called "RH Insurance" is available in a variety of permanent plans, as well as term insurance. Policies are issued for a maximum face amount of $10,000.

VI is open to veterans separated from the service on or after April 25, 1951, who receive a service-connected disability rating of 0% or greater. New policies are still being issued under this program.

To apply for Supplemental S-DVI, you must file "VA Form 29-4364, Application for Supplemental Service-Disabled Veterans (RH) Life Insurance" or send a letter requesting this insurance over your signature. You must apply for the coverage within one year from notice of the grant of waiver of premiums.

ELIGIBILITY FOR S-DVI INSURANCE ("RH")

Veterans are eligible to apply for S-DVI if they meet the following four criteria:
* They have received a rating for a service-connected disability (even if only 0%).
* They were released from active duty under any other condition than dishonorable on or after April 25, 1951.
* They are in good health except for any service-related condition.
* They apply for the insurance within two years from the date service-connection is established.

ELIGIBILITY FOR SUPPLEMENTAL S-DVI ("SUPPLEMENTAL RH")

The Veterans' Benefits Act of 2010, provided for $30,000 of supplemental coverage to S-DVI policyholders. Premiums may not be waived on this supplemental coverage. S-DVI policyholders are eligible for this supplemental coverage if:
* They are eligible for a waiver of premiums.
* They apply for the coverage within one year from notice of the grant of waiver.
* Are under age 65.

GRATUITOUS S-DVI ("ARH")

Congress enacted legislation in 1959 to protect veterans who become incompetent from a service-connected disability while eligible to apply for S-DVI, but who die before an application is filed. "ARH" insurance is:
* Issued posthumously;
* Payable to a preferred class of the veteran's relatives;
* Payable in a lump sum only.

PREMIUMS FOR S-DVI INSURANCE

The premiums charged for this coverage are:
* Based on the rates a healthy individual would have been charged when the program began in 1951.
* Insufficient to pay all of the claims because the program insures many veterans with severe disabilities.
* Waived for totally disabled veterans (27% of S-DVI policyholders).
* Supplemented on an annual basis by Congressional appropriations.

Effective November 1, 2000, the VA "capped" premium rates at the age 70 rate. This means that a term policyholder's premium will never increase over the age 70 -premium rate.

There are no reserves or surplus funds in this program. Therefore, dividends are *not* paid.

DISABILITY PROVISIONS

VI policies (except supplemental coverage) provide for the following disability benefits:
* A waiver of premiums at no extra premium based on the insured's total disability lasting six months or longer and starting before age 65;
* A total disability premium waiver in cases where the disability commenced prior to the effective date of the policy, providing the disability is service- connected.
* The optional Total Disability Income Provision is not available under this program.

FILING A DEATH CLAIM

To file a death claim, the beneficiary should complete "VA Form 29-4125, Claim for One Sum Payment."

The completed form should be mailed or faxed, along with a death certificate to:
Department of Veterans Affairs Regional Office and Insurance Center
PO Box 7208
Philadelphia, PA 19101
Fax: (215) 381-3561

If the beneficiary desires monthly payments instead of one lump sum, additional information is needed. The beneficiary should call the Insurance Center at (800) 669- 8477 for instructions.

CUSTOMER SERVICE

Any questions regarding USGLI should be directed to the VA Life Insurance Program at (800) 669-8477.

VETERANS' REOPENED INSURANCE

In 1964, Congress enacted legislation which provided for a limited one year reopening of the National Service Life Insurance (NSLI) and the Veterans Special Life Insurance (VSLI) programs.

From May 1,1965 until May 2, 1966, disabled veterans who had been eligible to obtain NSLI or VSLI between 1940 and 1956, could once again apply for Government life insurance. This coverage was available only to disabled veterans. Approximately 228,000 policies were issued. No term insurance policies were issued. Today there are still over 41,000 Veterans Reopened Insurance policies in force. Annual dividends are paid on these policies. The maximum face amount of a policy is$10,000.

However, this limit does not include paid-up additional insurance which can be purchased with the dividends that are paid annually on these policies. Certain disability benefits are available under these policies for policyholders who become totally disabled before their 65th birthday.

SERVICEMEMBERS' GROUP LIFE INSURANCE - SGLI (1965-PRESENT)

2017 Update: SGLI Online Enrollment System Now Live

Beginning October 1, 2017, Army members can manage their Servicemembers' Group Life Insurance (SGLI) coverage using the SGLI Online Enrollment System (SOES). Army members join the Navy and Air Force in using the new system. Navy began using SOES on April 5, 2017 and Air Force on August 2, 2017. Air Force, Navy, and Army members should look for information from their service about when they should access SOES to confirm and certify their SGLI elections.

SOES access for other branches of service is planned for release on the following schedule*:

Marine Corps   February 2018
Coast Guard, National Oceanic and Atmospheric Administration – March 2018

*This schedule is subject to change.

SGLI provides automatic life insurance coverage of $400,000 to Servicemembers upon enlistment. Members with SGLI also get automatic coverage for their dependent children and spouses (unless the child or spouse is insured under SGLI as a Servicemember) under the Family SGLI program and traumatic injury protection (TSGLI). Servicemembers with full-time SGLI coverage will no longer have to complete a paper SGLV-8286 to make changes to their coverage or beneficiary elections. Instead, these Servicemembers can use the online system, SOES, to manage the amount of their SGLI and spouse coverage and to designate or update beneficiaries.

To access SOES, go to www.dmdc.osd.mil/milconnect, sign in, and go to Benefits, Life Insurance SOES- SGLI Online Enrollment System. Servicemembers can log in with their CAC or with their DS Logon using Internet Explorer as soon as they receive notice that SOES access is available. Servicemembers can then make sure their SGLI coverage and beneficiaries are up-to-date.

SGLI is supervised by the Department of Veterans Affairs and is administered by the Office of Servicemembers' Group Life Insurance (OSGLI) under terms of a group insurance contract.

Effective December 1, 2005, a new program of insurance was created under SGLI, called Traumatic Servicemembers' Group Life Insurance (TSGLI). This coverage provides servicemembers protection against loss due to traumatic injuries and is designed to provide financial assistance to members so their loved ones can be with them during their recovery from their injuries. The coverage ranges from $25,000 to $100,000 depending on the nature of the injury.

(See following section for further information regarding Traumatic Injury Coverage.)

ELIGIBILITY FOR SGLI

Full-time coverage is available for:
- Commissioned, warrant and enlisted members of the Army, Navy, Air Force, Marine Corps and Coast Guard;
- Commissioned members of the National Oceanic and Atmospheric Administration and the Public Health Service;
- Cadets or midshipmen of the four United States Service Academies;
- Ready Reservists scheduled to perform at least 12 periods of inactive training per year.
- Members of the Individual Ready Reserves who volunteer for assignment to a mobilization category.
- Part-time coverage is available for eligible members of the Reserves who do not qualify for full-time coverage.

COVERAGE AMOUNTS

Effective September 1, 2005 coverage in the SGLI Program increased from $250,000 to $400,000. Coverage must be elected in $50,000 increments.
A special death gratuity of $150,000 was approved for survivors of servicemembers who:
- Died from October 7, 2001 to September 1, 2005, and
- Died while on active duty.

SGLI Coverage Is:

- Automatic at the time of entry into a period of active duty or reserve status.
- Available in $50,000 increments up to the maximum of $400,000 of insurance.

Members may decline coverage or may elect reduced coverage by contacting their personnel officer and completing "Form 8286, SGLI Election and Certificate." If such a member later wishes to obtain or increase coverage, proof of good health will be required.

NOTE: *Reservists called to active duty, are* **automatically** *insured for $400,000 regardless of whether or not they had previously declined coverage, or elected a lesser amount of coverage while on reserve duty.*

COVERAGE PERIODS

Full-time SGLI coverage for members on active duty or active duty for training and members of the Ready Reserve will terminate:

The 120th day after separation or release from duty, or separation or release from assignment to a unit or position of the Ready Reserve;

For members who are totally disabled on the date of separation or release, at the end of the last day of one year following separation or release or at the end of the day on which the insured ceases to be totally disabled, whichever is earlier, but in no event earlier than

- 120 days following separation or release from such duty; **(NOTE: Refer to important updated information following #4,below.)**
- At the end of the 31st day of a continuous period of: Absence without leave;
- Confinement by military authorities under a court-martial sentence involving total forfeiture of pay and allowances; or
- Confinement by civilian authorities under sentence adjudged by a civilian court.

*Note: Any insurance terminated as the result of the absence or confinement, together with any beneficiary designation in effect at the time the insurance was terminated, will be automatically restored as of the date the member returns to duty with pay.

The last day of the month in which the member files with the uniformed service, written notice of an election not to be insured.

SGLI DISABILITY EXTENSION INCREASED TO TWO YEARS

On June 15, 2006, the President signed P.L. 109- 233, the *Veterans' Housing Opportunity & Benefits Improvement Act of 2006.* The law extends the period of Servicemembers' Group Life Insurance (SGLI) coverage for totally disabled veterans following separation from active duty or active duty for training to the earlier of:

- The date on which the insured ceases to be totally disabled; or

- The date that is two years after separation or release,

The law makes identical changes with respect to certain reserve assignments in which the individual performs active duty or volunteers for assignment to a mobilization category.

The SGLI Disability Extension is available to you if you are totally disabled at time of

discharge. To be considered totally disabled, you must have a disability that prevents you from being gainfully employed OR have one of the following conditions, regardless of your employment status:

- Permanent loss of use of both hands Permanent loss of use of both feet
- Permanent loss of use of both eyes
- Permanent loss of use of one hand and one foot Permanent loss of use of one foot and one eye Permanent loss of use of one hand and one eye Total loss of hearing in both ears
- Organic loss of speech (lost ability to express oneself, both by voice and whisper, through normal organs for speech - being able to speak with an artificial appliance

is disregarded in determination of total disability)

PART-TIME COVERAGE TERMINATES AS FOLLOWS:

Part-time coverage is in effect only on the days of active duty or active duty for training, and the hours of inactive duty training, including period of travel to and from duty. A temporary termination of coverage occurs at the end of each such period of duty, including travel time, and coverage is resumed at the commencement of the next period of covered duty or travel.

When part-time coverage is extended for 120 days as the result of a disability, the extended coverage terminates at the end of the 120th day following the Reservist active or inactive period during which the disability was incurred or aggravated.

Unless extended for 120 days because of disability as referred to above, eligibility for part-time coverage terminates at the end of the last day of the member's obligation to perform such duty.

If a member files with the uniformed service a written notice of an election not to be insured, coverage terminates on the last day of the period of active duty or active duty for training, or at the end of the period of inactive duty training, including travel time while returning from such duty during which the election is filed. If the election is filed with a member's uniformed service other than during a period of active duty, active duty for training, or inactive duty the coverage is terminated immediately.

BENEFICIARY SELECTION

Any beneficiary can be named. If none is selected, the insurance is distributed, by law, in the following order:

- Spouse; or
- Children; or
- Parents; or
- Executor of estate; or
- Other next of kin.

An insured should designate a beneficiary by completing "Form SGVL 8286, Servicemembers' Group Life Insurance Election and Certificate." The completed form should be submitted to the individual's uniformed service.

OPTIONS FOR PAYMENT OF POLICY PROCEEDS

SGLI proceeds can be paid in a lump sum *or* over a 36-month period.

ALLIANCE ACCOUNT

If the proceeds are to be paid in a lump sum then beneficiaries of SGLI and VGLI will receive the payment of their insurance proceeds via an "*Alliance Account*". Rather than the traditional single check for the full amount of insurance proceeds, the beneficiary receives a checkbook for an interest-bearing account from which the beneficiary can write a check for any amount from $250 up to the full amount of the proceeds. The Alliance Account:
Earns interest at a competitive rate; Is guaranteed by Prudential;
Gives the beneficiary time to make important financial decisions while their funds are secure and earning interest ;
Gives them instant access to their money at all times.

ACCELERATED BENEFITS

On November 11, 1998, the President signed legislation authorizing the payment of

"Accelerated Benefits" in the SGLI and VGLI programs subject to the following:

- Terminally ill insureds will have access of up to 50% of the face amount of their coverage during their lifetime.
- This money will be available in increments of$5,000.
- An insured must have a medical prognosis of life expectancy of9 months or less.

INSURANCE OPTIONS AFTER SEPARATION FROM SERVICE

When released from active duty or the Reserve, members with full-time SGLI coverage can convert their coverage to Veterans Group Life Insurance *or* to an individual commercial life insurance policy with any one of 99 participating commercial insurance companies.

FILING DEATH CLAIMS

A beneficiary may file a claim for VGLI proceeds by submitting *Form SGLV 8283, Claim For Death Benefits*, to:

Office of Servicemembers' Group Life Insurance (OSGLI)
PO Box 70173
Philadelphia, PA 19176-9912
SGLI Traumatic Injury (TSGLI) Claims

TAXATION

SGLI proceeds that are payable at the death of the insured are excluded from gross income for tax purposes. (The value of the proceeds, however, may be included in determining the value of an estate, and that estate may ultimately be subject to tax.)

If SGLI proceeds are paid to a beneficiary in 36 equal installments, the interest portion included in these installments is also exempt from taxation. In addition, delayed settlement interest (interest accrued from the date of the insured's death to the date of settlement) is also exempt from taxation.

A beneficiary is not required to report to the Internal Revenue Service any installment interest or delayed settlement interest received in addition to the proceeds.

CUSTOMER SERVICE

Any questions regarding SGLI should be directed to the Office of Servicemembers' Group Life Insurance (OSGLI) at (800)419-1473.

TRAUMATIC INJURY PROTECTION UNDERSERVICEMEMBERS' GROUP LIFE INSURANCE (TSGLI)

TSGLI is a program that provides automatic traumatic injury coverage to all servicemembers covered under the Servicemembers' Group Life Insurance (SGLI) program. Every member who has SGLI also has TSGLI effective December 1, 2005. This coverage applies to active duty members, reservists, funeral honors duty and one-day muster duty. The premium for TSGLI is a flat rate of $1 per month for most service members This benefit is also provided retroactively for members who incur severe losses as a result of traumatic injury between October 7, 2001 and December 1, 2005 if the loss was the direct result of injuries incurred in Operations Enduring Freedom or Iraqi Freedom.

For the purposes of TSGLI only, "incurred in Operation Enduring Freedom or Operation Iraqi Freedom" means that the member must have been deployed outside the United States on orders in support of OEF or OIF or serving in a geographic location that qualified the service member for the Combat Zone Tax Exclusion under the Internal Revenue Service Code.

The service member is the beneficiary of TSGLI. The member cannot name someone other than himself or herself as the TSGLI beneficiary. If the member is incompetent, the benefit will be paid to his or her guardian or attorney-in-fact. If the service member is deceased, the TSGLI payment will be made to the beneficiary or beneficiaries of the member's basic SGLI.

TSGLI coverage will pay a benefit of between $25,000 and $100,000 depending on the loss directly resulting from the traumatic injury.

In 2011 the VA announced that servicemembers with severe injuries to the genitourinary organs are now eligible for Servicemembers' Group Life Insurance Traumatic Injury Protection (TSGLI). The first payments for eligible veterans and servicemembers began December 1, 2011. Eligibility is retroactive to injuries received on or after October 7, 2001.

EXPANSION OF COVERED LOSSES

Loss of Sight
Loss of Sight lasting 120 days or more is considered as "permanent", qualifying the service member for the same payment rate as for permanent loss of sight ($100,000 for both eyes, $50,000 for one eye).

Uniplegia
Uniplegia (complete and total paralysis of one limb) has been added to the schedule of losses with payment at $50,000.

Amputation of the Hand

The definition of amputation of the hand has been expanded to include loss of four fingers (on the same hand) or loss of thumb, with payment remaining at $50,000 for one affected hand and $100,000 for both hands.

Amputation of the Foot
The definition of amputation of the foot has been expanded to include loss of all toes, with the payment remaining at $50,000 for one affected foot and $100,000 for both feet.

Loss of Four Toes
A new category has been created for loss of four toes (on the same foot and not including the big toe) with payment at $25,000 for one affected foot and $50,000 for both feet.

Loss of Big Toe
A new category has been created for the loss of the big toe, with payment at $25,000 for one affected foot and $50,000 for both feet.

Limb Salvage
Coverage has been expanded to include limb salvage (multiple surgeries intended to save a limb rather than amputate) with payment equivalent to amputation.

Burns
The burn standard, currently 3rd degree (full thickness) burns to at least 30% of face or body, has been expanded to include 2nd degree (partial thickness) burns to at least 20% of the face or body.

Hospitalization as a Proxy for ADL Loss
Continuous 15-day inpatient hospital care is deemed a proxy for the first ADL eligibility

period for OTI (Other Traumatic Injury) and TBI (Traumatic Brain Injury) claims.

Facial Reconstruction
Facial Reconstruction, required as a result of traumatic avulsion of the face or jaw that causes discontinuity defects, has been added to the schedule of losses, with payment levels of $25,000 to $75,000, depending upon the severity of the injury.

Losses to the Genitourinary System
Effective beginning in 2011, the VA amended its regulations to add certain genitourinary system injuries to the Schedule of Covered Losses. These are injuries that occur to the genitals or urinary system. Payments range from $25,000 to $50,000 and are retroactive to October 7, 2001. The new losses added to the TSGLI Schedule of Covered Losses include the following:

- Anatomical loss of penis
- Permanent loss of use of the penis
- Anatomical loss of one or both of the testicles
- Permanent loss of use of both testicles
- Anatomical loss of the vulva, uterus or vaginal canal
- Permanent loss of use of the vulva or vaginal canal
- Anatomical loss of one or both ovaries
- Permanent loss of use of both ovaries
- Total and permanent loss of urinary system function

SCHEDULE OF LOSSES

For losses listed in Part I, multiple injuries resulting from a single traumatic event may be combined with each other and treated as one loss for purposes of a single payment (except where noted otherwise), however, the total payment amount MAY NOT exceed $100,000.

For losses listed in Part II, payment amounts MAY NOT be combined with payment amounts in Part I - only the higher amount will be paid. The total payment amount MAY NOT exceed $100,000 for multiple injuries resulting from a single traumatic event.

PART I

Loss	Payment Amount
1. Sight: Total and permanent loss of sight OR loss of sight that has lasted 120 days For each eye	$50,000
2. Hearing: Total and permanent loss of hearing For one ear For both ears	$25,000 $100,000
3. Speech: Total and permanent loss of speech	$50,000
4. Quadriplegia: complete paralysis of all four limbs	$100,000
5. Hemiplegia: complete paralysis of the upper and lower limbs on one side of the body	$100,000
6. Paraplegia: complete paralysis of both lower limbs	$100,000

7.	Uniplegia: complete paralysis of one limb* *Note: Payment for uniplegia of arm cannot be combined with loss 9, 10 or 14 for the same arm. Payment for uniplegia of leg cannot be combined with loss 11, 12, 13 or 15 for the same leg.*	$50,000
8.	Burns: 2nd degree or worse burns to at least 20% of the body including the face OR, at least 20% of the face	$100,000
9.	Amputation of hand: Amputation at or above the wrist For each hand* *Note: Payment for loss 9 cannot be combined with payment for loss 10 for the same hand.*	$50,000
10.	Amputation of 4 fingers on 1 hand OR thumb alone: Amputation at or above the metacarpophalangeal joint For each hand	$50,000
11.	Amputation of foot: Amputation at or above the ankle For each foot* *Note: Payment for loss 11 cannot be combined with payments for losses 12 or 13 for the same foot.*	$50,000
12.	Amputation of all toes including the big toe on 1 foot: Amputation at or above the metatarsophalangeal joint For each foot *Note: Payment for loss 12 cannot be combined with payments for loss 13 for the same foot.*	$50,000
13.	Amputation of big toe only, OR other 4 toes on 1 foot: Amputation at or above the metatarsophalangeal joint For each foot	$25,000
14.	Limb salvage of arm: Salvage of arm in place of amputation For each arm* *Note: Payment for loss 14 cannot be combined with payments for losses 9 or 10 for the same arm.*	$50,000
15.	Limb salvage of leg: Salvage of leg in place of amputation For each leg* *Note: Payment for loss 15 cannot be combined with payments for losses 11, 12 or 13 for the same leg.*	$50,000
16.	Facial Reconstruction – reconstructive surgery to correct traumatic avulsions of the face or jaw that cause discontinuity defects.	
	Jaw – surgery to correct discontinuity loss of the upper or lower jaw	$75,000

	Nose – surgery to correct discontinuity loss of 50% or more of the cartilaginous nose	$50,000
	Lips – surgery to correct discontinuity loss of 50% or more of the upper or lower lip For one lip For both lips	$50,000 $75,000
	Eyes – surgery to correct discontinuity loss of 30% or more of the periorbita For each eye	$25,000
	Facial Tissue – surgery to correct discontinuity loss of the tissue in 50% or more of any of the following facial subunits: forehead, temple, zygomatic, mandibular, infraorbital or chin. For each facial subunit	$25,000
	Note 1: Injuries listed under facial reconstruction may be combined with each other, but the maximum benefit for facial reconstruction may not exceed $75,000. Note 2: Any injury or combination of injuries under facial reconstruction may also be combined with other injuries listed in Part I and treated as one loss, provided that all injuries are the result of a single traumatic event.	
17.	Coma from traumatic injury AND/OR Traumatic Brain Injury resulting in inability to perform at least 2 Activities of Daily Living (ADL) at 15th consecutive day of coma or ADL loss	$25,000
	at 30th consecutive day of coma or ADL loss	An additional $25,000
	at 60th consecutive day of coma or ADL loss	An additional $25,000
	at 90th consecutive day of coma or ADL loss	An additional $25,000
18.	Hospitalization due to traumatic brain injury at 15th consecutive day of hospitalization Note 1: Payment for hospitalization replaces the first payment period in loss 17.	$25,000
	Note 2: Duration of hospitalization includes dates on which member is transported from the injury site to a facility described in § 9.20(e)(6)(xiii), admitted to the facility, transferred between facilities, and discharged from the facility.	

19.	Genitourinary Losses	
	Anatomical loss of the penis Anatomical loss of the penis is defined as amputation of the glans penis or any portion of the shaft of the penis above the glans penis (i.e. closer to the body) or damage to the glans penis or shaft of the penis that requires reconstructive surgery.	$50,000
	Permanent loss of use of the penis Permanent loss of use of the penis is defined as damage to the glans penis or shaft of the penis that results in complete loss of the ability to perform sexual intercourse that is reasonably certain to continue throughout the lifetime of the member.	$50,000
	Anatomical loss of one testicle Anatomical loss of the testicle(s) is defined as the amputation of, or damage to, one or both testicles that requires testicular salvage, reconstructive surgery, or both.	$25,000
	Anatomical loss of both testicles See above – Same definition as anatomical loss of one testicle	$50,000
	Permanent loss of use of both testicles Permanent loss of use of both testicles is defined as damage to both testicles resulting in the need for hormonal replacement therapy that is medically required and reasonably certain to continue throughout the lifetime of the member.	$50,000
	Anatomical loss of the vulva, uterus, or vaginal canal Anatomical loss of the vulva, uterus, or vaginal canal is defined as the complete or partial amputation of the vulva, uterus, or vaginal canal or damage to the vulva, uterus, or vaginal canal that requires reconstructive surgery.	$50,000
	Permanent loss of use of the vulva or vaginal canal Permanent loss of use of the vulva or vaginal canal is defined as damage to the vulva or vaginal canal that results in complete loss of the ability to perform sexual intercourse that is reasonably certain to continue throughout the lifetime of the member.	$50,000
	Anatomical loss of one ovary Anatomical loss of the ovary(ies) is defined as the amputation of one or both ovaries or damage to one or both ovaries that requires ovarian salvage, reconstructive surgery, or both.	$25,000

Anatomical loss of both ovaries See above – Same definition as anatomical loss of one ovary.	$50,000
Permanent loss of use of both ovaries Permanent loss of use of both ovaries is defined as damage to both ovaries resulting in the need for hormonal replacement therapy that is medically required and reasonably certain to continue throughout the lifetime of the member.	$50,000
Total and permanent loss of urinary system function Total and permanent loss of urinary system function is defined as damage to the urethra, ureter(s), both kidneys, bladder, or urethral sphincter muscle(s) that requires urinary diversion and/or hemodialysis, either of which is reasonably certain to continue throughout the lifetime of the member.	$50,000
Note 1: Losses due to genitourinary injuries may be combined with each other, but the maximum benefit for genitourinary losses may not exceed $50,000. Note 2: Any genitourinary loss may be combined with other (TSGLI) injuries listed in § 9.20(f)(1) through (18) and treated as one loss, provided that all losses are the result of a single traumatic event. However, the total payment may not exceed $100,000.	

PART II

	Loss	Payment Amount
20.	Traumatic injury resulting in inability to perform at least 2 Activities of Daily Living (ADL) at 30th consecutive day of ADL loss at 60th consecutive day of ADL loss at 90th consecutive day of ADL loss	$25,000 an additional $25,000
	at 120th consecutive day of ADL loss	an additional $25,000

| 21. | Hospitalization due to traumatic injury at 15th consecutive day of hospitalization

Note 1: Payment for hospitalization replaces the first payment period in loss 19.
Note 2: Duration of hospitalization includes dates on which member is transported from the injury site to a facility
Described in § 9.20(e)(6)(xiii), admitted to the facility, transferred between facilities, and discharged from the facility. | $25,000 | |

SERVICEMEMBERS' GROUP LIFE INSURANCE FAMILY COVERAGE

The *Veterans' Opportunities Act of 2001* extended life insurance coverage to spouses and children of members insured under the SGLI program, effective November 1, 2001.

AMOUNT OF COVERAGE

SGLI coverage is available in $50,000 increments up to the maximum of $400,000. Covered members receive 120 days of free coverage from their date of separation. Coverage can be extended for up to two years if the Servicemember is totally disabled at separation. Part-time coverage is also provided to Reserve members who do not qualify for full-time coverage (members covered part-time do not receive 120 days of free coverage).

If you are totally disabled at the time of separation (unable to work), you can apply for the SGLI Disability Extension, which provides free coverage for up to two years from the date of separation. At the end of the extension period, you automatically become eligible for VGLI, subject to premium payments.

ELIGIBILITY

Family coverage is available for the spouses and children of:

* Active duty servicemembers; and
* Members of the Ready Reserve of a uniformed service.

Note: *Family coverage is available only for members insured under the SGLI program. Family coverage is not available for those insured under the VGLI program.*

PREMIUMS

SGLI coverage for children is free. For monthly premiums for spouses, individuals should call (800) 419-1473.

DEPENDENT CHILD COVERAGE EXTENDED TO INCLUDE STILLBORN CHILDREN

Public law 110-389 expanded the Servicemembers' Group life Insurance (SGLI) program to include a member's "stillborn child" as an insurable dependent. SGLI dependent coverage provides for a $10,000 payment to the insured service member upon the death of the member's dependent child. The law was enacted October 10, 2008, and on November 18, 2009, regulations implementing section 402 of the *Veterans' Benefits Improvement Act of 2008*, were published in the Federal Register, and immediately went into effect. This change applies only for stillbirths on or after October 10, 2008, the effective date of PL110-389

DECLINING COVERAGE

If an individual does not want insurance coverage for a spouse, or wants a reduced amount of coverage, he or she must complete "form SGLV-82861, Family Coverage Election", and submit it to his or her personnel officer.

TERMINATION OF COVERAGE

Coverage for a spouse ends 120 days after any of the following events:
- The date elected in writing to terminate a spouse's coverage;
- The date elected in writing to terminate the service member's own coverage;
- The date of the service member's death;
- The date the service member's coverage terminates;
- The date of divorce.

A spouse can covert his or her coverage to a policy with a commercial company within 120 days following one of the events listed above. He or she should contact the Office of Servicemembers' Group Life Insurance at (800) 419-1473.

Coverage for a service member's children ends 120 days after any of the following events:
- The date elected in writing to terminate the service member's own coverage;
- The date the service member separates from service;
- The date of the service member's death;
- The date the child is no longer the service member's dependent.

No conversion options are available to children.

PAYMENT OF PROCEEDS

The service member is paid the proceeds due to the death of a spouse or child. If the service member were to die before payment could be made, the proceeds of a spouse or child claim would be paid to the member's beneficiary, as designated by the member.

VETERANS' GROUP LIFE INSURANCE – VGLI (1974- PRESENT)

VMLI is issued to those severely disabled veterans and servicemembers who have received grants for specially adapted housing from VA. These grants are issued to veterans and servicemembers whose movement or vision is substantially impaired because of their disabilities.

Policyholders have three options for their VMLI coverage. They may decline the increase and retain their pre-October level of VMLI coverage and premium, accept the maximum amount of VMLI coverage for which they are eligible, or select a different amount of VMLI coverage. Coverage may not exceed the maximum allowed by law, or their mortgage balance, whichever is less.

VGLI, like SGLI, is supervised by the Department of Veterans Affairs, but is administered by the Office of Servicemembers' Group Life Insurance (OSGLI). VGLI provides for the conversion of Servicemembers' Group Life Insurance to a five-year renewable term policy of insurance protection after a service member's separation from service.

Effective April 11, 2011, VGLI insureds who are under age 60 and have less than $400,000 in coverage can purchase up to $25,000 of additional coverage on each five-year anniversary of their coverage, up to the maximum $400,000. No medical underwriting is required for the additional coverage.

ELIGIBILITY FOR VGLI

Full-time coverage is available for the following members:
- Full-time SGLI insureds that are released from active duty or the Reserves, or;
- Ready Reservists who have part-time SGLI coverage, and who, while performing active duty or inactive duty for training for a period of less than 31 days, incur a

disability or aggravate a preexisting disability that makes them uninsurable at standard premium rates, or;
* Members of the Individual Ready Reserve (IRR) and Inactive National Guard (ING), or;
* A member of the Public Health Service (PHS) or Inactive Reserve Corps (IRC), or;
* A member who had part-time SGLI and who, while performing duty (or traveling directly to or from duty), suffered an injury or disability which renders him/her uninsurable at standard premium rates.

COVERAGE AMOUNTS

VGLI is issued in multiples of $10,000 up to a maximum of $400,000, but not for more than the amount of SGLI coverage the member had in force at the time of separation from active duty or the reserves.

VGLI RENEWAL

Members may renew their VGLI coverage under the following conditions:
* Members who have separated from service may renew their VGLI coverage for life in 5-year term periods.
* Members of the IRR or ING may renew their VGLI for additional 5-year term periods, as long as they remain in the IRR or ING.
   Rather than renew, a member also has the right at any time to **convert** VGLI to an individual commercial life insurance policy with any one of 99 participating commercial insurance companies.

INCREASING VGLI COVERAGE

You can increase your VGLI coverage by up to $25,000 on the five-year anniversary date of your coverage policy if you meet all of the following criteria:
* You have an active VGLI policy.
* You currently have less than $400,000 of VGLI.
* You will be under age 60 on your next policy anniversary date.

You must request the increase during the 120-day period prior to the 5-year anniversary of your policy

For more information on increasing your VGLI coverage, contact the Office of Servicemembers' Group Life Insurance online at osgli.osgli@prudential.com or by calling 1-800-419-1473.

HOW TO APPLY FOR VGLI

VGLI applications are mailed to eligible members, generally within 60 days after separation, and again shortly before the end of the 16-month application period. Applications are mailed to the address shown on the member's DD-Form 214 or equivalent separation orders. *It is the member's responsibility, however, to apply within the time limits, even if they do not receive an application in the mail.*

Applications should be mailed to:

Office of Servicemembers Group Life Insurance (OSGLI)
PO Box 70173
Philadelphia, PA 19176-9912

TIME LIMITS TO APPLY FOR VGLI

To be eligible, a member must apply for VGLI within the following time limits:

Ordinarily, a member must submit an application to the OSGLI with the required premium within 120 days following separation from service.

If a member is totally disabled at the time of separation from active duty and is granted extended free SGLI coverage, he or she may apply for VGLI anytime during the one-year period of extension.

Individuals who are assigned to the IRR and ING have 120 days after assignment to apply, without evidence of good health, and one year after that with evidence of good health. If an application or the initial premium has not been submitted within the time limits above, VGLI may still be granted if an application, the initial premium and **evidence of insurability** (good health) are submitted to OSGLI within 1 year and 120 days following termination of SGLI. **Applications will not be accepted after one year and 120 days.**

An application for an incompetent member may be made by a guardian, committee, conservator or curator. In the absence of a court appointed representative, the application may be submitted by a family member or anyone acting on the member's behalf.

VGLI PREMIUMS RATES

VGLI premium rates are determined by age group and amount of insurance. To lessen the high cost of term insurance at the older ages, a Decreasing Term Option is available, starting at age group 60 to 64. Under this option an insured pays a level premium for life, while the insurance amount declines by 25% for three subsequent five-year renewals. At that point, coverage remains level at 25% of the original insurance amount.

PAYMENT OF PREMIUMS

Once the VGLI application is approved, the OSGLI will send the insured a certificate and a supply of monthly premium payment coupons.

Premiums may be paid:

- Monthly;
- Quarterly;
- Semiannually;
- Annually;
- By monthly allotment from military retirement pay;
- By monthly deduction from VA compensation payments.

If the insured does not pay the premium when it is due, or within a grace period of 60 days, the VGLI coverage will lapse. If VGLI lapsed due to failure to pay the premiums on time, the insured will receive a notification of the lapse and a reinstatement form. The insured may apply to reinstate coverage at any time within 5 years of the date of the unpaid premium. If the insured applies for reinstatement within 6 months from the date of lapse, the individual only needs to provide evidence that he or she is in the same state of health on the date of reinstatement as on the date of lapse. Otherwise, the individual may need to provide proof of good health.

BENEFICIARY SELECTION

Any beneficiary can be named. If none is selected, the insurance is distributed, by law, in the following order:

- Spouse, or
- Children, or
- Parents, or

- Executor of estate, or
- Other next of kin.

To name a beneficiary, the insured must submit "Form SGLV 8712, Beneficiary Designation-Veterans' Group Life Insurance." The completed form should be sent to:

Office of Servicemembers Group Life Insurance (OSGLI)
PO Box 70173
Philadelphia, PA 19176-9912

When an insured converts SGLI to VGLI following separation from service, a new beneficiary designation form must be completed. If a new form is not filed, the SGLI beneficiary designation will be considered the VGLI designation for up to 60 days after the effective date of the VGLI. If a new beneficiary is not designated after this 60-day period, the proceeds would be paid "By Law" under the order of precedence in the law

ALLIANCE ACCOUNT

VGLI proceeds can be paid in a lump sum or over a 36-month period.
If the proceeds are to be paid in a lump sum then beneficiaries of SGLI and VGLI will receive the payment of their insurance proceeds via an "Alliance Account".

Rather than the traditional single check for the full amount of insurance proceeds, the beneficiary receives a checkbook for an interest-bearing account from which the beneficiary can write a check for any amount from $250 up to the full amount of the proceeds.

The Alliance Account:
- Earns interest at a competitive rate;
- Is guaranteed by Prudential;
- Gives the beneficiary time to make important financial decisions while their funds are secure and earning interest;
- Gives them instant access to their money at all times.

ACCELERATED BENEFITS

On November 11, 1998, the President signed legislation authorizing the payment of "Accelerated Benefits" in the SGLI and VGLI programs subject to the following:
- Terminally ill insureds will have access of up to 50 percent of the face amount of their coverage during their lifetime.
- This money will be available in increments of $5,000.
- An insured must have a medical prognosis of life expectancy of 9 months or less.

TAXATION

VGLI proceeds are exempt from taxation. Any installment interest or delayed settlement interest that a beneficiary receives in addition to the proceed is also exempt from taxation, and does not need to be reported to the IRS.

CUSTOMER SERVICE

Any questions regarding VGLI should be directed to the office of Servicemembers' Group Life Insurance (OSGLI) at (800) 419-1473.

VETERANS' MORTGAGE LIFE INSURANCE – VMLI (1971- PRESENT)

The Veterans' Mortgage Life Insurance (VMLI) program began in 1971, and is designed to provide financial protection to cover eligible veterans' home mortgages in the event of death. VMLI is issued to those severely disabled veterans, under age 70, who have received grants for Specially Adapted Housing from VA. (Refer to Chapter 6 of this book for information regarding Specially Adapted Housing.) **Veterans must apply for VMLI before their 70th birthday.**

The *Veterans Benefits Act of 2010* increased the maximum amount of VMLI coverage from $90,000 to $150,000, which became effective October 1, 2011. On January 1, 2012, the amount increased from $150,000 to 200,000, under the same law. The insurance is payable if the veteran dies before the mortgage is paid off. VA will pay the amount of money still owed on the mortgage up to $200,000.

The insurance is payable only to the mortgage lender. The day-to-day operations of the program are handled by the Philadelphia VAROIC.

COVERAGE AMOUNTS

VMLI coverage decreases as the insured's mortgage falls below $90,000. This reduced coverage cannot be reinstated. However, if the home is sold and a new home is purchased the veteran becomes eligible once again for the maximum amount of coverage.

PAYMENT OF VMLI PROCEEDS

Certain conditions apply to the payment of VMLI benefits:
- The insurance is payable at the death of the veteran only to the mortgage holder.
- If the title of the property is shared with anyone other than the veteran's spouse, the insurance coverage is only for the percentage of the title that is in the veteran's name.
- No insurance is payable if the mortgage is paid off before the death of the insured or if it was paid off by other mortgage insurance before the VMLI payment is made.

The insurance will be canceled for any of the following conditions:
- The mortgage is paid in full.
- Termination of the veteran's ownership of the property securing the loan.
- The request of the veteran.
- Failure of the veteran to submit timely statements or other required information.

PREMIUMS

Premiums are determined by the insurance age of the veteran, the outstanding balance of the mortgage at the time of application, and the remaining length of time the mortgage has to run. Veterans who desire insurance will be advised of the correct premium when it is determined.

Premiums *must* be paid by deduction from the veteran's monthly compensation or pension payments, if the veteran is receiving such payments. If such payments are not being received the veteran may make direct payments, on a monthly, quarterly, semiannual, or annual basis, to the VA Insurance Center in Philadelphia, Pennsylvania.

DIVIDEND OPTIONS

If a policyholder is eligible for a dividend, he or she may choose from several dividend options that are available:

Cash, paid to policyholder by US Treasury check.
Credit, held in account for the insured with interest. Can be used to prevent policy lapse. Will be refunded upon the insured's request, or will be included in the award to the beneficiary(ies) at the time of the insured's death.
Paid-Up Additions (PUA'S), used as a net single premium to purchase additional paid-up insurance. Available only on "V," "RS," "W," "J," "JR," and "JS" policies. PUA's will be whole life insurance if the basic insurance is an endowment policy.
Deposit, held in account for insured with interest. Available only on permanent plan policies. Considered part of the policy's cash value for the purpose of purchasing reduced paid-up insurance, or if the policy lapses, extended insurance (except for "K" or "JS" policies). Will be refunded upon the insured's request. Will be included in the award to the beneficiary(ies) at the time of the insured's death.
Premium, applied to pay premiums in advance.
Indebtedness, applied toward a loan or lien on a policy.
Net Cash, used to pay an annual premium with any remainder paid to the policyholder under the cash option.
Net PUA, used to pan an annual premium with any remainder used to purchase paid-up additional insurance.
Net Loan-Lien, used to pay an annual premium with any remainder used to reduce an outstanding loan or lien.

To change the method in which dividends are paid, individuals should speak with an Insurance Specialist at (800) 669-8477

MISCELLANEOUS INFORMATION ABOUT GOVERNMENT LIFE INSURANCE POLICIES

Power of Attorney is not acceptable for executing a change of beneficiary for government life insurance, even if certain state statutes allow it. Only a court appointed guardian that is recognized by state statutes can execute a beneficiary designation. If the state statute does not give the guardian broad powers to authorize a beneficiary change, a specific court order is needed to effectuate a change.

Assignment of government life insurance is not allowed, for any reason, nor can ownership of a policy be transferred. Only the insured can exercise the rights and privileges inherent in the ownership of the policy.

Policy Loans are available on permanent plans of insurance. The policyholder can take up to 94% of the reserve value of the policy, less any indebtedness. The policy cannot be lapsed, and premiums must be paid or waived at least one year before a policy has a loan value. Changes in interest rates are made on October 1 of each year, if warranted. Rate changes are tied to the "ten year constant maturities", U.S. Treasury securities index.

A policyholder can apply for a loan by filing *VA Form 29-1546, Application for Policy Loan.*

The completed form can be faxed to (215) 381-3580, or mailed to:

Department of Veterans Affairs Regional Office and Insurance Center
PO Box 7327
Philadelphia, PA 19101

An Annual Insurance Policy Statement is mailed to the insured on the policy anniversary date of each policy. The statement provides the insured with information about his or her VA insurance. The statement should be reviewed for accuracy each year, and the VA should be contacted immediately if there are any discrepancies.

CHAPTER 25

HOME LOAN GUARANTIES

BENEFITS

Purchase Loans help veterans purchase a home at a competitive interest rate, often without requiring a down payment or private mortgage insurance. Cash Out Refinance loans let eligible veterans take cash out of their home equity to pay off things such as debt, to make home improvements or to fund education. To be eligible veterans must have satisfactory credit, sufficient income to meet the expected monthly obligations, and a valid Certificate of Eligibility (COE).

Interest Rate Reduction Refinance Loans (IRRRL) are also called the Streamline Refinance Loan, and they can help veterans obtain a lower interest rate by refinancing an existing VA loan. This can be used only for veterans with an existing VA guaranteed loan on a property.

> **Key Takeaways**
>
> VA home loans are made by private lenders and guaranteed by the government if the veteran fails to repay the obligation
>
> There are service requirements for veterans to qualify for VA-backed home loans
>
> The Certificate of Eligibility (COE) is what's used to confirm eligibility for a VA home loan. To obtain a COE, veterans separated after 1979 should apply using DD Form 214

Native American Direct Loan (NADL) Program helps eligible Native American veterans finance the purchase, construction or improvement of homes on Federal Trust Land or reduce the interest rate on a VA loan. The veterans' tribal organization must participate in the VA direct loan program, and the veteran must have a valid COE.

Adapted Housing Grants help veterans with a permanent and total service-connected disability purchase or build an adapted home or to modify an existing home to account for their disability.

Other resources may be available to veterans depending on their state of residency, including property tax reductions.

GENERAL INFORMATION

The purpose of the VA loan guaranty program is to help veterans and active duty personnel finance the purchase of homes with competitive loan terms and interest rates.

The VA does not actually lend the money to veterans. VA guaranteed loans are made by private lenders, such as banks, savings & loans, or mortgage companies. The VA guaranty means the lender is protected against loss if the veteran fails to repay the loan.

The VA Loan Guaranty Service is the organization within the VA that has the responsibility of administering the home loan program.

In 2011 the VA announced that those veterans who qualify and submit to a short sale or deed in-lieu of foreclosure may be eligible to receive $1,500 in relocation assistance. The VA has instructed mortgage lenders to provide the funds in order to help borrowers cover the cost of moving or other expenses incurred during the process.

In 2012 Under *Public Law 112-154*, veterans in specially adapted housing or those in receipt of VA home loans, which have property hindered or destroyed by a natural disaster, became eligible to receive VA assistance. The law also extended the VA's authority to extend the guarantee of timely payment of principal and interest of mortgage loans. The VA's authority was also extended with regard to the collection of loan fees and adjustment of maximum home loan guarantee amounts.

VA GUARANTEED LOANS OFFER THE FOLLOWING IMPORTANT FEATURES:

- Equal opportunity for all qualified veterans to obtain a VA guaranteed loan.
- No down payment (unless required by the lender or the purchase price is more than the reasonable value of the property).
- Buyer's interest rate is negotiable.
- Buyer has the ability to finance the VA funding fee (plus reduced funding fees with a down payment of at least 5%, and exemption for veterans receiving VA compensation).
- Closing costs are comparable with other financing types (and may be lower).
- No mortgage insurance premiums are necessary.
- An assumable mortgage may be available.
- Buyer has the right to prepay without penalty.

VA GUARANTEED LOANS DO NOT DO THE FOLLOWING:

- Guarantee that a home is free of defects
- VA only guarantees the loan. It is the veteran's responsibility to assure that he or she is satisfied with the property being purchased. Veterans should seek expert advice as necessary, before legally committing to a purchase agreement.
- If a veteran has a home built, VA cannot compel the builder to correct construction defects, although VA does have the authority to suspend a builder from further participation in the VA home loan program.
- VA cannot guarantee the veteran is making a good investment.
- VA cannot provide a veteran with legal service.

USES FOR VA LOAN GUARANTIES

VA loan guaranties can be used for the following:

- To purchase, construct, or improve a home.
- To purchase and improve a home concurrently.
- To purchase a residential condominium or townhouse unit in a VA approved project. (If one veteran is purchasing the property, the total number of separate units cannot be more than 4.)
- To purchase a manufactured home or a manufactured home and manufactured home lot.

- To purchase and improve a manufactured home lot on which to place a manufactured home which the veteran already owns and occupies.
- To refinance an existing home loan.
- To refinance an existing VA loan to reduce the interest rate, and make energy-efficient improvements.
- To refinance an existing manufactured home loan in order to acquire a lot.
- To improve a home by installing a solar heating and/or cooling system, or other energy efficient improvements.

Veterans must certify that they plan to live in the home they are buying or building in order to qualify for a VA loan guaranty.

VA loan guaranties are available only for property located in the United States, its territories, or possessions (Puerto Rico, Guam, Virgin Islands, American Samoa, and Northern Mariana Islands).

VA loan guaranties are not available for farm loans, unless there is a home on the property, which will be personally occupied by the veteran. Non-realty loans for the purchase of equipment, livestock, machinery, etc. are not made. Other loan programs for farm financing may be available through the Farmers Home Administration, which gives preference to veteran applicants. (Interested veterans should refer to the local telephone directory for the phone number of a local office.)

Although business loans are not available through VA, the Small Business Administration (SBA) has a number of programs designed to help foster and encourage small business enterprises, including financial and management assistance. Each SBA office has a veteran's affairs officer available to speak with. (Interested veterans should refer to the local telephone directory for the phone number of a local SBA office, or call (800) 827- 5722.)

ELIGIBILITY REQUIREMENTS

Individuals may qualify for VA home loan guaranties if their service falls within any of the following categories:

WORLD WAR II ELIGIBILITY REQUIREMENTS:

- Active duty on or after September 16, 1940 and prior to July 26, 1947; and
- Discharge or separation under other than dishonorable conditions; and
- At least 90 days of total service, unless discharged earlier for a service- connected disability.
- Unremarried widows of above-described eligible individuals who died as a result of service.
- Widows of above-described eligible individuals who died as a result of service who remarried after age57.

POST WORLD WAR II ELIGIBILITY REQUIREMENTS:

- Active duty on or after July 26, 1947 and prior to June 27, 1950; and
- Discharge or separation under other than dishonorable conditions; and
- At least 181 days continuous service, unless discharged earlier for a service-connected disability.
- Unremarried widows of above-described eligible individuals who died as a result of service.
- Widows of above-described eligible individuals who died as a result of service who remarried after age57.

KOREAN CONFLICT ELIGIBILITYREQUIREMENTS:

- Active duty on or after June 27, 1950 and prior to February 1, 1955; and
- Discharge or separation under other than dishonorable conditions; and
- At least 90 days of total service, unless discharged earlier for a service- connected disability.
- Unremarried widows of above-described eligible individuals who died as a result of service.
- Widows of above-described eligible individuals who died as a result of service who remarried after age 57.

POST-KOREAN CONFLICT ELIGIBILITY REQUIREMENTS:

- Active duty on or after February 1, 1955 and prior to August 5, 1964; and
- Discharge or separation under other than dishonorable conditions; and
- At least 181 days continuous service, unless discharged earlier for a service-connected disability.
- Unremarried widows of above-described eligible individuals who died as a result of service.
- Widows of above-described eligible individuals who died as a result of service **who remarried after age 57**. (This provision is effective January 1, 2004.)

VIETNAM ELIGIBILITY REQUIREMENTS:

- Active duty on or after August 5, 1964, and prior to May 8, 1975. (For those serving in the Republic of Vietnam, the beginning date is February 28, 1961.); and
- Discharge or separation under other than dishonorable conditions; and
- At least 90 days of total service, unless discharged earlier for a service- connected disability.
- Unremarried widows of above-described eligible individuals who died as a result of service.
- Widows of above-described eligible individuals who died as a result of service who remarried after age57.

POST-VIETNAM ELIGIBILITY REQUIREMENTS FOR VETERANS WITH ENLISTED SERVICE BETWEEN MAY 8, 1975 AND SEPTEMBER 7, 1980 (IF ENLISTED) OR OCTOBER 16, 1981 (IF OFFICER):

- At least 181 days of continuous service, all of which occurred on or after May 8, 1975, unless discharged earlier for a service-connected disability; and
- Discharge or separation under other than dishonorable conditions.
- Unremarried widows of above-described eligible individuals who died as a result of service.
- Widows of above-described eligible individuals who died as a result of service who remarried after age 57.

POST-VIETNAM ELIGIBILITY REQUIREMENTS FOR VETERANS SEPARATED FROM ENLISTED SERVICE BETWEEN SEPTEMBER 7, 1980 (OCTOBER 17, 1981 FOR OFFICERS) AND AUGUST 1, 1990:

- At least 24 months of continuous active duty, or the full period (at least 181 days) for which individual was called or ordered to active duty, and discharged or

separated under other than dishonorable conditions; or
- At least 181 days of continuous active duty, and discharged due to:
- a hardship; or
- aservice-connected, compensable disability; or
- a medical condition which preexisted service, and has not been determined to be service-connected; or
- the convenience of the government as a result of a reduction in force; or
- a physical or mental condition not characterized as a disability, and not the result of misconduct, but which did interfere with the performance of duty.
- Early discharge for a service-connected disability.
- Unremarried widows of above-described eligible persons who died as the result of service.
- Widows of above-described eligible individuals who died as a result of service who remarried after age 57.

PERSIAN GULF WAR ELIGIBILITY REQUIREMENTS:

- At least 24 months of continuous active duty on or after August 2, 1990, or the full period for which the individual was called or ordered to active duty, and discharged or separated under other than dishonorable conditions; or
- At least 90 days of continuous active duty, and discharged due to:
- A hardship; or
- A service-connected, compensable disability; or
- A medical condition which preexisted service, and has not been determined to be service-connected; or
- The convenience of the government as a result of a reduction in force; or
- A physical or mental condition not characterized as a disability, and not the result of misconduct, but which did interfere with the performance of duty.
- Early discharge for a service-connected disability.
- Unremarried widows of above-described eligible individuals who died as the result of service.
- Widows of above-described eligible individuals who died as a result of service who remarried after age57.

When law or Presidential Proclamation ends the Persian Gulf War, a minimum of 181 days of continuous active duty will be required for those who did not serve during wartime.

Members of the Reserve and National Guard are eligible if activated after August 1, 1990, served at least 90 days, and discharged or separated under other than dishonorable conditions.)

ACTIVE DUTY PERSONNEL ELIGIBILITY REQUIREMENTS:

Individuals who are now on regular duty (not active duty for training) are eligible after having served 181 days (90 days during the Gulf War), unless discharged or separated from a previous qualifying period of active duty service.

ELIGIBILITY REQUIREMENTS FOR MEMBERS OF THE SELECTED RESERVE:

- At least 6 years in the Reserves or National Guard, or discharged earlier due to a service-connected disability; and
- Discharged or separated under other than dishonorable conditions; or
- Placed on the retired list; or
- Transferred to an element of the Ready Reserve other than the Selected Reserve; or
- Continue to serve in the Selected Reserve.
- Unremarried widows of above-described eligible persons who died as the result of

302

service.
- Widows of above-described eligible individuals who died as a result of service who remarried after age 57.

ELIGIBILITY REQUIREMENTS FOR OTHER TYPES OF SERVICE:

- Certain U.S. citizens who served in the armed forces of a U.S. ally in World War II. Members of organizations with recognized contributions to the U.S. during World War II (Questions about this type of service eligibility can be answered at any VA regional office.)

- Spouses of American servicemen who are listed as missing-in-action, or prisoners-of-war for a total of 90 days or more.

CERTIFICATE OF ELIGIBILITY

The Certificate of Eligibility is the medium by which VA certifies eligibility for A VA loan guaranty.

Individuals may request a Certificate of Eligibility by completing "VA Form 26-1880 Request for a Certificate of Eligibility for VA Home Loan Benefits." The completed form should be submitted to a VA Eligibility Center along with acceptable proof of service.

Veterans separated after January 1, 1950 should submit DD Form 214, Certificate of Release or Discharge from active Duty.

Veterans separated after October 1, 1979 should submit copy 4 of DD Form 214.

Since there is no uniform document similar to the DD Form 214 for proof of service in the Selected Reserve a number of different forms may be accepted as documentation of service in the Selected Reserve:

- For those who served in the Army or Air National Guard and were discharged after at least 6 years of such service, NGB Form 22 may be sufficient.
- Those who served in the Army, Navy, Air Force, Marine Corps or Coast Guard Reserves may need to rely on a variety of forms that document at least 6 years of participation in paid training periods, or have paid active duty for training.
- Often it will be necessary to submit a combination of documents, such as an Honorable Discharge certificate together with a Retirement Points Statement. It is the reservist's responsibility to obtain and submit documentation of 6 years of honorable service.

In addition, if an individual is now on active duty, and has not been previously discharged from active duty service, he or she must submit a statement of service that includes the name of the issuing authority (base or command), and is signed by or at the direction of an appropriate official. The statement must identify the individual, include the social security number, provide the date of entry on active duty and the duration of any lost time.

The Certificate of Eligibility should be presented to the lender when completing the loan application. (However, if an individual does not have a Certificate, the lender may have the forms necessary to apply for the Certificate of Eligibility.)

PROCEDURES FOR OBTAINING LOANS

- Find a real estate professional to work with.
- Locate a lending institution that participates in the VA program. You may want to get "pre-qualified" at this point - that is, find out how big a loan you can afford.

Lenders set their own interest rates, discount points, and closing points.

- Obtain your Certificate of Eligibility. The lender can probably get you a certificate online. Or, you can apply online yourself. To get your Certificate of Eligibility (COE) online, please go to the eBenefits portal at this link. If you need any assistance, please call the eBenefits Help Desk at 1-800-983-0937. Their hours are Monday-Friday, 8am to 8pm EST.
- You find a home you want to buy.
- When you negotiate, make sure the purchase and sales agreement contains a "VA option clause."
- You may also want the agreement to allow you to "escape" from the contract without penalty if you can't get a VA loan.
- You formally apply to the lender for a VA-backed loan. The lender will complete a loan application and gather the needed documents such as pay stubs and bank statements.
- The lender orders a VA appraisal and begins to "process" all the credit and income information.
- The lending institution reviews the appraisal and all the documentation of credit, income, and assets. The lender then decides whether the loan should be granted.
- Finally, the closing takes place and the property is transferred. The lender chooses a title company, an attorney, or one of their own representatives to conduct the closing. This person will coordinate the date and time.
- If a lender cannot be located, the local VA regional office can provide a list of lenders active in the VA program.

A VA loan guaranty does not guarantee approval of a loan. The veteran must still meet the financial institution's income and credit requirements. If a loan is approved, the VA guarantees the loan when it's closed.

VA ELIGIBILITY CENTERS

Regional Loan Center	Jurisdiction	Mailing Address	Telephone Number
Atlanta	Georgia North Carolina South Carolina Tennessee	Department of Veterans Affairs VA Regional Loan Center 1700 Clairmont Rd. Decatur, GA 30033-4032 (Mail: P.O. Box 100023, Decatur, GA 30031-7023)	(888) 768-2132
Cleveland	Connecticut Delaware Indiana Maine Massachusetts Michigan New Hampshire New Jersey New York Ohio Pennsylvania Rhode Island Vermont	Department of Veterans Affairs VA Regional Loan Center 1240 East Ninth Street Cleveland, OH 44199	(800) 729-5772

Denver	Alaska Colorado Idaho Montana Oregon Utah Washington Wyoming	Department of Veterans Affairs VA Regional Loan Center 155 Van Gordon Street Lakewood, CO 80228 (Mail: Box 25126, Denver, CO 80225)	(888) 349-7541
Honolulu	Hawaii Guam American Samoa Commonwealth of the Northern Marianas	Department of Veterans Affairs VA Regional Loan Center Loan Guaranty Division (26) 459 Patteson Rd. Honolulu, HI 96819 *Although not an RLC, this office is a fully functioning Loan Guaranty operation for Hawaii.	(888) 433-0481
Houston	Arkansas Louisiana Oklahoma Texas	Department of Veterans Affairs VA Regional Loan Center 6900 Almeda Road Houston, TX 77030-4200	(888) 232-2571
Phoenix	Arizona California New Mexico Nevada	Department of Veterans Affairs VA Regional Loan Center 3333 N. Central Avenue Phoenix, AZ 85012-2402	(888) 869-0194
Roanoke	District of Columbia Kentucky Maryland Virginia West Virginia	Department of Veterans Affairs VA Regional Loan Center 210 Franklin Road, SW Roanoke, VA 24011	(800) 933-5499
St. Paul	Illinois Iowa Kansas Minnesota Missouri Nebraska North Dakota South Dakota Wisconsin	Department of Veterans Affairs VA Regional Loan Center 1 Federal Drive, Ft. Snelling St. Paul, MN 55111- 4050	(800) 827-0611
St. Petersburg	Alabama Florida Mississippi Puerto Rico U.S. Virgin Islands	Department of Veterans Affairs VA Regional Loan Center 9500 Bay Pines Blvd. St. Petersburg, FL 33708 (Mail: P.O. Box 1437, St. Petersburg, FL 33731)	(888) 611-5916

GUARANTY OR ENTITLEMENT AMOUNT

The *Honoring America's Veterans and Caring for Camp Lejeune Families Act of 2012* was signed into law and includes a number of changes to the Department of Veterans Affairs' (VA) Loan Guaranty program, including reverting back to the previous method of calculating maximum guaranty.

This resulted in some loan limits increasing. While VA does not have a maximum loan amount, county "limits" must be used to calculate VA's maximum guaranty amount for a particular county.

Should the loan limit for a county decrease in 2017, VA will guarantee a loan using the previous higher limit if there is proof of a pre-approval based on a sales contract or URLA executed on or before December31, 2016.

The maximum guaranty amount (available for loans over $144,000) is 25 percent of the 2017 VA Limit, which is based on the location and county where a veteran is buying a home. Therefore, a veteran with full entitlement available may borrow up to the 2017 VA Limit and VA will guarantee 25 percent of the loan amount. If a veteran has previously used entitlement that has not been restored, the maximum guaranty amount available to that veteran must be reduced accordingly. Lenders should check their own.

HYBRID ADJUSTABLE RATE MORTGAGES (ARM)

An Adjustable Rate Mortgage is means the interest rate changes with changes in the market. The first-year rate, which is also referred to as a teaser rate, is generally a couple of percentage points below the market rate. The "cap" is the upper limit of the interest rate. If a teaser rate is 4%, and there is a five-point cap, then the highest that an interest rate could go would be 9%. The amount that the interest rate can rise each year is usually limited to one or two percentage points per year, but the frequency at which the rate adjusts can vary. If interest rates go up, an ARM will adjust accordingly.

DOWN PAYMENTS

The VA does not require a down payment be made, provided that:

- The loan is not for a manufactured home or lot (a 5% down payment is required for manufactured home or lot loans); and
- The purchase price or cost does not exceed the reasonable value of the property, as determined by VA; and
- The loan does not have graduated payment features. (Because with a graduated payment mortgage, the loan balance will be increasing during the first years of the loan, a down payment is required to keep the loan balance from going over the reasonable value or the purchase price.)

Even though the VA may not require a down payment, the lender may require one.

LOSING COSTS AND FEES

The VA regulates the closing costs that a veteran may be charged in connection with closing a VA loan. The closing costs and origination fees must be paid in cash, and cannot be included in the loan itself, except in the case of refinancing loans. Although some additional costs are unique to certain localities, the closing costs generally include:

VA appraisal Credit report Survey

Title evidence Recording fees
A 1% loan origination fee Discount points

A veteran is charged the customary fees for title search, credit report, appraisal and transfer fees, etc., the same as any other borrower, but he is not required to pay commission or brokerage fees for obtaining the loan. In home loans, the lender may also charge a reasonable flat charge, called a funding fee, to cover the costs of originating the loan.

FUNDING FEES

A VA funding fee is payable at the time of loan closing. This fee may be included in the loan and paid from the loan proceeds. The funding fee does not have to be paid by veterans receiving VA compensation for service-connected disabilities, or who but for the receipt of retirement pay, would be entitled to receive compensation for service- connected disabilities, or surviving spouses of veterans who died in service or from a service-connected disability.

The funding fee rates are as follows:

Loan Purpose	Percent Of Loan For Veterans	Percent Of Loan For Reservists
Purchase or construction loan with down payment of less than 5%; or Refinancing loan; or Home improvement loan	2.15%	2.4%
Purchase or construction loan with down payment between 5% and 10%	1.5	1.75
Second or subsequent use without a down payment	3.3	3.3
Assumption of VA guaranteed loan	0.5	0.5
Interest rate reduction loan	0.5	0.5
Manufactured home loan	1.0	1.0
Purchase or construction loan with downpayment of 10% or more	1.25	1.5

FLOOD INSURANCE

If the dwelling is in an area identified by the Department of Housing and Urban Development as having special flood hazards, and the sale of flood insurance under the national program is available, such insurance is required on loans made since March 1, 1974. The amount of insurance must be equal to the outstanding loan balance, or the maximum limit of coverage available, whichever is less.

INTEREST RATES

The interest rate on VA loans varies due to changes in the prevailing rates in the mortgage market. One a loan is made, the interest rate set in the note remains the same for the life of the loan. However, if interest rates decrease, a veteran may apply for a new VA loan to refinance the previous loan at a lower interest rate.

REPAYMENT PERIOD

The maximum repayment period for VA home loans is 30 years and 32 days. However, the exact amortization period depends upon the contract between the lender and the borrower.

The VA will guarantee loans with the following repayment terms:

- Traditional Fixed Payment Mortgage
- Equal monthly payments for the life of the loan
- Graduated Payment Mortgage – GPM
- Smaller than normal monthly payments for the first few years – usually 5 years, which gradually increase each year, and then level off after the end of the "graduation period" to larger than normal payments for the remaining term of the loan. The reduction in the monthly payment in the early years of the loan is accomplished by delaying a portion of the interest due on the loan each month, and by adding that interest to the principal balance.

BUYDOWN

The builder of a new home or seller of an existing home may "buy down" the veteran's mortgage payments by making a large lump sum payment up front at closing that will be used to supplement the monthly payments for a certain period, usually 1 to 3 years.

GROWING EQUITY MORTGAGE(GEM)

Provides for a gradual annual increase in monthly payments, with all of the increase applied to the principal balance, resulting in early payoff of the loan.

PREPAYMENT OF LOAN

A veteran or serviceman may pay off his entire loan at any time without penalty or fee, or make advance payments equal to one monthly installment or $100, whichever is the lesser amount. Individuals should check with the mortgage holder for the proper procedure.

LOAN DEFAULTS

If a veteran fails to make payments as agreed, the lender may foreclose on the property. If the lender takes a loss, the VA must pay the guaranty to the lender, and the individual must repay this amount to the VA. If the loan closed on or after January 1, 1990, the veteran will owe the VA in the event of default, only if there was fraud, misrepresentation, or bad faith on the veteran's part.

The US Department of Veterans Affairs urges all Veterans who are encountering problems making their mortgage payments to speak with their loan servicers as soon as possible to explore options to avoid foreclosure.

Depending on a Veteran's specific situation, servicers may offer any of the following options to avoid foreclosure:

- Repayment Plan: The borrower makes regular installment each month plus part of the missed installments.
- Special Forbearance: The servicer agrees not to initiate foreclosure to allow time for borrowers to repay the missed installments. An example would be when a borrower is waiting for a tax refund.
- Loan Modification: Provides the borrower a fresh start by adding the delinquency to the loan balance and establishing a new payment schedule.
- Additional time to arrange a private sale: The servicer agrees to delay foreclosure to allow a sale to close if the loan will be paid off.
- Short Sale: When the servicer agrees to allow a borrower to sell his/her home for a lesser amount than what is currently required to payoff the loan.
- Deed-in-Lieu of Foreclosure: The borrower voluntarily agrees to deed the property to the servicer instead of going through a lengthy foreclosure process.

RELEASE OF LIABILITY

Any veteran who sells or has sold a home purchased with a VA loan guaranty may request release from liability to the VA. (If the VA loan closed prior to March 1, 1988, the application forms for a release of liability must be requested from the VA office that guaranteed the loan. If the VA loan closed on or after March 1, 1988, then the application forms must be requested from the lender to whom the payments are made.) The loan must be current, the purchaser must assume full liability for the loan, and the purchaser must sign an Assumption of Liability Agreement. The VA must approve the purchaser from a credit standpoint.

For loans closed on or after March 1, 1988, release of liability is not automatic. To approve the assumer and grant the veteran release from liability, the lender or VA must be notified, and release of liability must be requested.

If the loan was closed prior to March 1, 1988, the purchaser may assume the loan without approval from VA or the lender. However, the veteran is encouraged to request a release of liability from VA, regardless of the loan's closing date. If a veteran does not obtain a release of liability, and VA suffers a loss on account of a default by the assumer, or some future assumer, a debt may be established against the veteran. Also, strenuous collection efforts will be made against the veteran if a debt is established.

The release of a veteran from liability to the VA does not change the fact that the VA continues to be liable on the guaranty.

RESTORATION OF ENTITLEMENT

Veterans who have used all or part of their entitlement may restore their entitlement amount to purchase another home, provided:

- The property has been sold, and the loan has been paid in full; or
- A qualified veteran buyer has agreed to assume the outstanding balance on the loan, and agreed to substitute his entitlement for the same amount of entitlement the original veteran owner used to get the loan. (The veteran buyer must also meet the occupancy, income, and credit requirements of the VA and the lender.)
- If the veteran has repaid the VA loan in full, but has not disposed of the property securing that loan, the entitlement may be restored ONE TIME ONLY.

Restoration of entitlement does not occur automatically. The veteran must apply for restoration by completing "Form 26, 1880." Completed forms may be returned to any VA regional office or center (A copy of the HUD-1, Closing Statement, or other appropriate evidence of payment in full should also be submitted with the completed Form 26, 1880.) Application forms for substitution of entitlement can be requested from the VA office that guaranteed the loan.

If the requirements for restoration of entitlement cannot be met, veterans who had a VA loan before may still have remaining entitlement to use for another VA loan. The current amount of entitlement available to eligible veterans has been increased over time by changes in the law.

For example, in 1974 the maximum guaranty entitlement was $12,500. Today the maximum guaranty entitlement is $36,000 (for most loans under $144,000). So, if a veteran used the $12,500 guaranty in 1974, even if that loan is not paid off, the veteran could use the $23,500 difference between the $12,500 entitlement originally used and the current maximum of $36,000 to buy another home with a VA loan guaranty.

DIRECT HOME LOANS

VA direct home loans are only available to:

- Native American veterans who plan to buy, build, or improve a home on Native American trust land; or
- Certain eligible veterans who have a permanent and total service-connected disability, for specially adapted homes.

NATIVE AMERICAN VETERANS LIVING ON TRUST LANDS

A VA direct loan can be used to purchase, construct, or improve a home on Native American trust land. These loans may also be used to simultaneously purchase and improve a home, or to refinance another VA direct loan made under this program in order to lower the interest rate. VA direct loans are generally limited to the cost of the home or $80,000, whichever is less.

To qualify for a VA direct loan, the tribal organization or other appropriate Native American group must be participating in the VA direct loan program. The tribal organization must have signed a *Memorandum of Understanding* with the Secretary of Veterans Affairs that includes the conditions governing its participation in the program.

Veterans should contact their regional VA office for specific information regarding direct home loans.

RESALE OF REPOSSESSED VA HOMES

The VA sells homes that it acquires after foreclosure of a VA guaranteed loan. These homes are available to veterans and non-veterans.

The properties are available for sale to the general public through the services of private sector real estate brokers. The VA cannot deal directly with purchasers. Real estate brokers receive the keys to the properties and assist prospective purchasers in finding, viewing, and offering to purchase them.

Participating brokers receive instructional material regarding the sales program, and are familiar with VA sales procedures. VA pays the sales commission. Offers to purchase VA acquired properties must be submitted on VA forms. Offers cannot be submitted on offer forms generally used in the real estate industry.

VA financing is available for most, but not all, property sales. The down payment requirements are usually very reasonable, the interest rate is established by VA based on market conditions. Any prospective purchaser who requests VA financing to purchase a VA-owned property must have sufficient income to meet the loan payments, maintain the property, and pay all other obligation. The purchaser must have acceptable credit, and must also have enough funds remaining for family support.

Anyone interested should consult a local real estate agent to find out about VA-acquired properties listed for sale in the area.

HUD / FHA LOANS

Veterans are not eligible for VA financing based on service in World War I, Active Duty for Training in the Reserves, or Active Duty for Training in the National Guard (unless "activated" under the authority of Title 10, U.S. Code). However, these veterans may qualify for a HUD / FHA veteran's loan.

The VA's only role in the HUD / FHA program is to determine the eligibility of the veteran, and issue a *Certificate of Veteran Status*, if qualified. Under this program, financing is available for veterans at terms slightly more favorable than those available to non-veterans.

A veteran may request a "Certificate of Veteran Status" by completing "VA form 26-8261a." The completed form and required attachments should be submitted to the veteran's regional VA office for a determination of eligibility.

SERVICEMEMBERS CIVIL RELIEF ACT (SCRA)

The Servicemembers Civil Relief Act expanded and improved the former Soldiers' and Sailors' Civil Relief Act (SSCRA). It is designed to provide a wide range of protections for people entering the military, being called to active duty, and deployed servicemembers. The goal of the SCRA is to postpone or suspend particular civil obligations, in order for the servicemember to devote full attention to service duties. It is also designed to relieve stress on family members of deployed servicemembers. Among these obligations, a servicemember may be exempt from are mortgage payments.

The new law expands the current law in place to protect servicemembers and their families from eviction from housing while the servicemember is on active duty.

Based on provisions of a recent SCRA Foreclosure Settlement completed by the Federal government, five major servicers (Bank of America, JPMorgan Chase, Ally (GMAC), CitiMortgage, and Wells Fargo) must provide the following relief to service members and veterans:

- Conduct a review of every servicemember foreclosure since 2006 and provide any who were wrongly foreclosed with compensation equal to a minimum of lost equity, plus interest and $116,785;
- Refund money lost because they were wrongfully denied the opportunity to reduce their interest rates to the 6% cap;
- Provide relief for service members who are forced to sell their homes for less than the amount they owe on their mortgage due to a Permanent Change in Station.

Extend certain foreclosure protections afforded under the Servicemember Civil Relief Act to service members serving in harm's way.

CHAPTER 26

OVERSEAS BENEFITS

MEDICAL BENEFITS

The Foreign Medical Program (FMP) is a healthcare benefits program for U.S. veterans with VA-rated service-connected conditions who are residing or traveling abroad (except Canada and the Philippines). Services provided in Canada and the Philippines are under separate jurisdictions, as indicated later in this chapter.

Under the FMP, VA assumes payment responsibility for certain necessary medical services associated with the treatment of service-connected conditions.

The Foreign Medical Program Office in Denver, Colorado has jurisdiction over all foreign provided services, with the exception of medical services received in Canada and the Philippines. It is responsible for all aspects of the program, including application processing, verification of eligibility, authorization of benefits, and payments of claims.

> **Key Takeaways**
>
> Veterans who may live outside the U.S. after discharge include veterans working at American embassies and consulates abroad, those who work for multi-national companies or those who do so by choice or for family reasons
>
> VA benefits are payable regardless of a veteran's place of residence or nationality
>
> Some differences apply to veterans living abroad for certain benefits programs

In September 2011, the VA announced the creation of a new program to provide comprehensive compensation and pension (C&P) examinations to U.S. veterans living overseas. The program includes providing a medical assessment to evaluate veterans' current disabilities that may be related to their military service.

If VA has previously determined a veteran has a service-connected medical condition, the examination helps determine the current severity of the condition, which could affect the amount of VA disability compensation payable or entitlement to additional benefits. During this time, the VA also conducted its first C&P examinations using telehealth technology, which is designed to ease the burden of travel for U.S. veterans living overseas. The VA plans to provide these services in various locations in Europe and Asia.

Individuals who are traveling to or reside in one of the following countries should use the following number to contact the FMP Office in Denver, Colorado: (877) 345-8179

Germany; Panama; Australia; Italy; UK; Japan; Spain

For individuals who are in Mexico or Costa Rica, first dial the U.S.A code and then (877) 345-8179. The number also works from the United States.

Generally, as long as the service is medically necessary for the treatment of a VA rated service-connected condition, it will be covered by the FMP. Additionally, the services must be accepted by VA and / or the U.S. Medical community (such as the American Medical Association and the U.S. Food and Drug Administration.)

EXCLUSIONS TO MEDICAL BENEFITS

The following services are not covered by the Foreign Medical Program:

- Procedures, treatments, drugs, or devices that are experimental or investigational;
- Family planning services and sterilization;
- Infertility services;
- Plastic surgery primarily for cosmetic purposes;
- Procedures, services, and supplies related to sex transformations;
- Non-acute institutional care such as long-term inpatient psychiatric care and nursing home care;
- Day care and day hospitalization;
- Non-medical home care (aid and attendance);
- Abortions
- Travel, meals, and lodging (including transportation costs to return to the United States)

PROSTHESIS

If an individual residing in a foreign country requires a prosthesis for a VA rated service-connected condition, and the cost of the prosthetic appliance is less than $300 (U.S. currency), the individual may purchase the prosthetic appliance from a local healthcare provider, and send the invoice to the FMP Office for reimbursement, or the healthcare provider may bill the VA.

If the cost of the prosthetic appliance exceeds $300 (U.S. currency), the individual must obtain preauthorization for the VA Foreign Medical Program Office (see address below).

APPLICATION PROCESS – REGISTRATION

Although pre-registration for eligible veterans is not necessary, veterans who are permanently relocating to a country under the FMP's jurisdiction are encouraged to notify the FMP once a permanent foreign address is established. At that time, FMP will provide detailed program material, such as benefit coverage, benefit limitations, selecting healthcare providers, and claim filing instructions.

Veterans who are simply traveling, and are not planning a permanent relocation do not need to notify the FMP of their travel plans. Program materials are available, however, upon request.

The FMP can be contacted at:

VA Health Administration Center Foreign Medical Program (FMP)
P.O. Box 65021
Denver, CO 80206-9021
Phone: (303) 331-7590
Fax: (303) 331-7803

MEDICAL SERVICES IN CANADA

The VA Medical and Regional Office Center in White River Junction, Vermont, is responsible for determining eligibility of U.S. veterans for reimbursement of medical treatment while traveling or residing in Canada. The local offices of Veterans' Affairs-Canada assists veterans in obtaining authorizations for treatment, arranging for treatment (if necessary), and providing information about the medical treatment program.

The same exclusions listed earlier in this chapter also apply to medical services in Canada, and VA assumes payment responsibility only for certain necessary medical services associated with the treatment of service-connected conditions.

To receive reimbursed medical treatment, an authorization must be obtained from the White River Junction office prior to treatment (unless an emergency situation exists).

When required by the VA to support a claim for disability benefits, Veterans' Affairs-Canada will make arrangement for disability examinations for veterans residing in Canada. In some instances, arrangements will be made locally in Canada. In other instances, arrangements will be made at bordering VA medical facilities.

Information on how to obtain medical services in Canada, including procedures for filing claims, can be obtained by contacting the following office:

VAM & RO Center (136FC)
North Hartland Road
White River Junction, VT 05009-0001
Fax: (802) 296-5174

Or

Veterans Affairs-Canada Foreign Countries Operations
Room 1055
264 Wellington Street
Ottawa, Ontario, Canada K1A 0P4
(613) 943-7461

MEDICAL SERVICES IN THE PHILLIPINES

The Republic of the Philippines is the only foreign country in which the VA operates a regional office and outpatient clinic.

The same exclusions listed earlier in this chapter also apply to medical services in the Philippines, and VA assumes payment responsibility only for certain necessary medical services associated with the treatment of service-connected conditions.

To receive reimbursed medical treatment, an authorization must be obtained prior to treatment (unless an emergency situation exists).

Information on how to obtain medical services in the Philippines, including procedures for filing claims, can be obtained by contacting the following office:

VA Department of Veterans Affairs Manila Regional Office & Outpatient Clinic
1501 Roxas Boulevard 1302
Pasay City, Philippines
TEL: 011-632-318-8387

Virtually all VA monetary benefits, including compensation, pension, educational assistance, and burial allowances, are payable regardless of an individual's place of residence.

However, there are some program limitations in foreign jurisdictions, including:

• Home-loan guaranties are available only in the United States and selected territories and possessions.
• Educational benefits are limited to approved degree-granting programs in institutions of higher learning
• Information and assistance are available to U.S. veterans worldwide at American embassies and consulates. In Canada, the local offices of Veterans Affairs-Canada provide information and assistance. Individuals may call toll- free within Canada, (888) 996-2242.

In the Philippines, service is available at the VA Regional Office and Outpatient Clinic in Manila:

VA Regional Office
1131 Roxas Boulevard
Manila, Philippines
TEL: 011-632-521-7521

DIRECT DEPOSIT

The conventional method of direct deposit is not available outside of the U.S. However, there are foreign banks with branches in the United States, through which direct deposit can be established. Once the funds are received in the U.S. branch through electronic funds transfer, the U.S. branch transfers the money to the foreign branch.

While this process may take a few days longer than direct deposit within the United States, it is still quicker than having checks mailed overseas through the Department of State or International Priority Airmail.

CHAPTER 27

AGENT ORANGE, MUSTARD GAS, RADIATION AND PROJECT 112 / SHAD

AGENT ORANGE OVERVIEW

Veterans who were exposed to Agent Orange or other herbicides during military service may be eligible for a variety of VA benefits, including disability compensation for diseases associated with exposure. Dependents and survivors may also be eligible.

Agent Orange is a blend of herbicides that were sprayed by the U.S. Military in Vietnam and around the Korean demilitarized zone to remove trees and foliage that could provide cover to the enemy. Herbicides were also used by the U.S. military to defoliate facilities domestically and in other countries dating back to the 1950s.

The VA has also determined there is evidence Air Force and Air Force Reserve members were exposed to Agent Orange if they served between 1969 and 1986, and regularly and repeatedly operated, maintained, or served onboard C-123 aircraft, which were known to have been used to spray and herbicide during the Vietnam era.

According to the VA and federal law, there is a presumption that certain diseases are a result of

> **Key Takeaways**
>
> Veterans who were exposed to Agent Orange or other herbicides during military service may be eligible for VA benefits
>
> VA and federal law presumes certain diseases are a result of exposure to these herbicides
>
> Monthly payment rates are based on the veteran's combined rating for his or her service-connected disabilities
>
> The Department of Veterans Affairs recognizes presumptive illnesses for service members who served outside the Vietnam or Korean demilitarized zone in some instances

exposure to these herbicides. This policy of presumption intends to simplify how exposed veterans receive compensation for these diseases, because the VA eliminates the normal requirements of proving an illness began during or was worsened by military service.

A veteran who believes he or she has a disease caused by exposure to Agent Orange that is not one of the conditions listed as presumptive is required to show a connection between the disease and herbicide exposure during military service.

ELIGIBILITY—SERVICE IN VIETNAM OR KOREA

VA presumes that veterans were exposed to Agent Orange or other herbicides if they served:

- In Vietnam anytime between January 9, 1962 and May 7, 1975 including brief visits ashore or service aboard a ship that operated on the inland waterways of Vietnam
- In or near the Korean demilitarized zone anytime between April 1, 1968 and August 31, 1971

If a veteran falls into the categories listed above, they don't have to show they were exposed to Agent Orange to be eligible for disability compensation for diseases VA presumes are associated with it.

ELIGIBILITY—SERVICE OUTSIDE OF VIETNAM OR KOREA

Even if a veteran didn't serve in Vietnam or the Korean demilitarized zone during the specified time periods, they can still apply for disability compensation if they were exposed to an herbicide while in the military, and believe it led to the onset of a disease.

This includes:

- Veterans who served on or near the perimeters of military bases in Thailand during the Vietnam Era
- Veterans who served where herbicides were tested and stored outside of Vietnam
- Veterans who were crew members on C-123 planes flown after the Vietnam War
- Veterans associated with Department of Defense (DoD) projects to test, dispose of, or store herbicides in the U.S.

If eligible, you are required to prove you were exposed to Agent Orange or other herbicides during your military service to be eligible for service-connection for diseases VA presumes are related to exposure to Agent Orange.

Exception: Blue Water Veterans with non-Hodgkin's lymphoma may be granted service-connection without showing inland waterway service or that they stepped foot in Vietnam. This is because the VA recognizes non-Hodgkin's lymphoma as related to service in Vietnam or the waters offshore of Vietnam during the Vietnam Era.

VETERANS' DISEASES ASSOCIATED WITH AGENT ORANGE

VA assumes that certain diseases can be related to a Veteran's qualifying military service. We call these "presumptive diseases." VA has recognized certain cancers and other health problems as presumptive diseases associated with exposure to Agent Orange or other herbicides during military service. Veterans and their survivors may be eligible for benefits for these diseases.

AL Amyloidosis
A rare disease caused when an abnormal protein, amyloid, enters tissues or organs

Chronic B-cell Leukemias
A type of cancer which affects white blood cells

Chloracne (or similar acneform disease)
A skin condition that occurs soon after exposure to chemicals and looks like common forms of acne seen in teenagers. Under VA's rating regulations, it must be at least 10 percent disabling within one year of exposure to herbicides.

Diabetes Mellitus Type 2
A disease characterized by high blood sugar levels resulting from the body's inability to respond properly to the hormone insulin

Hodgkin's Disease
A malignant lymphoma (cancer) characterized by progressive enlargement of the lymph nodes, liver, and spleen, and by progressive anemia

Ischemic Heart Disease
A disease characterized by a reduced supply of blood to the heart, that leads to chest pain

Multiple Myeloma
A cancer of plasma cells, a type of white blood cell in bone marrow

Non-Hodgkin's Lymphoma
A group of cancers that affect the lymph glands and other lymphatic tissue

Parkinson's Disease
A progressive disorder of the nervous system that affects muscle movement

Peripheral Neuropathy, Early-Onset
A nervous system condition that causes numbness, tingling, and motor weakness. Under VA's rating regulations, it must be at least 10 percent disabling within one year of herbicide exposure.

Porphyria Cutanea Tarda
A disorder characterized by liver dysfunction and by thinning and blistering of the skin in sun-exposed areas. Under VA's rating regulations, it must be at least 10 percent disabling within one year of exposure to herbicides.

Prostate Cancer
Cancer of the prostate; one of the most common cancers among men

Respiratory Cancers (includes lung cancer)
Cancers of the lung, larynx, trachea, and bronchus

Soft Tissue Sarcomas (other than osteosarcoma, chondrosarcoma, Kaposi's sarcoma, or mesothelioma)
A group of different types of cancers in body tissues such as muscle, fat, blood and lymph vessels, and connective tissues

Veterans with Lou Gehrig's Disease
VA presumes Lou Gehrig's Disease (amyotrophic lateral sclerosis or ALS) diagnosed in ALL veterans who had 90 days or more continuous active military service is related to their service, although ALS is not related to Agent Orange Exposure

Evidence Needed

If you are seeking service connection for one of the diseases presumed by the VA to be associated with herbicide exposure during service, the VA needs the following:

- A medical diagnosis of a disease which the VA recognizes as being associated with Agent Orange
- Competent evidence of service in Vietnam or at or near the Korean demilitarized zone during the dates shown above or exposure to herbicides in a location other than the Vietnam or the Korean demilitarized zone
- Competent medical evidence that the disease began within the deadline

If you believe you have a disease caused by exposure to herbicides but it's not listed on the presumptive diseases for Agent Orange, you will need all of the following to apply for service connection:

- Competent medical evidence of a current disability
- Competent medical evidence of an actual connection between herbicide exposure and the current disability and
- Competent evidence of service in Vietnam at or near the Korean demilitarized zone during the dates shown above or exposure to herbicides in a location other than Vietnam or the Korean demilitarized zone

VA ISSUES LIST OF SHIPS WITH AGENT ORANGE EXPOSURE

In 2010, the Department of Veterans Affairs Compensation and Pension (C&P) Service initiated a program to collect data on Vietnam naval operations for the purpose of providing regional offices with information to assist with development of claims based on herbicide exposure from Navy Veterans.

To date, the Department of Veterans Affairs (VA) has received verification from various sources showing that a number of offshore "blue water naval vessels" conducted operations on the inland "brown water" rivers and delta areas of Vietnam. The VA also has identified certain vessel types that operated primarily or exclusively on the inland waterways.

Veterans whose military records show they were on the ships or boats with the following designations or ships that were part of the Mobile Rivervine Force or Inshore Fire Support (ISF) Division 93 mean the veteran qualifies for presumption of Agent Orange exposure:

LCM (Landing Craft, Mechanized) LCU (Landing Craft, Utility) LCVP (Landing Craft, Vehicle, Personnel) LST (Landing Ship, Tank) PBR (Patrol Boat, River)

PCF (Patrol Craft, Fast or Swift Boat) PG (Patrol Gunboat) WAK (Cargo Vessel) WHEC (High Endurance Cutter) WLB (Buoy Tender) WPB (Patrol Boat) YFU (Harbor Utility Craft)

If a veteran's vessel is not included in the Mobile Rivervine Force or the Inshore Fire Support (ISF) Division 93, the veteran should check the following alphabetized list of ships that qualify for Agent Orange presumption (updated January 2012):

Ship Name	Activities in Vietnam
Ajax (AR-6)	Anchored in Vung Tau area for repair duties with evidence of shore- based repairs during June 1968, September to October 1969, April to May 1970, and August to November 1971
Alamo (LSD-33)	Conducted numerous troop, supply, and equipment landings with smaller boats at Da Nang and elsewhere between 1965 and 1972 with evidence that crewmembers went ashore for beach parties
Aludra (AF-55)	Conducted in-port replenishments at Cam Ranh Bay, Vung Tau and An Thoi during March 1969 and docked to pier at Da Nang April 17- 18, 1969
Antelope (PG-86)	Operated primarily or exclusively on Vietnam's inland waterways
Asheville (PG-84)	Operated primarily or exclusively on Vietnam's inland waterways
Askari (ARL-30)	Operated primarily or exclusively on Vietnam's inland waterways
Ault (DD-689)	Operated on Mekong River Delta and Soirap River May 26, 1967
Barracks Barge (APL- 26)	Operated primarily or exclusively on Vietnam's inland waterways
Barracks Barge (APL-30)	Operated primarily or exclusively on Vietnam's inland waterways
Barry (DD-933)	Operated on Saigon River during December 1965
Basilone (DD-824)	Operated on Saigon River, May 24-25, 1966
Bayfield (APA-33)	Conducted troop on loading and "mike boat" landings at Da Nang, Chu Lai, Baie de My Han, and Cua Viet River from July through October 1965 and Febru ary throu gh May 1967
Belle Grove (LSD-2)	Operated primarily or exclusively on Vietnam's inland waterways
Benewah (APB-35)	Operated primarily or exclusively on Vietnam's inland waterways
Benner (DD-807)	Operated on inland Ganh Rai Bay and Rung Sat Special Zone during June 26-July 1, 1968
Bexar (APA-237)	Operated primarily or exclusively on Vietnam's inland waterways
Bigelow (DD-942)	Docked to pier at Da Nang for one hour on April 19, 1967
Black (DD-666)	Operated on Saigon River July 13-19, 1966
Blue (DD-744)	Anchored in Da Nang Harbor on April 21, 1968, with crew members going ashore for a picnic
Bolster (ARS-38)	Crew operated on land to extract USS Clark County (LST-601) from beach after grounding at Duc Pho from November 18 to December 1, 1967
Boxer (LPH-4)	Docked to pier at Cam Ranh Bay on September 9, 1965
Braine (DD-630)	Docked to pier at Da Nang on November 27, 1966
Brownson (DD-868)	Operated on Song Nha Be and Ganh Rai Bay areas of Mekong River Delta during February 1967
Bru le (AKL-28)	Operated primarily or exclusively on Vietnam's inland waterways
Buck (DD-761)	Operated on Mekong River delta and Saigon River during October 1966
Cabildo (LSD-16)	Delivered equipment to Nha Be via the Long Tau River during June 1968. Conducted numerous troop, supply, and equipment landings at Da Nang, Cam Ranh Bay, and Vung Tau from July 1965 to November 1968

Ship Name	Activities in Vietnam
Card (ACV-11)	Mined, sunk, and salvaged in Saigon River Harbor during May 1964
Canberra (CAG-2)	Operated on Saigon River from March 31 through April 1, 1966, on Cua Viet River during December 15, 1966 and on Mekong Delta Ham Luong River during January 15, 1967
Canon (PG-90)	Operated primarily or exclusively on Vietnam's inland waterways
Carronade (IFS 1)	Operated primarily or exclusively on Vietnam's inland waterways
Carter Hall (LSD-3) (Landing Ship Dock)	Conducted troop-landing operations with "mike boats" at Da Nang, Dong Ha onCua Viet River, and Nha Be on Saigon River, as well as three-month duty as "boat repair ship" at Da Nang, from July 1965 through November 1968
Castor (AKS-1) (General Stores Ship)	Docked to pier at Da Nang on October 7, 1966
Catamount (LSD-17)	Operated on Song Nah Be River during April 1969
Cavalier (APA-37)	Conducted troop landings at Chu Lai and served as Da Nang station ship, with crew members going ashore, from March-August 1966
Charles S. Sperry (DD-	Docked at Da Nang during January 1966
Chicago (CG-11)	Deck logs show a utility boat went ashore for one hour with eight crew members aboard while anchored in Da Nang Harbor on May 22, 1969
Chevalier (DD-805)	Operated on Saigon River during June 15-21, 1966 and on Vung Ganh Rai area of Mekong River delta during January 25, 1968
Clarion River (LSMR 409)	Operated primarily or exclusively on Vietnam's inland waterways
Cleveland (LPD-7)	Operated on Cua Viet River and at Dong Ha, as well as Hue River, with "mike boats" from November 1967 through 1968 and on the Saigon River during September 1969
Cohoes (AN-78)	Operated primarily or exclusively on Vietnam's inland waterways
Colleton (APB-36)	Operated primarily or exclusively on Vietnam's inland waterways
Colonial (LSD-18) (Landing Ship Dock)	Traveled on Saigon River to Nha Be on June 22 and September 25-30,1969
Comstock (LSD-19)	Operated primarily or exclusively on Vietnam's inland waterways
Conway (DD-507)	Operated on Saigon River during early August 1966
Conflict (MSO-426) (Minesweeper-Ocean)	Operated on Saigon River April 1, 1966 and Song Huong River (Perfume River) May 14, 1966 and docked to piers at Cam Ranh Bay on September 30, October 7, 27, 28, and 31
Core (ACV-13)	Traveled on Saigon River to delivered aircraft to Saigon during June 1965
Crockett (PG-88)	Operated primarily or exclusively on Vietnam's inland waterways
Current (ARS-22) (Salvage Ship)	Conducted salvage operations on Saigon River during July 1964 and April 1967 and inland waterway of Qui Nhon Bay/Harbor during May 1967 and August 1971
Currituck (AV-7)	Traveled up Saigon River to Saigon during early 1964; operated inMekong River delta during June 1965; anchored at Cam Ranh Bay for month-long periods during 1966 and 1967 to repair and tend to Navy sea planes, with the likelihood that crewmembers went ashore on liberty leave
Dahlgren (DLG-12) (Guided Missile	Sent motorized whaleboat and captain's gig ashore while anchored in Da Nang Harbor on June 4, 1967
Damato (DD-871)	Operated on Saigon River from December 12-13, 1967
Davidson (DE-1045) (Destroyer Escort)	Operated on Vung Ganh Rai and Rung Sat Special Zone of Mekong River Deltafrom September 16 to October 5, 1967.Sent motorized whaleboat ashore while anchored off coast of Tan My on September 20, 1972
De Haven (DD-727)	Operated on Saigon River during early March 1967
Dennis J. Buckley (DD-808)	Operated on Mekong River Delta, Saigon River and Ganh Rai Bay from December19, 1966 to January 16, 1967
Denver (LPD-9)	Docked to pier at Da Nang to load troops and vehicles on March 24 and June 1,1971
Dubuque (LPD-8)	Docked at Da Nang on March 15, 1970

Ship Name	Activities in Vietnam
Duluth (LPD-6) (Amphibious Transport Dock)	Docked topier at Da Nang during December 1968 and March, April, and October1971
Duncan (DDR-874)	Operated on Saigon River during September and October1965
Du Pont (DD-941)	Operated on Mekong River Delta during October 1968
Durham (LKA-114) (Amphibious Cargo)	Docked to piers at Da Nang during March 20-21, July 20-21, August 18-19, and September 7, 1970
Dyess (DD-880)	Operated on Saigon River and Rung Sat Special Zone from June 19-July 1,1966
Eldorado (AGC-11) (Amphibious Force Flagship)	Sent crewmembers ashore for beach party at Cam Ranh Bay during July1970
Elkhorn (AOG-7)	Operated primarily or exclusively on Vietnam's inland waterways
Epperson (DD-719)	Docked to Da Nang Pier on October 4, 1970
Epping Forest (MCS-7)	Conducted "goodwill" tours at Cam Ranh Bay and Nha Trang with crewmembers going ashore and Vietnamese coming aboard during September-October 1964, and mine sweep of Cua Viet River using smaller vessels from main ship during May 1968
Esteem (MSO-438)	Crewmembers painted a Vietnamese orphanage while docked at inland waterway Qui Nhon Bay/Harbor during December 1967
Estes (AGC-12)	Anchored in mouth of Mekong River during January 1967 Conducted troop and supply beach landings during March and July-August 1965, at Chu Lai, Da Nang, and Qui Nhon and conducted small boat landings and a beach picnic at Vung Tau during April 1968
Eversole (DD-789)	Sent motorized whaleboat ashore to Chu Laifrom offshore anchorage totransfer two crewmembers on July 25, 1972
Finch (DER-328)	Crewmembers painted a Vietnamese orphanage while docked at inland waterwayQui Nhon Bay/Harbor during December 1967
Fiske (DD-842)	Operated on Mekong River, June 16-21, 1966
Floyd B. Parks (DD-884)	Operated on Saigon River and Ganh Rai Bay during February and March 1968
Force (MSO-445)	Docked to pier at Cam Ranh Bay March 13-15, 1972 and at Vung Tau April 25-May 3, 1972
Fortify (MSO-446)	Traveled up the Saigon River to Saigon September 19-22, 1964
Francis River (LSMR 525)	Operated primarily or exclusively on Vietnam's inland waterways
Gallop (PG-85)	Operated primarily or exclusively on Vietnam's inland waterways
Geiger (T-AP-197)	Docked at Qui Nhon November 23-26, 1965
General R M Blatchford (AP-153)	Landed elements of 1st Infantry Division at Vung Tau by small boats during October 1965
Genessee (AOG-8)	Operated primarily or exclusively on Vietnam's inland waterways
George Clymer APA-27) (Amphibious Attack Transport)	Conducted troop and supply "mike boat" beach landings during July 1965 and March to July, 1966, at Da Nang and Chu Lai. Navigated Saigon River to Saigon Port during January 1963.
George K. Mackenzie (DD-836)	Operated in Ganh Rai Bay area north of Vung Tau during February1969
Graffias (AF-29) (Stores Ship)	Docked to pier at Da Nang for resupply on February 20 and November 25, 1967, and conducted other in-port replenishments at An Thoi and Vung Tau during 1967
Grapple (ARS-7) (Salvage Ship)	Conducted numerous repair and salvaging operations while moored to piers inDa Nang, Chu Lai, Cam Ranh Bay, and Tan Myfrom November 1970 through April 1971 and August 1972 through January 1973
Grasp (ARS-24)	Conducted salvaging operations on Song Cua Dia River and other inland waters from February through April 1969

Ship Name	Activities in Vietnam
Gunston Hall (LSD-5)	Delivered equipment to Saigon via Saigon River during March 1968 Conducted numerous troop, supply, and equipment landings at Da Nang, Chu Lai, etc. during 1966 and from March 1968 to February 1970
Gurke (DD-783)	Operated on Ganh Rai Bay, Saigon River, and Mekong River during October 1966
Hamner (DD-718)	Operated onSong Lon Taoand LongSong Tao Rivers, August 15 toSeptember 1, 1966
Hanson (DD-832)	Anchored in Saigon River on September 13,1966
Harbor Tug 84 (YTB-84)	Operated primarily or exclusively on Vietnam's inland waterways
Harbor Tug 85 (YTB-85)	Operated primarily or exclusively on Vietnam's inland waterways
Hector (AR-7)	Anchored in Vung Tau Harbor repairing other vessels from July 20 to August 16, 1970, with deck logs stating that crew members went ashore on liberty leave
Henrico (APA-45)	Conducted numerous troop landings at Da Nang, Chu Lai, and Hue from March through May 1965 and from August 1966 through March1967
Henry B. Wilson	Docked at Da Nang pier on April 2, 1967
Herbert J Thomas (DD-833)	Operated in Mekong River Delta during December 1966
Hermitage (LSD-34)	Conducted numerous troop landings in Da Nang area from June through October 1967 and docked to Da Nang pier June 2-3, 1967
Higbee (DD-806)	Operated on Vung Ganh Rai area of Mekong River Delta from March 1-12, 1969
Holder (DD-819)	Operated on Vung Ganh Rai and Saigon River August 5, 1966
Hugh Purvis (DD-709)	Operated on the inland waters of Qui Nhon Bay during January1969
Indra (ARL-37)	Operated primarily or exclusively on Vietnam's inland waterways
Ingersoll (DD-652)	Operated on Saigon River October 24-25, 1965
Ingraham (DD-694)	Operated 10 miles up Saigon River on November 12, 1965
Inflict (MSO-456)	Traveled up the Saigon River to Saigon from September 19-22, 1964
Isle Royale (AD-29) (Destroyer Tender-Repair Ship)	Salvaged the beached USS Mahnomen County (LST-912) at Chu Lai during January 1967 with crewmembers going ashore for stripping operations
Jamestown (AGTR-3)	Conducted numerous month-long deployments along the Vietnam coast collecting data, with photographic evidence that crewmembers went ashore, between January 1966 and September 1969
John R. Craig (DD- 885)	Anchored off Nha Trang during summer 1968 with crewmembers going ashore for beach party
John W. Thomason (DD-760)	Operated on Nga Be River during 1969
Joseph Strauss (DDG-16)	Operated on Mekong River Delta March 4, 1966 and Ganh Rai Bay during November 7 and December 7, 1968
Kishwaukee (AOG-9)	Operated primarily or exclusively on Vietnam's inland waterways
Krishna (ARL-38)	Operated primarily or exclusively on Vietnam's inland waterways
Kula Gulf (CVE-108)	Used as helicopter and troop transport docked at Cam Ranh Bay, November 13-16,
Lang (DE-1060)	Docked topier #4 in Da Nang Harbor for 38 minutes on January 5, 1972, and sent whaleboat to and from shore with "briefing personnel" on January 8,1973
Leary (DD-879)	Operated on Baie de Ganh Rai of the Mekong River Delta on October 9, 1967
Lenawee (APA-195)	Conducted troop and supply landings at Da Nang and Chu Lai from April 1965 to December 1966
Leonard F. Mason (DD-852)	Operated on Vung Ganh Rai Bay and channels during August1969
Lloyd Thomas (DD- 764)	Operated on Ganh Rai Bay and Saigon River area during December 28,1970
Loftberg (DD-759)	Operated on Song Nha Be River from February 18-21 and April 14-15, 1969 and on Song Cua Dai River from April 10-12, 1969

Ship Name	Activities in Vietnam
Long Beach (CGN-9) (Guided Missile Cruiser, Nuclear)	While anchored in Da Nang Harbor, deck logs show that utility boats went ashore with passengers on May 5, 1968 and the Captains Gig went ashore on September 4, 1969
Lowe (DE-325)	Anchored in Saigon Harbor during April1966
Loyalty (MSO-457)	Traveled up the Saigon River to Saigon September 19-22, 1964, and docked to a pier at Cam Ranh Bay on April 9 and 25, 1971
Lucid (MSO-458)	Docked topier at Da Nang for off-loadingand on loading equipment during May1967
Lyman K. Swenson (DD-729)	Traveled up Saigon River for a 4-day visit to Saigon in May 1964
Mahan (DLG-11)	Visited Saigon via Saigon River October 24-28, 1962 and sent a "group of personnel" ashore at Da Nang for a short tour of Monkey Mountain on October 6, 1968
Mahopac(ATA-196)	Moored in Saigon during October 6-9, 1965, and operated on Mekong River from October 30-November 3, 1966
Mansfield (DD-728)	Operated on Saigon River August 8-19, 1967 and December 21-24, 1969
Marathon (PG-89)	Operated primarily or exclusively on Vietnam's inland waterways
Mark (AKL-12)	Operated primarily or exclusively on Vietnam's inland waterways
Mars (AFS-1) (Combat Stores Ship)	Operated on Mekong River July 8, 1966 Conducted numerous on shore supply replenishments at Da Nang, Cam Ranh Bay, Vung Tau, and An Thoi from May 1965 to November 1972 with evidence of crewmembers going ashore
Mathews (AKA-96)	On loaded supplies at Da Nang and delivered them up to the Cua Viet River to Dong Ha with "mike boats" from August through December 1967
Maury (AGS-16)	Conducted surveys of Mekong River Delta and other coastal area and rivers from November 1965-1969
McKean (DD-784)	Operated on Mekong and Saigon River Deltas during March 14-15, 1967
Mercer (APB-39)	Operated primarily or exclusively on Vietnam's inland waterways
Merrick (AKA-97) (Attack Cargo Ship)	Participated in Operation Jackstay amphibious landings while on inland Saigon River Delta during March 1966 Conducted troop and cargo beach landing with small boats at Hue, Chu Lai,Saigon River Delta, and Da Nang from July 1965 through November1968
Montrose (APA-212)	Operated on Song Hue River December 1965, operated on Long Tau River during March 1967, and operated on Cua Viet River and at Dong Ha during May1967
Morton (DD-948)	Operated on Vung Ganh Rai and Saigon River during April 1966 and February1969
Mullinnix (DD-944)	Operated on Vung Ganh Rai and Saigon River from August 5-6, 1966
Myles C. Fox (DD-829)	Anchored off Qui Nhon and Nha Trang with crew members going ashore from February 5-20, 1967
Navarro (APA-215)	Conducted troop on and off loading operations from May 1965 to February 1968 at Da Nang, Chu Lai, and Quang Ngai Province
Newell (DER-322)	Docked at Port of Nha Trang from December 22-24, 1965
Newman K. Perry (DD-883)	Operated on Mekong River Delta and Saigon River from November 23-28,1966
New Orleans (LPH-11)	Docked to pier at Da Nang on March 12, 1970
Niagara Falls (AFS-3)	Unloaded supplies on Saigon River and Cam Ranh Bay, April 22-25, 1968 Conducted on shore supply replenishments with helicopters and small boats at Da Nang, Cam Ranh Bay, Vung Tau, and An Thoi from April 1968 to March 1973
Nicholas (DD-449) (Destroyer)	Operated on Mekong River Delta during January 1967 and Ganh Rai Bay and Mekong River Delta during August 1968
Norris (DD-859)	Conducted operations on inland Song Nga Bay during November-December 1966
Noxubee (AOG 56)	Operated primarily or exclusively on Vietnam's inland waterways

325

Ship Name	Activities in Vietnam
Nueces (APB-40)	Operated primarily or exclusively on Vietnam's inland waterways
Oak Hill (LSD-7)	Served as station and repair ship in Da Nang Harbor with evidence of crewmembers going ashore from January through March 1966
O'Bannon (DD-450)	Operated on Saigon River during May 22-24, 1966
Okanogan (APA-220)	Operated primarily or exclusively on Vietnam's inland waterways
Okinawa (LPH-3) (Landing Platform Helicopter)	Docked to pier at Cam Ranh Bay to offload aircraft during May 1971
Oklahoma City (CLG- 5)	Docked in Saigon during 21-24 July 1964
Orleck (DD-886)	Operated on Mekong River Delta during July 1969
Oxford (AGTR-1)	Conducted numerous month-long deployments along the Vietnam coast collecting data, with likelihood that crew members went ashore, between 1965 and1969
Ozbourn (DD-846)	Conducted fire support missions on Saigon River October-November 1965 and August- October 1966
Patapsco (AOG-1)	Operated primarily or exclusively on Vietnam's inland waterways
Paul Revere (APA- 248)	Assisted with salvage of the USS Card (ACV-11) in Saigon Harbor on Saigon River during May 1964 Conducted small boat troop landings at Qui Nhon, Quang Ngai Province, and elsewherefrom August 1965 through April 1966 and August through November 1967.
Perkins (DD-877)	Operated on Saigon River during June 1969
Picking (DD-685)	Operated on Saigon River during November 16, 1965
Pictor (AF-54)	Delivered supplies by small boat to Dong Ha on Cua Viet River during September 1967 and docked to the pier at Da Nang during 1969
Pine Island (AV-12)	Anchored at Da Nang during August 1964, and Cam Ranh Bay for month-long periods during 1965 and 1966, to repair and tend to Navy sea planes, with the likelihood that crew members went ashore on liberty leave
Point Defiance (LSD-31)	Operated on Saigon River during March 1967 and conducted several operations on Saigon River to Saigon Port during October and November 1968 Conducted numerous troop and supply landings with small boats at Da Nang, Qui Nhon, Van Tuong, and Kien Hoa from May 1965 through October 1972.
Ponchatoula (AO-148)	Operated on Mekong River Delta during July 1971
Preston (DD-795)	Operated on Mekong River Delta, Ganh Rai Bay and Saigon River from September 28- 29 and December 27-29, 1965, and on Mekong River Delta June 3,1967
Prichett (DD-561)	Operated on Mekong River Delta and Saigon River during August1969
Prime (MSO-466)	Docked to pier at Da Nang on February 16, 1967
Providence (CLG-6)	Operated on Saigon River 3 days during January 1964 and on Cua Viet River during August 1972
Ready (PG-87)	Operated primarily or exclusively on Vietnam's inland waterways
Reclaimer (ARS-42)	Operated in Saigon Harbor to salvage USS Card (ACV-11) from sinking in Saigon River during May 1964 and in Rung Sat Special Zone of Mekong River delta salvaging ships during early 1966.
Repose (AH-16) (Hospital Ship)	Operated continuously on close coastal waters from 1966-1970, with the likelihood that crew members went ashore on liberty leave
Richard B. Anderson (DD- 786)	Docked to pier at Da Nang on August 29, 1972
Richard E. Kraus (DD-849)	Operated on coastal inlet north of Da Nang from June 2-5, 1966, protecting Marine holding a bridge
Richard S Edwards (DD-950)	Operated on Mekong River Delta in Province of Kien Hoa during February 28 and March 1, 1969

326

Ship Name	Activities in Vietnam
Rowan (DD-782)	Operated on Song Tra Khuc River and inland waterway Qui Nhon Bay from April through July 1965
Rupertus (DD-851)	Operated on Saigon River during May 1969
Safeguard (ARS-25)	Operated on Ganh Rai Bay and Mekong River Delta during December 8,1965
Saint Paul (CA-73) (Cruiser)	While anchored in Da Nang Harbor on May 9, 1969 and May 25, 1970, decklogs show limited small boat operations to shore
Salisbury Sound (AV-13)	Traveled up Saigon River to Saigon during June 1964, and anchored at Cam Ranh Bay for month-long periods during 1966, to repair and tend to Navy sea planes, with the likelihood that crew members went ashore on liberty leave
Samuel Gompers (AD-	Multiple dockings to piers at Da Nang during April 1972
Satyr (ARL-23)	Operated primarily or exclusively on Vietnam's inland waterways
Sanctuary (AH-17)	Operated continuously on close coastal waters from 1967-1971, with the likelihood that crew members went ashore on liberty leave
Serrano (AGS-24)	Conducted mapping surveys of Mekong River Delta and other coastal and river areas from 1966 through 1969
Shelton (DD-790)	Operated on Saigon River during January 16, 1966
Skagit (AKA-105)	Conducted troop and cargo beach "mike boat" landings at Da Nang, Chu Lai, and Quang Ngai from November 1965 to November 1967
Southerland (DD-743)	Operated on Song Nga Bay and Saigon River July 1966
Sphinx (ARL-24)	Operated primarily or exclusively on Vietnam's inland waterways
Sproston (DD-577)	Operated on Mekong River Delta and Ganh Rai Bay during January 1966
Steinaker (DD-863)	Anchored off Phan Thiet July 25- August 3, 1968 with crewmembers going ashore to visit Junk Base
Strong (DD-758)	Operated in Mekong River Delta and Rung Sat Special Zone during April 1968
Talladega (APA-208)	Operated on Saigon River during October 1967
Tanner (AGS-15)	Conducted surveys of Mekong River Delta and other coastal areas and rivers from October 1966 through 1968
Taussig (DD-746)	Operated on Soirap River in Mekong River Delta during June 15-26, 1966
Tawakoni (ATF-114)	Operated in Saigon Harbor to salvage USS Card (ACV-11) from sinking in Saigon River during May 1964
Tillamook (ATA-192)	Operated on Long Tau branch of Saigon River during January 1966
	Conducted dredge lift on Saigon River during November 1964
Thomaston (LSD-28)	Conducted numerous troop and supply landings with small boats at Da Nang, Cam Ranh Bay, Song Co Chien River area, and Cua Viet River area from 1965 to 1972 (Note: No Agent Orange exposure for 1975 operations)
Tolovana (AO-64) (Fleet Oiler)	Sent crew ashore for beach party at Phu Quoc during May 1971
Tombigbee (AOG-11)	Operated primarily or exclusively on Vietnam's inland waterways
Tortuga (LSD-26)	Operated primarily or exclusively on Vietnam's inland waterways
Towers (DDG-9)	Operated on Saigon River and Rung Sat Special Zone during July 1966
Tulare (AKA/LKA-112)	Conducted troop and cargo "mike boat" beach landings at Da Nang, Chu Lai, Cam Ranh Bay and Vung Tau from 1966 to 1972
Tutuila (ARG-4)	Operated primarily or exclusively on Vietnam's inland waterways
Union (AKA/LKA-106)	Anchored in mouth of the Hue River while conducting operations during April 1965 and conducted troop and cargo "mike boat" beach landings at Da Nang and Cam Ranh Bay from 1965 to 1969
Ute (ATF-76) (Fleet Ocean Tug)	Conducted numerous salvaging operations on beached vessels from April 1966 through April 1971 with crewmembers going ashore and all attended beach party at CamRanh Bay on April 12, 1969

Ship Name	Activities in Vietnam
Valley Forge (LPH-8) (Landing Platform Helicopter)	Operated as helicopter and troop transport with helicopters and smaller vessels transporting troops on and off shore from September 1964 to September1969
Vancouver (LPD-2)	Conducted numerous amphibious troop beach landingswith smaller "mike boats" in the areas of Da Nang, Cam Ranh Bay, Cua Viet River, and Mekong River Delta, from August 1966 through 1971
Vega (AF-59)	Conducted resupply operation inthe Mekong River delta area onSeptember 13, 1966, on loaded supplies at An Thoi, Vung Tau, Cam Ranh Bay, and Da Nang during June 1969, and delivered supplies to Da Nang, Cam Ranh Bay, Con Son, An Thoi, and Hon Choi during Novemberto December 1970
Walke (DD-723)	Operated on Mekong River Delta at Vung Ganh Rei September 2, 1969
Warbler (MSC-206) (Minesweeper-Coastal)	Docked to pier at Cam Ranh Bay July 22-25, 1964 and June 18 and July 6, 1970
Warrington (DD-843)	Operated on Mekong River Delta, Rung Sat Special Zone, north of Vung Ganh Rai Bay during March 1967
Washburn (AKA/LKA-108)	Conducted numerous small boat beach landings at Da Nang, Thon My Thuy, Hue on erfume River, and Dong Ha on Cua Viet River from 1965 to 1969
Weiss (APD/LPR-135)	Conducted troop-landing operations withMarine and SEAL units at various locations in the Mekong River Delta, Rung Sat Special Zone, and Saigon River and routinely surveyed river mouths and canal entrances for amphibious landings from November 1965 through February 1969
Whetstone (LSD-27)	On loaded and delivered troops to D Nang, Hue, Phu Bai, Dong Ha with beach landings and "mike boats" and served as long-term "boat havens" for repairs of smaller vessels at Da Nang and Qui Nhon during 1965, 1966, 1968 and 1969
Whippoorwill (MSC-207)	Docked to pier at Cam Ranh Bay during July 22-25,1964
White Plains (AFS-4)	Conducted on shore supply replenishments with helicopters and small boats at Da Nang, Cam Ranh Bay, Vung Tau, and An Thoi from January 1969 to March 1973
White River (LSMR 536)	Operated primarily or exclusively on Vietnam's inland waterways
Wiltsie (DD-716)	Operated on Saigon River during July 1966. While operating in close coastal waters during September 1970, two officers and five sailors were sent ashore by helicopter for one night
Winnemucca (YTB- 785)	Operated primarily or exclusively on Vietnam's inland waterways

MUSTARD GAS EXPOSURE AND LONG-TERM HEALTH EFFECTS

In 1991, the Department of Veterans Affairs (VA) relaxed requirements for evaluating mustard gas-related compensation claims because of the confidentiality of some of the World War II testing and a lack of military medical records and follow-up. At that time, a review of studies of the effects of mustard gas exposure led VA to publish regulations authorizing service-connection and disability compensation payments to veterans who were exposed to significant levels of mustard gas and who suffer from chronic forms of certain diseases.

An estimated 4,000 servicemen participated in tests using significant concentrations of mustard gas either in chambers or field exercises in contaminated areas during World War II. This secret testing was conducted in order to develop better protective clothing, masks and skin ointments. There is no central roster of World War II participants in either the laboratory or field tests. The Army conducted tests on Army personnel in the laboratory and in the field. The test sites included:

Edgewood Arsenal, Maryland;
Camp Sibert, Alabama;
Bushnell, Florida;
Dugway Proving Ground, Utah;
and San Jose Island, Panama Canal Zone

Military personnel from the U.S. Navy Training Center Bainbridge, Maryland also were sent to the Naval Research Lab in Washington, D.C., to participate in tests. Gas testing facilities also were located at Great Lakes Naval Training Center in Illinois and Camp Lejeune, North Carolina.

VETERANS WHO MAY BE ELIGIBLE FOR COMPENSATION

VA policies generally authorize service-connection and compensation payments to veterans who were exposed to mustard gas and/or Lewisite and who suffer from a number of diseases or conditions, including:

• Full-body exposure to nitrogen or sulfur mustard together with the subsequent development of chronic conjunctivitis, keratitis, corneal opacities, scar formation, or the following cancers: nasopharyngeal; laryngeal; lung (except mesothelioma); or squamous cell carcinoma of the skin;
• Full-body exposure to nitrogen or sulfur mustard -- or exposure to Lewisite -- and the subsequent development of a chronic form of laryngitis, bronchitis, emphysema, asthma or chronic obstructive pulmonary disease;
• Full-body exposure to nitrogen mustard with the subsequent development of acute nonlymphocytic leukemia.

Service-connection is not allowed if the claimed condition is due to the veteran's own willful misconduct or if there is affirmative evidence that establishes some other nonservice-related condition or event as the cause of the claimed disability.

Veterans who were exposed to significant amounts of mustard gas and have health problems that may be compensable (or their survivors) may contact the nearest VA regional office at (800) 827-1000 for more information about benefits.

VA PROGRAMS FOR VETERANS EXPOSED TO RADIATION

VA provides special priority for enrollment for health-care services to any veteran exposed to ionizing radiation in connection with:

• Onsite participation in a test involving the atmospheric detonation of a nuclear device (without regard to whether the nation conducting the test was the United States or another nation).
• The American occupation of Hiroshima and Nagasaki, Japan, during the period beginning August 6, 1945, and ending July 1, 1946.
• Internment as a prisoner of war in Japan (or service on active duty in Japan immediately following such internment) during World War II which (as determined by the Secretary of the VA) resulted in an opportunity for exposure to ionizing radiation comparable to that of veterans described above.
• The definition of radiation-risk activities was expanded in March 2002 to include service at Amchitka Island, Alaska, prior to January 1, 1974, if a veteran was exposed while performing duties related to certain underground nuclear tests.
• The new definition also includes service at gaseous diffusion plants located in Paducah, Ky., Portsmouth, Ohio and an area known as K25 at Oak Ridge, Tenn.

In addition, these veterans are eligible to participate in the VA ionizing radiation registry examination program. VA also pays compensation to veterans and their survivors if the veteran is determined to have a disability due to radiation exposure while in service.

RADIATION STATISTICS

Some 195,000 service members have been identified as participants in the post-World War II occupation of Hiroshima and Nagasaki, Japan. In addition, approximately 210,000 mostly military members are confirmed as participants in U.S. atmospheric nuclear tests between 1945 and 1962 in the United States and the Pacific and Atlantic oceans prior to the 1963 Limited Test Ban Treaty. The Defense Threat Reduction Agency's Nuclear Test Personnel Review program since 1978 has maintained a database of participants in atmospheric nuclear test activities. About one-fourth of the participants received no measurable dose of ionizing radiation, with fewer than one per cent of the nuclear test participants identified as having a dose of 5 rem or higher. (The current federal guideline for U.S. workplace exposure is 5 rem per year.)

DETERMINATION OF SERVICE-CONNECTED DISEASES

VA may pay compensation for radiogenic diseases under two programs specific to radiation- exposed veterans and their survivors:

STATUTORY LIST

Veterans who participated in nuclear tests by the U.S. or its allies, who served with the occupation forces in Hiroshima or Nagasaki, Japan, between August 1945 and July 1946, or who were similarly exposed to ionizing radiation while a prisoner of war in Japan, are eligible for compensation for cancers specified in legislation.

The types of cancer covered by these laws are:
All forms of leukemia;
Cancer of the thyroid;
Cancer of the breast;
Cancer of the pharynx;
Cancer of the esophagus;
Cancer of the stomach;
Cancer of the small intestine;
Cancer of the pancreas;
Cancer of the bile ducts;
Cancer of the gall bladder;
Cancer of the salivary gland;
Cancer of the urinary tract;
Lymphomas (except Hodgkin's disease);
Multiple myeloma;
Primary liver cancer;
Bone Cancer;
Brain Cancer;
Lung Cancer;
Colon Cancer;
Ovary Cancer

In 2011, the VA expanded the definition of non-Hodgkin's lymphoma to include:
Chronic lymphocytic leukemia;

Small-cell lymphocytic lymphoma

The new rules apply to those veterans who participated in "radiation-risk activities" while on active duty, during active duty for training or inactive duty training as a member of a reserve component.

REGULATORY LIST

Disability compensation claims of veterans who were exposed to radiation in service and who develop a disease within specified time periods not specified in the statutory list are governed by regulation. Under the regulations, various additional factors must be considered in determining service-connection, including amount of radiation exposure, duration of exposure, and elapsed time between exposure and onset of the disease. VA regulations identify all cancers as potentially radiogenic, as well as certain other non- malignant conditions: posterior subcapsular cataracts; non-malignant thyroid nodular disease; parathyroid adenoma; and tumors of the brain and central nervous system.

A final rule that expanded the regulatory list from more than a dozen specific cancers to add "any other cancer" (any malignancy) was published Sept. 24, 1998. The rulemaking began following a 1995 review of the radiogenicity of cancer generally by the Veterans Advisory Committee on Environmental Hazards. It concluded that, on the basis of current scientific knowledge, exposure to ionizing radiation can be a contributing factor in the development of any malignancy. VA also will consider evidence that diseases other those specified in regulation may be caused by radiation exposure.

RATES OF DISABILITY COMPENSATION

Rates of compensation depend upon the degree of disability and follow a payment schedule that is adjusted annually and applies to all veterans. Please refer to the charts in Chapter 4 of this book.

IONIZING RADIATION REGISTRY PROGRAM

In addition to special eligibility to enroll for VA healthcare for radiation-related conditions, atomic veterans are eligible to participate in VA's Ionizing Radiation Registry examination. Under the Ionizing Radiation Registry program, VA will perform a complete physical examination, including all necessary tests, for each veteran who requests it if the veteran was exposed to ionizing radiation while participating in the nuclear weapons testing program, or if he or she served with the U.S. occupation forces in Hiroshima or Nagasaki. Veterans need not be enrolled for general VA care to be eligible for the Ionizing Radiation Registry.

PROJECT 112 / PROJECT SHAD VETERANS

Project SHAD, an acronym for Shipboard Hazard and Defense, was part of a larger effort called Project 112, which was a comprehensive program initiated in 1962 by the Department of Defense (DoD).

Project SHAD encompassed a series of tests by DoD to determine the vulnerability of U.S. warships to attacks with chemical and biological warfare agents, and the potential risk to American forces posed by these agents.

Project 112 tests involved similar tests conducted on land rather than aboard ships.

Project SHAD involved service members from the Navy and Army and may have involved a small number of personnel from the Marine Corps and Air Force. Service members were not test subjects, but rather were involved in conducting the tests. Animals were used in some, but not most, tests.

DoD continues to release declassified reports about sea-and land-based tests of chemical and biological materials known collectively as "Project 112." The Department of Veterans Affairs (VA) is working with DoD to obtain information as to the nature and availability of the tests, who participated, duration and agents used.

To date, there is no clear evidence of specific, long-term health problems associated with a veteran's participation in Project SHAD, but the VA is conducting a follow-up study to a 2007 Institute of Medicine Study.

Veterans who believe their health may have been affected by these tests should contact the SHAD helpline at (800) 749-8387.

CHAPTER 28

SPINA BIFIDA PROGRAM

OVERVIEW

Spina bifida is the most frequently occurring permanently disabling birth defect. It affects approximately one of every 1,000 newborns in the United States. Neural tube defects (NTD) are birth defects that involve incomplete development of the brain, spinal cord, and/or protective coverings for these organs. Spina bifida, the most common NTD, results from the failure of the spine to close properly during the first month of pregnancy. (Anencephaly and encephalocele are less common types of NTDs). In severe cases, the spinal cord protrudes through the back of and may be covered by skin or a thin membrane.

Some Vietnam veterans, and certain other veterans have children with spina bifida. While Vietnam veterans and their mates are now moving out of the age category usually associated with childbirth, it is anticipated that some future births will occur and that some of these children may have birth defects, including spina bifida. Some research efforts have suggested that there may be a relationship between exposure to Vietnam veterans to Agent Orange and/or other herbicides used in Vietnam and the subsequent development of spina bifida in some of their children

> **Key Takeaways**
>
> Spina Bifida is a type of neural tube birth defect
>
> Some Vietnam veterans and other certain veterans have children with Spina Bifida
>
> The VA pays a monthly allowance based on the level of disability to or for a child with Spina Bifida who is a child of a Vietnam Veteran
>
> Vocational training programs may also be available as well as healthcare benefits

For the purpose of the Spina Bifida Program, the term *Vietnam Veteran* means an individual who performed active military, naval, or air service in the Republic of Vietnam during the period beginning on January 9, 1962, and ending May 7, 1975, without regard to the characterization of the individual's service. Service in the Republic of Vietnam includes service in the waters offshore and service in other locations if the conditions of service involved duty or visitation in the Republic of Vietnam.

Please note, the Spina Bifida Program does not include spina bifida occult

Children who have spina bifida and meet the following requirements may be eligible for VA benefits, including healthcare, compensation and vocational training:
- Are biological children of Veterans who served:
- In Vietnam during the period from January 9, 1962 through May 7, 1975, or
- In or near the Korean demilitarized zone between September 1, 1967 and August 31, 1971 and were exposed to herbicides. Veterans who served in a unit in or near the Korean demilitarized zone anytime between April 1, 1968 and August 31, 1971 are presumed to have been exposed to herbicides.
- Were conceived after the date on which the Veteran first entered Vietnam or the Korean demilitarized zone during the qualifying service period
- The term "herbicide agent" means a chemical in a herbicide used in support of United States and military operations in or near the Korean demilitarized zone, during the period beginning on September 1, 1967, and ending on August 31, 1971.

TOLL-FREE SPINA BIFIDA HOT LINE

In June 2001, VA opened a hot line for Vietnam veterans with questions about health care benefits for their children who have spina bifida.
The number for the hot line is (888) 820-1756.

Callers can speak to a benefits advisor Monday through Friday, from 10:00 a.m. to 1:30 p.m., and from 2:30 p.m. to 4:30 p.m., Eastern time. An after-hours phone message will allow callers to leave their names and telephone numbers for a return call the next business day.

The hot line is managed by VA's Health Administration Center in Denver, Colorado.

MONETARY BENEFITS

VA shall pay a monthly allowance based upon the level of disability to or for a child who is suffering from spina bifida, and who is a child of a Vietnam veteran. Receipt of this allowance shall not affect the right of the child, or the right of any individual based on the child's relationship to that individual, to receive any other benefit to which the child, or that individual, may be entitled under any law administered by VA. If a child suffering from spina bifida is the natural child of two Vietnam veterans, he or she is entitled to only one monthly allowance.

The monthly allowance is set at three levels, depending upon the degree of disability suffered by the child. VA shall determine the level of disability suffered by the child in accordance with the following criteria:

LEVEL I

- The child is able to walk without braces or other external support (although gait may be impaired); and
- Has no sensory or motor impairment of upper extremities; and
- Has an IQ of 90 or higher; and
- Is continent of urine and feces.

LEVEL II

Provided that none of the child's disabilities are severe enough to be evaluated at Level III, and the child is:
- Ambulatory, but only with braces or other external support; or
- Has sensory or motor impairment of upper extremities but is able to grasp pen,

334

feed self, and perform self-care; or
- Has an IQ of at least 70 but less than 90; or
- Requires drugs or intermittent catheterization or other mechanical means to maintain proper urinary bladder function, or mechanisms for proper bowel function.
-

LEVEL III

- The child is unable to ambulate;or
- Has sensory or motor impairment of upper extremities severe enough to prevent grasping a pen, feeding self, and performing self-care; or
- Has an IQ of 69 or less; or
- Has complete urinary or fecal incontinence

SPINA BIFIDA BENEFIT RATE TABLE (EFFECTIVE 12-01-2017)	
Disability Level	Monthly Allowance
Level I	$321.00
Level II	$1097.00
Level III	$1,869.00

VOCATIONAL TRAINING FOR CHILDREN WITH SPINA BIFIDA

To qualify for entitlement to a vocational training program an applicant must be a child:

- To whom VA has awarded a monthly allowance for spina bifida and;
- For whom VA has determined that achievement of a vocational goal is reasonably feasible.
- A vocational training program may not begin before a child's 18th birthday, or the date of completion of secondary schooling, whichever comes first. Depending on the need, a child may be provided up to 24 months of full-time training

HEALTHCARE BENEFITS

In addition to monetary allowances, vocational training and rehabilitation, the Department of Veterans Affairs (VA) also provides VA-financed healthcare benefits to Vietnam veterans' birth children diagnosed with spina bifida. For the purpose of this program, spina bifida is defined as all forms or manifestations of spina bifida (except spina bifida occulta), including complications or associated medical conditions related to spina bifida according to the scientific literature.

Healthcare benefits available under this program are limited to those necessary for the treatment of spina bifida and related medical conditions. Beneficiaries should be aware that this program is not a comprehensive healthcare plan and does not cover care that is unrelated to spina bifida.

Administration of the program is centralized to VA's Health Administration Center (HAC) in Denver, Colorado. HAC is responsible for all aspects of the spina bifida healthcare program, including the authorization of benefits and the subsequent processing and payment of claims. All inquiries regarding healthcare benefits should be made directly to HAC.

Healthcare benefits may be claimed for services and supplies starting on the effective date specified in the VA regional office award letter.

Beneficiaries in receipt of a VA regional office spina bifida award will receive an identification card from the Health Administration Center.

There are no beneficiary co-payments or deductibles. VA is the exclusive payer for services provided to beneficiaries under this program, and billing should be sent directly to the Health Administration Center. The determined allowable amount for payment is considered payment in full, and the provider may not bill the beneficiary for the difference between the billed amount and the VA-determined allowed amount.

COVERED BENEFITS

This program provides comprehensive health care for covered services and supplies that are considered medically necessary and appropriate.

GENERAL EXCLUSIONS

- Care as part of a grant study or research program
- Care considered experimental or investigational
- Care that is not medically necessary or appropriate
- Drugs not approved by the FDA for commercial marketing
- Services provided outside the scope of the provider's license or certification
- Services rendered by providers suspended or sanctioned by a federal agency
- Services, procedures or supplies for which the beneficiary has no legal obligation to pay, such as services obtained at a health fair
- Treatment for spina bifida occulta

PREAUTHORIZATION REQUIREMENTS

Although most health care services and supplies do not require approval in advance (preauthorization), some do.
Preauthorization is NOT required for routine health care services and supplies.
Preauthorization IS required for:
- Attendants Dental services
- Durable medical equipment (DME) with a total rental or purchase price in excess of $2,000
- Mental health services Hospice care
- Substance abuse treatment Training of family members
- Transplantation services
- Travel (other than mileage for privately owned automobiles for local travel) Note: When in doubt, contact the HAC.

SELECTING HEALTHCARE PROVIDERS

Beneficiaries may select the provider of their choice, as long as the provider is an approved health care provider. The provider must be approved by the Centers for Medicare and Medicaid Services (CMS), Department of Defense TRICARE program, CHAMPVA, JCAHO or may be a health care provider approved for providing services pursuant to a state license or certificate. A provider is not required to contract with the HAC; the HAC does not maintain a list of providers.

CLAIMS

Claims are to be mailed directly to VA's Health Administration Center at the following address.
VA Health Administration Center
PO Box 469065
Denver CO 80246-906

As a safeguard against claims getting lost in the mail, beneficiaries should keep copies of all claim documents submitted.

FILING DEADLINES

Claims must be filed with the Health Administration Center no later than:

- One year after the date of service; or
- In the case of inpatient care, one year after the date of discharge; or
- In the case of a VA regional office award for retroactive eligibility, 180 days following beneficiary notification of the award.

PAYMENTS

Approved healthcare providers will be paid 100% of the VA-determined allowable charge for covered services. VA payment for covered services constitutes payment in full. Federal regulations prohibit providers from seeking any additional monies from beneficiaries and third party payers such as private insurers, for services paid by VA.

Note: If the beneficiary pays for care and subsequently files a claim for reimbursement, VA payment to the beneficiary will be limited to the VA-allowed amount. For this reason, beneficiaries are advised not to pay their providers-but instead, have the providers bill HAC directly.

OTHER HEALTH INSURANCE

While VA assumes full responsibility for the cost of services related to the treatment of spina bifida and associated conditions, third-party insurers including Medicare and Medicaid, assume payment responsibility for services unrelated to the VA-covered conditions.

EXPLANATION OF BENEFITS

Upon completion of claim processing, an EOB will be mailed to the beneficiary. If a provider files the claim, an EOB will be mailed to them also. The EOB is a summarization of the action taken on the claim and contains, at a minimum, the following information.

- Beneficiary name;
- Description of services and/or supplies provided; Dates of service or supplies provided;
- Amount billed;
- VA-allowed amount;
- To whom payment, if any, was made; Reasons for denial (if applicable).

RECONSIDERATION OF CLAIMS / APPEALS

If a healthcare provider, beneficiary or beneficiary's representative disagrees with a claim determination, including the VA-allowed amount, a request for reconsideration of the disputed determination may be made. To do so, the request must:

- Be in writing;
- Be accompanied by a copy of the EOB in question; and

- State the specific issue that is being disputed, why the VA determination is considered to be in error, and include any new and relevant information not previously considered.

To meet the filing deadline, requests for reconsideration are to be mailed to the following address within one year of the date of the initial EOB:

VA Health Administration Center Reconsideration/Appeals
PO Box 460948
Denver CO 80246-0948

Upon complete review of the request and all the relevant documentation and evidence, a written determination will be mailed to the claimant.

CHAPTER 29

BENEFITS FOR POST-TRAUMATIC STRESS DISORDER AND SEXUAL TRAUMA

POST-TRAUMATIC STRESS DISORDER (PTSD)

PTSD is a condition resulting from exposure to direct or indirect threat of death, serious injury, or a physical threat. The events that can cause PTSD are called "stressors" and may include combat or war exposure, sexual or physical abuse, terrorist attacks, serious accidents or natural disasters such as fire, tornado, hurricane, flood or earthquake.

Symptoms of PTSD can include recurrent thoughts of the traumatic event, reduced involvement in work or outside interests, emotional numbing, hyper-alertness, anxiety and irritability. The disorder can be more severe and longer lasting when the stress is human initiated action (example: war, rape, terrorism).

> **Key Takeaways**
> PTSD is a mental health problem that some people develop after experiencing or witnessing a life-threatening event
>
> People with PTSD may also have other problems including feelings of hopelessness, shame or despair, depression or anxiety, drinking or drug problems, physical symptoms or chronic pain, or employment problems
>
> Medications including SSRIs and SNRIs can be helpful for treating PTSD

There are many types of treatment for PTSD, including counseling and medicines known as SSRIs.

CLAY HUNT ACT

The *Clay Hunt Suicide Prevention for American Veterans (SAV) Act* will help reduce military and veteran suicides and improve access to quality mental health care. The following are goals of the legislation.

- Increase access to mental health care by, among other things, creating a peer support and community outreach pilot program to assist transitioning servicemembers as well as a one-stop, interactive website of available resources.

339

- Better meet the demand for mental health care by starting a pilot program to repay the loan debt of students in psychiatry so it is easier to recruit them to work at the VA.

- Boost the accountability of mental health care by requiring an annual evaluation of VA mental health and suicide-prevention programs.

PRESUMPTIVE ELIGIBILITY FOR PSYCHOSIS AND OTHER MENTAL ILLNESS

Certain Veterans who experienced psychosis within a specified time- frame are to have their psychosis presumed to be service-connected for purposes of VA medical benefits. In addition, VA will presume that Persian Gulf War Veterans are service-connected for purposes of VA medical benefits if such Veterans develop mental illness other than psychosis within two years after discharge or release from service and before the end of the 2-year period beginning on the last day of the Persian Gulf War. Under this authority Veterans who are not otherwise eligible for VA health care and meet the description stated can receive treatment only for psychosis or mental illness and other conditions directly related to psychosis or mental illness at no cost.

Psychosis

Eligibility for treatment of psychosis, and such condition is exempted from copayments for any Veteran who served in the United States active duty military, naval, or air service and developed such psychosis within two years after discharge or release from the active military duty, naval or air service; and before the following date associated with the war or conflict in which the Veteran served:

- **World War II** July 26, 1949
- **Korean Conflict** February 1, 1957
- **Vietnam Era** May 8, 1977
- **Persian Gulf War** Date To Be Determined

Mental Illness (other than Psychosis)

Eligibility for benefits is established for treatment of an active mental illness (other than psychosis), and such condition is exempted from copayments for any Veteran of the Persian Gulf War who developed such mental illness:

- Within two years after discharge or release from the active duty military, naval, or air service; and
- Before the end of the two-year period beginning on the last day of the Persian Gulf War (end date not yet determined).

DISABILITY COMPENSATION

The Veterans Service Organizations provide Service Officers at no cost to help veterans and family members pursue VA disability claims. Service Officers are familiar with every step in the application and interview process, and can provide both technical guidance and moral support. In addition, some Service Officers particularly specialize in assisting veterans with PTSD disability claims. Even if a veteran has not been a member of a specific Veterans Service Organization, the veteran still can request the assistance of a Service Officer working for that organization. In order to get representation by a qualified and helpful Service Officer, you can directly contact the local office of any Veterans Service Organization or ask for recommendations from other veterans who have applied for VA disability, or from a PTSD specialist at a VA PTSD clinic or a VetCenter.

Once the VA has awarded service connection for PTSD, it will then review the most current clinical evidence of record to determine how the severity of your symptoms impairs your social and industrial (ability to work) capacity.

The VA has a schedule of rating disabilities, located in title 38 C.F.R., Part 4. The VA has established "Diagnostic Codes" (DC) for various medical and psychiatric disorders, which include a description of the severity of related symptoms and a corresponding disability percentage (called a "rating" or "evaluation").

Although there are different DCs for covered psychiatric disorders, the VA evaluates the level of disability due to psychiatric disorders under the same criteria, regardless of the actual diagnosis. 38 C.F.R. §4.130, DC 9411, governs PTSD ratings. This regulation provides graduated ratings of 0%, 10%, 30%, 50%, 70% or 100%. A 0% rating is noncompensable this means that you have service-connected PTSD, however, there is little or no impairment as a result. VA compensation payments begin at 10% and increase at each rating level.

GENERAL RATING FORMULA FOR MENTAL DISORDERS:

Disability Rating	Description of Disability
100%	Total occupational and social impairment, due to such symptoms as: gross impairment in thought process or communication; persistent delusions or hallucinations; grossly inappropriate behavior; persistent danger of hurting self or others; intermittent inability to perform activities of daily living (including maintenance of minimal personal hygiene); disorientation to time or place; memory loss for names of close relatives, own occupation, or own name
70%	Occupational and social impairment, with deficiencies in most areas, such as work, school, family relations, judgment, thinking, or mood, due to such symptoms as: suicidal ideation; obsessional rituals which interfere with routine activities; speech intermittently illogical, obscure, or irrelevant; near-continuous panic or depression affecting the ability to function independently, appropriately and effectively; impaired impulse control (such as unprovoked irritability with periods of violence); spatial disorientation; neglect of personal appearance and hygiene; difficulty in adapting to stressful circumstances (including work or a work-like setting); inability to establish and maintain effective relationships

50%	Occupational and social impairment with reduced reliability and productivity due to such symptoms as: flattened affect; circumstantial, circumlocutory, or stereotyped speech; panic attacks more than once a week; difficulty in understanding complex commands; impairment of short- and long-term memory (e.g., retention of only highly learned material, forgetting to complete tasks); impaired judgment; impaired abstract thinking; disturbances of motivation and mood; difficulty in establishing and maintaining effective work and social relationships
30%	Occupational and social impairment with Occasional decrease in work efficiency and intermittent periods of inability to perform occupational tasks (although generally functioning satisfactorily, with routine behavior, self-care, and conversation normal), due to such symptoms as: depressed mood, anxiety, suspiciousness, panic attacks (weekly or less often), chronic sleep impairment, mild memory loss (such as forgetting names, directions, recent events)
10%	Occupational and social impairment due to mild or transient symptoms which decrease work efficiency and ability to perform occupational tasks only during periods of significant stress, or; symptoms controlled by continuous medication
0%	A mental condition has been formally diagnosed, but symptoms are not severe enough either to interfere with occupational and social functioning or to require continuous medication

VA SIMPLIFIES ACCESS TO HEALTH CARE AND BENEFITS FOR VETERANS WITH PTSD

In July 2010, VA simplified the process for a veteran to claim service connection for PTSD. VA reduced the evidence needed if the trauma claimed by a veteran is related to "fear of hostile military or terrorist activity," and is consistent with the places, types, and circumstances of the veteran's service.

Previously, unless the veteran was a combat veteran, claims adjudicators were required to undertake extensive record development to corroborate whether a veteran actually experienced the claimed in-service stressor.

The rule applies to claims:

- Received by VA on or after July 13, 2010;
- Received before July 13, 2010 but not yet decided by a VA regional office;
- Appealed to the Board of Veterans' Appeals on or after July 13, 2010;
- Appealed to the Board before July 13, 2010, but not yet decided by the Board; and
- Pending before VA on or after July 13, 2010, because the Court of Appeals for
- Veterans Claims vacated a Board decision and remanded for re-adjudication. VA MEDICAL CENTER PROGRAMS

While PTSD treatment is available through all of VA's 171 medical centers, a VA network of 124 facilities offers specialized inpatient and outpatient treatment. One notable program consists of PTSD clinical teams that provide outpatient treatment but also work closely with other VA treatment programs, including Vet Centers, to coordinate services and provide information on PTSD throughout the medical center and the community.

In addition to 83 PTSD clinical teams, VA operates 22 specialized inpatient units around the country, plus 13 brief-treatment units, 11 residential rehabilitation programs, and four PTSD day hospitals. There also are four outpatient Women's Stress Disorder and Treatment Teams and eight outpatient-based PTSD Teams Substance Use Disorder demonstration projects. A special focus in the program expansions has included underserved and minority populations, such as African Americans, Hispanics and Native Americans. A specialized PTSD inpatient treatment unit serves women veterans at the Palo Alto, Calif., VA Medical Center's Menlo Park Division.

Each PTSD program offers education, evaluation, and treatment. Program services include:
- One-to-one mental health assessment and testing
- Medicines
- One-to-one psychotherapy and also family therapy
- Group therapy (covers topics such as anger and stress, combat support, partners, or groups for Veterans of specific conflicts)
- The VA provides treatments shown by research to be effective in treating Veterans
- Services are conducted by mental health care workers

MOBILE APPS

The VA announced the development of mobile applications (apps) to provide self-help, education and support. The VA also has treatment companion apps, for use with a health care provider, to make treatment easier. There are apps for iOS and Android devices.

In 2012 the Department of Veterans' Affairs and the Department of Defense announced a new smart phone application designed to help veterans manage PTSD. The app, entitled the

PTSD Coach, is aimed at helping to enhance the care of veterans already receiving treatment for PTSD, but can also be helpful for those who want to learn more about PTSD or are considering seeking help for their symptoms.

The PTSD Coach allows users to track symptoms, connect with local support services, locate information about PTSD and learn individualized strategies for managing symptoms. The PTSD Coach is free, and can be downloaded at the iTunes store

HELP FOR FAMILIES

In 2011, the Department of Veterans' Affairs launched a new telephone service to assist family members and friends of veterans to encourage them to seek healthcare for readjustment and mental health issues. The telephone service is called Coaching Into Care and is available by calling **(888) 823-7458.**

MILITARY SEXUAL TRAUMA (MST)

Both women and men can experience sexual harassment or sexual assault during their military service. VA refers to these experiences as military sexual trauma, or MST. Like other types of trauma, MST can negatively impact a person's mental and physical health, even many years later. Some problems associated with MST include:
Disturbing memories or nightmares; Difficulty feeling safe;
Feelings of depression or numbness; Problems with alcohol or other drugs; Feeling isolated from other people; Problems with anger or irritability; Problems with sleep;
Physical health problems.

VA defines sexual trauma as any lingering physical, emotional, or psychological symptoms resulting from a physical assault of a sexual nature, or battery of a sexual nature. Examples of this are:

- Rape;
- Physical assault;
- Domestic Battering; and
- Stalking.

TREATMENT FOR MST

People can recover from trauma. To help veterans do this, VA provides free, confidential counseling and treatment for mental and physical health conditions related to experiences of MST. You do not need to be service-connected and may be able to receive this benefit even if you are not eligible for other VA care. You do not need to have reported the incidents when they happened or have other documentation that they occurred.

Every VA facility has a designated MST Coordinator who serves as a contact person for MST-related issues. This person is your advocate and can help you find and access VA services and programs, state and federal benefits, and community resources.

Every VA facility has providers knowledgeable about treatment for the aftereffects of MST. Many have specialized outpatient mental health services focusing on sexual trauma. Vet Centers also have specially trained sexual trauma counselors.

Nationwide, there are programs that offer specialized sexual trauma treatment in residential or inpatient settings. These are programs for Veterans who need more intense treatment and support.

To accommodate veterans who do not feel comfortable in mixed-gender treatment settings, some facilities throughout VA have separate programs for men and women. All residential and inpatient MST programs have separate sleeping areas for men and women.

Disability Compensation is a monthly payment to a veteran disabled by an injury or a disease incurred or aggravated on active service. The veteran must have been discharged under other than dishonorable conditions to be eligible. The individual must currently be suffering from disabling symptoms to receive compensation. Refer to Chapter 4 of this book for information regarding Disability Compensation.

CHAPTER 30

BENEFITS FOR FORMER PRISONERS OF WAR (POWS)

Former American POWs are eligible for special veterans' benefits from the VA, including medical care in VA hospitals and disability compensation for injuries and disease presumed to be caused by internment. Studies have shown that the physical deprivation and psychological stress endured as a captive have life-long effects on subsequent health, social adjustment, and vocational adjustment.

Former prisoners of war (POW) are veterans who, while on active duty in the military, air, or naval service, were forcibly detained or interned in the line of duty by an enemy government or its agents or a hostile force. Periods of war include: World War II, the Korean War, the Vietnam War, and the Persian Gulf War (service after August 2, 1990).

Veterans who, while on active duty during peacetime, were forcibly detained or interned by a foreign government or its agents or a hostile force are also considered former POWs, if the circumstances of the internment were comparable to wartime internment (for example: Iran, Somalia or Kosovo).

> **Key Takeaways**
>
> Former POWs are veterans who during active military service were forcibly detained or interned in the line of duty by an enemy government or its agents or a hostile force
>
> Former Prisoners of War veterans may be eligible for a wide variety of benefits available to all U.S. Military veterans
>
> Each VA Regional Office has a POW Veterans Outreach Coordinator

A POW Coordinator has been designated at each VA regional office. The POW Coordinator can furnish former POWs with information about the benefits and services available to them.

HEALTHCARE

Former POWs are recognized as a special category of veterans, and will be placed on one of the top three Priority Groups established for VA healthcare by Congress. Those who have a service–connected disability are eligible for VA health care. This includes hospital, nursing home, and outpatient treatment. Former POWs who do not have a service- connected disability are eligible for VA hospital and nursing home care, regardless of the veterans' ability to provide payment. They are also eligible for outpatient care on a priority basis. Public Law 108-170, which became law December 6, 2003, eliminated prescription drug co-payments for former POWs.

Veterans who were POWs may receive complete dental care.

Former POWs are eligible for any prosthetic item, including eyeglasses and hearing aids. A VA physician must order the prosthetic items, when medically indicated, for eligible veterans.

Veterans may enroll in VA healthcare by completing VA Form 10-10EZR, "Application for Medical Benefits."

DISABILITY COMPENSATION

Veterans are encouraged to apply for VA Disability Compensation for any disabilities related to service, whether they were a POW or not. Some disabilities are presumptive, which means that if a veteran is diagnosed with certain conditions, and the veteran was a POW for at least 30 days (certain conditions do not include the 30-day requirement), the VA presumes the captivity caused the disability.

PRESUMPTIONS OF SERVICE-CONNECTION RELATING TO CERTAIN DISEASES AND DISABILITIES FOR FORMER PRISONERS OF WAR

Public Law 108-183, The Veterans Benefits Act of 2003, eliminated the requirement that a veteran was a POW for at least 30 days for certain conditions. Therefore, there are now two categories of presumptive conditions – those that include the 30-day requirement, and those that do not.

In the case of any veteran who is a former prisoner of war, and who was detained or interned for thirty days or more, any of the following which became manifest to a degree of 10% or more after active military, naval or air service, shall be considered to have been incurred in or aggravated by such service, notwithstanding that there is no record of such disease during the period of service:

- Avitaminosis
- Beriberi (Including beriberi heart disease, which includes Ischemic Heart Disease- coronary artery disease-for former POWs who suffered during captivity from edema- swelling of the legs or feet- also known as "wet" beriberi)
- Chronic dysentery Helminthiasis
- Malnutrition (including optic atrophy associated with malnutrition)
- Pellagra
- Any other nutritional deficiency
- Peripheral neuropathy, except where directly related to infectious causes Irritable bowel syndrome
- Peptic ulcer disease Cirrhosis of the liver
- Osteoporosis, on or after September 28, 2009

In the case of any veteran who is a former prisoner of war, and who was detained or interned for any period of time, any of the following which became manifest to a degree of 10% or more after active military, naval or air service, shall be considered to have been incurred in or aggravated by such service, notwithstanding that there is no record of such disease during the period of service:

- Psychosis
- Dysthymic disorder, or depressive neurosis
- Post-traumatic osteoarthritis

- Any of the Anxiety States Cold Injury
- Stroke and complications
- Heart Disease and complications
- Osteoporosis, on or after October 10, 2008, when Post Traumatic Stress Disorder is diagnosed

Former POWs should file a claim by completing "VA Form 21-526, Application for Compensation or Pension." The VA also offers a POW protocol exam. This is a one-time exam available to all former POWs, and is conducted at a VA medical facility to help determine if any presumptive disabilities exist.

SURVIVORS OF POWS

There are benefits for survivors of POWs. The major benefit is Dependency and Indemnity Compensation (DIC) which is a monthly benefit payable to the surviving spouse (and the former POW's children and parents in some cases) when the former POW:

- Was a service member who died on active duty; or
- Died from service-related disabilities; or
- Died on or before September 30, 1999 and was continuously rated totally disabled for a service connected condition (including individual unemployability) for at least 10 years immediately preceding death; or
- Died after September 30, 1999, and was continuously rated totally disabled for a service-connected condition (including individual unemployability) for at least 1 year immediately preceding death.

DIC is terminated for a surviving spouse who remarries, but can be resumed if the remarriage ends in death, divorce, or annulment. However, a surviving spouse who remarries on or after attaining age 57, and on or after December 16, 2003, can continue to receive DIC.

PRISONER OF WAR MEDAL

A Prisoner of War Medal is available to any member of the U.S. Armed Forces taken prisoner during any armed conflict dating from World War I.

CHAPTER 31

VETERANS CHOICE PROGRAM

Overview of the Veterans Choice Program

If you are already enrolled in VA health care, you may be able to receive care within your community, instead of waiting for a VA appointment or traveling to a VA facility.

WHAT TO KNOW ABOUT THE CHOICE PROGRAM

The Choice Program enables eligible veterans to receive medical care in the community. It supplements several existing statutory authorities that allow the Veterans Health Administration (VHA) to provide health care services to veterans outside of the Department of Veterans Affairs (VA) facilities. Generally, all medical care and services (including inpatient, outpatient, pharmacy, and ancillary services) are provided through the VCP—institutional long-term care and emergency care in non-VA facilities are excluded from the VCP and are provided under different authorities. The VCP is not a health insurance plan for veterans, nor does it guarantee health care coverage to all veterans.

> **Key Takeaways**
> To be eligible for participation in the choice program, veterans have to meet certain criteria
>
> The Choice Program is designed to make it easier to access care through an integrated health network.
>
> A continuing resolution for the program was signed in December 2017, allowing the program to continue into 2018

Eligibility and Choice of Care

Veterans must be enrolled in the VA health care system to request health services under the VCP. A veteran may request a VA community care consult/referral, or his or her VA provider may submit a VA community care consult/referral to the VA Care Coordination staff within the VA.

Veterans may become eligible for the VCP in four ways. First, a veteran is informed by a local VA medical facility that an appointment cannot be scheduled within 30 days of the clinically determined date requested by his or her VA doctor or within 30 days of the date requested by the veteran (this category also includes care not offered at a veterans' primary

VA facility and a referral cannot be made to another VA medical facility or other federal facility). Second, the veteran lives 40 miles or more from a VA medical facility that has a full-time primary care physician. Third, the veteran lives 40 miles or less (not residing in Guam, America Samoa, or the Republic of the Philippines) and either travels by air, boat, or ferry to seek care from his or her local facility or incurs a traveling burden of a medical condition, geographic challenge, or an environmental factor. Fourth, the veteran resides 20 miles or more from a VA medical facility located in Alaska, Hawaii, New Hampshire (excluding those who live 20 miles from the White River Junction VAMC), or a U.S. territory, with the exception of Puerto Rico.

Once found eligible for care through the VCP, veterans may choose to receive care from a VA provider or from an eligible VA community care provider (VCP provider). VCP providers are federally-qualified health centers, Department of Defense (DOD) facilities, or Indian Health Service facilities, and hospitals, physicians, and non-physician practitioners or entities participating in the Medicare or Medicaid program, among others. A veteran has the choice to switch between a VA provider and VCP provider at any time.

Program Administration and Provider Participation

The VCP is administered by two third-party administrators (TPAs): Health Net and TriWest. Generally, Health Net and TriWest manage veterans' appointments, counseling services, card distributions, and a call center. The TPAs contract directly with the VA. Then, Health Net or TriWest will contract with eligible non-VA community care providers interested on participating in the VCP.

Payments

Generally, a veteran's out-of-pocket costs under the VCP are equal to VHA out-of-pocket costs. Veterans do not pay any copayments at the time of their medical appointments. Copayment rates are determined by the VA after services are furnished. Usually, the VHA becomes the secondary payer when certain veterans with other health insurance (OHI) receive care for nonservice-connected conditions under VCP. Participating community providers are reimbursed by their respective TPA, and VA pays the TPAs.

Medical Services under VCP

Once an eligible veteran is authorized to receive necessary treatment, including follow-up appointments and ancillary and specialty medical services, under the VCP, a veteran may receive similar services that are offered through their personalized standard medical benefits package at a VA facility. VA's standard medical benefits package includes (but is not limited to) inpatient and outpatient medical, surgical, and mental healthcare; pharmaceuticals; pregnancy and delivery services; dental care; and durable medical equipment, and prosthetic devices, among other things.

However, institutional long-term care and emergency care in non-VA facilities are excluded from the VCP. These services are authorized and provided under separate statutory authorities outside the scope of VCP.

Eligibility

All veterans have to be enrolled in the VA health care system to receive care under the VCP, and then once this is met, qualified veterans can choose to receive care through VCP. There are four different pathways by which a veteran can become eligible for care.

The first is a 30-day wait list. A veteran is eligible for care through the VCP when they are informed by a local VA medical facility that an appointment can't be scheduled within 30 days of the date when the veteran's provider determines he or she needs to be seen. This includes care not offered at the veteran's primary VA medical facility, and when a referral can't be made to another federal or VA facility, or within thirty days of when the veteran wants to be seen.

With the mileage eligible option, a veteran is eligible for care through the VCP when they live 40 miles more away from a VA medical facility with a full-time primary care physician.

A veteran is also eligible for care when he or she lives somewhere other than Guam, American Samoa, or the Republic of the Philippines and travels via air, boat or ferry to get care from the local VA facility or incurs a traveling burden based on a medical condition, geographic challenges or environmental factors.

Another option occurs when the veteran lives in a state or territory without a full-service VA medical facility. A veteran may be eligible to receive care through the Veterans Choice Program when their residence is more than 20 miles from a VA medical facility and located in Alaska, Hawaii, New Hampshire or a U.S. territory excluding Puerto Rico.

Local VA facility staff members are to review clinical and administrative records of the veteran to determine the appropriate medical benefits package and clinical criterion. Confirmation of the veteran's eligibility status is generally determined within 10 business days from when the request for confirmation was submitted. Veterans who are found ineligible to participate in the VCP are to be given instructions, in their notification letters, on how to appeal the VA's decision.

Choice of Care

When veterans are eligible for health care services under the Veterans Choice Program they have two options. They can choose to receive their medical care rom a VA provider, or they may choice to receive medical care from a VA community care provider.

If a veteran opts for a VA community care provider who accepts eligible VCP patients, they then have their names and medical authorization information sent to that provider.

VCP Providers

Under the VCP program, entities and providers are eligible to provide care and services including federally-qualified health centers, Department of Defense medical facilities, Indian Health Service outpatient health facilities, hospitals, physicians, and non-physician practitioners or entities participating in the Medicare or Medicaid program, an Aging and Disability Resource Center, or a state agency for independent living.

VA employees are excluded from providing care or services under VCP, unless the provider is an employee of VA, and is not acting within the scope of such employment while providing hospital care or medical services through the VCP. Generally, VCP providers "must maintain at least the same or similar credentials and licenses as those required of VA's health care providers."

Program Administration

The Veterans Choice Program (VCP) is not a health insurance plan for veterans. Under the VCP, veterans are given the option of receiving care in their local communities instead of waiting for a VA appointment and/or enduring traveling burdens to reach a VA facility.

All veterans who are enrolled in the VA health care system are to be mailed a VCP card. The card lists relevant information about the VCP. Many veterans have attempted to use the VCP card as an insurance card. The VCP card may not be used to pay for medical services performed outside of or within the VA.

The VCP card doesn't replace a veteran's ID card, guarantee eligibility under the VCP or provide health insurance-like benefits.

Third-Party Administrators

In September 2013 the VA awarded contracts to Health Net and TriWest to expand access to non-VA health care in the community under something called the Patient-Centered Community Care initiative.

In November 2014 those contracts were changed to support services under the *Veterans Access, Choice and Accountability Act of 2014.*

Under the Veterans Choice Program, Health Net and TriWest manage the appointments, counseling services, card distributions and a call center. They're also responsible for overseeing providers, medical services reporting, billing processes, and coordination of care with private health insurance.

Consults/Referrals

Consults and referrals are handled in two different ways. First, a VA physician might submit a VA community care consult/referral through the Computerized Patient Record System on behalf of a veteran, when there is a clinical need for the veteran to receive timely medical services.

A veteran may also request a VA community care consult or referral from his or her VA provider or local VA staff to receive timely medical care.

No matter how a consult or referral is initiated they are all to be processed by the VA Community Care Coordination staff within the VA, and they are processed based on whether or not a veteran needs emergency or urgent care. When a consult/referral can't be approved, the local VA staff is responsible for notifying the veteran. If this happens, the veteran may continue having their care coordinated through the medical services within the VA, or the provider may be able to look for other community care options available from the Veterans Health Administration.

Once a veteran is found to be eligible to access care through the Choice Program, the VA community Care Coordination staff is responsible for electronically uploading their consult/referral and medical documentation in the Contractor Portal, which can be accessed by Health Net and TriWest. Once Helath Net or TriWest receives the documents, the TAP contacts the veteran and then he or she can confirm their choice to receive medical services under the VCP.

If a veteran reiterates his or her choice to receive medical care under the VCP, the veteran may select his or her VA community care provider and coordinate with a TPA to schedule an appointment.

In addition, the veteran is to be asked to provide other health insurance information, if applicable, and is made aware of possible copayments and deductibles. A veteran with a clinical need for a service-connected and/or special authority condition (SC/SA) is to have his or her screening information reviewed by Revenue Utilization Review (R-UR) nurses. The veteran's appointment is then to be entered in the Contractor Portal so that it can be viewed by the VA Community Care Coordination staff.

Daily, the VA Community Care Coordination staff is to check the Contractor Portal for appointment statuses and other updates. After the appointment is scheduled, the VA Community Care Coordination staff are to enter the appointment information into the Appointment Management system (within the VA) and update the veteran's status to "scheduled."

Unusual or Excessive Burden Determination

Along with environmental factors, geographic challenges and medical conditions, veterans may also be evaluated by the nature or simplicity of the hospital care or medical services required, how frequently hospital care or medical services are needed, and whether or not there is a need for an attendant for clinical service.

Authorization of Care and an Episode of Care

Prior to delivering medical services to veterans under the Veterans Choice Program (VCP), such services are to be authorized by the VA.36 If a veteran requires services beyond those authorized, his or her VCP provider may request another authorization. The delivery and usage of unauthorized medical services could result in non-reimbursement. Under the VCP, over 2 million authorizations have been validated by the third-party administrators (TPAs) Health Net and TriWest.

The VA defines an episode of care (EOC) as "a necessary course of treatment, including follow-up appointments and ancillary and specialty services, which last no longer than one calendar year from the date of the first appointment with a non-VA health care provider." This one-year Choice EOC period of validity begins when the first appointment is scheduled. VA community care providers may request an authorization extension for a veteran's current EOC through the veteran's respective TPA.

Appointment Scheduling

Veterans and VCP providers need to verify eligibility status before scheduling clinical medical appointments. Appointments are scheduled based on clinical appropriateness. Veterans who are eligible for VCP receive a call from their third-party administrator, whether that's Health Net or TriWest, and that TPA then provides the veteran with information and schedules their appointments. After the appointment is scheduled, the contractor informs the VA. Emergent or urgent care authorizations should be done quickly.

Emergent Care and Urgent Care Determination

VA community care consults/referrals are prioritized based on urgency levels. Urgency levels to deliver care are different under the VCP, and generally emergent care under the VCP doesn't mean an emergency medical condition requiring immediate medical attention (emergency treatment furnished by non-VA providers are authorized under separate statutory authorities and not the VCP). Emergent consultants/referrals are to be scheduled within five days from the veteran's consultant date with his or her third-party administrator. Urgent consults/referrals have a timeframe that is within 24 hours. VA providers may bypass the Choice Program process and contact the VA Community Care Coordination staff directly to schedule an urgent appointment with a VCP provider for their veterans.

After receiving a notification, a veteran's local VA facility staff should cancel his or her appointment at the VA. Veterans can choose to schedule their own appointments after receiving an authorization of care under the VCP. If veterans choose to do this, they're asked to provide their appointment information to Health Net or TriWest.

Appointment information provided to TPAs is uploaded into the Contractor's Portal so the VA Community Care coordination staff can see it, and the Community Care Coordination staff should check the Contractor Portal for veterans' appointment statuses and other updates. After receiving the notification, the local VA staff should cancel his or her appointment at the VA.

Medication

Veterans may have their prescriptions filled at local VA pharmacies, non-VA pharmacies and through the Consolidated Mail Outpatient Pharmacy (CMOP). If the VA can't fill a medication request within a prescribed timeframe, or one that is not within the VA formulary, a non-VA pharmacy can fill the initial 14-day supply without refills.

For veterans requiring prescriptions for more than 14 days, the VCP prescribing clinician must have the remaining supply of medicine filled at a VA pharmacy. Medications filled at non-VA pharmacies require prior authorizations from the VA.

The VA is required to provide reimbursement to veterans for out-of-pocket expenses related to the purchase of medications that treat service-connected conditions. For nonservice-connected conditions, veterans might be reimbursed as well for their out-of-pocket expenses, including ones with other health insurance plans. For reimbursement, veterans should submit a copy of their prescriptions, authorizations and original receipts to their local VA Community Care Office. The VA also allows non-VA pharmacies to process medication claims on a veteran's behalf.

Processing Medical Claims

Medical claims under the Veterans Choice Program are processed through the veteran's third-party administrator. Health Net and TriWest are responsible for uploading and managing veterans' medical claims via the Contractors Portal. Through this web portal, the VA Community Care Coordination staff retrieve a veteran's documentation of clinical need and upload it to the veteran's medical records.

The VA community care provider submits medical claims to a veteran's third-party administrator. Once the administrator receives the claim they submit it through the web portal.

Based on Federal authority, VA is the primary and exclusive payer for medical care it authorizes. Because of this, non-VA medical care providers can't bill the veteran or any other party for any portion of care authorized by the VA. Federal law also prohibits payments by more than one Federal agency for the same episode of care, so any payments made by the veteran, Medicare or any other Federal agency have to be refunded to the payer from the VCP provider, upon acceptance of VA payment.

Medical Services Not Previously Authorized

Under the Veterans Choice Program, medical claims for unauthorized non-VA health care services may be submitted to the VA for payment consideration. Veterans, VA community care providers and people who paid for services on behalf of the veteran must submit certain documentation to the VA for consideration.

This documentation includes a standard billing form or an invoice (e.g. Explanation of benefits), and or a receipt of services paid and/or owed, as well as an explanation of services of the circumstance that led to the veteran receiving unauthorized care outside of the VA. Also included should be any statements or supporting documentation, and VA Form 10-583, Claim for Payment of Cost and Unauthorized Medical Services.

Payments

Veterans Out-of-Pocket Costs

Veterans who are enrolled in VA health care don't pay premiums, deductibles or co-insurances for medical services, but they may be required to pay a fixed co-payment amount for non-service connected disabilities. When a veteran receives care at a VA facility they don't pay copayments at the time of their appointment and copayment rates are determined by the VA after medical services, based on whether the care was service-connected or not. Veterans' out-of-pocket costs under the VCP are the same as if they were receiving care from a VA provider in a VA facility. If a veteran doesn't pay copays at a VA health care facility, they won't pay them under the VCP.

Under the Veterans Choice Program, veterans with Medicare, Medicaid, or TRICARE, who are authorized care in the community are not required to pay any deductibles, coinsurances, or copayments for non-service connected medical care, even if Medicare, Medicaid or TRICARE requires a certain level of cost-sharing under plans.

VCP providers bill private health insurers for medical care, supplies and prescriptions provided to veterans for their nonservice-connected conditions.

The final rule states that the veteran may owe some copayment, cost share or deductible amount from their other health insurance to the other health insurance to the provider. VA can't completely eliminate any potential copayment liability because under the program, VA is a secondary payer, while under other non-VA care, the VA is the primary payer and their payment to the non-VA health care provider is payment in full.

Cost Shares for Veterans with Other Health Insurance (OHI)

The VA defines other health insurance (OHI) as commercial insurance. Commercial insurance, often referred to as private insurance, is not funded by federal and state taxes. This type of insurance is offered by companies such as Blue Cross and Blue Shield, Aetna, Cigna, and the Kaiser Foundation. Plans purchased through the state health exchanges are also considered as OHI. In addition, veterans who purchase commercial insurance plans agree to cost-sharing responsibilities. Such cost-sharing obligations include copayments, deductibles and coinsurance (e.g., 80/20 rule: 80% insurer responsibility/20% patient responsibility).

When veterans receive health care services for nonservice-connected conditions/diseases and have OHI, they may have to share the cost of the rendered services with the OHI company. Furthermore, veterans who receive VA community care services and have an OHI plan may also incur cost-sharing responsibilities. However, veterans may have their copayment responsibilities paid by the VA.

After [the] VA has paid for the non-VA care under Choice, and if there are funds available to reimburse the veteran, VA will apply a dollar-for-dollar offset to the Veteran's applicable VA copayment responsibility. In addition, VA can reimburse the Veteran for any payments made by the veteran to cover the cost of copayments, deductibles, or cost shares required by their OHI. Unless an exception applies, the VA payment is capped at the Medicare (or other allowable) rate. If the OHI payment does not completely satisfy the veteran's VA copayment responsibility, VA will bill the veteran for the remainder of the VA copayment amount.

As stated previously Medicare, Medicaid, or TRICARE are not considered "other health insurance" plans under the VCP. Therefore, veterans with these plans will not incur any deductibles, coinsurances, or copayments costs.

Provider Payment Methodologies

Guidance on rates for the delivery of care are outlined in the table below. The Veterans Choice Program providers are directed to receive their reimbursements from either Health Net or TriWest. Then, the VA reimburses the third-party administrator. Eligible VA community care providers who participate under the PC3 network as opposed to the Choice network may receive lower reimbursement rates than those of Medicare. If providers go to the Choice network they might be able to negotiate rates similar to what's contracted under the PC3 network.

	Service-Connected Condition	Non-Service Connected Condition
Payment Responsibility	VA is solely responsible	The primary payer is the veterans' other health insurance; the second is the VA
Payment Rates	Rates are not to exceed those in the "Medicare Fee Schedule" with exceptions in highly rural areas, Alaska, All-Payer Model Agreements, and when there are no available rates	

Care	Rates
Highly rural areas	Higher rates that exceed the "Medicare Fee Schedule" may be negotiated
Alaska	Rates are computer under 38 C.F.R. §§17.55(j), 17.56(b).
All-Payer Model Agreements	Rates are calculated based on the rates within the agreement
No available rates	In this, the Secretary will follow the methodology outlined in 38 C.F.R. §§17.55, 17.56.
Authorized Care	Health Net or TriWest, on behalf of the VA, will authorize services. The VA requires that all rendered services delivered to veterans receive prior authorizations. Medical services are delivered by an eligible entity or provider after a veteran chooses to receive care under the Veterans Choice Program.

A "highly rural area" is defined as a county having fewer than seven individuals residing per square mile.

Veterans and VA community care providers may call the Community Care Call Center to discuss billing issues. These issues range from the need to resolve a debt collection to inappropriately billed services.

VA Care In the Community—Existing Statutory Authorities

Program Title	Description
Veterans Choice Act (Veterans Choice Program) [38 U.S.C. §1701 note]	Temporary program to furnish hospital care and medical services to eligible veterans through eligible VA community care providers
Traditional VA Care in the Community (Formerly called Non-VA Medical Care) [38 U.S.C. §1703]	Authority to contract for hospital care and medical services when VA facilities are not capable of furnishing care due to geographic inaccessibility or are not

	capable of furnishing care; can also furnish counseling and related mental health services under 38 U.S.C. Section 1712A(e)(1).
Project Access Received Closer to Home (ARCH) [38 U.S.C. §1703 note]	Pilot program in five Veterans Integrated Service Networks to provide by contract covered health care services to covered veterans. The pilot expired in August 2016.
Enhanced Sharing Authority [38 U.S.C. §8153]	Authority to make arrangement by contract or other forms of agreement, for the mutual use, or exchange of use, of health care resources between VA facilities and any health care provider, or other entity or individual. Sharing agreements with academic medical affiliates are executed under this authority.
Indian Health Service (IHS)/Tribal Health Program (THP) [25 U.S.C §1645]	Authorizes the Secretary of Department of Health and Human Services (HHS) to enter into or expand sharing arrangements between IHS, tribes, and tribal organizations, and VA and Department of Defense (DOD). This authority is cited in VA's Direct Care Services reimbursement agreements with IHS and THP.
Sharing of VA and Department of Defense (DOD) Health Care Resources [38 U.S.C. §8111]	Authority to enter into sharing agreements and contracts with DOD for the mutual use or exchange of use of hospital and domiciliary facilities, and such supplies, equipment, material, and other resources as may be needed.
Emergency Care for Certain Veterans with Service-Connected Conditions [38 U.S.C. §1728]	Authority to pay or reimburse charges of emergency treatment furnished in a non-VA facility where such treatment was needed for/related to a service-connected condition or in certain instances vocational rehab or provided to a veteran permanently and totally disabled.
Emergency Care for Nonservice-connected Conditions [38 U.S.C. §1725]	Authority to pay or reimburse charges of emergency treatment furnished in a non-VA facility under certain circumstances to certain eligible veterans.

History of Choice Program Legislation

In August 2014, Then-President Obama signed into law the *Veterans Access, Choice and Accountability Act*. Included in that legislation was the Veterans Choice Program or the VCP. The VCP expands availability of medical services for eligible veterans with community providers.

In September 2014, The Department of Veterans Affairs Expiring Authorities Act of 2014 was signed into law, which made some technical changes to the *Veterans Access, Choice, and Accountability Act of 2014.*

In April 2015, the VA changed the distance rules. The Department of Veterans Affairs issued interim final rules changing how the VA measures the distance from a veteran's residence to the nearest VA medical facility. The change considered the distance the veteran must drive to the nearest VA medical center from their residence, as opposed to the straight line distance to the facility.

In May 2015 the Department of Veterans Affairs issued a Memorandum to Veterans Integrated Service Network (VISN) Directors, outlining that a specific hierarchy of care would be put into place when a veteran's primary VA medical facility couldn't provide needed care to a veteran, either because the care is unavailable or the facility can't meet VHA wait time criteria.

In June 2015, the Surface Transportation and Veterans Health Care Choice Improvement Act was signed into law. This allowed all veterans to be eligible for the Veterans Choice Program by changing the August 1, 2014 enrollment date restriction. It also defined the nearest VA medical facility as a Community Based Outpatient Clinic (CBOC) with no full-time primary physician, removed the 60-day limitation on an episode of care, included clinically indicated date as a wait time eligibility criteria, and expanded provider eligibility.

In May 2016, the VA launched the Community Care Call Center, designed to help veterans with credit and billing issues .

In April 2017 Congressed passed Public Law 115-26, which continued the program.

In August 2017, President Trump signed the *VA Choice and Quality Employment Act*. This authorized $2.1 billion in additional funds for the Veterans Choice Program, as a short-term temporary funding solution allowing the VA to increase the number of scheduled appointments and ensure payments are made to community providers.

CHAPTER 32

VETERAN FEDERAL HIRING

OVERVIEW

Veterans' Preference gives eligible veterans preference in appointment over many other applicants. Veterans' preference applies to almost all new appointments in both the competitive and excepted service. Veterans' preference does not guarantee veterans a job and it does not apply to internal agency actions like promotions, transfers, reinstatements, and reassignments.

In accordance with title 5, U.S. Code, Section 2108 (5 USC 2108), veterans' preference eligibility is based on dates of active duty service, receipt of a campaign badge, Purple Heart, or a service-connected disability. Not all active-duty service may qualify for veterans' preference.

Only veterans discharged or released from active duty in the armed forces under honorable conditions are eligible for veterans' preference. That means you must have been discharged under an honorable or general discharge. If you are a "retired member of the armed forces" you are not included in the definition of preference eligible unless you are a disabled veteran OR you retire below the rank of major or its equivalent.

> **Key Takeaways**
>
> The government fills vacancies in two ways: competitively and noncompetitively.
>
> Through the noncompetitive process, positions don't have to be announced to a large pool of applicants and it gives special consideration to eligible veterans.
>
> Veterans' Preference awards points to veterans during the application process, providing an advantage in placement. To be engaged, veterans must meet certain eligibility requirements.

There are three types of preference eligible, disabled (10-point preference eligible), non-disabled (5-point preference eligible), and sole survivorship preference (0-point preference eligible).

You are 0-point Preference eligible—no points are added to the passing score or rating of a veteran who is the only surviving child in a family in which the father or mother or one more siblings:

- Served in the armed forces; and
- Was killed, died as a result of wounds, accident or disease, is in captured or missing in action status, was permanently 100 percent disabled or hospitalized on a continuing

basis and is not gainfully employed because of the disability or hospitalization where the death, status or disability did not result from the intentional misconduct or willful neglect of the parent or sibling and was not incurred during a period of unauthorized absence.

You are a 5 point preference eligible if your active duty service meets any of the following:

- For more than 180 consecutive days, other than for training, any part of which occurred during the period beginning September 11, 2001, and ending on August 31, 2010, the last day of Operation Iraqi Freedom, OR
- Between August 2, 1990 and January 2, 1992, OR
- For more than 180 consecutive days, other than for training, any part of which occurred after January 31, 1955 and before October 15, 1976, OR
- In a war, campaign or expedition for which a campaign badge has been authorized or between April 28, 1952 and July 1, 1955.

You are 10-point preference eligible if you served at any time and you:

- Have a service-connected disability, OR
- Received a Purple Heart.

Preference eligibles are divided into five basic groups as follows:

CPS - Disability rating of 30% or more (10 points)
CP - Disability rating of at least 10% but less than 30% (10 points)
XP - Disability rating less than 10% (10 points)
TP - Preference eligibles with no disability rating (5 points)
SSP – Sole Survivorship Preference (0 points)

Disabled veterans receive 10 points, regardless of their disability rating.

When agencies use a numerical rating and ranking system to determine the best qualified applicants for a position, an additional 5 or 10 points are added to the numerical score of qualified preference eligible veterans.

When an agency does not use a numerical rating system, preference eligibles who have a compensable service-connected disability of 10 percent or more (CPS, CP) are placed at the top of the highest category on the referral list (except for scientific or professional positions at the GS-9 level or higher). XP and TP preference eligibles are placed above non-preference eligibles within their assigned category.

You must provide acceptable documentation of your preference or appointment eligibility. Acceptable documentation may be:

- A copy of your DD-214, "Certificate of Release or Discharge from Active Duty," which shows dates of service and discharge under honorable conditions.
- A "certification" that is a written document from the armed forces that certifies the service member is expected to be discharged or released from active duty service in the armed forces under honorable conditions not later than 120 days after the date the certification is signed.

You may obtain a letter from the Department of Veterans Affairs reflecting your level of disability for preference eligibility by visiting a VA Regional Office, contacting a VA call center or online.

NOTE: Prior to appointment, an agency will require the service member to provide a copy of the DD-214.

If claiming 10 point preference, you will need to submit a Standard Form (SF-15Adobe Acrobat Version [152 KB]) "Application for 10-point Veterans' Preference."

VOW (Veterans Opportunity To Work Act)

On November 21, 2011, the President signed the VOW (Veterans Opportunity to Work) Act. (Public Law 112-56). The VOW Act amends chapter 21 of title 5, United States Code (U.S.C.) by adding section 2108a, "Treatment of certain individuals as veterans, disabled veterans, and preference eligibles." This new section requires Federal agencies to treat certain active duty service members as preference eligibles for purposes of an appointment in the competitive or excepted service, even though the service members have not been discharged or released from active duty.

Because many service members begin their civilian job search prior to being discharged or released from active duty service, they may not have a DD form 214, Certificate of Release or Discharge from Active Duty, when applying for Federal jobs. The VOW Act was enacted to ensure these individuals do not lose the opportunity to be considered for Federal service (and awarded their veterans' preference entitlements if applicable) despite not having a DD form 214 to submit along with their résumés.

Agencies are required to accept, process, and grant tentative veterans' preference to those active duty service members who submit a certification (in lieu of a DD-form 214) along with their job application materials. Agencies must verify the individual meets the definition of 'preference eligible' under 5 U.S.C. 2108 prior to appointment.

A "certification" is any written document from the armed forces that certifies the service member is expected to be discharged or released from active duty service in the armed forces under honorable conditions within 120 days after the certification is submitted by the applicant. The certification letter should be on letterhead of the appropriate military branch of the service and contain (1) the military service dates including the expected discharge or release date; and (2) the character of service.

If the certification has expired; an agency must request other documentation (e.g., a copy of the DD form 214) that demonstrates the service member is a preference eligible per 5 U.S.C. 2108, before veterans' preference can be awarded.

Filling a Position Through the Competitive Examining Process

Announcing the Vacancy

To fill a vacancy by selection through the competitive examining process, the selecting official requests a list of eligibles from the examining office. The examining office must announce the competitive examining process through USAJOBS. OPM will notify the State employment service where the job is being filled. Subsequently, the examining office determines which applicants are qualified, rates and ranks them based on their qualifications, and issues a certificate of eligibles, which is a list of eligibles with the highest scores from the top of the appropriate register. A certificate of eligibles may be used for permanent, term, or temporary appointment.

Category Rating

Category rating is an alternative ranking and selection procedure authorized under the Chief Human Capital Officers Act of 2002 (Title XIII of the Homeland Security Act of 2002) and codified at 5 U.S.C. § 3319. Category rating is part of the competitive examining process. Under category rating, applicants who meet basic minimum qualification requirements established for the position and whose job-related competencies or knowledge, skills and abilities (KSAs) have been assessed are ranked by being placed in one of two or more predefined quality categories instead of being ranked in numeric score order. Preference eligibles are listed ahead of non-preference eligibles within each quality category. Veterans' preference is absolute within each quality category. For more detailed information on Category Rating please visit Chapter 5 of the Delegated Examining Operations Handbook.

The "Rule of Three" and Veteran pass overs

Selection must be made from the highest three eligibles on the certificate who are available for the job--the "rule of three." However, an agency may not pass over a preference eligible to select a lower ranking nonpreference eligible or nonpreference eligible with the same or lower score.

Example: If the top person on a certificate is a 10-point disabled veteran (CP or CPS) and the second and third persons are 5-point preference eligibles, the appointing authority may choose any of the three.

Example: If the top person on a certificate is a 10-point disabled veteran (CP or CPS), the second person is not a preference eligible, and the third person is a 5-point preference eligible, the appointing authority may choose either of the preference eligibles. The appointing authority may not pass over the 10-point disabled veteran to select the nonpreference eligible unless an objection has been sustained.

Category Rating

Category rating is an alternative ranking and selection procedure authorized under the Chief Human Capital Officers Act of 2002 (Title XIII of the Homeland Security Act of 2002) and codified at 5 U.S.C. § 3319. Category rating is part of the competitive examining process. Under category rating, applicants who meet basic minimum qualification requirements established for the position and whose job-related competencies or knowledge, skills and abilities (KSAs) have been assessed are ranked by being placed in one of two or more predefined quality categories instead of being ranked in numeric score order. Preference eligibles are listed ahead of non-preference eligibles within each quality category. Veterans' preference is absolute within each quality category. For more detailed information on Category Rating please visit Chapter 5 of the Delegated Examining Operations Handbook.

Disqualification of Preference Eligibles

A preference eligible can be eliminated from consideration only if the examining office sustains the agency's objection to the preference eligible for adequate reason. These reasons, which must be recorded, include medical disqualification under 5 CFR Part 339, suitability disqualification under 5 CFR Part 731, or other reasons considered by the Office of Personnel Management (OPM) or an agency under delegated examining authority to be disqualifying .

OPM must approve the sufficiency of an agency reason to medically disqualify or pass over a preference eligible on a certificate based on medical reasons to select a nonpreference eligible. Special provisions apply to the proposed disqualification or pass over for any reason of a preference eligible with a 30 percent or more compensable disability. See Disqualification of 30 Percent or more Disabled Veterans below.

Agencies have delegated authority for determining suitability in accordance with 5 CFR Part 731.

The preference eligible (or his or her representative) is entitled on request to a copy of the agency's reasons for the proposed pass over and the examining office's response.

An appointing official is not required to consider a person who has three times been passed over with appropriate approval or who has already been considered for three separate appointments from the same or different certificates for the same position. But in each of these considerations, the person must have been within reach under the rule of three and a selection must have been made from that group of three. Further, the preference eligible is entitled to advance notice of discontinuance of certification.

U.S.C. 3317, 3318 and 5 CFR 332.402, 332.404, 332.405, 332.406, and Parts 339 and 731

Disqualification of a 30 Percent or More Disabled Veteran

- If an agency proposes to pass over a disabled veteran on a certificate to select a person who is not a preference eligible, or to disqualify a disabled veteran based on the physical requirements of the position, it must at the same time notify both the Office of Personnel Management (OPM) and the disabled veteran of the reasons for the determination and of the veteran's right to respond to OPM within 15 days of the date of the notification.
- The agency must provide evidence to OPM that the notice was timely sent to the disabled veteran's last known address.
- OPM must make a determination on the disabled veteran's physical ability to perform the duties of the position, taking into account any additional information provided by the veteran.
- OPM will notify the agency and the disabled veteran of its decision, with which the agency must comply. If OPM agrees that the veteran cannot fulfill the physical requirements of the position, the agency may select another person from the certificate of eligibles. If OPM finds the veteran able to perform the job, the agency may not pass over the veteran.
- OPM is prohibited by law from delegating this function to any agency. U.S.C. 3312, 3318.

Filing Late Applications

A veteran may file a late application under the following circumstances by contacting the employing agency. Agencies are responsible for accepting, retaining, and considering their applications as required by law and regulation regardless of whether the agency uses case examining or maintains a continuing register of eligibles.

- Applications from 10-point preference eligibles must be accepted, as described below, for future vacancies that may arise after a case examining register or continuing register is closed. Agencies must accept applications from other individuals who are eligible to file on a delayed basis only as long as a case examining register exists.
- A 10-point preference eligible may file a job application with an agency at any time. If the applicant is qualified for positions filled from a register, the agency must add the candidate to the register, even if the register is closed to other applicants. If the applicant is qualified for positions filled through case examining, the agency will ensure that the applicant is referred on a certificate as soon as possible. If there is no immediate opening, the agency must retain the application in a special file for referral on certificates for future vacancies for up to three years. The Office of Personnel Management's Delegated Examining Operations Handbook provides detailed instructions.
- A preference eligible is entitled to be reentered on each register (or its successor) where previously listed if he or she applies within 90 days after resignation without delinquency or misconduct from a career or career-conditional appointment.
- A preference eligible is entitled to be entered on an appropriate existing register if he or she applies within 90 days after furlough or separation without delinquency or misconduct from a career or career-conditional appointment or if found eligible to apply after successfully appealing a furlough or discharge from career or career-conditional appointment.

- A person who lost eligibility for appointment from a register because of active duty in the Armed Forces is entitled to be restored to the register (or its successor) and receive priority consideration when certain conditions are met. See 5 CFR 332.322 for more details.
- A person who was unable to file for an open competitive examination or appear for a test because of service in the Armed Forces or hospitalization continuing for up to 1 year following discharge may file after the closing date if the register of eligibles still exists.
- A Federal employee who was unable to file for an open competitive examination or appear for a test because of active Reserve duty continuing beyond 15 days may file after the closing date of an existing register. 5 U.S.C. 3305, 3314, 3315, and 5 CFR 332.311, 332.312, 332.321, 332.322

Preference in Federal Employment

Veterans' preference is a tool to assist in the placement of veterans in federal government positions, providing a "first consideration." Veterans' preference was established by the Veterans' Preference Act of 1944, as amended and is found in certain provisions of 5 U.S.C. 2108.

Veterans' preference applies to permanent and temporary positions in both the competitive and excepted services, which are two class of jobs in the federal government. For the competitive service, applicants must compete with other individuals for positions that are posted on the USAJOBS website through a structured process. In the excepted service, applicants such as veterans with disabilities may be noncompetitively considered and hired through special appointing authorities that agencies may utilize to fill jobs. The excepted service contains certain agencies and entitles groups of individuals and positions that are outside the competitive service.

The methods used for the competitive and excepted services differ.

For competitive service, veterans' preference gives eligible veterans additional points toward passing examination score or rating. Eligible veterans are also placed at the top of hiring certificates for positions, except for professional and scientific positions at grate GS-09 and above. Eligible veterans who apply for professional or scientific positions still receive points and are listed ahead of other applicants having the same rating.

Regarding Excepted Service, veterans' preference allows eligible veterans to apply noncompetitively under special appointing authorities.

Veterans must be discharged from active duty under an honorable or general discharge to be eligible for veterans preference. Veterans preference does not guarantee a veteran will be selected for employment, apply to internal agency agencies, or apply to Senior Executive Service, positions in the legislative and judicial branches of the federal government, or positions in certain exempted agencies like the Central Intelligence Agency.

VA partners with the Vocational Rehabilitation and Employment Office and its Regional Veteran Employment Coordinators (RVECs) to support the Department's National Veterans Employment Program. VESO was designed to be a strategic management program that oversees VA Veteran employment initiatives and manages VA for Vets, its flagship initiative. VA for Vets is a comprehensive career support and management program for Veterans, National Guard, Reserve members and VA employees. Services include employment counseling, assistance in identifying transferable military skills (skills matching), qualifications and career assessment, assistance in drafting competitive resumes, instruction in developing comprehensive job search strategies, and direct job placement assistance. RVECs also advocate on behalf of Veterans, promoting the values, work ethic, leadership, dedication, skills, and qualifications Veterans possess, all of which make them ideal candidates to fill any position in the federal sector.

VR&E staff members must be thoroughly familiar and current with Veterans' preference regulations and documentation requirements.

Vocational Rehabilitation Counselors (VRCs) and Employment Coordinators (ECs) act as resources to perform the following tasks:

- Provide guidance on Veterans' preference and assist job ready Veterans in completing federal vacancy applications.
- Review applications and ensure Veterans have complete packages including appropriate Veterans' preference and required documentation.
- Educate Human Resources (HR) personnel and managers on the importance of hiring Veterans with disabilities and Veterans' preference regulations and rules. Hiring managers have at their discretion the ability to select applicants from various lists, some of which may not contain any Veteran applicants.
- Develop a basic understanding of the Office of Personnel Management's (OPM) Delegated Examining Operating Handbook (DEOH) and its regularly occurring memoranda, which provide updated information on Veterans' preference. The DEOH provides operational procedures for agencies to use in the staffing and placement process for competitive examining of positions.

OPM Role

The Office of Personnel Management is responsible for prescribing and enforcing regulations in the administration of veterans' preference in the competitive and excepted services. OPM is the deciding agency in requests for selecting non-veterans over veterans in the job selection process.

Required Documentation

Veterans who claim veterans' preference must submit the following documentation with their federal job applications. If a veteran doesn't submit the require documentation, the veterans' preference doesn't apply.

For Claiming 5-Points Preference

DD214, Certificate of Release or Discharge from Active Duty (must show Veteran's character of service upon discharge).

For Claiming 10-Points Preference

- DD214, Certificate of Release or Discharge from Active Duty (must show Veteran's character of service upon discharge).
- Purple Heart Recipients, which is listed on the DD214 or other official documentation
- SF-15, Application for 10-Point Veteran' Preference form
- Letter from the VA Regional Office or on eBenefits stating the veteran's percentage of disability

For Claiming To Be a Spouse or Child of a Qualifying Veteran (10-Points Preference)

- DD214, Certificate of Release or Discharge from Active Duty (must
- show the Veteran's character of service upon discharge)
- SF-15, Application for 10-Point Veterans' Preference form
- Letter from the VA Regional Office or on eBenefits showing that the veteran is unemployable or 100-percent service-connected
- If veteran is deceased, a copy of the death certificate

Veterans must contact their local VA Regional Office to obtain a veterans' preference letter at 800-827-1000, or the letter can be obtained on eBenefits.

Special Appointing Authorities

Special appointing authorities are noncompetitive and excepted service appointing authorities, which federal agencies can use entirely at their discretion. These authorities provide flexibility in staffing hard-to-fill positions and overcoming underrepresentation, and allow for quick and easy hiring. The following is a chart showing the overview of authorities.

VRA	VRA gives agencies the discretion to appoint eligible Veterans to positions in the federal government without competition. Veterans may be appointed to any grade level in the General Schedule through GS-11 or equivalent. This authority also allows applicants with disabilities rated at 30 percent or more, or rated at 10 or 20 percent and determined to have a "serious employment handicap" to be employed by VA as Veterans benefits counselors, Veterans claims examiners, Veterans representatives at educational institutions and counselors at readjustment centers. Applicants must meet the basic qualifications for the position to be filled.
30 Percent or More Disabled Veterans' Authority	Veterans may be initially appointed noncompetitively to a temporary or term position. Then, as early as day 61 of employment under this authority, hiring managers may convert veterans to a career or career-conditional appointment. There is no grade-level limitation for this authority. Applicants must meet all qualification requirements for the position to be filled.
Disabled Veterans Enrolled in a VA Training Authority	This authority is the equivalent to the Non-Paid Work Experience (NPWE) program. Veterans eligible for training through VR&E may enroll in training or work experience under an agreement between any government agency (local, state or federal) and VA. Veterans are not considered government employees for most purposes. Training is tailored to the individual's needs and goals. Certificates of Training are provided at the end of the training/work experience, which allows agencies to appoint Veterans noncompetitively under status quo appointments. Those appointments may be converted to career or career conditional at any time
VEOA	This authority, unique to the competitive service, allows Veterans to apply to positions under merit promotion procedures (inside the federal government) when the agency is recruiting outside of its own workforce. Veterans' preference is not a consideration when selections are made for these appointments.
Schedule A for Persons with Disabilities	This excepted service authority is an alternative to authorities specifically designed for Veterans. Schedule A provides a way to hire individuals with physical, psychiatric or cognitive impairments

	without competition. Schedule A employees can be converted to permanent positions in the competitive service after completing two years on the job demonstrating satisfactory performance, with or without reasonable accommodation
Employment of Veterans with Disabilities Who Have Completed a Training Course Under Chapter 31	This authority, unique to the competitive service, allows any agency to appoint a Veteran with a disability noncompetitively to positions or class of positions for which he/she is trained. Veterans with disabilities must satisfactorily complete an approved course of training prescribed by VR&E.

Noncompetitive Hiring

Eligible veterans may be appointed to federal positions without competing with the general public and federal agencies can hire veterans without posting a vacancy announcements. Veterans who are eligible for Special Hiring Authorities may be noncompetitively hired if they meet eligibility and qualification requirements for the position.

The following highlights the differences between competitive and noncompetitive hiring.

Competitive Hiring	Noncompetitive Hiring
Positions must be announced to a pool of job seekers in USAJOBS	Positions don't require public announcement
The applicant doesn't have to meet the same eligibility requirements as a noncompetitive job posting	The applicant must meet the requirements for noncompetitive status and be able to perform the essential duties of the job with or without reasonable accommodation
The applicant is rated based on qualifications	The applicant will not be subject to the usual requirement to determine the most qualified candidate and rating of qualification
All veterans have the option to apply	Veterans must provide proof of eligibility for Veterans' Preference or special appointments in order to be considered for noncompetitive placement. Documents may include SF-15, Application for 10-Point Veterans Preference, DD214, Certification of Job Readiness, and other medical documentation as requested

Veterans Recruitment Appointment (VRA) Authority

The VRA is a special authority by which agencies can, if they wish, appoint eligible veterans without competition to positions at any grade level through General Schedule (GS) 11 or equivalent. (The promotion potential of the position is not a factor.) VRA appointees are hired under excepted appointments to positions that are otherwise in the competitive service. There is no limitation to the number of VRA appointments an individual may receive, provided the individual is otherwise eligible.

If the agency has more than one VRA candidate for the same job and one (or more) is a preference eligible, the agency must apply the Veterans' preference procedures prescribed in 5 CFR Part 302 in making VRA appointments. A veteran who is eligible for a VRA appointment is not automatically eligible for Veterans' preference.

After two years of satisfactory service, the agency must convert the veteran to career or career-conditional appointment, as appropriate.

Eligibility Criteria

The Jobs for Veterans Act, Public Law 107-288, amended title 38 U.S.C. 4214 by making a major change in the eligibility criteria for obtaining a Veterans Recruitment Appointment (VRA). Those who are eligible:

- Disabled veterans; or
- Veterans who served on active duty in the Armed Forces during a war, or in a campaign or expedition for which a campaign badge has been authorized; or
- Veterans who, while serving on active duty in the Armed Forces, participated in a United States military operation for which an Armed Forces Service Medal was awarded; or
- Recently separated veterans.
- Veterans claiming eligibility on the basis of service in a campaign or expedition for which a medal was awarded must be in receipt of the campaign badge or medal.

In addition to meeting the criteria above, eligible veterans must have been separated under honorable conditions (i.e., the individual must have received either an honorable or general discharge).

Note: Under the eligibility criteria, not all 5-point preference eligible veterans may be eligible for a VRA appointment. For example, a veteran who served during the Vietnam era (i.e., for more than 180 consecutive days, after January 31, 1955, and before October 15, 1976) but did not receive a service-connected disability or an Armed Forces Service medal or campaign or expeditionary medal would be entitled to 5 pt. veterans' preference. This veteran, however, would not be eligible for a VRA appointment under the above criteria.

As another example, a veteran who served during the Gulf War from August 2, 1990, through January 2, 1992, would be eligible for veterans' preference solely on the basis of that service. However, service during that time period, in and of itself, does not confer VRA eligibility on the veteran unless one of the above VRA eligibility criteria is met.

Lastly, if an agency has 2 or more VRA candidates and 1 or more is a preference eligible, the agency must apply Veterans' preference. For example, one applicant is VRA eligible on the basis of receiving an Armed Forces Service Medal (this medal does not confer veterans' preference eligibility). The second applicant is VRA eligible on the basis of being a disabled veteran (which does confer veterans' preference eligibility). In this example, both individuals are VRA eligible but only one of them is eligible for Veterans' preference. As a result, agencies must apply the procedures of 5 CFR 302 when considering VRA candidates for appointment.

Making Appointments

Ordinarily, an agency may simply appoint any VRA eligible who meets the basic qualifications requirements for the position to be filled without having to announce the job or rate and rank applicants. However, as noted, Veterans' preference applies in making appointments under the VRA authority. This means that if an agency has 2 or more VRA candidates and 1 or more is a preference eligible, the agency must apply Veterans' preference. Furthermore, an agency must consider all VRA candidates on file who are qualified for the position and could reasonably expect to be considered for the opportunity; it cannot place VRA candidates in separate groups or consider them as separate sources in order to avoid applying preference or to reach a favored candidate.

Terms and Conditions of Employment

A VRA appointee may be promoted, demoted, reassigned, or transferred in the same way as a career employee. As with other competitive service employees, the time in grade requirement applies to the promotion of VRAs. If a VRA-eligible employee is qualified for a higher grade, an agency may, at its discretion, give the employee a new VRA appointment at a higher grade up through GS-11 (or equivalent) without regard to time-in-grade.

Agencies must establish a training or education program for any VRA appointee who has less than 15 years of education. This program should meet the needs of both the agency and the employee.

Appeal Rights

During their first year of employment, VRA appointees have the same limited appeal rights as competitive service probationers, but otherwise they have the appeal rights of excepted service employees. This means that VRA employees who are preference eligibles have adverse action protections after one year (see Chapter 7). VRA's who are not preference eligibles do not get this protection until they have completed 2 years of current continuous employment in the same or similar position.

Nonpermanent Appointment Based on VRA Eligibility

Agencies may make a noncompetitive temporary or term appointment based on an individual's eligibility for VRA appointment. The temporary or term appointment must be at the grades authorized for VRA appointment but is not a VRA appointment itself and does not lead to conversion to career-conditional.

Refer To: 38 U.S.C. 4214; Pub. L. 107-288; 5 CFR Part 307; 5 CFR 752.401 (c)(3)

CHAPTER 33

HOMELESS VETERANS

OVERVIEW

Approximately one-third of the adult homeless population living on the streets or in shelters has served their country in the armed services. Many other veterans are considered at risk because of poverty, lack of support from family and friends and precarious living conditions in overcrowded or substandard housing.

The VA describes their mission to end veteran homelessness as having three core goals and approaches. First, the VA conducts outreach to seek out veterans proactively if they might need assistance. The VA also works to connect homeless and at-risk veterans with housing, health care, community employment services and other support services. The VA also collaborates with federal, state and local agencies, employers, housing providers, faith-based and community non-profits with the goal of expanding employment and affordable housing options for veterans who are exiting homelessness.

> **Key Takeaways**
>
> The VA provides resources for homeless veterans or veterans at-risk to become homeless.
>
> Veterans can call 1-877-4AID-VET to learn more about relevant services
>
> The VA has a collaborative program between HUD and VA combining HUD housing vouchers with VA supportive services to help veterans and their families find and maintain permanent housing

In 2012 as part of Public Law 112-154, there were a number of changes in homeless and housing programs for veterans. These include:
* Authorization of grant funds for the construction of transitional housing for homeless veterans. It also ensures the matching of funds from private and public sources for transitional housing.
* Extension of funding for programs designed to assist homeless veterans, including homeless veterans' reintegration programs and support services for low-income veteran families.
* Public Law 112-154 increases case management and coordination of care for homeless veterans through state and local agencies.

HOMELESS PROVIDERS GRANT AND PER DIEM PROGRAM

VA's Homeless Providers Grant and Per Diem Program is offered annually (as funding permits) by the Department of Veterans Affairs Health Care for Homeless Veterans (HCHV) Programs to fund community agencies providing services to homeless veterans. The purpose is to promote the development and provision of supportive housing and/or supportive services with the goal of helping homeless veterans achieve residential stability, increase their skill levels and/or income, and obtain greater self-determination.

HOTLINE FOR HOMELESS VETERANS

In March 2010, VA announced a new hotline for homeless veterans: **(877) 4AID-VET.**

Well trained expert responders will staff the hotline 24 hours a day, seven days a week. Responders can provide emergency support and resources to homeless veterans, as well as family members, community agencies and non-VA providers.

LOAN GUARANTEE PROGRAM FOR HOMELESS VETERANS MULTIFAMILY HOUSING

This initiative authorizes VA to guarantee no more than 15 loans with an aggregate value of $100 million within 5 years for construction, renovation of existing property, and refinancing of existing loans, facility furnishing or working capital. No more than 5 loans could be guaranteed under this program prior to November 11, 2001. The amount financed is a maximum of 90% of project costs.

Legislation allows the Secretary to issue a loan guarantee for large-scale self-sustaining multifamily loans. Eligible transitional project are those that:
1) Provide supportive services including job counseling;
2) Require veteran to seek and maintain employment;
3) Require veteran to pay reasonable rent;
4) Require sobriety as a condition of occupancy; and,
5) Serves other veterans in need of housing on a space available basis.

STAND DOWNS

Stand Downs are one part of the Department of Veterans Affairs' efforts to provide services to homeless veterans. Stand Downs are typically one to three day events providing services to homeless veterans such as food, shelter, clothing, health screenings, VA and Social Security benefits counseling, and referrals to a variety of other necessary services, such as housing, employment and substance abuse treatment. Stand Downs are collaborative events, coordinated between local VAs, other government agencies, and community agencies who serve the homeless.

For additional information on Stand Down dates and locations, please contact the Homeless Veterans Programs Office at (202) 273-5764.

COMPENSATED WORK THERAPY/TRANSITIONAL RESIDENCE (CWT/TR) PROGRAM

In VA's Compensated Work Therapy/Transitional Residence (CWT/TR) Program, disadvantaged, at-risk, and homeless veterans live in CWT/TR community-based supervised group homes while working for pay in VA's Compensated Work Therapy Program (also known as Veterans Industries). Veterans in the CWT/TR program work about 33 hours per week, with approximate earnings of $732 per month, and pay an average of $186 per month toward maintenance and up-keep of the residence. The average length of stay is about 174 days. VA contracts with private industry and the public sector for work done by these veterans, who learn new job skills, relearn successful work habits, and regain a sense of self- esteem and self-worth.

CHALENG

Community Homelessness Assessment, Local Education, and Networking Groups (CHALENG) for veterans is a nationwide initiative in which VA medical center and regional office directors work with other federal, state, and local agencies and nonprofit organizations to assess the needs of homeless veterans, develop action plans to meet identified needs, and develop directories that contain local community resources to be used by homeless veterans.

More than 10,000 representatives from non-VA organizations have participated in Project CHALENG initiatives, which include holding conferences at VA medical centers to raise awareness of the needs of homeless veterans, creating new partnerships in the fight against homelessness, and developing new strategies for future action.

For more information, please contact CHALENG at (404) 327-4033.

DCHV

The Domiciliary Care for Homeless Veterans (DCHV) Program provides biopsychosocial treatment and rehabilitation to homeless veterans. The program provides residential treatment to approximately 5,000 homeless veterans with health problems each year and the average length of stay in the program is 4 months. The domiciliaries conduct outreach and referral; vocational counseling and rehabilitation; and post-discharge community support.

DROP-IN CENTERS

These programs provide a daytime sanctuary where homeless veterans can clean up, wash their clothes, and participate in a variety of therapeutic and rehabilitative activities. Linkages with longer-term assistance are also available.

HUD-VASH

This joint Supported Housing Program with the Department of Housing and Urban Development provides permanent housing and ongoing treatment services to the harder-to- serve homeless mentally ill veterans and those suffering from substance abuse disorders. HUD's Section 8 Voucher Program has designated 1,780 vouchers worth $44.5 million for homeless chronically mentally ill veterans. VA staff at 35 sites provide outreach, clinical care and ongoing case management services. Rigorous evaluation of this program indicates that this approach significantly reduces days of homelessness for veterans plagued by serious mental illness and substance abuse disorders.

SUPPORTED HOUSING

Like the HUD-VASH program identified above, staff in VA's Supported Housing Program provides ongoing case management services to homeless veterans. Emphasis is placed on helping veterans find permanent housing and providing clinical support needed to keep veterans in permanent housing. Staff in these programs operates without benefit of the specially dedicated Section 8 housing vouchers available in the HUD- VASH program but are often successful in locating transitional or permanent housing through local means, especially by collaborating with Veterans Service Organizations.

COMPREHENSIVE HOMELESS CENTERS

VA's Comprehensive Homeless Centers (CHCs) place the full range of VA homeless efforts in a single medical center's catchment area and coordinate administration within a centralized framework. With extensive collaboration among non-VA service providers, VA's CHCs in Anchorage, AK; Brooklyn, NY; Cleveland, OH; Dallas, TX; Little Rock, AR; Pittsburgh, PA; San Francisco, CA; and West Los Angeles, CA, provide a comprehensive continuum of care that reaches out to homeless veterans and helps them escape homelessness.

VBA-VHA SPECIAL OUTREACH AND BENEFITS ASSISTANCE

VHA has provided specialized funding to support twelve Veterans Benefits Counselors as members of HCMI and Homeless Domiciliary Programs as authorized by *Public Law 102-590*. These specially funded staff provides dedicated outreach, benefits counseling, referral, and additional assistance to eligible veterans applying for VA benefits. This specially funded initiative complements VBA's ongoing efforts to target homeless veterans for special attention. To reach more homeless veterans, designated homeless veterans coordinators at VBA's 58 regional offices annually make over 4,700 visits to homeless facilities and over 9,000 contacts with non-VA agencies working with the homeless and provide over 24,000 homeless veterans with benefits counseling and referrals to other VA programs. These special outreach efforts are assumed as part of ongoing duties and responsibilities. VBA has also instituted new procedures to reduce the processing times for homeless veterans' benefits claims.

VBA'S ACQUIRED PROPERTY SALES FOR HOMELESS PROVIDERS

This program makes all the properties VA obtains through foreclosures on VA-insured mortgages available for sale to homeless provider organizations at a discount of 20 to 50 percent, depending on time of the market.

VA EXCESS PROPERTY FOR HOMELESS VETERANS INITIATIVE

This initiative provides for the distribution of federal excess personal property, such as hats, parkas, footwear, socks, sleeping bags, and other items to homeless veterans and homeless veteran programs. A Compensated Work Therapy Program employing formerly homeless veterans has been established at the Medical Center in Lyons, NJ to receive, warehouse, and ship these goods to VA homeless programs across the country.

SUPPORTIVE SERVICES FORVETERAN FAMILIES (SSVF)

In July 2011, the VA announced the award of $60 million in grants to serve homeless and at-risk veterans and their families as part of the Supportive Services for Veteran Families (SSVF) program. The SSVF program awards grants to private non-profits and consumer cooperatives that provide a range of services to eligible low-income veteran families.

VA has been authorized to offer community-based grants through the Supportive Services for Veteran Families (SSVF) Program, which will provide supportive services to very low-income Veteran families in or transitioning to permanent housing. Funds are granted to private non- profit organizations and consumer cooperatives who will assist very low-income veteran families by providing a range of supportive services designed to promote housing stability.

Through the SSVF Program, VA aims to improve very low-income Veteran families' housing stability. Grantees (private non-profit organizations and consumer cooperatives) will provide eligible Veteran families with outreach, case management, and assistance in obtaining VA and other benefits, which may include:

- Health care services
- Daily living services
- Personal financial planning services
- Transportation services
- Fiduciary and payee services
- Legal services
- Child care services
- Housing counseling services

In addition, grantees may also provide time-limited payments to third parties (e.g., landlords, utility companies, moving companies, and licensed child care providers) if these payments help Veterans' families stay in or acquire permanent housing on a sustainable basis.

HEALTHCARE FOR HOMELESS VETERANS PROGRAM (HCHV)

HCHV programs now serve as the hub for a myriad of housing and other services which provide VA a way to outreach and assist homeless Veterans by offering them entry to VA care.

Outreach is the core of the HCHV program. The central goal is to reduce homelessness among Veterans by conducting outreach to those who are the most vulnerable and are not currently receiving services an reengaging them in treatment and rehabilitative programs. Contract Residential Treatment Program ensures that Veterans with serious mental health diagnoses can be placed in community-based programs which provide quality housing and services.

PROGRAM MONITORING AND EVALUATION

VA has built program monitoring and evaluation into all of its homeless veterans' treatment initiatives and it serves as an integral component of each program. Designed, implemented, and maintained by the Northeast Program Evaluation Center (NEPEC) at VAMC West Haven, CT, these evaluation efforts provide important information about the veterans served and the therapeutic value and cost effectiveness of the specialized programs. Information from these evaluations also helps program managers determine new directions to pursue in order to expand and improve services to homeless veterans.

CHAPTER 34

BENEFITS FOR FEMALE VETERANS

Females veterans are entitled to the same benefits that are available to male veterans (see below list), and the VA has also designed a number of programs aimed specifically at female veterans, including healthcare benefits and programs.

Female veterans are entitled to all of the benefits available to male veterans, including:

- Disability Compensation For Service-Related Disabilities;
- Disability Pension For Non-Service Related Disabilities;
- Education Assistance Programs;
- Work-Study Allowance;
- Vocational Rehabilitation And Counseling;
- Insurance;
- Home Loan Benefits;
- Medical Inpatient And Outpatient C
- Substance Abuse Treatment And Counseling;
- Sexual Trauma And Assault Counseling;
- Nursing Home Care;

Burial Benefits;
- Burial In A VA National Cemetery
- Employment Assistance;
- Survivors' Benefit Programs

Key Takeaways

Women veterans may be eligible for a wide variety of benefits available to all veterans including disability compensation, pension, education and training, health care, home loans and more

The VA's Center for Women Veterans monitors and coordinates VA's administration of services and programs for women veterans

There are Women Veteran Coordinators located in every regional office who serve as the primary contact for women veterans

At every VA medical center nationwide, a Women Veterans Program Manager advises and advocates for women veterans

HEALTHCARE FOR FEMALE VETERANS

In the spring of 2012 the VA announced a new partnership with the American Heart Association to combat heart disease in female veterans. The program, entitled "Go Red for Women," is working to actively address the issues associated with heart disease in women, including smoking, poor diet and obesity, all of which are risk factors. Heart disease has been identified as the leading cause of death among women, and a third of female veterans suffer from high cholesterol or high blood pressure.

Women Veterans Health Care works to make certain that all eligible women Veterans requesting VA care are assured of:
- Comprehensive primary care by a proficient and interested primary care provider
- Privacy, safety, dignity, and sensitivity to gender-specific needs
- The right care in the right place and time
- State-of-the-art health care equipment and technology
- High-quality preventive and clinical care, equal to that provided to male veterans

SERVICES PROVIDED TO WOMEN VETERANS INCLUDE:

Primary Care
General care includes health evaluation and counseling, disease prevention, nutrition counseling, weight control, smoking cessation, and substance abuse counseling and treatment as well as gender-specific primary care, e.g., cervical cancer screens (Pap smears), breast cancer screens (mammograms), birth control, preconception counseling, Human Papillomavirus (HPV) vaccine, menopausal support (hormone replacement therapy).

Mental Health Care
Mental health includes evaluation and assistance for issues such as depression, mood, and anxiety disorders; intimate partner and domestic violence; sexual trauma; elder abuse or neglect; parenting and anger management; marital, caregiver, or family-related stress; and post-deployment adjustment or post-traumatic stress disorder (PTSD).

Sexual Trauma
Military Sexual Trauma (MST). Women—and men as well—may experience repeated sexual harassment or sexual assault during their military service. Special services are available to women who have experienced MST. VA provides free, confidential counseling and treatment for mental and physical health conditions related to MST.

Specialty Care
Management and screening of chronic conditions includes heart disease, diabetes, cancer, glandular disorders, osteoporosis, and fibromyalgia as well as sexually transmitted diseases such as HIV/AIDS and hepatitis.

Reproductive health care includes maternity care, infertility evaluation and limited treatment; sexual problems, tubal ligation, urinary incontinence, and others. VA is prohibited by legislative authority from providing either in-vitro fertilization or abortion services.

Rehabilitation, homebound, and long-term care. VA referrals are given to those in need of rehabilitation therapies such as physical therapy, occupational therapy, speech-language therapy, exercise therapy, recreational therapy, and vocational therapy. Homebound and long-term care services are available as well, limited to those meeting specific requirements

The VA has placed a strategic priority on six pillars, which are designed to give women veterans the best possible health care services. These include:

Comprehensive Primary Care: Women Veterans Health Care works closely with Primary Care Services to redesign the way primary care is delivered, which tailors it to the specific needs of women.

Women's Health Education: Women Veterans Health Care has partnered with the VA

Employee Education Services to create mini-residencies in women's health, which will allow providers to be more educated in the advanced topics regarding women's health.

Reproductive Health: Women Veterans Health Care is working to implement safe prescribing measures for female veterans of childbearing age. Other efforts include improving follow-up of abnormal mammograms, tracking the timeliness of breast cancer treatment, and ensuring the care women receive from non-VA, maternity and emergency department care.

Communication and Partnerships: Women Veterans Health Care is working to develop a VA-wide communication plan to enhance the language, practice and culture of the VA to be more inclusive of female veterans.

Women's Health Research: Women Veterans Health Care has partnered with the Women's Health Evaluation Initiative based in Palo Alto, CA to develop a series of Sourcebooks with key descriptive information about women Veterans including demographics, population growth over time, diagnoses, utilization and cost of care.

Special Women Veteran Populations: The Women's Veteran Health Strategic Healthcare Group (WVHSHG) is working to ensure that the needs of all women Veterans are addressed, including those populations that require special attention.

Rural and homebound veterans can benefit from emerging technology that will deliver care remotely through "e-clinics", mobile clinics, and home-based care services.

Women veterans with mental illnesses can benefit through integration of mental health services within primary care, so that necessary treatment is provided in a comprehensive and coordinated way. Women Veterans Health Care is also working to enhance the availability of woman-safe inpatient psychiatric acute units.

Aging women veterans can benefit from the latest advances in medical science and technology to identify and address cardiovascular disease as well as advances in treatments for diabetes, osteoporosis, and menopause.

Referrals are made for services that VA is unable to provide. Women Veterans' Program Managers are available in a private setting at all VA facilities to assist women veterans seeking treatment and benefits.

VA has also established a division within the National Center for Post-Traumatic Stress Disorder, the Women's Health Science Division. The center is based at the Boston VA Medical Center, and conducts clinical research addressing trauma-related problems of female veterans. Veterans may contact the Center at:

VA Medical Center Women's Health Sciences Division
150 South Huntington Avenue
Boston, MA 02130
(617) 232-9500

WOMEN VETERANS COMPREHENSIVE HEATH CENTERS

Eight Women Veterans Comprehensive Health Centers have been established to develop and enhance programs focusing on the gender-specific healthcare needs of female veterans. The locations are as follows:

Boston VA Medical Center Boston, Massachusetts (617) 232-9500, extension 4276
Chicago Area Network (Hines, Lakeside, North Chicago, and West Side VA Medical

Centers) (312) 569-6168
Durham VA Medical Center Durham, NC (919) 286-0411
Minneapolis VA Medical Center Minneapolis, Minnesota (612) 725-2030
Southeast Pennsylvania Network (Coatesville, Lebanon, Philadelphia and Wilmington VA Medical Centers) (215) 823-44496
San Francisco VA Medical Center San Francisco, California (415) 221-4810, extension 2174
Sepulveda / West Los Angeles VA Medical Centers Sepulveda, California and Los Angeles, California (415) 221-4810
Tampa VA Medical Center Tampa, Florida (813) 972-2000, extension 3678

STATE WOMEN VETERANS COORDINATORS

In addition to the Department of Veterans Affairs' Women Veterans Coordinators that are located at local regional offices and medical centers, there may be an Office of State Veterans Affairs, or a State Commission for Veterans Coordinator available within the State government veterans program. These State offices are part of the veteran-advocate community and their staff may assist female veterans in accessing State and Federal entitlements. For specific information on availability in your state, contact your local VA office.

CHAPTER 35

BENEFITS FOR GULF WAR VETERANS

The first Gulf War, an offensive led by U.S. and coalition troops in January 1991, followed the August 1990 Iraqi invasion of Kuwait. The war was over on February 28, 1991, and an official cease-fire was signed in April 1991. The last U.S. troops who participated in the ground war returned home on June 13, 1991. In all, about 697,000 U.S. troops had been deployed to the Gulf region during the conflict.

Operation Iraqi Freedom, a military campaign which began on March 20, 2003, and Operation New Dawn, named for the reduced role of U.S. troops in Iraq, have created a new group of Gulf War veterans.

With variation in exposures and veterans' concerns ranging from oil well fire smoke to possible contamination from Iraqi chemical/biological agents, VA has initiated wide-ranging research projects evaluating illnesses as well as environmental risk factors.

Key Takeaways

More than 650,000 servicemembers served in Operation Desert Storm and Desert Shield.

For the purpose of VA benefits, the Gulf War period is still in effect.

Any veteran who served on active military service for any period from August 2, 1990 to the present meets the wartime service requirement.

The Department of Veterans Affairs (VA) offers Gulf War veterans physical examinations and special eligibility for follow-up care, and it operates a toll-free hotline at (800) 749-8387 to inform these veterans of the program and their benefits. Operators are trained to help veterans with general questions about medical care and other benefits. It also provides recorded messages that enable callers to obtain information 24 hours a day. Beginning in 2012, it was announced Veterans of the Persian Gulf War, with an undiagnosed illness, will have an additional five years to qualify for benefits from the VA. These changes also affect veterans of the Southwest Asia conflict. The change will apply to those veterans who may be eligible to claim VA disability compensation, as well as the ability of survivors to qualify for Dependency and Indemnity Compensation. Under previous VA guidelines, any undiagnosed illness used to establish eligibility for VA benefits had to be apparent by December 31, 2011. The change in rules pushed this date to December 31, 2016.

GULF WAR SERVICE

Gulf War service is active duty in any of the following areas in Southwest Asia during the Gulf War, which began in 1990 and continues to the present:
Iraq Kuwait
Saudi Arabia

The neutral zone (between Iraq and Saudi Arabia) Bahrain
Qatar
The United Arab Emirates Oman
Gulf of Aden Gulf of Oman
Waters of the Persian Gulf, the Arabian Sea, and the Red Sea The airspace
above these locations

PERSIAN GULF REGISTRY PROGRAM

A free, complete physical examination with basic lab studies is offered to every Gulf War veteran, whether or not the veteran is ill. Veterans do not have to be enrolled in VA healthcare to participate in registry examinations. Results of the examinations, which include review of the veteran's military service and exposure history, are entered into special, computerized registries. The registries enable VA to update veterans on research findings or new compensation policies through periodic newsletters. The registries could also suggest areas to be explored in future scientific research. Registry participants are advised of the results of their examinations in personal consultations and by letters.

SPECIAL ACCESS TO FOLLOW-UP CARE

VA has designated a physician at every VA medical center to coordinate the special registry examination program and to receive updated educational materials and information as experience is gained nationally. Where an illness possibly related to military service in the Southwest Asia Theater of operations during the Gulf War is detected during the examination, follow-up care is provided on a higher-eligibility basis than most non-service-connected care.

STANDARDIZED EXAM PROTOCOLS

VA has expanded its special registry examination protocol as more experience has been gained with the health of Gulf veterans. The protocol elicits information about symptoms and exposures, calls the clinician's attention to diseases common to the Gulf region, and directs baseline laboratory studies including chest X-ray (if one has not been done recently), blood count, urinalysis, and a set of blood chemistry and enzyme analyses that detect the "biochemical fingerprints" of certain diseases. In addition to this core laboratory work for every veteran undergoing the Gulf War program exam, physicians order additional tests and specialty consults as they would normally in following a diagnostic trail -- as symptoms dictate. If a diagnosis is not apparent, facilities follow the "comprehensive clinical evaluation protocol." The protocol suggests 22 additional baseline tests and additional specialty consultations, outlining dozens of further diagnostic procedures to be considered, depending on symptoms.

GULF WAR ILLNESS

Gulf War veterans have reported a variety of medically unexplained symptoms, such as fatigue, headache, joint pains, sleep disturbances and memory problems since serving in the Gulf. VA has recognized certain health problems as associated with Gulf War service or military service

VA has recognized that certain health problems for Gulf War Veterans are associated with Gulf War service or military service. These Veterans may be eligible for disability compensation and health care for these illnesses. Surviving spouses, children and dependent parents of Gulf War Veterans who died as the result of illnesses associated with Gulf War service may be eligible for survivors' benefits.

For the purposes of these benefits, Gulf War Veterans are Veterans who served on active duty in the Southwest Asia theater of operations any time during the first Gulf War starting August 2, 1990 through the current conflict in Iraq. This includes Veterans who served in Operation Iraqi Freedom (2003-2010) and Operation New Dawn (2010 and continuing).

Illnesses that are associated with Gulf War service include:
- Medically Unexplained Chronic Multi-Symptom Illnesses
- Gulf War Veterans have reported a variety of medically unexplained symptoms, such as fatigue, headache, joint pains, sleep disturbances and memory problems since serving in the Gulf. VA presumes certain medically unexplained symptoms existing for six months or more are associated with military service in the Gulf. The illnesses must have appeared during active duty in the Southwest Asia theater of operations or by December 31, 2016, and be at least 10 percent disabling.
- Illnesses include medically unexplained multi-symptom illnesses that have existed for six months or more, such as:
  o Chronic fatigue syndrome
  o Fibromyalgia
- Functional gastrointestinal disorders, a group of conditions marked by chronic or recurrent symptoms related to any part of the gastrointestinal tract. Functional condition refers to an abnormal function of an organ, without a structural alteration in the tissues. Examples include irritable bowel syndrome (IBS), functional dyspepsia, and functional abdominal pain syndrome. VA's final rule specifying that functional gastrointestinal disorders are covered as presumptive illnesses took effect on August 15, 2011.
- Undiagnosed illnesses with symptoms that may include but are not limited to: abnormal weight loss, cardiovascular symptoms, fatigues, gastrointestinal symptoms, headache, joint pain, menstrual disorders, muscle pain, neurologic symptoms, neuropsychological symptoms, skin conditions, upper and lower respiratory system symptoms, and sleep disturbances
- Infectious Diseases

In late 2010, VA established new presumptions of service connection for nine specific infectious diseases associated with military service in Southwest Asia during the first Gulf War starting August 2, 1990, through the conflict in Iraq and on or after September 19, 2001, in Afghanistan. Veterans must have the diseases within the time frames shown below and have a current disability as a result of that disease in order to receive disability compensation:
- Brucellosis
- Campylobacter jejuni
- Coxiella burnetii (Q fever)
- Malaria
- Mycobacterium tuberculosis
- Nontyphoid Salmonella
- Shigella
- Visceral leishmaniasis
- West Nile virus

A veteran now only has to show service in Southwest Asia or Afghanistan and that he or she had one of the nine diseases within a certain time after service, and has a current disability as a result of that disease, subject to certain time limits for seven of t he diseases.

Amyotrophic Lateral Sclerosis (ALS)

VA does not presume that amyotrophic lateral sclerosis (ALS) is associated with hazardous exposures during the Gulf War. However, VA has recognized ALS diagnosed in Veterans with 90 days or more of continuously active service in the military was caused by their military service.

OBTAINING COPIES OF HOSPITAL RECORDS

A program is in place to help Gulf War veterans obtain copies of their in-patient hospital records from hospitals established during the Persian Gulf War.

Although these records were always located in the National Personnel Records Center in St. Louis, MO, they were stored only by the name of the hospital and the date of treatment.

An electronic database has been created to cross-reference patient names and social security numbers with their theater hospitals and admission dates.

Veterans may call (800) 497-6261 to find out if their inpatient record has been added to the database, and to obtain the paperwork necessary to request a copy.

CHAPTER 36

SERVICEMEMBERS' CIVIL RELIEF ACT

OVERVIEW

Congress and state legislatures have long recognized that military service can often place an economic and legal burden on servicemembers. *The Soldiers' and Sailors' Civil Relief Act of 1918* was passed in order to protect the rights of service members while serving on active duty.

Servicemembers were protected from such things as repossession of property, bankruptcy, foreclosure or other such actions while serving in the military. This Act remained in effect until shortly after World War I when it expired. The Soldiers' and Sailors' Civil Relief Act of 1940 (SSCRA) was passed in order to protect the rights of the millions of service members activated for World War II. The SSCRA has remained in effect until the present day and has been amended many times, since 1940 to keep pace with the changing military.

> **Key Takeaways**
>
> Veteran borrowers who are called to active duty may be able to request relief pursuant to the Servicemembers Civil Relief Act
>
> The SCRA provides eligible servicemembers with a variety of rights and benefits.
>
> The SCRA protects servicemembers and their families from eviction if they leave a house or apartment and can't make rent

In December 2003, Congress passed legislation renaming SSCRA as the Servicemembers' Civil Relief Act (SCRA). The SCRA updates and strengthens the civil protections enacted during World War II.

The SCRA is designed to protect active duty military members, reservists who are in active federal service, and National Guardsmen who are in active federal service. Some of the benefits under the SCRA extend to dependents of active duty military members as well.

Public Law 107-330 extended protections under the SCRA to members of the National Guard who are called to active service authorized by the President or the Secretary of Defense, or a state governor for a period of more than 30 consecutive days, for purposes of responding to a national emergency declared by the President, and supported by Federal funds.

The SCRA can provide many forms of relief to military members. Below are some of the most common forms of relief.

PROTECTION FROM EVICTION

If a military member is leasing a house or apartment and his or her rent is below a certain amount, the SCRA can protect the individual from being evicted for a period of time, usually three months. The dwelling place must be occupied by either the active duty member or his or her dependents and the rent on the premises cannot exceed $2,932.31a month (rate as of 2016). This rent ceiling will be adjusted annually for consumer price index (CPI) changes. Additionally, the military member must show that military service materially affects his or her ability to pay rent. If a landlord continues to try to evict the military member or does actually evict the member, he or she is subject to criminal sanctions such as fines or even imprisonment.

TERMINATION OF PRE-SERVICE RESIDENTIAL LEASES

The SCRA also allows military members who are just entering active duty service to lawfully terminate a lease without repercussions. To do this, the service member needs to show that the lease was entered into prior to the commencement of active duty service, that the lease was signed by or on behalf of the service member, and that the service member is currently in military service or was called to active-duty service for a period of 180 days or more. Proper written notice with a copy of orders must be provided to the landlord.

TERMINATION OF RESIDENTIAL LEASES DURING MILITARY SERVICE

The SCRA allows military members who receive permanent change of station (PCS) orders or are deployed for a period of 90 days or more to terminate a lease by providing written notice to the landlord along with a copy of the military orders. The termination of a lease that provides for monthly payment of rent will occur 30 days after the first date on which the next rental payment is due and payable after the landlord receives proper written notice.

MORTGAGES

The SCRA can also provide military members temporary relief from paying their mortgage. To obtain relief, a military member must show that their mortgage was entered into prior to beginning active duty, that the property was owned prior to entry into military service, that the property is still owned by the military member, and that military service materially affects the member's ability to pay the mortgage.

Mortgage foreclosures or lien actions initiated during your military service or within nine months after the end of your military service must be stayed upon your request. This applies only to obligations that you have undertaken before entering active duty. A court may instead "adjust the obligations in a way that preserves the interests of all parties." Note that the nine-month period reverts to 90 days as of January 1, 2013, unless further extended.

No sale, foreclosure, or seizure of property for a breach of a pre-service mortgage-type obligation is valid if made during or within 9 months after the period of active duty, unless pursuant to a valid court order. This provides the service member tremendous protections from foreclosure in the many states that permit foreclosures to proceed without involvement of the courts. Service members who miss any mortgage payments should immediately see a legal assistance attorney.

MAXIMUM RATE OF INTEREST

Under the SCRA, a military member can cap the interest rate at 6% for all obligations entered into before beginning active duty if the military service materially affects his or her ability to meet the obligations. This can include interest rates on credit cards, mortgages, and even some student loans (except for Federal guaranteed student loans), to name a few. To qualify for the interest rate cap the military member has to show that he or she is now on active duty, that the obligation or debt was incurred prior to entry on active duty, and that military service materially affects the members' ability to pay. To begin the process, the military member needs to send a letter along with a copy of current military orders to the lender requesting relief under the SCRA. The interest rate cap lasts for the duration of active duty service. The interest rate cap will apply from the first date of active-duty service. The military member must provide written notice to the creditor and a copy of military orders not later than 180 days after the servicemember's termination or release from military service.

TERMINATION OF AUTOMOBILE LEASES DURING MILITARY SERVICE

The SCRA allows military members to terminate pre-service automobile leases if they are called up for military service of 180 days or longer. Members who sign automobile leases while on active-duty may be able to terminate an automobile lease if they are given orders for a permanent change of station outside the continental United States or to deploy with a military unit for a period of 180 days or longer.

STAY OF PROCEEDINGS

If a military member is served with a complaint indicating that they are being sued for some reason, they can obtain a "stay" or postponement of those proceedings if the military service materially affects their ability to proceed in the case. A stay can be used to stop the action altogether, or to hold up some phase of it. According to the SCRA, military members can request a "stay" during any stage of the proceedings. However, the burden is on the military member to show that their military service has materially affected their ability to appear in court. In general, individuals can request a stay of the proceedings for a reasonable period of time (30-60 days). For example, if they are being sued for divorce, they can put off the hearing for some period of time, but it is unlikely that a court will allow the proceedings to be put off indefinitely. The stay can be granted in administrative proceedings.

DEFAULT JUDGMENTS

A default judgment is entered against a party who has failed to defend against a claim that has been brought by another party. To obtain a default judgment, a plaintiff must file an affidavit (written declaration of fact) stating that the defendant is not in the military service and has not requested a stay. If someone is sued while on active duty, and fails to respond, and as a result a default judgment is obtained against them, they can reopen the default judgment by taking several steps. First, they must show that the judgment was entered during their military service or within 30 days after they've left the service. Second, they must write to the court requesting that the default judgment be reopened while they are still on active duty or within 90 days of leaving the service. Third, they must not have made any kind of appearance in court, through filing an answer or otherwise, prior to the default judgment being entered. Finally, they must indicate that their military service prejudiced their ability to defend their case and show that they had a valid defense to the action against them.

INSURANCE

Under SCRA, the U.S. Department of Veterans Affairs (VA) will protect, from default for nonpayment of premiums, up to $250,000 of life insurance for servicemembers called to active duty. (This amount was previously $10,000.) The protection provided by this legislation applies during the insured's period of military service and for a period of two years thereafter. The following are conditions for eligibility for protection:

- The policy must be whole life, endowment, universal life or term insurance.
- The policy must have been in force on a premium-paying basis for at least six months at the time the servicemember applies for benefits.
- Benefits from the policy cannot be limited, reduced or excluded because of military service.
- Policies for which an additional amount of premium is charged due to military service are not eligible for protection under SCRA.

The servicemember must apply for protection of their life insurance by filing "VA Form 29-380 "Application For Protection Of Commercial Life Insurance Policy" with his/her insurance company and forwarding a copy of the application to VA.

BENEFITS OF SCRA LIFE INSURANCE PROTECTION

Once the servicemember has applied for protection of their life insurance policy and VA determines that the policy is eligible for protection under SCRA:

- The servicemember is still responsible for making premium payments. However, the policy will not lapse, terminate, or be forfeited because of the servicemember's failure to make premium payments or to pay any indebtedness or interest due during their period of military service or for a period of two years thereafter.
- The rights of the servicemember to change their beneficiary designation or select an optional settlement for a beneficiary are not affected by the provisions of this Act.

LIMITATIONS OF SCRA LIFE INSURANCE PROTECTION

Once the servicemember has applied for protection of their life insurance policy and VA determines that the policy is eligible for protection under SCRA:

- Premium payments are deferred only, not waived. During this period, the government does not pay the premiums on the policy but simply guarantees that the premiums will be paid at the end of the servicemember's period of active duty.
- A servicemember cannot receive dividends, take out a loan, or surrender the policy for cash without the approval of VA. (Dividends or other monetary benefits shall be added to the value of the policy and will be used as a credit when final settlement is made with the insurer.)
- If the policy matures as a result of the insured's death, or any other means, during the protected period, the insurance company will deduct any unpaid premiums and interest due from the settlement amount.

TERMINATION OF PERIOD UNDER SCRA

The servicemember has up to two years after their military service terminates to repay the unpaid premiums and interest to the insurer. If the amount owed is not paid before the end of the two years, then:

- The insurer treats the unpaid premiums as a loan against the policy.
- The government will pay the insurer the difference between the amount due and the cash surrender value (if the cash surrender value of the policy is less than the

amount owed.)

o   The amount the United States government pays to the insurance company under the SCRA Act becomes a debt due the government by the insured.

o   If the policy matures as a result of the insured's death, or any other means, during the protected period, the insurance company will deduct any unpaid premiums and interest due from the settlement amount.

TAXATION

A service member's state of legal residence may tax military pay and personal property. A member does not lose residence solely because of a transfer to another state pursuant to military orders.

For example, if an Illinois resident who is a member of Illinois Army National Guard is activated to federal military service and sent to California for duty, that person remains an Illinois resident while in California. The service member is not subject to California's authority to tax his/her military income. However, if the service member has a part-time civilian job in California, California will tax his/her non-military income earned in the state.

The Servicemembers Civil Relief Act also contains a provision preventing servicemembers from a form of double taxation that can occur when they have a spouse who works and is taxed in a state other than the state in which they maintain their permanent legal residence. The law prevents states from using the income earned by a servicemember in determining the spouse's tax rate when they do not maintain their permanent legal residence in that state.

Public Law 111-98, which became law on November 11, 2009, provides that when a service member leaves his or her home state in accord with military or naval orders, the service member's spouse may retain residency in his or her home state for voting and tax purposes, after relocating from that state to accompany the service member.

RIGHT TO VOTE

In addition to the protections involving debt payments and civil litigation, the act guarantees service members the right to vote in the state of their home of record and protects them from paying taxes in two different states.

CAUTION

The SSCRA does not wipe out any of an individual's obligations. Rather, it temporarily suspends the right of creditors to use a court to compel an individual to pay, only if the court finds that the inability to pay is due to military service. The obligation to honor existing debts remains, and some day the individual must "pay up."

It is important to remember that the SSCRA affords no relief to persons in the Service against the collection of debts or other obligations contracted or assumed by them after entering such Service.

The Servicemembers' Civil Relief Act is highly technical. The above summary is intended only to give a general overview of the protection available. The specific nature of all the relief provided under the law is a matter about which an individual may need to contact an attorney. The Act is designed to deal fairly with military personnel and their creditors. While relief is very often available, individuals are expected and required to show good faith in repayment of all debts.

VETERANS BENEFITS ACT OF 2010

Amends the *Servicemembers Civil Relief Act* (SCRA) to prohibit lessors from charging early termination fees with respect to residential, business, agricultural, or motor vehicle leases entered into by servicemembers who subsequently enter military service or receive orders for a permanent change of station or deployment in support of a military operation.

Allows a servicemember to terminate a contract for cellular or home telephone service at any time after receiving military orders to deploy for at least 90 days to a location that does not support the contract. Requires the return of any advance payments made by a deploying servicemember under such a contract.

Allows the Attorney General to bring a civil suit against any violator of the SCRA. Also gives servicemembers a "private right of action" to file their own lawsuits against those who violate their legal rights.

CHAPTER 37

APPEALS

OVERVIEW

Veterans and other claimants for VA benefits have the right to appeal decisions made by a VA regional office or medical center.

If a claimant wishes to appeal a VA decision, the appeal is first reviewed by the BOARD OF VETERANS APPEALS. If, after review by the Board of Veterans' Appeals, the claimant is still dissatisfied, he or she may appeal to the UNITED STATES COURT OF VETERANS APPEALS. Both entities, along with specific guidelines for the filing of appeals, are discussed in the remainder of this chapter.

> **Key Takeaways**
>
> Any decision made by the VA on a benefit claim including disability, health care and cemetery claims, can be appealed for any reason
>
> Appeals begin at the VA office that made the initial decision
>
> Veterans have one full year to decide if they will appeal a VBA final claims decision

2017 Update: Rapid Appeals Modernization Program (RAMP)

What is RAMP?

In November 2017, the VA launched RAMP with the goal of providing eligible appellants with the earliest possible resolution of their disagreement with VA's decision on their claim.

RAMP is voluntary and will provide you with the opportunity to enter the new, more efficient review process outlined in the historic Veterans Appeals Improvement and Modernization Act of 2017 (Appeals Modernization Act), which the President signed into law on August 23, 2017.

Under RAMP, you can expect to receive a review of the decision on your claim much faster than if you remain in the legacy appeals process. The program will allow participants the option to have their decisions reviewed in the Higher-Level Review or Supplemental Claim Lane outlined in the new law.

RAMP will run through February 2019, when the VA plans to fully implement the Appeals Modernization Act. Further, the VA will continue to process RAMP elections as long as necessary to continue to accelerate resolution of legacy appeals.

Appeals Modernization Plan

RAMP is part of the larger Appeals Modernization Plan. The legacy appeal process, which was set in law, split jurisdiction over appeals in compensation claims between Veterans Benefits Administration (VBA) and the Board of Veterans' Appeals (Board), adding more complexity to the appeal process.

The Appeals Modernization Act establishes a new review process for VA claims that is timely, transparent, and fair, and thus allows the VA to improve the delivery of benefits and services to you and your family.

RAMP gives you the opportunity for early participation in the new Supplemental Claim and Higher-Level Review lanes.

Review Lanes

Supplemental Claim Lane

Select this option if you have additional evidence that is new and relevant to support granting your benefit claim. VA's goal is to complete these supplemental claims in an average of 125 days. The VA will assist you in gathering new and relevant evidence to support your claim. The VA will review any new and relevant evidence submitted since we last decided your claim.

If desired, you can continue to submit supplemental claims with new and relevant evidence or use the Higher-Level Review Lane after you receive a decision in the Supplemental Claim Lane by making an election for further review within one year of the date on your decision notice.

Higher-Level Review Lane

Select this option if you have no additional evidence to submit in support of your claim but you believe that there was an error in the initial decision. VA's goal is to complete these higher-level reviews in an average of 125 days.

A higher-level review consists of an entirely new review of your claim by a senior claims adjudicator.

The Higher-Level Reviewer will only consider evidence that was in VA's possession at the time you opt-in. You and/or your representative will NOT be able to add new evidence during this process.

The VA cannot assist you in developing additional evidence. However, if the Higher-Level Reviewer discovers an error in the VA's duty to assist in the prior decision, your claim will return to initial decision makers for additional processing to correct the error.

You or your representative can request an optional one time telephonic informal conference with the Higher-Level Reviewer to identify specific errors in the case. Requesting an informal conference may cause some delay in the processing of your higher-level review.

If necessary, you can use the Supplemental Claim Lane after you receive a decision in the Higher-Level Review Lane, by making an election for further review within one year of the date on your decision notice. However, you will not have immediate access to the Higher-Level Review after receiving a decision in the Higher-Level Review Lane.

RAMP Eligibility

You are eligible if you have a disability compensation appeal pending in one of the following legacy appeal stages:
- Notice of Disagreement (NOD)
- Form 9, Appeal to Board of Veterans' Appeals
- Certified to the Board but not yet activated for a Board decision
- Remand from the Board to VBA
- Those who have been waiting the longest in each of the above appeal stages for a resolution of their appeal will receive a letter giving them the opportunity to participate in RAMP first.

BOARD OF VETERANS APPEALS

The Board of Veterans' Appeals (Board) is a part of the Department of Veterans Affairs (VA), located in Washington, D.C. The Board's mission is to conduct hearings and decide appeals properly before the Board in a timely manner. 38 United States Code (U.S.C.) § 7101(a). The Board's jurisdiction extends to all questions in matters involving a decision by the Secretary under a law that affects a provision of benefits by the Secretary to Veterans, their dependents, or their Survivors. 38 U.S.C. §§ 511(a); 7104(a). Final decisions on such appeals are made by the Board based on the entire record in the proceeding and upon consideration of all evidence and applicable provisions of law and regulation. 38 U.S.C. § 7104(a).

The Board consists of a Chairman, a Vice Chairman, and such number of members as may be found necessary to conduct hearings and dispose of appeals properly before the Board in a timely manner. 38 U.S.C. § 7101(a). "Members of the Board," also known as "Veterans Law Judges" (VLJ), are supported by a large staff of attorneys and administrative personnel. 38 Code of Federal Regulations (CFR) § 19.2(b). After the end of each fiscal year, the Chairman is required to prepare a report on the activities of the Board during that fiscal year and the projected activities of the Board for the current and subsequent fiscal years. 38 U.S.C. § 7101(d)(1). To read the current and past Annual Reports click here.

The appeals process in VA is a complex, multi-step adjudication process, which utilizes an open record – that is, it allows a Veteran to submit medical and lay evidence at any point from the beginning to the end of the process, including while the claim is pending on appeal, which may in turn require VA to develop further evidence on the Veteran's behalf. Appeals are initiated at the Agency of Original Jurisdiction (AOJ), which includes the Veterans Benefits Administration (VBA) Regional Offices (RO), Veterans Health Administration (VHA) medical facilities, the National Cemetery Administration (NCA), and the Office of General Counsel (OGC). While the vast majority (98 percent) of appeals considered by the Board involves claims for disability compensation, the Board also reviews appeals involving other types of Veterans benefits, to include insurance benefits, educational benefits, home loan guaranties, vocational rehabilitation, dependency and indemnity compensation, health care delivery, burial benefits, pension benefits, and fiduciary matters. If an appeal is not resolved at the AOJ level to the Veteran's (or Appellant's) satisfaction, he or she may formally continue that appeal to the Board for a de novo review (i.e., new look) and the issuance of a final decision.

VLJs review benefit claims determinations made by local VA offices and issue decision on appeals. These VLJs, attorneys experienced in Veterans law and in reviewing benefit claims, are the only ones who can issue Board decisions. Staff attorneys, also trained in Veterans law, review the facts of each appeal and assist the Board members. 38 U.S.C. §§ 7103, 7104.

Overview of the Appeals Process

Anyone who has filed a claim for benefits with VA and has received a determination from a local VA office is eligible to appeal to the Board of Veterans' Appeals. Some decisions, such as eligibility for medical treatment, issued by VA medical centers can also be appealed to the BVA. An appeal can be made based on a complete denial of a claim, or based on the level of benefit granted. For example, if a veteran files a claim for disability, and the local VA office awards a 10% disability, but the veteran feels he or she is more than 10% disabled, the veteran can appeal that determination to the Board of Veterans' Appeals.

Decisions concerning the need for medical care or the type of medical treatment needed (such as a physician's decision to prescribe or not to prescribe a particular drug, or whether to order a specific type of treatment) are not within the BVA's jurisdiction.

On December 22, 2006 then-President Bush signed *Public Law 109-461*, the *Veterans' Benefits, Healthcare, and Information Technology Act of 2006*. The law allows veterans to hire an agent or attorney to represent them after a Notice of Disagreement has been filed. (A Notice of Disagreement is the written statement submitted by the veteran stating he or she disagrees with the claim decision made by the VA regional office.) Veterans will still have the option of utilizing the representation services provided without charge by many veterans' organizations, but in addition they will have the option of hiring an attorney if they so choose. Until now, the United States Code has not allowed a veteran to hire an attorney until the veteran has received a final Board of Veterans' Appeals (BVA) decision – a process that often takes years from a veterans' initial application.

HOW TO FILE AN APPEAL AND IMPORTANT TIME LIMITS

After the local VA office reviews a Notice of Disagreement, it is possible that the local office will agree with the NOD (VA Form-21-0958), and will change its original decision. However, if the local VA office does not change its decision, it will prepare and mail the veteran a *Statement of the Case*, which includes a VA Form 9 -Substantive Appeal, which the veteran must complete and return. The Statement of Case will summarize the evidence and applicable laws and regulations, and provide a discussion of the reasons for arriving at the decision.

Within 60 days of the date the local VA office issue the Statement of Case, the veteran must submit a completed VA Form 9-Substantive Appeal. Please note that if the one-year period from the date the VA regional office or medical center mailed its original decision is later than this 60-day period, the veteran has until that later one-year date to file the VA Form 9-SubstantiveAppeal.

Completion of the VA Form 9-Substantive Appeal is very important. The form should include a clear statement of the benefit being sought, as well as any mistakes the veteran feels VA made when issuing its decision. VA Form 9-Substantive Appeal should also identify anything in the Statement of Case the veteran disagrees with. In addition to VA Form 9, any additional evidence, such as records from recent medical treatments or evaluations may be included as part of the appeal.

In most instances, a veteran can obtain civilian medical records and other non- government documents supporting his or her case by calling or writing directly to the office that keeps those records. VA regional office personnel and VSO representatives are experienced in locating many items that can support your case, such as service medical records, VA treatment records, and other government records. The VA does have a duty to assist veterans in the developing of their cases. However, individual veterans need to assist the VA in identifyingthe evidence that can prove the case.

If new information or evidence is included with VA Form 9, the regional office will prepare a Supplemental Statement of the Case (SSOC). The SSOC is similar to the Statement of the Case, but addresses the new information or evidence. If a veteran is not satisfied with the SSOC, a written statement must be mailed to the regional office within 60 days from the mailing date of the SSOC.

It is important to realize the importance of submitting the VA Form 9-Substantive Appeal on a timely basis, otherwise, the right to appeal may be lost. Remember, the VA Form 9 is due the later of:

1 year from Regional Office determination mailing date or 60 days from Statement of Case (SOC) mailing date

An extension of the 60-day period for filing VA Form 9-Substantive Appeal or the 60-day period following a Supplemental Statement of the Case **may** be approved if a written request is filed with the local VA office handling the appeal. An extension will only be approved if the veteran can show "good cause" (can offer a valid reason why the extra time is needed).

DOCKET

A veteran's VA Form 9-Substantive Appeal becomes part of his or her claims folder, and is the basis for adding the appeal to the Board's *docket*.

The Board's docket is the record of all appeals awaiting review by the Board, listed in the order that appeals (VA Form 9) are received.

When an appeal is placed on the Board's docket, it is assigned the next higher number than the one received before it. The Board reviews appeals in the order in which they were placed on the docket. Thus, the lower the docket number, the sooner the appeal will be reviewed

LAWYERS AND OTHER REPRESENTATIVES

A veteran may represent himself or herself. However, over 90% of all people who appeal to the Board of Veterans' Appeals obtain representation. The majority choose to be represented by Veterans' Service Organizations (VSOs) or their state's veterans department.

A lawyer may also be hired for representation. There are strict guidelines about what a lawyer may charge for services, as well as restrictions on fees that a lawyer may charge for work performed prior to issuance of the Board's final decision.

In addition to VSOs and attorneys, some other agents are recognized by VA to represent appellants.

To authorize a VSO for representation, VA Form 21-22 must be completed. To authorize an attorney or recognized agent for representation, VA Form 22a must be completed. Both forms are available at all VA offices.

LENGTH OF APPEAL PROCESS

No one can determine exactly how long it will take form the time an appeal is filed until receipt of the Board's decision. However, veterans can expect an average of two years from the time an appeal is placed on the Board's docket until issuance of a BVA decision.

If a veteran believes his or her case should be decided sooner than others filed earlier, a *motion to advance on the docket* can be submitted. The motion should explain why the appeal should be moved ahead. Because most appeals involve some type of hardship, before a case can be advanced, there needs to be convincing proof of exceptional circumstances (i.e. terminal illness, danger of bankruptcy or foreclosure, or an error by VA that caused a significant delay in the docketing of an appeal. Veterans should be aware that, on average, fewer than 3 out of every 20 requests for advancement on the docket are granted.

To file a motion to advance on the docket, a written request should be sent to:

Board of Veterans' Appeals (014)
PO Box 27063
Washington DC 20038
(202) 495-6803

PERSONAL HEARINGS

A personal hearing is a meeting between the veteran (and his/her representative) and an official from VA who will decide the case. During the hearing, the veteran presents testimony and other evidence supporting the case. There are two types of personal hearings:

- Regional office hearings (also called RO hearing or local office hearings); and BVA hearings.
- A regional office hearing is a meeting held at a local VA office with a "hearing officer" from the local office's staff. To arrange a regional office hearing, a veteran should contact the local VA office or appeal representative as early in the appeal process as possible.
- In a BVA hearing, the veteran presents his or her case in person to a member of the Board. Appellants in most areas of the country can choose whether to hold the BVA hearing at the local VA regional office, called a "Travel Board Hearing," or at the BVA office in Washington, D.C. Some regional offices are also equipped to hold BVA hearings by videoconference. (Check with the regional office for availability.)

The VA cannot pay for any lodging or travel expenses incurred in connection with a hearing.

The VA Form 9-Substantive Appeal has a section for requesting a BVA hearing. VA Form 9 is not used, however, to request a local office hearing. Even if a BVA hearing is not requested on the VA Form 9, a request can still be requested by writing directly to the Board. If a BVA hearing is requested, the request must clearly state where the hearing is requested – at the VA regional office, or at the Board's office in Washington, D.C. A BVA hearing cannot be held in both places. (Travel Board hearings may not be available at regional offices located near Washington, D.C.)

The requested type and location of the hearing determines when it will be held. Generally, regional office hearings are held as soon as they can be scheduled on the hearing officer's calendar.

The scheduling of BVA hearings held at regional offices (Travel Board hearings) is more complicated, since Board members must travel from Washington, D.C. to the regional office. BVA video-conferenced hearings are less complicated to arrange, and can be scheduled more frequently than Travel Board hearings.

Hearings held at the Board's offices in Washington, D.C. will be scheduled for a time close to when BVA will consider the case – approximately three months before the case is reviewed by the BVA.

LOCATION OF CLAIMS FOLDER

If a BVA hearing is not requested, the claims folder remains at the local VA office until shortly before the BVA begins its review, at which time it is transferred to the BVA.

If a Travel Board hearing is requested, the claims folder remains at the local VA office until the hearing is completed, at which time it is transferred to the BVA

If a video-conferenced BVA hearing or a hearing held at the Board's office in Washington, is requested, the claims folder remains at the local VA office until shortly before the BVA hearing is held. It is transferred to the BVA in time for the hearing and the Board's review. When a claims folder is transferred from the local VA office to Washington, D.C., the local VA office will send the claimant a letter advising that he or she has 90 days remaining (from the date of that letter) during which more evidence can be added to a file, a hearing can be requested, or a representative can be selected (or changed).

The BVA cannot accept items submitted after the 90-day period has expired, unless a written explanation (called a "motion") is also submit, explaining why the item is late and showing why the BVA should accept it (called "showing good cause"). A motion to accept items after the 90-day period will be reviewed by a Board member who will issue a ruling either allowing or denying the motion.

CHECKING ON THE STATUS OF AN APPEAL

To check on the status of an appeal, veterans or their representatives should contact the office where the claims folder is located (see previous section).

If a claims file is at the Board, veterans or their representatives may call (202) 565-5436 to check on its status (be sure to have the claim number available).

THE BOARD REVIEW PROCESS

When the VBA receives an appeal from a local VA office, the veteran and/or representative will be notified in writing. The Board will then examine the claims folder for completeness, and will provide an opportunity to submit additional written arguments. The case is then assigned to a Board member for review. If a BVA hearing was requested, the Board member assigned the case will conduct the hearing prior to reaching a decision.

When the docket number for an appeal is reached, the file will be reviewed by a Board member and a staff attorney, who will check for completeness, review all evidence and arguments, as well as the regional office's Statement of the Case (and Supplement Statement of the Case, if applicable), the transcript of the hearing (if applicable), the statement of any representative, and any other information included in the claims folder. The staff attorney, if directed to do so by the Board member, may also conduct additional research and prepare recommendations for the Board member's review.

When, in the judgment of the Board member, expert medical opinion, in addition to that available within the VA, is warranted by the medical complexity or controversy involved in an appeal, the Board may secure an advisory medical opinion from one or more independent medical experts who are not employees of the VA.

The VA shall make necessary arrangements with recognized medical schools, universities, or clinics to furnish such advisory medical opinions at the request of the Chairman of the Board. Any such arrangement shall provide that the actual selection of the expert or experts to give the advisory opinion in an individual case shall be made by an appropriate official of such institution.

The Board shall furnish a claimant with notice that an advisory medical opinion has been requested, and shall furnish the claimant with a copy of such opinion when it is received by the Board.

Prior to reaching a decision, the Board member must thoroughly review all materials and recommendations. The Board member will then issue a decision.

The Board member's decision will be mailed to the home address that the Board has on file, so it is extremely important that the VA be kept informed of any address changes.

The BVA must attempt to make its decisions as understandable as possible. However, due to the nature of legal documents, laws, court cases, and medical discussions, decisions can be confusing. If an appeal is denied , the Board will send a "Notice of Appellate Rights" that describes additional actions that can betaken.

The Board annually produces a CD-ROM with the text of its decisions. Most VA regional offices have these CD-ROMS available for review, or the CD-Rom may be purchased from the Government Printing Office. For further information, contact:

REMANDS
Department of Veterans Affairs Board of Veterans' Appeals (01B)
Washington, D.C. 20420

Sometimes when reviewing a claims folder, the Board member determines additional development of the case is necessary. The appeal is then returned to the local VA office. This is called a "remand." After performing the additional work, the regional office may issue a new decision. If the claim is still denied, the case is returned to the Board for a final decision. (The case keeps its original place on the Board's docket, so it is reviewed soon after it is returned to the Board.)

Depending on the reason for the remand, the regional office may provide the veteran with a Supplement Statement of the Case (SSOC). The claimant then has 60 days from the date the local VA office mails the SSOC to comment on it.

APPEALING THE BOARD OF VETERANS' AFFAIRS DECISION

MOTION FOR RECONSIDERATION

If it can be demonstrated that the Board made an obvious error of fact or law in its decision, a written "motion to reconsider" can be filed. Any such motions should be sent directed to the Board, not to the local VA office. A motion to reconsider should not be submitted simply because of disagreement with the BVA's decision. The claimant must be able to show that the Board made a mistake, and that the Board's decision would have been different if the mistake had not been made. A motion to reconsider should be sent directly to the Board, not to the local VA office.

REOPENING

If a claimant has "new and material evidence," he or she can request that the case be re-opened. To be considered "new and material," the evidence submitted must be information related to the case that was not included in the claims folder when the case was decided.

To re-open an appeal, the claimant must submit the new evidence directly to the local VA office that handled the claim.

CUE MOTION

The law was amended in 1997 to provide one more way to challenge a Board decision. A Board decision can be reversed or revised if the claimant is able to show that the decision contained "clear and unmistakable error"(CUE).

The written request for the Board to review its decision for CUE is called a "motion." CUE motions should be filed directly with the Board, and not with the local VA office.

Because CUE is a very complicated area of law, most claimants seek help from a representative to file a CUE motion.

A motion for CUE review of a prior Board decision must meet some very specific requirements, described in the Board's Rules of Practice. If the motion is denied a claimant can't ask for another CUE review of the way the Board decided the issues raised in the first CUE motion, so it is very important that the motion be prepared properly the first time out.

Not many CUE motions are successful, because CUE is a very rare kind of error, the kind that compels a conclusion that the Board would have decided the claimant's case differently but for the error. A difference of opinion is not enough.

A motion to review a Board decision for CUE can be filed at any time, but if it is filed after filing a timely Notice of Appeal with the Court, the Board will not be able to rule on your CUE motion.

UNITED STATES COURT OF VETERANS' APPEALS

The United States Court of Veterans' Appeals was created under Public Law 100-687, on November 18, 1988. The Court has seven judges, appointed by the President and confirmed by the Senate. Judges are appointed for a 15-year term.

If a claimant is not satisfied with the Board of Veterans' Appeals decision, an appeal can be filed with the United States Court of Veterans Appeals (referred to as the "Court"). The Court is an independent court that is not part of the Department of Veterans Affairs. The Court does not hold trials, receive new evidence, or hear witnesses. It reviews the BVA decision, the written record, and the briefs of the parties. Claimants do not need to appear in Washington, D.C. for an appeal. (In approximately 1% of decided cases, the Court holds oral arguments in its Washington courtroom, or occasionally, by telephone conference call.)

A claimant may represent himself or herself, but may want to get advice from an attorney or from a service officer in a veterans organization or a state or county veterans' affairs office. The VA will be represented by its attorney, and a claimant's case may be better presented if he or she is represented.

The Court does not recommend or appoint attorneys to represent claimants. However, the Court does have a Public List of Practitioners which shows who is allowed to represent appellants in the Court, and have said that they are available. Most attorneys charge a fee.

To appeal a Board of Veterans' Appeals decision, a claimant must file a "Notice of Appeal" with the Court within 120 days from the date the Board's decision is mailed. (The first day of the 120 days a claimant has to file an appeal to the Court is the day the BVA's decision is postmarked, not the day the decision is signed.)

If a claimant filed a motion to reconsider with the Board of Veterans' Appeals within the 120 day time-frame, and that motion was denied, the claimant has an additional 120 days to file the "Notice of Appeal" with the Court. (This 120 day period begins on the date the Board mails a notification that it has denied the motion to reconsider.) If the Board denies the motion to reconsider, a "Notice of Appellate Rights" will be mailed to the claimant.
In addition to the above 120 day limit, in order for the Court to consider an appeal, a Notice of Disagreement must have been filed with the VA regional office handling the case on or after November 18, 1988.

An original "Notice of Appeal" must be filed directed with the Court at:

United States Court of Veterans Appeals
625 Indiana Avenue, NW, Suite 900
Washington, D.C. 20004
Fax: (202) 501-5848
(Appeals cannot be filed by e-mail)

The fee for an appeal is $50.00, and should be included with the "Notice of Appeal." If a claimant is unable to pay this fee, a "Motion to Waive Filing Fee" form must be completed and returned with the "Notice of Appeal."

If a claimant appeals to the Court, a copy of the "Notice of Appeal" must also be filed with the VA General Counsel at:

Office of the General Counsel (027) Department of Veterans Affairs
810 Vermont Avenue, NW
Washington, D.C. 20420

Please note that the original "Notice of Appeal" that is filed with the Court is the only document that protects a claimants right to appeal a BVA decision. The copy sent to the VA General Counsel does not protect that right, or serve as an official filing.

If the Court accepts an appeal, it will send a printed copy of the rules of practice and procedure to the claimant and his/her representative, if applicable.

To obtain more specific information about the "Notice of Appeal," the methods for filing with the Court, Court filing fees, and other matters covered by the Court's rules, a claimant should contact the Court directly at:

United States Court of Veterans Appeals
625 Indiana Avenue, NW, Suite 900
Washington, D.C. 20004
(800) 869-8654

If either party disagrees with the Court's ruling, an appeal may be filed with the U.S. Court of Appeals for the Federal Circuit, and, thereafter, may seek review in the Supreme Court of the United States.

DEATH OF APPELLANT

According to the law, the death of an appellant generally ends the appellant's appeal, and the Board normally dismisses the appeal without issuing a decision. The rights of a deceased appellant's survivors are not affected by this action. Survivors may still file a claim at the regional office for any benefits to which they may be entitled.

GENERAL GUIDELINES FOR EFFICIENT PROCESSING OF CLAIMS

The following guidelines may help ensure that an appeal is not unnecessarily delayed:

- Consider having an appeal representative assist with the filing of the appeal.
- Be as specific as possible when identifying the issues the Board should consider.
- Be as specific as possible when identifying sources of evidence for the VA to obtain. (For example, provide the full names and addresses of physicians, along with dates of treatment, and reasons for treatment.)
- Keep VA informed of current address, phone number, and number of
- dependents.
- When possible, provide clinical treatment records, rather than simply a

statement from a physician.

- Include the claim number on any correspondence with the VA.
- Do not submit material that is not pertinent to the claim. This will only delay the process.
- Do not use the VA Form 9 to raise new claims for the first time. (VA Form 9 is only to be used to appeal decisions on previously submitted claims.)
- Do not use the VA Form 9 to request a local office hearing.
- Do not raise additional issues for the Board's review late in the appeal process. This may cause the appeal to be sent back to the regional office for additional work, and may result in a longer delay.
- Do not submit evidence directly to the Board unless a written or typed statement is included, stating that consideration by the regional office is waived. The statement must clearly indicate that the Board is to review the evidence, even though the regional office has not seen it. If a waiver is not included with any additional evidence submitted directly to the Board, the case may be remanded to the regional office for review, and may result in further delays.
- Do not submit a last minute request for a hearing or a last minute change to the type or location of a hearing unless it is unavoidable. Such a request will likely result in a delay in reaching a final decision.
- Do not miss a scheduled VA examination or hearing.

CHAPTER 38

VA REGIONAL OFFICES & BENEFITS OFFICE

Department of Veterans Affairs
Headquarters
810 Vermont Avenue NW
Washington, DC 20420
(202) 273-5400

Alabama (SDN 5) Montgomery Regional
Office
345 Perry Hill Road
Montgomery, AL 36109

Alaska (SDN 8) Anchorage Regional
Office
1201 North Muldoon Road
Anchorage, AK 99504

Arizona (SDN 9) Phoenix Regional
Office
3333 North Central Avenue
Phoenix, AZ 85012

Arkansas (SDN 7)
North Little Rock Regional Office
2200 Fort Roots Drive Building 65
North Little Rock, AR 72114

California (SDN 9)
Los Angeles Regional Office Federal
Building
11000 Wilshire Boulevard
Los Angeles,
CA 90024

Oakland Regional Office
1301 Clay Street
Room 1400 North
Oakland, CA 94612

San Diego Regional Office
8810 Rio San Diego Drive
San Diego, CA 92108

Colorado (SDN 8) Denver Regional
Office
155 Van Gordon Street
Lakewood, CO 80228

Connecticut (SDN 1) Hartford Regional
Office
555 Willard Avenue
Newington, CT 06111
Mailing Address:
P.O. Box 310909
Newington , CT 06131

Delaware (SDN 3) Wilmington Regional
Office
1601 Kirkwood Highway
Wilmington, DE 19805

Florida (SDN 5)
St. Petersburg Regional Office
9500 Bay Pines Boulevard Bay Pines, FL
33708 Mailing Address:
P.O. Box 1437
St. Petersburg , FL 33731

Georgia (SDN 4) Atlanta Regional Office
1700 Clairmont Road
Decatur, GA 30033
Mailing Address:
P.O. BOX 100026
Decatur, GA
30031-7026

Hawaii (SDN 9) Honolulu Regional
Office
459 Patterson Road E-Wing
Honolulu, HI 96819-1522

Idaho (SDN 8)
Boise Regional Office
444 W. Fort Street
Boise, ID 83702-4531

Illinois (SDN 6)
Chicago Regional Office
2122 West Taylor Street
Chicago, IL 60612

Indiana (SDN 2) Indianapolis Regional
Office
575 North Pennsylvania Street
Indianapolis, IN 46204

Iowa (SDN 6)
Des Moines Regional Office
210 Walnut Street
Des Moines, IA 50309

Kansas (SDN 6) Wichita Regional Office
5500 East Kellogg
Wichita, KS 67211

Kentucky (SDN 3) Louisville Regional
Office
321 West Main Street, Suite 390
Louisville, KY 40202

Louisiana (SDN 7)
New Orleans Regional Office
1250 Poydras Street
New Orleans, LA 70113

Maine (SDN 1) Togus VA Med/
Regional Office
1 VA Center
Augusta, ME 04330

Maryland (SDN 3) Baltimore Regional
Office
31 Hopkins Plaza Federal Bldg
Baltimore, MD 21201

Massachusetts (SDN 1)
Boston VA Regional Office

JFK Federal Building
15 New Sudbury St. Government Center
Boston, MA 02114

Michigan (SDN 2) Detroit Regional
Office Federal Building
477 Michigan Avenue
Detroit, MI 48226

Minnesota (SDN 6)
St. Paul Regional Office
1 Federal Drive
Fort Snelling
St. Paul, MN 55111-4050

Mississippi (SDN 5) Jackson Regional
Office
1600 East Woodrow Wilson Ave.
Jackson, MS 39216

Missouri (SDN 6)
St. Louis Regional Office Federal
Building
400 South, 18th Street
St. Louis, MO 63103

Montana (SDN 8)
Fort Harrison Regional Office
3633 Veterans Drive
Fort Harrison, MT 59636-0188

Nebraska (SDN 6) Lincoln Regional
Office
3800 Village Drive
Lincoln, NE 68516
Mailing Address: PO Box 85816
Lincoln, NE 68501-5816

New Hampshire (SDN 1) Manchester
Regional Office Norris Cotton Federal
Bldg
275 Chestnut Street
Manchester, NH 03101

New Jersey (SDN 2) Newark Regional
Office
20 Washington Place
Newark, NJ 07102

New Mexico (SDN 8) Albuquerque
Regional Office
Dennis Chavez Federal Building
500 Gold Avenue,
S.W. Albuquerque, NM 87102

Nevada (SDN 9) Reno Regional Office
5460 Reno Corporate Dr.
Reno, NV 89511-2250

New York (SDN1) Buffalo Regional Office
130 South Elmwood Avenue
Buffalo, NY 14202

New York Regional Office
245 West Houston Street
New York, NY 10014

North Carolina (SDN 4) Winston-Salem Regional Office Federal Building
251 North Main Street
Winston-Salem, NC 27155

North Dakota (SDN 6)
Fargo Regional Office
2101 Elm Street
Fargo, ND 58102

Ohio (SDN 2)
Cleveland Regional Office
A.J. Celebrezze Federal Building
1240 East 9th Street
Cleveland, OH 44199

Oklahoma (SDN 7)
Muskogee Regional Office
125 South Main Street
Muskogee, OK 74401

Oregon (SDN 8) Portland Regional Office
100 SW Main Street, Floor 2
Portland, OR 97204
Mailing Address:
100 SW Main St FL 2
Portland, OR 97204

Pennsylvania (SDN 2) Philadelphia Regional Office
5000 Wissahickon Avenue
Philadelphia, PA 19101

Pittsburgh Regional Office
1000 Liberty Avenue
Pittsburgh, PA 15222

Rhode Island (SDN 1) Providence Regional Office
380 Westminster St.
Providence, RI 02903

South Carolina (SDN 4) Columbia Regional Office
6437 Garners Ferry Road
Columbia, SC 29209

South Dakota (SDN 6) Sioux Falls Regional Office
2501 West 22nd Street
Sioux Falls, SD 57117

Tennessee (SDN 4) Nashville Regional Office
110 9th Avenue South
Nashville, TN 37203

Southern Area Office
3322 West End, Suite 408
Nashville, TN 37203

Texas (SDN 7)
Houston Regional Office
6900 Almeda Road
Houston, TX 77030

Waco Regional Office
1 Veterans Plaza
701 Clay Avenue
Waco, TX 76799

Utah (SDN 8)
Salt Lake City Regional Office
550 Foothill Drive
Salt Lake City, UT 84158

Vermont (SDN 1)
White River Junction Regional Office
215 N. Main St.
White River Junction, VT 05009

Virginia (SDN 3) Roanoke Regional Office
116 N. Jefferson St.
Roanoke, VA 24016

Washington (SDN 8) Seattle Regional Office Federal Building
915 2nd Avenue
Seattle, WA 98174

West Virginia (SDN 3) Huntington Regional Office
640 Fourth Avenue
Huntington, WV 25701

Wisconsin (SDN 6) Milwaukee Regional Office
5400 West National Avenue
Milwaukee, WI 53214

Wyoming (SDN 8) Cheyenne Regional Office
2360 East Pershing Blvd.
Cheyenne, WY 82001

District of Columbia (SDN 3)
Washington DC Regional Office
1722 I Street N.W.
Washington, DC 20421

Puerto Rico (SDN 5)
San Juan Regional Office
50 Carr 165
Guaynabo, PR 00968-8024

Philippines (SDN 9) Manila Regional
Office
1501 Roxas Boulevard
Pasay City, PI 1302

Note: SDN = Service Delivery Network

*In order to reach any of the above offices by phone, call (800) 827-1000 and your call will be directed appropriately.

CHAPTER 39

STATE BENEFITS

Many states offer services and benefits to veterans in addition to those offered by the Department of Veterans' Affairs. To find out more about a particular state's programs, individuals should contact the following

Alabama Department of Veterans'
Affairs RZA Plaza
770 Washington Ave,
Suite 530
Montgomery, AL 36102-1509
(334) 242-5077

Alaska Department of Veterans' Affairs
P.O. Box 5800
Fort Richardson, AK 99505- 5800
(907) 428-6031

Arizona Department of Veterans'
Services 3839 North Third
Street, Suite 209
Phoenix, AZ 85012
(602) 248-1554

Arkansas Department of Veterans'
Affairs
2200 Fort Roots Drive Room 119 –
Bldg 65
North Little Rock, AR 72114
(501) 370-3820

California Department of Veterans'
Affairs
1227 O Street, Suite 300
Sacramento, CA 95814
(800) 952-5626

Colorado Division of Veterans' Affairs
6848 South Revere Parkway
Centennial, CO 80112

(720) 250-1500

Connecticut Department of Veterans'
Affairs
287 West Street
Rocky Hill, CT 06067
(860) 616-3603

Delaware Commission of Veterans'
Affairs
Robbins Building
802 Silverlake Blvd, Suite 100
Dover, DE 19904
(302) 739-2792
(800) 344-9900 (in state only)

Florida Department of Veterans' Affairs
Mary Grizzle Building, Room 311-K
11351 Ulmerton Road
Largo, FL 33778
(727) 518-3202

Georgia Department of Veterans' Affairs
Floyd Veterans Memorial Building Suite
E-970
Atlanta, GA 30334
(404) 656-2300

Hawaii Office of Veterans' Services
Mailing Address:
459 Patterson Road
E-Wing, Room 1-A103
Honolulu, HI 9681 Location:
Tripler Army Med Center (Ward Road)

VAMROC, E-Wing, Room 1-A103
Honolulu, HI 96819
(808) 433-0420

Idaho Division of Veterans' Affairs
351 Collins Road
Boise, ID 83702
(208) 577-2310

Illinois Department of Veterans' Affairs
362 North Linwood Rd.
Galesburg, IL 61401
(309) 343-2510

Indiana Department of Veterans' Affairs
302 West Washington, Room E120
Indianapolis, IN 46204-2738
(317) 232-3910

Iowa Commission of Veterans' Affairs
7105 N.W. 70th Avenue Camp Dodge -
Building 3663
Johnston, IA 50131-1824
(515) 242-5331

Kansas Commission on Veterans' Affairs
Jayhawk Towers Suite 1004
700 S.W. Jackson Street
Topeka, KS 66603-3714
(785) 296-3976

Kentucky Department of Veterans'
Affairs
1111 Louisville Road NGAKY Building
Frankfort, KY 40601
(502) 564-9203

Louisiana Department of Veterans'
Affairs
P.O. Box 94095 Capitol Station
1885 Wooddale Blvd. 10th Floor,
Room 1013
Baton Rouge, LA 70806
(225) 219-5000

Maine Bureau of Veterans' Services
117 State House Station
Camp Keyes Building 7, Room 115
Augusta, ME 04333
(207) 430-6035

Maryland Department of Veterans'
Affairs
16 Francis St. 4th Floor
Annapolis, MD 21401
(410) 260-3838

Massachusetts Department of Veterans'
Services
600 Washington Street,
Suite 1100
Boston, MA 02111
(617) 210-5480

Michigan Department of Veterans'
Affairs
7109 W. Saginaw
Lansing, MI 48913
(517) 335-6523

Minnesota Department of Veterans'
Affairs
State Veterans Service Building
20 West 12th Street, 2nd Floor Rm. 206
St. Paul, MN 55155-2079
(651) 296-2562

Mississippi State Veterans' Affairs Board
3466 Highway 80 East
P.O. Box 5947
Pearl, MS 39288-5947
(601) 576-4850

Missouri Veterans' Commission Mailing
Address:
205 Jefferson Street
12th Floor Jefferson Building
P.O. Drawer 147
Jefferson City, MO 65102
(573) 751-3779

Montana Veterans' Affairs Division
P.O. Box 5715
1900 Williams Street
Helena, MT 59604
(406) 324-3740

Nebraska Department of Veterans'
Affairs
State Office Building
301 Centennial Mall South
P.O. Box 95083
Lincoln, NE 68509-5083
(402) 471-2458

Nevada Commission for Veterans'
Affairs
5460 Reno Corporate Dr.Suite 131
Reno, NV 89511
(775) 688-1656

New Hampshire Office of Veterans' Service
275 Chestnut Street Room 517
Manchester, NH 03101-2411
(603) 624-9230
1-800-622-9230 (in state only)

New Jersey Department of Veterans' Affairs
Eggert Crossing Road PO Box 340
Trenton, NJ 08625-0508
(800) 624-0508

New Mexico Veterans' Service Commission
Bataan Memorial Building
407 Galisteo St. Rm. 142
Santa Fe, NM 87504
(866) 433-8387

New York Division of Veterans' Affairs
2 Empire State Plaza 17th Floor
Albany, NY 12223-1551
(518) 474-6114

North Carolina Division of Veterans' Affairs
325 N. Salisbury Street
Raleigh, NC 27601
(919) 807-4250

North Dakota Department of Veterans' Affairs
4201 38th St S # 104
Fargo, ND 58104
(701) 239-7165

Ohio Governor's Office of Veterans' Affairs
77 South High Street
Columbus, OH 43215
(614) 644-0898

Oklahoma Department of Veterans' Affairs
2311 N. Central Avenue
Oklahoma City, OK 73105
(405) 521-3684

Oregon Department of Veterans' Affairs
100 South Main St.
Portland, OR 97204
(503) 412-4777

Pennsylvania Department of Veterans' Affairs
Fort Indiantown Gap Building S-O-47
Annville, PA 17003-5002
(717) 861-2000

Rhode Island Division of Veterans' Affairs
480 Metacom Avenue
Bristol, RI 02809
(401) 462-0324

South Carolina Office of Veterans' Affairs
1205 Pendleton Street, Suite 463
Columbia, SC 29201
(803) 734-0200

South Dakota Division of Veterans' Affairs
425 East Capitol Avenue
c/o 500 East Capitol Avenue
Pierre, SD 57501
(605) 773-3269

Tennessee Department of Veterans' Affairs
312 Rosa Parks Ave.
Nashville, TN 37243-1010
(615) 741-2931

Texas Veterans' Commission
1700 Congress Ave.
Austin, TX 78701
(512) 463-5538

Utah Division of Veterans' Affairs
550 Foothill Blvd, Room 202
Salt Lake City, UT 84113
(801) 326-2372

Vermont State Veterans' Affairs
118 State Street
Montpelier, VT 05602
(802) 828-3379

Virginia Department of Veterans' Affairs
900 East Main Street
Richmond, VA 23219
(804) 786-0286

Washington Department of Veterans' Affairs
P.O. Box 41150
1011 Plum Street
Olympia, WA 98504-1150
(800) 562-0132

West Virginia Division of Veterans' Affairs
1514-B Kanawha Blvd.
Charleston, WV 25311
(304) 558-3661

Wisconsin Department of Veterans'
Affairs
201 West Washington Avenue
Madison, WI 53703
(800) 947-8387

Wyoming Veterans' Affairs Commission
Wyoming ANG Armory
5905 CY Avenue - Room 101
Casper, WY 82604
(307) 265-7372

American Samoa Veterans' Affairs
P.O. Box 982942
Pago Pago, American Samoa 96799
(001) 684-633-4206

Guam Veterans' Affairs Office Mailing
Address:
Box 3279 Agana,
Guam 96932
(671) 475-4222
Location: "M" Street HSE
#105 Tiyan, Guam

Puerto Rico Public Advocate for
Veterans' Affairs
Mailing Address:
Apartado 11737 Fernandez Juncos
Station
San Juan, PR 00910-1737
Location:
Mercantile Plaza Bldg, Fourth Floor,
Suite 4021
Hato Rey, PR 00918-1625
(787) 758-5760

Government of the Virgin Islands
Division of Veterans' Affairs
1013 Estate Richmond Christiansted
St. Croix VI 00820-4349
(340) 773-6663

CHAPTER 40

MILITARY PERSONNEL RECORDS

The U.S. Department of Veterans Affairs does not maintain veterans' military service records.

The personnel records of individuals currently in the military service, in the reserve forces, and those completely separated from military service are located in different offices. A nominal fee is charged for certain types of service. In most instances service fees cannot be determined in advance. If your request involves a service fee you will be notified as soon as that determination is made.

A veteran and spouse should be aware of the location of the veteran's discharge and separation papers. If a veteran cannot locate discharge and separation papers, duplicate copies may be obtained (further information regarding who to contact is included later in this chapter).

Use "Standard Form 180, Request Pertaining To Military Records," which is available from VA offices and veterans organizations. Specify that a duplicate separation document or discharge is needed. The veteran's full name should be printed or typed so that it can be read clearly, but the request must also contain the signature of the veteran or the signature of the next of kin, if the veteran is deceased. Include branch of service, service number or Social Security number and exact or approximate date and years of service.

> **Key Takeaways**
>
> If you've been discharged from military service, your personnel files are stored at the National Archives and Record Administration.
>
> Recent military service and medical records are not online, but most veterans and their next-of-kin can get free copies of their DD Form 214 and other records by using the eVetRecs System to create a request or mailing a fax or standard form SF-180

It is not necessary to request a duplicate copy of a veteran's discharge or separation papers solely for the purpose of filing a claim for VA benefits. If complete information about the veteran's service is furnished on the application, VA will obtain verification of service from the National Personnel Records Center or the service department concerned.

WHO TO CONTACT

The various categories of military personnel records are described in the tables below. Please read the following notes carefully, to make sure an inquiry is sent to the right address. Please note especially that the record is not sent to the National Personnel Records Center as long as the person retains any sort of reserve obligation, whether drilling or non-drilling.

SPECIAL NOTES FOR FOLLOWING TABLES:

Records at the National Personnel Records Center: Note that it takes at least 3 months, and often 6 or 7, for the file to reach the National Personnel Records Center after the military obligation has ended (such as by discharge). If only a short time has passed, please send the inquiry to the address shown for active or current reserve members. Also, if the person has only been released from active duty, but is still in a reserve status, the personnel record will stay at the location specified for reservists. A person can retain a reserve obligation for several years, even without attending meetings or receiving annual training.

If there were two or more periods of service within the same branch, send your request (only one is necessary) to the office having the records for the LAST PERIOD OF SERVICE

LOCATION OF AIR FORCE MILITARY PERSONNEL & HEALTH RECORDS

Status of Service Member or Veteran	Location of Personnel Record	Location of Health Record
Discharged, deceased or retired from active duty on or after October 1, 2004	AFPC/DP2SSM Military Records 550 C. St. West Suite 19 Randolph AFB, TX 78150 (800) 525-0102	Department of Veterans Affairs Records Management Center P.O. Box 5020 St. Louis, MO 63115-5020 (800) 827-1000
Active (including National Guard on active duty in the Air Force), TDRL, or general officers retired with pay	AFPC/DP2SSM Military Records 550 C. St. West JBSA-Randolph, TX 78150 Fax: (800) 525-0102	
Reserve, retired reserve in nonpay status, current National Guard officers not on active duty in the Air Force, or National Guard released from active duty in the Air Force	Air Reserve Personnel Center HQ AFPC/DPSSRP 550 C Street West Suite 19 Randolph AFB, TX 78150-4721 (800) 525-0102	

Current Air National Guard enlisted not on active duty in the Air Force	Adjutant General of your state	
Discharged, deceased, or retired before 5/1/1994	National Personnel Records Center 1 Archives Drive St. Louis, MO 63138 (314) 801-0800 Note: Personnel records are Archival 62 years after the service member's separation	
May 1, 1994 to September 30, 2004	National Personnel Records Center 1 Archives Drive St. Louis, MO 63138 (314) 801-0800	Department of Veterans Affairs Records Management Center PO Box 5020 St Louis, MO 63115 (888) 533-4558

LOCATION OF ARMY MILITARY PERSONNEL & HEALTH RECORDS

Status of Service Member or Veteran	Location of Personnel Record	Location of Health Record
Discharged, deceased, or retired (Enlisted) before 11/1/1912	Old Military and Civil Records (NWCTB-Military) Textual Services Division 700 Pennsylvania Ave., N.W. Washington, DC 20408-0001	
Discharged, deceased, or retired (Officer) before 7/1/1917	Old Military and Civil Records (NWCTB-Military) Textual Services Division 700 Pennsylvania Ave., N.W. Washington, DC 20408	
Discharged, deceased, or retired (Enlisted) 11/1/1912 – 10/15/1992	National Personnel Records Center 1 Archives Drive St. Louis, MO 63138 (314) 801-0800	National Personnel Records Center 1 Archives Drive St. Louis, MO 63138 (314) 801-0800
Discharged, deceased, or retired (Officer) 7/1/1917 – 10/15/1992	National Personnel Records Center Military Personnel Records 9700 Page Avenue St. Louis, MO 63132 (314) 801-0800	National Personnel Records Center Military Personnel Records 9700 Page Avenue St. Louis, MO 63132 (314) 801-0800
Discharged, deceased, or retired 10/16/1992 to 9/30/2002	National Personnel Records Center 1 Archives Drive St. Louis, MO 63138 (314) 801-0800	Department of Veterans Affairs Records Management Center PO Box 5020 St. Louis MO 63115-5020 (314) 538-4500

411

Reserve; or active duty records of current National Guard members who performed service in the U.S. Army before 7/1/1972	Commander U.S. Army Personnel Command ATTN: ARPC-ZCC-B 1 Reserve Way St. Louis, MO 62132-5200	
October 16, 1992 to September 30, 2002 (All Personnel)	National Personnel Records Center, NARA 1 Archives Drive St. Louis, MO 63138 (314) 801-0800	Department of Veterans Affairs Records Management Center P.O. Box 5020 St. Louis, MO 63115-50 (800) 827-1000
Discharged, deceased or retired on or after October 1, 2002 (All Personnel)	U.S. Army Human Resources Command Attn: AHRC-PDR-VIB 1600 Spearhead Division Ave. Depart 420 Fort Knox, KY 40122-5402 (888) 276-9472	Department of Veterans Affairs Records Management Center P.O. Box 5020 St. Louis, MO 63115-5020 (800) 827-1000
Active enlisted (including National Guard on active duty in the U.S. Army) or TDRL enlisted	U.S. Army Human Resources Command AHRC-PDR-VIB 1600 Spearhead Division Avenue Dept 420 Fort Knox, KY 40122-5402 (800) 318-5298	
Active officers (including National Guard on active duty in the U.S. Army) or TDRL officers	U.S. Army Human Resources Command Attn: AHRC-PDR-VIB 1600 Spearhead Division Avenue Dept 420 Fort Knox, KY 40122-5402 (800) 318-5298	

LOCATION OF COAST GUARD MILITARY PERSONNEL & HEALTH RECORDS

Status of Service Member or Veteran	Location of Personnel Record	Location of Health Record
Discharged, deceased, or retired before 1/1/1897	The National Archive's Old Military and Civil Records Branch (NWCTB-Military) Textual Services Division 700 Pennsylvania Ave., N.W. Washington, DC 20408 (202) 357-5000	
Discharged, deceased, or retired: 1/1/1898 – 3/31/1998	National Personnel Records Center Military Personnel Records National Personnel Records Center, NARA 1 Archives Drive St. Louis, MO 63138 (314) 801-0800	
Discharged, deceased, or retired on or after: 4/1/1998 to 9/30/2014	National Personnel Records Center Military Personnel Records Records Center, NARA 1 Archives Dr. St. Louis, MO 63138 (314) 801-0800	Department of Veterans Affairs Records Management 1 Archives Dr. St. Louis, MO 63138 (314) 801-0800
Active, reserve, or TDRL	Commander, CGPC-adm-3 USCG Personnel Command 4200 Wilson Blvd. Suite 1100 Arlington, VA 22203-1804 (703) 872-6392	

413

LOCATION OF MARINE CORPS MILITARY PERSONNEL & HEALTH RECORDS

Status of Service Member or Veteran	Location of Personnel Record	Location of Health Record
Discharged, deceased, or retired before 1/1/1905	National Archives & Records Administration Old Military and Civil Records (NWCTB-Military) Textual Services Division 700 Pennsylvania Ave., N.W. Washington, DC 20408-0001 (202) 357-5000	
Discharged, deceased, or retired (Enlisted): 1905 – 4/30/1994	National Personnel Records Center, NARA 1 Archives Drive St. Louis, MO 63138 (314) 801-0800	National Personnel Records Center, NARA 1 Archives Drive St. Louis, MO 63138 (314) 801-0800
Discharged, deceased, or retired (All Personnel): 1/1/1905 – 4/30/1994	National Personnel Records Center Military Personnel Records 9700 Page Avenue St. Louis, MO 63132-5100 (314) 801-0800	National Personnel Records Center Military Personnel Records 9700 Page Avenue St. Louis, MO 63132-5100 (314) 801-0800
Discharged, deceased, or retired from May 1, 1994 to December 31, 1998	National Personnel Records Center 1 Archives Drive St. Louis, MO 63132-5100 (314) 801-0800	Department of Veterans Affairs Records Management Center PO Box 5020 St Louis MO 63115-5020 (314) 538-4500

Status of Service Member or Veteran	Location of Personnel Record	Location of Health Record
Discharged, deceased or retired on or after January 1, 1999 to December 31, 2013	Headquarters U.S. Marine Corps Personnel Management Support Branch (MMSB) 2008 Elliot Road Quantico, VA 22134-5030 (800) 268-3710	Department of Veterans Affairs Records Management P.O. Box 5020 St. Louis, MO 63115-5020 (800) 827-1000
Discharged, deceased or retired on or after January 1, 2014	HQ U.S. Marine Corps Personnel Management Support Branch (MMSB-10) 2008 Elliot Rd. Quantico, VA 22134 (800) 268-3710	Navy Medicine Records Activity BUMED Detachment 4300 Goodfellow Blvd. Bldg. 103 St. Louis, MO 63120
Individual Ready Reserve or Fleet Marine Corps Reserve	Headquarters U.S. Marine Corps Personnel Management Support Branch (MMSB) 2008 Elliot Road Quantico, VA 22134-5030 (800) 268-3710	

LOCATION OF NAVY MILITARY PERSONNEL & HEALTH RECORDS

Status of Service Member or Veteran	Location of Personnel Record	Location of Health Record
Discharged, deceased, or retired (Enlisted) before 1/1/1885	National Archives & Records Administration Old Military and Civil Records (NWCTB-Military) Textual Services Division 700 Pennsylvania Ave., N.W. Washington, DC 20408-0001 (202) 357-5000	
Discharged, deceased, or retired (Officer) before 1/1/1903	National Archives & Records Administration Old Military and Civil Records (NWCTB-Military) Textual Services Division 700 Pennsylvania Ave., N.W. Washington, DC 20408-0001 (202) 357-5000	
Discharged, deceased, or retired (Enlisted): 1885 – 1/30/1994	National Personnel Records Center, NARA 1 Archives Drive St. Louis, MO 63138 (314) 801-0800	National Personnel Records Center, NARA 1 Archives Drive St. Louis, MO 63138 (314) 801-0800
Discharged, deceased, or retired (Officer) 1902– 1/30/1994	National Personnel Records Center, NARA 1 Archives Drive St. Louis, MO 63138 (314) 801-0800	National Personnel Records Center Military Personnel Records 9700 Page Avenue St. Louis, MO 63132-5100 (314) 801-0800
January 31, 1994 to December 31, 1994 (All Personnel)	National Personnel Records Center, NARA 1 Archives Drive St. Louis, MO 63138 (314) 801-0800	

Discharged, deceased, or retired on or after: 1/1/1995 (* see note on Navy Records from 1995 on)	Navy Personnel Command (PERS-312E) 5720 Integrity Drive Millington, TN 38055-3120 (901) 874-4885	Department of Veterans Affairs Records Management Center PO Box 5020 St Louis MO 63115-50204 (314) 538-4500
Active, reserve, or TDRL	Navy Personnel Command (PERS-313C1) 5720 Integrity Drive Millington, TN 38055 (901) 874-4885	

NOTE: Beginning in 1995, the United States Navy no longer retires military personnel records to the NPRC (MPR). For the conversion period between 1995 and 1997, either the NPRC or the Navy may hold the record, but it is recommended that all requests relating to Navy personnel discharged, deceased, or retired from 1995 to the present contact:

Navy Personnel Command PERS-313C1,
5720 Integrity Drive
Millington, TN 38055-3130

FACTS ABOUT THE 1973 ST. LOUIS FIRE AND LOST RECORDS

A fire at the NPRC in St. Louis on July 12, 1973, destroyed about 80 percent of the records for Army personnel discharged between November 1, 1912, and January 1, 1960. About 75 percent of the records for Air Force personnel with surnames from "Hubbard" through "Z" discharged between September 25, 1947, and January 1, 1964, were also destroyed

WHAT WAS LOST

It is hard to determine exactly what was lost in the fire, because:

- There were no indices to the blocks of records involved. The records were merely filed in alphabetical order for the following groups:
  - o World War I: Army November 1, 1912 - September 7, 1939World War II: Army September 8, 1939 - December 31,1946
  - o Post World War II: Army January 1, 1947 - December 31,1959
  - o Air Force September 25, 1947 - December 31,1963

- Millions of records, especially medical records, had been withdrawn from all three groups and loaned to the Department of Veterans Affairs (VA) before the fire. The fact that one's records are not in NPRC files at a particular time does not mean the records were destroyed in the fire.

RECONSTRUCTION OF LOST RECORDS

If veterans learn that their records may have been lost in the fire, they may send photocopies of any documents they possess -- especially separation documents -- to the NPRC at:
National Personnel Records Center Military Personnel Records
9700 Page Blvd.
St. Louis, MO 63132-5100.

ALTERNATE SOURCES OF MILITARY SERVICE DATA

When veterans don't have copies of their military records and their NPRC files may have been lost in the St. Louis fire, essential information about their military service may be available from a number of other sources including:

The Department of Veterans Affairs (VA) maintains records on veterans whose military records were affected by the fire if the veteran or a beneficiary filed a claim before July 1973.

Service information may also be found in various kinds of "organizational" records such as unit morning reports, payrolls and military orders on file at the NPRC or other National Archives and Records Administration facilities.

418

There also is a great deal of information available in records of the State Adjutants General, and other state "veterans services" offices.

By using alternate sources, NPRC often can reconstruct a veteran's beginning and ending dates of active service, the character of service, rank, time lost on active duty, and periods of hospitalization. NPRC can issue NA Form 13038, "Certification of Military Service," considered the equivalent of a Form DD-214, "Report of Separation From Active Duty," to use in establishing eligibility for veterans benefits.

NECESSARY INFORMATION FOR FILE RECONSTRUCTION

The key to reconstructing military data is to give the NPRC enough specific information so the staff can properly search the various sources. The following information is normally required:

- Full name used during military service;
- Place of entry into service;
- Branch of service;
- Last unit of assignment;
- Approximate dates of service;
- Place of discharge;
- Service number or Social Security number.

CHAPTER 41

CORRECTION OF RECORDS BY CORRECTION BOARDS

Retirees may feel that their records need correcting or amending for any number of reasons. Correction boards consider formal applications for corrections of military records.

Each service department has a permanent Board for Correction of Military (Naval) records, composed of civilians, to act on applications for correction of records.

In order to justify correction of a military record, the applicant must prove to a Corrections Board that the alleged entry or omission in the record was in error or unjust. This board considers all applications and makes recommendations to the appropriate branch Secretary.

An application for correction of record must be filed within three years after discovering the error or injustice. If filed after the three-year deadline, the applicant must include in the application reasons the board should find it in the interest of justice to accept the late application.

> **Key Takeaways**
>
> The secretary of a military department has the authority to change any military record when necessary to correct an error or remove an injustice
>
> A correction board may consider applications for correction of a military record including a review of a discharge issued by courts martial
>
> The veteran, survivor or legal representative must file a request for correction within three after discover of an alleged error or injustice

Evidence may include affidavits or signed testimony executed under oath, and a brief of arguments supporting the application. All evidence not already included in one's record must be submitted. The responsibility for securing new evidence rests with the applicant.

To justify any correction, it is necessary to show to the satisfaction of the board that the alleged entry or omission in the records was in error or unjust. Applications should include all available evidence, such as signed statements of witnesses or a brief of arguments supporting the requested correction. Application is made with DD Form 149, available at VA offices, from veterans organizations or from the Internet

Each of the military services maintains a discharge review board with authority to change, correct or modify discharges or dismissals that are not issued by a sentence of a general courts-martial. The board has no authority to address medical discharges. The veteran or, if the veteran is deceased or incompetent, the surviving spouse, next of kin or legal representative may apply for a review of discharge by writing to the military department concerned, using DoD Form 293. This form may be obtained at a VA regional office, from veterans organizations or from the Internet. However, if the discharge was more than 15 years ago, a veteran must petition the appropriate service Board for Correction of Military Records using DoD Form 149, which is discussed in the "Correction of Military Records" section of this booklet. A discharge review is conducted by a review of an applicant's record and, if requested, by a hearing before the board.

Discharges awarded as a result of a continuous period of unauthorized absence in excess of 180 days make persons ineligible for VA benefits regardless of action taken by discharge review boards, unless VA determines there were compelling circumstances for the absence. Boards for the correction of military records also may consider such cases.

Veterans with disabilities incurred or aggravated during active military service may qualify for medical or related benefits regardless of separation and characterization of service. Veterans separated administratively under other than honorable conditions may request that their discharge be reviewed for possible recharacterization, provided they file their appeal within 15 years of the date of separation. Questions regarding the review of a discharge should be addressed to the appropriate discharge review board at the address listed on DoD Form 293.

JURISDICTION

Correction boards are empowered to deal with all matters relating to error or injustice in official records. The boards cannot act until all other administrative avenues of relief have been exhausted. Discharges by sentence of Special Court-Martial and administrative discharges cannot be considered by correction boards unless:

- Application to the appropriate Discharge Review Board has been denied and rehearing is barred; or
- Application cannot be made to the Discharge review Board because the time limit has expired.

APPLICATION

DD Form 149, Application for Correction of Military or Naval record, must be used to apply for correction of military records. It should be submitted, along with supporting evidence, to one of the review boards listed below:

Army
Army Review Boards Agency (ARBA)
ATTN: Client Information and Quality Assurance
251 18th Street South, Suite 385
Arlington, VA 22202

Navy & Marine Corps
Board for Correction of Naval Records
701 S. Courthouse Road
Bldg 12, Suite 1001
Arlington, VA 22204-2490
(703) 604-6884

Coast Guard
DHS Office of the General Counsel
Board for Correction of Military Records

245 Murray Lane, Stop 0485
Washington, DC 20528
(202) 447-4099

Air Force
Board for Correction of Air Force Records
SAF/MRBR
550-C Street West, Suite 40
Randolph AFB, TX 78150-4742

DECISIONS

In the absence of new and material evidence the decision of a correction board, as approved or modified by the Secretary of the Service Department, is final. Adverse decisions are subject to judicial review in a U.S. District Court. Decisions of the Boards for Correction of Military or Naval Records must be made available for public inspection. Copies of the decisional documents will be provided on request.

CHAPTER 42

DISCHARGE REVIEW

DISCHARGE REVIEW BOARDS

Each branch of service has discharge review boards to review the discharge or dismissal of former service members. (The Navy Board considers Marine Corps cases.)

2017 Update: Liberal Consideration for Veterans' Discharge Upgrade Requests

The Defense Department released guidance in 2017 to clarify the liberal consideration given to veterans who request upgrades of their discharge saying they had mental health conditions or were victims of sexual assault or sexual harassment.

> **Key Takeaways**
>
> Veterans who received less than an honorable discharge can apply to the Discharge Review Board for an upgrade of their discharge character
>
> To receive a discharge upgrade or a change in discharge reason, the individual has to prove to the Discharge Review Board that the reason or characterization was inequitable or improper

The new guidance clarifies that the liberal consideration policy includes conditions resulting from post-traumatic stress disorder, traumatic brain injury, sexual assault or sexual harassment.

The policy is meant to ease the burden on veterans and give them a reasonable opportunity to establish the extenuating circumstances of their discharge

Under new guidance, the following are some of the key things involved in discharge relief:

- Evidence may come from sources other than a veteran's service record and may include records from the DoD Sexual Assault Prevention and Response Program (DD Form 2910, Victim Reporting Preference Statement), and/or DD Form 2911 (DoD Sexual Assault Forensic SAFE Report), law enforcement authorities, rape crisis centers, mental health counseling centers, hospitals, physicians, pregnancy tests, tests for sexually transmitted diseases, and statements from family members, friends, roommates, co-workers, fellow servicemembers, or clergy.

- Evidence may also include changes in behavior, requests for transfer to another military duty assignment, deterioration in performance, inability of the individual to conform their behavior to the expectations of a military environment, substance abuse, periods of depression, panic attacks or anxiety without an identifiable cause, unexplained economic or social behavior changes, relationship issues or sexual dysfunction

- Evidence of misconduct, including any misconduct underlying a veteran's discharge may be evidence of a mental health condition, including PTSD, TBI or of behavior consistent with experiencing sexual assault or sexual harassment

- The veteran's testimony alone, written or oral, may establish the existence of a condition or experience, that the condition or experience existing during or was aggravated by military service, and that the condition or experience causes or mitigates the discharge

- Absent clear evidence to the contrary, a diagnosis from a licensed psychiatrist or psychologist is evidence the veteran had a condition that could excuse or mitigate the discharge

- Evidence that may reasonably support more than one diagnosis should be liberally considered as supporting a diagnosis, where applicable, that could excuse or mitigate the discharge

- A veteran asserting a mental health condition without a corresponding diagnosis of such condition from a licensed psychiatrist or psychologist will receive liberal consideration of evidence that may support the evidence of such a condition

- Review Boards are not required to find that a crime of sexual assault or an incident of sexual harassment occurred in order to grant liberal consideration to a veteran that the experience happened during military service, was aggravated by military service, or that it excuses or mitigates the discharge

AUTHORITY

Discharge review boards can, based on the official records and such other evidence as may be presented, upgrade a discharge or change the reason and authority for discharge. Discharge review boards cannot grant disability retirement, revoke a discharge, reinstate any person in the service, recall any person to active duty, act on requests for re-enlistment code changes or review a discharge issued by sentence of a general court- martial. Discharge review boards have no authority to address medical discharges.

Discharges awarded as a result of a continuous period of unauthorized absence in excess of 180 days make persons ineligible for VA benefits regardless of action taken by discharge review boards, unless VA determines there were compelling circumstances for the absence. Boards for the correction of military records also may consider such cases.

APPLICATION

DD Form 293, "Application for Review of Discharge or Dismissal from the Armed Forces of the United States," is used to apply for review of discharge. (If more than 15 years have passed since discharge, DD Form 149 should be used.) The individual or, if legal proof of death is provided, the surviving spouse, next-of-kin, or legal representative can apply. If the individual is mentally incompetent, the spouse, next-of-kin, or legal representative can sign the application, but must provide legal proof of incompetence. The instruction for completing DD Form 293 must be read and complied with.

TIME LIMITATION

Initial application to a discharge review board must be made within 15 years after the date of discharge.

PERSONAL APPEARANCE

A personal appearance before the Discharge Review Board is a legal right. A minimum 30-day notice of the scheduled hearing date is given unless the applicant waives the advance notice in writing. Reasonable postponements can be arranged if circumstances preclude appearance on the scheduled date. All expenses of appearing before the board must be paid by the applicant. If no postponement of a scheduled hearing date is requested and the applicant does not appear on the date scheduled, the right to a personal hearing is forfeited and the case will be considered on the evidence of record.

HEARINGS

Discharge review boards conduct hearings at various locations in the U.S. Information concerning hearing locations and availability of counsel can be obtained by writing to the appropriate board at the address shown on DD Form 293. Those addresses are listed at the end of this chapter.

PUBLISHED UNIFORM STANDARDS FOR DISCHARGE REVIEW

A review of discharge is conducted to determine if an individual was properly and equitably discharged. Each case is considered on its own merits.

A discharge is considered to have been proper unless the discharge review determines:

- That there is an error of fact, law, procedures, or discretion which prejudiced the rights of the individual, or
- That there has been a change of policy which requires a change of discharge.

A discharge is considered to have been equitable unless the discharge review determines:
- That the policies and procedures under which the individual was discharged are materially different from current policies and procedures and that the individual probably would have received a better discharge if the current policies and procedures had been in effect at the time of discharge; or
- That the discharge was inconsistent with the standards of discipline; or
- That the overall evidence before the review board warrants a change of discharge. In arriving at this determination, the discharge review board will consider the quality and the length of the service performed, the individual's physical and mental capability to serve satisfactorily, abuses of authority which may have contributed to the character of the discharge issued, and documented discriminatory acts against the individual.

An authenticated decisional document is prepared and a copy provided to each applicant and council. A copy of each decisional document, with identifying details of the applicant and other persons deleted to protect personal privacy, must be made available for public inspection and copying. These are located in a reading room in the Pentagon, Washington, DC.

To provide access to the documents by persons outside the Washington, D.C. area, the documents have been indexed. The index includes case number of each case; the date, authority and reason for, and character if the discharge, and the issues addressed in the statement of findings, conclusions and reasons.

Interested parties may contact the DVARO or the State veterans Agency for the location of an index. A copy of the index will be made available at the sites of traveling board hearings during the period the board is present.

An individual can go through the index and identify cases in which the circumstances leading to discharge are similar to those in the individual's case. A copy of these case decisional documents can be requested by writing to:

DA Military Review Boards Agency
ATTN: SFBA (Reading Room) Room 1E520
The Pentagon Washington, D.C. 20310.

Examination of decisional documents may help to identify the kind of evidence that was used in the case, and may indicate why relief was granted or denied. Decisional documents do not set precedence - each case is considered on its own merits.

RECONSIDERATION

An application that has been denied can be reopened if:

- The applicant submits newly discovered evidence that was not available at the time of the original consideration.
- The applicant did not request a personal hearing in the original application and now desires to appear before the board. If the applicant fails to appear at the hearings, the case will be closed with no further action.
- The applicant was not represented by counsel in the original consideration and now desires counsel and the application for reconsideration is submitted within 15 years following the date of discharge.
- Changes in policy, law or regulations have occurred or federal court orders have been issued which substantially enhance the rights of the applicant.

SERVICE DEPARTMENT DISCHARGE REVIEW BOARD ADDRESSES ARMY

ARMY DISCHARGE REVIEW BOARD
Attention: SFMR-RBB
251 18th St. South Suite 385
Arlington, VA 22202-4508

NAVY & USMC
Secretary of the Navy Council of Review Boards
720 Kennon St. SE Suite 309
Washington, DC 20374

AIR FORCE
Air Force Military Personnel Center Attention: DP-MDOA1
Randolph AFB, TX 78150-6001

COAST GUARD
DHS Office of the General Counsel Board for Correction of Military Records
Mailstop # 485
245 Murray Lane
Washington, DC 20528

CHAPTER 43

PENAL AND FORFEITURE PROVISIONS

The first section of this chapter outlines basic information for veterans with questions concerning the effect of incarceration on VA benefits. The later sections of this chapter provide detailed information regarding misappropriation by fiduciaries, fraudulent acceptance of payments, forfeiture for fraud, forfeiture for treason, and forfeiture for subversive activities.

BASIC INFORMATION

VA benefits are restricted if a veteran, surviving spouse, child, or dependent parent is convicted of a felony and imprisoned for more than 60 days. VA may still pay certain benefits, however, the amount paid depends on the type of benefit and reason for imprisonment. Following is information about the benefits most commonly affected by imprisonment.

> **Key Takeaways**
>
> VA benefits are restricted if a veteran, surviving spouse, dependent parent or child is convicted of a felony and imprisoned more than 60 days
>
> Any person who fraudulently accepts money is fined or may be imprisoned for a maximum of one year

Please note that overpayments due to failure to notify VA of a veteran's incarceration results in the loss of all financial benefits until the overpayment is recovered.

VA DISABILITY COMPENSATION

VA disability compensation payments are reduced if a veteran is convicted of a felony and imprisoned for more than 60 days. Veterans rated 20 percent or more are limited to the 10 percent disability rate. For a veteran whose disability rating is 10 percent, the payment is reduced by one-half. Once a veteran is released from prison, compensation payments may be reinstated based upon the severity of the service connected disability(ies) at that time.

The disability compensation paid to a veteran incarcerated because of a felony is limited to the 10% disability rate, beginning with the 61st day of imprisonment. For a surviving spouse, child, dependent parent or veteran whose disability rating is 10%, the payment is at the 5% rate. This means that if a veteran was receiving $188 or more prior to incarceration, the new payment amount will be $98. If a veteran was receiving $98 before incarceration, the new payment amount will be $49.

If a veteran resides in a halfway house, participates in a work release program, or is on parole, compensation payments will not be reduced.

*Increased compensation during incarceration - the amount of any increased compensation awarded to an incarcerated veteran that results from other than a statutory rate increase may be subject to reduction due to incarceration

VA DISABILITY PENSION

VA will stop a veteran's pension payments beginning on the 61stday of imprisonment for conviction of either a felony or misdemeanor. Payments may be resumed upon release from prison if the veteran meets VA eligibility requirements.

VA MEDICAL CARE

While incarcerated veterans do not forfeit their eligibility for medical care, current regulations restrict VA from providing hospital and outpatient care to an incarcerated veteran who is an inmate in an institution of another government agency when that agency has a duty to give the care or services.

However, VA may provide care once the veteran has been unconditionally released from the penal institution. Veterans interested in applying for enrollment into the VA health care system should contact the nearest VA health care facility upon their release.

EDUCATIONAL ASSISTANCE / SUBSISTENCE ALLOWANCE

Beneficiaries incarcerated for other than a felony can receive full monthly benefits, if otherwise entitled. Convicted felons residing in halfway houses (also known as "residential re-entry centers"), or participating in work-release programs also can receive full monthly benefits.

Claimants incarcerated for a felony conviction can be paid only the costs of tuition, fees, and necessary books, equipment, and supplies.
VA cannot make payments for tuition, fees, books, equipment, or supplies if another Federal State, or local program pays these costs in full.
If another government program pays only a part of the cost of tuition, fees, books, equipment, or supplies, VA can authorize the incarcerated claimant payment for the remaining part of the costs.

CLOTHING ALLOWANCE

In the case of a veteran who is incarcerated in a Federal, State, or local penal institution for a period in excess of 60 days and who is furnished clothing without charge by the institution, the amount of any annual clothing allowance payable to the veteran shall be reduced by an amount equal to 1/365 of the amount of the allowance otherwise payable under that section for each day on which the veteran was so incarcerated during the 12-month period preceding the date on which payment of the allowance would be due.

PAYMENT TO DEPENDENTS

VA may be able to take part of the amount that the incarcerated veteran is not receiving and pay it to his or her dependents, if they can show need. Interested dependents should contact the nearest VA regional office for details on how to apply. They will be asked to provide income information as part of the application process.

VA will inform a veteran whose benefits are subject to reduction of the right of the veteran's dependents to an apportionment while the veteran is incarcerated, and the conditions under which payments to the veteran may be resumed upon release from incarceration.

VA will also notify the dependents of their right to an apportionment if the VA is aware of their existence and can obtain their addresses.

No apportionment may be made to or on behalf of any person who is incarcerated in a Federal, State, or local penal institution for conviction of a felony.

An apportionment of an incarcerated veteran's VA benefits is not granted automatically to the veteran's dependents. The dependent(s) must file a claim for an apportionment.

RESTORATION OF BENEFITS

When a veteran is released from prison, his or her compensation or pension benefits may be restored. Depending on the type of disability, the VA may schedule a medical examination to see if the veteran's disability has improved or worsened.

MISAPPROPRIATION BY FIDUCIARIES

Whoever, being a guardian, curator, conservator, committee, or person legally vested with the responsibility or care of a claimant or a claimant's estate, or any other person having charge and custody in a fiduciary capacity of money heretofore or hereafter paid under any of the laws administered by the VA for the benefit of any minor, incompetent, or other beneficiary, shall lend, borrow, pledge, hypothecate, use, or exchange for other funds or property, except as authorized by law, or embezzle or in any manner misappropriate any such money or property derived wherefrom in whole or in part, and coming into such fiduciary's control in any matter whatever in the execution of such fiduciary's trust, or under color of such fiduciary's office or service as such fiduciary, shall be fined in accordance with Title 18, or imprisoned not more than 5 years, or both.

Any willful neglect or refusal to make and file proper accountings or reports concerning such money or property as required by law shall be taken to be sufficient evidence prima facie of such embezzlement or misappropriation.

FRAUDULENT ACCEPTANCE OF PAYMENTS

Any person entitled to monetary benefits under any of the laws administered by the VA whose right to payment ceases upon the happening of any contingency, who thereafter fraudulently accepts any such payment, shall be fined in accordance with Title 18, or imprisoned not more than one year, or both.

Whoever obtains or receives any money or check under any of the laws administered by the VA without being entitled to it, and with intent to defraud the United States or any beneficiary of the United States, shall be fined in accordance with Title 18, or imprisoned not more than one year, or both.

FORFEITURE FOR FRAUD

Whoever knowingly makes or causes to be made or conspires, combines, aids, or assists in, agrees to, arranges for, or in any way procures the making or presentation of a false or fraudulent affidavit, declaration, certificate, statement, voucher, or paper, concerning any claim for benefits under any of the laws administered by the VA (except laws pertaining to insurance benefits) shall forfeit all rights, claims, and benefits under all laws administered by the VA (except laws pertaining to insurance benefits).

Whenever a veteran entitled to disability compensation has forfeited the right to such compensation under this chapter, the compensation payable but for the forfeiture shall thereafter be paid to the veteran's spouse, children, and parents. Payments made to a spouse, children, and parents under the preceding sentence shall not exceed the amounts payable to each if the veteran had died from service-connected disability. No spouse, child, or parent who participated in the fraud for which forfeiture was imposed shall receive any payment by reason of this subsection. Any apportionment award under this subsection may not be made in any case after September 1, 1959.

Forfeiture of benefits by a veteran shall not prohibit payment of the burial allowance, death compensation, dependency and indemnity compensation, or death pension in the event of the veteran's death.

After September 1, 1959, no forfeiture of benefits may be imposed under the rules outlined in this chapter upon any individual who was a resident of, or domiciled in, a State at the time the act or acts occurred on account of which benefits would, but not for this subsection, be forfeited unless such individual ceases to be a resident of, or domiciled in, a State before the expiration of the period during which criminal prosecution could be instituted. The paragraph shall not apply with respect to:

- Any forfeiture occurring before September 1, 1959; or
- An act or acts that occurred in the Philippine Islands before July 4, 1946.

The VA is authorized and directed to review all cases in which, because of a false or fraudulent affidavit, declaration, certificate, statement, voucher, or paper, a forfeiture of gratuitous benefits under laws administered by the VA was imposed, pursuant to this section or prior provisions of the law, on or before September 1, 1959. In any such case in which the VA determines that the forfeiture would not have been imposed under the provisions of this section in effect after September 1, 1959, the VA shall remit the forfeiture, effective June 30, 1972. Benefits to which the individual concerned becomes eligible by virtue of any such remission may be awarded, upon application for, and the effective date of any award of compensation, dependency and indemnity compensation, or pension made in such a case shall be fixed in accordance with the facts found, but shall not be earlier than the effective date of the Act or administrative issue. In no event shall such award or increase be retroactive for more than one year from the date of application, or the date of administrative determination of entitlement, whichever is earlier.

FORFEITURE FOR TREASON

Any person shown by evidence satisfactory to the VA to be guilty of mutiny, treason, sabotage, or rendering assistance to an enemy of the United States or its allies shall forfeit all accrued or future gratuitous benefits under laws administered by the VA.

The VA, in its discretion, may apportion and pay any part of benefits forfeited under the preceding paragraph to the dependents of the person forfeiting such benefits. No dependent of any person shall receive benefits by reason of this subsection in excess of the amount to which the dependent would be entitled if such person were dead.

In the case of any forfeiture under this chapter, there shall be no authority after September 1, 1959 to:

- Make an apportionment award pursuant to the preceding paragraph; or
- Make an award to any person of gratuitous benefits based on any period of military, naval, or air service commencing before the date of commission of the offense.

431

FORFEITURE FOR SUBVERSIVE ACTIVITIES

Any individual who is convicted after September 1, 1959, of any offense listed below shall, from and after the date of commission of such offense, have no right to gratuitous benefits (including the right to burial in a national cemetery) under laws administered by the VA based on periods of military, naval, or air service commencing before the date of commission of such offense, and no other person shall be entitled to such benefits on account of such individual. After receipt of notice of the return of an indictment for such an offense, the VA shall suspend payment of such gratuitous benefits pending disposition of the criminal proceedings. If any individual whose rights to benefits has been terminated pursuant to this section, is granted a pardon of the offense by the President of the United States, the right to such benefits shall be restored as of the date of such pardon.

The offenses referred to in the previous paragraph are:
Sections 894, 904 and 906 of Title 10 (articles 94, 104, and 106 of the Uniform Code of Military Justice);
Sections 792, 793, 794, 798, 2381, 2382, 2383, 2384, 2385, 2387, 2388, 2389, 2390, and chapter 105 of Title 18;
Sections 222, 223, 224, 225 and 226 of the Atomic Energy Act of 1954 (42 U.S.C. 2272, 2273, 2274, 2275, and 2276);
Section 4 of the Internal Security Act of 1950 (50 U.S.C. 783).
The Secretary of Defense, the Secretary of Transportation, or the Attorney General, as appropriate, shall notify the VA in each case in which an individual is convicted of an offense mentioned in this chapter.

CHAPTER 44

PERIODS OF WAR

Military service is classified either as wartime or peacetime service. This is important because there are significant advantages specifically accruing only to veterans with wartime service.

The following list sets out the periods of wartime designated by Congress for pension purposes. To be considered by the VA to have served during wartime, a veteran need not have served in a combat zone, but simply during one of these designated periods.

Indian Wars:
The period January 1, 1817 through December 31, 1898. Service must have been rendered with the United States military forces against Indian tribes or nations.

Spanish-American War:
The period April 21, 1898 through July 4, 1902. In the case of a veteran who served with the United States military forces engaged in hostilities in the Moro Province the ending date is July 15, 1903.

Mexican Border Period:
The period May 9, 1916 through April 5, 1917, in the case of a veteran who during such period served in Mexico, on the borders thereof, or in the waters adjacent thereto.

World War I:
The period April 6, 1917, through November 11, 1918. In the case of a veteran who served with the United States military forces in Russia, the ending date is April 1, 1920. Service after November 11, 1918 and before July 2, 1921 is considered World War I for compensation or pension purposes, if the veteran served in the active military, naval, or air service after April 5, 1917 and before November 12, 1918.

World War II:
The period December 7, 1941 through December 31, 1946. If the veteran was in service on December 31, 1946, continuous service before July 26, 1947 is considered World War II service.

Korean Conflict:
The period June 27, 1950 through January 31, 1955.

Vietnam Era:
The period August 5, 1964 (February 28, 1961 for Veterans who served "in country" before August 5, 1964), and ending May 7, 1975.

Persian Gulf War:

The period August 2, 1990 through a date to be set by law or Presidential Proclamation.

Future Dates:

The period beginning on the date of any future declaration of war by the Congress, and ending on a date prescribed by Presidential Proclamation or concurrent resolution of the Congress. (Title U.S.C. 10)

CHAPTER 45

COMMON FORMS

General Administration Forms	
Form #	**Purpose**
20-572	Request For Change Of Address / Cancellation Of Direct Deposit

Compensation and Pension Forms	
Form #	**Purpose**
21-22	Appointment Of Veterans Service Organization As Claimant's Representative
21-0304	Application For Spina Bifida Benefits
21P-534EZ	Application for DIC, Death Pension, and/or Accrued Benefits
21-526EZ	Application for Disability Compensation Benefits
21-526c	Pre-Discharge Compensation Claim
21P-527EZ	Application for Pension
21P-530	Application for Burial Benefits
21P-601	Application for Accrued Amounts Due a Deceased Beneficiary
21-686c	Declaration of Status of Dependents
Form 9	Appeal to Board of Veterans Appeals
21-0958	Notice of Disagreement
21-0966	Intent to File a VA Claim

21-2680	Request for Aid and Attendance/Housebound Status
21-4138	Statement in Support of Claim
21-4142	Authorization for Release of Information
21-8940	Application for Increased Compensation Due Unemployability

Vocational Rehabilitation and Employment Forms

Form #	Purpose
22-1190	Application for VA Education Benefits
22-5490	Dependent's Application for VA Education Benefits
28-1900	Disabled Veterans Application for Vocational Rehabilitation

VA Insurance Forms

Form #	Purpose
29-336	Designation Of Beneficiary – Government Life Insurance
29-1546	Application For Cash Surrender Value / Application For Policy Loan
29-4125	Claim For One Sum Payment
29-4364	Application For Service-Disabled Insurance

Finance and Budget Forms

Form #	Purpose
24-0296	Direct Deposit Enrollment

Miscellaneous Forms

Form #	Purpose
DD 149	Application For Correction Of Military Record
DD 214	Report of Separation From Active Duty

DD 293	Application For The Review Of Discharge OR Dismissal From The Armed Forces Of The United States
SF 15	Application For 10-Point Veteran's Preference
SF 180	Request Pertaining To Military Records
SGLV8283	Claim For Death Benefits – Form Returned To Office Of Servicemembers' Group Life Insurance
SGLV8285	Request For Insurance (Servicemembers' Group Life Insurance)
SGLV8286	Servicemembers' Group Life Insurance Election And Certificate
SGLV8714	Application For Veterans' Group Life Insurance
VAF 8	Certification To Appeal
VAF 9	Appeal To Board Of Veterans' Appeals
10 –10ez	Instructions For Completing Application For Health Benefits
VAF 3288	Request For And Consent To Release Of Information From Claimant's Records
VAF 4107	Notice Of Procedural And Appellate Rights
VAF 4107b	Notice Of Procedural And Appellate Rights (Spanish Version)
40-1330M	Application For Standard Government Headstone Or Marker For Installation In A Private Or State Veterans' Cemetery

CHAPTER 46

APPLICATION AND CHARACTER OF DISCHARGE

APPLYING FOR BENEFITS AND YOUR CHARACTER OF DISCHARGE

Generally, in order to receive VA benefits and services, the Veteran's character of discharge or service must be under other than dishonorable conditions (e.g., honorable, under honorable conditions, general). However, individuals receiving undesirable, bad conduct, and other types of dishonorable discharges may qualify for VA benefits depending on a determination made by VA.

> **Key Takeaways**
> Generally to receive VA benefits and services the veteran's character of discharge must be under other than honorable discharge
>
> Discharge requirements for compensation benefits and services include discharge under other than dishonorable conditions including honorable, under honorable conditions, or general

Basic eligibility for Department of Veterans Affairs (VA) benefits depends upon the type of military service performed, the duration of the service, and the character of discharge or separation. VA looks at the "character of discharge" to determine whether a person meets the basic eligibility requirements for receipt of VA benefits under title 38 of the United States Code. Any discharge under honorable conditions satisfies the character of discharge requirement for basic eligibility for VA benefits. Certain types of discharges, along with the circumstances surrounding those discharges, bar an individual from basic eligibility for VA benefits. Other types of discharges require VA to make a character of discharge determination in order to assess basic eligibility for VA benefits.

Under the law (38 U.S.C. § 5303), a release or discharge for any of the following reasons constitutes a statutory bar to benefits, unless it is determined that the Servicemember was insane at the time he/she committed the offense that resulted in the discharge:

- Sentence of a general court-martial
- Being a conscientious objector who refused to perform military duty, wear the uniform, or otherwise comply with lawful orders of competent military authority

- Desertion
- Absence without official leave (AWOL) for a continuous period of 180 days or more, without compelling circumstances to warrant such prolonged unauthorized absence (as determined by VA)
- Requesting release from service as an alien during a period of hostilities, or This means that if an individual is discharged for any of the above reasons, the law prohibits VA from providing any benefits
- Resignation by an officer for the good of the service

VA reviews military service records, including facts and circumstances surrounding the incident(s) leading to the discharge. VA also considers the following when making its determination:

- Any mitigating or extenuating circumstances presented by the claimant
- Any supporting evidence provided by third parties who were familiar with the circumstances surrounding the incident(s) in question
- Length of service
- Performance and accomplishments during service
- Nature of the infraction(s), and
- Character of service preceding the incident(s) resulting in the discharge.

VA considers whether an individual was insane when determining whether a statutory bar to benefits exists. When no statutory bar to benefits exists, the impact of disabilities may be considered during the analysis of any mitigating or extenuating circumstances that may have contributed to the discharge.

SPECIFIC BENEFIT PROGRAM CHARACTER OF DISCHARGE REQUIREMENTS

DISCHARGE REQUIREMENTS FOR COMPENSATION BENEFITS

To receive VA compensation benefits and services, the Veteran's character of discharge or service must be under other than dishonorable conditions (e.g., honorable, under honorable conditions, general).

DISCHARGE REQUIREMENTS FOR EDUCATION BENEFITS

To receive VA education benefits and services through the Montgomery GI Bill program or Post-9/11 GI Bill program, the Veteran's character of discharge or service must be honorable.

To receive VA education benefits and services through any other VA educational benefits program, including the Survivors' and Dependents' Educational Assistance (DEA) program, the Veteran's character of discharge or service must be under other than dishonorable conditions (e.g., honorable, under honorable conditions, general).

DISCHARGE REQUIREMENTS FOR HOME LOAN BENEFITS

To receive VA home loan benefits and services, the Veteran's character of discharge or service must be under other than dishonorable conditions (e.g., honorable, under honorable conditions, general).

DISCHARGE REQUIREMENTS FOR INSURANCE BENEFITS

Generally, there is no character of discharge bar to benefits to Veterans' Group Life Insurance. However, for Service Disabled Veterans Insurance and Veterans' Mortgage Life

Insurance benefits, the Veteran's character of discharge must be other than dishonorable.

DISCHARGE REQUIREMENTS FOR PENSION BENEFITS

To receive VA pension benefits and services, the Veteran's character of discharge or service must be under other than dishonorable conditions (e.g., honorable, under honorable conditions, general).

REVIEW OF DISCHARGE FROM MILITARY SERVICE

Each of the military services maintains a discharge review board with authority to change, correct or modify discharges or dismissals not issued by a sentence of a general court-martial. The board has no authority to address medical discharges.

The Veteran or, if the Veteran is deceased or incompetent, the surviving spouse, next of kin or legal representative, may apply for a review of discharge by writing to the military department concerned, using DD Form 293, "Application for the Review of Discharge from the Armed Forces of the United States." This form may be obtained at a VA regional office, or from Veterans organizations.

However, if the discharge was more than 15 years ago, a Veteran must petition the appropriate Service's Board for Correction of Military Records using DD Form 149, "Application for Correction of Military Records Under the Provisions of Title 10, U.S. Code, Section 1552." A discharge review is conducted by a review of an applicant's record and, if requested, by a hearing before the board.

Discharge Related to Mental Health Conditions, Sexual Assault, or Sexual Harassment

In December 2016, the Department announced a renewed effort to ensure that veterans are aware of the opportunity to have discharges and military records reviewed. Following a review, it was determined that clarifications were needed regarding mental health conditions, sexual assault and sexual harassment. New guidance was issued.

Clarifying Guidance to Military Discharge Review Boards and Boards for Correction Requests by Veterans for Modification of Their Discharge Due to Mental Health Conditions, Traumatic Brain Injury, Sexual Assault or Sexual Harassment

Requests for discharge relief usually involve four questions, which include:

- Did the veteran have a condition or experience that may excuse or mitigate the discharge?
- Did that condition exist/experience occur during military service?
- Does that condition or experience actually excuse or mitigate the discharge?
- Does that condition or experience outweigh the discharge?

Liberal consideration will be given to veterans for petitioning for discharge relief when the application for relief is based in whole or in part on matters relating to mental health conditions including PTSD, TBI, sexual assault or sexual harassment.

Evidence may come from sources other than a veteran's service record and may include records from the DoD Sexual Assault Prevention and Response Program (DD Form 2910, Victim Reporting Preference Statement) and/or DD Form 2911, DoD Sexual Assault Forensic Examination (SAFE) Report, law enforcement authorities, rape crisis centers, mental health and counseling centers, hospitals, physicians, pregnancy tests, tests for sexually transmitted diseases and statements from family members, friends, roommates, co-workers, and fellow servicemembers or clergy.

Evidence may also include changes in behavior, requests for transfer to another military assignment, deterioration in work performance, inability of the individual to conform their behavior to expectations of a military environment, substance abuse, episodes of depression or panic attacks, anxiety without an identifiable cause, unexplained economic or social behavior changes, relationship issues, or sexual dysfunction.

Evidence of misconduct, including any misconduct underlying a veteran's discharge may be evidence of a mental health condition, including PTSD, TBI or behavior consistent with experience sexual assault or sexual harassment.

The veteran's testimony alone, oral or written, may establish the existence of a condition or experience, that the condition or experience existed during or was aggravated by military service, and that the condition or experience excuses or mitigates the discharge.

The Department of Defense today announced a renewed effort to ensure veterans are aware of the opportunity to have their discharges and military records reviewed. Through enhanced public outreach, engagement with Veterans Service Organizations (VSOs), Military Service Organizations (MSOs), and other outside groups, as well as direct outreach to individual veterans, the department encourages all veterans who believe they have experienced an error or injustice to request relief from their service's Board for Correction of Military/Naval Records (BCM/NR) or Discharge Review Board (DRB).

Additionally, all veterans, VSOs, MSOs, and other interested organizations are invited to offer feedback on their experiences with the BCM/NR or DRB processes, including how the policies and processes can be improved.

In the past few years, the department has issued guidance for consideration of post-traumatic stress disorder (PTSD), as well as the repealed "Don't Ask, Don't Tell" and its predecessor policies. Additionally, supplemental guidance for separations involving victims of sexual assault is currently being considered.

The department is reviewing and consolidating all of the related policies to reinforce the department's commitment to ensuring fair and equitable review of separations for all veterans. Whether the discharge or other correction is the result of PTSD, sexual orientation, sexual assault, or some other consideration, the department is committed to rectifying errors or injustices and treating all veterans with dignity and respect.

To request an upgrade or correction:

Veterans who desire a correction to their service record or who believe their discharge was unjust, erroneous, or warrants an upgrade, are encouraged to apply for review.

For discharge upgrades, if the discharge was less than 15 years ago, the veteran should complete DD Form 293 and send it to their service's DRB (the address is on the form). For discharges over 15 years ago, the veteran should complete the DD Form 149 and send it to their service's BCM/NR (the address is on the form).

For corrections of records other than discharges, veterans should complete the DD Form 149 and submit their request to their service's BCM/NR (the address is on the form).

Key information to include in requests:

There are three keys to successful applications for upgrade or correction. First, it is very important to explain why the veteran's discharge or other record was unjust or erroneous—for example, how it is connected to, or resulted from unjust policies, a physical or mental health condition related to military service, or some other explainable or justifiable circumstance.

Second, it is important to provide support, where applicable, for key facts. If a veteran has a relevant medical diagnosis, for example, it would be very helpful to include medical records that reflect that diagnosis.

Third, it is helpful, but not always required, to submit copies of the veteran's applicable service records. The more information provided, the better the boards can understand the circumstances of the discharge.

BCM/NRs are also authorized to grant relief on the basis of clemency. Veterans who believe their post-service conduct and contributions to society support an upgrade or correction should describe their post-service activity and provide any appropriate letters or other documentation of support.

Personnel records for veterans who served after 1997 should be accessible online and are usually retrievable within hours of a request through the Defense Personnel Records Information Retrieval System (DPRIS). Those who served prior to 1997 or for whom electronic records are not available from DPRIS, can request their records from the National Personnel Records Center (NPRC).

452

W

Y

Would You Like Additional Copies Of
<u>What Every Veteran Should Know?</u>

Simply tear out this form, and:

Phone 309-757-7760 or Fax 309-278-5304

Mail To: VETERANS INFORMATION SERVICE
P.O. Box 111
East Moline, IL 61244-0111

ORDER ONLINE AT: www.vetsinfoservice.com

☐ Yes! Send me _____ copies of *"What Every Veteran Should Know"*, at $25.00 each (shipping & handling included). I request the _____ (specify: <u>current already released 2018,</u> or <u>pre-reserve 2019</u>) edition. New annual books are published every March 1st.

☐ Yes! I would like to subscribe to *"What Every Veteran Should Know"* monthly supplement (an 8 page newsletter which keeps your book up to-date), and receive _____ copies of all 12 monthly issues (1 year) for $35.00 per subscription (shipping & handling included).

☐ Yes! I want to save money, and receive both the book and the monthly supplement. I would like _____ sets, at $55 per set (shipping & handling included).

Name   Current Customer ID?

Address

City / State / Zip Code

Telephone Number   E-mail Address

Amount Enclosed   Daytime Phone # (including area code)

Method of Payment:

☐ Check   ☐ Visa   ☐ MasterCard   ☐ Money Order

Credit Card #   3-digit CVV   Expiration Date
(Month/Year)

Signature

Thank you for your order!
If you have any questions, feel free to contact us at
(309) 757-7760
www.vetsinfoservice.com - Email: help@vetsinfoservice.com

Would You Like Additional Copies Of
What Every Veteran Should Know?

Simply tear out this form, and:

Phone 309-757-7760 or Fax 309-278-5304

Mail To: VETERANS INFORMATION SERVICE
P.O. Box 111
East Moline, IL 61244-0111

ORDER ONLINE AT: www.vetsinfoservice.com

☐ Yes! Send me _____ copies of "*What Every Veteran Should Know*", at $25.00 each (shipping & handling included). I request the _____ (specify: <u>current already released 2018,</u> or <u>pre-reserve 2019</u>) edition. New annual books are published every March 1st.

☐ Yes! I would like to subscribe to "*What Every Veteran Should Know*" monthly supplement (an 8-page newsletter which keeps your book up-to-date), and receive _____ copies of all 12 monthly issues (1 year) for $35.00 per subscription (shipping & handling included).

☐ Yes! I want to save money, and receive both the book and the monthly supplement. I would like _____ sets, at $55 per set (shipping & handling included).

Name   Current Customer ID?

Address

City / State / Zip Code

Telephone Number   E-mail Address

Amount Enclosed   Daytime Phone # (including area code)

Method of Payment:

☐ Check   ☐ Visa   ☐ MasterCard   ☐ Money Order

Credit Card #   3-digit CVV   Expiration Date
(Month/Year)

Signature

Thank you for your order!
If you have any questions, feel free to contact us at
(309) 757-7760
www.vetsinfoservice.com - Email: help@vetsinfoservice.com